J. S. Bach's Johannine Theology

J. S. Bach's Johannine Theology

THE *ST. JOHN PASSION* AND THE CANTATAS FOR SPRING 1725

Eric Chafe

OXFORD UNIVERSITY PRESS

OXFORD
UNIVERSITY PRESS

Oxford University Press is a department of the University of Oxford. It furthers the University's objective of excellence in research, scholarship, and education by publishing worldwide.

Oxford New York
Auckland Cape Town Dar es Salaam Hong Kong Karachi
Kuala Lumpur Madrid Melbourne Mexico City Nairobi
New Delhi Shanghai Taipei Toronto

With offices in
Argentina Austria Brazil Chile Czech Republic France Greece
Guatemala Hungary Italy Japan Poland Portugal Singapore
South Korea Switzerland Thailand Turkey Ukraine Vietnam

Oxford is a registered trade mark of Oxford University Press in the UK and certain other countries.

Published in the United States of America by
Oxford University Press
198 Madison Avenue, New York, NY 10016

Chafe, Eric Thomas, 1946–
J. S. Bach's Johannine theology : the St. John Passion and the Cantatas for spring 1725 / Eric Chafe.
pages cm
Includes bibliographical references and index.
ISBN 978-0-19-977334-3 (hardback) — ISBN 978-0-19-977347-3 (electronic text) 1. Bach, Johann Sebastian, 1685–1750—Criticism and interpretation. 2. Bach, Johann Sebastian, 1685–1750. Johannespassion. 3. Bach, Johann Sebastian, 1685–1750. Cantatas. 4. John, the Apostle, Saint—Songs and music—History and criticism. 5. Sacred vocal music—18th century—History and criticism. I. Title.
ML410.B13C45 2014
782.23—dc23 2013016012

BB 9780199773343
DG 9780199773473

1 3 5 7 9 8 6 4 2

Printed in the United States of America on acid-free paper

Publication of this book was supported by the
Margarita Hanson Endowment of the American Musicological Society.

{ ACKNOWLEDGMENTS }

I have been involved with the *St. John Passion* for a long time, and there are a great many individuals to whom I owe a debt of gratitude that can never be adequately repaid. My earliest systematic thought on the Passion goes back to a seminar of Christoph Wolff's at the University of Toronto during the 1969–70 academic year. There I and my fellow students were introduced to the sources and literature of the Bach Passions and encouraged to develop research projects. Mine was on the *St. Matthew Passion*, but my colleague and longtime friend, Gregory Butler, set forth as his project a version of overall tonal symmetry for the *St. John Passion* that, after a decade during which our research paths had diverged, awakened my desire to explore the subject further. On bringing the matter up with him, Greg very kindly left me a clear field, for which I am eternally grateful. From that time to the present, I have had many friends, colleagues, and students who have given me help in molding my various writings on the *St. John Passion* and the cantatas discussed in this book. I cannot possibly adequately thank them all, but the following persons were instrumental: Don Franklin, Robert Marshall, Paul Brainard, Laura Schechter, Robin Leaver, Betsy Joyce, Jacquelyn Sholes, Michael Marissen, Joseph Morgan, Alfred Dürr, Werner Breig, Annegret Klaua, Gilad Harel, Markus Rathey. Martina Rebmann, of the Stattsbibliothek zu Berlin-Preußischer Kulturbesitz, was of great assistance in acquiring the photograph of Bach's autograph page from the *St. John Passion* that I have reproduced as figure 5.1. For several years I have corresponded with John Eliot Gardiner, exchanging ideas on Bach, the *St. John Passion* in particular, and have benefitted greatly from this exchange with one of the foremost Bach conductors of our time, not to mention the performances themselves. Gardiner's own book on Bach, embodying the insights of a lifetime of Bach performances, will be published around the same time as this one. The experience of publishing this book with Oxford University Press has been a fulfilling one. Music editor Suzanne Ryan shepherded it through all the early stages, giving much encouragement and advice when it was needed, Adam Cohen, Erica Woods Tucker, and Jessen O'Brien coordinated production details very skillfully. And copy editor Mary Sutherland was pure pleasure to work with; her interactive style, attention to detail and expertise in music and theology were instrumental in getting this book to its present state. In the final analysis, however, it is to Christoph Wolff that I owe the very great debt of that initial introduction to Bach research, something that has shaped my life in incalculable ways.

{ CONTENTS }

{ LIST OF FIGURES AND ILLUSTRATIONS }

Figures

Illustrations

{ A NOTE ON TRANSLATIONS, SPELLING, ORTHOGRAPHY, AND PITCH DESIGNATIONS }

This book makes extensive use of citations from theological sources from the sixteenth to the eighteenth centuries. Except for relatively short passages, all such citations are given in the main text in English translation and in the notes in the original language (usually German). All translations are mine unless noted differently. Citations from the Bible are, generally, from the King James Version (KJV). I have striven for clarity and literalness rather than elegance (which is often not to be found in the originals and was certainly not their authors' primary concern). Since the sources used are not always the original editions (which Bach probably did not have in most cases), their spelling and orthography varies considerably. German spelling of many words changed greatly from the sixteenth century to the eighteenth century, as did punctuation and capitalization. So eighteenth-century editions of Luther, Chemnitz, and others were modernized at the time. I have kept as close as possible to the original sources used (not necessarily the first editions) in the notes. Variant spellings within the notes are owing to the sources themselves; they are sometimes not consistent even within a single source. In the translations, however, I have modernized punctuation and for the most part changed the most common form of emphasis in the old sources from boldface type to italics. German orthography commonly distinguished word roots by changing type: Latin type for the root, German for the remainder. In transcribing the originals I have used Roman type and italics to convey this difference, for example, temper*irte*. In title pages changing ink colors (red versus black) have not been preserved.

Pitches are designated in the text according to the following system:

CC, C, c, c′ [middle C], c″, c‴.

When specific tonalities are mentioned, upper case designates major (G), lower case is minor (g).

Abbreviations and musical symbols

NBA = Neue Bach-ausgabe
BWV = Bach Werke-Verzeichnis (index to Bach's works)

Books of the Bible

Exodus	Ex
Genesis	Gen

Numbers	Num
Matthew	Mt
Mark	Mk
Luke	Lk
John	Jn
Corinthians	1 Cor, 2 Cor
Romans	Rom
1 John (etc.)	1 Jn
1 Peter	1 Pet
Revelation	Rev
Jeremiah	Jer

Cited in text, the name of the biblical book is spelled out in full John 1:2–3; as cited in parentheses, I use the abbreviated form (Jn 1:12–34).

King James translation/version KJV

sharp ♯, natural ♮, flat ♭

v. and vv. = verse/verses
ch. chs. = chapters (abbreviations in parentheses)

SDG = Soli Deo Gloria
JJ = Jesu Juva

J. S. Bach's Johannine Theology

Introduction: Bach and John

Problems and Objectives

One of the most interesting and rewarding endeavors in the study of music is that of understanding the intricate relationship between music and extramusical ideas, especially in music with words, and more particularly so when the verbal texts embody extensive reference to belief systems associated with the composers and their times. That quality is prominent in the music of Wagner, whose adoption of fundamental elements of the philosophy of Schopenhauer in his greatest works amounted to a kind of religion. This kind of situation is even more true of Bach, in whose case the belief system to which the texts of his cantatas and Passions refer, that of the orthodox Lutheranism of the sixteenth through the eighteenth centuries, was shared by his Lutheran predecessors and contemporaries, and was articulated in many hundreds of treatises spanning the two centuries between Luther and Bach. It literally formed the framework for his life and work.[1]

Those beliefs are not fundamental to the lives of many who are drawn to Bach's music today, any more than the frequency of infant mortality, candlelight, and the huge number of other disparities between his era and our own.[2] In countless ways, both subtle and sweeping, even those who hold to religious beliefs that are nominally or actually close to those of Bach's time cannot experience existence in the same way that he did. Yet the works have arguably lost none of their force from his time to ours, despite enormous changes in the ways they have been understood. When we consider how nineteenth-century critics recognized enduring qualities

---

[1] I do not mean to imply that the beliefs associated with orthodox Lutheranism remained completely unchanged from Luther's time to Bach's. Nevertheless, there is a core of basic dogmatic ideas that changes very little or not at all during that time, whereas sensibilities and emphases do. The student of such literature must read it in that light.

[2] For a very perceptive study devoted to Bach's "distance" in this respect, see Wolfgang Hildesheimer, *Der ferne Bach* (Frankfurt am Main: Insel Verlag, 1985).

in Bach's music, describing them in terms wholly other than ours, and on the basis of cantata performances with choirs numbering in the hundreds of voices and very few if any of the instruments Bach actually called for, we are acutely aware of the capacity of great music to transcend its historical surroundings and of just how important historical understanding is for us. Hopefully we recognize not that we have finally got it right, or that taste is relative, but that continuing interaction with the history of ideas—including, of course, musical ideas—is what is particularly valuable in the study of great musical thinkers. In such study we inevitably have to deal with disparities between the composer, her ideals, visions, and intentions, and the various historical circumstances that conditioned, but at times even opposed those ideals. Such disparities carry over into modern scholarship as well. In this context, the reader may consider, how, for the two most prestigious editions of Bach's work, a century apart, Wilhelm Rust (1822–92) and Arthur Mendel (1905–79) represented the modulation associated with Peter's denial in Part 1 of the *St. John Passion*, a detail that is vital to our understanding of the structure and meaning of the work (see discussion with facsimile and transcription in ch. 5). What Bach actually wrote in the score of ca. 1740 perhaps reflects some lingering notational uncertainty on his part (even though the passage had been composed nearly two decades earlier). It is clearly unsuitable for a modern edition. Its very irregularity, however, points up the highly symbolic nature of a modulation that in their editorial interventions, Rust and Mendel approached from divergent, almost opposite standpoints, the one seeking to highlight its significance and the other not recognizing it (and not discussing it in the critical commentary to the edition itself).

Through the interaction with history (which would involve Bach's original notation as well as consideration of why and how the passage in question is both meaningful and problematic), we open new windows on our subject matter. And the more we study Bach's works, the clearer it becomes that his own interaction with the religious ideas of his time and surroundings is an intricate one. This study aspires to awaken further recognition of that fact. And if it is to pay more than lip service to the historical character of his cantatas and Passions, a considerable degree of identification with beliefs that now demand the suspension of disbelief is necessary. Probing their meaning is in large part a historical study, but one that is guided and inspired by the compositions themselves, which, whatever their problems in understanding, comprise one of the very high peaks of human civilization.

It may be that no scholarly monograph can do justice to the enduring value of Bach's work as a whole, or the full scope of its relationship to the belief system in which it is grounded. This book attempts to focus on one aspect of that work as a kind of microcosm of the nature of Bach's interaction with the Lutheran Christian theological tradition, with particular reference to one of that tradition's most characteristic topics. Primarily it comprises a musico-theological investigation of J. S. Bach's response to the Gospel of John as revealed in compositions produced in his first two years in Leipzig, above all in the springs of 1724 and 1725. But it also attempts to delineate the broad conceptual background for those works and their liturgical meaning, topics that sometimes take us back to authors many centuries before Bach's time. Increasingly, it seems, this subject has emerged as a symbol for all that is most problematic in Bach studies from a "global" perspective. This book does not address those issues—John's anti-Judaism, for example—as its direct subject matter, although it does take seriously the question of their reflection in Bach's work. It aspires, rather, to provide a basis in historically oriented musical analysis for better understanding of how music and religion (or theology) interact in a selection of works whose musical designs are reflective of the kind of deep thought we associate with Bach.

Foremost among the works in question are the *St. John Passion* (composed and first performed in 1724, then re-performed with significant changes in 1725) and the Easter and post-Easter cantatas of 1725. In spring 1724 Bach probed the meaning of John's account of the Passion to a truly extraordinary degree, producing a setting that remains a milestone to this day. His involvement with John must have been an absorbing one in light of the many Johannine qualities that are closely mirrored in his Passion. However, the cantatas for the 1723–24 liturgical year, most of which preceded the Passion performance, do not exhibit a corresponding degree of interest in the characteristics of the particular Gospels on which their texts are based. Nevertheless, a significant number of those cantatas—especially the newly composed ones—feature a quality that relates directly to the *St. John Passion* and might well have awakened Bach's interest in exploring the meaning of John's Passion account in the manner that he did: they begin with biblical excerpts (*dicta*), often drawn from the psalms, that their subsequent movements expound upon in a systematic and sequential manner. In many of those cantatas Bach's interest in the interpretation of scripture through musical means is prominent, perhaps stimulating him to create a Passion setting on the same basis. Since—apart from the inserted meditative movements—the Passion text drew entirely on a single biblical narrative from the Gospel of John, Bach was stimulated by the challenge of mirroring its special characteristics throughout an extended setting. At the head of the work a carefully chosen biblical *dictum* drawn from Psalm 8 (slightly modified, expanded, and given a Christological twist) set the tone for the entire work.

For most of the following year Bach was occupied with a cantata cycle of a wholly different kind. Based on a series of Lutheran chorales, this cycle—the so-called chorale cantatas—retains the idea of sequential interpretation, but now in a form that is dictated by the chorales in question. In the spring of 1725, however, Bach re-performed the *St. John Passion* with modifications that might in part have been influenced by the chorale cantata cycle. From that point on the composition of chorale cantatas breaks off. Then, soon after Easter, we find once again that Bach engages deeply with John's Gospel, this time in a sequence of post-Easter cantatas that extend to the end of the 1724–25 cycle, on Trinity Sunday. This occurrence is remarkable in that the aforementioned modifications to the *St. John Passion* that year substantially lessened its Johannine qualities. From a purely liturgicotheological standpoint it seems anomalous, but from the perspective of Bach's awakened interest in the special qualities of John's Gospel we can, in fact, speak of qualities that are shared by the 1724 *St. John Passion* and the 1725 post-Easter cantatas. Although not temporally contiguous, those works are bonded by theological and musical qualities that derive specifically from John and the placement of readings from the Fourth Gospel in the liturgical year. Those readings aid in articulating the particular character of the post-Easter season.

More specifically, after what was in Leipzig the musically silent season of Lent, the period from Good Friday through Easter and the weeks that followed, including Ascension Day, Pentecost and Trinity Sunday—a fifty-nine-day stretch in toto—was the most concentrated of the liturgical year in terms of musical performances, rivaled only by the Christmas/Epiphany season. Spanning two of the three principal feasts of the year, Easter and Pentecost, each of which was celebrated with cantata performances for three consecutive days, this time period involved the performance of a Passion and fourteen cantatas. And because there are an unusually large number of Gospel readings from John in the liturgy of the post-Easter season—the eight-week period extending from Easter through Trinity Sunday—it is highly unified theologically. We might therefore expect a measure of consistency in the cantatas for those occasions. And this would apply, of course, to any year in which cantatas were produced (since the feast days and their readings remain the same from year to year). This is what we find in 1725. In 1724, however, we have only sporadic signs of what might be called "Johannine" qualities in the post-Easter cantatas. During his first year in Leipzig, 1723–24, Bach, whether because of the need to build up a body of cantatas for weekly performance (*Jahrgang*) or because of external pressures, drew extensively on works composed at earlier times, and sometimes for other occasions, reworking them as necessary for their new purposes. The 1723–24 cantata cycle therefore does not exhibit a sense of overall consistency, and the post-Easter cantatas are no exception.

The cycle of the following year, 1724–25, however, contains what is certainly one of the most consistent sustained projects of Bach's creative life, the aforementioned chorale cantatas, which extend from the beginning of the cycle through a period of about nine-and-a-half months, from the first Sunday after Trinity 1724 (June 11) until the feast of the Annunciation 1725 (March 25). Thus, for about three-quarters of the liturgical year Bach was involved primarily with an ongoing compositional project, producing an amazing series of cantatas of a single basic type, cantatas that have long been recognized as crowning achievements in the genre and his work as a whole. Inexplicably, however, those cantatas came to an end just before Easter. On Good Friday Bach re-performed the *St. John Passion* with alterations that have never been completely explained. After that, his cantata for Easter Day was a parody of a secular work (and was later revised as the *Easter Oratorio*, BWV 249), whereas the next three surviving cantatas, for Easter Monday and the first and second Sundays after Easter, reverted to a textual type that had appeared four times in the post-Easter cantatas of the previous year (the cantata for Easter Tuesday has not survived). Then, for the remaining nine Sundays and feast days, Bach set cantata texts written by the Leipzig poetess Mariane von Ziegler, producing a group of cantatas now known widely as the "Ziegler" cantatas. Significantly, those cantatas extend only to what for Bach was the end of the annual cycle, Trinity Sunday, so their texts were presumably contracted in some manner to complete the cycle. Since the end of the cycle was determined by the time that Bach began composing cantatas in Leipzig (the first Sunday after Trinity, 1724), and not by the beginning of the liturgical year in Advent, the fact that the Ziegler cantatas extended only to Trinity Sunday must probably be understood, at least partially, in pragmatic terms. That is, they completed two-years-worth of cantatas, but not two unified cantata cycles.

Nevertheless, as it happens, Trinity Sunday also marks a point of liturgical division in the year—between the post-Easter/Pentecost season and the Trinity season—so that Ziegler's "commission" has a distinct liturgical aspect as well. It is probably significant, therefore, that some of the traits of the first three post-Easter cantatas (those whose texts were *not* written by Ziegler) are shared with the Ziegler cantatas, a situation that leads one to suspect that Ziegler, knowing those texts, accommodated her own poetry to them in some respects. For this reason, it seems logical to include the cantata for Easter Day and the three cantatas just mentioned within the framework of the works for the season from Easter to Pentecost/Trinity, which is liturgically unified. In addition, Bach's music for these non-Ziegler cantatas fits very well with that of the Ziegler cantatas for the remainder of the season (including the appearance of the rarely used *violoncello piccolo* in the cantatas of both authors). Perhaps Bach, knowing that Ziegler could produce texts only from the third Sunday after Easter (Jubilate) on, attempted to create a degree of consistency throughout the season by musical means. The impression created by these events is that Bach intended a full chorale-cantata cycle for 1724–25, but for reasons that have never been discovered—such as the death or illness of the author of the texts—had to discontinue the project just before Easter. Mariane von Ziegler was presumably engaged to write texts for the remainder of the season, but for some reason (perhaps insufficient advance notice or because the first few cantata texts for the post-Easter season had already been prepared the preceding year but not set to music that year) did not begin her texts until the third Sunday after Easter.

Whatever the reasons for that situation, we are arguably none the poorer; Mariane von Ziegler produced a set of texts that project a striking indebtedness to the Gospel of John, drawing frequently on excerpts (*dicta*) from the Fourth Gospel for the texts of the opening movements and in several cases for other movements as well. And Bach responded to those texts with musical settings that, although very different in character from the monumental nature of the chorale cantatas, present us with some of his most subtle compositions. The Ziegler cantatas are often highly intimate in character, frequently utilizing instruments, above all the *violoncello piccolo*, which mirror aspects of the Johannine Gospel readings closely. This quality invites us to consider them from the liturgical standpoint, to broaden our understanding of how Bach interpreted the unique character of the post-Easter season and its close association with John's Gospel, for which we already have considerable evidence in the *St. John Passion*.

With the *St. John Passion* we have a different set of "problems" owing to the fact that while the 1725 revision survives in full, the 1724 original version survives in a form that must be reconstructed in part from later versions.[3] This reconstruction, although secure in its presentation of the basic structure of the work (e.g., its movement sequence and their keys), nevertheless leaves numerous questions regarding precise details of instrumentation, melodic elaboration, and the like, in doubt. Bach's further revision of the Passion around 1730, however, restores most of the movements that had been replaced in 1725, while introducing new changes; his fourth major involvement with the Passion, near the beginning and ending of the last decade of his life, restores the basic structure of the work as it existed in 1724: that is, its sequence of movements and keys. This fourth version survives in a set of parts from near the end of Bach's life as well as in a new score whose first twenty pages were copied ca. 1739–40 by Bach himself, after which it was continued to the end by a copyist, perhaps as late as the last year of the composer's life. As Alfred Dürr remarks, the version presented by the final set of parts is "to all intents and purposes" a return to the first version of 1724.[4] And the new score preserves essentially the same version, the autograph portion presumably embodying Bach's considered reflection on its prior performance history, whereas the remainder must have been copied directly from a lost score, probably the original one (which might well have contained many alterations in Bach's hand). In the differences between this score and the final set of parts we find numerous revisions of detail and instrumentation, even of the text, some of which reveal that here, as in many other works, Bach continued to elaborate the basic original conception of the work. Since the score was not fully overseen by Bach, we cannot take it without question as his final word. But that its completion was left to a copyist surely indicates that by the last decade of his life Bach had a "settled" conception of the Passion in his mind, one that corresponds closely to that of 1724.

Modern performances, and the prestigious edition prepared by Arthur Mendel for the new Bach edition, greatly favor a "version" of the Passion that was never heard as such in Bach's lifetime, but which is rooted in the structural correspondences between the first and fourth versions. It incorporates changes from the end of Bach's life that are viewed as improvements to the original version, but not those

---

[3] The basic work on which our knowledge of the versions of the *St. John Passion* is based was that of Arthur Mendel, *Kritischer Bericht* to NBA Series 2, vol. 4 (*Johannes-Passion*), Leipzig: Deutscher Verlag für Musik, 1974. For English-language summaries of the implications of this research see Alfred Dürr, *Johann Sebastian Bach's "St. John Passion": Genesis, Transmission and Meaning* (1988), trans. Alfred Clayton (Oxford: Oxford University Press, 2000); Daniel Melamed, *Hearing Bach's Passions* (New York: Oxford University Press, 2005).

[4] Dürr, *Johann Sebastian Bach's "St. John Passion,"* 9. On the versions and the text revisions, see the penultimate section of ch. 1: "The 1725 version of the St. John Passion in outline."

that are viewed, at least implicitly, as having been altered for external reasons. It therefore involves aesthetic rather than purely historical judgments on the value of some of the revisions. The issue is not that of unilateral preference for an early or late version of the work but of seeking out what appears to be the most satisfactory (but not by any means the only) version of any given movement or passage, from a multiplicity of standpoints, historical, aesthetic, and theological. Unsatisfactory as this may sound, especially from the standpoint of strict historical fidelity to the individual performances (insofar as they can be reconstructed), it is possible that it is the closest we can come to Bach's intentions for the work.

Within this uncertain environment it may seem that speaking of the *St. John Passion* as a concrete entity, separate from its various performances, is a questionable undertaking. Daniel Melamed expresses this view in his survey of the versions of the work, pronouncing that the second version represents a "new setting." At the same time, both Melamed and Alfred Dürr point out that "version IV, undertaken many years later, musically speaking was essentially a return to Version I" (except for some instrumental and textual changes).[5] And Arthur Mendel, who edited the Passion for the New Bach Edition, makes the same point.[6] For this reason, but also—and principally—because of its far greater integrity as a setting of John's Passion account than the version of 1725, I view the first and last versions of the *St. John Passion* as representing a single primary form of the work. Although it was revised in the final version in numerous matters of detail (particularly instrumental usages and, in a few cases, the text), those revisions do not in any sense seriously alter the Johannine character of the original 1724 conception of the work.[7]

From the fact that the fourth version of the *St. John Passion* is essentially a return to that of the first in concept, as well as the fact that the third version moves significantly in the direction of that restoration, it is important to recognize that the correspondence in basic structure between the first and fourth versions articulates a conception that is considerably more Johannine in character than does that of 1725. The third version might be thought the most Johannine of all, in that it restores much of the original version that had been altered in 1725, and it removes the two recitative additions from the Synoptic Gospels that appear in the other versions. But the latter feature, while it may appear to have arisen from a desire to be faithful to John's exact narrative, led to changes in the structure of the work that seriously modify its character at the points in question—in my view adversely,

---

[5] Dürr, *Johann Sebastian Bach's "St. John Passion,"* 9; Daniel Melamed, *Hearing Bach's Passions* (New York: Oxford University Press, 2005), 74–75.

[6] Arthur Mendel, *Kritischer Bericht* to NBA Series 2, 4:117–20.

[7] As Christoph Wolff remarks (*Johann Sebastian Bach: The Learned Musician* [New York: W. W. Norton, 2000], 294), the revision that Bach began around 1739 was "intended to preserve the work in an autograph fair copy and to restore the basic structure of the original version." The key words here are "basic structure," meaning that the movement sequence (including the keys) is the same for both the first and fourth versions. The ongoing revision of details of text and instrumentation did not affect that in any way.

at least in the first of the two instances. From this position, we may say that the second version is the truly anomalous one, standing apart from the others in its altered character, whereas the third version represents an imperfect restoration, aesthetically speaking. It appears that there were at least two entirely different kinds of revision over the two-and-a-half decades of its performance history. One involved the kinds of changes that Bach might have been expected to make in the way of elaborating and amplifying the original conception, especially if that original form had been produced somewhat in haste. The other seems more likely to have been produced in response to outside influences, whether because of the interruption of the chorale cantata cycle, or of theological considerations, or (most likely) both. Some (presumed) outside influences, especially those of 1725, lessened the theological and aesthetic unity of the work, whereas others were probably merely the result of musical exigencies, such as the lack of lute or viole d'amore players for the arioso "Betrachte, meine Seele" and the aria "Erwäge."

For these and other reasons I have elected to discuss the *St. John Passion* in what I consider to be its primary form, that of the combined first and last versions—that is, the 1724 performance—which Bach restored in the 1740s, albeit with changes in the elaboration of melodic details, the instrumentation and revision of a few texts (so that, as Daniel Melamed remarks, the restoration was not total). Some present-day Bach scholarship inclines toward the view that we do not know enough about the purpose of the revisions and changes to proclaim any one version as the "true" *St. John Passion*. However, that the *Fassung erster Hand* of 1724 and the *Fassung letzter Hand* of the 1740s are in essence the same version speaks strongly to me, especially when taken in conjunction with the markedly more unified Johannine character of that version, a conception that was probably modified in the intervening versions for external rather than artistic reasons. The different emphases among the versions of the *St. John Passion* (primarily two) are considerable enough for us to say that the one projects a consistent and unified vision of the Passion in John much more than the other. Admittedly, we do not know what prompted the revisions that began in 1725 and continued (with still other changes and modifications) for at least one other performance. But from a famous remark of Bach's concerning one of his Passions (which one is unknown, although the *St. John Passion* is the prime candidate), it is clear that at some time objections had been made on account of its text. Without knowing exactly what he was referring to, we can certainly imagine that something of this kind was involved in some of the revisions to the *St. John Passion*.

Thus, we may note that the 1725 version of the Passion is tantalizingly suggestive that it was in part modified from its original form so as to fit more closely within the chorale cantata cycle. To some extent, the two versions of the *St. John Passion* mirror some of the prominent characteristics of the two very different cycles within which they were first performed. But the 1725 version of the Passion was surely not considered as a permanent component of the chorale cantata cycle, or even an independent form of the work. Not only did Bach continue to modify the work, returning to something very close to the 1724 version near the end of his life, but also one of the most telling of the 1725 alterations—the introduction of the aria dialog with chorus, "Himmel reiße, Welt erbebe"/"Jesu, deine Passion" in Part 1—is so illogically placed in terms of its text (which responds to events at Golgotha in Part 2), that it must have been conceived as a temporary measure from the start. Ulrich Leisinger's view of the 1725 *St. John Passion* as "nur ein Notbehelf" suggests as much.[8]

The problems surrounding the versions of the *St. John Passion* and the breaking off of the chorale cantatas are of considerable historical interest. At the same time, however, the *St. John Passion* and the cantatas that followed it in spring 1725 invoke another, very different, set of ideas broader in scope than those just described and more interesting as a field of investigation. For the liturgical season in question, from the Holy Week/Passiontide and Easter to Pentecost/Trinity—traditionally known as the "great fifty days" (the seven weeks from Easter to Pentecost)—is not only unified in its theological character, but it is also the oldest and most fundamental part of the Christian liturgy, embodying the very core of Christian belief as it arose in relation to Judaism in the first century and reflected in the books of the New Testament (hereafter NT). This was well understood in Bach's time. In addition, the post-Easter weeks comprise the only time period in the liturgical year when the majority of the Gospel readings for the individual Sundays and feast days are drawn from John, the Gospel that has been known since ancient times as the "spiritual" one because of its focus on the ideas embodied in Jesus's often extended discourses rather than on the narrative of historical events. With this aspect of John's Gospel as its central theme, the great fifty days, as a symbolic transition from the era of Jesus and the disciples to that of the church under the Holy Spirit, has always been understood to embody, more than any other time of the year, the core questions around which Christianity arose, questions that are particularly prominent in John.

In addition, John had a special resonance within Lutheranism: not only was it Luther's favorite Gospel but also the part of the Gospel known as the Farewell Discourse (Jn 14–17, directly before the Passion) was his favorite part, on which he preached a set of sermons between Easter and Pentecost 1537 and which he later declared his best book.[9] From this extended discourse, comprising Jesus's last

---

[8] Ulrich Leisinger, "Die zweite Fassung der Johannes-Passion von 1725: Nur ein Notbehelf?" in *Bach in Leipzig/Bach und Leipzig*, Leipzig Beiträge zur Bach-Forschung, vol. 5, ed. Ulrich Leisinge, 29–44 (Hildesheim: Georg Olms Verlag, 2002).

[9] For some authors, including most theologians of Bach's time, the Farewell Discourse proper includes only chs. 14–16, whereas ch. 17, addressed to God rather than to the disciples, is treated separately, as Jesus's prayer to the Father, in his role as high priest. See, for example, Johann Anastasius Freylinghausen's twenty-six chapter study *Das Hohepriesterliche Gebeth unsers hochgelobten Heilandes JEsu CHristi aus dem XVII Capitel Johannis . . .* (Halle, 1719).

words to the disciples, spoken at the Last Supper, five of the spring Gospel readings were taken; the other Johannine readings were chosen from other chapters so as to address the same or very similar themes, most of them centering on the words of Jesus. In light of the fact that it was John's emphasis on Jesus's words that led Luther to praise the Gospel so highly, it is significant that of the 1725 Bach cantatas for this time period, eight begin (and one ends) with a motto-like excerpt (a *dictum*) drawn from John. Another begins with a chorale paraphrase of such a *dictum*, while several of the cantatas have either paraphrases or second *dicta* based on John in other movements. Moreover, eleven of those *dicta* are the words of Jesus (more if we count paraphrases); this, too, is a unique occurrence among the Bach cantatas. It reflects that the sequence of Gospel readings for the great fifty days is occupied with the crucial question for the disciples and the church of life in the world when Jesus is no longer physically present, a theme that leads to Pentecost and the celebration of the role of the Holy Spirit within the church.

Thus the Sunday that initiates the sequence of post-Easter Johannine readings, Quasimodogeniti (the Sunday after Easter), establishes, with the aid of both Gospel and epistle readings from John, the analogy between the disciples and the church. Quasimodogeniti is traditionally the Sunday associated with Jesus's "breathing" the Spirit into the disciples and giving them their mission, as told in the Gospel for the day. In this context it is significant that Bach's 1725 cantata for this Sunday, *Am Abend aber desselbigen Sabbats* (BWV 42), is the only cantata in his oeuvre to directly mention the Jews, which it does in the context of the long-established practice of drawing an analogy between the situation of the disciples in first-century Jerusalem and the place of the Christian church in the world. That context dictated much of what follows in the remainder of the 1725 cantata sequence, which further alludes to the interaction of Jews and Christians in the first century. The cantata for Exaudi (the sixth Sunday after Easter), *Sie werden euch in den Bann tun* (BWV 183), for example, refers to the disciples being excluded from the synagogue, and was widely interpreted by Lutherans as excommunication by the pope. And the cantata for Trinity Sunday, *Es ist ein trotzig und verzagt Ding um aller Menschen Herzen* (BWV 176), takes Nicodemus, named by John "a high official among the Jews," and described as such toward the end of John's Passion narrative as well, as symbol for human qualities that are viewed pejoratively, but at the same time related to the need for spiritual rebirth through baptism, the subject of the Gospel for Trinity Sunday. Ultimately, as some Lutherans believed, Nicodemus became a symbol for early Christianity in his eventual emergence from the "darkness" of Judaism. In this respect Cantata 176 looks back to the meaning of Quasimodogeniti ("as newborn babes"), which, taking its name from the Mass introit (1 Pet 2:2), was known from ancient times as the *Domenica in albis*, the Sunday on which new members, baptized on Easter Day, were confirmed and admitted to participation in the Holy Eucharist (taking off the white baptismal robes—hence the name, meaning "white Sunday"). In Bach's time the memory of such ancient associations, bound up with the very origins of the church, was still very much alive and generated analogies to the Lutheran church. In the 1725 Bach cantatas for this time period we have a unique opportunity of considering how the most fundamental tenets of Lutheranism and its inheritance from the ancient church were mirrored in a sequence of musical art works.

It is clear that the concurrence of unusual features surrounding this group of works involves some that are ancient, some that go back to the Reformation era, some that are particular to Mariane von Ziegler's texts, and some that are entirely attributable to Bach. It seems possible, therefore, that a factor behind at least some of the anomalous features mentioned earlier was the unique liturgical character of the great fifty days—that is, that Bach and his librettists, perhaps influenced by the Leipzig theological establishment, intended to create a sequence of works that would mirror the traditional character of the season as a whole. Although the interruption of the chorale cantata cycle was most likely the result of external circumstances, Bach and Ziegler seized on the opportunity in a positive manner, emphasizing the qualities mentioned earlier, especially the focus on Jesus's words, as primary characteristics of the weeks that form the transition from Easter to Pentecost. From this standpoint we may consider that Bach (with input from Ziegler, perhaps, and the Leipzig authorities), knowing that the chorale cantatas could not be completed as a cycle within the 1724–25 time frame, and perhaps already with the plan in mind of completing the cycle in the future, formed the conception of creating a subcycle to mirror the character of the liturgically most ancient and central part of the year.[10]

Whatever the historical circumstances relating to the revisions to the *St. John Passion* and the breaking off of the chorale cantatas—and, again, we may never

---

[10] At the spring 2011 meeting of the Cambridge Bach Colloquium, Stephen Crist made the interesting suggestion that Bach might have intentionally ended the chorale cantatas of 1724–25 with BWV 1, *Wie schön leuchtet der Morgenstern*, for the feast of the annunciation (March 25), rather than having that decision forced upon him by external circumstances. Crist made the point that Cantata 1, the fortieth cantata of the cycle, was performed just four days after Bach's fortieth birthday. And, with an unusually long opening chorale fantasia, it might be viewed as Bach's ending the series with a tour de force, so to speak. Although there is no evidence for this suggestion, and the fact that Bach in later years wrote chorale cantatas that seem obviously intended to expand the cycle of 1724–25 by filling in gaps would seem to deny it, a couple of further points may be mentioned. First, if Bach was conscious of Cantata 1 as number forty in the series, then perhaps the biblical resonance of that number came into play. The annunciation (which sometimes coincided with Palm Sunday) comes toward the end of the forty-day Lenten season; at the same time, it marks a new beginning because of its celebrating the conception of Jesus. Based on Nicolai's eschatological chorale, it ends with the lines "Komm, du schöne Freudenkrone, bleib nicht lange, deiner wart ich mit Verlangen," that Nicolai used to end the first book of his *Praxis Vitae Aeternae*, and that Heinrich Müller used to end the first book of his *Himmlischer Liebes-Kuß*, in both cases books that culminated in the vision of eternity. Bach's Cantata 61, *Nun komm, der Heiden Heiland* (Weimar, 1714), for the first Sunday in Advent, also ends with these lines, where they culminate the most pronounced reflection of the four senses of scripture in all his cantatas. There is, admittedly, not enough evidence for Crist's hypothesis. But if it were true, it would lend support to the idea that the 1725 post-Easter cantatas might have been intended to form a coherent sequence.

know just what they were—the Passion, in its first/last version/s, and the 1725 post-Easter cantatas offer us a unique opportunity to consider Bach's response, in a sustained manner, to the special qualities associated throughout the centuries with the Gospel of John. Many questions, often of unusual breadth regarding the subject of Bach and theology, are involved in the study of these works and their historical circumstances. This book is my response to those questions, which I set forth in Part One, before undertaking an extended study of the *St. John Passion* (Part Two) and the 1725 post-Easter cantatas (Part Three).

I have written about the *St. John Passion* several times before. I hope that the present new study of the work, which retains the basic outlook of my earlier studies but goes more deeply into many questions, both musical and theological, will confirm my view that the *St. John Passion* (primarily in its first/last version) is a virtuoso piece in the musical allegorizing of theological themes. What makes it such is an understanding on Bach's part of John's particular vision of the significance of the Passion and, of course, the translation of that understanding into music. For Bach the entire process might well have been primarily intuitive, but for us it necessarily involves much historical investigation of various kinds.

The question of the purpose of, and methodology involved in, such historical investigation is one that needs to be clarified. My approach follows the conception of history according to which it is often not so much documents or sources of a direct kind that bear the meaning of history as it is the background to those sources: the underlying thoughts and thought patterns to which the documents refer. In this view, it is often not so much what the authors of documents stated directly that is of greatest importance but what they took for granted. To choose an example from the subject of theology that is relevant to our understanding of Bach: in Lutheran theological treatises from the time of Luther to that of Bach and beyond we find ubiquitous references to God's *Rath* (sometimes *Raht*, in the most common spellings of the time; the word is now spelled *Rat*), which is often casually spoken of simply to mean God's will or counsel. (In order to preserve the usage of most Lutheran treatises from Bach's time and earlier, I retain the spelling *Rath* throughout). The word in German has a wide range of meanings, encompassing advice, authority, counsel, and the like, and these are common meanings in the theological literature. But, in a manner somewhat analogous to the way scientists speak of a "strong" and "weak" anthropic principle, God's *Rath* (sometimes *Rathschluß* or *Rathschlag*) can mean something much more specific than we may immediately suspect. And in theological contexts the more common, or "weaker" meanings always refer in some way to the larger, or "stronger" meaning: that of God's plan for the salvation of humanity, not only in its meaning as God's will in general, which is not fully accessible to humankind, but according to its objective aspect, which involves a sequence of events taking place in history and recounted in scripture. This objective aspect, sometimes described by the Lutheran authors with the term *Vorsatz* (plan, intention) or *oikonomia* ("economy," meaning God's "disposition" of history) is very close to the modern concept of salvation history, one of the primary scriptural sources for which is bound up with the Greek word that Luther translated as God's *Rat.*[11]

I take up this concept in chapter 2, with particular reference to a full study of the subject by the theologian Johann Jacob Rambach (1693–1735) that Bach had in his collection of theological books. There and throughout this book I argue that the concept of God's plan for the redemption of humankind is fundamental to the design of the *St. John Passion*, underlying Bach's treatment of classic Johannine themes such as irony, dualism, and determinism, and providing explanation not only for the well-known symmetrical aspects of the work, but also for why Bach set the chorus of the Roman soldiers who divide and cast lots for Jesus's cloak as a permutation fugue, why he used the music associated in Part 1 with the name "Jesus of Nazareth" in five choruses with four different texts, and a host of other musical decisions. As we will see, the succession of eight meditative movements that are added to the biblical narrative in Part 1 follows closely that of the themes associated with discussions of God's plan, described by theologians of the time as the "Ordnung des Heils" (ordering of salvation). That is, after an introductory chorus that proclaims the equivalence of Jesus and the God of the Hebrew Bible or Old Testament (OT hereafter), it first outlines stages that center on Jesus and which correspond to the plan itself—Jesus' divinity and foreknowledge, love as having brought him to the Passion, his obedience to God's will, the purpose of the Passion—then further stages that center on Peter as representative of the response of sinful humanity: following Jesus, acknowledgment of sin and guilt, penitence and prayer. In its principal structural divisions, especially the shift from the tonal *ambitus* of g/B♭ to that of A/f♯ (see ch. 5), Part 1 of the Passion was molded so as to embody this well-known pattern, which is suggested already in John's narrative and amplified in Bach's setting. Thus Part 1 takes on the character of an introduction to the trial that comes in Part 2.

I set this forth in greater detail in chapters 4–8. In the present context the main point is that in order to understand Bach's setting of sacred texts we often need to range well beyond their immediate contexts to discover the meaning that lies behind them. And this very quality of layered meaning is a foremost principle behind the composition of the texts—a version of the ancient principles of scripture inter-

---

[11] A useful study of salvation history is that of Hans Conzelmann, *The Theology of St. Luke* (originally published in German as *Die Mitte der Zeit* [Tübingen: J. C. B. Mohr, 1953]), trans. Geoffrey Buswell (Philadelphia: Fortress Press 1961). See 151, n. 3 for references to the appearance of the word in question in Luke/Acts and elsewhere in scripture. Conzelmann associates the concept of salvation history with Luke. For a study that brings out its particular applicability to John, see Oscar Cullmann, *Christ and Time,* trans. Floyd V. Filson, rev. ed. (London: SCM Press, 1962), xxiii–xxiv. See also Catherine Mowry LaCugna, *God for Us: The Trinity and Christian Life* (New York: Harper Collins, 1991), 21–52. For Luther's translation, as it first appeared, see *Biblia, das ist, die gantze Heilige Schrifft Deudsch. Mart. Luth. Wittemberg . . . 1534*. (The Luther Bible of 1534, complete facsimile edition); two vols. plus a cultural-historical introduction by Stephan Füssel (Cologne: Taschen, 2003); vol. 2, Acts 20 (n.p.): "denn ich habe euch nichts verhalten / das ich nicht verkündiget hette / alle den rat Gottes" (in modern Bibles Acts 20:21).

pretation that are commonly known as the "four senses of scripture" (see ch. 2). In acquiring knowledge of such schemes of thought we need to remember that in Bach's surroundings no such extensive research as we may have to undertake was required. The concepts in question were embodied in the thought of the time and its inheritance from prior centuries of religious thought. Often it was only learned theologians who thought about such concepts directly or systematically (or consciously); but the ideas themselves were central to the daily lives and beliefs of countless individuals of the time, regardless of their learning. It is a fallacy to confuse the effort and complexity of our scholarly endeavor to understand the theological concepts of Bach's time with the nature of his own understanding. Not only the theological subject matter of Bach's cantatas but also their musical structures necessitate investigating the background concepts according to which the more variegated immediate subjects were presented and depicted musically.

Some scholars will, of course, disagree with this perspective on Bach and theology. But I wish to be up front about what the reader can expect to find here. I have divided it into three parts, the first of which (chs. 1–3) introduces the reasons for this study, including aspects of Bach's cantata cycles that relate to the works under discussion and how the versions of the *St. John Passion* relate to the cantata cycles (ch. 1). Chapter 2 takes up a broad range of themes relating to the concept of God's *Rath* and the hermeneutic principles that underlie the Bach cantatas; and chapter 3 the liturgical year, with special reference to the great fifty days from Easter to Pentecost, and the role of the Gospel of John both within it and within Lutheranism. Part Two is a five-chapter study of the *St. John Passion*, viewed in part in conjunction with the theologian August Hermann Francke's 1716 set of sermons on John's Passion narrative. The last of these chapters (ch. 8) is designed to place the Passion and its central issues in the context of a broader spectrum of Bach's work. It extends beyond the Passion to include other works, such as the Credo of the *Mass in B minor*, that relate, in the "background" sense I have described, to the concept of God's *Rath* as it appears in the *St. John Passion*. Finally, chapters 9–14 take up the 1725 post-Easter cantatas in some detail, including a separate chapter (ch. 11) on their instrumental characteristics.

This study centers, therefore, on what is perhaps the most interesting as well as problematic instance of a potential, or ideal musico-theological subgrouping among the Bach cantata cycles: that comprised by the *St. John Passion* (in its 1724 original form), the 1725 Easter cantata that eventually became the *Easter Oratorio*, and the sequence of twelve cantatas that directly followed in the spring of 1725 (the cantatas from Easter to Trinity Sunday 1725, minus the cantata for Easter Tuesday, which has not survived). Although it did not exist as a performance sequence at any time during Bach's lifetime, and might never have been intended to, Bach's restoration of something close to the original version of the *St. John Passion* near the end of his life does seem to reflect an "ideal" conception of the work, one whose closest equivalent among Bach's various performances was that of 1724.

Although this book occasionally offers hypotheses concerning Bach's cycles, they do not constitute its main theme, which centers on the individual works themselves. That would remain the case even if every hypothesis could be proven true. I believe that the study of individual works—the true center of our involvement with Bach—embodies profounder kinds of information regarding the spirit of their time and its claims for universality than does the purely historical focus on their cultural, historical, or even religious surroundings and trappings. Regardless of whether an external event caused the change in the cantata type after Easter 1725, the season from the Passion and Easter to Pentecost/Trinity is a highly interesting and important one that drew very detailed responses from Bach. Certain of the cantatas from this time period are of truly extraordinary subtlety, grappling with such questions as the nature of the experience of the Spirit within. In contrast to the majestic, monumental character of many of the chorale cantatas, these works often mirror, expecially in their instrumental characteristics (taken up in ch. 11), the intimacy that belongs to the original contexts of Jesus's words, and to the event whose celebration is the goal of the sequence as a whole, the coming of the Holy Spirit. In all cases the musical qualities that distinguish these cantatas derive directly from the character of the great fifty days and its indebtedness to the fourth evangelist. Focusing directly on the works immediately brings out the fact that distinguishable theological (and musical) qualities derive from multifarious sources. Considering the texts of the 1725 post-Easter cantatas, we recognize input from the author/s of John's Gospel and its countless interpreters through the centuries, from the many anonymous figures of different eras who created and established the liturgical year, from the authors who formed the Lutheran tradition as Ziegler and Bach received it, from the Leipzig theological establishment (a presumed influence), from Mariane von Ziegler, and finally from Bach himself. Bach, however, operated in a dual capacity, since his was the only stage to embody another set of influences: those embracing inherited musical traditions and contemporary practices. At the same time, certain of the musical traditions in question had many points of contact with the theological ones via what I call the Lutheran "metaphysical" tradition in music theory, whose principal exponents, following Luther himself, saw distinct connections between music and theology. They therefore articulated forms of musical hermeneutics that had a considerable impact on musical composition. In the long chain of influences surrounding the cantatas of spring 1725, Bach is the end point, the final "filter" through which these many influences pass; the fact that we understand the cantatas as primarily "his" works is the result of his special ability as a composer of music to weave the many strands he inherited from numerous identifiable and unidentifiable sources into the forms we know as his church cantatas.

The cantatas of spring 1725 illustrate, perhaps more than any other group of his works, that Bach's cantata cycles sometimes feature successions whose musico-theological meaning is greatly illuminated by our considering them within the context of the season of the liturgical year to which they belong. It might be said, of course, that *all* Bach's sacred cantatas profit from being viewed in this way; but working within reasonable practical limitations demands that we identify the principles that cause some successions of cantatas to link up with those that precede and follow to a much greater extent than is true of others. Nevertheless, paradoxical as it sounds, the highest level of Bach's activity as cantata composer remains the ground level of the individual work. We cannot value the placement of cantatas within cycles or series, their statistical or comparative features, above our recognition that as individual works (often produced under constrained circumstances) they are among the monuments of human achievement. But, that said, it must be maintained that those individual works are often enormously illuminated by the distant, or not so distant, light of the overarching firmament of the year as a whole.

This book, therefore, follows the principles I set forth in an earlier study, *Analyzing Bach Cantatas* (2000), in which I attempted to illustrate how we might analyze the conjunction of music and theology in the Bach cantatas. Although I did not state the fact baldly there, that book was conceived in large part as an argument that the Bach cantatas lend themselves to close musical analysis as much as any repertoire of multimovement works in the Western musical canon—the Beethoven symphonies, to choose an obvious, and perhaps obviously provocative, example. I do not expect, on the basis of published analyses, that this statement will go unresisted. There is, in fact, very little in the Bach literature to suggest that such a view is widely accepted, or even acceptable in principle, and much that goes against it, at least implicitly. Following the great successes surrounding the philological study of the Bach works in the twentieth century, the study of their history has all too often been whittled down to that of speculation regarding earlier versions and the like, not infrequently on the basis of insufficient evidence from the manuscript sources. In the play with source evidence the works are sometimes lost in the shuffle. Continued argument remains necessary in order to show that the designs of the Bach cantatas are not merely the accidental products of external circumstances, however much some of them might have been conceived or—as in the case of the *St. John Passion*—modified subsequent to their composition in relation to such circumstances. More than is true of any other of the "first tier" composers, a major part of Bach's work—the cantatas—has suffered from the belief that as "occasional" music it is inherently separate from aesthetic questions, of which analysis is the primary one (and *tonal* analysis a crucial aspect). We may not completely accept Donald Francis Tovey's view that "the main lesson of the analysis of great music is a lesson of organic unity," but the unquestioned acceptance of heterogeneity as the inevitable product of circumstances beyond the composer's control is a far more blatant error.

In the case of the Bach cantatas, the "object" of analysis is not merely the notes, a point that I emphasized in *Analyzing Bach Cantatas*. In that book there was not the scope to fully explore the theological aspects of the works; I was intent on making points regarding the relationships of the notes of the separate movements of particular Bach cantatas. I did not argue for "organic unity" as such; but hoped to show not only that the cantatas in question formed highly integrated and consistent sequence of movements (from an analytical standpoint), but also that investigating their origins and theological associations led us to understand something of the unity, both musical and theological, behind the impulse to meditation in the language of the Bach cantatas.

I have given considerably more space here to investigation of the theological background ideas that, in my view, served as the "matrix" for Bach's cantata composition. That is, the Bach cantatas and Passions are not simply responses to the biblical narratives on which their Gospels center. They are "reductive" in the sense that they refer constantly to a story that underlies all the others: the aforementioned objective aspect of God's *Rath* (or *Vorsatz*) for the salvation of humanity. Bach's early cantatas often center directly on this idea, and their overall designs, which may be very different from one another, can be shown to descend from it.

This book and a forthcoming one on Cantata 21 are cross-disciplinary in nature, drawing extensively on Lutheran theological writings from Bach's time and before and citing as much as possible from the authors themselves. Despite considerable research into this subject over the past two or three decades, it is not at all well known to Bach scholars, and most definitely not to the general reader or Bach lover. Moreover, a considerable amount of the research that has been done in this area with respect to Bach has not been directed toward showing how deeply it relates to the music. Often there are no musical examples or discussions of the intricate manner in which Bach "allegorized" in musical tones the theological ideas that he knew intimately and probably served as a powerful directing force in his life. The reasons for this lack are many, but one is certainly the unusual complexity of the subject itself, by which I mean not only the effort that is required for us to come to terms with the terminology and thought patterns of an enormous body of erudite theological literature, and the necessary suspension of disbelief it involves for many of us as historians, but also the musical expertise that enables us to imagine *how* Bach might have conceived of the relationship between theology and music.

In this connection, I have decided after considerable reflection not to pursue one of the perennial topics of Johannine theology—that of anti-Judaism—in this study. This decision does not reflect any particular dissatisfaction with either the topic of itself or the manner in which it has been taken up in Bach studies. However, the context of such discussions has never been either sufficiently broad or detailed to make clear the distinction between anti-Judaism and anti-Semitism, or to deal with the question of how the choruses of the crowd in the *St. John Passion* (to choose the aspect that most represents this topic) function within the work as a whole. Many of the anti-Judaic aspects of the Passion stand completely on the surface, immediately recognizable even to those with little or no musical understanding. This is especially true of the so-called *turba* choruses, above all those associated with Jesus's trial, the very movements of the Passion that exhibit a strong sense of internal organization as well. In many of those choruses Bach projects a very pejorative view of Jesus's antagonists, sometimes the Roman soldiers but more often the Jews, by means of frenzied musical styles, chromaticism, and the like. And in another set of choruses, five in all—whose music is initially assigned to the arresting party in search of "Jesus of Nazareth" and afterwards to choruses of the Jews in the trial—Bach confronts two conflicting viewpoints, that of the Jews as presented in the historical narrative and that of the Christians of later times up to and including Bach's and beyond. This type of conflict, for which John's Gospel is famous, is a prominent feature of the *St. John Passion* in both its text and its musical styles. The meaning of Bach's repeating the music of what I call the "Jesus of Nazareth" choruses is not obvious at all, but is in fact a very direct reflection of John's literary style and anti-Judaic perspective. It is also related to Luther's concept of the "hidden" God (*Deus absconditus*) who lays the cross upon the faithful for the purpose of leading them to salvation, the view that Christian believers become "conformable" to Christ in his human sufferings. Although it is historically demonstrable, arguing for it is easily misinterpreted as adherence to the beliefs of sixteenth- to eighteenth-century Lutheranism. For that reason I must emphasize that I am not a theologian nor an advocate or critic of theology. Rather, as a historian-musician, I attempt to set forth how Bach's understanding of John, filtered through the perspective of Lutheran orthodoxy, influenced the design of one of his most prominent works. In such an endeavor suspending disbelief is a constant state of mind. If that sounds too negative, let me add that I hold to Woodrow Wilson's belief that "few things are more benighting than the condescension of one age for another."[12]

To go more deeply into the question of John's anti-Judaism, as it relates to Bach, is another matter, fraught with problems surrounding the relationship of the historical (anti-Judaism) and the contemporary (anti-Semitism). Fundamentally, it involves making clear distinctions between John's writings as they are interpreted by scholars today and by those of Bach's time, as well as considering carefully how passages from John are interpreted by the Lutheran traditions Bach may be presumed to have known and by his librettists—that is, through analysis of the texts of the cantatas and Passions—then considering how Bach's music responds to all this. Without setting forth a convincing conception of the structure of the work as a whole, by limiting our discussions to present-day theological perspectives on John in the absence of detailed musical analysis of the *St. John Passion*, we cannot hope to distinguish between Bach's treatment of the Jews and that of the Roman soldiers, for example, or to understand how they fit within the larger religious purpose of the "use" of the Passion for the individual believer, as is stated in virtually every Lutheran theological treatise of the time. The *St. John Passion* is a work whose sense of musical design, or structure, is unusually prominent, to the extent

[12] Woodrow Wilson, "The Variety and Unity of History," in *International University Lectures* (New York: University Alliance Inc., 1909), 42.

that it forms in itself a central part of the musico-allegorical nature of the work. Not merely the well-known repetition of the music of the *turba* choruses, some in symmetrical arrangement, but also many other aspects of the work, such as the key design, melodic interconnectedness between arias and recitatives, and within the recitatives themselves, attest to this quality. In fact, we can speak of a range of interrelationships that extends from the very definite and indisputable to the uncertain and highly questionable. Drawing the line between the two is no easy matter. At the same time, so-called imbalances within the design, such as the very close proximity of certain arias ("Von den Stricken" and "Ich folge dir gleichfalls" in Part 1, "Es ist vollbracht" and "Mein teurer Heiland" in Part 2) seem to cry out for more than purely musical interpretation, to the extent that we may feel a split between the musical structure and its theological correlatives, between the dramatic and the meditative, one that is not nearly as apparent in the *St. Matthew Passion*. In my view there has been a serious gap in the musicological literature between the discussion of topics such as anti-Judaism and that of how the structural design of the Passion reflects the thought of its time.

Again, this book attempts to fill that gap, in order to provide a resource for those who are interested in how one of the greatest of all musical minds shaped his compositions, in his typically very detailed manner, so as to have them function on two levels simultaneously: (1) to fulfill the ideals of the many (but not all) theologians and musicians of his time who believed in such notions as that music could provide a "foretaste" of eternal life, uplift the "spirit" in a more concrete sense than we are accustomed to, even give pleasure to God; and (2) to demonstrate the intricate aesthetic possibilities within the art itself, its tonal and contrapuntal complexities, its structural stability and enduring capacity to arouse affective response. Within that framework Bach's response to John's anti-Judaism has a definite place, but one that demands understanding of the design of the Passion as a whole, an undertaking that involves discussion of numerous intricacies in the construction of individual movements. Bach was a lover of detail, famous in his own time for his complexity of thought; and I have tried to capture as much of it as possible without overburdening the reader. The reader will find discussions of some complexity throughout the book, at times purely theological or musical, but at others with the two intertwined or in tandem. It is not an easy read, but one that will, hopefully, bring the rewards of sustained involvement, especially for those who are prepared to get to know the works themselves, preferably consulting the scores wherever possible.

The post-Easter cantatas that followed the second, altered performance of the *St. John Passion* in 1725 have been investigated once before: in Walter F. Hindermann's 1975 book, *Die nachösterlichen Kantaten des Bachschen Choralkantaten-Jahrgangs*. In going over some of the same ground, I am conscious of considerable indebtedness to a study that, although its focus and some of its more general conclusions are often very different from mine, makes many significant contributions to our understanding of the cantatas for spring 1725. It is not my intention to replace that study. Rather, I encourage the reader to consult Hindermann's book for differing perspectives on many of the same questions. Where we differ most is first of all in the area of musical analysis, which from the standpoint of tonality I attempt to understand in the terms of eighteenth-century theory and terminology (in particular, the circle-of-keys of Johann David Heinichen and the concept of *ambitus* in which it is rooted). We also differ on the interpretation of the relatedness of cantatas one to another, which I do not perceive, as Hindermann does, in terms of underlying motivic elements; these I view as fundamentally ahistorical in nature and in the long run not capable of separating Bach's musical language in general from any specific intentions he might have had for these particular cantatas. And another difference in our outlooks is that I give great weight to understanding the spring 1725 cantata sequence in theological and liturgical terms, which as my title indicates, I perceive as flowing from the Johannine characteristics of the *St. John Passion*.

I have also found useful another, more recent, study of the nine cantatas from spring 1725 whose texts were composed by Mariane von Ziegler, that of Mark Peters's *A Woman's Voice in Baroque Music: Mariane von Ziegler and J. S. Bach* (Burlington, VT: Ashgate, 2008). Although basically limited to the Ziegler cantatas, and centered primarily on the poetess' career and her texts, Peters's close analyses of the 1725 and 1728 versions of Ziegler's texts provide considerable insight into the changing theological emphases and authorship of the revisions that although it cannot claim definitiveness serves as a necessary corrective to the older view that Bach himself was their author. Peters's assessment of Mariane von Ziegler's work and career is unquestionably the best that has been done. In focusing on Ziegler, however, Peters's book has little to say regarding the liturgical character of the post-Easter season and how it is reflected in the Bach cantatas for that time period; his approach to the cantatas therefore involves comparative musical qualities much more than close analysis of individual works. In addition, Peters does not include discussion of the Passion or the first four cantatas that followed it. What I attempt here is something very different from both Peters and Hindermann—namely, to examine each of the works in question closely from both the historico-liturgical and musico-theological standpoints. I argue that, owing to the accidental breaking off of the chorale cantatas, Bach and Ziegler decided to mirror the liturgically unified character of the great fifty days in a set of cantatas that exhibit many of the same qualities, even though, as a last-minute decision, it could not fulfill that ideal in all respects. As individual works, however, the cantatas for this time period often attest, as does the *St. John Passion*, to an astonishing degree of detailed thought of a musico-theological character. In the final analysis that quality, associated with Bach rather than Ziegler, is the key to their equally astonishing artistry.

{ PART I }

Introductory Themes

{1}

Spring 1724 and 1725

The *St. John Passion*: Identity of the Messiah

Any study of Bach's response to the Gospel of John must begin with the *St. John Passion*. Therefore, although that work will be the focus of study for part 2 of this book, we must consider, as an introduction to the themes of the book as a whole, how the *St. John Passion*, in its original version of 1724, sets forth what is John's principal theme: the messianic identity of Jesus. First of all, from almost any standpoint the *St. John Passion*, especially as first performed in spring 1724, exhibits a very substantial sense of musico-theological purpose. And that purpose relates directly to the particular theological, literary, even structural characteristics associated with the Fourth Gospel, qualities that are the root of its being viewed as the spiritual Gospel. It appears that Bach and his librettist/s took pains to project the traditional "Johannine" character of the Passion—always, of course, in the terms according to which the individual characteristics of the various Gospels were understood in the Lutheranism of the seventeenth and early-eighteenth centuries. In itself, this quality in Bach's first Leipzig Passion is striking and unexpected, given that the era of Lutheran orthodoxy was one in which, unlike our own, the harmonizing, rather than the distinguishing, of the characteristics of the four Gospels was the main concern.[1] In that era the historico-philological side of biblical schol-

[1] This quality is particularly the case with the monumental commentary on the Gospels produced in the era of early Lutheran orthodoxy by three scholars, representing the three generations from Luther to the first half of the seventeenth century, the *Harmonia Quattuor Evangelistarum* of Martin Chemnitz (1522–86), Polycarp Leyser (1552–1610), and Johann Gerhard (1582–1637). I have used three editions of the various parts of this commentary: (1) that of the first and second parts of the commentary (those completed by Chemnitz and Leyser), as published under the title *Harmoniae Evangelicae, A praestantissimo Theologo D. Martino Chemnitio primum inchoatae et per D. Polycarpum Lyserum continuatae, Libri Quinque*, . . . (Frankfurt, 1622); (2) the first volume of a projected six-volume German translation, *Die Harmonie derer Heiligen vier Evangelisten, angefangen vom D. Martinus Chemnitius, fortgesetzet vom D. Polycarpus Lyserus, und zu Ende gebracht vom D. Johann Gerhard*, trans. D. Otto

arship, which was very substantial, took second place to the belief that scripture was God's word, unified in its purpose, which was nothing other than the redemption of humanity. It is virtually indisputable that Bach and his librettist/s held this view. Yet, within that framework, it was still possible to bring to the fore the particular characteristics of one evangelist, to emphasize the distinctiveness of one author's account of the Gospel events, not in isolation from other accounts but with an intensified focus on its meaning. The impulse for this quality actually arose from the belief that led to the harmonizing of the Gospels, that God's word, as transmitted with variations, even contradictions among its various human (and therefore fallible) authors, exhibited two dimensions, the historical and the spiritual, though it had but one purpose: the salvation of humanity. This unique characteristic of scripture, which Erich Auerbach highlights from a literary standpoint in the first and second chapters of his book *Mimesis*, permitted the view that one Gospel, that of John, was more "spiritual" than the others, at least in its style, which was widely recognized as unique and unified in outlook.[2] It was to a considerable extent this quality that engaged Bach and his librettists in the creation of the *St. John Passion*.

John's Gospel is celebrated for its literary qualities and its sense of structure, both of which qualities lend it a striking sense of unity and purpose. The Gospel of John is the one that most embodies what was known as the *Christus victor* theory of the atonement, the one that is most concerned with dividing the world into stark oppositions, light and darkness, good and evil, spirit and flesh, truth and falsehood, worlds "above" and "below," and the like. This incorporates a quality that, whatever the thinking of those who originally determined the Gospel readings for the spring liturgy, inevitably sets the followers of Jesus (i.e., the disciples, viewed as analogous to the Christian church) apart from those whom John calls "the Jews" and who in his perspective are not of the "truth." Jesus and the disciples were themselves Jews, of course, and the very framework of their lives, the church they instituted, and the Gospels that formed its cornerstones was entirely that of the Jewish religion. But, in speaking pejoratively of the Jews, John intends a particular distinction, based on only one fact to which, ultimately, all else reduces: the acceptance or non-acceptance of Jesus as the Messiah. Thus, when we consider what it is in John that most underlies its striking sense of unity and purpose—its center—we find that it is the question of the identity of Jesus that John grapples with constantly, the "signs" of and witnesses to that identity and the response of

Nathanael Nicolai, *Erster Theil* (Magdeburg und Leipzig, 1764); (3) a German-language edition published in the United States in a form that was reorganized (and abbreviated) so as to follow the Gospel readings of the liturgical year: *Echt evangelische Auslegung der Sonn- und Festtags-Evangelien des Kirchenjahrs*, 7 vols. (St. Louis, 1872). An English translation in fifteen volumes has been announced by The Center for the Study of Lutheran Orthodoxy (Repristination Press); to date the first three volumes have been published.

[2] Erich Auerbach, *Mimesis: The Representation of Reality in Western Literature*, trans. Willard R. Trask (Princeton, NJ: Princeton University Press, 1953).

the world to it. This thesis was well recognized in the Lutheran tradition of Bach's time and before. August Hermann Francke, for example, devoted his treatise *Christus, der Kern heiliger Schrifft* to a detailed exegesis of the prolog to John's Gospel, addressing in what is by far the most extended of its nine "meditations" the arguments for Jesus's divinity as presented in the prologue. The other eight meditations take up many of the traditionally recognized themes of the Gospel, including the opposition of light and darkness, John's language and vocabulary, and above all, in the final meditation, the means by which the faithful can "know" Christ through scripture.[3] In another treatise, written as an introduction to the reading of scripture, Francke names the purpose of John's Gospel, which he contrasts with Luke's very different one, as that of "demonstrating the divine nature of Christ, on account of which purpose he relates many discourses and deeds of Christ, from which we can recognize the divine majesty of Christ more clearly than from the other evangelists."[4] Francke's pupil, Joachim Lange, likewise identifies the goal of John's Gospel as that of "testifying that Jesus of Nazareth was the true promised Messiah and the Son of God," a purpose named, as both Francke and Lange point out, by the evangelist himself (Jn 20:31).[5] John's literary style, the traditional perception of John as the spiritual Gospel, Luther's love for John, John's hostility toward "the Jews," and many other themes associated with the Fourth Gospel, all rotate around this one central issue. It provides a ready explanation for the appearance of the five-stringed *violoncello piccolo* in five of the post-Easter cantatas of 1725, as we will see.

And when we study Bach's *St. John Passion* and the cantatas that followed its second performance in 1725, we find the same issue squarely in the foreground. The opening chorus of the Passion (in its original version) is a case in point. Its initial line, "Herr, unser Herrscher, dessen Ruhm in allen Landen herrlich ist" (Lord, our Master, whose fame is glorious in all lands), is based, like many of the *dicta* that begin the 1723–24 cantatas, on a line from the Psalms: in this case the verse that begins and ends Psalm 8: "Herr, unser Herrscher, wie herrlich ist dein Nam' in allen Landen" (Lord, our Master, how glorious is your name in all lands). And the remaining text of the chorus makes clear that the psalm paraphrase was not included merely as praise of God of some generic kind, as it may appear today.

---

[3] August Hermann Francke, *CHRISTUS / Der Kern heiliger Schrifft / Oder / Einfältige Anweisung / wie man Christum / als den Kern der gantzen heiligen Schrifft / recht suchen / finden / schmäcken / und damit seine Seele nähren / sättigen und zum ewigen Leben erhalten solle.* Halle, 1702. This treatise was published in English translation in 1732 as *Christ: The Sum and Substance of all the Holy Scriptures in the Old and New Testament* (London: J Downing, 1732).

[4] August Hermann Francke, *Einleitung zur Lesung der H. Schrifft / insonderheit des Neuen Testaments* (3rd ed., Halle, 1699), 17–18: "Johannes aber nach dem Zeugniß der Alten / sonderlich sein Evangelium zur Beweisung der Göttlichen Natur CHristi geschrieben / und von wegen solches Zwecks viele Reden und Thaten Christi erzehlet / aus welchen wir die göttliche Herrlichkeit Christi klärer als aus den andern Evangelisten erkennen können; . . ."

[5] Joachim Lange, *Evangelisches Licht und Recht, Oder Richtige und Erbauliche Erklärung der heiligen Vier Evangelisten, und die Apostel-Geschichte, . . .* (Halle, 1735), 506–7.

Addressing first the God of the Hebrew Bible (OT), it makes the point that stands forth in the celebrated prologue to John's Gospel, that the creator God of Israel is present in and equated with the historical Jesus of Nazareth. Bach's setting, beginning with a threefold address to the deity, "Herr, Herr, Herr," set to the descending minor triad in the soprano, projects a striking sense both of the majesty of the Trinity and the descent—the *Niedrigkeit*—of Jesus that reaches its end point and its goal in the Passion. Only after this does the melodic line continue with the rising figure of "unser Herrscher," the line as a whole anticipating the juxtaposition of Jesus's *Niedrigkeit* (abasement) and his *Verherrlichung* (glorification) that is the goal of the text as a whole. This is entirely in keeping with the Christological interpretation of all the psalms in the Lutheran tradition. Johann Arndt, for example, titled each of the three sermons that formed his commentary on Psalm 8 with Christological titles, centering them on, respectively, the majesty, the *Niedrigkeit*, and the glorification of Jesus; and in this context he gives special emphasis to the name of Jesus.[6] Likewise, Johann Olearius, author of the important commentary owned by Bach, says the following of John 18:4 ("Als nun Jesus wusste alles, was Ihm begegnen solte, ging Er hinaus, und sprach zu ihnen: Wen suchet ihr?"):

> Jesus. This dear name "Jesus" is the key to the entire history of the suffering and death of Christ, which points to the principal purpose of the entire action. For no martyr, prophet or saint, only Jesus, is the one whom Matthew (Mt 1) and Luke (Lk 2) [call] the true Messiah and mediator (1 Tim 2). His suffering is the suffering of the Son of God (1 Jn 1), who purchased us with his own blood (Acts 20), so that we believe it and have eternal life through him (Jn 20).[7]

The name of Jesus is of central importance in the *St. John Passion*, where it has particular associations to the cross. That the opening chorus "Herr, unser Herrscher" speaks of God's *Ruhm* rather than of his name, is in fact a means of establishing the focus on Jesus's person and name in the narrative that follows. For the writings of Lutheran orthodoxy give great emphasis to the equivalence of "Ruhm" and "Name," as was also the case in Bach's cantatas for New Year's Day, traditionally bound up with the naming of Jesus (and his circumcision, which was usually

---

[6] See Johann Arndt, *Auslegung des gantzen Psalters Davids des Königlichen Propheten. . .* (Jena, 1624), fol. 42v.: "Christi Name / das ist / Person / Ampt und Wolthaten sollen in aller Welt offenbahr werden." Arndt's commentary brings out the meaning of Psalm 8 in a manner that relates very closely to Bach's "Herr, unser Herrscher" (see pp. 151–155).

[7] Johann Olearius, *Biblischer Erklärung / Fünfter und letzter Theil* (Leipzig, 1681), 775: "Jesus. Dieser werthe Jesus-Nahme ist der Schlüssel zu der gantzen Historia deß Leidens und Sterbens Christi / welcher den Haupt-Zweck dieser gantzen Handlung weiset. Denn kein Märtyrer / Prophet oder Heiliger / sondern JEsus ists / davon Matth. I. Luc. 2. Der einige Meßias Mat. II. Und Mittler I. Tim. 2. Sein Leiden ist das Leiden deß Sohnes GOttes I. Joh. I. der uns mit seinem eigenen Blut erworben hat Ap. Gesch. 20. daß wirs gläuben / und durch ihn das Leben haben. Joh. 20."

omitted). The opening chorus of Cantata 171, "Herr, wie dein Name, so ist auch dein Ruhm," based on Psalm 48, expresses the meaning succinctly.[8]

In German the verb "rühmen" means to glorify, praise, or proclaim the glory of someone. Within the *St. John Passion* the greatest expression of this meaning is the "royal inscription" that was placed over the cross, "Jesus of Nazareth, King of the Jews," which proclaimed the unity of Jesus's name and cross.[9] Looking ahead to this event, the text of the middle section of "Herr, unser Herrscher": "Zeig' uns durch deine Passion, daß du, der wahre Gottessohn, zu aller Zeit, auch in der größten Niedrigkeit, verherrlicht worden bist" (Show us through your Passion that you, the true Son of God, at all times, even in the greatest humiliation, have been glorified) announces the "goal" of the Passion as the one that is particularly associated with John: recognition of Jesus's divine identity within the framework of the adverse events of the narrative. It proclaims the equivalence of Jesus and the Father immediately with "deine Passion," expanding on it with "Gottessohn." Ultimately the "du" of the text refers to both Jesus and the God of the OT. In fact, the quality of differentiation plus oneness between Jesus and the Father is exactly the way John presents Jesus, one of the primary theological supports for the doctrine of the Trinity, especially as Luther viewed it. And the continuation, "at all times, even in the greatest humiliation," articulates the primary thrust of Luther's *theologia crucis*, that God is to be recognized in Jesus above all, and particularly in terms of his crucifixion and treatment as a criminal by the world. The crucifixion is the begin-

---

[8] A good example of this can be found in Valerius Herberger's commentary on Psalm 8 in his 1598 *Paradies Blümlein* (new edition published as *Valerius Herberger's Paradies-Blümlein aus dem Lustgarten der 150 Psalmen*. . . Mit einem Vorwort von C. W. Otto, . . . Neue wortgetreue Ausgabe. Halle, 1857), 129: "Des Herrn Jesu Name ist sein Ruhm; das bezeugt der Psalm 48, 11: Gott, wie dein Name, so ist auch dein Ruhm, bis an der Welt Ende." Herberger's commentary, like that of Johann Arndt (see ch. 4), views Psalm 8 entirely in Christological terms (122–23: "dem achten Psalm, welcher ganz vom Anfang bis zu Ende von Jesu Christo redet." . . . "Jesus ist dieses Psalms Kern und Stern, ja Sonne und Glanz," etc.). And Herberger, likewise, sees the fifth and sixth verses as referring to Jesus's work of redemption in the Passion: "Er erniedrigte sich selbst, und ward gehorsam bis zum Tode, ja zum Tode am Kreuz. Darum hat ihn auch Gott erhöhet, und hat ihm einen Namen gegeben, der über alle Namen ist, . . ." etc.) Herberger's extended commentary, in particular his analysis of the first verse, makes clear many themes that resound throughout the *St. John Passion*, not merely the name of Jesus and the process of *Erniedrigung* and *Erhöhung* but also the association of Jesus's "Ruhm" with the spread of his name "in allen Landen," the victorious nature of the Passion and its eschatological goal, praising and thanking God in eternity. In this light, the choice of "Herr, unser Herrscher" for the introductory chorus to a Johannine Passion account is entirely in keeping with the thought of sixteenth- to eighteenth-century Lutheranism.

[9] See the commentary of Chemnitz, Leyser, and Gerhard (see n. 1), where we read (in the German-language edition published in the United States, 313): "durch Gottes wunderbaren Rath geschieht es, daß durch diese Gelegenheit [the royal inscription] Christi Ehre um so weiter ausgebreitet wurde, sintemal Gott, . . . das Herz und die Hand Pilati so regiert, daß jener Titel, der dem Ruhm Christi diente, in jenen drei Sprachen, die damals die vorzüglichsten und verbreitetesten auf dem Erdkreis waren, geschrieben und somit angezeigt wurde, daß die Herrlichkeit Christi werde ausgebreitet werden unter allen Völkern, Sprachen und Zungen."

ning of his glorification, the fulfillment of his predictions in John regarding his glorious "lifting up."

Thus both "Herr, unser Herrscher" and the royal inscription project the fact that the messianic identity of Jesus is revealed through his *Niedrigkeit*. "Herr, unser Herrscher" announces, in the striking contrast between its proclamation of the glory of God and its minor-key projection of an aura of suffering and lamentation, that the meaning of the Passion is to be understood within the context of opposition and adversity. In this regard, the trial of Jesus before Pilate embodies the central question of Jesus's divinity, which it sets forth in terms of the Christological title "King" or "King of the Jews," heard eight times and finally culminating only after the trial with the royal inscription. And, with the addition of the name "Jesus of Nazareth" (which appears only in John's version of the inscription), John refers back to the opening scene of the Passion, directly following "Herr, unser Herrscher," where the arresting party specifies "Jesus of Nazareth" in response to Jesus's words "Whom do you seek?"

Bach's treatment of this point in the narrative is one of the most striking occurrences in the Passion, perhaps its strongest evidence for the fact that Bach should be ranked with other artistic interpreters of the Gospel—Leonardo da Vinci, as Leo Steinberg has interpreted his *Last Supper*, for example.[10] In his setting of Jesus's name, Bach composed a very compact and distinctively patterned chorus setting ("Jesum von Nazareth"), which is sung twice, once before and once after Jesus identifies himself with the words "Ich bin's." Those words, traditionally understood by Christian theologians as an expression of messianic self-revelation, have enormous significance in John, as countless commentators have recognized through the centuries. In John's Gospel Jesus begins many sayings with the words "I am" ("I am the way, the truth and the life"; "I am the good shepherd"; "I am the true vine"; "I am the door to the sheepfold"; and the like). And several similar expressions, including Jesus's "Ich bin's" in the *St. John Passion*, simply say "I am" in a particularly emphatic manner, that is, as a predicate nominative, as do certain expressions of God in the OT. John, it appears, uses them as a special means of pointing to Jesus's divinity, a quality that was well recognized by Bach's contemporaries, since they are interpreted as such in some of the theological books that Bach owned or might have consulted.[11] Two of the most prominent of Jesus's "I am" sayings appear in the Gospel readings from the Farewell Discourse that belong to the great

[10] See ch. 8 for full citation and further discussion of Steinberg's study of Leonardo's *Last Supper*.

[11] Thus Johann Olearius, like many others, links Jesus's "Ich bin's" with the various OT passages in which God speaks similarly, the most widely cited of which was Ex 3:14 ("Ich werde sein, der ich sein werde. Und sprach: also sollt du zu den Kindern Israel sagen: Ich werde sein, der hat mich zu euch gesandt"). Olearius also links both passages with Rev 1:8, where Jesus refers to himself as Alpha and Omega. See Olearius, *Biblische Erklärung*, 5:776. As is well known, Bach owned a copy of the Olearius commentary. For titles and descriptions of Bach's collection of theological books, see Robin Leaver, *Bach's Theological Library* (Neuhausen-Stuttgart: Hänssler, 1983). For August Hermann Francke's and Johann Jacob Rambach's interpretations of Jesus's "Ich bin's" see ch. 4, 156–157 and 170, n. 56.

fifty days, while two others appear in Gospel readings for that time period and which were chosen from elsewhere in John's Gospel. In addition, there are many related expressions in the discourse, in which Jesus affirms his messianic identity and his oneness with the Father, the best known of which is the one that Luther particularly loved: Jesus's words to Philip, "He who has seen me has seen the Father" (Jn 14:9). From this standpoint alone they link up with the kind of equivalence of Jesus and the Father that underlies the text of "Herr, unser Herrscher." In the Gospel Jesus's last "I am" saying appears in the Passion narrative, where it is explicitly linked to the name "Jesus of Nazareth" for the only time in the Gospel, a reflection of John's linking the incarnate "word," who was equivalent to the creator God, with the historical Jesus of Nazareth in the first chapter of his Gospel. As if to underscore this meaning, John narrates that upon Jesus's words the arresting party drew back and fell to the ground, an occurrence that Bach's contemporary, August Hermann Francke, for example, interpreted entirely as a sign of Jesus's divinity.

The remarkable point about Bach's setting of Jesus's name is that he repeats the music of the two "Jesus of Nazareth" choruses three additional times throughout the Passion—making five appearances in all—and those later appearances, now sung to different texts, are all associated with *denial* of Jesus's messianic identity by the crowd in the segment that deals with the Roman trial. We might say that such a denial lies beneath the words of the arresting party as well, as, indeed, at some level it does. But John takes great pains to make clear in this scene that the all-important issue is that Jesus be recognized by the faithful as the Messiah, that this identity shine forth despite the fact that the events must also be understood as the beginning of his *Erniedrigung* (humiliation). Lutheran commentaries from the sixteenth to the eighteenth centuries emphasize this without fail. And, as a clear indication that Bach intended his setting of the name "Jesus of Nazareth" to embody proclamation of Jesus's divinity, note that in the *Christmas Oratorio* he modeled his chorus setting of the words, "Wo ist der neugeborne König der Juden," sung by the Magi (and certainly without any pejorative associations), on the same music (in particular, as it sets the words "Wir haben keinen König denn den Kaiser" in the Passion.)[12] For August Hermann Francke the word "neugeborne" in the passage just cited from the *Christmas Oratorio* linked up with Jesus's words to Pilate regarding his messianic identity later in the Passion: "Du sagests, ich bin ein König. Ich bin dazu geboren und in die Welt kommen, daß ich die Wahrheit zeugen sollen." Although there is disagreement about the exact meaning of these words, for Francke, and most others in Bach's time (and even today), they have been understood as Jesus identifying himself as the Messiah.[13] And this seems clearly to

[12] Without noting this fact, Gerhard Freiesleben argued, on the basis of what he called its "Passion-like character," that "Wo ist der neugebornen König der Juden" was the original from which the chorus "Pfui dich" of Bach's lost *St. Mark Passion* was parodied. See Freiesleben, "Ein neuer Beitrag zur Entstehungsgeschichte von J. S. Bachs Weihnachtsoratorium." *Neue Zeitschrift für Musik* 83 (1916): 237–38.

[13] See ch. 6, 239, n. 10, 11. Johann Olearius (*Biblische Erklärung*, 5:787) relates the "ich bin der Juden König" of the High Priest's rejection of the wording of the royal inscription to Jesus's "Du sagest's. Ich

have been Bach's interpretation, in which the initial "du sagest's" reiterates at pitch the rising fourth of Jesus's "Ich bin's" in Part 1 (but with the harmony changed, very significantly, from minor to major). In other words, in Bach's settings the three appearances of the "Jesus of Nazareth" music to different texts also embody the original association to Jesus's name and messianic identity, and all appearances must be understood as projecting what Leo Steinberg calls, with reference to Leonardo's *Last Supper*, a "duplex" quality, that is, a double meaning embodying both the spiritual and the physical, which is one of John's foremost literary traits. Commentators from the earliest Christian times to that of Bach have understood this quality as central to John, where it is more focused than in the Synoptic Gospels.

I expand on the meaning of the "Jesus of Nazareth" choruses and the various related questions, such as symmetry, in later chapters. But here, to extract conclusions in advance from that discussion, their significance in this context is that Bach was willing to set certain textual passages with music associated with the opposite meaning, to separate two conflicting points of view in the understanding of a single text. This is part and parcel of John's style, which Luther describes, in his commentary on the Farewell Discourse, as involving "two kinds of sight and of hearing. The one is performed with physical eyes and ears, entirely without the Spirit. . . . The second is a spiritual sight, which only Christians have and which takes place by means of faith in the heart. . . . This is a way of looking at Christ that is far different from the way all the world does and the disciples did up to this time. But now their eyes are made clear by faith; this is a new insight."[14] Among Lutheran theologians before and during Bach's lifetime it was common to cite Joseph's words to his brothers in Genesis 50:20, "Ihr gedachts böse mit mir zu machen, aber Gott gedachts gut zu machen" ("ye thought evil against me; but God meant it unto good," KJV), for the purpose of affirming that scripture contained double meanings and perspectives, as well as antitheses between its divine purpose, which was entirely salvific—the redemption of humanity—and the adverse worldly events it narrated. And nowhere was this sense of opposition as great as in the Passion. Thus August Hermann Francke paraphrases Joseph's words, replacing "Ihr" with Caiphas.[15] It is absolutely essential to understand the "Jesus of Naza-

---

bin ein König," whereas Johann Jacob Rambach relates the inscription itself to Jesus's "Ich bin's" and to Ex 3:14. Many other authors made these or similar connections, sometimes drawing the contrast with Peter's "Ich bin's nicht," and thereby emphasizing the central issue of Jesus's identity.

[14] *Luther's Works*, vol. 24: *Sermons on the Gospel of St. John, Chapters 14–16*, ed. Jaroslav Pelikan and Daniel E. Poellot, 33–35 (St. Louis: Concordia, 1961).

[15] See ch. 4, n. 62; among the authors referred to in this study, Johann Heermann, Heinrich Müller, and Johann Jacob Rambach cite it also (see ch. 6, n. 50; ch. 8, n. 26). It may be mentioned that in the entire first meditation of the source cited in n. 3. Francke emphasizes the simplicity of John's language in the prologue to the Gospel, arguing against those who would make it seem more complicated by ingenious overinterpretations and the like. The thrust of his arguments is that John's language is simple if we read directly for the "faith" interpretation, its *Scopus*; that is, we must read "through" the irony and other literary qualities.

reth" choruses in this way as projecting the "duplex" meaning of Jesus's divinity or glorification and his human suffering that is announced in "Herr, unser Herrscher."

This occurrence suggests considerable musico-theological reflection on Bach's part. And at the same time it is entirely in keeping with the theological interpretation of the Gospel text in his time. Ultimately, it traces to the concept introduced in the Introduction, which was known to Bach's contemporaries as God's "Rath" (sometimes God's "vorbedachter Rath" or "Rathschluß"), which referred to God's predetermining the events of history according to his plan for the salvation of humanity. All the Lutheran theologians of Bach's time refer to this concept, some extensively and in particular relation to John, as we will see. Bach had books on the subject among his collection. In their double association with the name "Jesus of Nazareth," on the one hand, and the rejection of Jesus by the crowd, primarily on the basis of the Christological title "King of the Jews" on the other, these choruses linked up conceptually (as Bach's contemporary Johann Jacob Rambach said of the initial demands for "Jesus of Nazareth") with the royal inscription placed over the cross in John's account of the Passion. In the inscription, which appears with the full name "Jesus of Nazareth" only in John, the historical name and the Christological title that is debated throughout the trial are finally joined. Culminating the scene that follows the trial before Pilate, the scene of the crucifixion itself, the royal inscription (like the aforementioned "Ich bin's") is one of the key occurrences for all who investigate the special character of John's Gospel, since it embodies the quintessential instance of Johannine irony, making a true statement under the guise of its opposite. This quality was recognized in virtually every theological commentary of the sixteenth through the eighteenth centuries. Pilate, who has vacillated between his own inclination to set Jesus free and the demand of the crowd for execution, places a sign over the cross that simultaneously echoes and contradicts the outcry that had caused him—not according to his own intentions, but as the outcome of God's *Rath*—to order Jesus's crucifixion, "Wir haben keinen König denn den Kaiser" (We have no king but Caesar), which in Bach's design is the last of the choruses to utilize the "Jesus of Nazareth" music.[16] Thus the inscription relates the ending of John's trial, in which Jesus's divine identity is denied by the crowd and "veiled" beneath its opposite, his *Erniedrigung* (as Rambach and countless others said of the Passion), to the public, albeit ironic, proclamation of Jesus's messianic identity. Responding to the adverse judgment of the trial, the inscription is so reflective of John's well-known literary devices, those of irony, hidden and double meaning, misunderstanding, contradiction, "circular" repetition, and the like, that

[16] See Lothar Steiger, "'Wir haben keinen König denn den Kaiser!' Pilatus und die Juden in der Passionsgeschichte nach dem Johannesevangelium mit Bezug auf Heinrich Schütz und Johann Sebastian Bach. Oder die Frage nach dem Antijudaismus." In *"Wie freudig ist mein Herz, da Gott versöhnet ist." Die Lehre von der Versöhnung in Kantaten und Orgelchorälen von Johann Sebastian Bach*, ed. Renate Steiger, 25–36 (Internationale Arbeitsgemeinschaft für theologische Bachforschung, Bulletin 5 [Heidelberg, 1995].

it is truly difficult to understand it in any other way. The same is true of Bach's "Jesus of Nazareth" choruses as a "series" within the Passion. Bach's settings suggest a hidden meaning (but not one that is so hidden that the more intelligent among his contemporaries could not have readily understood it), that is, an ironic affirmation of Jesus's divine identity behind the adverse events. In culminating the extended and largely symmetrical musical substructure within Part 2 of the Passion with the chorale that meditates on the uniting of Jesus's name and the cross in the royal inscription—"In meines Herzens Grunde dein Nam' und Kreuz allein"—Bach brings out what August Hermann Francke would have called the "perfect simplicity" of John's language (see n. 15).

We do not know to what extent Bach might have been influenced, or even instructed by his theologian colleagues as to certain of the theological emphases in his setting; it is entirely feasible, though, that his treatment of the "Jesus of Nazareth" choruses was the outcome of his own study of the Gospel and reading of theological literature. By the end of Bach's life, if not before, he possessed a collection of theological books in which these questions are addressed. The brilliant interpretation of the chorus, however, can only have been his, for its musical ramifications, linking up not only with Jesus's "Ich bin's" but also with Peter's "Ich bin's nicht," and ultimately with the design of Part 1 as a whole, are enormous (see chs. 4–8). In the end, the design of the *St. John Passion* (in its 1724 version) suggests deep theological reflection on Bach's part; it is a formidable challenge to all who take a purely literal-minded or pragmatic view of Bach's text setting.

The 1725 version of the *St. John Passion* in outline

Bach's 1725 revisions to the *St. John Passion* affected a relatively small number of movements, but ones that were pivotal in defining the Johannine character of the work. Once thought, erroneously, to represent the original version of the Passion, the 1725 form replaced the G-minor chorus, "Herr, unser Herrscher," with the E♭ chorale fantasia, "O Mensch, bewein," known primarily today as the closing movement of the *St. Matthew Passion*, Part 1 (where it is transposed to E major). It also replaced the final E♭ chorale, "Ach Herr, lass dein lieb' Engelein," with a three-verse setting of "Christe, du Lamm Gottes," in C minor, otherwise known as the final movement of the Quinquagesima cantata, *Du wahrer Gott und Davids Sohn* (BWV 23), composed in 1723 and first performed at Bach's audition for the Leipzig position early that year. In addition, Bach removed the f♯ aria, "Ach, mein Sinn," associated with Peter toward the end of Part 1, replacing it with the A-major aria, "Zerschmettert mich," and he inserted the f♯ bass dialog with soprano chorale, "Himmel reiße, Welte erbebe"/"Jesu, deine Passion" earlier in the same scene, directly following the A-major chorale "Wer hat dich so geschlagen." As Alfred Dürr pointed out, this latter alteration created a correspondence with the bass dialog with chorale, "Mein teurer Heiland"/"Jesu, der du warest tot," which followed the narrative of Jesus's death in Part 2.[17] Both segments now featured two settings of verses from the same chorale, "Jesu, Leiden, Pein und Tod," one in a straightforward four-part setting, and the other for solo bass in dialog with the chorale verse. In the former scene the keys in question were f♯ and A, in the latter one A and D. It suggested a symmetrical order but one attained at the expense of logical ordering of the inserted text. And, in Part 2, at what is a point of enormous symbolic importance, the meditation on Jesus's scourging that begins the substructure I call the "symbolic trial," Bach replaced the E♭ arioso "Betrachte, meine Seele" and its companion aria, "Erwäge" (in C minor), with the C-minor tenor aria, "Ach, windet euch nicht so, geplagte Seelen." Additionally, following the aria dialog with chorale, "Mein teurer Heiland"/"Jesu, der du warest tot," that meditates on Jesus's death, Bach inserted a new recitative from Matthew describing the outbreaks of nature that followed Jesus's death in the Synoptic Gospels. In the 1724 version, which is lost, he had apparently set Mark's similar but shorter version. John has no narrative of these events.

It is difficult to believe that these changes were motivated by either artistic or theological considerations, since they affect the Johannine character of the Passion and its mirroring in music adversely. Over the next twenty or more years, Bach re-performed the *St. John Passion* at least twice more, once in the early 1730s and once in the late 1740s, in the former "version" rescinding most of the 1725 substitutions and making further modifications of a different kind. "Herr, unser Herrscher," "Betrachte, meine Seele," and "Erwäge, wie sein blutgefärbter Rükken" were restored and "Himmel reiße, Welt erbebe"/"Jesu, deine Passion" and "Christe, du Lamm Gottes" removed in this "third" version, while a new and unknown aria replaced "Zerschmettert mich." In this version the two recitative interpolations from Matthew (one originally from Mark) were excised. The latter one (describing the outbreaks of nature following Jesus's death), plus the arioso and aria that followed, was replaced by an instrumental *Sinfonia*, which is now lost. In important respects, therefore, this version moves in the direction of restoring the 1724 version. Within this version another kind of revision takes place, one that has largely gone unnoticed in interpretation of the Passion. The removal of the narrative of Peter's repentance (the last eight measures of no. 12c) meant that the final recitative of Part 1 ended with John's narrative of the cock's crow following Peter's third denial, not with the narrative of Peter's repentance, as in all other versions. The recitative now ended in B minor, rather than F-sharp minor. And this difference meant that the unknown aria that followed was probably in e or G, instead of f♯ or A, in addition to which, as we know for certain, the chorale "Petrus, der nicht denkt zurück," ending Part 1, was in G instead of A. The third version, therefore,

---

[17] Alfred Dürr, "Zu den verschollenen Passionen Bachs," *Bach-Jahrbuch* 64 (1957): 5–162. In order to bring this out, I have incorporated "Himmel reiße, Welte erbebe" into fig. 4.1, ch. 4.

deviated from what was otherwise virtually the same key plan in all other versions.[18] It may be significant to note, however, that G major is (in all versions) the key in which Peter's first denial ("Ich bin's nicht") appears, where it is bound up with the modulation to sharp keys that ends Part 1 (and where it is a kind of "opposite" to Jesus's G-minor "Ich bin's"). In this version, therefore, Part 1 apparently ended in G major instead of A, amplifying the g/G contrast of Jesus's avowal of his messianic identity and Peter's denial of his discipleship. Thus Peter's "fall" is given greater emphasis, as it is in John, than his repentance (which, as I argue in ch. 5, is mirrored in the A-major original ending of Part 1). In this instance what we have in Bach's revision is perhaps a response to an external influence, one that retains elements of the Petrus/Christus symbolism that was already present, but that realizes it somewhat differently, as a result of the removal of the part of the recitative that did not originate with John.[19]

Then, around 1740, Bach began to prepare a new score, copying the initial twenty pages himself but not continuing the project, which was completed by a copyist in the last years of Bach's life. This "fourth" version, essentially a restoration of the 1724 original one, but with numerous further revisions and elaborations, primarily of melodic, instrumental, and textual details, is close enough to the 1724 version for us to take the two together, as the great majority of scholars have done, as representing Bach's primary conception of the *St. John Passion*.

The big question is why he revised the work in 1725, since from virtually any perspective the 1724 version is more consistent and convincing. And immediately the conjecture comes to mind that the version of 1725 was made so as to reflect the 1724–25 chorale cantata cycle more closely. Not only were elaborate chorale settings placed at the beginning and ending of the work, but the addition of "Himmel reiße"/"Jesu, deine Passion" augmented the symmetrical aspect of the Passion with chorale settings, as Dürr recognized (see ch. 4, fig. 4.1). Beyond this, the substitutions seem almost to anticipate features of the *St. Matthew Passion*. "O Mensch, bewein" was actually added to the *St. Matthew Passion* at some time after what was

---

[18] See Mendel, *Kritischer Bericht* to NBA Series 2, 4:84–88. A page from the original first violin part showing the G-major version of "Petrus, der nicht denkt zurück" (which is then crossed out and replaced below, after the words "Fine della Parte 1ma," by the A-major version), is reproduced in facsimile in Annette Oppermann, "Zur Quellenlage . . . *Johannes-Passion* BWV 245," in *Bachs Passionen, Oratorien und Motetten: Das Handbuch,* ed. Reinmar Emans and Sven Hiemke, 91 (Laaber: Laaber-Verlag, 2009). See ch. 5 for further discussion of this matter.

[19] That is, in the other versions of the Passion, the chorales "Petrus, der nicht denkt zurück" (ending Part 1 in A), and "Christus, der uns selig macht" (beginning Part 2 in E Phrygian, sounding like A minor) exhibit parallels that mirror the shift of focus from Peter's repentance to Jesus's sufferings. In the version of ca. 1730 the G major of "Petrus, der nicht denkt zurück" relates back to Peter's "Ich bin's nicht" (modulating to G) as an opposite number to Jesus's "Ich bin's" (in g). With the G ending of Part 1 in the third version, therefore, Bach might have intended a g/G overall design related to the Christus/Petrus shift in the design of Part 1 as a whole; Part 1 of the *St. Matthew Passion* outlines a minor/major overall shift (e/E) that, although it does not relate to Peter's repentance, may be considered to articulate the necessity of penitence at the end ("O Mensch, bewein dein Sünde groß"), and in a context that reflects on the fleeing of the disciples (the ending of the Part 1 narrative).

probably its original version; there it is remarkably well-suited to its new role, which provides a balance at the end of Part 1 to the chorale fantasia with madrigal-texted dialog that begins that work, "O Lamm Gottes unschuldig"/"Kommt, ihr Töchter." And "Christe, du Lamm Gottes" is a German paraphrase of the Agnus Dei, as is "O Lamm Gottes unschuldig." Also, the idea of creating a "series" of verses of the same chorale, with internal parallels among them, is common to the 1725 *St. John Passion*, with its four verses of "Jesu, Leiden, Pein und Tod," and the *St. Matthew Passion*, with its five settings of the melody "Herzlich tut mich verlangen" (or "O Haupt voll Blut und Wunden"). It is possible that the *St. Matthew Passion* was originally conceived to form a component of the chorale cycle, while the 1725 *St. John Passion* was a temporary solution.

The questions surrounding this impression cannot be definitively settled on the basis of present evidence. Nevertheless, the 1725 modifications to the *St. John Passion*, which as Ulrich Leisinger argues (see Introduction, n. 8), probably arose as an "emergency aid" (*Notbehelf*) because of the unexpected breaking off of the chorale cantata cycle, might have been conceived not only as augmenting the chorale character of the Passion but also as reinterpreting some of its theological qualities. In keeping with Jaroslav Pelikan's and Elke Axmacher's view that the *St. Matthew Passion* reflects a different perspective on the atonement, that of the satisfaction theory, we note, as Pelikan did, that most of the changes to the *St. John Passion* text bring it more closely in line with the main themes of that theory, themes that are often conspicuous by their absence in the *St. John Passion*.[20] Thus, "O Mensch, bewein dein Sünde groß" brings the acknowledgment of the guilt of humanity over Jesus's Passion into the foreground, at least in its hortatory first line. That theme runs throughout the *St. Matthew Passion*, mirroring the aspect of Luther's theology that derives most conspicuously from the satisfaction theory. In the *St. John Passion* it is hardly present at all (except for the second verse of "Wer hat dich so geschlagen?"). Rather, the earlier work gives enormous weight to the benefit of Jesus's Passion for humanity, passing over the process by which the believer becomes "conformable" to Christ in his suffering, as Luther expressed it. This latter quality is also prominent in "Himmel reiße," where the bass sings "sehet meine Qual und Angst, was ich, Jesu, mit dir leide" and "weil ich in Zufriedenheit mich in deine Wunden senke" (See my torment and anxiety, which I, Jesus, with you suffer" and "since I sink with contentment into your wounds"). "Zerschmettert mich" introduces the image of God as "strict judge" that runs throughout the *St. Matthew Passion*, but is entirely missing from the 1724 *St. John Passion*; the aria also emphasizes acknowledgment of sin, as does "Ach, windet euch nicht so" ("Ach, windet euch nicht so, geplagte Seelen, bei eurer Kreuzes Angst und Qual. Könnt ihr die unermess'ne Zahl der harten Geisselschläge zählen: so zählet euch die Menge eurer Sünden, ihr werdet diese grösser finden" [Ah, writhe not so, tormented souls, in the pain and anxiety of your cross. If you could count the innumerable

[20] Jaroslav Pelikan, *Bach Among the Theologians* (Philadelphia: Fortress Press 1986), 110–11.

number of scourging blows, then count the quantity of your sins; you will find it greater]). The contrast of this movement to those it replaced—"Betrachte, meine Seele" and "Erwäge, wie sein blutgefärbter Rucken"—both of which emphasize not human sin but the benefit of Jesus's sufferings for the faithful, could hardly be greater.

In this light it may be significant that among the revisions for the fourth version of the Passion are additional textual changes to the two movements just mentioned. In that version the reference to the crown of thorns, taken over from the Brockes poem from which "Betrachte"/"Erwäge" and several other madrigal texts of the Passion were developed, is removed, and with it the imagery of the "Himmelsschlüsselblume" (primrose: literally "flower that is the key to heaven") and the believer's plucking of "sweet fruit" from Jesus's "wormwood." The immediate reason might have been that John narrates the scourging before the crown of thorns, so the replacement lines refer to the scourging instead.[21] But this alone is hardly sufficient to explain the removal of the imagery. Authors have differed in whether the changes constitute an improvement or the reverse. Considered from the standpoint of the Johannine character of the Passion, they must certainly be judged as the latter. For the new version lessens one of the primary characteristics of the *St. John Passion* text considered as a whole, the reinterpretation of Jesus's sufferings in wholly salvific terms (see ch. 4). What "blooms" forth in the new version is not the flower that is the key to heaven but hyssop, a symbol of the purging of sin, based on passages from the OT, such as in Psalm 51:7. The latter is a theme that the revised version brings out but is entirely absent from the earlier one. Similarly, in "Erwäge" the imagery of the rainbow patterns formed from the mixture of blood and water on Jesus's back is expunged and replaced by the message that Jesus's sufferings in general bring joy and the removal of sin; now the believer's terror ("Schrecken"), implying God's judgment, gives way to the awakening of joy in freedom from hell and death. In both movements, therefore, the revisions bring out the benefit of Jesus's sufferings in terms of the removal of sin, a message that the earlier versions do not project and that are mirrored less well in Bach's settings.

In this fourth version of the Passion, the text of the aria "Ich folge dir gleichfalls" was also revised. One change is the replacing of reference to the believer's joyful steps ("mit freudigen Schritten"), by the words "mein Heiland, mit Freuden" (my savior, with joy), a decision it is difficult to imagine Bach making without some external influence, since the "steps" are suggested by the music. And the original reference to Jesus as "mein Leben, mein Licht" is replaced by "Mein Heiland, mein Licht," which introduces a clumsy reiteration of the word "Heiland." But it is the removal of "Leben" that is most damaging. For "life" and "light" belong together in John's prologue, and throughout the Gospel, as Francke went to great

[21] Arthur Mendel makes this point (*Kritischer Bericht*, 170).

lengths to bring out in his commentary.[22] One might imagine that some outside authority not at all concerned with John's characteristic language found "Heiland" to be more fundamentally reflective than "Leben" of Jesus's redemptive work. In the remaining lines the alteration of "befördre den Lauf und höre nicht auf, selbst an mir zu ziehen, zu schieben, zu bitten" (promote my path and do not cease to draw, to urge, to beg me) to "mein sehnlicher Lauf hört eher nicht auf, bis daß du mich lehrest, geduldig zu leiden" (my longing path will not cease until you teach me to suffer patiently) replaces the believer's petitioning of Jesus with a simple statement of resolve, adding a reference to the believer's own suffering. This change at once takes away the sense that it is the all-powerful Jesus of John's Gospel who is the active force in the believer's redemption, along with the Johannine expression "ziehen," associated with Jesus's saying "When I am lifted up from the earth I will *draw* (ziehen) all men unto me" (Jn 12:32). It is nearly impossible to imagine Bach's making these changes without some outside theological influence, since in all cases they lessen the text–music relationships in ways that a number of scholars have noted.

The one remaining textual change in the fourth version, to the burial chorus, "Ruht wohl, ihr heilige Gebeine," was made after Bach's death for a performance by C. P. E. Bach.[23] Although this change might reflect an intention of Bach's that was not carried out at the time of his death, there is no very compelling reason to take it into account. Nevertheless, the shift of emphasis from Jesus's burial to that of the believer in lines four and five of the original versus three and four of the revision ("Das Grab, so euch bestimmet ist und ferner keine Not umschließt" versus "Ich weiß, einst gibt der Tod mir Ruh, nicht stets umschließet mich die Gruft") removes the reference to the predetermining of Jesus's death according to God's plan ("so euch bestimmet ist") as well as that to Jesus's death involving "keine Not," both of which allude to the voluntary, glorious nature of Jesus's work in John. Likewise, the change in the second line—from "die ich nun weiter nicht beweine" to "um die ich nicht mehr trostlos weine"—lessens (through the qualifying nature of "trostlos") the original sense that the believer does not need to weep over Jesus's death.

If the textual revisions just described reflect an impulse related to the 1725 modifications to the Passion, then we must probably conclude that they were the result of theological considerations imposed from outside. Along with the deletion of the biblical recitatives not from John in the third version, they certainly seem to involve questions that relate directly to the Johannine character of the Passion. Thus, while some of the alterations appear to have been motivated by an attempt to make the *St. John Passion* "fit" temporarily with the chorale cantata cycle, the

[22] See Francke, *Christ: The Sum and Substance . . .*, 69–78. Many commentaries, from Bach's time to the present, bring this out. See, for example, C. H. Dodd, *The Interpretation of the Fourth Gospel* (Cambridge: Cambridge University Press, 1953), 201–12.

[23] Mendel, *Kritischer Bericht*, 171.

suspicion arises that some of the changes of other kinds, especially the textual alterations that continued right to the end of Bach's life, might have been the result of a kind of "decree" from Bach's employers, who might have demanded a closer attention to the basic doctrine of Lutheran orthodoxy than they felt was provided in the *St. John Passion*. This is pure speculation, but we do know that the Passion performance was cancelled in 1739 and that Bach, upon being told, remarked that "if an objection were made on account of the text, . . . it had already been performed several times."[24] We do not know which Passion was being referred to, but it seems clear that Bach had encountered objection on the basis of the text/s before, and only the *St. John Passion* is known to have undergone the kind of textual changes that might relate to such a situation. Perhaps Bach's beginning the copying of a new score around that time was related to this event.

It is possible, therefore, that the artistic and doctrinal aspects of Bach's works might not always have converged perfectly and that objections might occasionally have arisen from very theologically punctilious quarters. We know that as a part of his taking up the Leipzig position Bach had to submit to a formal questioning regarding his "theological competence," although he was already hired and had even performed his first Leipzig cantata before the questioning took place.[25] This may not mean, however, that it was a mere formality. Since Bach had put in his candidacy for the Leipzig position before the end of 1722, it may be significant that on the autograph title page of the *Clavier-Büchlein* for Anna Magdalena Bach, dated 1722, there appear the titles of three books by the theologian August Pfeiffer, written in a manner that might be understood to indicate that Bach did not yet own the books, but had been recommended them, perhaps in order to prepare for his Leipzig interview or the abovementioned questioning.[26] An interesting fact concerning the three books is that in keeping with Pfeiffer's regard for pure doctrine, they all take up questions about which there was theological dispute between Calvinists and Lutherans, such as predestination, usually discussed under the heading of the "Absolutum Decretum," which referred to whether God predetermined absolutely the salvation or damnation of individuals. The first of the three books, Pfeiffer's *Anti-Calvinism*, is entirely devoted to such issues; the second, his *[Apostolische] Christen-Schule*, takes them up in more limited form; and the third, his

---

[24] Arthur Mendel (*Kritischer Bericht*, 75) suggested this possibility, which Dürr (*Bach's Johannespassion*, 11) entertains, while suggesting other possibilities. For the documents relating to the 1739 Passion performance, see Werner Neumann and Hans-Joachim Schulze, eds., *Bach-Dokumente, Band II: Fremdschriftliche und gedruckte Dokumente zur Lebensgeschichte Johann Sebastian Bachs*, 1685–1750 (Kassel: Bärenreiter, 1969), 338–39. See also Hans T. David and Arthur Mendel, eds., *The New Bach Reader*, rev. exp. ed. by Christoph Wolff (New York: W. W. Norton, 1998), 204.

[25] David, Mendel, Wolff, *New Bach Reader*, 105.

[26] On the document in question, which was published in facsimile in vol. 44 of the *Bach-Gesellschaft* edition of Bach's works (Leipzig, 1895), Bach writes the first word of the title of Pfeiffer's *Anti Calvinismus* as "Ante" rather than "Anti," an error that would more naturally arise if it were being written down from a spoken recommendation rather than copied from the book itself; likewise another of the titles written by Bach, "Christen Schule," is not the complete title of the book.

Antimelancholicus, treats them at considerable length with series of dialogs between the idealized Lutheran believer and the Calvinist minister.[27] Since the official religion at the Köthen court, where Bach held a secular position for the six years preceding his Leipzig tenure, was Calvinist, Bach (or whoever recommended the Pfeiffer books to him) might have wanted to make sure the abovementioned theological questioning raised no doubts concerning his religious allegiance. This is, again, pure speculation; but the question of God's predestining the elect and the damned, around which the "Absolutum Decretum" pivots, might well have been a factor in Bach's interpretation of the *St. John Passion* text.

In short, since the cantata texts were printed well in advance, they would presumably have caused no theological concerns. But perhaps the Passion, being Bach's first one in Leipzig, had not been composed under such strict control. We know that in 1724 Bach had scheduled the first performance of the *St. John Passion* at St. Thomas rather than the Nikolaikirche, and that, upon receiving a complaint from the pastor of the latter church, the council had ordered that the performance take place in the Nikolaikirche, even though the libretto with the wrong announcement had been printed and had to be done again.[28] Since the council minutes begin with the statement that Bach had been notified in advance regarding the principle of alternating the Passion performance between the two Leipzig churches and therefore that it should take place in the Nikolaikirche, it is possible that Bach underestimated the seriousness of the original notification and made an unacceptably independent decision on the basis of musical considerations. Perhaps the text of the *St. John Passion* was seen to exhibit similar traits. We may never know the actual circumstances. But it does seem likely that the council demanded at least some of the textual changes that run through the different performances of the work. For this reason the common preference for performing the Passion in a combination of the first and fourth versions does not seem misguided.

The post-Easter cantatas of 1724 and 1725

When we reflect on Bach's work as a whole, one of its most prominent characteristics is large-scale projects, often of a systematic nature, such as the forty-eight preludes and fugues of the *Well-Tempered Clavier*, the four parts of the *Clavier-Übung*, and numerous other collections.[29] In the case of one of the most extensive such collections—the *Orgelbüchlein*—Bach dealt with the entire liturgical year in a projected set of more than 160 chorale preludes of a single basic type, of which only

[27] August Pfeiffer, *Antimelancholicus oder Melancholey Vertreiber* (Leipzig, 1688), 413–22, 665–87.

[28] David, Mendel, Wolff, *New Bach Reader*, 116.

[29] Martin Geck ("The Ultimate Goal of Bach's Art," *Bach: Journal of the Riemenschneider Bach Institute* 35, no. 1 [2004]): 29–41) links this quality in Bach's oeuvre to the composer's famous 1708 statement regarding his "final purpose" of a "regulated church music to the Glory of God." In this interpretation the word "regulated" is its primary reflection.

forty-six are copied into the manuscript. Bach's desire and capacity to order his compositions this way is not in any way unique for the time; we find much larger collections in the works of other composers, some of whom were far more prolific than Bach in terms of the numbers of compositions produced, and some who were even more systematic in ordering their collections internally. Nor is this aspect of Bach's work the principal key to its much higher standing today than those collections of other composers. Rather, it is the individual works, the depths of the musical thought processes they involve and Bach's very characteristic attention to musical detail within the collections that make Bach unique. It seems likely in some instances—especially the cycles of the most extensive scope, such as the *Orgelbüchlein* and even more the cantata cycles—that the very depth and intricacy of the individual compositions, and not just the hurried circumstances under which they were often composed, prevented the degree of consistency—or what Bach called "regulation"—we find in Bach's other cycles.

Bach's obituary, written jointly by his son Carl Philipp Emanuel Bach and his son-in-law and pupil, Johann Friedrich Agricola, refers to five cantata cycles and five Passions composed by Bach, thereby giving the distinct impression that the two went hand in hand. However, since we are missing fully one-third of the presumed corpus of cantatas and have only two surviving Passions, plus the text of a third, any arguments for matching up cantata cycles and Passions must remain tentative. Moreover, the date of the *St. Matthew Passion* is not established beyond any doubt; even if it were, that would not necessarily indicate its place within an annual cycle, since it is by no means certain that the rate at which Bach composed his Passions was equivalent to that at which he composed the cantatas.

Even if Bach's presumed five cycles and five Passions had survived, it might be difficult to make associations between the Passions and the cycles, since the complex dramatic and variegated nature of the Passions could not be expected to fall completely under the categories to which the cantatas belong. That said, there is one instance in which we *do* see a close conjunction (at least a temporal one) between a Passion and a cantata cycle: Bach's first year in Leipzig, 1723–24, for which most of the cantatas have survived, as has the *St. John Passion*, first produced in spring 1724. And although Bach's first Leipzig cantata cycle does not exhibit the same consistency of cantata type as the chorale cantatas of his second Leipzig cycle, we nevertheless find from time to time within that cycle groupings of cantatas (particularly among the newly composed ones) that suggest Bach's thinking in terms of a larger design than the individual Sunday. Those groupings, which range from two to, in one instance, seven cantatas, relate to the *St. John Passion* in one very important respect: they all begin with introductory choruses that cite or are based closely on excerpts from scripture (usually called biblical *dicta*), most often from the psalms.[30] Figure 1.1 illustrates this quality for the cantatas of the 1723 Trinity

[30] Of the sixty liturgical occasions on which cantatas were performed in the 1723–24 cycle (and for only three of which occasions the cantatas are unknown), Bach produced one (occasionally two) new

Trin. 1	5/30	75: *Die Elenden sollen essen*	*ch., r, a, r, a, r, c. // sinf., r, a, r, a, r, c.
Trin. 2	6/6	76: *Die Himmel erzählen die Ehre Gottes*	*ch., r, a, r, a, r, c. // sinf., r, a, r, a, r, c.
Trin. 3	6/13	21: *Ich hatte viel Bekümmernis*	Weimar, 1714
Trin. 4	6/20	185: *Barmherziges Herze der ewigen Liebe* 24: *Ein ungefärbt Gemüte*	Weimar, 1715 a, r, *ch., r, a, c.
John the Baptist	6/24	167: *Ihr Menschen, rühmet Gottes Liebe*	Weimar, 1715
Trin. 5	6/27	?	–
Visitation of Mary	7/2	147: *Herz und Mund und Tat und Leben*	Weimar, 1716
Trin. 6	7/4	?	–
Trin. 7	7/11	186: *Ärgre dich, o Seele, nicht*	Weimar, 1716
Trin. 8	7/18	136: *Erforsche mich, Gott, und erfahre mein Herz*	*ch., r, a, r, a, c.
Trin. 9	7/25	105: *Herr, gehe nicht ins Gericht mit deinem Knecht*	*ch., r, a, r, a, c.
Trin. 10	8/1	46: *Schauet doch und sehet, ob irgend ein Schmerz sei*	*ch., r, a, r, a, c.
Trin. 11	8/8	179: *Siehe zu, daß deine Gottesfurcht nicht Heuchelei sei*	*ch., r, a, r, a, c.
Trin. 12	8/15	69a: *Lobe den Herrn, meine Seele*	*ch., r, a, r, a, c.
Trin. 13	8/22	77: *Du sollt Gott, deinen Herren, lieben*	*ch., r, a, r, a, c.
Trin. 14	8/25	25: *Es ist nichts Gesundes an meinem Leibe*	*ch., r, a, r, a, c.
Ratswechsel	8/30	119: *Preise, Jerusalem, den Herrn*	*ch., r, a, r, a, r, *ch. r, c.
Trin. 15	9/5	138: *Warum betrübst du dich, mein Herz*	cch.+r, r, cch.+r, r, a, r, c.
Trin. 16	9/12	95: *Christus, der ist mein Leben*	cch+r+cch, r, c, r, a, r, c.
Trin. 17	9/19	148(?): *Bringet dem Herrn Ehre seines Namens*	*ch., a, r, a, r, c.
Trin. 18	9/26	?	–
St. Michael	9/29	?	–
Trin. 19	10/3	48: *Ich elender Mensch, wer wird mich erlösen*	*ch., r, c, a, r, a, c.
Trin. 20	10/10	162: *Ach! Ich sehe, itzt, da ich zur Hochzeit gehe*	Weimar, 1716?
Trin. 21	10/17	109: *Ich glaube, lieber Herr, hilf meinem Unglauben*	*ch., r, a, r, a, c.
Trin. 22	10/24	89: *Was soll ich aus dir machen, Ephraim?*	*a, r, a, r, a, c.
Trin. 23	10/31	163(?): *Nur jedem das Seine*	Weimar, 1715
Reformation	10/31	?	–
Trin. 24	11/7	60: *O Ewigkeit, du Donnerwort*	*+c., r, a, r, c.
Trin. 25	11/14	90: *Es reiffet euch ein schrecklich Ende*	a, r, a, r, ch.
Trin. 26	11/21	70: *Wachet! betet! betet! wachet!*	Weimar, 1716
Trin. 27	none	–	–

FIGURE 1.1 **The cantatas for Trinity 1723** *Cantatas enclosed within boxes exhibit the same or very similar textual designs. Formal designations in column four are for newly composed cantatas only. Asterisks indicate movements based on biblical* dicta. *Ch = chorus, r = recitative, a = aria, sinf = sinfonia, c = simple chorale, cch = chorale chorus, // = the division between parts one and two of two-part cantatas*

season. In many of these cantatas the *dictum* in question proclaims a central theme for the work as a whole that is then interpreted throughout the subsequent movements. This is also the case with "Herr, unser Herrscher," the opening movement of the *St. John Passion*. This quality bonds the 1724 *St. John Passion* to the first cycle to some degree.

In spring 1724 the first performance of Bach's *St. John Passion* lent a singularly Johannine character to the Good Friday service. Yet, while most of the six newly composed cantatas performed in the weeks that followed also featured Johannine elements, they were outnumbered by works that were either parodies of secular works or re-performances of earlier cantatas, generally with no particular connection to John (see fig. 1.2).[31] Owing, perhaps, to the production of a new Passion in

---

cantatas on thirty-eight feast days, making a total of about forty cantatas composed specifically for that cycle. On a few feast days the dating of the cantata in question is uncertain, but on some sixteen occasions Bach produced compositions written either in Weimar or Mühlhausen, or parodied from secular cantatas. Of the new cantatas, twenty-eight feature a biblical motto as text of the opening movement, that is, approximately three-quarters of the new cantatas. Seven new cantatas do not; but four other new cantatas feature biblical mottoes in a movement other than the first. Also, seven of the Weimar cantatas have biblical mottoes, two in the opening movement. From all this it seems that Bach noticeably favored biblical-motto cantatas for the 1723–24 cycle. Interesting in this regard, is the fact that at a few times among the 1723–24 cantatas we find sequences of cantatas, newly composed for the cycle, that resemble one another closely, both in their textual designs and their theological subject matter, a quality suggesting subgroupings within the cycle. These works nearly always begin with OT *dicta* chosen to connect up with the Gospel for the day and serving as springboards to multifaceted interpretation in the movements that follow. This occurrence is most prominent in the pairing of the first two cantatas of the cycle, for the first and second Sundays after Trinity (BWV 75 and 76), and the cantatas performed on the eighth through the fourteenth Sundays after Trinity. At a few other points similar, less pronounced, parallels occur. Thus, near the true beginning of the liturgical cycle that year we find that the librettist/s of the cantatas for the second and third days of Christmas, *Darzu ist erschienen der Sohn Gottes* (Cantata 40) and *Sehet, welch eine Liebe* (Cantata 64), reached outside the prescribed readings for those feast days, apparently so as to bring out Johannine themes more fully. Bach's settings respond to the texts very closely and sensitively in terms of their Johannine qualities, to the extent that they, like Cantatas 75 and 76, form a continuity in their theological message, one culminating in a striking expression of John's realized eschatology; but there is otherwise nothing in the two cantatas (at least in musical terms) that might suggest a pairing. It appears that the anomalous but very meaningful deviations from the prescribed Gospel readings in these cantatas were the creation of the librettist.

[31] See Alfred Dürr, *The Cantatas of J. S. Bach*, trans. Richard D. P. Jones rev. ed. (Oxford: Oxford University Press 2005), 26–29. The six new cantatas were 67, *Halt im Gedächtnis Jesum Christ*, for Quasimodogeniti; 104, *Du Hirte Israel, höre*, for Misericordias Domini; 166, *Wo gehst du hin*, for Cantate; 86, *Wahrlich, wahrlich, ich sage euch*, for Rogate; 37, *Wer da gläubet und getauft wird*, for Ascension Day; and 44, *Sie werden euch in den Bann tun*, for Exaudi. Of these works, three (166, 86, and 44) begin with mottoes from John, while one other (67) contains as its fourth movement an "aria" with chorus that cites Jesus's words "Friede sei mit euch!" from John's Gospel for the day four times in alternation with the chorus. Cantata 37, for Ascension Day, has, understandably, no connection with John, while Cantata 104, beginning with a motto from Psalm 80, sticks close to the subject matter from John; its emphasis on the "foretaste" of eternity in the present life—especially in the aria "Beglückte Herde Jesu Schafe, die Welt ist euch ein Himmelreich. Hier schmeckt ihr Jesu Güte schon und hoffet noch des Glaubens Lohn nach einem sanften Todesschlafe"—expresses the extent to which Lutheranism approached John's "realized" eschatology. Some eleven other cantatas have been documented, with varying degrees of certainty, as having been heard between Easter and Trinity 1724 (sometimes two per feast day): 31, *Der Himmel lacht, die Erde jubiliret*, 4, *Christ lag in Todesbanden* (both on Easter Day); 66, *Erfreut euch, ihr Herzen* (Easter Monday); 134, *Ein Herz, das seinen Jesum lebend weiss* (Easter Tuesday);

Good Friday (4/3)	*St. John Passion*: original version	Based on Jn 18–19	first performance
Easter Sunday (4/9)	Cantata 4: *Christ lag in Todesbanden*; and 31: *Die Himmel lacht! Die Erde jubilieret*	BWV 4: chorale cantata; BWV 31: no *dictum*	re-performances of cantatas written in Mühlhausen (4?) and Weimar (31)
Easter Monday (4/10)	Cantata 66: *Erfreut euch, ihr Herzen*	no *dictum*	parody of Köthen secular cantata
Easter Tuesday (4/11)	Cantata 134: *Ein Herz, das seinen Jesum lebend weiß*	no *dictum*	parody of Köthen secular cantata
Quasimodo-geniti (4/16)	Cantata 67: *Halt im Gedächtnis Jesum Christ*	two *dicta*: nos. 1 (Tim) & 6 (Jn 20:19)	new
Misericordias Domini (4/23)	Cantata 104: *Du Hirte, Israel, höre*	*dictum* (no. 1), from Ps 80:1	new
Jubilate (4/30)	Cantata 12: *Weinen, Klagen, Sorgen, Zagen*	*dictum* (no. 2) from Acts 14:22	re-performance of Weimar cantata
Cantate (5/7)	Cantata 166: *Wo gehest du hin*	*dictum* (no. 1) from Jn 16:5	new
Rogate (5/14)	Cantata 86: *Wahrlich, wahrlich, ich sage euch*	*dictum* (no. 1) from Jn 16:23	new
Ascension Day (5/18)	Cantata 37: *Wer da gläubet und getauft wird*	*dictum* (no. 1) from Mk 16:16	new
Exaudi (5/21)	Cantata 44: *Sie werden euch in den Bann tun*	*dictum* (no. 1) from Jn 16:2	new
Pentecost: Sunday (5/28)	Cantata 172, *Erschallet, ihr Lieder* and (?) Cantata 59: *Wer mich liebet, der wird mein Wort halten*	172: *dictum* (no. 2) from Jn 14:23; 59: *dictum* (no. 1) from Jn 14:23	re-performance of Weimar cantata (172); possibly also BWV 59 (composed 1723)
Pentecost: Monday (5/29)	Cantata 173: *Erhöhtes Fleisch und Blut*	no *dictum*	parody of Köthen secular cantata
Pentecost: Tuesday (5/30)	Cantata 184: *Erwünschtes Freudenlicht*	no *dictum*	parody of Köthen secular cantata
Trinity Sunday (6/4)	Cantata 194 *Hocherwünschtes Freudenfest* and 165?: *O heilges Geist- und Wasserbad*	no *dicta*	re-performances of dedicatory cantata (194) and Weimar cantata (165?)

FIGURE 1.2 **The Passion and cantata performances of spring 1724**

1724, Bach might not have had time to compose new works for all the feastdays to the end of the cycle. In the corresponding weeks of 1725, however, the focus on cantatas with Johannine mottoes in their texts was particularly strong (fig. 1.3).

12, *Weinen, Klagen, Sorgen Zagen* (Jubilate); 172, *Ershallet ihr Lieder, erklinget, ihr Saiten*, 59, *Wer mich lieber, der wird mein Wort halten* (both on Whitsunday); 173, *Erhöhtes Fleisch und Blut* (probably on the second day of Pentecost); 184, *Erwünschtes Freudenlicht* (the third day of Pentecost); and 194, *Höchsterwünschtes Freudenfest*, and 165, *O heiliges Geist- und Wasserbad* (presumably both on Trinity Sunday). Of these works only the cantatas for Whitsunday (172 and 59) feature mottoes or other conspicuous elements from John.

Good Friday (3/3)	St. John Passion	Based on John, chapters 18–19	second performance, with alterations
Easter Sunday (4/1)	Cantata 249: *Kommt, gehet und eilet*	Dramatic nonbiblical text; characters Mary Magdalene, Mary, mother of James, Peter, John	parody of Shepherd cantata (249a: 1725)
Easter Monday (4/2)	Cantata 6: *Bleib bei uns, denn es will Abend werden*	*dictum* (no. 1) from Luke 24:29	new: text possibly written in 1724
Easter Tuesday (4/3)	Cantata unknown	–	–
Quasimodo-geniti (4/8)	Cantata 42: *Am Abend aber desselbigen Sabbats*	*dictum* (no. 2) from John 20:19	new: text possibly written in 1724
Misericordias Domini (4/15)	Cantata 85: *Ich bin ein guter Hirt*	*dictum* (no. 1) from John 10:12 (Jesus)	new: text possibly written in 1724
Jubilate (4/22)	Cantata 103: *Ihr werdet weinen und heulen*	*dictum* (No. 1) from John 16:20 (Jesus)	new: Ziegler
Cantate (4/29)	Cantata 108: *Es ist euch gut, daß ich hingehe*	2 *dicta* (nos 1 & 4) from John 16 (both Jesus)	new: Ziegler
Rogate (5/6)	Cantata 87: *Bisher habt ihr nichts gebeten in meinem Namen*	2 *dicta* (nos. 1 & 5) from John 16 (both Jesus)	new: Ziegler
Ascension Day (5/10)	Cantata 128: *Auf Christi Himmelfahrt allein*	No *dictum*	new: Ziegler
Exaudi (5/13)	Cantata 183: *Sie werden euch in den Bann tun*	*dictum* (no. 1) John 16:2 (Jesus)	new: Ziegler
Pentecost: Sunday (5/20)	Cantata 74: *Wer mich liebet, der wird mein Wort halten*	2 *dicta* (nos. 1 & 4) from John 14 (Jesus): *dictum* (no. 6) from Rom 8:1	movements 1 and 2 reworked from Cantata 59. Ziegler
Pentecost: Monday (5/21)	Cantata 68: *Also hat Gott die Welt geliebt*	*dictum* (no. 5) from John 3:18 (Jesus); chorale paraphrase (no. 1) of John 3:16	both arias (nos. 2 & 4) reworked from 1713 (?) Shepherd cantata (208) 1713 (?). Ziegler
Pentecost: Tuesday (5/22)	Cantata 175: *Er rufet seinen Schafen mit Namen*	2 *dicta* from John 10 (nos. 1 [Jesus] & 4)	new: Ziegler
Trinity Sunday (5/27)	Cantata 176: *Es ist ein trotzig und verzagt Ding*	2 *dicta* from Jer (1) and John 3 (4: Jesus)	new: Ziegler

FIGURE 1.3 **The Passion and cantata performances of spring 1725**

Apart from the second performance of the *St. John Passion*, now in revised form, and the dramatic cantata that later became the *Easter Oratorio* (BWV 249), we have cantatas for twelve of the thirteen feast days from Easter through Trinity Sunday 1725: nos. 6, 42, 85, 103, 108, 87, 128, 183, 74, 68, 175, and 176 (as mentioned, only the cantata for Easter Tuesday is missing).[32] Of these twelve works, ten—the

[32] Bach's three surviving cantatas for Easter Tuesday, BWV 134, 145, and 158, all offer problems of one kind or another regarding their dating and sources (145 and 158), versions (134), and even the intended performance occasion/s (158); see Dürr, *Cantatas*, 284–90.

cantatas from Quasimodogeniti (42) to Rogate (87) and from Exaudi (183) to Trinity (176)—have one or more excerpts from the Gospel reading from John for the day in question. The exceptions are the cantatas for Easter Monday, *Bleib bei uns, denn es will Abend werden*, (Cantata 6) and Ascension Day, *Auf Christi Himmelfahrt allein* (Cantata 128), two feasts that do not have Gospel or epistle readings from John. Those two cantatas, however, do have certain specific connections to John, as does the original form of the *Easter Oratorio* (these features will be addressed in chs. 9 and 10).

In addition to their emphasis on John, the cantatas of spring 1725 reflect the apparently coincidental situation that the cycle of chorale cantatas that had begun after Trinity Sunday the preceding year came suddenly to an end one week before Easter 1725. Bach continued to produce new cantatas, though no chorale cantatas, through the Sunday (Trinity) that officially ended the cycle, but after that, so far as we know, he might have ceased to produce cantatas at the regular pace he had followed for exactly two years. The reasons for these events are unknown, although a variety of tentative explanations have been offered.[33] The most obvious explanation for a break in cantata composition (if there really was one) is that having completed the composition of two years' worth of cantatas (if not exactly two cycles, at least in the "ideal" sense), Bach could re-perform them without repeating cantatas on successive years. This does not explain the change in cantata *type* from Easter to Trinity 1725, however.

With respect to the latter situation, the best-known feature of the cantatas of spring 1725 is that nine successive works (beginning with Jubilate and continuing through Trinity: nos. 103 through 176) form a group set to texts of Mariane von Ziegler, which were published by her in Leipzig a few years later.[34] Since the anonymous texts of the first three surviving cantatas after Easter Day 1725, those for Easter Monday (6), Quasimodogeniti (42), and Misericordias Domini (85), resemble one another very closely in certain respects—the first beginning with a motto from the Gospel for that day (Lk 24:29) and the other two with mottoes from John—and since the Ziegler cantatas, beginning on the following week (Jubilate), mostly carry forward the idea of beginning with biblical mottoes, now from John, it is possible that the succession of works reflects a design for the post-

---

[33] With regard to the breaking off of the chorale cantatas, Dürr (*Die Kantaten,* 1:53) speculates that either the author of the texts of the chorale cantatas discontinued for some reason or that the cantatas corresponded to a cycle of chorale-based sermons that changed its theme. With regard to the lack of cantatas immediately following the end of the cycle on Trinity Sunday, Gerhard Herz suggests that Bach might have withdrawn from church composition as early as 1725 in part because of dissatisfactions that became clear only a few years later, and in part because he wanted to reach a wider public through the printing of keyboard music. See Herz, "Toward a New Image of Bach," *Bach: Quarterly Journal of the Riemenschneider Bach Institute* 1, no. 4 (October 1970): 11–16.

[34] Mariane Ziegler, *Versuch in gebundener Schreib-Art* (Leipzig, 1728). The pages from Ziegler's publication that contain the nine texts set by Bach are reproduced in facsimile in Werner Neumann, ed., *Sämtliche von Johann Sebastian Bach vertonte Texte* (Leipzig, 1974), 358–65. See Mark A. Peters, *A Woman's Voice in Barogue Music: Mariane von Ziegler and J. S. Bach* (Burlington, VT: Ashgate, 2008).

Easter cantatas as a whole and not merely a situation forced on the composer by external circumstances. If so, we might consider the most conspicuous part of that design as follows: after the two non-Ziegler cantatas that begin with mottoes from John, seven (or eight) of the "series" of nine cantatas by Ziegler that follows draw upon mottoes from John, several of them, in fact, upon more than one such motto (see fig. 1.3).[35]

Since Ziegler published only these nine cantatas in her 1728 collection of poetry, we might speculate that their production was done specifically for spring 1725, perhaps as a special one-time "commission," planned in advance.[36] If so, we might wonder why she did not compose chorale cantata texts, especially since there is evidence, from her producing some of the texts to fit preexistent music by Bach, that she must have worked closely with the composer at least some of the time. If the conception of a chorale cantata cycle was Bach's, why was it altered after Easter, so close to its point of completion? In the discussion that follows I consider that whatever the reason for the breaking off of the chorale cantatas, Ziegler's texts were perhaps intended to complete a design originally intended for the *preceding* year, when the *St. John Passion* was heard in its original version. In other words, the 1725 post-Easter cantatas might have been thought of as normally following the *St. John Passion* in its original 1724 version. It is extremely unlikely, however, that this situation ever took place, since none of the known later performances of the *St. John Passion* was that of the original version; nor were the 1725 cantatas ever performed, so far as we know, in the context of a re-performance of the 1723–24 cycle.[37] The only real link among the two would therefore have to

---

[35] Ziegler's publication (see n. 41) identifies biblical mottoes with the word *Dictum*. Cantata 128, for Ascension Day (which had no reading from John) has no motto beginning and no texts derived from John. Cantata 176, for Trinity Sunday, begins with a motto from Jeremiah; in Ziegler's printed version it has no motto or paraphrase from John, but in Bach's setting a paraphrase is added, possibly by Bach himself, to the end of the only recitative (the fourth movement). See Dürr, *Cantatas*, 377. The remaining seven Ziegler cantatas all have at least one motto from John, all but one (BWV 68) beginning with such a motto. Cantatas 108, 87, 74, and 175 all have two mottoes from John, one at the beginning and one as the fourth (108, 74) or fifth (87, 175) movement. Cantata 74 also features a third biblical motto, from Paul (the sixth movement); Cantata 68 *ends* with its Johannine motto (the fifth movement), and contains chorale and recitative paraphrases from John's Gospel for the day as its first and part of its third movement.

[36] Gunther Stiller's *Johann Sebastian Bach and Liturgical Life in Leipzig*, trans. Herbert J. A. Bouman, Daniel F. Poellot, and Hilton C. Oswald, ed. Robin A. Leaver, 210 (St. Louis: Concordia, 1984), argues that Mariane von Ziegler's statement of "final purpose" as set forth by her in the publication of poetry that contains the cantata texts set by Bach expresses a "totally different frame of mind" from that of Bach as set forth in his statements of "final purpose" and concludes that "this was very likely also the reason why a lasting cooperation with Christiane Mariane von Ziegler was impossible for Bach." As Ferdinand Zander points out ("Die Dichter der Kantatentexte Johann Sebastian Bachs: Untersuchungen zu ihrer Bestimmung," *Bach-Jahrbuch* 1968: 25), in Ziegler's second volume of poetry (1729) she published an entire cantata cycle of which Bach, so far as we know, set nothing. Zander remarks that Bach apparently never altered texts of any librettist as much as he did those of Mariane von Ziegler, speculating that rivalry between Gottsched (to whose circle Ziegler belonged) and Picander played a role.

[37] Alfred Dürr's remark that at a later time Bach removed most of the cantatas from Easter to Pentecost 1725 from the chorale cantata cycle and included them in his third cycle (Dürr, *Cantatas*,35–36)

be considered as completely *ideal*; and this is something that would demand considerable evidence. Nevertheless, there remains such a possibility here; at the very least, it draws attention to the problems involved, and it has the potential to point up theological affinities between the *St. John Passion* and the 1725 post-Easter cantatas, especially as those cantatas relate to the biblical-motto cantatas of 1723–24.

As several commentators have pointed out, Cantatas 6, 42, and 85—the first three surviving cantatas after Easter Day 1725 and the only non-Ziegler texts of spring 1725, apart from the parodied cantata that was to become the *Easter Oratorio*—closely parallel the design of four cantatas from the spring of 1724 (nos. 166, 86, 37, and 44: see figs. 1.2 and 1.3). Each of these seven cantatas presents the same movement sequence (or a very close variation of it): biblical motto, aria, chorale, followed by recitative, aria, chorale.[38] Cantatas 6 and 85 follow the sequence exactly, while Cantata 42 precedes it by an instrumental Sinfonia (a decision of Bach's, of course, not of the librettist; the pattern of the text is the same). The fact that the spring 1725 works of this type all appear on different feast days from those of the preceding year (Easter Monday, Quasimodogeniti, and Misericordias Domini 1725, as opposed to Cantate, Rogate, Ascension Day, and Exaudi 1724), supports the idea that their texts form a "group" written by the same author and perhaps in the same year, 1724. In that year Bach's cantatas for all three days of Easter were either re-performances of works written in earlier years or parodies of secu-

---

does not contradict the possibility that at the time of their composition Bach was thinking of completing the *first* cycle. As Dürr indicates, the third cycle, as it survives today, is "no longer the result of continuous cantata composition in the course of a single year. Either it is a *mixtum compositum* of two cycles (or even three if we take account of the cantatas borrowed from Cycle II), or else suspension of Bach's creativity during the Trinity period of 1725 caused the composition of Cycle III to be spread out over several years so that gaps could be filled."

[38] Dürr, *Cantatas*, 27–28. Dürr differentiates this third "group" of cantatas from two other groups with somewhat different orderings of movement types that occur at other points within the first Leipzig cycle (but all beginning with biblical mottoes). In fact, Cantata 67 also follows the same sequence, except that its opening motto is not drawn from the Gospel for the day, that it features a recitative between the initial biblical motto and the first aria, and that its second "aria" is a hybrid form featuring a motto (from John's Gospel for the day) in alternation with chorus. Dürr (*Cantatas*, 27) places it with another group of cantatas (his second), which follow the sequence bible motto, recitative, chorale, aria, recitative, aria, chorale. Cantata 67, however, resembles that pattern less than it does the one followed by Cantatas 166, 86, 37, and 44 of the same season. It may be noted that all six of the newly composed spring cantatas of 1724 belong to one of the three groups (BWV 104 to group one, and 67 to either group two or three); also two other cantatas of the first cycle that feature mottoes from John (BWV 40 and 64) belong to the second group. Rudolf Wustmann (*Johann Sebastian Bachs Kantatentexte* [Leipzig: Breitkopf & Härtel, 1913], 75) noted that a number of texts of Bach's first cycle exhibited poetico-theological traits that seemed to originate with a theologian-author; he assigned eleven such works to Christian Weiß the elder (BWV 37, 44, 67, 75, 76, 81, 86, 104, 154, 166, 179). Interestingly, this group of works contains Bach's first two Leipzig cantatas of late spring 1723 (BWV 75 and 76) as well as the six newly composed cantatas of spring 1724. William Scheide ascribes Cantatas 166, 86, 37, 44, 6, 42, and 85 to a single author, adding the Reformation cantata, BWV 79, to the list. Scheide, "Johann Sebastian Bachs Sammlung von Kantaten, Part 2," *Bach-Jahrbuch* (1961): 10). Zander ("Die Dichter der Kantatentexte Johann Sebastian Bachs," 33–34) argues that the many verbal correspondences between the chorales of these cantatas and the madrigal-texted movements indicate that the chorales were chosen first and the madrigal texts composed around them.

lar cantatas. After that (on Quasimodogeniti and Misericordias) follow two new cantatas (67 and 104), one of which resembles the type just described in some respects, while the other does not. On the following week (Jubilate) Bach re-performed another Weimar cantata; and after that, the four cantatas mentioned above appear in succession, all of which begin with biblical mottoes from the Gospels for the days in question. For the remainder of the season, however, all the cantatas were either re-performances or parodies. The six new cantatas of 1724, therefore, all began with biblical mottoes, the first two (those not of the prevailing type) with mottoes *not* from the Gospels for the days on which they were heard, and the other four *with* such mottoes, three of which are therefore from John's Farewell Discourse (nos. 166, 86, and 44).

If Bach had the idea of a unified cycle in mind (presumably one with biblical motto beginnings), then only the *new* cantatas should be considered. Parodies and re-performances could not be expected to fit the pattern, although sometimes they do. That the first and second new cantatas of this time period, Cantatas 67 and 104 (for Quasimodogeniti and Misericordias 1724) begin with mottoes that are *not* drawn from the Gospel for the day, that of John, may mean that, as the first and second post-Easter cantatas of 1724, they were composed before the pattern of the remaining four new cantatas had been adopted.[39] In other words, the other four new cantatas of 1724 and the three surviving 1725 cantatas of the same textual type, taken together, may represent a series of seven texts created for the time between Easter and Pentecost (perhaps eight if the missing cantata for Easter Tuesday were of the same type). Those works all begin with biblical mottoes drawn from the Gospels for the days in question. One other cantata that might have been performed in spring 1724 also begins with a motto drawn from John, the Gospel for the day, *Wer mich liebet, der wird mein Wort halten* (BWV 59, for Pentecost); it was written no later than 1723 but was most likely not performed that year.[40] It shares with the cantatas of the group in question the motto beginning and placement of a chorale as the third movement; but it appears to be incomplete, consisting of only four movements and ending with an aria. Since Bach and Ziegler took over the first and fourth movements of this cantata into Cantata 74 of 1725 (re-arranging the first movement and supplying a completely new text for the fourth), it seems that they intended Cantata 74 as a replacement for Cantata 59.

From the foregoing details, it appears possible that in 1725 Bach, as Alfred Dürr hypothesizes, began the sequence of cantatas that interrupted the chorale cantata cycle by setting texts produced the year before but for unknown reasons not set to

[39] Remember, though, that they belong with the other new cantatas of spring 1724 to the group of cantatas whose texts Wustmann assigned to Christian Weiß the elder (see n. 42). Scheide ("Johann Sebastian Bachs Sammlung, Part 2", 11) points out that apart from the cantatas of the aforementioned "group," only Cantatas 67 and 104 are completely new, arguing that "there is reason to believe that their texts were delivered to Bach several months earlier."

[40] See Dürr, *Cantatas*, 349–50.n. 1.

music at that time.[41] If all the texts that form this group were indeed written by 1724, then we must probably presume that Bach planned a group of cantatas of the same type for the weeks immediately following Easter that year, but was unable to set them all at that time for external reasons, such as lack of time for any advance composition owing to the production of a new Passion. Hence the parodies and re-performances of that year. Since the *St. John Passion* was re-performed (in revised form) in 1725, the sequence of texts that make up this group, most of which feature mottoes from John, would follow easily from the *St. John Passion* in either year. But whereas in 1724 they would fit with the dominant cantata type, in 1725 they break with the pattern of the chorale cantatas. From that standpoint alone, we might speculate that in setting those texts in 1725 Bach was attempting to complete a project related to the cycle of the preceding year. That he composed new cantatas in 1725 for occasions for which he had produced new cantatas the preceding year might have been because, having already re-performed the Passion heard the preceding year, he did not want also to re-perform a group of cantatas from 1724. In relation to the chorale cantatas, the Ziegler cantatas have a noticeable increase in parodied movements; the incidence of completely parodied cantatas and of the re-performance of older works, however, is greatly lessened in relation to the corresponding feast days of the year before (perhaps because in 1725 Bach did not produce a new Passion). And from the fact that some of Mariane von Ziegler's texts had to have been created to fit preexistent music, we may speculate with reason that Bach himself had input into the theological character of the cantata sequence.

To summarize the hypothesis: In 1725, after the re-performance of the *St. John Passion* in its revised form, Bach produced for Easter Day a parody of the "Shepherd Cantata" (BWV 249a), written earlier that year. In several respects it appears that this cantata, later to become the *Easter Oratorio*, might have been designed or at least modified from its parody original so as to follow the *St. John Passion.*[42] He then composed a series of basically new works, of which the first three to survive (Cantatas 6, 42, and 85) utilized texts perhaps written, but not set to music, the preceding year. Then, having set the next four texts from that group the preceding year, Bach picked up with Mariane von Ziegler's cantata texts, which extended to the end of the cycle. This gave him a series of twelve or thirteen cantatas, nearly all of which begin with biblical mottoes. Since he presumably did not wish to re-perform works of the preceding year, the cantatas for Quasimodogeniti and Misericordias Domini (42 and 85) as well as four of Ziegler's cantatas (108, 87, 128, and 183) were heard on feast days for which the works of the preceding year had been newly composed. In addition, as mentioned, Cantata 74 replaces the incomplete 1723 work of the same title, Cantata 59, which would, presumably, have come next in the sequence.

---

[41] Ibid., 27–28.

[42] See the discussion of Cantata 249 in ch. 8.

Of the non-Ziegler works of 1725, Cantatas 42 and 85 both begin with mottos from John whereas the corresponding works of the preceding year (67 and 104) did not. And, setting aside the cantata for Ascension Day (128) for which there is no reading from John, four of the five Ziegler cantatas for those occasions on which new cantatas were produced in 1724 (108, 87, 183, and 74) all feature either the same motto or a very closely related one to the corresponding works from 1724 (166, 86, 44, and 59). In covering much the same ground as he had in 1724, but at the same time expanding ideas that the *new* works of that year had introduced, especially the emphasis on John, these cantatas give the impression that creating a sequence of cantatas to follow the *St. John Passion* might have been the intent. Although those cantatas might never again have followed a performance of the *St. John Passion*, and definitely not one of the Passion's original version, they can be considered to fulfill the theological purpose behind such a conception. That is, the Johannine view of Jesus's greatest work—emerging in the *Christus Victor* theology of the *St. John Passion*—would have been completed in the post-Easter cantatas, which articulated the fundamental message of scripture regarding Jesus's incarnation and sacrifice as the outcome of God's love and its immediate benefit for humanity.

{ 2 }

The Ordering of Salvation

ASPECTS OF SCRIPTURE AND THE LITURGICAL YEAR

Introduction: The "four senses," salvation history, and the liturgical year

In beginning with a paraphrase from one of the psalms, which it then places entirely in the context of Jesus and the New Testament (NT), Bach's *St. John Passion* evokes what is probably the most ubiquitous characteristic not only of the Lutheran religion but of Christianity as a whole: the Christocentric interpretation of all the scriptures, both OT and NT.[1] This practice, according to which the scriptures formed a unity rooted in God's revelation of his plan for the salvation of humankind, began with the NT authors themselves, and is very prominent in them all, including John. In the Middle Ages it found its most systematic expression in the multiple senses of medieval hermeneutics: the literal-historical (usually centered on a passage from the Hebrew Bible), allegorical (interpretation of the passage according to the NT or the church), tropological (faith-centered meaning, often focused on the individual believer), and eschatological (interpretation in light of eternity).

Since the discipline of hermeneutics arose in response to the often very different characteristics of the two parts of the Bible, its principles were rooted in the necessity of harmonizing the two and relating them to the faith experience of the believer. Luther's earliest psalm commentaries follow the ancient pattern quite closely. And, although his later hermeneutics, and that of many of his successors, voiced considerable rejection of the medieval scheme, the principles that they ar-

[1] Three works cited in this book make this point abundantly clear: Valerius Herberger, *DE JESU, Scripturae nucleo & medulla, MAGNALIA Dei. Das ist: Die grossen Thaten GOTTES von JEsu, Der gantzen Schrifft Kern und Stern, . . .* 5th ed. (Leipzig, 1700) (hereafter *De Jesu . . . Magnalia Dei*); Herberger heads each individual chapter with the name of Jesus as subject matter (e.g., "Jesus der edelste Weinstock in Noahs Weinberge und aller frommen Christan Herzgärtlein"); Francke, *CHRISTUS / Der Kern heiliger Schrifft* (Halle, 1702: see ch. 1, n. 3); Johan Jacob Rambach, *Christus in Mose* (Halle, 1728).

ticulated in its place were very obviously derived from and sometimes indistinguishable from it. The greatest point of difference was in the application of allegory, which had, in the Lutheran view, wandered away from the center, Christ, to the institutes of the church, monastic life, and the like.[2] In keeping with Luther's reforms, it is not at all usual for Lutheran theological books to set forth this pattern in the manner that centuries of (mostly Roman Catholic) authors did (except, sometimes, to criticize it). Nevertheless, they draw on that tradition extensively, frequently utilizing patterns that are unmistakably variations of it, in the terminology, the number of senses, their further subdivision, and so forth. Although such variants were common throughout the Middle Ages as well, in some Lutheran theoretical writings on hermeneutics during the seventeenth and eighteenth centuries (such as those of Johann Jacob Rambach), the discipline reached levels of complexity that seem at odds with the far more direct and immediate practice of exegesis in the writings of the same authors.[3]

---

[2] As is well known, Luther applied the four senses in many of his early writings; see *Luther's Works,* vol. 10, *First Lectures on the Psalms*, ed. Hilton C. Oswald, xi (St. Louis: Concordia, 1974). The question of his rejection of the medieval system centered on the allegorical sense, which had been used by Jesus and the disciples and could not be rejected, but which, as Luther felt, had been bowdlerized by many commentators. For an excellent summary by Luther of his own views, see *Luther's Works,* vol. 2, *Lectures on Genesis, Chapters 6–14*, ed. Jaroslav Pelikan, 150–64 ("Concerning allegories") (St. Louis: Concordia, 1960). In this discussion Luther refers to the "rule in use by the apostles" and the "rule of Paul, who enjoins in Romans 12:6 that prophecy of doctrine should be conformable to the faith" (151). This is the well-known "allegory [or analogy] of [the] faith that Luther referred to elsewhere and that was a common term in writings on hermeneutics before and after his time. See the final section of this chapter, "Johann Jacob Rambach on symmetry and the analogy of faith"). The basic study of medieval hermeneutics is Henri de Lubac's two-volume *Medieval Exegesis: The Four Senses of Scripture*; vol. 1, trans. Mark Sebanc (Grand Rapids, MI: Wm. B. Eerdmans, 1998); vol. 2, trans. E. M. Macierowski (Grand Rapids, MI: Wm. B. Eerdmans, 2000). The subject of "monastic exegesis" is discussed in de Lubac, 2:143–53.

[3] An interesting instance of how the senses survived and were reoriented toward ideas more amenable to Lutheranism than many of the traditional ones (to which Luther and many later Lutherans objected) is provided by comparison of Johann Jacob Rambach's discussion of the spiritual senses with Francke's discussion of baptism, cited in ch. 8. In Rambach's *Ausführliche und gründliche Erläuterung über seine eigene INSTITUTIONES HERMENEUTICAE SACRAE,* 2 vols. (Giessen, 1738), 1:218–19), he considers the division of the senses, criticizing those interpreters among the Jews, the church fathers, and the papists who err on the side of the excessive application of allegorical interpretation. Among the last category (which he explains as including the scholastics, who follow the fathers and precede the papists), are those who follow the threefold division of the "mystic" sense into the allegorical, tropological, and anagogical. As an illustration of such allegory Rambach selects the expression "de sabbato" (concerning the sabbath: God's resting on the seventh day after the work of creation), which according to the allegorical sense would be applied to faith (*ad credenda*), such as Christ's rest in the tomb (before the resurrection); according to the tropological sense (*ad agenda*), would be applied to cessation from sin; and according to the eschatological sense (*sensus anagogicus*: *ad speranda*) to the calm of eternal life. And in the passage from Francke we find a similar interpretation of baptism as the spiritual reenactment of Jesus's death, burial, and resurrection. Francke describes Jesus's burial as "pure stillness and quiet, nothing other than Sabbath, a peaceful awaiting of the resurrection" (Rambach's allegorical sense). This he compares to the peace of faith that comes through baptism, in which we are taken unto the peace of God, the rest of forgiveness of sins, justification, and blessedness. As Christ is buried, so are we in baptism dead to sin (Rambach's tropological sense); and as he is resurrected, so are we awakened to the peace of a new life through the Holy Spirit and ultimately to that of

Among musicians and musical settings, however, the patterns are understandably never as intricate or rationalized as those in the theological treatises, and may even reflect the basic underlying principles more directly. In a discussion headed "Von der Allegorischen und Moralischen Music" (allegorical and tropological music), for example, Bach's older contemporary, the music theorist Andreas Werckmeister, adapts the four senses to a discussion of the symbolic qualities associated with the basic materials of music, whereas Bach's predecessor in the Leipzig position, Johann Kuhnau, takes a more pragmatic stance, naming understanding of hermeneutics, which he subdivides into the *sensus*, *scopus*, and *pondus* of the text, as essential for the composition of sacred music.[4] The well-known theologian-poet Erdmann Neumeister sometimes embodies the senses in his cantata poetry in something close to their ancient form, whereas composers such as Telemann and Handel mirror them closely in certain of their works. Their appearance in Lutheran church works seems to expand on Luther's view of music as "next to theology" in its capacity to refresh the spirit.

In more concrete terms, a typical pattern for many Bach cantatas, usually rooted in a biblical story drawn from the Gospel for the day, is to explore its meaning from different sides—historical, doctrinal, collective, individual—ending with the ultimate hopes of the faithful, to live after death in God's presence. Often reaching back to draw on parallel passages from the OT, and frequently using one as a *dictum* or motto for the opening movement, then interpreting it from different sides in the movements that follow, many of Bach's texts articulate both the essential unity of scripture and an underlying progression through some version of the "senses," not necessarily the exact sequence that was favored in the Middle Ages but often one with very similar purpose and goals. That purpose, in its broadest sense, was to articulate the unity of the biblical scriptures as a single narrative centering on Christ and leading to the salvation of the faithful; hence the entirely Christological interpretation of the Psalms. Typological parallels between the Hebrew Bible and New Testaments abound in a language that is heavily permeated by biblical metaphors—Egypt as the world, Eden or Canaan as the Kingdom of God, Jerusalem nearly always in multiple senses, and the like—none of which needed

---

eternal life (Rambach's eschatological sense). Francke's interpretation would certainly have been approved by Rambach, who venerated Francke and cites from his writings often. Rambach (469) approves of the ancient interpretation of the *scopus* of the book of Judges in terms of the four senses ("scopum historicum, evangelicum, moralem & propheticum"). What seems like a contradiction between Rambach's disapproval of the traditional division of the spiritual senses and his practice in his own exegesis of interpretations comparable to Francke's (and the traditional divisions), derives, in fact, from Luther's acceptance or rejection of allegory according to whether such interpretation remained close to the historical sense, within which prophesy of the fundamental beliefs of Christianity, such as baptism, or the roles of law and gospel, could be clearly seen.

[4] See Andreas Werckmeister, *Musicae mathematicae hodegus curiosus* (Frankfurt and Leipzig, 1687), facsimile ed. (Hildesheim: Georg Olms Verlag, 1972), 141–54; Johann Kuhnau, preface to *Texte zur Leipziger Kirchen-Music* (Leipzig, 1710). Reprinted in B. F. Richter, "Eine Abhandlung Joh. Kuhnau's," *Monatshefte für Musik-Geschichte* 34 (1902): 148–54.

any explanation whatsoever. The patterns just described are especially prominent in certain of Bach's early cantatas, such as the *Actus tragicus* (Cantata 106), *Ich hatte viel Bekümmernis* (Cantata 21), and *Nun komm, der Heiden Heiland* (Cantata 61) Thus, in Cantata 21, not only the initial choral *dictum* but the whole of Part 1 (movements 1–6, all but the first of which are texted) is devoted to either psalm or psalm-derived texts that outline a state of mind that centers on tribulation, feelings of desertion by God, holding onto faith in the midst of adversity, and the like. The concluding chorus, setting a verse from Psalm 42, seems to summarize this viewpoint, voicing the believer's hopes in terms of the necessary awaiting of God's further revelation. After that, Part 2 begins immediately with the faith encounter with Jesus, symbolized in a pair of dialogs for soprano (the soul) and bass (Jesus). The believer, still feeling doubt and unrest, now receives assurance of God's comforting presence in Jesus, after which a double-texted choral movement combines a verse from Psalm 116, which was traditionally linked with the Psalm 42 verse that ended Part 1 with two verses of the chorale "Wer nur den lieben Gott läßt walten." Countering the spiritual unrest and tribulation voiced in Part 1, the two texts converge in a symbolic representation of the church's role in interpreting the scriptures, both OT and NT. The movement that follows, for soprano solo with *basso continuo*, the most intimately scored of the cantata, then calls for the transformation of tears ("Weinen") into the "wine of joy" ("Wein"), setting up the eschatological final chorus, the most fully scored of the work. Traditionally, the transformation of tears into wine (at the wedding at Cana) was interpreted as the progression from literal to spiritual interpretation.[5] Over the course of the movement sequence, a change from the initial C minor of Part 1 to the C major in which the cantata ends represents not only the transformation announced in the penultimate movement but also the stage by stage progression of the believer's consciousness from worldly tribulation to eschatological fulfillment.

Cantata 21 is only one of several early Bach cantatas that mirror the multiple senses of scripture. Undoubtedly the text that most *directly* reflects the ancient pattern is that of Erdmann Neumeister, which Bach used for Cantata 61, *Nun komm, der Heiden Heiland*, composed at Weimar in 1714 for Advent Sunday and reperformed in Leipzig for the beginning of the 1723–24 liturgical year. It was traditional at Advent to proclaim the various "senses" of Jesus's incarnation, in preparation for the liturgical year to follow, and Cantata 61 exhibits a movement sequence that was designed so as to outline those senses in a particularly straightforward manner, calling, over its succession of movements, for Jesus's advent to the world ("Nun komm, der Heiden Heiland"), to the church ("Komm, Jesu, komm zu deiner Kirche"), to the individual, internally ("Öffne dich, mein ganzes

[5] Thus, as E. Ann Matter indicates, in Book Four of Origen's *De Principiis*, the three or four measures of water that are miraculously turned into wine signify that "the words of scripture reveal three or four levels of meaning" (E. Ann Matter, *The Voice of My Beloved: The Song of Songs in Western Medieval Christianity* [Philadelphia: University of Pennsylvania Press, 1990], 28).

Herze, Jesus kömmt und ziehet ein"), and at the end of time ("Komm, du schöne Freudenkrone").

The liturgical year and God's plan of salvation

In the first chapter of his *Bach Among the Theologians*, Jaroslav Pelikan outlines for the general reader something I take to be axiomatic: the relevance of the seasons of the liturgical year to our understanding of J. S. Bach's composition of church music.[6] For anyone living within a religious community with a structured liturgy, such as the Leipzig of Bach's time, the individual characters of the seasons of the church year and the change from one to another were invested with a deep-rooted sense of meaning and purpose, one whose origins are not particular to Christianity and are undoubtedly as old as human civilization itself. That such a person could be unaware of those seasons is about as inconceivable as one being unaware of the seasons of the geophysical year. And, in fact, the four seasons Pelikan describes—centering on Christmas (Advent through Epiphany), Easter (including Lent), Pentecost (including Ascension Day), and Trinity (the entire series of up to twenty-seven Sundays)—parallel to a considerable degree the seasons of the geophysical year through the ancient alignment of Christmas with the winter solstice, and the Annunciation and Easter via the association of Jesus's Passion with Passover with the spring equinox. Pentecost (Whitsunday) and Trinity Sunday then occur one week apart in the late spring.[7] In general terms, therefore, the stretch from Christmas through Lent parallels the winter and that from Easter to Trinity the spring, while the long Trinity season coincides with summer and fall. The theological books of Bach's time often described the year in those terms.

It is natural, therefore, to think of the liturgical year as comprising two "halves" of about six months each and of markedly different characters. In the Lutheran version of the year, which was inherited with very few modifications from the

---

[6] Pelikan, *Bach Among the Theologians*, 2–12.

[7] More precisely, Easter can occur as early as March 22, roughly midway between Christmas and the summer solstice, and as late as April 25, whereas Pentecost, always the fiftieth day after Easter, ranges from May 10 to June 13, with Trinity one week later. Since the dates of the entire period from Easter to Trinity fluctuate within the span of a (lunar) month, Easter can be as early as one day after the Spring equinox and Trinity can be as late as one day before the summer solstice. The feast days whose dates are fixed so as to coincide with the spring equinox and the summer solstice (according to the Julian calendar) are those of the Annunciation (March 25) and John the Baptist (June 24). From ancient times the Easter season had begun with the feast of the Annunciation, in celebration not only of the Passion, but of the conception of Jesus, whose life thereby became a perfect thirty-three years from his conception to his death; accordingly, the dating of Christmas followed nine months later. See Peter G. Cobb, "The History of the Christian Year," in *The Study of Liturgy*, ed. Geoffrey Wainwright, Edward Yarnold, Paul Bradshaw, and Cheslyn Jones, 467: "The primitive Pascha celebrated the entire mystery of Christ including the incarnation with the moment of conception, which put the nativity nine months later." See also Thomas J. Talley, *The Origins of the Liturgical Year*, 2nd ed. (Collegeville, MN: Liturgical Press, 1986), 88–90.

Roman Catholic liturgy, the first half extends from Advent to Trinity Sunday and encompasses as its cornerstones the three principal feasts of the year, Christmas, Easter, and Pentecost, each of which was celebrated in Leipzig on three consecutive days.[8] This part of the year follows a well-known design that traces the principal events in the life of Christ in chronological outline, from the anticipation of his coming (Advent), followed by the nativity and the events surrounding Christmas and Epiphany, through a brief sequence of representative events (his appearance as a twelve-year-old in the temple, the first miracle and some later ones, a group of parables), then the journey to Jerusalem, followed by the Passion, resurrection, post-resurrection appearances, ascension, and the coming of the Holy Spirit. Directly following Pentecost, Trinity Sunday logically concludes the first half of the year by commemorating God's triune nature; in this sense it can be considered a symbolic "doxology" to the first half of the year.

Something of the flavor of this view of the first half of the year, at least in terms of its high points, can be gained from the following extracts from Martin Moller's *Praxis Evangeliorum* (1614), a set of meditative commentaries on the Gospels of the church year, published in the era of emerging orthodox Lutheranism by a theologian whose leanings were toward the kind of spirituality that would nearly a century later be identified with pietism. In his discussion of the meaning of Pentecost, Moller says (after explaining the meaning and origin of the word):

> For, beloved soul, just as there are three different persons in the one single divine being, so there are also three principal feasts in the year, which are celebrated for three days each, namely, Christmas, Easter, and Pentecost. On which high feast days the church preaches and proclaims the high inexpressible blessings which each of the divine persons has done, and still does, for our blessedness.
>
> (1) See, Christmas is the feast of God the Father, on which he has shared his father's heart with us, and has introduced his only Son as savior into this world.
> (2) Easter is the feast of the Lord Jesus Christ, on which he was victorious over all his and our enemies, and was resurrected from the dead with great triumph and joy.
> (3) Pentecost, however is the feast of the Holy Spirit, on which he filled the dear disciples with his grace and gifts, and prepared them for the holy office of apostles.
>
> Yes, my soul, Christmas and Easter are certainly beautiful, noble feasts. But they would bring us neither usefulness nor joy, if God had not also celebrated Pentecost. For Pentecost is the same feast on which the Lord ordained

[8] In some of the theological books of Bach's time, the division between the two halves of the year is made with Pentecost rather than Trinity, that is, with the second half of the year beginning with Trinity Sunday, occasionally even with Pentecost or Easter.

> his messengers, teachers and preachers, adorned them with art, speech and gifts and sent them forth so that they would disclose to us suffering humans the loving heart of the Father, reveal his beloved Son, proclaim all his good deeds, and point the way to heaven: so that we would properly know our God, and through true faith enjoy all his blessings. . . .

Moller's remarks on Pentecost bring out the crucial point that its meaning, like that of scripture as a whole, is bound up with its value, or use (*Nutz*, in the language of Lutheranism), for the contemporary believer and the church: the all-important *pro nobis* of Luther's theology. Later Moller links Trinity Sunday to the three principal feasts in a manner that makes clear that it celebrates what has already been expressed in them:

> This is, dear soul, the feast of the Holy Trinity. For, after those of Christmas, Easter and Pentecost, on which is made clear to us the inexpressible blessings of our God and what each person in the deity does for our blessedness, are past, then we also celebrate accordingly a kind of feast on which we may learn to recognize the being of our God, who and what he is, who does such great things for us.[9]

August Pfeiffer makes the same Trinitarian associations of the three principal feasts, linking them to the threefold "Sanctus" of Isaiah (6:3), and including Ascension Day along with Easter as the day on which Jesus upheld the victory against

---

[9] Martin Moller, *Praxis Evangeliorum: Einfeltige erklerung und nützliche betrachtung der Evangelien / so auff alle Sontage und vornemesten Fest Jährlich zu predigen verordnet sind* (Görlitz, 1614), 3:293–94, 351–52:

> Denn, liebe Seele, gleich wie drey unterschiedene Personen sind in dem einigen göttlichen Wesen: Also sind auch drey Haupt-fest im Jahr, die mit dreyen Tagen gehalten werden, nemlich Weyhenachten, Ostern und Pfingsten. An welchen hohen Festagen die Kirche prediget unnd rühmet die hohen unausprechlichen Wolthaten, die eine jede Person bey unser Seligkeit gethan hat, und noch thut. **1.** Sihe, Weyhenachten ist Gottes des Vaters Fest, daran er sein väterliches Herz mit uns getheilet, und seinen einigen Sohn zum Heilande in diese Welt eingeführet hat. **2.** Ostern ist des HErrn Jesu Christi Fest, daran er uber alle seine und unsere Feinde gesieget, und mit grossem Triumph unnd Freuden von den Todten aufferstanden ist. **3.** Pfingsten aber ist des heiligen Geistes Fest, an dem er die lieben Jünger mit seinen Gnaden und Gaben erfüllet, unnd zum heiligen Apostelampt bereitet hat. Ja, meine Seele, Weyhenachten und Ostern sind wol schöne herrliche Fest, aber sie brechten uns weder Nutz noch Freude, wenn Gott nicht auch hette Pfingsten gehalten. Denn Pfingsten ist dasselbe Fest, daran der Herr seine Boten, Lehrer und Prediger ordiniret, sie mit Kunst, Sprachen und Geben gezieret, und ausgesendet hat, daß sie uns elenden Menschen das liebreich: Vaterherz entdecken, seinen lieben Sohn offenbaren, alle seine Wohlthaten verkündigen, und deon Weg zum Himmel zeugen: Auff daß wir unsern Gott recht kennen, und durch wahren Glauben aller seiner Wolthaten geniessen. . . . Es ist, liebe Seele, das Fest der heiligen Dreyfaltigkeit. Denn noch dem nu Weyhenachten, Ostern und Pfingsten, fürüber, daran uns die unaussprechlichen Wolthaten unsers Gottes, unnd was eine jede Person in der Gottheit bey unser Geligkeit thut, erkläret ist: So halten wir nu auch billich ein solches Fest, daran wir das Wesen unsers Gottes, wer und was er ist, der solche grosse Ding an uns thut, mögen erkennen lernen.

all the gates of hell.[10] Thus, as Catherine Mowry LaCugna remarks, "the rhythm of the liturgy is unmistakably Trinitarian, structured according to the events of the economy of salvation."[11]

In keeping with the fact that Jesus's death and resurrection coincided with Passover, the season that followed—the "great fifty days" from Easter to Pentecost, the oldest part of the liturgy—had its origins in the Jewish Pentecost, that is, the fifty days from Passover to the feast of "first fruits," By the second century, if not earlier, the Hebrew Bible narrative of the "Israelite passover in Exod. 12" formed a principal lection for the original nocturnal Easter festival, an association that remained through the centuries:

> Nothing could more clearly indicate the close original connection of the christian with the jewish "passover" than the choice of this lesson. There followed a lection from the Gospel of S. John, the account of the death and resurrection of our Lord, extending from the trial before Pilate to the end of S. John's account of the resurrection, with its hint of an ascension on Easter Day itself. This choice of lessons is in the exact spirit of S. Paul's phrase "Christ our passover was sacrificed for us; therefore let us keep the feast with joy." . . . The primitive Pascha . . . therefore commemorated a deliverance from bondage, in the case of christians not from Egypt but from the bondage of sin and time and mortality into "the glorious liberty of the children of God; and the everlasting kingdom of our Lord and Saviour Jesus Christ."[12]

Noteworthy in this description is the fact that the Passion, resurrection, and ascension are all part of the Easter feast, a deliverance from bondage, which is more the way John presents those events than in the Synoptic Gospels. John's vision of the crucifixion as Jesus's triumphant "lifting up" that would draw all men to him describes the meaning of Easter and the forty days after the manner that modern authors have described as an "upswing," ending on Ascension Day. Thus Johann Arndt joins the Passion, Easter, and ascension as three aspects of the same work, the Passion confirming Jesus's love, and the resurrection and ascension the faith and hope of the faithful, respectively. For Arndt, Jesus's ascension was so that our spirits would be directed upward, to heavenly things.[13] In fact, much of the ancient

---

[10] August Pfeiffer, *Evangelisches Schatz-Kammer* (Nürnberg, 1697), 38.

[11] LaCugna, *God for Us*, 210.

[12] Dom Gregory Dix, *The Shape of the Liturgy* (London: Dacre Press), 338–39.

[13] Johann Arndt, *Postilla, Das ist: Geist-reiche Erklärung der Evangelischen Texte durchs gantze Jahr, . . . Sampt einer durchgehenden Betrachtung über die gantze Paßions-Historie . . .* (Frankfurt, 1713), pt. 2: *Passion, das ist: Geist-reiche Erklärung des Heil. und bittern Leydens und Sterbens unsers HERRN JEsu Christi*, 174–75:

> **wann ich erhöhet werde / wil ich euch alle nach mir ziehen** / und uns die selige Hoffnung gemacht / daß wir auch seine Herrlichkeit sehen mögen. Dann / gleichwie **wir alle mit ihm gestorben und begraben seyn** geistlich; und wie wir alle mit ihn aufferstanden / und durch seine Aufferstehung alle aus dem Tode gerissen; Also sind wir im Glauben und Hoffnung allbereit geistlich mit ihm gen Himmel gefahren / . . . . Daß Christus gen Himmel gefahren / ist auch

character of Easter can be clearly perceived in Bach's *St. John Passion*, especially in the aria "Es ist vollbracht" and the "centering" of Jesus's trial on the idea of liberation from the bondage of sin and death (the chorale, "Durch dein Gefängnis, Gottes Sohn, ist uns die Freiheit kommen").

The Lutheran writers of Bach's time and earlier were virtually unanimous in describing the post-Easter weeks as a forty-day period culminating in Jesus's ascension, in which Jesus's appearances to the disciples prepared them for the time to come, in terms of both their mission on earth (associated with Pentecost) and the coming of God's kingdom, which the forty days anticipated. For some the forty days provided a "mirror," "prefiguring," or "foretaste" of eternal life.[14] They were commonly viewed in relation to one or more time periods in scripture involving the number forty: the forty hours that Jesus was dead between the crucifixion and the resurrection, the forty days of Jesus's fasting in the wilderness (linked with Lent), the forty years of the Israelites wandering in the desert, and the forty days between Christmas and Jesus's presentation in the Temple (the feast of the Purification on February 2). In the liturgy the placement of Ascension Day was derived from Acts 1:1–11 (the epistle for Ascension Day), which narrates that Jesus showed himself to the disciples for forty days "speaking of the things pertaining to the kingdom of God" (v. 3), after which (v. 5) the evangelist reports Jesus as saying "but ye shall be baptized with the Holy Ghost not many days hence." Pentecost itself was, of course, derived from the Jewish Pentecost, or feast of "first fruits," fifty days after Passover. And the Lutheran church retained all the ancient associations. As Luther explained in the sermon on the epistle for Pentecost from the *Kirchenpostilla*, the original Pentecost commemorated the fact that the Jews, on the fiftieth day after the Exodus, reached Mount Sinai, where the law was given to Moses, and God commanded that the fiftieth day after Passover be celebrated annually.[15] The Christian Pentecost, then, commemorated the giving of a "new law," as described by St. Paul in 2 Corinthians 3:6, where the apostle juxtaposes it to the law of Moses in terms of the opposition of "letter" (or "flesh") and "spirit." After expounding on these two covenants and how they relate to "two kinds of people," Luther turns to the office of the Holy Spirit, which is to make God's word live in the heart and to

---

darum geschehen / daß er unsere Gemüther zum Himmlischen möchte auffrichten. In seinen Leyden haben wir eine Versicherung seiner Liebe / in seiner Auferstehung eine Versicherung unsers Glaubens / in seiner Himmelfahrt eine Versicherung unserer Hoffnung.

[14] See, for example, Johann Arndt, *Postilla*, Part 3 (Easter through Pentecost), 164–78; Joachim Lütkemann, *Apostolischer Hertzens-Wekker* (published along with Heinrich Müller's *Evangelischer Hertzens-Spiegel . . .* (Stade, 1736), 754; Heinrich Müller, *Apostolischer Schluß-Kette* (Frankfurt, 1671), 505–08; August Hermann Francke, *Predigten über die Sonn- und Fest-Tags Episteln* (Halle, 1724), 705–9; Johann Jacob Rambach, *Evangelische Betrachtungen über die Sonn- und Fest-Tags-Evangelia des gantzen Jahrs* (Halle, 1732), 646–48; Valerius Herberger, *Das Himmlische Jerusalem* (1609), newly edited by Dr. Friedrich Ahlfeld (Leipzig: Ernst Bredt, 1858), 1–4; Herberger, *Epistolische Herz-Postilla* (Leipzig, 1736), 46–54; Martin Moller, *Praxis Evangeliorum*, 2:258.

[15] Martin Luther, *The Complete Sermons of Martin Luther*, vol. 4.1, *Sermons on Epistle Texts for Epiphany, Easter, and Pentecost* (Grand Rapids, MI: Baker Books, 2000), 330.

instill the heart with love by making Christ present for the believer, as John described it in the Farewell Discourse. For some Lutheran authors, therefore, the readings from John that dominated the post-Easter weeks, and especially the five from the Farewell Discourse that directly preceded and followed Ascension Day, culminating on Pentecost, were viewed as representing the kind of discourse with the disciples described in Acts 1:2, where Jesus spoke for forty days with the disciples of things "pertaining to the kingdom of God."[16]

In the great fifty days, therefore, the season that formed the core of the year was also its climax, celebrating Jesus's completed work, the Passion, resurrection, and ascension, followed by the coming of the Holy Spirit, the symbolic birthday of the church. Beginning with Easter, it celebrated the new hope for humanity that began with the resurrection of Christ, recalling St. Paul's metaphoric description of Jesus's resurrection as the "firstfruits of them that slept" (1 Cor 15:20, KJV). In the ancient liturgy, the rites of baptism (closely associated with the death and resurrection of Christ) and confirmation "incorporated" new members into the "body" of Christ, the church, at Easter and the following Sunday, Quasimodogeniti, while at the end of the "great fifty days," Pentecost, the church celebrated "her own character as the 'People' of the New Covenant, and the fact that 'the law of the Spirit of life in Christ Jesus hath made' her members 'free from the law of sin and death' [Rom 8:2]."[17] Thus August Hermann Francke ends his series of lectures on John's Passion narrative with a discussion of how baptism reenacts the death and resurrection of Christ, which the Exodus of the Jews was traditionally considered to prefigure.[18] Symbolizing the birth of Christianity as the successor to Judaism, the great fifty days (a "great Sunday" or feast of weeks comprising 7 x 7 days, and including the Sunday at both ends) were viewed as the fulfillment of Jesus's prediction regarding the three days of his death and resurrection as the destruction and rebuilding of the Temple.[19] Pentecost was the key to the origins of the year as a whole, both in terms of the spiritual meaning of the liturgy and also in the more historical, pragmatic sense according to which from the association of Jesus's Passion and resurrection with Passover, other dates, such as the Annunciation, Christmas, and the

---

[16] Francke, for example, makes this point in his *Predigten über die Sonn- und Fest-Tags Episteln*, 704, interpreting Jesus's command that the disciples wait in Jerusalem for the "promise of the Father" as the promise made in John 14, 15, and 16, in which Jesus spoke of the Holy Spirit.

[17] Dix, *Shape of the Liturgy*, 341.

[18] Francke, *Oeffentliche Reden über die Paßions-Historie / Wie dieselbe vom Evangelisten Johanne im 19. u. 19. Cap. beschrieben ist* (1716; 2nd ed., Halle, 1719), 168–70; hereafter *Oeffentliche Reden*. As Francke mentions in his preface (5), these lectures (originally delivered between Quinquagesima and Easter 1716) were published along with a similar set of twelve lectures on Mark's Passion account, delivered originally between Quinquagesima and Easter 1712 and first published in 1714. I use a 1724 printing of the second edition of Francke's sermons on John as published in 1724, along with the third edition of the lectures on Mark.

[19] See Cobb, "The History of the Christian Year," 459–60, 463–64; Talley, *Origins of the Liturgical Year*, 1–77.

feast of John the Baptist, were calculated and set in place, the year eventually expanding so that its first half centered on the time of Jesus as celebrated in a microcosm of his life and work.

Traditionally, Advent, as the beginning of the liturgical year, anticipated over the course of its three or four weeks the multiple senses according to which Jesus came to the world, the church, and the faithful. The liturgical year, centered on the regular reading of scripture, outlined the very principles upon which its cycle of scriptural excerpts—the epistle and Gospel readings—was interpreted. As the point where the cycle renewed itself, Advent represented the overlap not only of chronological eras but also of the scriptural senses. Henri de Lubac's description makes this clear:

> After the long advent of the history of Israel [i.e., the OT], the object of the historical sense, "at the end of the age and at the evening of the world" [symbolized liturgically in the end of the year, the late-Trinity season followed by Advent], "the Word was made flesh and dwelt amongst us." Then was revealed the mystery that constituted the object of the mystical or spiritual sense. But this mystery could not receive its ultimate fulfillment all at once. It unfolded in three phases, or was elaborated in three successive states. In other words, as was announced in the ancient Scriptures, a threefold advent of Christ may be distinguished—and this requires correspondingly a distinction of a threefold mystic sense [that is, the three "spiritual" senses]. The first advent, "humble and hidden," on our earth, performs the work of redemption, which is pursued in the Church and in her sacraments: this is the object of allegory in the proper sense of the word. The second advent, entirely interior, takes place within the soul of each of the faithful, and is unfolded by tropology. The third and last advent is saved up for the "end of the age," when the Christ will appear in his glory and will come to look for his own to take them away with him: such is the object of anagogy.[20]

What de Lubac describes is the substance of the progression outlined earlier for Cantata 61. Not only does Advent articulate the multiple senses of Jesus's coming, but the seasons of the liturgical year outline a succession rooted in the four senses. That is, in a very broad sense, the year describes a motion from history and allegory, embodied in Jesus's life and work as the fulfillment of OT prophesy concerning the Messiah, through tropology, embodied in the spiritual incarnation that is the subject of Pentecost, to eschatology, toward which the end of the year moves increasingly. The "evening of the world," the "end of the age"—or as it was often expressed in Bach's time, the "letzte Zeit"—was the era inaugurated by the incarna-

---

[20] de Lubac, *Medieval Exegesis,* 2:179. In this passage de Lubac cites Jerome, Origen, and Bernard, including further related citations from other medieval sources within the notes (which I have omitted).

tion of Christ and continuing on into that of the church awaiting the Second Coming.[21] The year enacted the whole of salvation history within the liturgical cycle, beginning at Advent following weeks in which the Second Coming was anticipated (and was again celebrated on the second Sunday in Advent).[22] Martin Moller, on the title page of the *Praxis Evangeliorum*, gave the purpose of his cycle of Gospel meditations as "for all pious heart, who in the present last times separate themselves

---

[21] The ancient view of Jesus's incarnation taking place in the "evening of the world," was prominent in Lutheran orthodoxy as well, where it retained a form of "salvation history," which, as Heinrich Müller explains, was rooted in Judaism. In giving the various meanings of the expression "Abendmahl," he adds: "Ein Abendmahl / weil Christus das heyl am Abend der Welt hat erworben. So ward die Zeit von den Juden abgetheilet. Die Zeit vor Mose hieß der Welt Morgen, die Zeit unter Mose der Welt Mittag, die Zeit nach Mosen unter dem Messias / der Welt Abend / das Ende der Welt / die letzte Stunde / da starb Christus / und bracht der Welt das Heyl." See Heinrich Müller, *Geistlicher Danck-Altar / Zum täglichen Beth- und Lob-Opffer / In dem Hertzen der Christen aufgerichtet, . . .* Hanover, 1724, 269. In the same discussion Müller links the meaning of "Abendmahl" to God's walking in Eden in the cool of the evening, where after the Fall, the promise of Jesus's defeat of the serpent (i.e., Satan) was made: "Ein Abendmahl, weil Christus zur Abendzeit, da der Tag kühle worden, unsern ersten Eltern im Paradies versprochen. . . . Endlich aber ward das liebliche Abend-Gericht auffgetragen: Des Weibes Same sol der Schlangen den Kopff zutreten" (268–69). Similarly, August Hermann Francke, in his sermon on the Gospel for the second Sunday after Trinity (*Das Abendmahl des Lammes / In einer Predigt Uber das Evangelium Luc. XIV, vers. 16–24* [Halle, 1699]), explains the parable of God's *Abendmahl*:

> Es wird aber ein **Abendmahl** genennet / weil das Lamm Gottes am Abend dieser Welt solches sein Gastmahl anstellen will. Denn gleich wie am Abend / **da der Tag kühle ward** / das erste Evangelium nach dem kläglichen Sünden-Fall unsern ersten Eltern verkündiget ward / I. B. Mos. III. V. 8. 15. Und das Täublein Noah umb die Vesperzeit / d.i. umb den Abend kam / und ein Oelblat in ihrem Munde trug / Cap. X. II. Also soll auch dessen endliche Erfüllung am Abend dieser Welt geschehen / und die Zeit der Erquickung erfolgen / da sich Gott in seiner Freundligkeit und unendlichen Liebe seinen Gläubigen zu schmecken und völlig zu genießen geben wird (10–11) Die Stunde des Abendmahls ist die letzte grosse Welt-Stunde. Die erste währete von Adam biß auff die Sündfluth / die andere von Noah biß auf Christum; Die dritte und letzte von Christo biß zum Ende dieser gegenwärtigen Welt. Darum schreibet Johannes I. Epist. 2/18. **Kinder / es ist die letzte Stunde.** Diese wird aber die Stunde des Abendmahls genennet / weil sie die letzte ist vor dem Abendmahl des Lammes (36–37).

Both Müller's and Francke's discussions and even their language remind us of the arioso "Am Abend, da es kühle war" in the *St. Matthew Passion*, in which evening is the link among Jesus's burial, Gethsemane, God's walking in Eden in the cool of the evening, and the return of the dove to Noah with the olive branch in the evening. On the link of the *St. Matthew Passion* passage to traditional hermeneutics, see Paul Minear, "Matthew, Evangelist, and Johann, Composer," *Theology Today* 30 (1973): 243–55. On evening as the time of reconciliation with God, see Renate Steiger, "'O schöne Zeit! O Abendstunde!': Affekt und Symbol in J. S. Bachs Matthäuspassion," *Musik und Kirche* 46 (1976): 15–22. August Pfeiffer, likewise, explains why the "Gnaden-Mahl" or "Seelen-Mahl" that "we enjoy in the Christian church" was not called a "Mittags-Mahl": namely, "it goes back in part to the sorrowful paradise-breakfast (*Paradies-Frühstück*) at which the devil prepared the hellish poison meal (*Gifft-Koch*) for our first ancestors, at which they ate death for themselves and all their descendants, because of which it was toward evening, that is, in the last part of the world-time ("in dem letzten Theil der Welt-Zeit") that the Lamb of God, who bore all the sins of the world, was slaughtered and is now prepared for the evening meal" (*Evangelischer Schatz-Kammer*, 77). Pfeiffer also uses the expression "Vesper-Zeit der Welt" to characterize the New Testament era (79). On the relevance of the idea of the "evening of the world" to Cantata 6, *Bleib bei uns, denn es will Abend werden* (see 407–8).

[22] Thus Bach's eschatological cantata, written in Weimar for the second Sunday after Trinity, *Wachet, betet, betet, wachet*, was reworked and expanded in Leipzig for the twenty-sixth Sunday after Trinity.

from the sinful course of the world and await with joy the coming of our Lord Jesus."[23] Salvation history, which dictated the basic ordering of the books in the Bible, is at the same time the progression from history to anagogy; both are embedded within the church year.

In Leipzig, the absence of church cantatas between the first Sunday in Advent and Christmas lent that period the character of "waiting," mirroring, like Lent, the ancient custom of fasting before the principal joyful feasts of the year. Anticipation of Christmas colored the season of increasingly shorter days, until at the darkest time of the year, "the evening of the world" (as in de Lubac's description), just after the winter solstice, the celebration of the birth of Jesus marked a turning point and a new beginning, symbolically the coming of the light into the world as told in the preface to the Gospel of John, which recalls the beginning of Genesis. Advent and Christmas, therefore, took on the character of continuity with Israel, emphasizing Jesus's birth as the fulfillment of the Hebrew scriptures, exactly as it was viewed in the NT. This theme was further developed in the symbolism of the New Year and the Epiphany season, which in its introduction of eschatological themes mirrors the progression that is embodied in the four senses of scripture.

Parallel to the fasting season of Advent, the Lenten season (again without church cantatas in Leipzig) prepares for another great event, the completion of Jesus's work and time on earth, his death and resurrection, the Passion and Easter, whose date, like that of Passover, fluctuates within the lunar month that follows the spring equinox. As viewed by the Lutheran church, the liturgical span from Lent through Passiontide and Easter, then to Pentecost and Trinity, formed a sequence whose principal events provided the core of Lutheran theology. For Luther all true theology was theology of the cross (*theologia crucis*), centered on the paradox that Jesus's divinity was revealed in his incarnation and ignominious death on Good Friday, an expression of the antithesis of faith and experience (in Luther's view, God's "alien" work, his unfathomable greatness "hidden" behind the suffering and death of Jesus).[24] In Jesus's resurrection and ascension, the coming of the Spirit, and the final revelation of the Trinity, however, the season increasingly represented what Luther called God's "proper" work, brought to its completion in the final events of Jesus's life and thereby articulating more directly the hopes of the present-day congregation.

As Jesus's time drew to a close, following the completion of his work (the Passion and Easter) and his ascension, the feast that commemorated the coming of the Holy Spirit formed the basis for the shift to the era of the church. This is reflected in Moller's emphasis on the work of the ministers of the church in his characterization of Pentecost. Trinity Sunday follows logically from the feast that celebrates the

---

[23] Moller, *Praxis Evangeliorum*, title page to all three parts: "Für alle frome Hertzen, die sich in jetzigen letzten Zeiten vom Sündlichen Weltlaufft absondern, und auff die Erscheinung unsers HERRN Jesu mit frewden warten."

[24] Walther von Loewenich *Luther's Theology of the Cross*, trans.Herbert J. A. Bouman (Minneapolis: Augsburg Publishing House, 1976).

third person of the Trinity, but it nevertheless initiates a change in the character of the year in that it commemorates, as Pelikan remarks, not an event but a doctrine (albeit a doctrine that was fundamental to the Lutheran church).[25] Thus Trinity Sunday is both an end and a beginning. In the Lutheran division of the liturgical year it marked a point of culmination that corresponded to the stage of "salvation history" at which God's three-person nature was revealed, the ending of the "Time of Christ" (Ascension Day) and the beginning of the "Time of the church," or humanity under the guidance of the Holy Spirit. But, in keeping with its appearance in the liturgy centuries later than the establishment of the season that preceded it, Trinity Sunday symbolizes the beginning of an era dominated by the concerns of humanity living in the world without the physical presence of Christ, but guided by the presence of Jesus through the Spirit within. Throughout the season, therefore, the tropological or moral sense is carried forward from Pentecost, while the progression as a whole is directed increasingly toward "last things" (eschatology) meditation in light of eternity (anagogy).

The Trinity season no longer chronologically outlines events in the life of Christ and has no principal feast days like those of the first half of the year; it therefore exhibits no such sense of structure as that of the preceding seasons. The series of parables and miracle narratives that run throughout the Gospels of the Trinity season inspires a far greater emphasis on moral issues, as the trials of faith and life in the world come to the fore. The theological character of that season is therefore far more variegated and "doctrinal" than that of the first half of the year, a situation reflected in Bach's cantatas, which often feature warnings against hypocrisy, false doctrine, and prophets, reason, pride, self-love, and so on, intermingled with the command to love God and one's neighbor, assertion of the doctrine of justification by faith, and the like. In them there is an ever present sense of a split between the world, nearly always described in pejorative terms, and the life of faith, whose fulfillment lies in the future. In its projecting an increasing sense of dissatisfaction with the world, the Trinity season intensifies the preoccupation with Christian life in the world as a testing ground until, toward its close, it is dominated by the sense that the end of time is at hand. Metaphors of the world as "desert" or "hospital," such as we find in certain of Bach's Trinity cantatas, are now more closely aligned with the sense that the year is occupied with eschatological themes, anticipation of the end in both its hopeful and fearful aspects. Thus the end of the Trinity season has a distinctly eschatological character, emphasizing "last things," thoughts of death, the last judgment, and the coming Kingdom of God, giving particular focus to the hopes and fears of the Christian community.

Bach's cantatas for the last weeks of the Trinity season all reflect this quality. Some, such as Cantata 60, *O Ewigkeit, du Donnerwort*, for the twenty-fourth Sunday after Trinity, are dialogs between fear and hope, while others, such as Cantata 90,

---

[25] Pelikan, *Bach Among the Theologians*, 3.

Es reifet euch ein schrecklich Ende, for the twenty-fifth Sunday after Trinity, center on fear of God's judgment. Cantata 70, *Wachtet! betet!*, originally composed in Weimar for the second Sunday in Advent, then reworked in Leipzig for the twenty-sixth Sunday after Trinity, presents images of fear and destruction, on the one hand, and on the other, of progression from the metaphoric "Egypt" of the world to the "Eden" of the world to come, while Cantata 140, *Wachet auf, ruft uns die Stimme*, for the twenty-seventh Sunday after Trinity (based on the parable of the wise and foolish virgins) typifies the more positive aspect of this situation. The turning of the liturgical year at Advent, and the Christmas season as a whole, place those concerns in the perspective of Jesus's birth as the pivotal event in God's plan for the salvation of humanity, the birth of a new "economy" (*oikonomia*). In drawing parallels between the church's longing for Jesus's Second Coming and Israel's awaiting the birth of the Messiah, the rotation of the liturgical, geophysical, and civil years (Advent, Christmas, New Year/Epiphany) mirrors the continuity, fulfillment, and renewal of history in conjunction with the coming to fruition of God's plan for the salvation of humanity, the onset of the time of Jesus.

In this view the year is not only a chronological summary of Jesus's life but also a structured representation of God's plan for the redemption of humanity, fulfilled in Jesus's death, resurrection, and ascension, and followed by the coming of the Holy Spirit. In the Christian scriptures that plan was revealed gradually throughout the eras of Jewish and Christian history, reaching its climax in the final events of Jesus's life and the beginning of the third era, that of the church. Although the Time of Israel is substantially foreshortened in this sequence, the reinterpretation of OT events in terms of those of the NT runs continually throughout the year, emerging with particular force at key points such as the Passion, when it was traditional to rehearse the various prefigurations. Such passages, the story of Isaac, for example, were embodied in the liturgy; and the Lutheran sermon cycles of Bach's time and before typically include interpretations of such stories at the corresponding points in the year, often at great length.[26] Works such as Handel's *Messiah* and Telemann's 1728 *St. Luke Passion* are built largely or even entirely around this practice.[27] In the Lutheran theological books of Bach's time and earlier the three-

[26] For example, Johann Arndt, in his *Postille*, offers two sermons on Psalm 55 and four on Isaiah 53 as introduction to the Passion; see 484–507 of the first division of the treatise (the Passion narrative itself comprises the second division, numbered from 1 to 170 and comprising twenty sermons). And following his sermons on the three days of Easter in the third division of the book, Arndt provides lengthy sermons on the stories of Jonah, Samson, Joshua, and Job (55–86). Closer to Bach's time, August Pfeiffer published a treatise titled *Paßion- u. Oster-Spiegel / Aus Der Historia Isaacs Gen. XXII. In Sechs Predigten / und Aus der Weissagung Des Propheten Jonae / Durch richtige Erklärung Des gantzen Prophetischen Textes Und Vorzeigung Der ähnligkeit des Leidenden / Sterbenden und Erstandenden JESU Mit dem Propheten JONA In funffzig Puncten dargestellet*. . . (Leipzig, 1683).

[27] See Georg Philipp Telemann, *Musikalische Werke*, vol. 15, *Lukaspassion 1728*, ed. Hans Hörner and Martin Ruhnke (Kassel: Bärenreiter, 1964). Telemann divides the Passion into five segments, each of which is subdivided into three parts: (1) *Vorbereitung* (*zur ersten* [*zweiten*, etc.] *Abteilung* (a typo-

fold temporal sequence is therefore often expanded through subdivision of the "Time of Israel" into two or more distinct eras reflecting the multiple prophecies concerning Christ. Johann Jacob Rambach, in his two-volume treatise on hermeneutics, emphasizes the necessity of dividing the scriptures into time periods, or "intervals" in which "prophesies concerning Christ [*vaticinio de Christo*] were communicated," then describes *four* such intervals that have the character of marking new eras or stages of God's revelation: (1) the time of the destruction of the world in the great flood, after which a new world arose; (2) the time of the Exodus from Egypt, which was capped by the founding of a new order [*oeconomie*] on Mount Sinai [i.e., the giving of the law]; (3) the time of the birth of the savior [*nati servatoris*], which again marked the foundation of a new *oeconomie*; and, finally, (4) the era of the consummation of the centuries [*epocha consummationis seculorum*], that is, of the church awaiting the Second Coming.[28] Such divisions were sometimes viewed as tracing back to Jewish conceptions of salvation history. Heinrich Müller describes three (or four) eras that are analogous to the times of day: before Moses (morning), under Moses (midday), the time of the Messiah, which came after that of Moses (evening), and which led to the "end of the world, the last hour, when Christ died and brought salvation" (see n. 21), This meaning underlies the line "Die Trauernacht läßt nun die letzte Stunde zählen" in the aria "Es ist vollbracht" from the *St. John Passion.* The number and exact definition of the eras of salvation history varied according to the topic at hand. Thus Luther, interpreting the three (!) colors of the rainbow, saw in it a reflection of the three eras in which the world was (or would be) destroyed: that of Noah as a watery blue, the destruction of the Temple as the central yellow band, and the eventual destruction of the world by fire as the red uppermost band.[29] And, following from his four-fold division cited earlier, Rambach subdivides the OT into several further prefigurations of Jesus, affirming the general principle that throughout the various time intervals "the prophetic light of the knowledge of Christ became ever clearer and brighter by stages" ("wie in diesen *invervallis temporis* das prophetische Licht von der Erkenntniß Christi *per gradus* immer klärer und heller worden").[30]

What all this indicates is that although the exact division of the eras of scripture and history could vary, the principle that the entire story was a unified one, center-

---

logical prefiguration of the Passion drawn from the Old Testament [e.g., Joseph and his brothers]); (2) *Die gläubige Anwendung* (application of the Old Testament story to the contemporary believer); and (3) *Erste [Zweite, etc.] Abteilung* (the biblical narrative itself, with interspersed nonbiblical recitatives and chorales, and an occasional aria). The design as a whole is the same for all five parts.

[28] Rambach, *Ausführliche und gründliche Erläuterung über seine eigene INSTITVTIONES HERMENEVTICAE SACRAE,* 2:439–40. For a modern perspective on the divine "economy" see LaCugna, *God for Us*, 21–52.

[29] For Luther the blue and red bands were the primary ones, with the yellow resulting from the intermingling of the two. See *Luther's Works*, vol. 1, *Lectures on Genesis, Chapters 1–5*, ed. Jaroslav Pelikan, (St. Louis: Concordia, 1958), 359.

[30] Rambach, *Ausführliche und gründliche Erläuterung,* 1:439–40.

ing on or fulfilled in Jesus, never did. The fulfillment was, of course, Jesus's victory over death in the Passion, resurrection, and ascension; and in John it is viewed as one basic upward motion: the "lifting up" of the cross that drew all humanity to him. Thus, in a Lutheran chorale based on Jesus's final words in John, "Es ist vollbracht," we read "was Gottes Rath von Ewigkeit bedacht, daß ist durch seinen Tod vollbracht."[31] In the *St. John Passion*, the quintessential expression of this view is the aria "Es ist vollbracht," a projection of Jesus's victory as bringing to an end the *Trauernacht* of the many centuries during which humanity was held captive by sin, death, and the devil. As mentioned, this is the meaning of the line "Die Trauernacht läßt nun die letzte Stunde zählen" at the close of the slow opening section of the aria, before the triumphant proclamation of Jesus's victory, "Der Held aus Juda siegt mit Macht und schließt den Kampf." Thus the expression "letzte Stunde" does not refer only to Jesus's last hours or to those of the believer, but also (and primarily) to the fact that his death brought an end to the preceding era of salvation history, as in the passage from Müller cited in n. 21. Although the concept of "salvation history" might be interpreted differently from author to author, its tracing to what was usually called God's *Rath* remained constant. Similarly, viewed from the standpoint of strict chronological ordering, the scriptures, especially those from the Hebrew Bible, were not without many inconsistencies and inaccuracies. Rambach discusses these in detail, affirming that whereas the outline of scripture history is basically chronological, the many deviations from strict temporal order, both among the succession of books and within individual books, should not be understood in purely historical terms (as some of his contemporaries had done). Rather, God had introduced such irregularities because of God's larger purpose, which transcended the purely historical.[32]

Johann Jacob Rambach on God's "*Rath*"

What I have outlined to this point is a necessary background to the understanding of the writings of Lutheran theology from the time of the reformer to Bach. Salvation history and the senses of traditional hermeneutics frequently converge in the Bach cantata texts, sometimes directly, but more often in a manner according to which they are taken for granted. In order to illustrate this convergence in the theological thought of Bach's time, we need to consider at this time how Bach's contemporary, Johann Jacob Rambach, presents the ideas in question. Bach himself might have had more than a passing interest in such themes, for his collection

---

[31] Johann Anastasius Freylinghausen, *Neues Geist-reiches Gesang-Buch* (Halle, 1719), 90–95. Rambach cites this chorale in its entirety at the end of the discussion of "Es ist vollbracht" in his *Betrachtungen über die Sieben Letzten Worte des gecreutzigten JEsu* (Halle, 1728), 161–62.

[32] Rambach, *Ausführliche und gründliche Erläuterung*, 2:5–7.

of theological books contained several works in which these ideas are treated extensively, including the one of Rambach on which the following discussion is based.[33]

In a relatively short lifetime (1693–1735), Rambach produced many books (a considerable number of which were published posthumously, often edited by friends), nearly all of which center on the interpretation of scripture and the aspect that Rambach considered most important, understanding its *scopus*, or intention, which, as he proclaimed repeatedly, was Christ (*scopus communis totius scripturae*).[34] The *scopus*—usually described in German as the *Zweck*, *End-Zweck*, or *Haupt-Zweck* of scripture—was, of course, given by God and could be divided into the *scopus ultimus*, which was the salvation of humanity, and the *scopus intermedius*, which was faith in Christ, the means by which the "ultimate purpose" was attained. Rambach, like his teacher and colleague August Hermann Francke, identified the purpose, *Zweck* or *scopus* of scripture as the blessedness (*Seeligkeit*) of humanity, attained only through faith in Jesus Christ. As Francke summarized it (after citing passages from scripture in which its "purpose" was set forth):

> Because you know the Scriptures from childhood, they can instruct you towards blessedness through faith in Jesus Christ; for all scripture given by God is useful for doctrine, for punishing, for betterment, for discipline in righteousness, NB. that a person of God be perfect, capable of every good work. It is clear that in these and similar places [in scripture] not only the uses, but also of the purpose of holy scripture is taken up and illuminated throughout, that this principal purpose is: *our blessedness*.[35]

Francke then sets forth the means by which blessedness is attained:

> and because blessedness can be received only through faith in Jesus Christ, that therefore next in accordance with this, the purpose of holy scripture is also: *faith in Jesus Christ*. Because, however, a faith that truly leads to blessedness cannot exist without penitence and good fruits, all scripture is also given to this end: that it be of use (1) for instruction, (2) for punishment, (3) for improvement, (4) for discipline in righteousness, and (5) for consola-

---

[33] Johann Jacob Rambach, *Betrachtungen über den Rath Gottes von der Seeligkeit der Menschen, wie solche von dem seligen Auctore in der Stadt-Kirche zu Giessen in den ordentlichen Donnerstags-Predigten vorgetragen worden; nunmehro in zweyen Theilen ans Licht gestellet von Johann Philip Fresenius, . . .* (Giessen, 1737).

[34] Rambach, *Ausführliche und gründliche Erläuterung*, 1:419–23.

[35] Francke, *Einleitung zur Lesung*, 3–4:

> Weil du von Kind auff die H. Schrifft weissest / kann dich dieselbige unterweisen zur Seeligkeit durch den Glauben an CHRISTO JESU; Denn alle Schrifft von GOtt eingegeben / ist nütz zur Lehre / zur Straffe / zur Besserung / zur Züchtigung in der Gerechtigkeit / NB. daß ein Mensch GOttes sey vollkommen / zu allem guten Werck geschickt. Offenbar ist es / daß an diesen und dergleichen Orten nicht allein von dem Nutzen / sondern auch von dem Zweck der heiligen Schrifft gehandelt werde / und erhellet daraus / daß solcher Haupt-Zweck sey: **Unsere Seeligkeit; . . .**

tion (Rom 15:4), and, to be sure, that a person of God be perfectly directed to every good work, and that we amidst all cross and tribulation hold firmly to the hope of eternal life.[36]

Logically following from these descriptions is the division of scripture into two types, law and gospel, each with its own *End-Zweck*, (1) that of the law being bound up with the process of punishment, recognition, and acknowledgment of sin, all for the purpose of leading the believer to turn to Christ for aid, whereas (2) that of the Gospel was summarized in the words of John 20:31: "that we believe Jesus to be Christ, the Son of God, and that we through faith have life in his name." Later, Francke identifies John's words as the purpose behind all four evangelists' telling the history of Jesus's works and teachings. Within this context he differentiates Luke and John in the following manner:

> It is the case then, that one wants to perceive in addition a special purpose in this or that evangelist, such as that Luke, as he himself tells us at the outset, is particularly occupied with bringing everything into its proper order, as one thing follows after the other, and thus he also describes one thing or another in greater detail. John, however, according to the testimony of the ancients, particularly wrote his Gospel in order to demonstrate the divine nature of Christ, and because of such a goal relates many discourses and deeds of Christ, from which we can recognize the divine majesty of Christ more clearly than from the other evangelists; also he, on the other hand, passes over one thing or another that the others think of.[37]

Here we have the traditional view of Luke as the historian among the evangelists, concerned with chronology and historical detail (hence his serving for some as the primary source for the concept of salvation history), of John as the evangelist who is most concerned with Jesus's divine nature, his signs, and discourses. As

---

[36] Ibid.,4:

> . . . und weil die Seeligkeit allein durch den Glauben an JEsum Christum erhalten wird / daß dahero hiernächst auch der Zweck der Heil. Schrifft sey: der **Glaube an JEsum Christum.** Weil aber auch ein wahrer seeligmachender Glaube nicht seyn kann ohne Busse / und gute Früchte: So ist alle Schrifft zu dem Ende gegeben / daß sie nütz sey 1. zur Lehre / 2. zur Straffe / 3. zur Besserung / 4. zur Züchtigung in der Gerechtigkeit / und 5. zum Trost / Rom. XV. 4. und zwar daß ein Mensch GOTTes sey vollkommen zu allem guten Werck geschickt / und damit wir unter allem Creutz und Trübsal die Hoffnung des ewigen Lebens veste behalten.

[37] Ibid., 17–18:

> Es sey denn / daß man in diesem und jenem Evangelisten noch einen besondern Zweck beobachten wollte / als daß Lucas / wie er im Anfange selbst meldet / sich sonderlich beflissen alles in richtige Ordnung zu bringen / wie eines nach dem andern erfolget / und also auch ausführlicher ein und anders beschreibet; Johannes aber nach dem Zeugniß der Alten / sonderlich sein Evangelium zur Beweisung der Göttlichen Natur CHristi geschrieben / und von wegen solches Zwecks viele Reden und Thaten Christi erzehlet / aus welchen wir die göttliche Herrlichkeit CHristi klärer als aus den andern Evangelisten erkennen können; auch wol hingegen ein und anders übergehet / welches die andern gedencken.

Francke makes clear, here and throughout his writings on scripture, the story of God's will for the blessedness of humanity is the *scopus* not only of all four evangelists but of all scripture. And in this John's special role is that by virtue of his emphasizing Jesus's divine nature, his presence with the Father as divine word, before Creation, and his voluntary undertaking God's mission, he (John) provides most clearly the knowledge of Jesus's participation in the divine plan for salvation.[38] This quality is mirrored in Francke's lectures on John's Passion account as well as in Bach's *St. John Passion*.

Rambach, in his writings on hermeneutics, is far more detailed than Francke in presenting the *scopus* of scripture, which he further divides and subdivides in ways that do not concern us directly. What is important is that here, as in his other writings, Rambach understands God's purpose and the means of its accomplishment in terms of what he and many others called God's *Rath* (i.e., *Rat*, sometimes *Raht*) or *Rathschluß* (sometimes *Rathschlag*, or *Vorsatz*), that is, God's eternal or foreordained will for the salvation of humanity whose objective or historical dimension is the concept of salvation history, God's plan of salvation as progressively revealed in scripture. Rambach describes what he calls its *a priori* aspect as follows:

> Namely, the good Lord, in his revelation, since he revealed himself to humanity through His word (*per verbum*), can have had no other intention than to make humanity, which had fallen away from him, justified and blessed. Since, however, according to God's eternal will (*ewigen Rathschluß*), humanity can be made justified and blessed in no way other than through Jesus Christ, the only fountain of all justification that is valid for God, we see easily that the eye of God everywhere in the entire scriptures must have been directed towards Christ.[39]

The concept of God's *Rath*, his *ewiger* [or *vorbedachter*] *Rath*, *Rathschluß*, or *Wille*, is one of the broadest concepts of early Lutheranism, sometimes discussed openly but more often serving as a background to theological writings of various kinds. It encompasses various meanings, so that at times it is equivalent to God's counsel or will, unfathomable by humanity, at others to God's intention, design, or plan for

---

[38] Thus the traditional view of Luke as historian and John as the spiritual Gospel needs to be qualified where salvation history is concerned. Of the sources cited in Introduction, n. 11, Hans Conzelmann (*Theology of St. Luke*) centers his work on Luke, whereas, as Oscar Cullmann (*Christ and Time*) points out (xxiii), redemptive history is to be found "particularly" in John. From Martin Moller's remarks on this subject (see 78), it is clear that salvation history was associated closely with John in the era of emerging Lutheran orthodoxy.

[39] Rambach, *Erläuterung*. 2:419: "Nemlich der gütige GOtt kan in seiner *revelation*, da er sich den Mensch *per verbum* offenbaret hat, keine andere Intention gehabt haben, als die Menschen, die von ihm abgefallen waren, gerecht und selig zu machen. Da nun aber der Mensch nach dem ewigen Rathschluß GOttes nicht anders gerecht und selig gemacht werden kan, als durch JEsum Christum, den einigen Brunnen aller vor Gott geltenden Gerechtigkeit; so siehet man leicht, daß das Auge GOttes in der ganzen Schrift überall auf Christum müsse gerichtet gewesen sein." Rambach's *a posteriori* demonstration, which directly follows, is concerned with Jesus as *scopus* of scripture in its twofold aspects of law and gospel.

the salvation of humanity, revealed to humanity through scripture. As presented by Rambach, in his treatise, *Betrachtungen über den Rath Gottes von der Seeligkeit der Menschen* (published posthumously in 1737 but given as a series of 69 sermons from 1732 to 1734), it parallels very closely the chronology of scripture and the ordering of the liturgical year. In his introductory sermon on the general or overall meaning of God's *Rath*, Rambach first associates the concept with Paul's closing remarks to the Ephesians as told by Luke in the book of Acts 20:27: "Denn ich habe euch nichts verhalten, daß ich nicht verkündiget hätte alle den Rath Gottes" ("For I have not shunned to declare unto you all the counsel of God," [KJV]), a summary reference to the still more famous passage in Ephesians 1:3–17 in which Paul sets forth what Catherine Mowry LaCugna calls "the shape of salvation history."[40] That "shape" is, of course, that of the incarnation of Christ as "making tangible within human history and within human personality the ineffable mystery of God," while "the Spirit, present and active in creation from the very beginning, leads all of creation back to its origin, God."[41] In the first chapter of Ephesians Paul describes God's plan (*oikonomia*) as the fulfillment in history of God's will for the salvation of humanity, accomplished through Christ. In Luther's translation, cited by Rambach in conjunction with the abovementioned verse from Acts, Ephesians 1:11 ended "daß wir zum Erbtheil kommen seyen, nach dem Vorsatz deß, der alle Dinge wirket nach dem Rath seines Willens" (so that we would come to inheritance according to the plan of him, who works all things according to his counsel and will).[42] God's plan, will or counsel, is the "economy" or the story of salvation history that constitutes the objectification of God's will as manifested in Christ and the Holy Spirit, and told in scripture. It is intimately bound up, at least for the Lutherans of the sixteenth through the eighteenth centuries, with the activity of the Trinity throughout history.

Rambach next divides the concept of God's *Rath* into three parts: (1) God's decision to effect the salvation (Heil) of the sinful (made along with his son before the Creation); (2) the means ("Mittel") of that salvation; and (3) the process ("Ordnung," often called "Heilsordnung," occasionally "Gnadenordnung") by means of which the sinner will participate in this "Heil."[43] In the three parts the reader may discern a relationship to Martin Moller's association of Christmas with God the Father, Easter with God the Son, and Pentecost with the Holy Spirit. In other words, Christmas is associated with God's *Rath* itself, Easter with Christ as the means by which salvation was effected, and Pentecost with the Holy Spirit as the process or "Ordnung," according to which Christ's work becomes efficacious for the faithful.

Over the next sixteen sermons (2–17), Rambach discusses first the existence and nature of God (2–4), then the Creation (5–8), God's demand for innocence,

---

[40] LaCugna, *God for Us*, 21.

[41] Ibid., 21.

[42] Rambach, *Betrachtungen über den Rath Gottes*, 6.

[43] Ibid.,3–17.

the fall of humanity, and the ramifications and consequences of original sin (9–16), ending with humanity's inability to help itself in its misery (17). Here Rambach picks up again with the subject of God's *Rath*, first in terms of God's will toward fallen humanity (ch. 18), then of God's plan (*Vorsatz*) for its redemption (ch. 19), which as Rambach makes clear at many points in his entire series of sermons, took place before the Creation. Next comes a discussion of the "eternal contract" (*ewigen Vertrag*) between the Father and Son concerning the redemption of the human race (ch. 20), and finally a summary of God's *Rathschluß* itself (ch. 21), anticipating the new "economy" that began with the granting of the law. These topics are followed by God's promise of a redeemer (the so-called proto-Gospel of Gen 3 discussed in ch. 22) and its further clarification in the OT (see ch. 23), and finally by the granting of the law and the meaning of its strictness (chs. 24 and 25). Here Rambach leaps forward in time. His twenty-sixth sermon, "Die Sendung des längst versprochenen Erlösers" (The sending of the long promised redeemer), initiates a sequence of sixteen sermons (26–41) that tell the story of Christ's work of redemption up to the description of the work of the Holy Spirit (41). The forty-one sermons to this point, encompassing the two stages described above (i.e., the *Rath* itself and the *Mittel*), Rambach designates as Part 1, after which the remaining twenty-eight sermons comprise Part 2, under a separate heading.

Thus Rambach's threefold presentation of the concept of God's *Rath* at the outset of the book emerges also within the chronological ordering of his sermons into three eras: from before the Creation through the Time of Israel, culminating in the granting of the law; the Time of Christ, from the incarnation through the coming of the Holy Spirit; and, the era of the church under the guidance of the Spirit. At the same time his presenting the three eras within the framework of two large divisions with separate headings (the first and second eras are contained within division 1, whereas the third comprises division 2 in its entirety) corresponds to the two halves of the liturgical year, divided after Pentecost. Within the year itself, the first half alludes to the Time of Israel in the pre-Christmas weeks, then, in the period from Christmas to Pentecost/Trinity, presents the life of Christ in outline, culminating in the "means" of humanity's salvation, the Passion, Easter, and Pentecost. After that, the Trinity season mirrors the third era, that of the church under the inspiration of the Holy Spirit and awaiting the final consummation. Rambach's second part reflects this closely, not only in its dealing with the process by which contemporary humanity participates in God's plan, following the role of the Holy Spirit, but also in its sequence of themes, which corresponds closely in character, and sometimes in placement as well, to those of the Trinity season. At the end of the series of sermons Rambach turns to the eschatological themes that characterize the end of the Trinity season, "The blessed death of the faithful" (65), "The blessedness of the faithful on the day of the appearance of Jesus Christ" (66), "The eternal Glory" (67), and "A meditation on eternal damnation" (68). A concluding sermon, headed with a paraphrase of the passage from Acts that Rambach took as his starting point, places the entire sequence within the framework of God's plan of salvation: "The joy of a teacher who has revealed the entire plan of God" ("Die Freudigkeit eines Lehrers, der allen Rath Gottes verkündiget hat").

From all this we see that the principles of hermeneutics and the concept of salvation history are mutually interdependent and articulated in the form of the liturgical year as well. God's *Rath*, as Rambach presents it, is remarkably close in outline to the modern concept of salvation history, a three-period history, based primarily, as is Rambach's scheme, on the book of Acts, and centering the "Time of Christ" between the "Time of Israel" and the "Time of the church." In the liturgical year the Time of Israel is compressed within the weeks of Advent; that is, the church draws the parallel between that of Israel awaiting the coming of the Messiah and the church awaiting the Second Coming (Bach's reworking of Cantata 70 from its original association with the second Sunday in Advent to that of a cantata for the twenty-sixth Sunday after Trinity reflects this exactly). But since the whole of scripture was conceived as a unity, there are numerous references to it throughout the year. In Rambach's version the view of the Time of Christ as the center is reflected in the fact that the sixteen sermons from the incarnation to the coming of the Holy Spirit (Advent/Christmas to Pentecost) are "centered" between the initial twenty five (from before the Creation to the granting of the law), and the concluding twenty-eight (from the coming of the Holy Spirit to anticipation of the Second Coming). More prominent in Rambach than is usually brought out in modern versions of salvation history is the sense of purpose of such a history, its "use" for the contemporary believer in search of redemption. In keeping with this purpose, Rambach divides the "Heilsordnung" of the third division (which concerns the present-day believer and corresponds to the era of the church) into a double process, penitence and faith, the former offered to God (meaning God the Father) from the sinner who has transgressed the law, and the latter centered on Jesus and the Gospel of the forgiveness of sins.[44]

Rambach's descriptions make clear that this double process of penitence/forgiveness is basically one of descent followed by ascent, mirroring Jesus's twofold nature and work. In his initial sermon Rambach describes the "Ordnung" stage as one of penitence followed by faith, and within his third grouping of sermons (those of part 2), there is a basic division into two broad themes, the first centering largely on penitence, and the second on the process of faith. Similarly, at approximately the center of the sermons corresponding to the "Time of Christ" between the incarnation and ascension (32; the seventh of the sixteen that comprise this group), Rambach discusses what he calls "the twofold condition of our redeemer" ("Der doppelte Zustand unsers Mittlers"), describing it as "I. Der Stand seiner Erniedrigung" (the condition of his humiliation) and "II. Der Stand seiner Erhöhung" (the condition of his elevation). He then makes clear that this "doppelte Zustand," corresponds to the twofold "Ordnung" of penitence and faith that render it of

[44] Ibid., 770 ff.

"use" to the believer.[45] Thus the penitence/faith sequence of Rambach's third division (part 2), mirrors the process of the believer's "conformity" to Christ in his "Erniedrigung" and Erhöhung" that is the primary work of the Holy Spirit.[46] Its "dynamic" is that of Luther's conception of the "summary" of scripture: the work of law and gospel as destruction followed by restoration, historically as well as tropologically.[47] It presents the same descent/ascent pattern as that of the "shape of salvation history" or the "economy" of salvation as described by LaCugna.

Rambach does not utilize the word "*Oekonomie*" in the title of any of his many treatises; but the term itself appears in many of them, always in close association with God's *Rath*. Other authors used the term more widely. One of these was Rambach's father-in-law, Joachim Lange, who, like Rambach himself, was a pupil and colleague of August Hermann Francke's at Halle. In one of the largest of his treatises (published posthumously), Rambach bases his own treatment of the "economy of salvation" on a treatise of Lange's titled *Oeconomia Salutis Evangelica [Dogmatica]*.[48] In his introduction (1–9) Rambach discusses the terms in question as well as the "natural" ordering of the subject, which proceeds from God, the divine nature (i.e., the Trinity), the plan of salvation, and its implementation in history, and the like, to topics directly concerning humankind, involving prominently, of course, penitence. The direction is from theology in its strict sense (concerning God) to economy, the two aspects of trinitarian theology that LaCugna discusses as either united or polarized at different points in Christian history. At the end of Rambach's introduction, having explained the religious meaning of *oeconomia*, its original association with household hierarchy and ordering, and its application to God's ordering of salvation, he turns to the term *evangelica* as indicating the *Endzweck* of that ordering. He explains that the "evangelical economy" of salvation in the NT manifests the reality behind the prefigurings of the OT, "the salvation won through the death of Christ and dispensed and brought forward in word and sacrament."[49] Rambach's chosen ordering follows this pattern closely, in a thirty-

---

[45] Ibid., 549–56.

[46] And, as Rambach makes clear (*Betrachtungen über den Rath Gottes*, 547), Jesus's *Erniedrigung* was a form of penitence for the original sin of humanity, which the believer has to acknowledge as still present in himself/herself through penitence.

[47] See ch. 8, 85–86.

[48] Rambach's treatise, which was published posthumously, is titled *Dogmatische Theologie / oder / Christliche / Glaubens-Lehre / Vormals in einem* Collegio thetico / *Uber des / Hochberühmten Herrn D. Joachim Langens, . . .* OECONOMIAM SALUTIS / DOGMATICAM (Frankfurt und Leipzig, 1744). As Rambach states in his introduction, Lange's treatise was originally published as *Oeconomia salutis evangelica* (Halle, 1728) and only later with the addition of the word "dogmatica."

[49] Rambach, *Dogmatische Theologie*, 9: "Das dritte Wort ist *evangelica*, in *oppositione* gegen *oeconomiam salutis legalem*, da das wahre Heyl, seiner wircklichen Erwerbung und Erfüllung nach, noch ferne und zukünftig war, und da es unter mancherley *umbris* und Vorbildern *repraesentir*et wurde; da hingegen die **Evangelische Oeconomie** unterm N. T. Die *realit*ät jener Vorbilder *exhibir*et, und das durch Christi Tod erworbene Heyl im Wort und Sacramenten auf eine deutliche, reiche und herrliche Art in derselben *dispensir*et und vorgetragen wird." The verb "dispensiret" alludes to one of the commonest Latin/German equivalents of *oeconomia* (*dispositio*, *dispensatio*).

part (10 × 3) division ending with the "consummation of salvation" (*De consummatione salutis*). Although beginning from the divine being, the entire process is directed toward the salvation of the sinner: "Thus everything is concentrated on the salvation of the sinner, which is the final purpose of the whole of theology, on whose proper recognition and profit each person must be oriented to the utmost."[50]

Rambach's presentation of the concept of God's *Rath* is probably the most detailed of the time. But Bach also had another substantial work on the subject in his collection, Johannes Müller's *Absolutum Decretum, Das ist/Blosser Rathschluss Gottes. . .* (1652). And the subject tends to form a strong underlying presence in theological works of a comprehensive or summarizing nature even when it is not directly announced in the title. It permeates entire sections of the aforementioned harmony of the Gospels written by Chemnitz, Leiser, and Gerhard and is linked particularly with John in the introductory first chapter of that work.[51] Many other works, such as Nikolaus Hunnius's *Epitome Credendorum /Oder Innhalt der ganzen Christlichen Lehre* (1625) and Johann Anastasius Freylinghausen's *Grundlegung der Theologie* (1704) discuss the concept at some length; and the ordering of the subjects of their treatises is very close in outline to that of Rambach.[52] Others, such as Christian Scriver (*Evangelischer Seelen-Schatz*, 1687), work it into their treatises at various points.[53] And it even crops up in funeral sermons, such as the *Oeconomia Scholae Crucis* (1694) of Daniel-Ernst Jablonski, court preacher to the Elector of Brandenburg, where it is equated to God's "economy" as the way of the cross:

---

[50] Ibid., "Also concentrirt sich alles auf *salutem* peccatoris, als den Endzweck der gantzen Theologie, an dessen rechter Erkentniß und Genuß einem jeden aufs allerhöchste gelegen seyn muß."

[51] The first book of the Chemnitz/Leyser/Gerhard commentary begins with a chapter that sets forth, and to some extent compares, the beginnings of the Gospels of Luke and John, as the two NT authors who deal in their very different ways with those events that precede Jesus's ministry. The discussion of Luke, much shorter than that of John, points up Luke's concern for the historical ("narrative") character of those events. That of John centers, as we might expect, on John's prologue as introducing the entire subject matter of the account to follow. It therefore links John's emphasis on Jesus's divinity as divine *Logos* with God's plan of redemption ("decretum redemptionis" in the Latin original; "göttliche Rathschluß" or "Entschluß" in the 1764 German translation; "decree" in the English edition). See the sources cited in ch. 1, n. 1 (respectively, *Caput Primum*, col. 7; *Buch 1. Cap. 1*, 10; and 67).

[52] Nicolaus Hunnius, *Epitome Credendorum Oder Innhalt der gantzen Christlichen Lehre . . .* (Wittenberg, 1719), 132–58; Johann Anastasius Freylinghausen, *Grundlegung der Theologie* (Halle, 1703), facsimile ed. by Matthias Paul (Hildesheim: Olms-Weidmann, 2005), 47–60. In the preface to his *Dogmatische Theologie* (6), Rambach comments on the ordering of Freylinghausen's treatise, viewing it as an example of the "natural" order mentioned earlier.

[53] Already the full title, and of course the five-part ordering, of Scriver's enormous treatise indicates its occupation with the chronological ordering of salvation associated with God's economy: *Seelen-Schatz, Darinnen Von der menschlichen Seele hohen Würde, tieffen und kläglichen Sünden-Fall, Busse und Erneuerung durch Christum / göttlichen heiligen Leben / vielfältigen Creutz und Trost im Creutz, seligen Abschied aus dem Leibe, triumphirlichen und frölichen Einzug in dem Himmel, und ewiger Freude und Seligkeit, erbaulich und tröstlich gehandelt wird* (Schaffhausen edition, 1738). Scriver introduces the concept of God's *Rath* at key points, such as the introduction to book 4, "Vom Creutze der gläubigen Seelen," where he associates it with the way of the cross as presented in his view by passages from the psalms, and Isaiah, as well as citations of phrases of Solomon, in all of which the concept is associated with God's leading the faithful to blessedness (4:1–4). Later (5:139) Scriver cites Luther in the same way.

"Gottes Kreutz-Schule."[54] Jablonski discusses God's *Raht* [*sic*] as his *Ordnung* and *Vorsatz*, defining it as God's will as revealed in scripture, and linking it specifically to Jesus's acceptance of the "Kelch" (cup) given him by God in John's Passion account:

> However, we might also quite fittingly understand by God's will (*Raht Gottes*) his *eternal plan* and *foreordained ordering*, with which he wants to lead his own through much suffering to glory. In this sense it is said of Christ, *that he suffered what the will of God (Raht Gottes) had conceived beforehand should take place* (Acts 4:28). Accordingly, *God's will* would be just that which otherwise scripture calls *the cup* (*Kelch*) that the Father has given us to a certain degree that pleases him, and which we must drink in accordance with his will (*Raht*), as the Lord Jesus says of himself: *"Shall I not drink the cup that my Father has given me?"*[55]

In chapter 5 we learn that August Hermann Francke and Johann Anastasius Freylinghausen view this passage from John in the same terms, Freylinghausen linking it up with Jesus's "Es ist vollbracht" as well. And Bach in his setting of those words clearly understood them in exactly the same manner. Characteristic Johannine expressions, such as what God "gave" Jesus, or God's having "sent" Jesus, reflect the concept of God's *Rath* in numerous theological writings. Martin Moller, cited earlier, sees it as underlying passages from the Farewell Discourse in John, such as "Nun aber gehe ich hin zu dem, der mich gesandt hat . . ." (Jn 16:5, "But now I go my way to him that sent me," from the Gospel for Cantate, the fourth Sunday after Easter) and "Also hat Gott die Welt geliebt . . . " (Jn 3:16, "God so loved the world, . . ." from the Gospel for Pentecost), as well as from elsewhere in John, such as "Das ist der Wille des Vaters, der mich gesandt hat, daß ich nichts verliere von allem, das er mir gegeben hat, . . ." (This is the will of the Father, who sent me, that I lose none of those whom he gave me . . . ," a compound drawn from different points in John). Likewise, Moller paraphrases passages from John, such as Jesus's description of the Holy Spirit as speaking "not of himself but of what he hears" (Jn 16:13, from the Gospel for Cantate) in terms of God's revealing his will (*Rath*) through the "prophets, evangelists and apostles." In such passages, several of which are prominent in the Bach cantatas of spring 1725, Jesus explains God's

---

[54] Daniel-Ernst Jablonski, *Oeconomia Scholae Crucis, GOTTES Kreutz-Schule* (Cölln an der Spree, Berlin, 1694).

[55] Ibid., 17:

> Doch mögen wir auch gar füglich durch diesen **Raht** [*sic*] **Gott**es verstehen / Seinen **ewigen Vorsatz** und **beschlossene Ordnung** daß Er die Seinen durch viel Leiden führen wolle zur Herrlichkeit. In diesem Verstande wird von Christo gesagt / **daß Er gelitten / was der Raht Gottes zuvor becacht hatte / das geschehen solt** / Act. 4, 28. Wäre demnach **Gottes Raht** even das / was sonst die Schrift nennet **den Kelch** / den der Vater uns / unter gewisser / Ihme gefälliger Maaß eingeschencket hat / und den wir seinem Raht gemäß / trincken müssen : wir der HErr JEsus von sich sagte: **Sol ich den Kelch nicht trincken / den mir mein Vater gegeben hat?**

purpose, which Moller describes as God's *Rath* or God's *Vorsatz* (plan) to the disciples and others.[56]

From such passages it is clear that the Lutheran authors of the seventeenth and eighteenth centuries viewed the readings of the Farewell Discourse as particularly closely associated with Passiontide, Easter, and the great fifty days as the fulfillment of God's plan for human salvation. Thus Rambach uses the concept copiously to underscore the meaning of the Passion; and, as we will see (ch. 4), it underlies August Hermann Francke's 1716 lectures on John's Passion account. In their directly preceding and following Ascension Day, culminating in Pentecost, the Gospel readings from the Farewell Discourse mirror the quality that Rambach, in his commentary on the Gospel readings for the entire year, identifies with Ascension Day as the fulfillment of God's plan.[57]

The insistence, in most accounts of God's *Rath*, or *Vorsatz*, that it was conceived between the Father and the Son, before the creation of the world, mirrors John's presentation of Jesus as the divine Logos who was present from the beginning with God, indeed *as* God. Along with the well-known parallel of John's prologue to the beginning of Genesis, it goes hand in hand with the idea that God's plan encompasses the entire history of scripture as told in the Bible and understood as one single story. Often, in Lutheran theological books, however, the part of that story that represents the "Time of Israel" is foreshortened, as is the case within the liturgical year itself, for the purpose of concentrating and elaborating on the work of Jesus and its benefit for humankind in the present: the stage that Rambach identifies as the "Ordnung des Heils." This is the case in another extended treatise of Rambach, his *Erbauliche Betrachtungen über die Heils-Güter in Christo*, in which forty-eight out of fifty-nine sermons are devoted to the *Heils-Ordnung*.[58] At the

---

[56] Moller, *Praxis Evangeliorum*, 2:205–7, 218. A characteristic passage is the following (205): "Ja / Herr Jesu / in dem du sprichst: **Der mich gesandt hat:** zeigestu mir nicht alleine den Vater / der dich gesand hat: Sondern thust mir elenden Menschen gleich ein Fensterlin auff / unnd lessest mich hinein blicken in den ewigen Rhat der heiligen Dreyfaltigkeit / darinnen vor der Zeit der Welt dieser Vorsatz und Beschlus gemacht: Daß du / O Gott Vater / mir mein Heil aus lauter Gnaden unnd Barmhertzigkeit schencken: Dasselbe durch Jesum Christum deinen Sohn erwerben: Und mich durch den heiligen Geist im Glauben erleuchten / heiligen / und erbawen woltest."

[57] Rambach, *Evangelische Betrachtungen über die Sonn- und Fest-Tags-Evangelia*,638–56. Rambach's Ascension Day sermon is titled "Der Rath GOttes in der Himmelfahrt JEsu Christi."

[58] Rambach, *Erbauliche Betrachtungen über die Heils-Güter in Christo / Nach Anleitung des von dem sel. D. Philipp Jacob Spenern herausgegebenen Tractätlein, Die lauter Milch des Evangelii genannt: Vormals in einigen Erbauungs-Stunden auf dem Wäysenhause zu Halle angestellet; nun aber, als / Der andere Theil / Von des sel. Auctoris Betrachtungen über die Ordnung des Heils* (Frankfurt und Leipzig, 1737). As the preface to the *Erbauliche Betrachtungen* tells us, the work was published to serve as the second part of an earlier treatise of Rambach, his *Erbauliche Betrachtungen über den Catechismum Lutheri, wie auch über des Herrn Past. Freylinghausens Ordnung des Heils und dessen so genanntes Güldenes A. B. C.* (Frankfurt and Leipzig, 1736). The editor, Rambach's son J.[ohann] G.[otthilf] R.[ambach], refers to the two treatises together as *Rambachs Betrachtungen über die Ordnung und Wohlthaten des Heils*, explaining that the first volume encompassed sets of meditations on the catechism of Luther and on two treatises of Johann Anastasius Freylinghausen, whereas the organization of the second volume followed that of Spener's treatise *Die lautere Milch des Evangelii.*

outset Rambach takes God's love for humankind as the starting point for the understanding of God's plan of salvation, especially as told by John in such classic passages as 3:16 ("For God so loved the world . . . , ") and 1 John 4:10 ("Herein is love, not that we loved God, but that he loved us, and sent his Son to be the propitiation for our sins" [KJV]). Then, after presenting God's love as the first "principal benefit" (*Haupt-Gut*) for humanity, the motive for his plan of salvation, Rambach turns to God's plan or intention itself (*Vorsatz*) as the second, under the heading "The merciful plan of the heavenly Father, to send his son as a savior for the fallen human race" (**"Das andre Haupt-Gut** ist / Der barmhertzige Vorsatz des himmlischen Vaters, dem gefallenen menschlichen Geschlechte sein Sohn zu einem Erlöser zu schicken"):

> This is the next action of the eternal merciful love of God, as therefore they were then united with one another: *For God so loved the world, that he gave his only begotten Son*; where the giving of his Son also encompasses in itself, as the first fruit of God's love, *the plan to give him*; as can also be recognized from the passage adduced here: 1 John 4:10. . . . *The foundation* of this matter is this: God is equally as *just* as he is *full of love*, as a result of which it was impossible for him to have love for the stained, errant and rebellious sinners without injury to his holiness, if a means were not at hand to reconcile his demand for justice and, by means of an adequate satisfaction, to pacify himself on account of the offense it caused him. This means, however, which no creature would have found in an eternity, God found himself, since he, out of his gracious heart, conceived the plan of giving his only son as a redeemer for the fallen human race, which would pacify his demand for justice, free humankind from service to Satan, and, through his dear payment of the price of release, would lay a truly lasting foundation for God to be able to live once again in friendship with humankind and turn towards them with his grace and love. To this end a council was held, before the creation of the world, between the first two persons of the divine being, the Father and the Son, and at the same time, a contract between the two was established, in which *the Father* made a certain proposal, and *the Son*, however, accepted it and undertook it.[59]

---

[59] Ibid., 14–15:

> Dieses ist die nächste Wirkung der ewigen erbarmenden Liebe GOttes, wie sie dann auch daher mit einander verknüpfet werden Joh. 3, 16: **Also hat GOtt die Welt geliebet, daß Er seinen eingebornen Sohn gab;** alwo die Schenckung seines Sohnes auch **den Vorsatz ihn zu schencken,** als die erste Frucht der Liebe GOttes, mit in sich fasset; wie auch solches zu erkennen ist aus dem hierbey gefügten Ort 1. Joh. 4, 10. . . . **Der Grund** dieser Sache ist dieser: GOtt ist eben so **gerecht**, als Er **liebreich** ist, folglich konte Er den befleckten abtrünnigen und rebellischen Sünder unmöglich ohne Verletzung seiner Heiligkeit lieb haben, wo nicht ein Mittel vorhanden gewesen wäre, seine Gerechtigkeit zu befriedigen, und durch eine hinlängliche Satisfaction sich wegen der zugefügten Beleidigung zu beruhigen. Dieses Mittel aber, welches keine Creatur in Ewigkeit würde erfunden haben, hat GOtt selbst erfunden, da Er in seinem

Here Rambach couches the story of God's plan in the legalistic, or juridical terms of what is known as the "satisfaction theory" of redemption that is a recognized feature of Picander's text for Bach's *St. Matthew Passion*. God's love is equaled by his demand for justice, which can only be "satisfied" by the adequacy of Jesus's work of redemption, the payment of the price of human sin, a process that is described as a "contract" proposed by God and accepted by Jesus. As in the *St. Matthew Passion*, love remains paramount as God's motive, God's will that all sinners be saved. August Hermann Francke, in describing the "purposes" of law and gospel in scripture, describes the Gospel (in both the OT and NT) as the manifestation of God's "herabsteigende Liebe" (downward-tending love) for fallen humanity—the love that prompted Jesus's incarnation and *Erniedrigung*—and the work of the law as the "aufsteigende Liebe" (upward-tending love) by which humankind, through love of God and the neighbor, returns to God.[60] Thus God's plan had a descent/ascent character: God's love for humanity prompted the descent manifested in Jesus's incarnation and sufferings on earth, whereas humanity, brought down by the "cross" that was given by God out of love, and directed by the law toward consciousness of sin and repentance, was granted faith in that work and its upward course (the resurrection and ascension). In God's plan, therefore, the law as what Luther called God's "alien work" was subordinate to the Gospel, God's "proper work," founded in love; through the process of *Heils-Ordnung* humanity could thus produce the fruits of love that led to blessedness. God's love, as we will see, is announced in the first chorale of the *St. John Passion*, "O grosse Lieb," which, following emphasis on God's glory ("Herr, unser Herrscher") and Jesus's foreknowledge, initiates a sequence that follows the pattern of the ordering of salvation, culminating in Peter's repentance. Part 1 is structured around this sequence.

One of the main concerns for authors dealing with the concept of God's *Rath* was, of course, the fact that it invoked the idea of predestination, a topic that has considerable resonance in John as well. It was usually discussed in terms that long predated Lutheranism: of God's "vorhergehenden" will, that is, God's general or overall will for the salvation, or blessedness, of all humanity, and his "nachfolgenden" will, that is, God's ordaining particular means (Rambach's *Heilsordnung*) according to which only some of humanity (usually a small part) was saved. In the Lutheran view, humanity participated in a process that was foreseen but not arbitrarily decided by God. As mentioned earlier, Bach had several books in his collec-

gnädigen Hertzen von Ewigkeit den Vorsatz gefasset, seinen einigen Sohn dem gefallenen menschlichen Geschlecht zum Erlöser zu schencken, welcher seine Gerechtigkeit befriedigen, die Menschen aus dem Dienste des Satans befreyen und durch sein theures Lösegeld einen recht dauerhaften Grund legen solte, daß GOtt mit den Menschen wiederum in Freundschaft leben und ihnen seine Gnade und Liebe zuwenden könte. Zu dem Ende ist nun vor Erschaffung der Welt zwischen den beyden ersten Personen in der Gottheit, dem Vater und dem Sohn, ein Rath gehalten, und gleichsam ein Vertrag zwischen beyden aufgerichtet worden, darinnen **der Vater** einen gewissen Vorschlag gethan, **der Sohn** aber denselben acceptiret und angenommen hat.

[60] Francke, *Einleitung zur Lesung*, 6.

tion that take up this theme, which was a major point of dispute between Lutherans and Calvinists. Thus, after the discussion of God's "plan," the third chapter of Rambach's *Erbauliche Betrachtungen über die Heils-Güter in Christo* is devoted to God's "ewigen Gnadenwahl," after which the meditations turn to the narrative of Jesus's work. Chapter 4, "Von der Sendung des Sohnes Gottes" (On the sending of the Son of God), introduces a sequence outlining the stages of that work (chs. 5–10, from the incarnation to the founding of the "kingdom of grace" on earth through the Holy Spirit), after which Rambach takes up the *Heils-Ordnung* itself, beginning with baptism. The last seven chapters (53–59) have very much the eschatological character of the ending of the Trinity season, so that the sequence as a whole bears a considerable relationship to the ordering of the liturgical year.[61] Since God's "time" was not equivalent to that of humanity, and could not be understood by humanity, the question of the elect—God's *Gnadenwahl*—versus the damned was fraught with paradox and explanations that no longer seem compelling to many today. The best counsel given in the theology of the time was faith: for the individual to believe in his own election and act accordingly, in keeping with God's dictates, that is, to accept God's *Ordnung* as the framework of existence and to leave matters in God's hands. This, rather strikingly, is the subject of the largest single group of passages underlined by Bach in his copy of the so-called Calov Bible.[62]

In authors closely associated with Halle pietist circles discussion of the ordering of salvation ("Heils-Ordnung" or *Oekonomie*) is particularly prominent, and was considered essential to the education of children. Sometimes several treatises were bound together in collections oriented toward this subject and presented in catechism form. One such groups Rambach's *Erbauliches Handbüchlein für Kinder* (1726), which takes the "Ordnung des Heils" as its starting point, with Rambach's *Wohl-informirte Catechet* (1727), which likewise gives prominence to that theme. It also includes two treatises by Johann Anastasius Freylinghausen of similar purpose, as well as Christoph Lösecke's *Catechetische Einleitung / Die Haushaltung* (1720). Lösecke's treatise, as the author's preface informs us, was published in shorter form several years earlier and was itself an extract from a completed longer treatise. The latter treatise, published in 1724 under the title *Theologia Foederalis-Oeconomica*, combines the principles of Lutheran "Heils-ordnung" or the economy of salvation ("Heils-oeconomie") with the so-called federal theology (or covenant theology) widely associated with the reformed theologian Herman Witsius's *De oeconomia foederum Dei com hominibus* (1677). Lösecke's treatise attempts to cover at once God's "Haushaltung" or economy in terms of the succession of covenants made with humanity, the "Heils-Ordnung" as expressed in the chronologi-

---

[61] The principal themes of these chapters are, the "patient and longing awaiting of the consummation of the salvation of the faithful" (ch. 53); "The blessed death or falling asleep of the faithful" (ch. 54); "The blessed condition of the faithful souls in Abraham's bosom" (ch. 55); "The glorious coming of Christ for His revelation" (ch. 56); "The glorious resurrection of the faithful to eternal life" (ch. 57); "The presence of the faithful before the last judgment" (ch. 58); "The eternal glory" (ch. 59).

[62] See ch. 8, 328.

cal ordering of the articles of faith in scripture, the prefigurings of Christ in the OT and their fulfillment in the NT, and even the entire history of the church from the Creation to Lösecke's own time.[63] Needless to say, it was not necessary for Bach, or any similarly educated Lutheran of his time, to have direct knowledge of such treatises or the details of their contents and the disputes surrounding their acceptance or non-acceptance among the various reformed, pietist, or orthodox circles. Nor is it necessary for us to become deeply involved in their study in order to recognize resonances in Bach's works. But it is important, if we are interested in the interaction of music and theology in those works, to recognize that in many of them broad sets of background ideas converge, informing us regarding how to understand their designs, even if we cannot always pinpoint exactly how they were conceived.

Collections such as those just described ensured that the principles underlying the "ordering" of salvation formed a central part of Lutheran education from childhood on. Frequently presented in catechismal form, they were the embodiment of dogmatic, didactic theology (as in the titles of the Lange and Rambach treatises), branches of learning that did not yet possess the pejorative associations that have dominated those terms since the Enlightenment and romantic eras. What for us may seem entirely pedantic was entered into with a wholly other frame of mind, in which, ideally at least, the joy of religious consolation dominated over the excess of learning. Exactly this coupling of apparent opposites underlies a work such as the *Actus Tragicus*, BWV 106, in which an appealing simplicity and immediacy of tone forms a counterpoint to a text that, although limited to chorales and passages from scripture, embodies intricate reference to many of the ideas discussed here. The very positive affirmation of God's "time" at the outset encompasses the chosen theme of death, assuring the believer of God's control of human events, no matter how adverse, and offering that believer the means of accepting it, as outlined in the movement sequence that follows. Allusion to the old covenant and its association with the law (the tenor solo "Herr, lehre uns bedenken, daß wir sterben müssen, auf daß wir klug werden"), then to the necessity of putting one's house in order ("Bestelle dein Haus, denn du wirst sterben und nicht lebendig bleiben") perform the necessary work of educating the believer as to what was known as God's "alien" work, after which the fugue "Es ist der alte Bund," sums up what was known as the [old] "covenant of works." The sequence is chronological, from Psalm 90 to Isaiah and Jesus Sirach. Putting one's house in order might or might not have been associated in the mind of the librettist with the meaning of God's economy or "Haushaltung," but both "Herr, lehre uns bedenken" and "Bestelle dein Haus" refer to

---

[63] Albrecht Lösecke, *THEOLOGIA-FOEDERALIS-OECONOMICA, Die Haushaltung u. Wege GOttes mit den Menschen / Darin Die Lehre von den Bündnissen GOttes mit den Menschen verhandelt / die Theologie u. Ordnung des Heyls / wie alle Glaubens-Artickel in Biblischer Folge, Kettenweise an einander hangen, gezeiget, Die Vorbilder Altes Testaments in ihrem Gegen-Bilde erkläret, und die Kirchen-Historie von Anbegin der Welt bis an die gegenwärtige Zeit nebst dem allmähligen Anwachs der Ceremonien, vorgestellt wird* (Halle, 1724).

covenants: that with Moses, the supposed author of Psalm 90, and that with Hezekiah, both of which contained hidden promises that anticipated the "covenant of grace" whose coming underlies the soprano solo response to "Es ist der alte Bund" ("Ja, komm, Herr Jesu") and the movements with NT and chorale texts that follow. The texts of musical works cannot present those ideas in anything more than allusive, outline form; thus it is usually best if their affective rather than rational traits come to the fore. In fact, in numerous ways the *Actus tragicus* refers to sets of ideas that could never be presented directly in its text, ideas that underlie its "descent"/"ascent" sequence of keys; its antithesis of law and gospel (or covenant of works and covenant of grace, subsumed under the first and primary covenant the "covenant of redemption"—God's *Rath*); its pairs of solos in OT/NT prayer-response ordering (suggestive of typological prefiguration); and the like. What seems complex when subjected to historical and musical analysis is, like the "perfect simplicity" that August Hermann Francke attributed to John's literary style, a reflection of what is taken for granted in the belief system of the time.

The *St. John Passion* also exhibits the thematic succession associated with God's *Rath*, the divine *oecomomia*, to a high degree, especially in the choice and placement of the meditative movements in Part 1. Its overall progression from the majesty of God (the opening chorus, "Herr, unser Herrscher" and the emphasis on Jesus's divinity and love in the scene that follows) to the eschatological praise of God in eternity in the final chorale (ending "dich will ich preisen ewiglich") reflects an interpretation of the Passion in light of the very broad framework about which we have read. In this respect it is different from the *St. Matthew Passion* and close to the way that many Lutheran authors viewed the Gospel of John. In other words, the special character of the Passion is owing not only to the "Christus victor" theology that some authors have emphasized, but also to qualities in John that have a close affinity with the economy of salvation as presented by the Greek fathers.

Johann Jacob Rambach on symmetry and the analogy of faith

Among Bach's liturgical works in general, a significant number mirror such ideas closely. In them the prominence of musical *Ordnung*, especially when associated with the ordering of the history of salvation centered on Christ, may remind us that the Latin term that was most widely used from earliest times to describe God's plan—*dispositio* (a translation of *oikonomia*)—was also the term used by some music theorists of Bach's time and before to describe the process of *Ordnung* or pre-planning that is particularly conspicuous in their designs.[64] The most obvious

[64] On the translation of *oekonomie* as *dispositio*, see LaCugna, *God for Us*, 24. Johann Mattheson associates *dispositio* with pre-planning in his *Kern melodischer Wissenschaft* (Hamburg, 1737), 129, and his *Der vollkommene Capellmeister* (Hamburg, 1739), 235. One of the earliest music theorists to use the

instances of such ordering are unquestionably those that exhibit symmetrical qualities, of which the *Actus Tragicus* and the *St. John Passion* are the best known. In this connection, it is interesting that Rambach addresses this quality in relation to the ancient concept of the "analogy of faith" that Luther retained from medieval hermeneutics and associated with the relationship of law and gospel as the summary of scripture.[65] Bach could not have known Rambach's treatment of the subject at the time he wrote the *St. John Passion*, of course; but the principles on which it is based were widespread and rooted in concepts such as scripture as "mirror" (see ch. 8). In this sense Rambach's discussion relates to the association between the interrelatedness of theological themes derived from scripture and the kind of dovetailing of such themes that Bach presents in symmetrical form in the *St. John Passion*. Those themes—Jesus's messianic identity, law versus freedom, God's *Rath* (or the idea of power from "above"), the way of the cross, and several others—appear throughout the Gospel and are "centralized" in particularly concentrated form in the segment of Part 2 of the *Passion* that Friedrich Smend called the *Herzstück*.

One of Luther's most succinct references to the analogy of faith is the following extract. Here, Luther is commenting on the destruction of Jesusalem as told by Isaiah (1:21–28; 4:2–6):

> Faith must be built up on the basis of history, and we ought to stay with it [history] alone and not so easily slip into allegories, unless by way of metaphor we apply them to other things in accordance with the method [analogy] of faith. So here Jerusalem can allegorically be called our conscience, which has been taken and laid waste by the terror of the Law and then set free out of the remnant and the sprouts, and the restored conscience is saved by the Word of the Gospel, through which we grow up into mature manhood by the knowledge of God (cf. Eph 4:13). Such allegory must be used in accordance with the Word of the Law and the Gospel, and this is the explanation of different matters by the same Spirit. . . . This is the summary of Scripture: It is the work of the Law to humble according to history, externally and internally, physically and spiritually. It is the work of the Gospel to

term in this manner was Joachim Burmeister in *Musica Poetica* (Rostock, 1606), 71–72. See Hans Heinrich Unger, *Die Beziehungen zwischen Musik und Rhetorik im 16.–18. Jahrhundert* (Würzburg, 1941), facsimile ed. (Hildesheim: Georg Olms, 1969), 46–62; Rolf Dammann, *Der Musikbegriff im deutschen Barock* (Cologne: Arno Volk Verlag, 1967), 125–27.

[65] Rambach discusses the analogy of faith in at least three treatises, in two of which he relates it closely to symmetry. In his *INSTITUTIONES HERMENEUTICAE SACRAE* (4th ed., Jena, 1732), the discussion is very brief; in his two-volume *Ausführliche . . . Erläuterung über seine eigene INSTITUTIONES HERMENEUTICAE SACRAE* (Giessen, 1738), it occupies an entire chapter (313–43); in his *Dogmatische Theologie oder Christliche Glaubens-Lehre* (Frankfurt and Leipzig, 1744), a treatise that originated as a commentary on the *OECONOMIAM SALUTIS DOGMATICAM* of Rambach's father-in-law, the Halle theologian Joachim Lange (see n. 48), it is again treated at considerable length. Both the latter Rambach treatises discuss symmetry as an essential part of the analogy of faith, and in some detail.

> console, externally and internally, physically and spiritually. What our predecessors have experienced according to history externally and physically, this we experience according to our own history internally and spiritually.[66]

Luther's remarks are immensely reductive in nature, a quality that aids us in drawing parallels with Bach's musico-allegorical procedures. In particular, his view that "this is the explanation of different matters by the same Spirit" refers to the basic principle of pre-Enlightenment hermeneutics: the unity of scripture, according to which many different biblical stories revealed the same underlying meaning, and which Luther viewed in terms of the complementary opposites: law and gospel. The analogy between history and faith, event and experience thus involved what we might call the faith "dynamic," or "shape" behind narratives of the most diverse kinds, which for Luther was that of descent versus ascent, or destruction followed by restoration. Certain Bach cantatas, the *Actus Tragicus* and *Es ist das Heil uns kommen hier* (BWV 9), for example, conspicuously feature this quality.[67]

Inspired by Isaiah's account of the destruction and rebuilding of Jerusalem, Luther's commentary is intimately bound up with the Passion. For Jerusalem in all its aspects was not used throughout the Middle Ages and later only to illustrate the pattern of the four senses of scripture, but its destruction and rebuilding were also widely understood as prefiguring Jesus's Passion and resurrection, along with other OT texts, such as Psalm 22, which was cited by John. Jesus himself, in speaking of the destruction and rebuilding of the Temple in three days made the comparison to his death and resurrection on which such views were founded.[68] Thus, following traditional practice, Heinrich Müller included a detailed discussion of the destruction of Jerusalem as the final section of the set of Passion sermons that Bach's librettist Picander used in creating the madrigal texts of the *St. Matthew*

---

[66] Martin Luther, *Luther's Works*, vol. 16, *Lectures on Isaiah, Chapters 1–39*, trans. Herbert J. A. Bouman, ed. Jaroslav Pelikan (St. Louis: Concordia, 1969), 327. In this form, Luther's words, as the editors point out (Introduction, ix), are those of his lecture notes, the so-called Lauterbach manuscript, published for the first time in volume 31:2 of the modern Weimar edition (1914). However, Luther's lectures on Isaiah of 1527–29 were published in 1532–34 as *In Esaiam Scholia Ex D. Martini Lutheri praelectionibut collecta*. Georg Spalatin translated the commentary on chapters 36 and 37, source of my citation, into German in 1535, and it was reprinted in the Wittenberg, Eisleben, and Altenburg Luther editions (in vol. 6, 342–56 of the Altenburg edition). Although somewhat different from the version of the *Scholia*, it makes the same points, if anything even more emphatically.

[67] See Chafe, "Luther's 'Analogy of Faith' in Bach's Church Music." *dialog* 24 (Spring 1985): 96–101.

[68] See John 2:19–21 (KJV), where, in response to the Jews' request for a sign (v. 18) John narrates that "Jesus answered and said unto them, Destroy this temple, and in three days I will raise it up (v. 19)," whereupon the Jews said (v. 20) "Forty and six years was this temple in building, and wilt thou rear it up in three days?" upon which John remarks (v. 21) "But he spake of the temple of his body." Francke, (*Oeffentliche Reden über die Paßions-Historie / Wie dieselbe vom Evangelisten Johanne im 18. U. 19. Cap. beschrieben ist / gehalten Von Esto mihi bis Ostern 1716*, 2nd ed. [Halle, 1719], 165) cites this connection, remarking that Jesus's death was "nun ein wahrhaftiger Tod in Absicht auf seiner Auferweckung," thereby bridging to the theme of descent/ascent in baptism.

Passion.[69] In Leipzig during Bach's time the Vespers service on the tenth Sunday after Trinity, the Sunday on which Jesus's prediction of the destruction of Jerusalem was the Gospel reading, was devoted to the reading of Josephus's account of the destruction of Jerusalem in 70 C.E., and a Leipzig chorale book of the time included that reading as an appendix, along with Matthew's and John's Passion narratives.[70] In 1723 Bach's cantata for that Sunday, *Schauet doch und sehet, ob irgend ein Schmerz sei wie mein Schmerz* (BWV 46), binds together Jeremiah's words of lamentation over the destruction of Jerusalem in the OT with Jesus's prediction of its second destruction in the NT (in the Gospel for the day), giving the whole an extensive tropological orientation toward the contemporary believer, and bringing out the opposition of God's wrathful judgment and Jesus's loving protection of the faithful as the counterpart of the fate of Jerusalem. The final chorale makes clear that this destruction/restoration dynamic is the direct outcome of Jesus's "Marter, Angst und schwere Pein"—in other words, the Passion.

In certain Bach works, particularly the *Actus Tragicus*, the motet *Jesu, meine Freude*, and the *St. John Passion*, the relationship of law and gospel is presented in terms of symmetrical designs featuring a sense of both opposition (at the local level) and complementarity (at the "higher" level of the symmetry itself). In this light, it will be useful to consider Rambach's discussion of the analogy of faith, in which symmetry plays an important role. In his several treatises on hermeneutics Rambach assigns that role to the analogy of faith, and within three of his discussions of the subject he takes up the question of symmetry. Since Rambach's treatments of the subject are similar I give priority to that of his most extensive treatise on hermeneutics, the two-volume *Erläuterung über seine eigene INSTITUTIONES HERMENEUTICAE SACRAE* of 1737, in which the analogy of faith is the subject of an entire chapter.[71] There Rambach begins his definition by tracing the concept to the ideas of similitude set forth by Greek authors, explaining the derivation of the term from mathematical proportions (and citing Euclid and "other Greek mathematicians" as the origin). As he explains, numbers related proportionally in terms

[69] *D. Henrici Müllers Evangelischer Herzens-Spiegel, Und Paßions-Predigten; Imgleichen D. Joachimi Lütkemanns Apostolischer Herzens-Wekker* (Stade, 1736). In this edition the Passion sermons appear on 1403–1508, directly followed by the "Historia von Zerstöhrung der Stadt Jerusalem" (1509–12). Elke Axmacher, "Ein Quellenfund zum Text der Matthäus-Passion," *Bach-Jahrbuch* 64 (1978): 181–91; Axmacher, *"Aus Liebe will mein Heyland sterben": Untersuchungen zum Wandel des Passionsverständnisses im frühen 18. Jahrhundert* (Neuhausen-Stuttgart: Hänssler-Verlag, 1984).

[70] Robin Leaver, "Bach, Hymns and Hymnbooks," *Hymn* 36, no. 4 (October 1985): 7–13; Chafe, *Analyzing Bach Cantatas*, 132–35; Michael Marissen, "The Character and Sources of the Anti-Judaism in Bach's Cantata 46," *Harvard Theological Review* 96, no. 1 (2003): 65–99.

[71] In Rambach's *INSTITUTIONES HERMENEUTICAE SACRAE*, 4th ed. (Jena, 1732), discussion of the analogy of faith (87–106) occupies the first chapter of the second book; and the discussion of symmetry (along with *ordo, nexus,* and *relatio*) appears in a footnote only (90); in the corresponding discussion of his two-volume *Erläuterung über seine eigene INSTITUTIONES HERMENEUTICAE SACRAE* (Giessen, 1738, 313–43) the discussion of symmetry is considerably expanded and appears in the text itself; in his *Dogmatische Theologie*, it is again treated at considerable length.

of their quantities were "best expressed in the word symmetry, which consists of a proper and seemly proportion, such as, for example, the parts of a building have both in themselves and in relation to the building as a whole." The shift from numerical to architectural proportions parallels the well-known derivation of the latter from Pythagoras and Euclid in the foremost treatise on architecture of classical times, that of Vitruvius, whose aesthetic descriptions of symmetry, proportion, analogy and *dispositio* (including the Greek *oeconomia*) seem clearly to underlie (directly or indirectly) Rambach's discussion (and Rambach, like Vitruvius, draws the parallel with the human body as well).[72] Similar analogies had been drawn by earlier Lutheran authors at least as far back as Martin Chemnitz, who made the comparison of Paul's discussion of "canon" or "rule" with the doctrine of the apostles as a

> line or rope, which is held to a building or any other work in order that it may not err from the true plan or from the order which it ought to follow, but may be completed and finished according to a certain order and necessary plan. This is a most pleasing metaphor which is applied to the doctrine of the apostles. . . . In order that through the ministry of the Word, or the preaching of the doctrine, the building may be correctly begun and completed and finished in the right order and proper manner, a certain canon, or rule, is necessary, according to which the builders perform their work, in order that the building may not depart from the right order and proper plan. This rule is the doctrine of the apostles, Ps. 18.[73]

Chemnitz's preceding chapter had described the same concept as the "rule of faith," which he had equated to scripture itself.

Continuing, Rambach describes how such symmetry, transferred to hermeneutics and theology, was applied to the doctrines of the faith rather than to numbers and quantities. From that arose the term "analogy of faith," as reflected in Luther's translation of Romans 6:17 and 2 Timothy 1:13, respectively, as "Vorbilde der Lehre" (images of doctrine) and "Vorbilde der heilsamen Worte" (images of the healing words).[74] The two passages from scripture mentioned by Rambach are among those traditionally cited in connection with the analogy of faith; but it must be mentioned that at this point Rambach does not mention the one that is by far the most often cited—Romans 12:6—where Paul had used the Greek word *analogia* to express the fact that prophecy should conform to the faith (in Luther's trans-

---

[72] In the Renaissance such ideas again came to the fore, in Leonardo's *Vitruvian man*, Palladio's treatise on architecture, and Albrecht Dürer's treatise on symmetry, to name only a few of the best-known instances.

[73] See Chemnitz, *Examination of the Council of Trent*, translated by Fred Kramer (St. Louis: Concordia, 1971), 161, 169.

[74] Rambach, *Erläuterung über seine eigene INSTITUTIONES HERMENEUTICAE SACRAE*, p. 315.

lation, "Hat jemand Weissagungen so sei sie dem Glauben ähnlich").[75] In more modern German Bibles the expressions translated by Luther as the "Vorbilde" of scripture or doctrine have been translated as "Bild," and in English Bibles with "pattern," "model," "mirror," "form" or "image." It is significant that Rambach introduces the idea of symmetry at the very outset of his definition of the analogy of faith, moving from mathematics to architecture and choosing two passages from scripture that suggest the patterning or image of doctrine. He supports the analogy with passages from scripture itself, then subdivides it into four closely related qualities:

(1) "nexus" or "Verbindung," [meaning the joining of truths from scripture, so that] as in the beams of a house, no single one could be taken out without damaging the whole;
(2) "ordo" or "Ordnung" [meaning that every truth has its proper place in the sequence, some before and some after others];
(3) "relatio" or "da sich eine Wahrheit auf die andere beziehet" [meaning how] "in a building a story, a window, a beam relates to the others," in the same way that "the doctrine of the *unio mystica* has its foundation in the doctrine of the personal uniting of the divine and human natures in Christ";
(4) "symmetrie" (or *pulcherrima symmetria*), or "how all the fundamental truths together relate to the glory of God and the salvation of humanity. In this some truths have a mediated influence, others an unmediated influence, some a more remote influence, others a more adjacent influence, some a weaker, some a stronger. With one another, however, they all are oriented towards the salvation of humanity, which consists in the enjoyment of God's eternity as much as the highest good, which was interrupted through the fall and will be restored, which is inchoate here in the world, but complete in the world to come.
These, then, are the four parts that belong together to the harmony and analogy of divine truth. . . ."[76]

---

[75] In his earlier *INSTITUTIONES HERMENEUTICAE SACRAE*, however, Rambach introduces Romans 12:6 much earlier, before the other references; presumably the increased emphasis on the association between the analogy of faith and the visual symmetry of architecture underlay the change.

[76] Rambach, *Ausführliche und gründliche Erläuterung*, 316–17. I have abbreviated Rambach's discussion of the four qualities, in particular his choice of examples from scripture to illustrate them:

1. "die allergenaueste **Verbindung** mit einander, *nexum veritatis*, darin eine Wahrheit mit der andern stehet. Denn alle Glaubens-Artickel sind dergestalt in einander hinein gefüget und gepasset, wie die Balcken in einem Hause, da man keinen heraus reissen kann, ohne zugleich das gantze Gebäude zu beschädigen . . . . "
2. "Das zweyte, das dazu gehöret, ist *ordo*, die schönste **Ordnung.** Wie nemlich an einem Gebäude ein ieder Balcken und Träger an seinem Ort stehet, da er nach den Regeln der Bau-Kunst stehen soll, so stehet auch ein iedes Stück der himmlischen Wahrheiten in dem *systemate* der *veritatum caelestium* an seinem rechten Orte, wo es stehen soll. . . ."

Thus, for Rambach, symmetry, when applied to scripture, is both an overall concept and a subdivision of the analogy of faith, representing the interrelatedness of scriptural themes as well as their analogies with visual forms. Although at this point Rambach does not proclaim the relationship of law and gospel as the summary of scripture as clearly and succinctly as Luther did, his discussion of symmetry ends by giving as the basic truth of scripture the restoration of humanity from its "fall," which is essentially the same as Luther's destruction/restoration dynamic.

Directly following his discussion of symmetry, Rambach turns to the classic scriptural source for the term "analogy of faith," Romans 12:6, referring to Luther's translation of *analogia* as "similarity" (*Ähnlichkeit*), and arguing, as did the great majority of Lutheran authors, that Paul's reference to prophecies ("Weissagungen") could refer only to the interpretation of scripture.[77] Rambach acknowledges that the underlying meaning of scripture is summarized in "symbols," such as the

---

3. "*mutua relatio*, da sich eine Wahrheit auf die andere beziehet, wie sich in einem Gebäude ein Stockwerck, ein Fenster, ein Balcken auf den andern beziehet. . . . Die *doctrin de unione mystica* hat ihr Fundament in der *doctrin* von der persönlichen Vereinigung der göttlichen und menschlichen Natur in Christo."
4. "Gehöret dazu eine vollkommene *symmetrie, pulcherrima symmetria*, da sich alle Grund-Wahrheiten zusammen beziehen auf *gloriam Dei & salutem hominis*. Einige Wahrheiten haven dahin einen *influxum mediatum*, andere einen *influxum immediatum*, einige einen *influxum remotiorem*, andere einen *influxum propinquiorem*, einige *debiliorem*, andere *fortiorem*. Alle mit einander aber zielen sie dahin, daβ *salus hominum*, welches bestehet *in aeterna fruitione Dei tamquam summi boni*, welche durch den Fall unterbrochen worden ist, *restituiret* werde, hier in dieser Welt *inchoate*, dort in iener Welt *complete*. Das sind also die 4. *partes*, die zusammen *ad harmoniam & analogiam veritatum caelestium* gehören. . . . "

[77] Here, as in most of his discussion, Rambach is following what countless Lutheran authors had set forth as the meaning of Romans 12:6. See, for example, Aegidius Hunnius, *Postilla / Oder Auβlegung der Sontäglichen Episteln und Evangelien / von Ostern an biβ auff den Advent* (Frankfurt, 1591), 160; Herberger, *Epistolische Hertz Postilla, Erster Theil*, 101–2; Joachim Lütkemann, *Apostolische Aufmunterung zum lebendigen Glauben in Christo* (Erfurt, 1740), 203–4; Müller, *Apostolische Schluβ-Kette und Krafft-Kern*, 43; Francke, *Predigten / über die / Sonn- und Fest-Tags*, 225. Directly following the passage cited in the preceding note, Rambach refers to a dissertation *De analogia fidei* (the correct title is *Commentatio theologica de analogia fidei*) by Elias Bütow, completed under the supervision of Paul Anton (Magdeburg, 1724), in which the same matters are discussed (with references to numerous earlier writers); earlier Lutheran dissertations on the topic include M. Christophorus Zeller, *Jubilum Academicum, Seu Dissertatio Theologica De Analogia Fidei* (Wittenberg, 1672), supervised by Abraham Calov, and Benjamin Christopher Enzel, *Locum Rom. XII, 6. De Analogia Fidei* (Wittenberg, 1712), supervised by Gottlieb Wernsdorf. All three associate the analogy of faith with Romans 12:6. A treatise by Johann Wilhelm Zierold, *Analogia Fidei, Per Exegesin Epistolae ad Romanos Demonstrata* (Magdeburg, 1702), extends the concept to the epistle to the Romans as a whole, with obvious associations to the epistle that Luther described as "the Gospel in its purest form." In his commentary on Romans 12:6 (D Johann Jacob Rambachs, . . . *Ausführliche und gründliche Erklärung der Epistel Pauli an die Römer* [Bremen, 1738], 871–74) Rambach refers the reader to the Bütow dissertation, as well as to one by Michael Förtsch, completed in Giessen in 1682, and a study of Johann Georg Walch, as well as to two other studies of his own. Elsewhere in his commentary Rambach cites expressions used by Zierold as well.

creed, the catechism, the symbolic books, and even theological treatises; but only scripture itself is the source of the analogy of faith.[78] Understood by means of the analogy of faith, scripture has a duplex foundation: first, that it is the work of a single author, the Holy Spirit, "just as in a large organ there is one single wind that is compressed and driven through the bellows into all the pipes"; and second, that the same end—eternal life—and the same means—faith in Christ—are represented in scripture for the faithful in both the Hebrew Bible and the New Testament:

> The *substance* of the covenant of grace, which was established by God immediately after the fall, has always been one, only the *economy* and external disposition of that was different. *Before the coming of Christ* it was *beneath shadows and types*, but in the New Testament *without types*, which had been fulfilled by the death of Christ.[79]

Later, in countering possible objections to the view that the truths of scripture comprise a "system" ("daβ die *scriptores sacri* ein gewisses *systema veritatum* gehabt haben"), he concludes (after having affirmed that since scripture hangs together like the links on a chain, so must its truths form a system):

> Concerning this, the same *express system* can be found in holy scripture, namely the *analogy of faith in terms of belief* (*analogia fidei quoad credenda*), which is contained in the *proto-Gospel* (Gen 3:15), in which all principal truths of revealed religion lie, in part *explicitly*, in part *implicitly*, which afterwards were ever more enlightened by the servants of God. The *analogy of faith in terms of actions* (*analogia fidei* aber *quoad agenda*), however, is

---

[78] Rambach, *Ausführliche und gründliche Erläuterung*, 332–36. In speaking of scripture as the only source of the analogy of faith, but at the same time acknowledging its "symbolic" or summary forms, Rambach is perhaps thinking of the discussion of the analogy of faith in Matthias Flacius Illyricus's *Clavis Scripturae Sacrae* (Basel, 1580, 36), where the term is cited from Romans 12, expressed in terms of law and gospel, derived from mathematics and related to the scriptural symbols of the creed, catechism, and Lord's prayer. It is significant that Rambach gives, as his main instance of a theological treatise that exhibits the "summary" quality of scripture, Freylinghausen's *Grundlegung der Theologie.*—"**Freylinghausens** Grundlegung, item Ordnung des Heyls und einige kleine Schriften mehr." Rambach presumably means to refer also to Freylinghausen's shorter treatises on the same subject, such as his *COMPENDIUM, oder Kurtzer Begriff der gantzen Christlichen Lehre. . . nebst einer Summarischen Vorstellung der Göttlichen Ordnung des Heyls* (Halle, 1715). Like several of Rambach's treatises, and those of many other authors, such as Nicolaus Hunnius's *EPITOME CREDENDORUM, oder Innhalt der gantzen Christlichen LEHRE* (Wittenberg, 1719), Freylinghausen's *Grundlegung* is ordered very systematically according to the chronological "Ordnung des Heils." That is, it begins with discussion of the divine nature and proceeds through the creation, redemption, sanctification sequence associated with the Credo, then to humanity, ending up with eschatological themes, the last of which is "die Herrlichkeit selbst oder das ewige Leben."

[79] Rambach, *Erläuterung*, 1:322: "Die *substantia* des Gnaden Bundes, der gleich nach dem Fall von GOtt gemacht wurde, ist immer einerley gewesen, nur die *oeconomie* und äusserliche Verfassung desselben war unterschieden. *Ante Christi adventum* war sie *sub umbris & typie*, im neuen Testament *sine typis*, die durch den Tod CHRISTI erfüllet worden."

contained in the decalog, and is concentrated in the two great commandments: of the love of God and of the love of the neighbor.[80]

Here Rambach, like Luther, makes clear that law and gospel comprise the "system" that encompasses the truths of scripture, subtly bringing out the fact, emphasized by all Lutherans, that the Gospel came first (immediately after the Fall) and was later progressively enlightened by the servants of God (i.e., prophets and lawgivers; Moses is described as God's "servant" [*Knecht*] in Luther's hymn on the Ten Commandments "Dies sind die heiligen zehn Gebot"), then summarizing the meaning of the law in terms of the Gospel interpretation as given in the great commandment[s]. The expressions "ad credenda" and "ad agenda" refer to the first and second of the three "spiritual" senses of medieval hermeneutics, the allegorical and tropological, meaning here that the allegorical dimension of scripture is its centering on Jesus's work of redemption, foretold in Gen 3:15, whereas the tropological centers on the work of the law, in Luther's terms God's "proper" and "alien" works.[81]

In the passage just cited Rambach echos what his teacher and colleague, August Hermann Francke, had set forth in a sermon on the "nexus" or "Verbindung" of law and gospel, which for Francke, as for Luther, comprised "the entire content of the holy scriptures, according to which the same is divided into law and gospel."[82] This "nexus" revealed "how the one did not abolish the other and throw it on the heap, but rather how the one offered the other its hand, so to speak, and the Gospel raised up the law, in such a way, however, that humanity was made blessed not through the works of the law, but through faith in Christ Jesus."[83] Throughout his sermon, for the eighteenth Sunday after Trinity (whose Gospel reading is one of the principal sources of the "great commandment" to love God and one's neighbor), Francke treats the relationship of law and gospel as entirely complementary, the one (just as in the text of Bach's *Es ist das Heil*) concerned chiefly with bringing

---

[80] Ibid., 325: "über dieses findet sich auch dergleichen *systema expresse* in der heiligen Schrift, nemlich die *analogia fidei quoad credenda,* die ist in dem *protevangelio* enthalten, *Gen. 3, 15*. Darin alle Haupt-Wahrheiten der geoffenbarten Religion theils *explicite,* theils *implicite* liegen, welche nachgehends von denen Knechten GOttes immer mehr aufgekläret worden. Die *analogia fidei* aber *quoad agenda,* die ist in dem *decalogo* enthalten, und *concentrirt* sich in den 2. Grossen Geboten: von der Liebe ***GOttes*** und von der Liebe des **Nächsten.**" The metaphor of a chain for the unity of scripture was a widespread one that is embodied in two treatises of Heinrich Müller, his "Evangelical Chain of Conclusions" and his "Apostolic Chain of Conclusions."

[81] The senses were sometimes described in a Latin catchphrase: *Littera gesta docet, quid credas allegoria, Moralis quid agas, quo tendas anagogia.*

[82] Francke, "NEXUS LEGIS ET EVANGELII, Oder Die Verbindung des Gesetzes und des Evangelii," in *August Hermann Franckens / . . . Sonn- und Fest-Tags-Predigten* (Halle, 1724), 1495–1517.

[83] Ibid., 1497: "damit fänget der Mensch an, so wol dem Gesetz als dem Evangelio besser nachzudencken. Und solchen denn, . . . kömmt nun recht zu statten, daβ sie einigen nähern Unterricht empfangen, ja immer besser unterrichtet werden, wie das Gesetz und Evangelium zusammen hange, was für ein *nexus* oder für eine Verbindung zwischen beyden sey, wie eins das andere nicht aufhebe und übern Haufen werfe, sondern wie vielmehr eines dem andern gleichsam die Hand biete, und das Evangelium das Gesetz aufrichte, dennoch aber so, daβ der Mensch nicht durch die Wercke des Gesetzes, sondern durch den Glauben an Christum JEsum selig werde."

the believer to consciousness of sin and penitence, and the other with forgiveness of sins, freedom from sin and guilt, from God's wrath, the curse of the law and the judgment of death, and eternal damnation.[84] This relationship Francke describes in terms of God's twofold will, what Luther called God's "alien" and "proper" work.[85] Once the law has done its work of bringing the sinner "down," that sinner is ready, as Luther said, like the plowed field, for the seed of the Gospel. Francke uses the verbs "drücken" (press), "demuthigen" (humble), "zermalmen" (crush), "zerknirschen" (grind), "zerschlagen" (strike down), and the like, in order to express this quality of the law. The Gospel, on the other hand has the goal of making the sinner blessed and justified before God. Yet, paradoxically, the law, through its work of *Sündenerkenntnis* (acknowledgement of sin) and repentance, ultimately brings about the believer's ascent to blessedness.

Rambach's discussion of the analogy of faith is vastly more "theoretical" in presentation than Luther's, as befits an author writing on the underlying principles of hermeneutics rather than one whose life's work centered on commentary. In this respect it is indebted to learned, academic discussions of the concept (see n. 77). Johann Wilhelm Zierold's *Analogia Fidei, Per Exegesin Epistolae Ad Romanos Demonstrata* (1702), for example, takes the book of scripture that Luther called "the Gospel in its purest form," the Epistle to the Romans, as the subject of a "demonstration" of the analogy of faith, dividing the epistle into ten "chapters" whose sequence of topics follows from what Zierold names the "Scopus & Dispositio totius Epistolae" (the intention and disposition of the entire epistle). For Zierold, as for many others, including Luther, the scopus was that of the Gospel itself, embodied in Romans 1:16, where Paul defined it as "the power of God unto salvation to all who believe, to the Jew first and then the Greek." Flowing from this affirmation of justification by faith, the epistle, as Zierold sets it forth, covers all the core themes of Lutheranism, showing how they are linked together in the manner described by Rambach. The great majority of the chapters begin by naming the "nexus" (sometimes the "nexus realis") and the "scopus," returning frequently to 1:16 and always naming Jesus as the center of faith and the Gospel. Thus, at the head of his discussion of Romans 8, which supplied several verses for Bach's motet *Jesu, meine Freude*, in which they appear in alternation with the strophes of that chorale, Zierold names the "nexus" as Romans 1:16, the "propositio hujus Epistolae" (proposition of this Gospel): "Evangelium est potentiam DEI ad Salutem cuiuis credenti."

---

[84] Ibid., 1507–9.

[85] Ibid., 1498–1502. In his *Predigten über Sonn- und Fest-Tags*, Francke, exceptionally, included two sermons for the eighteenth Sunday after Trinity, of which the "*NEXUS LEGIS ET EVANGELII*," although written earlier (1713) is the second, preceded by a sermon titled "Der Wille GOttes nach dem Gesetz und Evangelio" (1717). The ordering reflects the fact that the theme of God's twofold will is very prominent in the latter (earlier) sermon, where it appears as if a recapitulation, leading to further expansion on the topic. In the later sermon Francke apparently expanded on the broad theme of God's will from the earlier one, generalizing and reiterating much of its treatment of that topic, perhaps so as to serve as an introduction to the idea of the "nexus" of law and gospel.

And a little later he names it the "scopus" as well, emphasizing that the phrase refers "not only to the power of God, but to the power of God for salvation." The heading of Zierold's chapter is the "salvific victory of the spirit over the flesh in the state of grace," and Zierold associates it with the victory of life over death, the law of the spirit over the flesh, as in Bach's motet. Perhaps, therefore, the well-known symmetrical design of the motet is also indebted to the kinds of associations that Rambach set forth in terms of the connection between symmetry and the analogy of faith.

Rambach's discussion of symmetry, it should be understood, does not attribute to scripture the kind of structure we find in the *Actus Tragicus*, in *Jesu, meine Freude* and the trial scene of the *St. John Passion*, in which there is a central pivot following which we hear the repetition of comparable elements (even nearly identical movements) in reverse order (although he does emphasize that beginnings and endings—like themes and conclusions—should correspond to one another). Rambach's is a symmetry of *ideas*, their relationships, proper ordering, foundational or "decorative" roles, and the like. At the same time, however, understanding the interrelatedness of the truths of scripture is analogous to recognizing aesthetic qualities in architecture. The quality that coordinates such truths on the largest scale is

> *Symmetria*, since on a building a story, a window, a beam, relates to the others, and all together stand in the most beautiful symmetry with one another. Thus one truth also relates to the other: for example, the *doctrina de renovatione* [doctrine of renewal] to the *doctrin de imagine Dei* [doctrine of the image of God] which is repeated in that of renewal [*renovatione*]. All together relate to the *glory of God and the salvation of humankind*, and therefore stand in a beautiful *symmetry* with one another.[86]

In the *St. John Passion*, symmetry is one of Bach's primary means of projecting the interrelatedness of John's principal theological themes. It is focused with particular intensity in the part of the trial that extends from the arioso "Betrachte, meine Seel'" in Part 2 to the chorale "In meines Herzens Grunde," and from there it spreads out to the setting as a whole. Ultimately, its center is Luther's *theologia crucis*, the point of convergence for the themes in question and the principal reference for Bach's overall design.

---

[86] Rambach, *Dogmatische Theologie*, 274–75: "*Symmetria*, da an einem Gebäude ein Stockwerck, ein Fenster, ein Balcke sich auf den andern beziehet, und alle zusammen in der schönsten *symmetrie* mit einander stehen. So beziehet sich auch eine Wahrheit auf die andere, z. E. *doctrina de renovatione* auf die *doctrin de imagine Dei*, welches in *renovatione instauriret* wird. Alle zusammen beziehen sich auf *gloriam Dei et salutem hominis*, und stehen also in einer schönen *symmetrie* mit einander."

{3}

Johannine Themes

John in the church year

Whereas the emphasis on longing for release from the world at the end of the church year paralleled the darkening of the geophysical year (the "evening of the world" in Henri de Lubac's phrase) and was followed by a new beginning, the message of the weeks following Easter linked the time of increasing light to emphasis on Jesus's completed work, preparing the believer for life *in* the world after Jesus's departure. The coming of the Holy Spirit at Pentecost initiated the "time of the church," symbolized by the Trinity season, the time when the Christian community, guided by the Holy Spirit and God's word, clung to faith and awaited the Second Coming.

From this standpoint, the ending of the first half of the year, celebrating Jesus's Passion, resurrection, and ascension, followed by the coming of the Holy Spirit, is very different in character from that of that of Trinity. That difference can be understood in terms of the two forms that eschatology takes in the NT and that have contributed to two different, though not mutually exclusive, theories of the atonement: "present" or "realized" eschatology, on the one hand, and "future" eschatology, on the other, the former widely associated with the Gospel of John and the latter with the Synoptic Gospels, particularly Matthew. That two such potentially conflicting views of eternity exist is due to various factors that for some authors center on the fact that Jesus's Second Coming, predicted in all four Gospels and widely believed to be immanent—that is, to take place within the lifetimes of those who wrote the scriptures—did not happen. In this view, the "delay of the *parousia*" ("presence" in Greek) affected the writers of the Gospels in different ways, the most obvious being that the latest of the four Gospels, chronologically, that of John, shifts the eschatological focus markedly toward present life rather than future hopes. In John, more than the division between a present existence of tribulation and the hope of future release, there is an opposition between two simultaneously existing "worlds," the one "above" of light and the spirit, the world toward which faith is directed, and the other "below," that of darkness and the absence of faith. For John eternity is a present reality, and the judgment awaited with Jesus's Second Coming takes place in the present; those who believe are not judged, whereas those who do not believe are judged *already*.

This thesis forms the text of the concluding movement of Bach's Cantata 68, *Also hat Gott die Welt geliebt*, first performed on the second day of Pentecost, 1725: "Wer an ihn gläubet, der wird nicht gerichtet; wer aber nicht gläubet, der ist schon gerichtet; denn er gläubet nicht an den Namen des eingebornen Sohnes Gottes" (Whoever believes in him, he will not be judged; however, he who does not believe is judged already; for he does not believe in the name of the only begotten Son of God). In chapter 12 we consider how full of purpose is Bach's setting of those words and how meaningful it is in the context not only of the cantata in which it appears but also in that of the other cantatas for the season in which it belongs. At this point we must recognize that the characters of the individual Sundays and feast days of the year and of the liturgical seasons had great impact on Bach's cantata composition. And one of the most significant ways that the church reinforced the meaning of the various seasons was in the cycle of scriptural readings for the successive Sundays and feast days. In this context one of the most useful observations regarding the liturgical year is that it sometimes features sequences of readings from one or another of the Gospels. This is particularly true in the case of the endings of the two halves of the year. Thus, at the end of the Trinity season the eschatological emphasis goes hand in hand with readings from Matthew's parables of the kingdom, especially from his "eschatological discourse," a segment of the Gospel (Mt 24:1–25:46) of unusually apocalyptic, end-oriented character (see fig. 3.1 for a summary of the readings for the Trinity season). The final three Sundays of the season and the year are drawn from this discourse, while six of the preceding seven Sundays feature readings from Matthew that—at least as they were understood by Bach's librettists—articulate dissatisfaction with and rejection of the world, on the one hand, and longing for eternity intermingled with fear of God's judgment, on the other. Awareness that it is the "letzte Zeit," as Cantata 70 puts it, that judgment is at hand, and that watchfulness and preparation for the end are necessary, runs throughout several of the Bach cantatas for this time period; dialogs between Fear and Hope voice the believer's wavering between two visions of the end: the one beatific, anticipating union with God, and the other terrifying, dominated by the possibility of God's rejection. Matthew's famous division of humanity into sheep and goats, or wise and foolish virgins, as in Cantata 140, *Wachet auf*, underlies all such twofold visions of the coming kingdom, the end of time, and the onset of eternity. In the final weeks of the year the believer is consumed by thoughts of the end, which the beginning of the new liturgical year in Advent, puts ultimately into the multiple perspectives of Jesus's coming, especially his incarnation and Second Coming.

The high incidence of readings from Matthew at the end of the Trinity season reflects that the entire season draws heavily from the Synoptic Gospels (especially Luke and Matthew) for its Gospel readings, and from the letters of Paul for the epistles. Only one Sunday in the Trinity season (the twenty-first) features a Gospel reading from John, and that single instance was perhaps chosen because it embodies a Johannine perspective on the miracle stories from the Synoptics that dominate the readings of the surrounding weeks.[1] Likewise, there are only two epistle readings from John during the Trinity season, for the first and second Sundays; and those readings derived from themes prominent in the season that precedes them and can be viewed as completing the transition between the time of Jesus and that of the church.[2] In fact, both Gospel and epistle readings from John are far more circumscribed throughout the Sundays and feast days of the church year than are those from any other of the evangelists, a situation undoubtedly due to the well-known differences between the Gospel of John and the Synoptic Gospels. This circumstance is so noteworthy as to invite more than a summary treatment, and we will see in later chapters that this is reflected closely in Bach's cantatas.

At some very early point in the fixing of the Gospel and epistle readings for the Sundays and principal feast days of the year, it became established that both the Gospel reading for Good Friday (the Passion narrative) and the majority of Gospel readings for the time between Easter and Pentecost/Trinity would be drawn from John. Although there exists no direct statement from early times on the purpose behind those decisions, the perception of John's Gospel from ancient times must have played a part, presumably as an equivalent of the kind of discourses Jesus had with the disciples during the time of the post-resurrection appearances, as some Lutheran authors have maintained. Since the author of the Fourth Gospel was believed to have been the disciple John, the "disciple whom Jesus loved," and witness to the accounts described in that Gospel, its particular characteristics have caused it to be viewed as spiritual, making it appropriate that readings from John follow

---

[1] As is reflected in Bach's cantatas *Ich glaube, lieber Herr, hilf meinem Unglauben* (BWV 109) and *Aus tiefer Not schre ich zu dir* (BWV 38), for the twenty-first Sunday after Trinity, Jesus's discourse on the meaning of "signs" or miracles in general (Jn 4:47–54) relates not only to the miracle story in the gospel for the day (the healing of a king's son), but also to the miracle stories of several of the preceding weeks (the twelfth, fourteenth, sixteenth, seventeenth, and nineteenth Sundays after Trinity), putting them in perspective, as it were. See Eric Chafe, *Tonal Allegory in the Vocal Music of J. S. Bach* (Berkeley: University of California Press 1991), 215–23.

[2] In 1723 something of that character emerged in Bach's first two Leipzig cantatas, for the first and second Sundays after Trinity, *Die Elenden sollen essen* (BWV 75) and *Die Himmel erzählen die Ehre Gottes* (BWV 76), whose emphasis on the gifts of the Holy Spirit, brotherly love, good works, and the land bringing forth fruit (an echo of the Jewish feast of "firstfruits, Shavuot") extended the tone of the post-Easter weeks into the beginning of the half of the year that dealt so extensively with the concerns of Christian life and that ended with the church awaiting the final consummation. I have taken up this question in "Bach's First Two Leipzig Cantatas: A Message for the Community," in *A Bach Tribute: Essays in Honor of William H. Scheide* (Kassel: Bärenreiter; Chapel Hill, NC: Hinshaw Music, Inc., 1993), 71–86.

Trin. 1	1 Jn 4:16–21 (God is love)	Lk 16:19–31 (parable of the rich man and poor Lazarus)
Trin. 2	1 Jn 3:13–18 (he who does not love is dead)	Lk 14:16–24 (parable of the great evening meal)
Trin. 3	1 Pet 5:6–11 (cast your cares on him, for he cares for you)	Lk 15:1–10 (parable of the lost sheep and lost silver piece)
Trin. 4	Rom 8:18–23 (the “creature” awaits the manifestation of God’s glory, the redemption of the body)	Lk 6:36–42 (Sermon on the Mount: show mercy, do not judge)
John the Baptist	Isa 40:1–5 (the voice in the wilderness)	Lk 1:57–80 (the birth of John the Baptist and Zacharias’s song of praise)
Trin. 5	1 Pet 3:8–15 (do good, not evil; sanctify Christ in your hearts)	Lk 5:1–11 (Peter and the great catch of fish)
Visitation of Mary	Isa 11:1–5 (prophecy of the Messiah)	Lk 1:39–56 (visit of Mary to Elizabeth; Magnificat)
Trin. 6	Rom 6:3–11 (through the death of Christ we are dead to sin)	Mt 5:20–26 (Christian righteousness versus the Pharisees’ fulfillment of the law)
Trin. 7	Rom 6:19–23 (the wages of sin is death, but God’s gift is eternal life)	Mk 8:1–9 (the feeding of the four thousand)
Trin. 8	Rom 8:12—17 (whoever are led by the Spirit of God are God’s children)	Mt 7:15–23 (Sermon on the Mount: warning against false prophets: from their fruits ye shall know them)
Trin. 9	1 Cor 10:6–13 (flee from idolatry, fornication, tempting, murmuring)	Lk 16:1– 9 (parable of the unjust householder)
Trin. 10	1 Cor 12:1–11 (gifts are many but the Spirit is one)	Lk 19:41–48 (Jesus predicts the destruction of Jerusalem and drives the merchants from the Temple)
Trin. 11	1 Cor 15:1–10 (the gospel of the death and resurrection of Christ)	Lk 18:9–14 (parable of the Pharisee and the tax collector)
Trin. 12	2 Cor 3:4–11 (the letter kills but the Spirit gives life)	Mk 7:31–37 (the healing of a deaf and dumb man)
Trin. 13	Gal 3:15–22 (God’s promise to Abraham precedes the law)	Lk 10:23–37 (love of God and one’s neignbor; parable of the good Samaritan)
Trin. 14	Gal 5:16–24 (the works of the flesh and the fruit of the Spirit)	Lk 17:11–19 (the healing of the ten lepers)
Ratswechsel	–	–
Trin. 15	Gal 5:25–26,10 (if we live in the Spirit, let us walk in the Spirit)	Mt 6:24–34 (Sermon on the Mount: take no thought for worldly needs but seek the kingdom of God)
Trin. 16	Eph 3:13–21 (Paul prays for the strengthening of faith in the community at Ephesus)	Lk 7:11–17 (the raising of the youth at Nain)
Trin. 17	Eph 4:1–6 (Paul urges oneness through the Spirit)	Lk 14:1–11 (healing of a man with dropsy on the Sabbath; whoever humbles himself shall be exalted and vice versa)
Trin. 18	1 Cor 1:4–9 (thanks for the blessing of the Gospel at Corinth)	Mt 22:34–46 (love of God and one’s neighbor as the principal commandment)
Trin. 19	Eph 4:22–28 (put on the new man who is created in the image of God)	Mt 9:1–8 (healing of a man with palsy)

Trin. 20	Eph 5:15–21 (walk circumspectly and be full of the Spirit)	Mt 22:1–14 (parable of the king's wedding feast)
Trin. 21	Eph 6:10–17 (put on the armor of God so that, when the evil day comes, you hold the field)	Jn 4:47–54 (healing of the son of a nobleman, who then believes)
Trin. 22	Phil 1:3–11 (thanks and prayer for the community in Philippi)	Mt 18:23–35 (parable of the wicked servant)
St. Michael	Rev 12:7–12 (battle between Michael and the dragon)	Mt 18:1–11 (the kingdom belongs to the children; their angels see God's countenance)
Trin. 23	Phil 3:17–21 (worldliness of the enemies of Christ vs Christian "conversation" in heaven)	Mt 22:15–22 (the Pharisees question Jesus "is it lawful to give tribute to Caesar?")
Reformation	2 Thess 2:3–8 (withstand opponents and deceivers)	Rev 14:6–8 (the everlasting gospel: fear God and give glory to him)
Trin. 24	Col 1:9–14 (Paul prays for the Colossians)	Mt 9:18–26 (Jesus raises the daughter of a ruler; a woman touches the hem of his garment and is healed)
Trin. 25	1 Thess 4:13–18 (the Second Coming of Christ)	Mt 25:15–28 (events preceding the end of the world)
Trin. 26	2 Pet 3:3–13 (we await a new heaven and a new earth)	Mt 25:31–46 (the last judgment)
Trin. 27	1 Thess 5:1–11 (preparation for the last judgment)	Matt 25:1–13 (parable of the wise and foolish virgins)

FIGURE 3.1 **The epistle and Gospel readings for the Trinity season**

those from the Synoptic Gospels, to put their narratives in perspective. Reflections of this view could be cited from centuries of Christian authors going back to the second century at least.[3] John Calvin, in his 1553 commentary, puts it as follows:

> The other three Gospels give fuller narrative of the life and death of Christ, but John dwells at greater length on the teaching about the role of Christ and the power of his death and resurrection. The others certainly say that Christ came to bring salvation to the world, to atone for the sins of the world by the sacrifice of his death, and, in short, to do everything that was required from the Mediator. John, likewise, devotes a portion of his work to historical details. But the teaching which points out to us the power and benefit of the coming of Christ is far more clearly shown by him than by the rest. They all had the same purpose: to point out Christ. The first three Gospels show his body, so to speak, but John shows his soul. For this reason I usually say that this Gospel is a key to understanding the rest; for whoever understands the power of Christ strikingly pictured here will then profit by reading what the others tell about the Redeemer who appeared.[4]

[3] As Raymond E. Brown points out (*An Introduction to the New Testament* [New York: Doubleday, 1996], 378), Clement of Alexandria (ca. 200 C.E.) so characterized the Gospel of John.

[4] John Calvin, *John*, ed. Alistair McGrath and J. I. Packer (Wheaton, IL: Crossway Books, 1994), xii.

That perception perhaps underlies the fact that John's Gospel follows Matthew, Mark, and Luke in the Bible, that the Johannine epistles are placed near the end of the epistles as a whole, that the book of Revelation, once ascribed to John, is the last book in the Bible, and that readings from John are placed at the end of the part of the liturgical year that deals with the life of Christ.[5] All these occurrences seem to reflect the ordering of the literal and spiritual senses of hermeneutics.

Apart from the time between Easter and Trinity Sunday, only six Sundays or feast days during the year have Gospel readings from John. Of these, three occur on Sundays during Advent or Lent, when there was no concerted church music in the Leipzig churches: the fourth Sunday in Advent, and the fourth (Laetare) and fifth (Judica) Sundays in Lent. The other three Sundays are widely separated in the year: the third day of Christmas (December 27, also celebrated as the feast of John), the second Sunday after Epiphany, and the twenty-first Sunday after Trinity. In all three cases the readings from John have particular symbolic significance.

Following three Sundays whose Gospels take up, respectively, Jesus's "royal" entry into Jerusalem (looking ahead to the Passion), his Second Coming, and Jesus's response to John the Baptist's query from prison regarding his identity as the Messiah, the Gospel for the fourth Sunday in Advent (Jn 1:19–28) turns to John the Baptist as precursor (this theme directly follows John's celebrated prologue). Bach's only cantata for that Sunday, *Bereitet die Wege, bereitet die Bahn* (BWV 132), written in Weimar, 1715, to a text by Salomo Franck, interprets John's witness to Jesus's divinity entirely in terms of the contemporary believer's faith, beginning with a poeticized reference to Isaiah's urging preparation for the coming of the Messiah. After that, two recitative/aria pairings apply a sequence of themes derived from the Gospel for the day directly to the contemporary believer: the need for the witness of faith, purification of the conscience through the *Sündenerkenntnis* (acknowledgment of sin) given by the law, and prayer for the renewal of the *Gnadenbund* (covenant of grace) with God, for which baptism provides the entranceway. The final chorale juxtaposes the "old" and "new" man (Adam and Christ) as symbolic representatives of the change of eras. Thus Cantata 132 amplifies the spiritual understanding of John the Baptist's witness, which is, of course, the primary thrust of the Gospel.

---

[5] Calvin continues:

> John is believed to have written chiefly in order to emphasize that Christ was God, as against the wicked blasphemies of Ebion and Cerinthus. This is what Eusebius and Jerome say, as did most of their contemporaries. But whatever his motive for writing at the time, there can be no doubt whatever that God intended something far greater for his church. He therefore dictated to the four evangelists what they should write, in such a way that while each had his own part, the whole might be collected into one. It is now our duty to blend the four together so that we may learn from all of them as if by one teacher. As for John being placed fourth, it was done because of when he wrote; but it would be better to read the Gospels in a different order: when we wish to read in Matthew and the others that Christ was given to us by the Father, we should first learn from John the purpose for which he appeared (xii).

Then, on the third day of Christmas, preceded by two feast days in which the Gospel readings together comprise the narrative of Jesus's birth as told in Luke 2:1–20, now the Gospel reading is most of the prologue to John 1:1–14. This, one of the most famous passages in the Fourth Gospel, tells of Jesus's incarnation in "cosmic" terms: as the "Word" that was in the beginning with God and that was God, that was the creator and life itself, born of God, that became flesh and came into the world bringing light, but that was not comprehended by the world of darkness and was rejected by that world. With vv. 12 and 13 the prologue brings out the benefit for humanity: that to those who accepted him and believed in his name he gave the power to become God's children. And v. 14 is the famous narrative that "the Word was made flesh and dwelt among us, (and we beheld his glory as of the only begotten of the Father,) full of grace and truth" (KJV). Thus the prologue announces central themes of the Gospel as a whole: the antithesis of light and darkness, the oneness of Jesus and the Father, the filial relationship of the faithful to God, and the attributes of glory, grace, and truth. Jesus's identity with the Father is particularly emphasized. John's initial "In Principio" was viewed, of course, as a parallel to the beginning of the creation narrative in Genesis, his opposition of light and darkness paralleling God's original division of light from darkness.[6]

In addition, the third day of Christmas was also celebrated as the feast day of the apostle and evangelist John, with 1 John 1 as its epistle reading; that chapter has distinct thematic affinities with the prologue to the John's Gospel, in that it refers again to the "Word" that was present with the Father at the beginning, to Jesus as God's only Son, to God as pure light, in contrast to those who walk in darkness, and to the kinship with God of those who are of the light. The Gospel reading for that day comes from just before the end of John's Gospel, where, in a famously debated passage, Jesus seems to say that John would not die before Jesus's Second Coming, a meaning that the evangelist himself seems to deny, although he acknowledges that it became current among the disciples (Jn 21:20–23). In the Middle Ages the passage was often understood to mean that John was taken up to glory without dying, a confirmation of the inspired and directly spiritual nature of his writings. In this Gospel the author then identifies himself as the disciple in question and attests to the truth of his testimony.

The placing of these two alternate sets of Gospel and epistle readings on the third day of Christmas acknowledges the traditionally perceived relationship of John's Gospel (spiritual) to those of the Synoptics (narrative).[7] It is fitting, therefore, that the readings for the first and second days of Christmas come from the Gospel that is most "historical" in character, that of Luke, telling the history of Jesus's physical birth, after which John's prologue provides what has been called a "poem" on Jesus's divine identity.

---

[6] August Hermann Francke makes this point in the source cited in ch. 1, n. 22.

[7] Brown, *Introduction to the New Testament*, 378 (see n. 3).

The third feast day on which the Gospel reading comes from John, the second Sunday in Epiphany, is one for which the Gospel narrative, the wedding at Cana, has unusually pronounced qualities of the kind just described. Jesus's first miracle, the changing of water into wine at the wedding in Cana, was narrated only by John, who presents it as the first manifestation of Jesus's glory. In the Middle Ages it was one of the most frequently cited models for the four senses of scripture, the six water jars symbolizing the literal sense, and the wine the spiritual senses. The transformation of the former into the latter allegorized the change from sorrow (water, tears) to joy and eschatological fulfillment. In this respect, as Henri de Lubac points out, "of all the symbols furnished by the Gospel, this is the one most often referred to in exegetical writings and in the liturgy."[8] And in the writings of seventeenth- and eighteenth-century Lutheranism the story of the wedding at Cana retained its eschatological associations, the wedding itself prefiguring the union of the soul (or the church) and Christ, and the "good wine" that was reserved for the end signifying eternal life.

The final two Sundays in Lent on which the Gospel reading comes from John, Laetare and Judica, take up, respectively, the miracle of the feeding of the five thousand (Jn 6:1–15) and Jesus's confrontation with the Jews over his divine identity, including one of John's famous "I am" sayings in which Jesus proclaims that identity: "Before Abraham was, I am" (Jn 8:46–59. There are no cantatas by Bach for those occasions, although we will consider his setting of one of Jesus's "I am" sayings within the context of the *St. John Passion*). Apart from the post-Easter season only one other occasion—the twenty-first Sunday after Trinity, features a Gospel reading from John 4:47–54: the healing of a royal official's son, after which the official believes—that brings out the question of "signs" and faith with one of John's "signs" narratives in which Jesus speaks directly to that topic.[9]

Within the readings from John cited to this point, we may well perceive a pattern centered on Jesus's divine identity and his manifesting his glory in the form of "signs" (miracles) of highly symbolic character, the changing of water into wine and the miracle of the loaves suggesting eucharistic associations (the latter associated with the discourse in which Jesus identifies himself as the "bread of life"), and the healing of the official's son addressing the meaning and purpose of "signs" in general. In all of them, the characteristic Johannine theme of spiritual meaning arising from the miracle and prompting discourse from Jesus is prominent.

The pattern of transformation from history and the literal sense to spiritual meaning emerges again at the end of the first half of the year, when, following Jesus's Passion and resurrection, and the first and second of the post-Easter appearances, the Gospel and epistle readings for the Sunday after Easter (Quasimodogeniti) shift to John (symbolically, as I argue, in light of the traditional associations of Quasimodogeniti). And from that point until Trinity Sunday, all but one of the

[8] De Lubac, *Medieval Exegesis*, 1:253.

[9] See n. 1.

Sundays and feast days draw their Gospel readings from John.[10] Within this sequence the sole exception is Ascension Day, for which, owing once again to the narrative or event-centered character of that occasion, the epistle and Gospel readings come from Acts and Mark. John, in fact, has no narrative of the ascension per se, but he deals with it in his usual "spiritual" way, a quality that emerges in Mariane von Ziegler's 1725 cantata texts.

In the liturgy for the great fifty days Ascension Day is aligned with the fortieth day, in keeping with Acts 1:3–5, which tells not only of Jesus speaking with the disciples about the kingdom of God for forty days after the resurrectionbut also refers to the disciples being baptized of the Holy Spirit "not many days hence" (i.e., Pentecost). (Thus, Ascension Day always falls on the fortieth day of Easter.) And, since John's Farewell Discourse was sometimes viewed as the kind of discourse described in Acts, the three Sundays before Ascension Day (Jubilate, Cantate, Rogate) and the two following that feast (Exaudi, Pentecost) all draw their Gospel readings from the Farewell Discourse. The spiritual content of those readings was then expanded by other Johannine readings for the Sundays that immediately preceded and followed those in turn. In short, between Quasimodogeniti and Trinity Sunday the Gospel readings for ten feast days, including those for all three days of Pentecost, come from John, while within them those from the Farewell Discourse form a secondary emphasis. This feature parallels a well-known characteristic of the Gospel of John itself: the association of "signs" and discourses, the former much more restricted in number (usually calculated as seven) and symbolic in character than those of the Synoptics, whereas the latter are often quite extended and replace the parables of the Synoptics.[11] John's favorite pattern is to follow Jesus's miracles or, as John terms them, "signs," by discourses that interpret their meanings, often in the characteristically circular, "spiritual" manner associated with John's literary style. The part of the Gospel that most exhibits such patterns—between the prologue and the Passion—is often called the "Book of Signs." Owing to John's close linking of the Passion and resurrection as Jesus's triumphant "lifting up," the events beginning with the Passion, and continuing in the resurrection, ascension, and coming of the Holy Spirit are viewed as the "Book of Glory," fulfilling the character of the final chapter of the Farewell Discourse.[12] For this concurrence of Jesus's greatest signs, the discourse necessarily *precedes* rather than follows the events it explains (although, as mentioned earlier, the discourse was understood by some to

---

[10] In addition to these principal feasts, the majority of feast days in the Roman Catholic liturgy for this time of the year featured readings from John: altogether, the fourth, fifth, and seventh days after Easter, the five consecutive Sundays after Easter, the Sunday after Ascension Day, the Saturday before Pentecost, the three days of Pentecost, Trinity Sunday (in the Lutheran, not the Catholic liturgy), and the feast that ended the first half of the year in the Catholic liturgy, Corpus Christi (the Thursday after Trinity).

[11] Brown, *Introduction to the New Testament*, 364–65. See also Raymond Brown, *The Gospel According to John I–XII*, vol. 29a, Anchor Bible Series (New York: Doubleday, 1966), 525–32.

[12] The "Book of Signs" encompasses everything from 1:19 to 12:50; the "Book of Glory" everything from 13:1 to 20:31. See Brown, *Gospel According to John*, cxxxviii–cxliv, 541–42.

represent the character of Jesus's post-resurrection discourses with the disciples). The long Farewell Discourse takes place at the Last Supper, in advance of the Passion, introducing in a form that has been described as a poetic masterpiece the principal themes and devices of the Gospel as a whole.[13] In it Jesus prepares the disciples for the coming events, which they, reacting as the modern congregation would, fail to understand. The spiraling character of the discourse, which moves among themes such as the Passion, resurrection, ascension, and coming of the Spirit, interweaving them with the elevated themes of truth, love, "the world," and the nature of God, eschews direct statement or narrative, so that the often bewildered response of the disciples creates a palpable sense of split between literal and "spiritual" meanings. The discourse is threaded throughout with references to the fuller understanding that would come later. Its final climactic chapter, John 17, which is sometimes considered not to be a part of the discourse proper, is Jesus's transcendent prayer to the Father, calling for his glorification, referring to his completion of the work given him by the Father and to his existence in glory with the Father before creation, as in the prologue. This chapter, called by Raymond Brown "one of the majestic moments in the Fourth Gospel," is the immediate background for the Passion, which it directly precedes.[14] For some modern authors it is the Johannine equivalent of the missing ascension narrative. It provides the theme of glorification and oneness with the Father that, in the opening chorus of Bach's *St. John Passion*, was merged with the address to God in majesty from Psalm 8. And it connects up with the theme of Jesus's announcement of his completion of the work given him by God (as reflected in the aria "Es ist vollbracht").

The five Gospel readings from the Farewell Discourse can be said to form the "core" of the readings between Quasimodogeniti and Trinity Sunday, in that three readings from the discourse immediately precede and two directly follow Ascension Day (see fig. 3.2). That John has no separate narrative of the ascension has been interpreted as following from his emphasis on Jesus's transfigured nature throughout the Gospel.[15] The readings from the Farewell Discourse, however, supply ample reference to the meaning of the ascension in typical Johannine spiritual terms. In the Lutheran tradition, these readings were frequently interpreted as a community of ideas that for some extended to the other Johannine readings as well. Thus Martin Moller, in his *Praxis Evangeliorum*, describes the relationship between Jubilate and Cantate as that of the first and last feasts of an octave: a single eight-day feast; Christian Marbach describes a continuity embracing Cantate and the two Sundays that follow, Rogate and Exaudi, while Valerius Herberger describes the six Sundays between Easter and Pentecost as an "artistic Easter sermon," envi-

[13] Brown, *Gospel According to John*, 581–603; see esp. 582.

[14] For a detailed study of this chapter from Bach's time, see Freylinghausen, *Das Hohepriesterliche Gebeth unsers hochgelobten Heilandes JEsu CHristi* (Halle, 1719).

[15] Stephen S. Smalley, *John Evangelist and Interpreter* (Exeter: Paternoster Press, 1978), 237.

sioning the life to come as a heavenly "Jubilate, Cantate and Vocem Jucunditatis" (Rogate).[16]

There is, therefore, a degree of structural ordering to the Johannine readings from Quasimodogeniti to Pentecost and Trinity Sunday, possibly the result of an attempt to compress the spiritual character of John's Gospel into a coherent framework. For the most part the five readings from the Farewell Discourse that surround Ascension Day appear in reverse order, with excerpts from the sixteenth and fifteenth chapters of John leading back toward Jesus's first reference to the Holy Spirit in John 14, the Gospel for Pentecost. Thus the first reading from the discourse (Jn 16:16–23) sets up the theme of Jesus's departure and return, the disciples' suffering and eventual joy, and the power of prayer in Jesus's name; the second reading (16:5–15), from earlier in the same chapter, likewise tells of Jesus's coming departure, and in addition announces the coming of the "Comforter," the "Spirit of truth"; the third (16:23–31) picks up from the power of prayer (reiterating the twenty-third verse from the Gospel reading of two weeks earlier) and leads it to Jesus's announcement of his return to the Father. After the celebration of that event on Ascension Day, the fourth reading from the Farewell Discourse (15:26–16:4) begins in the preceding chapter of the Gospel, picking up with another reference to the Comforter and further describes the coming persecution of the disciples; and on Whitsunday the fifth reading (14:23–31) speaks of the "Comforter, which is the Holy Ghost, whom the Father will send in my name, he shall teach you all things, and bring all things to your remembrance, whatsoever I have said unto you" (v. 26, KJV). Thus, toward the end of the liturgical sequence, one of John's earliest references to the coming of the Holy Spirit in the Farewell Discourse is given as the key to the fuller understanding of Jesus's words that would come later. It is as if the backward chronology shows how later knowledge illuminates earlier, more initially provocative or perplexing passages, a classic Johannine characteristic.

Directly preceding the readings from the Farewell Discourse (v. 12, Misericordias Domini) and on the third day of Pentecost are two excerpts from John 10, placed adjacent in the Gospel itself, in which Jesus calls himself the good shepherd; in context, these readings make clear that the coming of the Holy Spirit is equivalent to the return of Jesus in a comforting, protective role toward "his own." The second of these references (v. 27) to Jesus as the good shepherd is then preceded and followed by adjacent excerpts from the third chapter of John, Jesus's dialog, and discourse with Nicodemus, which takes up the theme of rebirth through water and the Spirit and addresses one of John's favorite oppositions, that of light

---

[16] Moller, *Praxis Evangeliorum*, 2:201; Christian Marbach, *Evangelische Singe-Schule* (Breslau and Leipzig, 1726), facsimile ed. (Hildesheim: Georg Olms Verlag, 1991), 5–7. See also Valerius Herberger, *Hertz-Postilla* (Leipzig, 1667), 1:425–26; Herberger, *Das Himmlische Jerusalem* (Leipzig: Ernst Bredt, 1858), 24.

and darkness. Thus the second day of Pentecost and Trinity Sunday are linked by their Gospel readings. Both themes just mentioned relate back to the first Johannine reading in the post-Easter sequence, that for the Sunday after Easter (Quasimodogeniti), in which the disciples hide behind closed doors in the evening, and Jesus appears in their midst. On that Sunday the epistle reading is also drawn from John (1 Jn 5:4–10). In very symbolic terms it refers to the faith as the hallmark of those who are "born of God" and therefore overcome the world, of the "three who bear record in Heaven, the Father, the Word and the Holy Spirit" and the "three who bear record in earth, the spirit and the water and the blood." Quasimodogeniti, as mentioned earlier, has great symbolic significance in the post-Easter sequence because of its ancient association with baptism and confirmation. The theme of rebirth through water and the spirit thus appears at the beginning and ending of the sequence of Johannine readings. And via the light/darkness theme, the dialog with Nicodemus also has the potential (which Bach and Ziegler seized on) to connect up with the reading from Luke for the second day of Easter, in which, after Jesus's post-resurrection appearance to the disciples on the road to Emmaus, they urge him to stay, "for it is toward evening and the day is far spent." The following diagram (fig. 3.2) outlines something of these interrelationships.

From this outline, it is clear that the post-Easter readings from John represent a structured presentation of his themes, which serves to unify the "great fifty days." And even the reading for Easter Monday, which is not from John, bears a symbolic relationship to the Fourth Gospel in its reference to "evening," which the unknown librettist expanded to the entire text of Cantata 6, *Bleib bei uns*. The theme of the darkness of the world "below" versus the light of the resurrection and the world "above" is, in fact, an underlying presence in the readings for this time period even when it is not directly expressed, since the coming of the Holy Spirit, the event toward which the entire season is directed, is viewed as a manifestation from the world above into the world below, an enlightening presence. But mostly what the thematic correspondences that run throughout the post-Easter weeks bring out is the circular, spiritual character of John's Gospel, its doubling back to clarify through varied restatement what has been introduced indirectly and was in many cases misunderstood (a theme directly expressed in Mariane von Ziegler's text for Cantata 175, *Er rufet seinen Schafen mit Namen*). And that quality, as Raymond Brown explains, is part and parcel of John's presentation of Jesus as being forced to impart, in the language and terms of the world below, higher "spiritual" truths of the world above that in the final analysis are incapable of being so conveyed.[17] The encounter with Jesus is a spiritual, not an intellectual, one, made through faith, not reason; and Jesus appears throughout the readings from John as a figure who can be understood only in this way.

For obvious reasons, the order of signs followed by discourses is reversed in the Gospel for the final events of Jesus's time on earth, whereas the ordering of the

---

[17] Brown, *Introduction to the New Testament*, 333–37.

OCCASION	GOSPEL READING	SUMMARY OF CONTENT
Good Friday	Jn 18–19	John's account of the Passion
Easter Sunday	Mk 16:1–8	Mark's resurrection narrative
Easter Monday	Lke 24:13–35	Jesus's appearance to the disciples on the road to Emmaus. "Abide with us: for it is toward evening and the day is far spent."
Easter Tuesday	Lk 24:36–47	Jesus appears to the disciples in Jerusalem; "Peace be unto you." Jesus affirms the fulfillment of scripture.
Quasimodogeniti	Jn 20:19–31	Jesus appears to the disciples, who hide for "fear of the Jews"; "Peace be unto you"; doubting Thomas.
Misericordias	Jn 10:12–16	Jesus, the "good shepherd."
Jubilate	Jn 16:16–23 (FD)	Jesus announces his departure and return; the disciples' sorrow will be turned into joy.
Cantate	Jn 16:5–15 (FD)	Jesus announces his departure and foretells the coming of the Spirit
Rogate	Jn 16:23–30 (FD)	Jesus speaks of the power of prayer; tells of his coming into the world from the Father and his coming return to the Father.
Ascension Day	Mk 16:14–20	Jesus instructs the disciples and ascends to heaven.
Exaudi	Jn 15:26–16:4 (FD)	Jesus speaks of the coming of the Holy Spirit and predicts the persecution of the disciples.
Pentecost:Sunday	Jn 14:23–31 (FD)	Jesus speaks of love; the "indwelling" of Jesus and the Father; the Holy Spirit will teach and bring remembrance of what Jesus has said.
Pentecost:Monday	Jn 3:16–21	Jesus speaks of love; those who believe are not judged, those who do not are already judged; light versus darkness.
Pentecost:Tuesday	Jn 10:1–11	The shepherd knows his sheep and they know his voice; Jesus as the door to the fold.
Trinity Sunday	Jn 3:1–15	Dialog with Nicodemus; Jesus speaks of rebirth through the Spirit; light versus darkness.

FIGURE 3.2 **Gospel readings for the period from Good Friday to Trinity Sunday** *(FD) = farewell discourse. Bracketing indicates thematic correspondences among the Johannine readings*

Gospel *readings* for this part of the church year restores the sequence of signs followed by discourses, beginning the series of excerpts from John *after* the two principal events (or signs) taken up in the Farewell Discourse: the Passion and resurrection. References to Jesus's departure and return, therefore, admit of multiple interpretations, mirroring the spiritual senses of scripture: as his death and resurrection (including the post-resurrection appearances), his ascension and the coming of the Holy Spirit, and his Second Coming. Similar to the first two days of Christmas, within the "great fifty days" the Gospel readings for the three days of Easter and that for Ascension Day draw upon the Synoptic Gospels because of their narrative character, while the following and surrounding excerpts from John provide a series of meditations on the meaning of Easter and the events of the post-Easter weeks, Jesus's last time on earth. At the same time, however, the Farewell Discourse is heavily occupied with the theme of Jesus's presence versus his absence, and the coming of the "Paraclete," the Holy Spirit, advocate or "comforter," who will ultimately replace Jesus's physical presence. What happened historically in the physical advent of Jesus is now viewed spiritually, the tropological advent of Jesus in the human heart (the Holy Spirit). This multilayered meaning is reflected closely in Cantata 68 for the second day of Pentecost. The running theme of this part of the year is very much bound up with how the community (i.e., the church, analogous to the disciples) must prepare for life in the world after Jesus's departure, must recognize the *Trost* (comfort) provided by Jesus's victory and the presence of the Spirit, holding on to them in faith and tribulation, and living in love for one another. These themes, reflected also in the Johannine letters, carry over into the epistles for the first and second Sundays after Trinity, so that the Trinity season takes John's presentation of the Spirit as a point of departure (see n. 2).

One of the apparent motives behind the placing of Gospel readings from John on the third day of Christmas and during the time between Easter and Pentecost (approximating the beginning and ending of the time of Christ), was, therefore, the perceived spiritual character of the prologue and the Farewell Discourse of the Fourth Gospel. John's well-known emphasis on Jesus's birth as the descent of God from the realm of the Spirit, light, and truth into a world of sin and darkness lent a "cosmic" tone to the message of the third day of Christmas; the references to Jesus's return to the Father in the Gospel readings for the weeks after Easter affirmed John's view of the crucifixion and resurrection as the triumphant "lifting up" that marked Jesus's return to the world "above" from which he came. In this view Jesus's life and work, and hence the symbolic "shape" of the first half of the year, can be understood in terms of elemental descent/ascent patterns of the kind that are often invoked to characterize the Gospel of John. Jesus's initial descent in the Incarnation, like the downswing of a pendulum, reaches simultaneously its "nadir" and its turning point in the Passion, while the return upswing, anticipated within the hymn for glorification that climaxes the Farewell Discourse and which C. H. Dodd viewed as Jesus's ascension to the Father, is manifested in the Passion, resurrection, and ascension, the triumphant completion of Jesus's work.[18] Hence Johann Jacob Rambach's association of Ascension Day with God's *Rath*, as mentioned earlier. Within this frame of reference Pentecost can be considered to fulfill the implications of Jesus's incarnation as introduced by John in the prologue to the

---

[18] Dodd, *Interpretation of the Fourth Gospel*, 419–20; Brown, *Gospel According to John XIII–XXI*, 541–42.

Fourth Gospel.[19] That is, the descent of the Holy Spirit at Pentecost represents another, now tropological, advent or incarnation of Jesus within the human heart, after which the Trinity season symbolizes life in the world under the direction of the spirit, a theme that is prominent in the Bach cantatas for this time period.

In the time from Easter to Pentecost, Jesus's words to the disciples in the Farewell Discourse exhibit the well-recognized character of seeming to transcend time and space.[20] In this respect the discourse is sometimes viewed as John's counterpart to the "Eschatological Discourse" of the Synoptic Gospels, of which Matthew's version served for the Gospel readings of the last weeks of the Trinity season (and the Bach cantatas for that time period). Yet there are major differences between the Synoptic and Johannine discourses that perhaps dictated the placing of readings from the two at "opposite" points in the liturgical year. Although the topic of Jesus's return after his death is shared with the Synoptic Gospels' version of the discourse, John's emphasis is oriented far more toward "realized" eschatology than that of Matthew, Mark, and Luke.[21] Whereas the language of the Synoptic Gospels is apocalyptic, emphasizing an intervening time of persecution and waiting that Jesus's second coming in glory will end (these events are mirrored in the Trinity season, culminating in its final weeks), John's references to Jesus's return intermingles his post-resurrection appearances: Jesus's return through the Holy Spirit and the Second Coming. As Raymond Brown remarks, the Farewell Discourse "may represent a non-apocalyptic Johannine form of the theme of the coming of the Son of Man that we find in the Synoptic Apocalypse."[22] From this standpoint, the late Trinity season anticipates Jesus's Second Coming as a future event, the onset of eternity, which merges at Advent with his birth and the rotation of the year once again, whereas the great fifty days, climaxing the time of Christ with his resurrection and ascension, anticipate and complete his coming through the Holy Spirit, the enlightening of humanity through the "indwelling" of God and the revelation of the Trinity, initiating the "time of the church." The Passion, resurrection, and ascension describe the pendular "upswing" that balances the Incarnation, while the descent of the Holy Spirit returns the perspective to that of the community living in the world (as reflected in the Johannine epistle readings for the first two Sundays after Trinity).

---

[19] As we will see in a later chapter (see 533–534), Bach's 1725 cantata for the second day of Pentecost, *Also hat Gott die Welt geliebt* (BWV 68) mirrors this conceptual link between Christmas and Pentecost as Jesus's physical and spiritual births.

[20] As Brown points out (*Gospel According to John* XIII–XXI, 581–82), "the Jesus who speaks here [in the Farewell Discourse] transcends time and space; he is a Jesus who is already on his way to the Father, and his concern is that he shall not abandon those who believe in him but must remain in the world [Jn 14:18; 17:11]. Although he speaks at the Last Supper, he is really speaking from heaven; although those who hear him are his disciples, his words are directed to Christians of all times. The Last Discourse is Jesus' last testament: it is meant to be read after he has left the earth."

[21] Ibid., 601.

[22] Ibid.

Luther and the Gospel of John

The selection and placing of the Gospel and epistle readings, like the ordering of the liturgical year as a whole, long pre-dated the Reformation, since essentially the Lutheran church carried the readings forward from the Roman Catholic church. In the case of Bach's understanding of John the obvious place to begin is with Luther, whose love of the Fourth Gospel was fundamental to his theology. Although Luther's theology was centered on Paul, whose Epistle to the Romans Luther called "the gospel in its purest form," the Gospel of John was also a cornerstone of that theology, pronounced by Luther as "unique in loveliness, and of a truth the principal gospel." Thus, in answer to the question "which are the true and noblest books of the New Testament," Luther named "John's Gospel and St. Paul's epistles, especially that to the Romans, and St. Peter's first epistle . . . the true kernel and marrow of all the books." A little later he added the well-known passage:

> If I had to do without one or the other—either the works or the preaching of Christ—then I would rather do without the works than without his preaching. For the works do not help me, but his words give life, as he himself says [Jn 6:63]. Now John writes very little about the works of Christ, but very much about his preaching, while the other evangelists write much about his works and little about his preaching. Therefore John's Gospel is the one, fine, true, and chief Gospel, and is far, far to be preferred over the other three and placed high above them.[23]

In addition, within the Fourth Gospel Luther's favorite part was the Farewell Discourse, on which he preached a series of sermons between Easter and Pentecost 1537, which he later published, and which he considered, next to his translation of the Bible, his best book.[24] For Luther, Paul and John were, more than any other of the NT authors, individual voices who spoke directly of the basis of God's message to mankind, albeit in very different tones. Luther found in John what many commentators before and after have brought out: an emphasis on Jesus's teachings (discourses) rather than his works (the miracles or signs), which lends the Fourth Gospel a spiritual, meditative, even mystical quality, as opposed to the more narrative character of the Synoptic Gospels. Whereas Paul provided Luther with the major conceptual lines of his theology—justification by faith, the theology of the cross, the opposition of law and gospel, and the like—John's principal contribution

---

[23] *Luther's Works*, vol. 35, *Word and Sacrament 1*, ed. E. Theodore Bachmann, 361–62 (Philadelphia: Muhlenberg Press, 1960). For a concise assessment of this topic, including the passage just cited, see Victor C. Pfitzner, "Luther as Interpreter of John's Gospel. With Special Reference to His Sermons on the Gospel of St. John," *Lutheran Theological Journal* 18, no. 2 (1984): 65–73.

[24] See *Luther's Works*, vol. 24, *Sermons on the Gospel of St. John, Chapters 14–16*), ix–x.

to that theology was as that of *Trost* (consolation), an idea that found its place in John's (and Luther's) emphasis on the person and sayings of Jesus.[25]

Yet certain well-known disparities between John and Paul, above all that of the role of faith versus love in the question of justification, were problematic for Luther, whose unmistakable tendency to view the fourth evangelist through the eyes of Paul was offset by a special attraction to John's more spiritual character.[26] Thus John came to represent the "other side" of Luther's Pauline theology, one in which the emphasis on faith as evidence of things not seen, or faith "in opposition to experience" was tempered by the "possessions" of faith, faith "realized in experience."[27] And experience, as the theologian Walther von Loewenich has argued, is for Luther the "school" of the Holy Spirit, bringing a "new life," the product of the "indwelling" of God in the faithful, teaching them to live in love and brotherhood, in the certainty of faith. Through the Holy Spirit the sharp antithesis between faith and experience is overcome.[28] The "realization of faith in reality" is, of course, a primary characteristic of John's "realized eschatology." And while Luther's theology is unmistakably one of future rather than realized eschatology, he nevertheless found means of reconciling the two, above all in the way he easily accommodated John's extraordinary emphasis on love, which he viewed as the "feeling quality" of faith.[29] Thus Luther's echoing the terms of the ancient "satisfaction" theory of redemption (see the discussion that follows), which portrayed God as a severe judge demanding the just sentence of death for human sins and Jesus as substitute for the sinner at the point of sentencing, was rooted not only in Paul's theology of justification but also in John's proclaiming God's love as the motive for the incarnation and for Jesus's act of atonement in the Passion.[30]

---

[25] Loewenich, *Luther und das Johanneische Christentum*, 15–22: "Johannes ist das Evangelium des Trostes. Es ist der eigentlich ursprüngliche und für Luther bezeichnende Zugang. Aber daneben drängt sich der Beobachtung deutlich noch ein Zweites auf. Johannes ist für ihn das Evangelium, das in ganz besonderer Weise die Person Christi in den Mittelpunkt stellt" (20). In the cantatas for spring 1725, Bach devised very particular means of bringing out these two ideas.

[26] Ibid., 16 ("der Trost, den Luther aus Johannes gewinnt, ist derselbe, den er aus der Verkündigung des Paulus reichlich geschöpft hat. *Der Weg zu Johannes geht für Luther über Paulus*"), 26–31, 62–63 (on faith and love), 61 (on Luther's response to John's *Christusmystik*), 70.

[27] Walther von Loewenich, *Luther's Theology of the Cross*, trans. Herbert J. A. Bouman (Minneapolis: Augsburg Publishing House, 1976), 94–99.

[28] Ibid., 109–11.

[29] Ibid., 94.

[30] Loewenich, *Luther und das Johanneische Christentum*, 65–68 (the distinction between John's and Luther's eschatological focuses). Jaroslav Pelikan has demonstrated in *Bach Among the Theologians*, (91–101), that the *St. Matthew Passion* text is indebted to the theology of Anselm of Canterbury's "satisfaction" theory, which is prominent in Luther's writings on meditation on the Passion. And Elke Axmacher shows that the severe stage that represents God's judgment of the sinner in that theory was offset in the *St. Matthew Passion* text by increased emphasis on love, which belonged properly only to the second stage. Axmacher, *"Aus Liebe will mein Heyland sterben,"* 170–85. The consequent lessening of the dialectical character of Luther's dynamic of faith in Bach's time can be said to represent a leaning

What Jesus accomplished in the Passion and Easter was the key to all true theology, the "theology of the cross" (*theologia crucis*); and for Luther it meant that Jesus's victory over the world, sin, death, hell, and Satan was the source of comfort (*Trost*) for the believer. Von Loewenich explains that the *Trost* that John promulgates as the outcome of Jesus's work is the bond between Paul and John for Luther, encapsulated in John's proclaiming "comfort for the tormented conscience" ("Trost fürs angefochtene Gewissen"). This phrase, it might be mentioned, echoes at two points in Bach's *St. John Passion* that are of great prominence in the structure of the work: the dialog aria, "Eilt, ihr angefocht'nen Seelen," which urges the faithful to seek solace in Jesus's crucifixion, and the aria, "Es ist vollbracht," whose message regarding the meaning of the cross, "O Trost für die gekränkten Seelen," is proclaimed as the outcome of Jesus's victorious death (the middle section of the aria, "Der Held aus Juda siegt mit Macht, uns schließt den Kampf") and "realized" in the dialog aria with chorale, "Mein teurer Heiland."[31] John's proclaiming the purpose of the Incarnation in terms of Jesus's defeat of Satan and as the manifestation of God's love is expressed in Bach's cantatas for the second and third days of Christmas, 1723, *Darzu ist erschienen der Sohn Gottes* (BWV 40) and *Also hat Gott die Welt geliebt* (BWV 68). Likewise, as von Loewenich points out, Jesus's words "In der Welt habt ihr Angst; aber seid getrost, ich habe die Welt überwunden" from the Farewell Discourse (Jn 16:33) resound throughout Luther's writings, characterizing the believer's relationship to the world. They too have a prominent place in a Bach cantata (*Bisher habt ihr nichts gebeten in meinen Namen*, BWV 87) to be taken up in chapter 10. Finally, the Gospel of John was the one that—because of its stressing the identity of Jesus and the Father and the "indwelling" of God in humankind through the Holy Spirit—provided Luther with the cornerstones of his Christology and his doctrine of the Trinity.[32] In Lutheran terms, therefore, the Gospel of John proclaims the full meaning of Jesus's work for humanity, so that by virtue of its series of Johannine readings, the period from Easter to Pentecost can be said to outline a progression from the dialectical or opposition centered aspects of the *theologia crucis* to the possibility of oneness with God through faith, love, and the Holy Spirit.

toward the kind of thinking represented by John; Loewenich in *Luther und das Johanneische Christentum*, 70 calls it "meditative" rather than "dialectical." .

[31] The last of these movements, "Mein teurer Heiland"/"Jesu, der du warest tot," expresses John's realized eschatology in its proclaiming the certainty of salvation *now* as the result of Jesus's victory. See Chafe, *Tonal Allegory*, 277–82.

[32] The classic work on the Lutheran doctrine of the Trinity, on which the Formula of Concord was based, was that of Martin Chemnitz, sometimes known as the "second Martin." A copy of Chemnitz's monumental four-volume *Examen Concilii Tridentini* (*Examination of the Council of Trent:* 1565–1573) was in Bach's collection of theological books. With reference to the present subject, the crucial work is Chemnitz's *De Duabus Naturis in Christo (The Two Natures in Christ*, 1578), which draws extensively from John in forming its arguments regarding the Trinity. See Chemnitz, *The Two Natures in Christ*, trans. J. A. O. Preus (St. Louis: Concordia, 1971).

Behind much of what I have just outlined lies a set of theological ideas that, although they are best known from twentieth-century scholarship on the atonement, provide us with a key to understanding not only the relationship of John to Paul in Luther's writings but also important aspects of Bach's response to the Gospel of John. Here I refer to the well-known distinction between the "*Christus victor*" and "satisfaction" theories of the atonement as set forth originally in 1931 by the Swedish theologian-historian, Gustav Aulén.[33] In Aulén's terms, the former theory, that of the early Greek fathers, is the classic or patristic one, sometimes called the "dramatic" or "dualistic" view of Jesus's work in combating the forces of sin, death, and the devil in the world. This view, which Aulén felt had been neglected over many centuries of theological thought, and particularly in the time from Lutheran orthodoxy through the nineteenth and early twentieth centuries, was overshadowed in the Lutheran orthodoxy of the seventeenth and early eighteenth centuries by a competing view, the "satisfaction" theory of the atonement, first set forth by Anselm of Canterbury in the eleventh century. This theory was prominent in the late Middle Ages, dominant in Lutheran orthodoxy, and a strong force in some quarters for much longer. Instead of emphasizing the triumphant, victorious character of Jesus's work of atonement, the satisfaction theory (Aulén's "Latin" type) treated the atonement in far more rationalistic, legalistic, or juridical manner.[34] According to that theory, God does not reconcile the world to himself solely through Jesus's defeat of the forces of evil; rather, his wrath toward sinful humanity is overcome by Jesus's offering himself for punishment on behalf of humankind. Thus redemption, instead of being a work of God alone and carried out by Jesus, is a work in which Jesus's humanity is the key. Whereas the "classic" view (*Christus Victor*) is a drama of stark oppositions: light versus darkness, good versus evil, and the like, with no possibility of compromise, the Latin theory has almost the character of a negotiation between God and humankind, a logical argument that convinces God, if not to relax his demand for strict justice, at least to soften his wrath toward human sinfulness, to be persuaded, as it were, by human logic. In the classic view Jesus overcomes the law (described as a "curse" or "wrath"), whereas in the Latin view he fulfills it to God's "satisfaction." In the classic view humankind is the beneficiary of a work carried out by God alone in the person of Jesus, to free it from bondage to Satan, whereas in the Latin view humanity participates through Jesus' humanity in its own salvation. Instead of stressing the divinity of Jesus, the Latin theory views Jesus's sacrifice as the offering made to God from the human side.

One of the most forceful and, for some, controversial aspects of Aulén's study is his claim that Luther's work had long been seriously misunderstood as adhering to the satisfaction theory, when in reality it represented a return of the classic view "with a greater intensity and power than ever before."[35] Aulén draws particular

---

[33] Gustav Aulén, *Christus Victor*, trans. A. G. Hebert (New York: Macmillan, 1969).

[34] For an instance, see the quote from Rambach in ch. 2, n. 59.

[35] Aulén, *Christus Victor*, 107.

attention to the "dualistic and dramatic" nature of Luther's description of the conflict and triumph of Jesus's victory over the forces of evil: "We have only to listen to Luther's hymns to feel how they thrill with triumph, like a fanfare of trumpets."[36] Aulén emphasizes that this dualistic character is "particularly prominent in the Johannine writings, with their constant antitheses, such as light and darkness, life and death."[37] In Aulén's view, therefore, Luther's retention of terms associated with the satisfaction theory is separate from the core meaning of his view of the atonement, which "can only be rightly understood as a revival of the old classic theme of the Atonement as taught by the Fathers, but with a greater depth of treatment."[38] Owing to his retention of those terms, though, Luther was misunderstood even by his contemporaries and immediate successors, and particularly during the era of Lutheran orthodoxy, which was thoroughly committed to the satisfaction theory.

Clearly, there was some form of coexistence and interaction of these two theories in Luther's work, though their exact relationship may never be fully agreed upon.[39] Had Luther set forth a systematic theology and been forced in that process to take a single stand on the atonement, a ready answer might have been forthcoming. But since his work was centered almost entirely on scriptural exegesis, its character tended to mirror the changing emphases of the scriptural sources. Just as Luther's work exhibits characteristics of what would at a later time become the split between Pietism and Orthodoxy, without the sense that the two are in sharp conflict, just as it reconciles the differing theological emphases of John and Paul, so it bypasses the necessity of unbreachable conflict between the classic and Latin views of the atonement. After Luther, however, this was less obviously the case. The rationalistic, methodological tendency of Lutheran orthodoxy, a necessary outcome of the Reformation emphasis on the authority and interpretation of scripture, very naturally inclined toward the satisfaction theory and those aspects of Luther's work that derived from the "theological" character of Paul, whose work, as Aulén also argued forcefully, nevertheless contained a great deal more of the classic view than was acknowledged by later Lutherans.

The point of all this for Bach is not that he took a reasoned and consistent position regarding such issues, or even that he was fully aware of their potential conflict. Nevertheless, in Bach's library we find foundation texts of both Pietism and Orthodoxy, as well as two editions of Luther's works, including a three-volume Bible with extensive commentary drawn from Luther's works, and a substantial number of underlinings and marginalia penned by Bach in his own copy; and this certainly suggests that Bach's study of such writings might have led him to an awareness (whether rationalized or intuitive is of less importance) of the two principal views of the atonement and their coexistence in Luther's work. They have been

---

[36] Ibid., 108.

[37] Ibid., 74. See p. 134, n. 20 for a more extended citation of this passage.

[38] Ibid., 102.

[39] This is the view set forth in Paul Althaus's critique of Aulén. See Althaus, *The Theology of Martin Luther*, trans. Robert C. Schulz, 218–23 (Philadelphia: Fortress Press, 1966). See also ch. 4, this book.

demonstrated to coexist in his own work. For, as both Elke Axmacher and Jaroslav Pelikan have pointed out, Bach's two surviving Passions exhibit very marked traits of the two theories, the classic view (*Christus Victor*) in the case of the *St. John Passion* and the Latin view (the satisfaction theory) in the case of the *St. Matthew Passion*.[40] This occurrence is unique among the Passions of Bach's time, an indication, perhaps, that Bach himself had greater input than is commonly supposed into their texts. That is, the texts of the two Passions seem to have had a significant part of their origins in sources particular to Bach's own interests rather than to what we would suppose to have been those of the Leipzig theological establishment.

[40] Pelikan, *Bach Among the Theologians*, 102–15.

{ PART II }

The *St. John Passion*

{4}

The *St. John Passion*: Introduction and Part 1

Two perspectives on the Passion: law versus freedom

One of the most interesting observations one can make about the texts of Bach's two surviving Passions is that, unexpectedly, they suggest two very different viewpoints on the atonement. Three decades ago Jaroslav Pelikan pointed out that much of the free poetry of the *St. Matthew Passion* derives from the satisfaction theory of the atonement first set forth in the late Middle Ages.[1] This viewpoint was all the more interesting in light of Elke Axmacher's discovery some years earlier that several of the texts of the Passion that most exhibit those traits are indebted to sermons of the seventeenth-century theologian Heinrich Müller, their theological emphases further modified by Bach's librettist Picander (C. F. Henrici), so as to reflect the outlook of early eighteenth-century Lutheranism.[2] Axmacher's discovery suggests something more far-reaching than the usual poeticizing of individual points of meditation; a significant number of the movements in question correspond to the stages in the process of faith that Luther set forth in various writings, including his widely published sermon on the meditation of Christ's Passion of 1519. In addition, they are keystones in the musical and textual design of the *St. Matthew Passion*.[3]

Thus, it seems, the *St. Matthew Passion* was conceived to a very considerable degree as a coherent representation of the prevailing view of the atonement in

---

[1] Pelikan, *Bach Among the Theologians*, 89–101.

[2] Elke Axmacher, "Ein Quellenfund zum Text der Matthäus-Passion." *Bach-Jahrbuch* 64 (1978): 181–91; Axmacher, *"Aus Liebe will mein Heyland sterben."*

[3] Chafe, *Tonal Allegory*, 337–59. So far as I know, the first scholar to view the text of the *St. Matthew Passion* in light of Luther's 1519 Passion sermon was Hans Ludwig Holborn, "Bach and Pietism: The Relationship of the Church Music of Johann Sebastian Bach to Eighteenth-Century Lutheran Orthodoxy and Pietism with Special Reference to the *St. Matthew Passion*." Ph D diss., School of Theology at Claremont, California, 1976.

Lutheran orthodoxy. In striking contrast, however, the *St. John Passion* text, in Pelikan's view, reflected a different outlook altogether, that of the far older *Christus Victor* theory of the atonement that originated among the Greek church fathers in the early Christian centuries.[4] The Swedish theologian Gustav Aulén had argued that Luther's theological focus, generally accepted as adhering to the satisfaction theory, was really that of the *Christus Victor* theory, although it retained much of the language of satisfaction. By drawing Aulén's controversial viewpoint on the roles of the two theories in Luther's writings into the discussion of Bach's two Passions, Pelikan sharpened our awareness of their underlying differences, which now might be taken to derive not merely from two narratives with differing emphases, structures, and language but also from modes of understanding the Passion that were fundamentally different, if not incompatible. In light of the prominence of the satisfaction theory in Lutheran orthodoxy, it appears that the *St. Matthew Passion* text articulates a viewpoint on the Passion that was closer to that of the Leipzig theological establishment than that of the *St. John Passion*, in which little or nothing of the satisfaction theory appears. This was, perhaps, a factor in the textual alterations made to the *St. John Passion* over the course of its various performances.

Nowadays, with the change from pre-Enlightenment to Enlightenment (or "precritical" to "critical") hermeneutics long behind us, we are thoroughly accustomed to literary, historical, and philological studies emphasizing the differences among the Gospels, and especially those involving John versus the Synoptics. Differences in the *ways* each of the evangelists recounted the events of Jesus's life and work were always recognized, of course; as we have seen, Luther was closely attuned to those between John and the Synoptic Gospels, and he was following long-established tradition in that respect. And the writers of Bach's time were by no means oblivious to the differences between the Johannine account of the Passion and those of the Synoptics. But in an age when harmonizing rather than differentiating the four Gospel accounts of the Passion was decidedly the norm, the extent to which both of Bach's Passions project something approaching two competing theories of the atonement is probably unique among musical settings.

Nevertheless, it is not necessary to hold the view that Bach deliberately and systematically embedded two conflicting views of the atonement in his two Passions. Paul Althaus asserts in his critique of Aulén's work that Luther unifies the two "theories" by viewing both the law (central to the satisfaction theory) and the powers of evil defeated by Jesus in the *Christus Victor* theory as God's "instruments against the sinner," thus placing the law "in a category with the other powers and tyrants" as "that one of all the powers which most directly and obviously carries out God's work and will and functions as an instrument of his wrath and judgment."[5] From this standpoint, Jesus's victory is the victory of the Gospel, of forgiveness of sins, of freedom from sin and the powers of evil, and above all it is victory over the

---

[4] Pelikan, *Bach Among the Theologians*, 102–15.

[5] Althaus, *Theology of Martin Luther*, 218–23.

tyranny of the law, which holds humanity in bondage to sin. The law, although viewed differently by the two theories, is Jesus's primary opponent in both, since its authority, like that of the demonic powers, is God's wrath toward sin, which must be stilled, or "satisfied."[6] And so the depiction of Jesus as *Christus Victor* is not at all incompatible with the satisfaction theory, for even when the dualistic language of victory rather than the legalistic approach of the satisfaction theory dominates, the difference is primarily one of emphasis.

However, the considerable differences between Bach's two Passions, and their tracing to those within the Gospels themselves, must be acknowledged. Within both Passions Jesus's triumph over the law and its ultimate goal, death as judgment for sin, finds symbolic expression in the trial before Pilate, a legal proceeding. But in John, not only is the trial considerably more extended than in the Synoptic Gospels (with Jesus's questioning before the Sanhedrin greatly curtailed), but also reference to the law is introduced more directly than in Matthew. In John it emerges at an early point in the trial in Pilate's response to the Jews' naming Jesus an evildoer, "So take him and try him according to your laws," which elicits the outcry, "we may not kill anyone" ("Wir dürfen niemand töten" in Bach's German version or "it is not lawful for us to put any man to death" [KJV]). As understood literally by generations of commentators, this response referred to the fact that the power of executing criminals had been taken from the Jews by the Romans; for, as many Lutheran authors brought out, the Jews, in fact, had laws that demanded the death of blasphemers. Behind it, therefore, lay two different kinds of laws: those of the Jews, given in scripture and religious in nature; and those of the Romans, political and secular. The real meaning of the exchange was embodied in the remark added by John—"That the saying of Jesus might be fulfilled, which he spake, signifying what death he should die" (i.e., crucifixion by the Romans in fulfillment of Jesus's earlier references to his "lifting up")—which was understood by many theologians, including Bach's older contemporary August Hermann Francke (1663–1727), as evidence that Jesus was the Messiah, put to death by both Jews and gentiles. Behind his death, therefore, lay human guilt; yet John's narrative did not invite meditation on guilt, since it moved on immediately to the more elevated themes of Jesus's kingship and "truth."

Later in the trial we hear a second, more explicit association of the law with death: in the chorus, "Wir haben ein Gesetz und nach dem Gesetz soll er sterben,

---

[6] Johann Heermann, in his *Heptalogus Christi, Das ist: Die Allerholdseligsten Sieben Worte unsers treuen und hochverdienten Heylandes JESU CHRISTI, Mit welchen Er am Creutze sein Leben geendet hat* (Braunschweig, 1670, 121–26), discusses, in order, Jesus's defeat of Satan, death, the law, hell, and God's wrath against sin as the *opus redemptionis* whose completion was symbolized in the cry "Es ist vollbracht," which Heermann calls Jesus's "Triumph-und Siegs-Worte." As is not uncommon for the time, Heermann intermingles the language of satisfaction and victory. This quality is reflected in his Passion hymn, "Herzliebster Jesu," three verses of which appear in the *St. Matthew Passion*, where they fit closely with the appearance of the satisfaction theory in that work, and three of which appear in the *St. John Passion*, where they articulate the themes of love, guilt/penitence, and Jesus's kingship. (See also Johann Jacob Rambach's view of satisfaction in relation to God's plan as cited in ch. 2, n. 59.)

denn er hat sich selbst zu Gottes Sohn gemacht" (We have a law and according to the law he should die, for he has made himself out to be the Son of God). And in the dialog that follows, Pilate professes the legal authority of the Roman governor, either to crucify or to set free, a claim that Jesus rejects, announcing that Pilate could have no power over him if it were not given from above (i.e., God's *Rath*). With the words "von oben herab gegeben" (given from above) in the recitative "Da Pilatus das Wort hörete . . . ", Jesus alludes to the various other points in the Gospel at which he had spoken of worlds "above" and "below," the best known, perhaps, being that of John 8:23, "Ye are from beneath; I am from above: ye are of this world; I am not of this world." Pilate would not, of course, have known such sayings, but, as the Lutheran commentators emphasized, he had heard Jesus speak of his kingdom being not of this world in the previous dialog; hence, for them, John's narrating that from then on Pilate sought to free Jesus (the ending of Bach's recitative "Da Pilatus das Worte hörete, fürchtet' er sich noch mehr"). In addition, Jesus's use of the word "gegeben" (given), has a particular Johannine resonance, linking up with many other places in the Gospel, including two earlier in the Passion narrative, where Jesus refers to what God "gave" him. At this point in the Passion poem from which Bach drew its text, the presumed author, Christian Heinrich Postel, introduced the theme of freedom in a context that made clear that God, who had given the law to humankind, now gave to humanity the means of attaining freedom from the law ("Durch dein Gefängnis, Gottes Sohn, ist uns die Freiheit kommen"). His imagery of Jesus as *Gnadenthron* and *Freistatt*, especially as understood by the Lutheran tradition, brought out through antithesis the central meaning of the Passion: that Jesus's imprisonment brought freedom from the law for humankind.[7]

Bach not only follows Postel in his placement of the text for "Durch dein Gefängnis" but also turns Postel's aria into a chorale by setting it to a melody of Johann Hermann Schein, "Mach's mit mir, Gott, nach deiner Güt." But Bach goes still farther, in that he makes this new "chorale" into the culmination of a substantial modulation from flat to sharp key areas (or *ambitus*, in the terms of the time) that follows from John's opposition of "above" and "below" in the preceding recitative, which begins in d and ends in E, setting up the key of "Durch dein Gefängnis." And he makes these events into a pivot in the structure of his symbolic version of the trial, reiterating the music of "Wir haben ein Gesetz," now transposed down a semitone from F to E, after "Durch dein Gefängnis," for the next of the choruses:

---

[7] Postel's authorship of the poem in question is not, however, absolutely certain (see n. 14). For convenience I will refer to it as his, as most scholars do. The theme of freedom was sometimes linked to the name "good Friday" ("gute *Frei*tag") as the day on which God turned evil into good (as in the widespread application to the passion of the words of Joseph to his brothers: "Ye thought to do evil against me; but God meant it unto good" Gen 50:20). Valerius Herberger, author of "In meines Herzens Grunde," discusses it in these terms in his *Evangelisches Herz-Postilla* (Leipzig, 1668), 1:347–48, naming Jesus as the "tröstliche Freystadt." On the meaning of *Gnadenthron* and *Freistatt* in "Durch dein Gefängnis" (particularly as explained by Johann Jacob Rambach) see ch. 8, this book; on "gegeben" see ch. 5.

"Lässest du diesen los, so bist du des Kaiser's Freund nicht; denn wer sich zum Könige machet, der ist wider den Kaiser" (If you set this man free, then you are no friend of the emperor; for whoever makes himself out to be a king is against the emperor). The reason for these structural emphases is not difficult to determine: in "Wir haben ein Gesetz" the Jews make an association between *their* law and death, giving as the reason for the demand for death that Jesus has made himself out to be the Son of God, a blasphemy from their standpoint. In "Lässest du diesen los," however, they oppose Jesus's being set free, giving now the reason that he has made himself out to be a king, and therefore in opposition to the emperor, that is, Roman law. Thus the two choruses in question articulate more explicitly than the earlier exchange a shift from religious to worldly interpretation of the law. Bach's confirming the sudden shift from flat to sharp keys with "Durch dein Gefängnis" represents another important event in the trial. The modulatory recitative marks the last time that Jesus speaks in the trial; and in the absence of further dialogs between Jesus and Pilate, events move swiftly to the point of judgment. Bach continues the new key area (*ambitus*), repeating the music of the previous two choruses to new texts, transposed down a semitone (from flat to sharp keys) and in reverse order. The new key area eventually culminates in the judgment of crucifixion with which the trial ends, directly following another reference to the emperor ("Wir haben keinen König denn den Kaiser"—We have no king but Caesar).

As many commentators have pointed out, for John the trial of Jesus before Pilate was the focal point not only for the Passion but also for the Gospel as a whole, which is permeated by forensic language and imagery, thus a kind of symbolic trial.[8] In the trial before Pilate the central issues of the Gospel come to a head, especially the all-important question of Jesus's identity and its meaning for humanity. In it John creates a narrative in which the truth, Jesus's divinity, emerges in contradictions and oppositions, one of the foremost characteristics of his celebrated literary style. The ability to see through appearances and oppositions to the truth beyond was, for John, the hallmark of faith, and the trial of Jesus was its touchstone. Throughout the trial, therefore, John keeps the question of worldly versus spiritual perspectives in the foreground, especially in the Christological title "king" or "king of the Jews." Pilate himself introduces that title in the first dialog with Jesus—"Bist du der Juden König?" (in the recitative "Auf dass erfüllet . . .")—which leads Jesus to the proclamation that his kingdom is not of this world. Although this is not the ending of the dialog in John, Bach divides it at this point by introducing two verses of the chorale "Herzliebster Jesu," beginning "Ach großer König." This gesture has the effect of making a caesura within the trial, a point of culmination in the affirmation of Jesus's kingship. After the chorale, the dialog continues with the theme of kingship, and this time Jesus's immediate response is "Du sagsts, ich bin ein König." This reply is sometimes interpreted today as mean-

[8] See, for example, Dodd, *Interpretation of the Fourth Gospel*, 435–37.

ing "*You* say I am a king," as if the title were merely Pilate's.[9] In the Lutheran tradition, however, the prevailing interpretation was that Jesus himself acknowledges his kingship at this point. And Bach's music makes this clear, as we will see in chapter 6. From this point, however, the course of events takes a downward turn that leads to the cry for release of Barrabas, and the beginning of Jesus's physical punishments, the scourging and crown of thorns. At this point Bach introduces a second point of meditation, with the paired arioso "Betrachte, meine Seele" and aria "Erwäge," now in a completely different tonal region from that of "Ach großer König."

After the second dialog between Pilate and Jesus (which is continuous with the preceding one in John) the title "king" or "king of the Jews" is heard several additional times in the trial. Pilate repeatedly refers to Jesus in this manner, at first in dialog with Jesus, then in his provocative remarks to the crowd. With the mocking and scourging the title is picked up by the soldiers, then by the Jews, sounding eight times in all. Ultimately, the worldly view of the law prevails in the trial, embodied in the high priests' "Wir haben keinen König denn den Kaiser" (We have no king but Caesar), pressuring Pilate into pronouncing the judgment of crucifixion. After the trial, however, Bach returns, for the shift of locale to Golgotha, introducing a segment in the key area or *ambitus* that begins and ends not only with the keys that begin and end the Passion as a whole (g and E♭), but that are also the keys of the scourging (g) and the meditative movement that directly follows it, "Betrachte, meine Seele" (E♭). Beginning after the modulation with the hortatory dialog, "Eilt, ihr angefocht'nen Seelen," the flat-key region that follows the trial centers on John's final pronouncement regarding Jesus's kingship in the sign placed by Pilate over the cross, "Jesus of Nazareth, King of the Jews." Corresponding to the ending of the third of the traditional five divisions of the Passion narrative ("Pilatus"), it marks, with the chorale "In meines Herzens Grunde dein Nam' und Kreuz allein" that Bach inserted at this point, another powerful structural caesura within the work.

We note that within the trial the chorales "Ach großer König" and "Durch dein Gefängnis" respond to Christological issues, introduced at the beginning of the trial in "Christus, der uns selig macht," whereas after the trial "In meines Herzens Grunde," meditating on the meaning of the "royal" inscription, places the seal, as it were, on this question. The four chorales just cited affirm Jesus's divinity at key points, reminding the listener of the true meaning of the trial and the crucifixion itself. One can therefore speak of the trial as having two outcomes: the worldly judgment of crucifixion with which the trial proper ends, directly following "Wir haben keinen König denn den Kaiser"; and the "spiritual" acknowledgment of Jesus's identity, which follows the trial and is associated with the internalizing of his name and cross in the culminating chorale "In meines Herzens Grunde."

---

[9] See, for example, Andreas J. Köstenberger, *A Theology of John's Gospel and Letters* (Grand Rapids, MI: Zondervan, 2009), 449; Brown, *Gospel According to John*, 853–54.

Whereas the chorales are associated with the Christian perspective on Jesus's trial and crucifixion, the *turba* choruses have exactly the opposite meaning, associated directly with the Passion drama itself and centered on Jesus's persecution. In Bach's design, therefore, the *turba* choruses do not culminate scenes, as some of the chorales do. At the ending of the trial, therefore, "Wir haben keinen König" is not given a climactic extended setting, and not only is its key, B minor, followed by D major for the brief narrative that ends the trial, but that D itself is immediately turned into the dominant of G minor for the segment that follows (the shift of locale to Golgotha). Nevertheless, Bach has taken care that the *turba* choruses exhibit a very substantial degree of ordering in the design as a whole. It is important to recognize, though, that this organization of the choruses does not represent the "highest" level of ordering but yields that role to another principle altogether. That principle is a directly audible one, while at the same time encompassing great time spans in the Passion: the tonal ordering of the entire work according to its key areas, or *ambitus*, to be discussed in chapter 5. In the fact that it is easily audible in its local impact (i.e., the points of change), whereas its more abstract overall design is not so, it can be said to function on two levels that center on the opposition of worlds "above" and "below" in John, as proclaimed in the recitative that precedes "Durch dein Gefängnis." In the structure of the Passion it coordinates the various other kinds of organization (substructures) within the work as a whole.

With respect to the arrangement and symbolism of the choruses, the pivotal musicological study was that of Friedrich Smend, who argued many years ago that both Bach Passions, despite their differences, embody symbolic representations of the law in the so-called *turba* choruses—that is, the choruses of the crowd, whether Jews or Romans—especially those that center on the trial before Pilate, and that exhibit elements of symmetrical organization in both works.[10] According to Smend, in each work Bach had contrived a symmetrical arrangement of *turba* choruses, which pivoted around a movement or grouping of movements (*Herzstück*) and which functioned as a central focal point for the meaning of the work. In the *St. Matthew Passion* there were ten, a representation, as in other Bach works, of the law (symbolized in the Ten Commandments).

In neither Passion narrative do we find ten *turba* choruses associated with the Roman trial, but in the *St. Matthew Passion* it was possible to argue for a set of ten that embraced all the *turba* choruses of Part 2 up to the point immediately before meditation on Golgotha takes place. There it marks a symbolic caesura in the de-

---

[10] Smend's articles on the two Bach Passions, originally published in the *Bach-Jahrbuch* in 1926 and 1928, respectively, have been republished in Friedrich Smend, *Bach-Studien*, edited by Christoph Wolff (Kassel: Bärenreiter, 1968), 11–23 ("Die Johannes-Passion von Bach. Auf ihren Bau untersucht") and 24–83 ("Bachs Matthäus-Passion: Untersuchungen zur Geschichte des Werkes bis 1750"). Smend used the term *Herzstück* to designate what he viewed as the symmetrical core of each work, centered on the *turba* choruses. Although I have followed this usage in earlier studies, I find the term not wholly appropriate since it is rooted more in musical correspondences (some of them very tenuous), rather than musico-theological purpose.

sign that is followed by a new perspective on the crucifixion.[11] In John's Passion narrative there are nine *turba* choruses in the trial itself plus an additional one that follows the trial and responds to Pilate's placing the royal inscription over the cross.[12] The latter corresponds in some respects to the point just described for the *St. Matthew Passion*, especially in its association with Golgotha and its marking a point of culmination. Bach's design, however, does not draw all ten *turba* choruses into a symmetrical design that is completed at this point, but instead features a more complex pattern of substructures. The first two choruses in the *St. John Passion*, "Wäre dieser nicht ein Übeltäter" and "Wir dürfen niemand töten," which are very closely related, appear within the scene that culminates in "Ach großer König." That scene is followed by a transitional recitative culminating in the narrative of the scourging (with which Postel's meditations on the Passion began) and in which the third chorus appears ("Nicht diesen . . . sondern Barabbam"). Next follows a primarily symmetrical grouping of choruses (four through nine) that begin within the segment that follows the recitative just described, and therefore articulates a substantial shift of key area from the scene ending with "Ach großer König." Within that segment a momentous shift to sharp keys occurs, followed by repetition of the fifth and sixth of the choruses, transposed down a semitone, with new texts and in reverse order (the seventh and eighth choruses). Complicating this picture is the fact that in addition three choruses within the trial repeat the music previously associated with the two "Jesus of Nazareth" choruses in Part 1, one of them in combination with the repetition of music from the first chorus within the second, and the other (the ninth and last of the trial) coming just before the judgment of crucifixion with which the trial ends ("Wir haben keinen König"). The tenth chorus, repeating the music of the fourth with a new text, and now untransposed, comes only after the trial proper, leading to the chorale "In meines Herzens Grunde," which marks a point of convergence for the themes of Jesus's identity and the meaning of the crucifixion.

In the *St. John Passion*, therefore, we can speak of a culminating point that is associated with the tenth of the *turba* choruses ("Schreibe nicht der Juden König"), as well as an extensive sense of their interrelatedness, but not of a symmetrical design that spans the set as a whole. Smend could not achieve this either; but in

---

[11] See Chafe, *Tonal Allegory*, 392–93.

[12] Interestingly, there are also ten choruses within the scenes of Jesus's questioning by the high priest in Part 1 and the trial in Part 2, taken together (and, of course, not including the tenth chorus of Part 2, which is outside both trials). The Part 1 chorus, "Bist du nicht seiner Jünger einer?" is, however, put to Peter, as is the chorus "Wahrlich du bist auch einer von denen" in the *St. Matthew Passion*. In the earlier work the division between Parts 1 and 2 ruled out any such tenfold arrangement. And, since the number ten is not a symbolic factor in either Gospel, it may be legitimately questioned whether it was for Bach. That is, the numerological aspect of the law is not the really important point, even though in the *St. John Passion*, as in other Bach works where the law is the central theme, such as Cantata 77 (*Du sollt Gott, deinen Herren lieben*), Bach has embedded it into the musical designs of individual movements (see ch. 8).

order to maximize the idea of a symmetrically conceived *Herzstück* rooted in the repetition of eight of the choruses, he was forced to describe pairings of choruses that were not only widely separated from each other in the design—"Nicht diesen, sondern Barabbam" (no. 3) with "Sei gegrüßet, lieber Judenkönig" (no. 4) and "Wir haben keinen König denn den Kaiser" (no. 9) with "Schreibe nicht der Juden König" (no. 10)—but that were in highly contrasted key areas, an aspect that Smend largely passes over. As a result, his *Herzstück* did not exhibit either a sense of tonal unity or even of textual unity, since it began with the recitative before "Ach, großer König," and extended beyond the chorale "In meines Herzens Grunde" to include the recitative that introduced the shift to the soldiers' dividing Jesus's robe, but nothing further of that scene itself. In other words, although it pointed to the principal of symmetrical organization, it failed to follow any consistent musical principle. And theologically its particular boundaries made no sense. Nevertheless, the concept marked a very important beginning point in understanding the design of the Passion, one that, when brought more sharply into focus, can be said to project the sense of a centralized tonal mirror, or "image" of the work as a whole, within which the arrangement of the choruses has a distinct theological role.

There are many differences between the roles of the choruses in the two Passions, owing to the somewhat different arrangement and pacing of events between Matthew and John. But the ones I have described bring about an even greater difference in pacing between Bach's two Passions than that between the two evangelists. Since the choruses are more widely separated in the *St. Matthew Passion* and are not all occupied with attaining the judgment of crucifixion, their association with the law is depicted in broader terms suggestive of its impact on all humanity, not just on Jesus's trial; hence the need for a unifying element that would relate the questions of human guilt and penitence to the trial. The Müller sermons and their articulation of the satisfaction theory provided exactly that. As a result, the meditative movements are greater in number, and the array of symbolic *turba* choruses is more spread out than in the *St. John Passion*. The meditative movements introduce the question of the guilt of humanity, providing reminders of the law by means of the legalistic aspect of the language of satisfaction.

The greatest differences between the two Passions, in this respect, are the result of the two evangelists' perspectives on the law (and the trial), as manifested in their emphases and their organization of the events of the Passion. John plays down Jesus's questioning by the Jewish authorities enormously in relation to the Synoptic Gospels, giving the Roman trial corresponding emphasis. In the *St. John Passion* Jesus's questioning by the high priest takes place in Part 1, and his trial before Pilate, in which the law is directly invoked, in Part 2, whereas in the *St. Matthew Passion,* because of the broad treatment of themes and narratives not contained in John (primarily Jesus's inner struggles in Gethsemane), the two scenes take place in Part 2, with the contrasted stories of Peter's denial and repentance and Judas's remorse and death (not told by John) coming between them.[13] This difference has two principal effects on Bach's designs. First, in the *St. Matthew Passion* the ten *turba* choruses that, in Smend's view, symbolized the law, span the scenes of Jesus's questioning by the Jewish authorities (more extensive than in John), as well as the trial before Pilate and the crucifixion itself, not just the latter two (as in the *St. John Passion*); in addition, two of the choruses are occupied with the intervening narratives of Peter and Judas. Second, in the *St. Matthew Passion,* owing to the prominence of Peter's and Judas's stories, the theme of human guilt, very prominent in Part 1, is picked up again between the two trials.

In John, however, the trial is much more compact; one of its main characteristics is its internal structure, which comprises two kinds of "scenes" for which John has arranged that they also involve shifting locations. John's trial alternates dialogs between Jesus and Pilate, which take place inside the governor's courtyard, and Pilate's interaction with the Jews who, as the initial words of the trial make clear, do not enter so as not to become impure and unable to eat Passover. Sometimes viewed as a sevenfold chiastic (symmetrical) design, in which the central episode involves the scourging by the soldiers, the trial in this view dramatizes the conflicts surrounding Jesus's identity. As a result, it enables the symbolism behind the choruses to come across particularly clearly, especially the sense that the law, which is referred to directly by both Pilate and the Jews, has become the primary expression of opposition to Jesus's messianic claims ("Wir haben ein Gesetz"). Bach brings this out this character throughout the trial in the frenzied character of certain of the choruses, which amplify John's dramatic contrasts, and the structural means by which he projects them. In the *St. Matthew Passion* only the two central "Laß ihn kreuzigen" choruses are sung to the same music, whereas in the *St. John Passion* the music of every chorus is repeated at least once to a different text (with the "Jesus of Nazareth" choruses featuring four different texts, three of them in the trial). Smend's arguments for symmetrically ordered musical parallels among the other choruses of the *St. Matthew Passion* are not entirely without merit, but the question of a symmetrical substructure is much less in evidence in that work. In the *St. John Passion*, however, by limiting the meditative movements to key points in the trial, and by linking the choruses musically in a highly patterned manner, Bach makes the trial a palpable presence within the work, projecting its own sense of structure and identity, one in which the law becomes a much more hostile force than in the *St. Matthew Passion.*

In this context it was all the more necessary to articulate the freedom from the law that was the outcome of Jesus's victory. And Bach does this by creating a substructure within the work whose sense of unity goes beyond the repetition of the

---

[13] Apart from Jesus's inner struggles in the garden of Gethsemane, the principal differences from John's Gospel seen in the *St. Matthew Passion*, Part 1, are Matthew's narratives of the woman of Bethany and the Last Supper, with Jesus's predictions of Judas's betrayal and Peter's denial and the institution of the sacrament.

choruses, and whose boundaries, defined substantially in musical (tonal) terms, are not aligned with those of John's trial. Instead, Bach creates subdivisions within the trial as John presents it, articulating those divisions by means of great differences in their key areas and limiting the symmetrical arrangement of choruses to fewer than ten. The first subdivision is that described earlier, including the initial dialogs between Jesus and Pilate, the initial pairing of choruses of the Jews, and the culmination in "Ach großer König." It establishes the Christian perspective on Jesus's kingship from the outset. The second, much larger subdivision begins with meditation on the scourging, as does Postel's Passion text from which the text of "Durch dein Gefängnis" was taken. At the same point in the *St. John Passion,* Bach introduces a pair of meditative movements, the arioso "Betrachte, meine Seele" and aria "Erwäge," that are not only the first such extended meditative movements of Part 2 but also involve "special" instrumentation. In addition, "Erwäge" is the longest meditative movement of the Passion. At this point,there is a very significant meditative break in the trial. In the Gospel this marks the division between John 18 and 19, beginning directly after the point at which, as the outcome of the Jews' demanding that Barrabas rather than Jesus be set free, Pilate has Jesus scourged. In Raymond Brown's view this point is the *center* of John's trial scene. Between it and Bach's next meditative insertion, "Durch dein Gefängnis," we hear three *turba* choruses ("Sei gegrüsset," "Kreuzige ihn," and "Wir haben ein Gesetz") making the association between the law and death. Then, following the shift of key area, the second and third of those three choruses ("Kreuzige ihn," and "Wir haben ein Gesetz") reappear with new texts, in reverse order and transposed down a semitone, leading to the ending of the trial, preceded by "Wir haben keinen König." Following the trial, Bach's next meditative insertion, the dialog aria "Eilt, ihr angefocht'nen Seelen," shifts the key area once more, enabling the tenth chorus ("Schreibe nicht") to repeat the music of the fourth ("Sei gegrüsset," like the others, with a new text) in its original key, to be followed, after a brief recitative, by the last meditative insertion, the chorale "In meines Herzens Grunde," in the key of "Betrachte, meine Seele."

Thus, from the point of meditation on the scourging to that of meditation on the royal inscription, Bach's design articulates a sense of return to its starting point in some respects, comprising a unit that encompasses seven of the *turba* choruses (4–10), in which the music of the first three of the seven is heard a second time in reverse order as the fourth, fifth, and seventh, with new texts. Between the third and fourth of these seven choruses ("Wir haben ein Gesetz" and "Lässest du diesen los") the aforementioned shift from flat to sharp key areas occurs. Here Bach makes a structural "pivot" around the chorale *contrafactum* "Durch dein Gefängnis, Gottes Sohn, ist uns die Freiheit kommen," which describes the antithesis of Jesus's imprisonment and the freedom it brings for humanity. Its reference to Jesus as Son of God echoes the final phrase of the last of the untransposed choruses, "Wir haben ein Gesetz, und nach dem Gesetz soll er sterben, denn er hat sich selbst zu Gottes Sohn gemacht." And its imagery, as we will see in chapter 8, embodied traditional Lutheran references to freedom from the law. "Durch dein Gefängnis" is therefore "centralized" within the symmetrical arrangement of the repeated choruses, its key, E major, presented as the outcome of the final dialog between Jesus and Pilate. No evidence has ever surfaced that anyone other than Bach was responsible for turning the aria text in question into a chorale; and, in light of its highly symbolic importance in the Passion and its possible source in a musical setting of the Passion, we must attribute it to Bach's own intention until such evidence does appear.[14] Placed between the *turba* choruses that also embody the question of law versus freedom ("Wir haben ein *Gesetz*" and "Lässest du diesen *los*"), and that shift the focus of the crowd's objections to Jesus from the law as a spiritual to a worldly force, as symbolized in the Christological titles *Gottessohn* and *König*, this chorale centralizes the theme of freedom.[15]

Again, Smend's "*Herzstück*" includes but, unfortunately, is not limited to the segment that extends from the scourging to the royal inscription, with which the third of the traditional fivefold divisions of the Passion narrative concludes. In attempting to extend the symmetry beyond that point so as to draw the movements that immediately preceded and followed into his *Herzstück*, Smend weakened the concept considerably, greatly lessening its sense of unification. I propose re-conceiving the concept somewhat, in order to emphasize that it begins with "Betrachte, meine Seele," in E♭, and extends to "In meines Herzens Gründe," also in E♭. The keys that immediately precede and follow belong to the aforementioned large-scale of the Passion as a whole, and do not form part of the unit itself. Whereas the designation *Herzstück* captures much of the role of this segment within the Passion, it is theologically neutral. I refer to it as a "symbolic trial" instead, one reason for which is that it centers on the theme of freedom from the law and how it is attained, a theme emphasized by the fact that its culminating point—the chorale "In meines Herzens Grunde"—is outside the trial proper.

Within John's trial the theme of freedom first emerges in the chorus "Nicht diesen, sondern Barrabam" (Not this man, but Barrabas) that directly precedes the scourging, on which the beginning of the symbolic trial meditates. That same theme reappears in the dialog preceding "Durch dein Gefängnis." In "Durch dein Gefängnis" its meaning is a spiritual one, whereas in the subsequent chorus, "Lässest du diesen los," it returns to the worldly frame of reference. But the theme of freedom is, in fact, proclaimed at two additional points in the Passion, the one earlier and the other later than the symbolic trial, so that the centralizing of that theme in

[14] Mendel (*Kritischer Bericht*, 4:163–64) points out that the text of Postel's poetry was not widespread and not printed, and that the only evidence for Postel's authorship is a 1706 remark of Christian Hunold, who published excerpts from the text, among which "Durch dein Gefängnis" was not included. A textbook for Mattheson's setting of this text was apparently published in Hamburg earlier in 1724 and, as Mendel conjectures, Bach might possibly have come across a copy either of that or of the earlier setting formerly attributed to Handel.

[15] It may be considered that, whereas the two *turba* choruses that precede and follow the shift of *ambitus* mark a point of opposition in their keys (corresponding to the shift from religious to worldly viewpoints on the law), the fact that they are based on the same music indicates equivalence of the two Christological titles, "Son of God" and "king."

"Durch dein Gefängnis" has still wider significance in the meaning of the whole. The first comes in Part 1, in the aria "Von den Stricken," the first aria of the Passion and one whose text was derived from the introductory movement of the Passion text of Barthold Heinrich Brockes where it announces a primary theme of the whole. It describes Jesus's capture and binding as freeing humanity from sin; and Bach makes clear in his modulatory design that this aria is the outcome of Jesus's earlier reference to what God "gave" him, the "cup" of the Passion. Much later in the Passion, the aria with chorale, "Mein teurer Heiland"/"Jesus, der du warest tot," a symbolic dialog between the believer and the dying Jesus, poses the question of freedom once more, "Bin ich vom sterben frei gemacht?" (Am I free from death), answering it in the affirmative in Jesus's bowing his head at the point of death.[16] If we think of the theme of freedom as centralized in "Durch dein Gefängnis," then it "spreads out" to the earlier and later scenes in a manner that lends unity to the overall design of the whole, and is comparable to the spreading out of the idea of the trial in John to the Gospel as a whole. Although the law is not directly invoked at the two points just mentioned, it was understood according to the Lutheran theology of the time. Thus the primary meaning of the Passion—its "use" or *Nutz* in Lutheran terms—is the freedom that comes to humanity as the result of Jesus's victory over sin, the law, and death, regardless of whether the sense of victory is projected openly, or whether there is emphasis on Jesus's sufferings, his conflict, or on human repentance.[17]

Whereas the theme of law versus freedom is expressed directly in the *St. John Passion* choruses, and only needed to be slightly amplified in Bach's structure, in the *St. Matthew Passion* it is not referred to directly but brought out in the forensic imagery of the satisfaction theory in the meditative movements. The theme of

---

[16] Smend ("Die Johannes-Passion von Bach," 16–17) pointed out a close melodic resemblance between the theme of "Von den Stricken" in Part 1 and the beginning of "Es ist vollbracht,"in Part 2 drawing it into an interpretation according to which his *Herzstück* was framed by correspondences of various kinds before and after. It is, in fact, not usual for Bach to introduce an inexact correspondence of this kind, which will suggest to many an ahistorical element, invoking ideas of Wagnerian leitmotifs and the like. As such, the correspondence is untenable; and it should be noted that very similar melodic patterns can be found in other Bach works in which no such connections exist. Nevertheless, Smend's observation is at least worthy of consideration in light of the theological connection between the two points: that is, the soteriological interpretation of Jesus's captivity, first introduced in "Von den Stricken" underlies the juxtaposition of musical styles in "Es ist vollbracht." This relationship would exist with or without any musical parallels.

[17] The Brockes Passion poem that served as a source for several of the poetic movements of the *St. John Passion* begins with a two-strophe aria-chorus for the believing souls (it is headed *Chor Gläubiger Seelen*) that presents the message of "Von den Stricken" as that of the Passion as a whole: "Mich / vom Stricke meiner Sünden zu entbinden / Wird mein Gott gebunden; . . . Ja / es will / ein Ewig Leben Mir zu geben / Selbst das Leben sterben." See Barthold Heinrich Brockes, *Der für die Sünde der Welt / Gemarterte und Sterbende JESUS Aus Den IV. Evangelisten. In gebundener Rede vorgestellet / Und In der Fasten-Zeit Musicalisch auffgeführet* (Hamburg, 1713). And much later in the poem we hear the "ARIA à II. Mit einer Gläubigen Seele" that served as the source of the non-chorale text of "Mein teurer Heiland": "Sind meiner Seelen tieffe Wunden / Durch Deine Wunden nun verbunden? / Kan ich durch Deine Quaal und Sterben / Nunmehr das Paradieß ererben? / Ist aller Welt Erlösung nah?"

Jesus's messianic *identity*, however, is articulated by both evangelists, especially at points that come *after* the trial and crucifixion. Owing to Bach's structural emphases, especially as manifested in the *turba* choruses, the trial seems in both Passions to extend beyond its literal boundaries, proclaiming Jesus's identity in ironic terms. In the *St. Matthew Passion* the two paired choruses, "Der du den Tempel Gottes zerbrichst" and "Andern hat er geholfen"—the last in what Smend viewed as a sequence of ten symbolizing the law—mock Jesus on the cross, culminating with terrible finality in a cadence in which all parts of both choruses move into parallel octaves to proclaim the reason for the crucifixion: ["Denn er hat gesagt:] Ich bin Gottes Sohn." This point, like "In meines Herzens Grunde" in the *St. John Passion*, describes a caesura in the work, after which the shift of key and the tone of the meditative movements that follow mark a new beginning associated symbolically with Golgotha. In both Passions the shift of location to Golgotha has enormous symbolic significance in terms of the "way of the cross." In the *St. John Passion* it directly follows the trial with return to the initial key of the Passion, in the dialog "Eilt, ihr angefochtenen Seelen," setting up the return to flat keys that culminates in "In meines Herzens Grunde."[18] In the *St. Matthew Passion* the caesura of "Ich bin Gottes Sohn" is followed by a complete shift of key area for the arioso "Ach Golgotha," whereas the *progression* to Golgotha itself is lifted out of its literal context (which occurred earlier on) and made into the introductory chorus of the Passion, with very close affinity to "Eilt, ihr angefochtenen Seelen." In both Passions the way of the cross receives highly emblematic treatment. Its dramatic presentation in the *St. John Passion* comes directly after the trial, marking simultaneously a new beginning and a new perspective on the outcome of the trial, now associated with John's ironic proclamation of Jesus's messianic identity. In the scene that follows "Ach Golgotha" in the *St. Matthew Passion*, the corresponding proclamation comes with the chorus of onlookers, in response to the outbreaks of nature on Jesus's death, "Wahrlich dieser ist Gottes Sohn gewesen" (Truly this man was the Son of God).

In the *St. John Passion* the theme of Jesus's identity is prominent right from the opening scene, his divinity proclaimed in "Herr, unser Herrscher" and in the subsequent dialog and choruses sung to the name "Jesus of Nazareth." There is a distinct echo of the meaning behind the celebrated prolog to John's Gospel in these events. And this scene connects up directly with the much later one in which the name "Jesus of Nazareth" is placed over the cross in multiple languages, his identity proclaimed to "all lands" as in "Herr, unser Herrscher." As in the *St. Matthew Passion*, Bach plays down the ending of the trial and the judgment of crucifixion,

---

[18] In the *St. Matthew Passion* the shift of locale to Golgotha took place earlier, but in Bach's design the large-scale shift of key comes only later, after the dramatic cadence on "Ich bin Gottes Sohn," which culminates the mocking of Jesus on the cross, giving the reason for his crucifixion. After the E-minor cadence Bach makes a striking modulation to C minor, setting up the flat keys of the arioso "Ach Golgatha" and dialog "Sehet, Jesus hat die Hand uns zu fassen ausgespannt." See Chafe, ch. 14, *Tonal Allegory*.

making it subordinate to the transition to the "scene" that follows. Bach avoids any strong point of articulation for the ending of the trial (that is, there is no meditative response). Instead, he modulates immediately to a new tonal region in which he defines a new beginning musically, that of the scene that follows—the shift of locale to Golgotha—by means of a hortatory dialog aria with chorus, "Eilt, ihr angefocht'nen Seelen." At the same time, the unit culminates soon afterwards with the narratives of the crucifixion and the "royal inscription," drawing the final chorus of the high priests (not a part of the trial in John) into the abovementioned symmetrical sequence, and ending with a chorale meditation on the meaning of the crucifixion and the inscription, "In meines Herzens Grunde dein Nam' und Kreuz allein." This is the culminating point of the third of the traditional five divisions of the Passion narrative. In both settings Bach's musical design seems to respond to the rejection of Jesus's messianic claims, whether as Son of God or king of the Jews, making the point that the crucifixion *itself* and its meaning as projected in the royal inscription form the point of resolution, not the *judgment* of crucifixion. Symbolically, the law as expression of God's wrath gives way to the cross as the route to freedom from the law, the means by which God proclaims Jesus's identity and brings about the redemption of humanity. In the *St. John Passion* the recitative that sets up the shift to sharp keys that culminate in "Durch dein Gefängnis" contains a highly symbolic association of the cross with the power that comes only from above (see ch. 6, ex. 6.2). From this standpoint, we may think of the shift to sharp keys at this point as pointing to the "center" of the whole, a point of convergence for three major themes of the Passion: (1) Jesus's divine (messianic) identity; (2) the cross as the means by which, according to God's *Rath*, that identity is revealed; and (3) the freedom that the Passion brings for the faithful.[19] The interdependency of these ideas is the root of what Johann Jacob Rambach described as the *nexus* and *relatio* of scriptural themes (see ch. 2, 89), whereas the quality of *symmetria* that Rambach associated with architecture and the aesthetic character of such ideas ("pulcherrima symmetria") is the most natural means of translating such correspondences into musical structure.

In light of the many parallels between the two Passions, their differences must be viewed as emphases arising from the Passion accounts, not as fundamental differences within the theology of the time, although they might have been perceived

[19] Martin Petzoldt's interesting study, "Zur theologischen Petrusexistenz in Bachs Johannes-Passion," in *Bachs Johannes Passion: Poetische, musikalische, theologische Konzepte*, ed. Michael Gassmann, 63–88 (Stuttgart: Internationale Bachakademie Stuttgart, 2012), raises the question of why Bach did not associate the center of the Passion with the crucifixion itself (i.e, in his terminology, the *Actus crux*) remarking that for commentators of Bach's time this was considerably less interesting than for us (79). That may be so, but in my view Pilate's reference to the power of crucifixion and Jesus's associating it with God's plan mark this point in the Passion as embodying the *meaning* of the cross: freedom from the law, the background for "Durch dein Gefängnis." The initiation of the move to sharp keys with Pilate's assertion of that power (with a tritone leap upward to g♯ on "kreuzigen" followed by the first sharp cadence in a recitative that begins in D minor) involved a rhetorical association of the "Kreuztonarten" (sharps as "cross" keys) with the center of the spectrum of *ambitus* of the Passion as a whole.

as such by some of Bach's contemporaries. The unique character of the *St. John Passion* is the result of the sheer intensity of its presentation of the Johannine worldview, which is closest of all the evangelists to the *Christus Victor* theory.[20] The *Christus Victor* perspective on the atonement is by no means absent in Bach's cantatas; and although it is sometimes associated particularly with John (as in Cantata 40, *Darzu is erschienen der Sohn Gottes*, for example), it is also prominent in other works, such as the *Christmas Oratorio*. Likewise, the satisfaction theory runs through much of Bach's work, especially certain of the cantatas of the Trinity season. Both theories give great emphasis to the theme of freedom: from God's wrath in the satisfaction theory and from the powers of evil in the *Christus Victor* theory.[21] In the *St. John Passion* Bach introduces the theme in forms that are not specifically identified with either theory, although there is a distinct sense in the pivotal modulation to sharps preceding "Durch dein Gefängnis" that the Jews, on account of having delivered Jesus over for crucifixion in the name of the law, bear the primary guilt. As a result, both kinds of freedom can be read into the Passion, without our necessarily viewing the absence of the satisfaction theory as a decisive and deliberate gesture. Nevertheless, the fact that it *is* absent, taken along with the character of the meditative texts, and the nature of the Passion's structural and symbolic devices, suggests that the specific character of the work might have been in part the product of Bach's own study of the Gospel and not a close expression of the prevailing theological outlook in Leipzig.

This does not in any way contradict the statements of those contemporaries of Bach (such as his pupil Lorenz Mitzler) that emphasize that Bach was a musician first and foremost, and not a man given to learned speculations. I very much doubt that by learned speculations Mitzler meant either theological influences or text-music relationships, especially in light of the manner in which he considers such erudite topics as the complex mathematical ratios of the musical intervals of well-tempered tuning. But even if Mitzler did in fact mean this, the evidence provided by Bach's collection of theological books and his embodying concepts from the Lutheran "metaphysical" tradition of music theory in his canons is clear enough. But this does not single Bach out among his contemporaries. What *does* single him out is the depth of his fusion of theology and music, a quality that could have been perceived then (as now) only in terms of its artistic end result, that is, in primarily musical terms. What we must do to uncover the thought processes that were sec-

[20] Aulén makes this point in *Christus Victor* (74–75): "The dualistic outlook is particularly prominent in the Johannine writings, with their constant antitheses, such as light and darkness, life and death."

[21] Althaus, *Theology of Martin Luther*, 221: "Luther himself has explicitly stated the way in which the two elements of stilling the wrath of God [i.e., the satisfaction theory] and setting men free from the demonic powers are related to each other. Therefore 'the freedom by which we are free from God's wrath forever is indescribable; it is greater than heaven and earth and all creation. From this there follows the other freedom by which we are made safe and free through Christ from the law, from sin, death, and the power of the devil, and hell.'"

ond nature for Bach is something different from the fact that he inhabited a world where such ideas were all around him. In other words, we should not confuse our own scholarly activities with what for Bach was a part of daily life.

Bach's study of John's Passion account probably involved simply the necessary responsible requirements for setting such a text, particularly in such a learned theological environment as Leipzig. In fact, the main sources we have for the free poetry of the *St. John Passion* all have distinct connections to musical settings that might have been known to the composer independently of his librettist.[22] A theological model for the overall textual design, such as Heinrich Müller's Passion sermons provided in the case of the *St. Matthew Passion*, has not yet come to light, nor has any concrete information regarding the input of a librettist. Several scholars have maintained that the design follows the traditional division of the Passion into episodes (or *actus*) corresponding to the five stages of the narrative: Alfred Dürr and Martin Petzoldt present them as (1) the garden (*Hortus:* the events up to Jesus's arrest); (2) the questioning by the high priest (*Pontifices:* up to the end of Bach's Part 1); (3) the events involving Pilate (*Pilatus:* the trial, crucifixion, and placing of the royal inscription); (4) the cross (*Crux:* Jesus's death, the piercing of Jesus's side, and predictions of his legs not being broken); and (5) the burial (*Sepulchrum*).[23] However, while the fivefold division of the Passion was of ancient pedigree and well known in Bach's time, it was by no means the only one. And it is

---

[22] See Mendel, *Kritischer Bericht*, 4:162–72; also Alfred Dürr, *Johann Sebastian Bach's "St. John Passion,"* 41–56, esp. 42–43. The Brockes Passion text that influenced several of Bach's texts is primarily known today in the context of musical settings (those by Keiser, Telemann, Handel, and Mattheson), for which it was written. In Bach's time the printed poem went through several editions, beginning in 1712, with additions to the 1713 edition that were adopted in Bach's *St. John Passion*. See Henning Friedrichs, *Das Verhältnis von Text und Musik in den Brockes-Passionen Keisers, Händels, Telemanns und Matthesons*. Musikwissenschaftliche Schriften, vol. 9 (Munich and Salzburg, 1975). The aria "Ach, mein Sinn" is modeled after a poem by Christian Weise, which as Dürr points out (43) was written specifically to illustrate how to add a text to an instrumental work. And other movements, most notably the chorale "Durch dein Gefängnis," have been traced to Christian Heinrich Postel, who wrote at least three movements that appear in the setting once believed to be a *St. John Passion* by Handel (now thought to be a work of Christian Ritter, composed around 1700). In *Critica Musica: Des fragende Componisten/Erstes Vehör/über ein gewisse Passion*, (Hamburg, 1725), 2:1–29, 33–56, Johann Mattheson published a critique of the anonymous setting, taking his own setting, titled *Das Lied des Lammes*, as a model. "Durch dein Gefängnis" is an aria text, placed by Postel in exactly the same position as it is in Bach's *St. John Passion*, where it is set as a chorale to Johann Hermann Schein's melody for the chorale "Machs mit mir, Herr, nach deiner Güt." In light of the latter occurrence, as well as the pivotal importance of "Durch dein Gefängnis" in Bach's design, it seems reasonable to conclude that Bach had considerable input into the text of the *St. John Passion*.

[23] See Martin Petzoldt, "Theologische Überlegungen zum Passionsbericht des Johannes in Bachs Deutung," in *Johann Sebastian Bach: Johannes-Passion*, BWV 245, Schriftenreihe der Internationalen Bachakademie Stuttgart (Kassel, 1994), 5:142–65; Dürr, *Johann Sebastian Bach's "St. John Passion,"* 51–52; Don Franklin, "The Libretto of Bach's John Passion and the Doctrine of Reconciliation: An Historical Perspective," in *Das Blut Jesu und die Lehre von der Versöhnung im Werk Johann Sebastian Bachs*, ed. A. A. Clement(proceedings of the Royal Netherlands Academy of Arts and Sciences, no. 164, Amsterdam: North-Holland, 1995), 179–203. For the most part, the five-part division of the Passion is indebted to that of Johannes Bugenhagen's *Historia des leidens und Aufferstehung unsere Herrn Jhesu Christi / aus den vier Evangelisten* (Wittenberg, 1530).

much too general in outline to account for Bach's structure, which features internal divisions and correspondences that are highly individual and owing to substantial interaction of musical and theological considerations. Alfred Dürr's statement that "it seems that Bach and his librettists included it [the fivefold division] in their plan inasmuch as each *actus* is brought to an end by a simple chorale movement" is true as far as it goes, that is, it can be thought to account for the placement of five of the Passion's eleven simple chorales. But it is unsatisfactory as an overall explanation of Bach's design, if for no other reason than its failure to differentiate culminating chorales from others that do not fulfill that role.[24] In fact, several of the chorales that culminate musical "units" in the Passion(i.e., "O große Lieb," and "Ach, großer König") do not coincide at all with the traditional divisions, whereas others (i.e., "Dein Will gescheh" and "Durch dein Gefängnis") complete modulations to new keys but do not culminate units at all.[25] The placement of the chorales has a more complicated functioning, in light of which we can say that Bach interacted with tradition, but modified it substantially for his own purposes. The view of the Passion as divided into five parts has, in my view, the more serious disadvantage of implying that Bach's setting is comprised of discrete units with distinct boundaries, something of the kind we find in a *St. Luke Passion* setting of Telemann, for example, where each of the five cantata-like segments follows exactly the same plan and where the idea of separate units is integral to the conception.[26]

The design of the *St. John Passion*, although it is constructed around discrete key areas (*ambitus*), has little or nothing to do with clear-cut boundaries or cantata-like divisions (except for that between Parts 1 and 2), and although it incorporates traditional elements and divisions in the placement of some chorales, most of its structural design—and hence the organization of the text, including the placement of at least some of the free poetry—was Bach's own, can only, in fact, have been his, owing to its close dependence on factors of musical composition. For this reason, I have incorporated a modern scheme of the Passion narrative, that of Raymond Brown, into my diagrams of the structure of the work (see figs. 4.1 and 4.2).[27] While Brown's "division one" of the Passion is equivalent to the first and second of the traditional five divisions, or *actus* (including their internal dividing points), his "divisions" two (the trial) and three (Jesus's death and burial) do

---

[24] Dürr, *Johann Sebastian Bach's "St. John Passion,"* 51.

[25] Alfred Dürr's view that the chorale "Dein Will gescheh" culminates the first *actus* of the passion (*Hortus*) is certainly incorrect from a musical standpoint (see. n.23). For reasons discussed in ch. 5, it is clear that "Dein Will gescheh" is not a point of culmination but of confirming modulation to a new key, D minor. On the other hand, the equation of the third *actus* (*Pilatus*) with everything from the beginning of Part 2 up to the chorale "In meines Herzens Grunde" means that the obviously culminating character of "Ach großer König" and the tremendous modulatory shift that follows it is completely ignored. In these and several other instances the five-part scheme fails to account for many details of the musical structure.

[26] On Telemann see ch. 2, n. 27.

[27] Raymond Brown, *The Gospel According to John* (XIII–XXI), vol. 29b, Anchor Bible Series, (New York: Doubleday, 1970), 785–86.

not correspond to the remaining three *actus*. Instead, Brown's division three begins with the shift of locale to Golgotha. Its title, "Introduction: The way of the cross and the crucifixion," points up a very important facet of the meaning of the Passion that Bach brings out clearly and unmistakably in his setting. At the point corresponding to the beginning of Brown's "division three," the *St. John Passion* has a substantial shift of key that immediately turns the D-major cadence that marks the judgment of crucifixion, and the ending of the trial proper, into the dominant of G minor (see ex. 6.4 and the accompanying discussion in ch. 6), leading to the hortatory dialog aria with chorus, "Eilt, ihr angefocht'nen Seelen." That movement is similar in concept to the opening movement of the *St. Matthew Passion* (but with differences that are the result of the diverse character of John's narrative). The fact that it returns to the beginning key of the Passion is probably significant, since in a real sense it marks a new beginning, but one that articulates what "Herr, unser Herrscher" had petitioned for from the deity: it urges the faithful, as "Betrachte, meine Seele" and "Erwäge" had, to seek out their salvation in Jesus's sufferings.[28] Although it introduces a segment that eventually culminates in what is the end of the traditional third *actus* (*Pilatus*), if we ignore the fact that a change of locale and the sense of a new beginning appear within the *actus*, we overlook one of the most significant features of Bach's design: that he respects what Brown calls "the way of the cross" in terms of its broad tropological meaning for the Passion as a whole. This is the root of the connection of "Eilt, ihr angefocht'nen Seelen" to the opening chorus of the *St. Matthew Passion*, where the progression to Golgotha is depicted as a symbol for the meaning of the Passion.[29]

Thus Bach's design creates an interaction or overlap between the ending of his "symbolic trial" and the tropological meaning of Golgotha and the cross that was of paramount importance in the Lutheran view of the purpose of the Passion. It is entirely possible that Bach himself developed this aspect of the structure with or without the aid of specific theological study. This is a separate question from that of the indebtedness of individual movement texts to earlier sources and from the likelihood that a librettist was also involved. Bach might well have used both the texts of earlier Passion poems, such as those of Postel and Brockes, as well as Passion sermons of the time in mapping out an overall structural design, and these may have accounted for traditional divisions of the narrative in forming his own conception, without, however, drawing on the kinds of one-to-one correspondences that exist between the *St. Matthew Passion* text and the Müller sermons. And even

---

[28] "Eilt, ihr angefocht'nen Seelen" derives from the Brockes Passion poem cited in n. 17, which does not in any way articulate the fivefold division of the Passion. It appears that in all instances in which Bach's aria or chorus texts were derived from that poem they were drawn into a new, highly individual, structure. In fact, the particular movements derived from Postel and Brockes all seem to have served such a function in the design of the work.

[29] "Eilt, ihr angefocht'nen Seelen" was derived, as was the opening chorus of the *St. Matthew Passion* from a dialog for the "daughter of Zion" (*Tochter Zion*) and the "chorus of believing souls" (*Chor der gläubigen Seelen*) in the Brockes Passion poem.

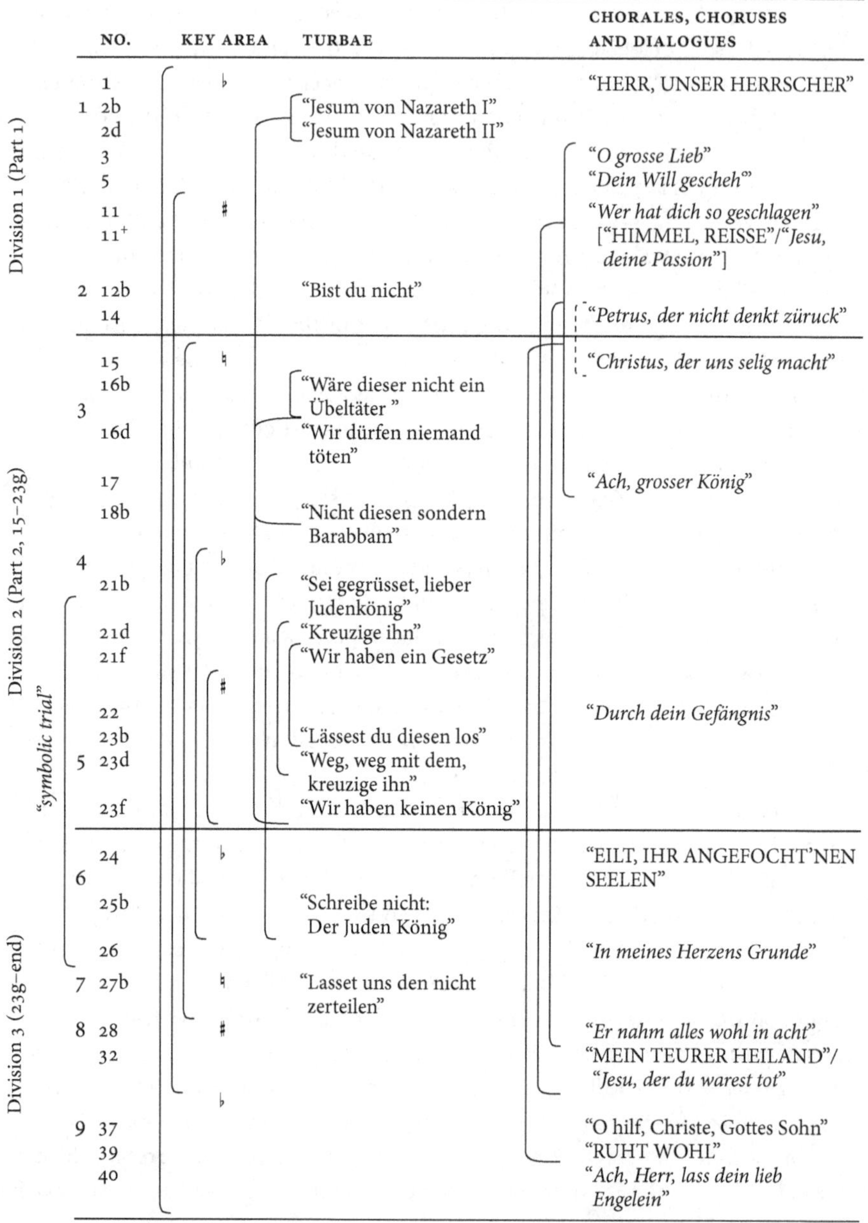

NO.
KEY AREA
TURBAE
CHORALES, CHORUSES AND DIALOGUES
Division 1 (Part 1)
1
1 2b
2d
3
5
11
11+
2 12b
14
"HERR, UNSER HERRSCHER"
"Jesum von Nazareth I"
"Jesum von Nazareth II"
"O grosse Lieb"
"Dein Will gescheh"
"Wer hat dich so geschlagen"
["HIMMEL, REISSE"/"Jesu, deine Passion"]
"Bist du nicht"
"Petrus, der nicht denkt zürück"
Division 2 (Part 2, 15–23g)
"symbolic trial"
15
16b
3
16d
17
18b
4
21b
21d
21f
22
23b
5 23d
23f
"Christus, der uns selig macht"
"Wäre dieser nicht ein Übeltäter"
"Wir dürfen niemand töten"
"Ach, grosser König"
"Nicht diesen sondern Barabbam"
"Sei gegrüsset, lieber Judenkönig"
"Kreuzige ihn"
"Wir haben ein Gesetz"
"Durch dein Gefängnis"
"Lässest du diesen los"
"Weg, weg mit dem, kreuzige ihn"
"Wir haben keinen König"
Division 3 (23g–end)
24
6
25b
26
7 27b
8 28
32
9 37
39
40
"EILT, IHR ANGEFOCHT'NEN SEELEN"
"Schreibe nicht: Der Juden König"
"In meines Herzens Grunde"
"Lasset uns den nicht zerteilen"
"Er nahm alles wohl in acht"
"MEIN TEURER HEILAND"/"Jesu, der du warest tot"
"O hilf, Christe, Gottes Sohn"
"RUHT WOHL"
"Ach, Herr, lass dein lieb Engelein"
N.B.: capital/lower case = biblical texts; italics = chorale texts; capitals = madrigal texts.

FIGURE 4.1 ***St. John Passion*** *"symbolic" plan of movement correspondences and key areas, following Raymond Brown's three-division structure of the Gospel account Recitative and non-dialog arias omitted. The aria with chorale, "Himmel Reisse"/"Jesu, deine Passion," from the 1725 version of the Passion has been included. Capital/lower case = biblical texts; italics = chorale texts; capitals = poetic texts*

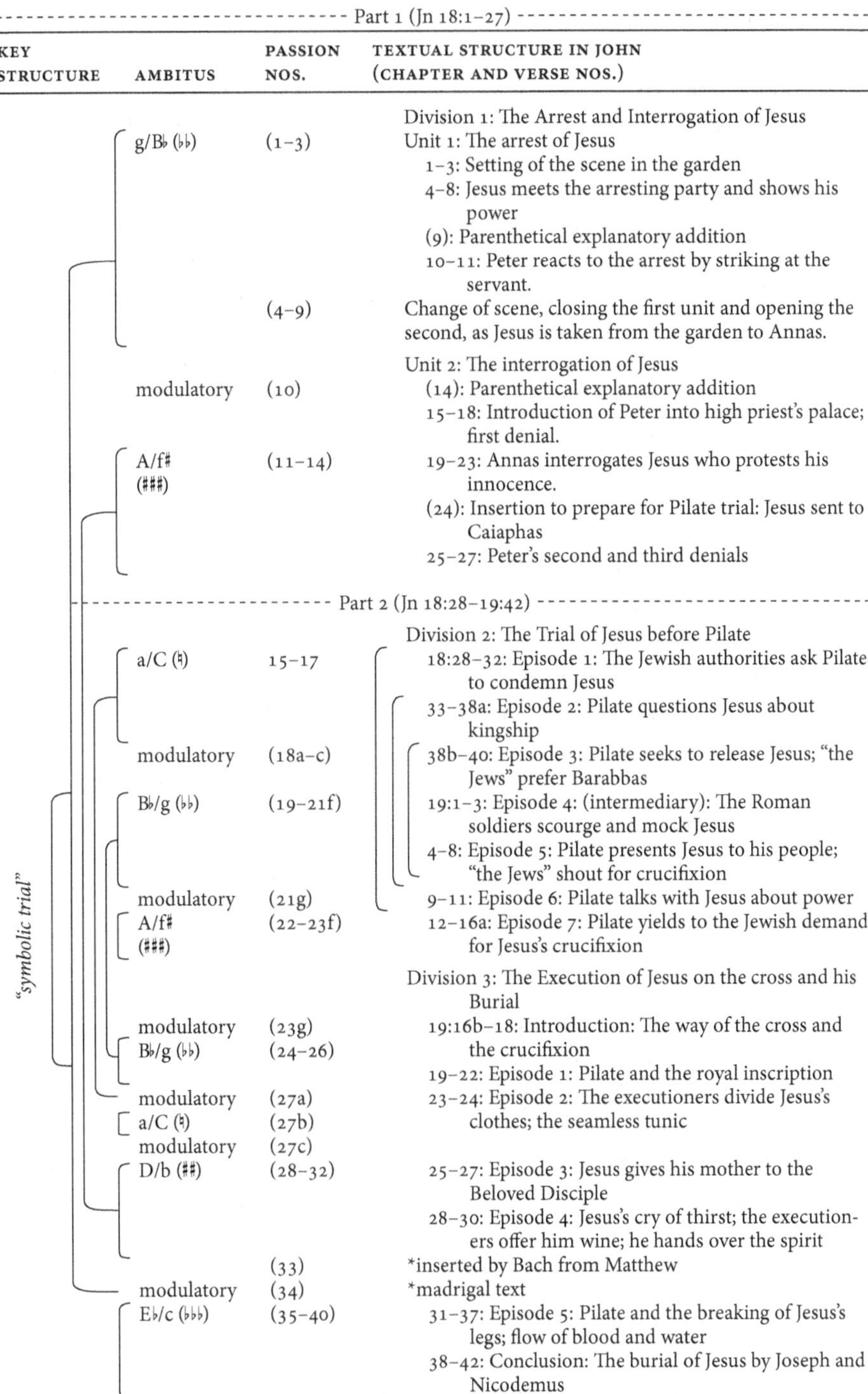

KEY STRUCTURE	AMBITUS	PASSION NOS.	TEXTUAL STRUCTURE IN JOHN (CHAPTER AND VERSE NOS.)
			Part 1 (Jn 18:1–27)
			Division 1: The Arrest and Interrogation of Jesus
	g/B♭ (♭♭)	(1–3)	Unit 1: The arrest of Jesus
			1–3: Setting of the scene in the garden
			4–8: Jesus meets the arresting party and shows his power
			(9): Parenthetical explanatory addition
			10–11: Peter reacts to the arrest by striking at the servant.
		(4–9)	Change of scene, closing the first unit and opening the second, as Jesus is taken from the garden to Annas.
			Unit 2: The interrogation of Jesus
	modulatory	(10)	(14): Parenthetical explanatory addition
			15–18: Introduction of Peter into high priest's palace; first denial.
	A/f♯ (♯♯♯)	(11–14)	19–23: Annas interrogates Jesus who protests his innocence.
			(24): Insertion to prepare for Pilate trial: Jesus sent to Caiaphas
			25–27: Peter's second and third denials
			Part 2 (Jn 18:28–19:42)
			Division 2: The Trial of Jesus before Pilate
"symbolic trial"	a/C (♮)	15–17	18:28–32: Episode 1: The Jewish authorities ask Pilate to condemn Jesus
			33–38a: Episode 2: Pilate questions Jesus about kingship
	modulatory	(18a–c)	38b–40: Episode 3: Pilate seeks to release Jesus; "the Jews" prefer Barabbas
	B♭/g (♭♭)	(19–21f)	19:1–3: Episode 4: (intermediary): The Roman soldiers scourge and mock Jesus
			4–8: Episode 5: Pilate presents Jesus to his people; "the Jews" shout for crucifixion
	modulatory	(21g)	9–11: Episode 6: Pilate talks with Jesus about power
	A/f♯ (♯♯♯)	(22–23f)	12–16a: Episode 7: Pilate yields to the Jewish demand for Jesus's crucifixion
			Division 3: The Execution of Jesus on the cross and his Burial
	modulatory	(23g)	19:16b–18: Introduction: The way of the cross and the crucifixion
	B♭/g (♭♭)	(24–26)	19–22: Episode 1: Pilate and the royal inscription
	modulatory	(27a)	23–24: Episode 2: The executioners divide Jesus's clothes; the seamless tunic
	a/C (♮)	(27b)	
	modulatory	(27c)	
	D/b (♯♯)	(28–32)	25–27: Episode 3: Jesus gives his mother to the Beloved Disciple
			28–30: Episode 4: Jesus's cry of thirst; the executioners offer him wine; he hands over the spirit
		(33)	*inserted by Bach from Matthew
	modulatory	(34)	*madrigal text
	E♭/c (♭♭♭)	(35–40)	31–37: Episode 5: Pilate and the breaking of Jesus's legs; flow of blood and water
			38–42: Conclusion: The burial of Jesus by Joseph and Nicodemus

FIGURE 4.2 ***St. John Passion*** *key structure in relation to Raymond Brown's three-division structure of the Passion narrative*

were such a single source to come to light, we would still have to acknowledge, as we do in the case of the *St. Matthew Passion*, that Bach's musical design goes way beyond its inherited elements. That is, if we do not satisfactorily account for the musical design, then our proclaiming Bach's indebtedness to the traditional five-fold division of the Passion is a hollow exercise.

Although much of the musico-theological uniqueness of the work has been described elsewhere, the main points are outlined here, with a view toward illustrating how Bach, perhaps with the aid of a librettist, might have formed such a striking conception. I draw on a comparison of Bach's text and structural design for the Passion with a theological source that has hitherto not been considered in Bach scholarship: a set of ten public lectures on John's Passion account by August Hermann Francke, who is usually considered the foremost representative of the Lutheran pietist movement in Halle, where he taught at the university. Francke delivered these lectures between Quinquagesima (Estomihi) and Easter 1716, publishing them that year as well as in a second edition in 1719.[30] Since Francke's lectures focus only on John, they afford us with an excellent opportunity to consider how a major theologian responded to the Fourth Gospel during Bach's time. These lectures influenced the well-known *Betrachtungen über das ganze Leiden Christi* (1721–30) of Johann Jacob Rambach, who also taught at the university of Halle, and whose work I also refer to.[31] I will not argue that Bach used Francke's work directly in composing the *St. John Passion*, or even that he read it (although those are distinct possibilities). Rather, I play off the emphases of the one against those of the other with a view to coming closer to understanding the musico-theological design of Bach's setting.

The 1724 first version: Johannine characteristics

The most striking indication of difference between the *St. John Passion* and its successor is evident immediately from the characters of the two opening choruses. Whereas the *St. Matthew Passion* begins with a chorus of lamentation, "Kommt, ihr Töchter, helft mir klagen," that is based on the progression of Jesus and the crowd to Golgotha, presenting Jesus as Matthew's "suffering servant" (derived from Isaiah), the *St. John Passion*'s introductory chorus proclaims Jesus's divine status in no uncertain terms: "Herr, unser Herrscher, dessen Ruhm in allen Landen herrlich ist! Zeig' uns durch deine Passion dass du, der wahre Gottessohn, zu aller Zeit, auch in der grössten Niedrigkeit, verherrlicht worden bist" (Lord, our Master, whose

---

[30] Francke, *Öffentliche Reden*. (see ch. 2, n. 18).

[31] Among Bach's collection of theological books, the only one listed of Francke was a *Haus Postilla*, whose exact identity is not known. A listing also occurs for Rambach's *Betrachtungen;* but since Rambach published several collections titled *Betrachtungen*, it is not known to which source it refers. Rambach published the five parts of his meditations on the Passion in 1730, but the first two parts (corresponding to Part 1 of Bach's *St. John Passion*) were published separately in 1722.

fame is noble in all lands! Show us through your Passion that you, the true son of God, at all times, even in the greatest adversity, are glorified). "Kommt, ihr Töchter" is a dialog between the church and the community of believers—"Zion und die Gläubigen," as Picander headed it in his printed poem—making clear that it is their sins that have brought about the events now being lamented (a theme that is echoed throughout the entire setting). It is derived from the words spoken by Jesus, while carrying the cross to Golgotha, to the "daughters of Jerusalem," who followed him "and bewailed and lamented," (Lk 23:27–28): "Daughters of Jerusalem, weep not for me, but weep for yourselves, and for your children." Traditionally understood as Jesus's final call to penitence—his "letzte Buss-Predigt," as Johann Jacob Rambach put it—its thrust is far more in keeping with Matthew than with John; and, indeed, Rambach links it up with the high priests' "Sein Blut komme über uns und unser Kinder" in Matthew 27:25.[32] In the *St. Matthew Passion* its purpose is to bring out the all-pervading theme of the sin and guilt of humanity in Jesus's death, which is offset by the simultaneous sounding of the chorale "O Lamm Gottes unschuldig" and the hortatory character of the chorus as a whole. In its urging the faithful to come, see, lament, it is a necessary corrective to what Rambach calls the "natural compassion" of the women of Jerusalem, which was rooted in failure to understand God's *Rath.*[33] "Herr, unser Herrscher," on the other hand, projects the other, ultimate, meaning of the Passion, petitioning an all-powerful deity who here is equated to the Jesus of the Passion to "show" the process of his glorification to the faithful. Alluding to one of the most pronounced OT hymns to God's glory, Psalm 8 (whose first and last verses are "Herr, unser Herrscher, wie herrlich ist dein Name in allen Landen"), the chorus places the emphasis on Jesus himself, downplaying the participation of the community of the faithful, their guilt, and the necessity of repentance. Both choruses point ahead to the crucifixion; but whereas Golgotha is symbolic of suffering and horror in the *St. Matthew Passion* ("unsel'ges Golgatha"), witnessing, in Matthew's Gospel, Jesus's final words, "My God, My God, why hast thou forsaken me?" in John it is ultimately the locus

---

[32] Johann Jacob Rambach, *Betrachtungen über das gantze Leiden Christi* (Jena, 1730) 926–27.

[33] Ibid., 926–27:

> Allein, warum verbietet denn der Heyland diesen Weibern, daß sie nicht über ihn weinen sollen? Es geschiehet solches 1) darum, weil er einen wichtigen Fehler an ihren Thränen erblickte. Nemlich diese Töchter Jerusalems sahen nur auf die äusserliche Schmach, Wunden und Schmertzen des HErren JEsu, und wurden dadurch zu einem natürlichen Mitleiden bewegt; aber sie gedachten nicht an den darunter verborgenen Rath Gottes, und an die wahre Ursach aller dieser Leiden. Sie erkanten nicht, daß die Sünde der Welt, folglich auch ihre eigene Sünden, diesem Lamm Gottes auf dem gebeugten Rücken lagen, und daß er dieselbe hinaus an die Schädelstätt schleppen, sie an seinem Leibe auf das Creutz hinauf tragen, und sie daselbst öffentlich abthun und versohnen solle.

In the phrase "die wahre Ursach aller dieser Leiden" Rambach may be alluding to the verse of Johann Heermann's "Herzliebster Jesu" ("Was ist die Ursach aller solchen Plagen") that appears in the *St. Matthew Passion* in dialog with tenor solo in the arioso "O Schmerz," where it gives voice to the response of the faithful to Jesus's sufferings in Gethsemane.

of Jesus's triumph, given forth in his last words in that Gospel, "Es ist vollbracht (It is accomplished), a cry of victory, of the deity's completed voluntary work, not of human forsakenness.

There is, in fact, a connection between "Herr, unser Herrscher" and "Es ist vollbracht" that arises from parallels in John that define his outlook on the Passion and were well known in the Passion literature of Bach's time. Near the beginning of John's narrative, as the arresting party comes in search of Jesus, John 18:4 informs us that "since Jesus knew everything that would happen to him, he went forth and said to them: 'Whom do you seek?'" (Als nun Jesus wusste Alles, was ihm begegnen sollte, ging er hinaus, und sprach zu ihnen: Wen suchet ihr?). Much later in the Passion, John 19:28 refers again to Jesus's foreknowledge and voluntary undergoing of the Passion: "Thereupon, since Jesus knew that everything was already accomplished, that the scriptures had been fulfilled, he said 'I thirst'" (Darnach, als Jesus wusste, dass schon alles vollbracht war, dass die Schrift erfüllet würde, spricht er: Mich dürstet!). And after that narrative, John recounts that "After Jesus had drunk the vinegar, he said 'It is accomplished!' And bowed his head and departed" (Da nun Jesus den Essig genommen hatte, sprach er: Es ist vollbracht! Und neigte das Haupt und verschied). The two passages make clear Jesus's foreknowledge of the events of the Passion and his carrying them out voluntarily through the completion of the plan they represented: God's *Rath*.[34] Between these two passages Bach, like many others before and since, perceived a relationship that, as we will see, is instrumental in defining the meaning of the Passion narrative in John.

To understand the nature of that relationship we must ask a basic question that is seldom, if ever, raised about "Herr, unser Herrscher," namely, given its theme of the majesty and glorification of the deity, why it is in minor, exhibiting many of the traits of the lamenting style of the time. And the immediate answer—that it introduces a Passion setting—is not satisfactory without further consideration. First of

---

[34] August Hermann Francke (*Öffentliche Reden*, 142) connects up these two passages, making clear their use (*Nutz*) for the faithful: "sintemal uns eben hiedurch seine Herrlichkeit mitten in seinem Leiden und in seiner grössesten Erniedrigung, samt seiner unaussprechlichen Liebe zu uns, durch welche er alles Leiden williglich übermonnen, offenbar wird." In his commentary on the seven last words, cited in ch. 2, n. 31, Johann Jacob Rambach names God's "ewigen Rathschluß" as the first of a sequence of seven meanings for what was fulfilled by Jesus: "so war 1) vollbracht, **was GOTT in seinem weisen Rathschluß von der Erwerbung unsers Heyls beschlossen hatte,** . . . Denn das war bisher die Speise des Sohnes Gottes gewesen, diesen Willen seines Vaters zu thun, und sein Werck zu vollenden, wie er selbst Joh. 4, 34. von sich bezeuget. In dieser Vollbringung des Willens Gottes war er nun bis auf die unterste Stufe herabgestiegen, und gehorsam worden bis zum Tode, ja zum Tode am Creutz, nach Philip. 2, 8" (see Rambach, *Betrachtungen über die sieben letzten Worte*, 146–52). The remaining six meanings—fulfillment of prophesy concerning the Messiah, fulfillment of the demands of the law, fulfillment of everything concerning the reconciliation of humanity with God, fulfillment of what was necessary for the restoration of the image of God in the souls of humankind, fulfillment of the destruction of the kingdom of Satan, and fulfillment of what God in his justice had decided that the enemies of Jesus Christ impose upon the life of this holiest of persons—all flow from the first one; and Rambach concludes "Sie hatten nun alles vollendet, was nach dem vorbedachten Rath und Willen GOttes geschehen solte, und es war nun nichts mehr übrig, als daß der Sohn sein Haupt neigen, und seine Seele in die Hände seines himmlischen Vaters empfehlen solte" (ibid.).

all, the principal section of its ABA design is devoted entirely to addressing God in his majesty; and even the contrasting expressions of the middle section, referring to the Passion and to Jesus's *Niedrigkeit*, are subsumed under the larger theme of the glorification *at all times* of the "true Son of God." The Passion itself is defined as the vehicle of making that glorification manifest to the faithful. We do not expect that Bach will set such a text in a style comparable to the first movement of the *Ascension Oratorio*, for example, where the liturgical occasion itself demanded a festive, celebratory setting. But that the chorus projects a sense of opposition between the prominence of musical elements associated with lamentation and the divine glory projected in its text is not something that can be overlooked. And that opposition is a core part of the work's Johannine meaning, especially as it was understood in the Lutheran tradition. The key idea is that of the *theologia crucis*—theology of the cross—-according to which Jesus's glorification in *Niedrigkeit* represents the means by which, according to God's plan of redemption, Jesus's divinity was to be revealed. In this light "Herr, unser Herrscher" projects an opposition that will hold for the Passion as a whole, that will be manifested in the double meaning behind the "Jesus of Nazareth" choruses, the royal inscription, and much of the text in general. And the fulfillment referred to in "Es ist vollbracht" is of just that quality, the "inverted" nature of God's means of revealing Jesus's divinity.

After Jesus's trial, Bach leads by stages to "Es ist vollbracht." As introduction to the segment of the Passion that deals with Jesus's crucifixion, death, and burial (named "Division Three" by Raymond Brown, but beginning within the third of the five traditional *actus*), Bach places the hortatory dialog with chorus, "Eilt, ihr angefocht'nen Seelen," which bears distinct resemblances to "Kommt, ihr Töchter," especially in its identifying Golgotha as focal point for what might be called the tropological meaning of the Passion. In dialog with reiterated cries of "Wohin? Wohin?" (Where? Where?) from the chorus, all depicted with dramatic leaps upward, the solo bass urges the faithful to "go forth from your caves of martyrdom, take on the wings of faith, fly to the hill of the cross, your pilgrimage blooms there" ("geht aus euren Martyrhöhlen, nehmet an des Glaubens Flügel, flieht zum Kreuzes Hügel, eure Wolhfahrt blüht allda"). With sweeping upward scales in the violins, Bach depicts the dramatic motion of the pilgrimage to the "Kreuzes Hügel" as one of faith for the believer.

With such a dramatic dialog movement, suggestive of a new beginning, and one that completes a large-scale tonal shift within the work, marking a return to the key of "Herr, unser Herrscher," Bach articulates not only the shift of locale to Golgotha but also the very meaning of the Passion. Again, in the Lutheran tradition the Passion was vastly more than a dramatic story. A favorite expression in Luther's writings on the Passion and those of his successors up to Bach's time and beyond was *Nutz*, referring to the "use" or "purpose" of the Passion, which was always, of course, centered on the redemption of humanity and therefore embodied the concerns of the faithful living in the world at the present moment. After the adverse judgment of the trial, "Eilt, ihr angefocht'nen Seelen" points onward to its primary meaning, especially for Lutherans: that of the cross not only as the fulfillment of Jesus's work on earth but also as the key to Christian life. Is there a Lutheran theological work of the time that does not make that point over and again? That Bach based the opening movement of the *St. Matthew Passion* on the progression to Golgotha attests to that fact. It may even have been considered a justification for the otherwise inappropriate insertion of "Himmel reiße, Welt erbebe" (which follows the chorale "Wer hat dich so geschlagen" in the 1725 version) in Part 1 of the *St. John Passion.* Golgotha, as Walter Benjamin stated, is the place where allegorical reversal takes place; that is, where the salvific viewpoint that runs throughout the Passion comes to a head, the place where, as Bach's text tells us, the "pilgrimage" of the faithful blooms forth.[35] It is the perfect symbol for the meaning of the Passion.

For Johann Jacob Rambach, Golgotha was, likewise, a locale signifying reversal, an "impure" place of death, where Jesus took on the curse of human sin outside the city of Jerusalem in order to lead humanity to the heavenly Jerusalem. It was, therefore, one of the "high" places ordained by God for great events, such as the story of Isaac, the granting of the law, the deaths of Moses and Aaron; and, above all, it was a sublime place, fulfilling Jesus's predictions in John (3:14; 8:28; 12:32–33) regarding his "lifting up."[36] In Bach's design the upward motion depicted in "Eilt, ihr angefocht'nen Seelen" is finally brought to fulfillment with Jesus's death, meditated upon in "Es ist vollbracht" and "Mein teurer Heiland"/"Jesu, der du warest tot." Jesus's final words are the springboard to the Passion's most overt expression of victory, the middle section of the aria "Es ist vollbracht." In that aria, after responding to the tormented concerns of the faithful in "Eilt, ihr angefocht'nen Seelen," in the text of its opening segment ("O Trost für die gekränkten Seelen"/"O comfort for the diseased souls"), Bach sets the strings in highly dramatic trumpet-like rising fanfares for "Der Held aus Juda siegt mit Macht, und schliesst den Kampf" (The hero from Judea conquers with might, and ends the battle). Thus, the petition of the middle section of "Herr, unser Herrscher" for Jesus to show through the Passion his divinity and glorification at all times, even at the point of greatest humiliation ("Zeig' uns durch deine Passion, dass du, der wahre Gottessohn, zu aller Zeit, auch in der grössten Niedrigkeit, verherrlicht worden bist") is answered in "Es ist vollbracht." And, following almost immediately after "Es ist vollbracht," the dialog aria with chorale, "Mein teurer Heiland"/"Jesu, der du warest tot," responds to the believer's deepest concerns, effecting the all-important shift from Jesus's work to its benefit for the faithful.

These are among the most telling moments in the Passion for the theme of Jesus's *Herrlichkeit* (majesty, glory); but there are others, especially in John's narrative, which depicts Jesus at many points as undertaking the Passion willingly, with

---

[35] Walter Benjamin, *The Origin of German Tragic Drama*, trans. John Osborne (London: New Left Books, 1977), 232.

[36] Rambach, *Betrachtungen über das gantze Leiden Christi*, 5, 946–48.

complete foreknowledge, and with the power to overcome his persecutors should he so choose. Jesus's dialogs with Pilate in the trial scene center on his claim to kingship, which emerges as the truth (although expressed ironically) in the royal inscription, "Jesus of Nazareth, King of the Jews." It is already proclaimed by the community of believers in the first scene of the trial in the chorale "Ach grosser König, gross zu aller Zeiten," echoing the "zu aller Zeit" of the opening chorus (as the multiple languages of the "royal" inscription echo "in allen Landen"). Likewise, the final chorale of the Passion, "Ach Herr, lass dein lieb' Engelein," in E♭ major, takes the last verse of a chorale associated in Bach's cantatas with the feast of St. Michael, the defeat of Satan and his followers by God's angels. The verse selected by Bach anticipates seeing and praising Jesus in eternity. The contrast with the ending of the *St. Matthew Passion*—in C minor, with a dissonance that resolves on the final chord itself, and no chorale—could hardly be greater. Whereas the *St. Matthew Passion* does not incorporate the perspective of Easter and the resurrection overtly into its frame of reference, the *St. John Passion* does, although only momentarily, as is evident from parallels to the Easter Oratorio of 1725 (see ch. 9).

The prologue to John's Gospel describes Jesus in "cosmic" terms as the Word that was with God at the creation and that was God. This opposition of worlds above and below, light and darkness is of great importance for our understanding, not only of the presentation of Jesus by the evangelist but also of the allegorical aspect of Bach's musical structure. "Herr, unser Herrscher," despite its minor key (g) and conspicuous signs of the lamenting style of the eighteenth century, does not project a predominant effect of lamentation, but rather one of awe, in such devices as the off-the-beat cries of "Herr, Herr" from the chorus and the rising choral lines for "unser Herrscher." The minor key is the framework of the world, into which, in Johannine terms, the light came and was rejected (the *Niedrigkeit* of the middle section). The descending minor triad that accompanies the threefold "Herr, Herr, Herr" from the chorus, and the immediately following rising sequences for "unser Herrscher," outline the "shape" of the work of redemption. Likewise, "Es ist vollbracht" dramatizes the opposition between "the world" and the life of faith, or, in John's terms, of worlds "below" and "above," darkness and light, an opposition that centers on the encounter between Jesus and all around him. That opposition usually involves, as here, a split between the literal and spiritual senses of scripture. In the Gospel recitative Bach sets Jesus's dying words, "Es ist vollbracht," in minor and in a manner suggestive of death, as a downward scalar motion to the cadential tone (see ex. 4.1) Suppressed for the moment is the fact that John's Greek, *tetelestai*, is a cry of triumph, of accomplishment.[37] And, in the aria that follows, "Mein theurer Heiland," Bach sets the outermost segments in B minor, introducing a solo viola da gamba, whose restrained, somewhat archaic sound affirms the elegaic character

[37] Johann Jacob Rambach, in his commentary on the seven last words (see n. 34, this chapter), cites this word numerous times, usually in John's Greek (τετέλεϛαι), emphasizing the force and simplicity of the single word as symbol of the multiple levels of completion or fulfillment embodied in Jesus's work.

EXAMPLE 4.1 ***St. John Passion*** *no. 29, recitative, ending*

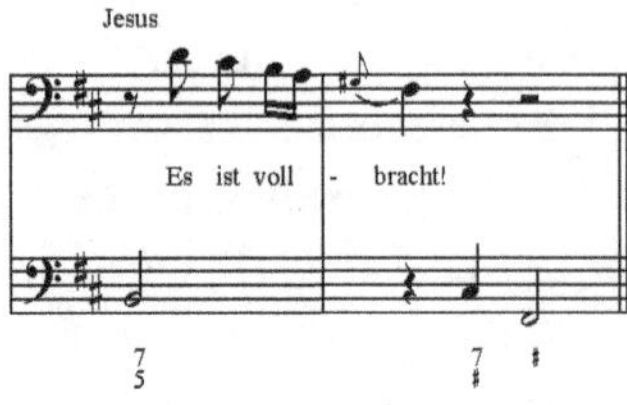

of its melodic head motive, a variant of the ending of the recitative (see ex. 4.2).

The message is not pessimistic, though, but of "comfort for the tormented souls," that is, for the faithful who remain in the world "below": "Es ist vollbracht, o Trost für die gekränkten Seelen." Through faith the believer perceives the counting off of the "last hour" of the "night of sorrow": "die Trauernacht lässt nun die letzte Stunde zählen." These words, which are often taken to refer to the believer's thinking ahead to his own death, allude literally to the three hours of darkness that came over the land before Jesus's death, which are not told by John. John, likewise, does not narrate the rending of the veil of the Temple and

EXAMPLE 4.2 ***St. John Passion*** *no. 30, aria "Es ist vollbracht," beginning*

EXAMPLE 4.3 ***St. John Passion*** *no. 30, aria "Es ist vollbracht," mm. 17–44 and following recitative*

EXAMPLE 4.3 (*continued*)

EXAMPLE 4.3 (*continued*)

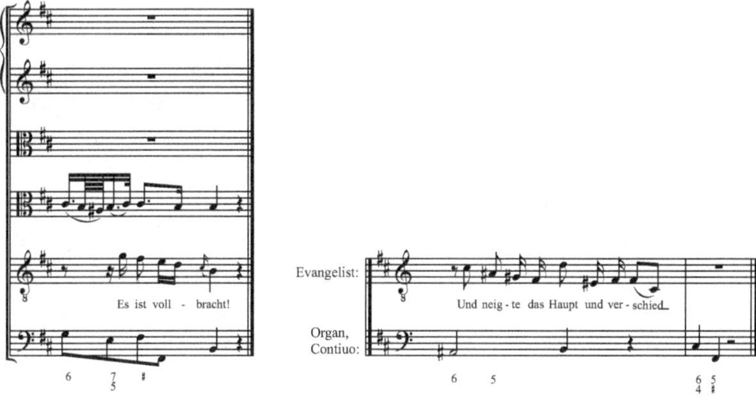

the miraculous outbreaks of nature that took place at Jesus's death. In the 1724 *St. John Passion*, however, they were added to his account in the recitative from Matthew (or Mark) that follows "Es ist vollbracht" and "Mein teurer Heiland." And after that, the arioso "Mein Herz" links the darkness and the other events together, introducing the imagery of the sun veiling itself in sorrow at Jesus's death (see ch. 7). In "Es ist vollbracht" the "Trauernacht" whose last hour can now be counted off, embodies the multiple senses according to which Jesus's last words in John were interpreted. Foremost among them was, for many authors, the sense that Jesus's victory ended the darkness of humanity's long enslavement to sin, death and the law: that it was the central event in the fulfillment of scripture as the record of God's *Rath*, his plan for the salvation of humanity. A chorale devoted to the words "Es ist vollbracht" proclaims this aspect of Jesus's words, "Es ist vollbracht am creutze dort gesetz und der Propheten wort, . . ; was GOttes rath von ewigkeit bedacht, das ist durch seinen tod vollbracht."[38] Bach's setting seems to depict the numbering, or counting of the "last night of sorrow," in terms of the regularity of the slow dotted rhythm that pervades the gamba line (see exx. 4.2 and 4.3) Then, with the change of tone for "Der Held aus Juda siegt mit Macht," the entire metric character of the music is suddenly altered, from the slow, minor-key character of the *Trauernacht* to a rapid major-key *alla breve*, an eruption of what Monteverdi called the *stile concitato*, or excited style. Bach initiates it with a well-known fanfare melody, which was often an emblem of divine majesty associated in the seventeenth and eighteenth centuries with trumpet music, and which was cited by Bach in several other works with primarily eschatological associations.[39] Here, with the

[38] Cited as it appears in the *Neues Geist-reiches Gesang-Buch* (Halle, 1713), 91. See pp. 298–9; ch. 2, n. 31.

[39] These associations emerge particularly clearly in Cantata 127, *Herr Jesu Christ, wahr' Mensche und Gott*, movement 4, "Wenn einstens die Posaunen schallen," in which Bach depicts the last judg-

utmost dramatic contrast, the night of sorrow gives way to the light of Jesus's victory, an anticipation of the resurrection, but even more importantly, an expression of the triumph of the crucifixion itself.

Although not presented elsewhere with such dramatic force as in "Es ist vollbracht," antithesis of various kinds runs throughout the entire *St. John Passion* text, which iterates and reiterates the dichotomy between Jesus's work, his sufferings, trial, and death, culminating in the crucifixion and the benefit of this work for humanity. It is rooted, of course, in the antitheses within the Gospel itself, for which John is well known, but it permeates the nonbiblical texts as well. In Part 1, it progresses from the opposition of Jesus's glorification and the "grössten Niedrigkeit" of his death ("Herr, unser Herrscher") through that between Jesus's "Marter Strasse" and the believer's "Lust und Freude" in the world (the final line of the chorale "O grosse Lieb'") to its most significant form for the contemporary believer, in the aria "Von den Stricken." "Von den Stricken" sets in opposition Jesus's bonds and the believer's freedom from bondage, making the point that Jesus's Passion was undergone for the benefit of a sinful humanity. This is the central meaning of the Passion, appearing again at the center of the trial in the chorale "Durch dein Gefängnis," which describes Jesus's imprisonment as the source of the believer's release from sin, his prison as the "throne of grace," and in the believer's question regarding freedom in "Mein teurer Heiland."

There are thus three types of antithesis: (1) between Jesus's divine nature and his human suffering; (2) between Jesus's suffering and human guilt; and (3) between Jesus's suffering and its benefit for humanity. The particular one chosen for any given circumstance depends on the nature of the narrative; but as the Passion proceeds, the third type becomes the most prominent.The aria "Ich folge dir gleichfalls," which follows "Von den Stricken" after the briefest of recitatives, contains no antithesis. After that, however, virtually all the meditative movements of the Passion center on antithesis. The chorale "Wer hat dich so geschlagen" juxtaposes Jesus's innocent suffering and the sin and guilt of humanity, prompting the response of acknowledgment of sin, both in its second verse and in the aria "Ach, mein Sinn." The chorales that end Part 1 and begin Part 2, respectively, juxtapose Peter's denial (in A major) and Jesus's sufferings (in E Phrygian, sounding like A minor). The chorale in Part 2, "Ach, grosser König," sets Jesus's greatness and love for humanity up against the incapacity of human understanding to fathom it. The arioso "Betrachte, meine Seele" introduces the double image of the crown of thorns and the primrose (*Himmelsschlüsselblume*, literally "flower that is the key to heaven," and a symbol of redemption) that blooms from it. The aria "Erwäge" interprets the blood and water on Jesus's back as the rainbow of the covenant with Noah after the flood, now renewed in Jesus. The aria dialog with chorus, "Eilt, ihr

---

ment, and in Cantata 70, *Wachet! betet!*, movement 1, which urges the faithful to watch and pray in expectation of the last judgment.

angefocht'nen Seelen" reinterprets Golgotha as the fulfillment of the believer's pilgrimage, and the chorale "In meines Herzens Grunde" interprets Jesus's bleeding to death as providing *Trost* and joy for the believer. After "Es ist vollbracht," the aria dialog with chorale, "Mein teurer Heiland," interprets Jesus's bowing his head in death as an affirmative response to the believer's questions regarding his salvation. The aria "Zerfließe" interprets the believer's tears as honoring Jesus. And the burial chorus, "Ruht wohl, ihr heiligen Gebeine," describes the grave that encloses Jesus as the opening up of heaven for the believer.

This aspect of Bach's *St. John Passion* text, centered on opposition, is its most characteristic and remarkable quality. In the *St. John Passion* the theme of penitence, which pervades the *St. Matthew Passion*, is present but enormously played down in order to emphasize that the work of redemption is Jesus's alone, flowing from John's interpretation of the cross as Jesus's triumphant "lifting up." Significantly, its point of articulation in the *St. John Passion* is in the closing scene of Part 1, where, in order to complete the message of Peter's denial and repentance, Bach's text borrows from Matthew for the latter. John contains no narrative of Peter's repentance, only of his denial. But Bach's treatment of Peter's repentance has the character of ending Part 1 with the positive outcome of repentance, as manifested in the turn from f♯ to A in the final chorale. In addition, Bach makes clear in his modulatory design that it is Jesus who brings about this outcome. In the *St. John Passion* antitheses of the kinds I have described tend to make the division between God and humankind, worlds above and below, all the greater, to impart to the Passion much of its well-known dramatic character. The structure of the *St. John Passion* is rooted in dramatic contrast, as manifested in its oppositions between the persecuting crowd and the spiritual meaning of the events, especially Jesus's trial. Analogous to the spiritual interpretation of scripture, we are asked to understand all such details in terms of meaning that goes beyond the immediate affect, a quality that Bach introduces by means of musical correspondences that articulate a "higher level" design rooted in symmetry.[40]

"Herr, unser Herrscher" and Johann Arndt on Psalm 8

Undoubtedly, the greatest manifestation of the idea of opposition in the *St. John Passion* is that given right from the outset in the opening chorus, where it is cast in terms of Jesus's *Herrlichkeit*, his *Niedrigkeit,* and his glorification, one of the most common juxtapositions in seventeenth- and eighteenth-century Passion commentaries. Psalm 8 was surely cited in "Herr, unser Herrscher" because of its association with this threefold descent/ascent dynamic. Johann Arndt provides us with the underlying meaning: here Arndt divides his commentary on Psalm 8 into three

---

[40] See ch. 8 for more on this subject.

sermons, announcing in his introduction that they reflect the threefold division of the psalm. The following comparison with the text of the first chorus makes this clear:

Arndt: commentary on Psalm 8[41]	"Herr, unser Herrscher"
1. The description of his kingdom of grace in the first three verses	Herr, unser Herrscher, dessen Ruhm in allen Landen herrlich ist,
2. By what means is this kingdom established? Through the deep humiliation of the son of God on the cross, through his suffering and death	Zeig' uns durch deine Passion, daß du, der wahre Gottessohn, zu aller Zeiten, auch in der größten Niedrigkeit,
3. Through the raising up of Christ, and the rule in heaven and on earth given to him, so that he is our only head, and has everything under his feet.	Verherrlicht worden bist.

Arndt's first division is then subdivided into three parts, whose headings emphasize first Jesus's *name* as equivalent to the spread of his kingdom throughout the world. Arndt's heading for the psalm as a whole is "Christi Name / das ist / Person / Ampt unnd Wolthaten sollen in aller Welt offenbahr werden" (Christ's name, that is, [his] person, office and good deeds shall be proclaimed in all the world). Arndt continues:

> For, speaks the Lord, my name shall be glorious among the Gentiles. Now just as this saying is a beautiful clear prophesy of the kingdom of our Lord Jesus Christ, which shall be spread throughout the whole world, so that the knowledge of God and of the glorious good deeds of Christ will be praised, which the prophet here calls God's name, . . . so also this psalm is a beautiful outstanding prophesy of the kingdom of the true Messiah, Christ Jesus our Lord, and how the same shall be spread through the gospel.[42]

[41] Arndt, *Auslegung des gantzen Psalters Davids*, fol. 43r.: "I: Die Beschreibung seines Gnadenreichs in den ersten dreyen Verslein. II: Wodurch dieses Reich gestifftet? durch die tieffe Erniedrigung des Sohnes Gottes am Creutz / durch sein Leiden und Sterben. III. "Durch die Erhöhung Christi / und ubergebene Herrschafft im Himmel und auff Erden / daß er unser einiges Heupt sey / und alles unter seinen Füßen habe."

[42] Arndt, *Auslegung des gantzen Psalters Davids*, fol. 42v.–43r.: "Denn mein Name soll herrlich werden unter den Heyden / spricht der Herr. Gleich wie nun dieser Spruch eine schöne klare Weissagung ist vom Reich unsers Herrn Jesu Christi / welches in der gantzen Welt solle ausgebreitet werden / darin Gottes Erkentnüß und die herrlichen Wolthaten Christi gepreiset werden wollen / welches der Prophet allhie Gottes Namen nennet / . . . Also ist auch dieser Psalm eine schöne vortreffliche Weissagung von dem Reich des wahren Messiae CHRISTI JEsu unsers Herrn / wie dasselbige durchs Evangelium soll ausgebreitet werden."

And Arndt's headings for the three subdivisions of his first sermon reflect this closely:[43]

I. Wie Christus unser Herr und Herrscher sey? und von seinem wunderbarlichen und herrlichen Namen im Himmel und Erden. (How is Christ our Lord and Master? And of his wondrous and glorious name in heaven and earth)
II. Die ander Eigenschafft des Reichs Christi / wie Christi wunderbarlicher und herrlicher Name geoffenbaret werde / und wie in Gottes Lob der Sieg stehe uber unsere Feinde. (The second characteristic of the kingdom of Christ, how Christ's wondrous and glorious name is revealed, and how in praise of God the victory over our enemies consists)
III. Der natürliche Himmel ist ein schön Bilde des geistlichen Himmels / der heiligen Christlichen Kirchen. (The natural heaven is a beautiful image of the spiritual heaven, the holy Christian church)

As mentioned earlier, Christ's *Name* and *Ruhm* are equivalent. In the opening scene of Bach's *St. John Passion*, therefore, the arresting party's demand for Jesus of Nazareth is pregnant with implications for the later point in the Passion when that name will be proclaimed to the world in the royal inscription, the point where Jesus's *Erniedrigung* (humility) and his glorification, or in Johannine terms, his "lifting up," converge.

In his second sermon on Psalm 8 Arndt takes up the meaning of Jesus's *Erniedrigung*, which in Arndt's view, is the subject of verse 4, "What is man that thou art mindful of him? and the son of man, that thou visitest him?" (KJV). This second sermon begins by posing the question of what moved God to give his son for humanity, that God, through his "wunderliche Vorsehung und göttlichen Rath" (miraculous foreseeing and divine will) led humanity through so much "Creutz und Elend" (cross and misery), then sustained him, not condemning him but leading him through chastisement to blessedness. This leads Arndt to divide his sermon into two parts: (1) "Wohin die gantze Schrifft gerichtet sey: Nemlich auff zwey Stück / unser Elend / und Gottes Gnade" (What the entire scriptures are directed toward: namely two things, our misery and God's grace); and (2) "Von der Ernidrigung Christi" (On the humiliation of Christ). Regarding the first part, Arndt concludes,

> Now this is the proper foundation of our conversion, yes the goal of the entire holy scripture, that we be led away from our strengths and capacities, our worthiness and merit, to recognition of our misery and nothingness, and then further brought to recognition of grace; toward these two things must the office of the preacher be directed. Humanity can not recognize the

[43] Ibid., fol. 43r., 43v., 44r.

> grace of God, nor properly take it to heart, unless it recognizes its nothingness beforehand, and in itself is made into nothing. It is, however, difficult for a person to bring himself to that, so that he learns to hold himself as nothing, and to accept the proper fundamental humility. For it is born and bred into humanity to be always noble and proud, and the evil, poison root of original sin bears daily evil fruits, so that it is difficult to check; yes, that is itself the kingdom of Satan in humanity, which is difficult to destroy; it must, however, be destroyed through the word of God, through God's Spirit and power. These are the weapons of our spiritual knighthood, of which St. Paul says (1 Cor 10), they are powerful for God to destroy the fortress and all the heights that rise up against the recognition of God. Therefore we must daily have God's word before our eyes, which holds up our misery to us.[44]

And on the second theme of his sermon, Arndt makes clear that it was Jesus's "tieffe Erniedrigung" that earned God's grace for humanity. Therefore, although we must conform to his image and participate as members in the suffering of our "head," we must believe, in the midst of our "cross," that Jesus has earned for us reconciliation with God, freedom from God's wrath, forgiveness of sin, justification in Christ, and eternal blessedness. "For without such a cross we cannot comprehend the power of sins, and the great beneficial deeds of Christ, our Lord; therefore the dear cross is only a lesson and revelation both of our misery and the great good deeds of Christ, and a sign that we belong to Christ, and are his members, to die with him so that we may live with him."[45]

Thus Arndt understands Psalm 8 not only in terms of the descent/ascent character of Jesus's work but also as that of the Lutheran dynamic of faith, acknowledg-

---

[44] Ibid., fol. 45r.:

> Diß ist nu das rechte Fundament unser Bekehrung / ja das Ziel der gantzen heiligen Schrifft / daß wir von unsern Krefften und Vermögen / Wirdigkeit und Verdienst abgeführet werden zur Erkentnüß unsers Elendes unnd Nichtigkeit / unnd denn ferner gebracht werden zur Erkentnüß der Gnaden / auff diese beyde Stücke muß das Predigampt gerichtet seyn. Der Mensch kan die Gnade Gottes nicht erkennen / noch recht zu Hertzen nehmen / wenn er nicht zuvor seine Nichtigkeit erkennet / und in ihm selbst gar zu nichte gemacht wird. Es ist aber sehr schwer einen Menschen dahin zu bringen / daß er sich lerne für nicht halten / und die rechte gründliche Demut annehme. Denn es ist Fleisch und Blut angeboren / immer herrlich und hoch zu seyn / und gebieret die böse gifftige Wurtzel die Erbsünde / teglich böse Früchte / daß ihr schwerlich zu stewren ist / ja dasselbe ist das Reich des Satans im Menschen / welches schwer ist zu zerstören / es muß aber durchs Wort Gottes / durch Gottes Geist und Krafft zustöret werden. Das sind die Waffen unser geistlichen Ritterschafft / davon S. Paulus sagt I. Corinth.10 die sing mechtig für Gott zu berstöhren die Festung und alle Höhe / so sich erhebt wider das Erkentnüß Gottes. Darumb müssen wir Gottes Wort teglich für Augen haben / welches uns unser Elend fürhelt.

[45] Ibid., fol. 45v.–46r.: "denn ohne solch Creutz können wir nicht verstehen die Krafft der Sünden / und die grosse Wolthaten Christi unsers HErrn / darumb ist das liebe Creutz nur eine Unterweisung und Offenbarung beydes unsers Elendes und der grossen Wolthaten Christi / und ein Zeugniß / daß wir Christum angehören / und seine Glieder seyn / mit ihm sterben / auff daß wir mit ihm leben mögen."

ment of sin followed by recognition of God's grace. Like Luther, Arndt sees it as the purpose of the entire scriptures, duplicating the descent/ascent pattern underlying the meaning of law and gospel, Jesus's death and resurrection.[46] From Jesus's name in the first sermon and the cross in the second, Arndt's third sermon now deals with "the raising up, majesty and unending power of Christ," which follow from Jesus's ascension, completing the "Erhöhung" that for Arndt leads humanity as Christ's "members" to the faith that overcomes the world (1 Jn, 5:4–5) and raises them to glory as well:

> The suffering of this time is not equal to the glory that shall be revealed to us, and through the cross and shame we must also in Christ be raised up to this glory. Because now Christ is raised up for our good, we should at all times take comfort in this glory and rejoice, for the raised up and glorious Christ is as much ours as the humiliated, degraded, crucified Christ, . . . This is the faith that overcomes the world; who is he who overcomes the world unless he believes now that Jesus is God's son, this faith is the victory that overcomes the world. Lord our master, how glorious is your name in all lands.[47]

The "Jesus of Nazareth" choruses

In light of Johann Arndt's Christological understanding of Psalm 8, Bach's treatment of Jesus's name in the *St. John Passion* (above all in the "Jesus of Nazareth" choruses and the royal inscription) seems to flow from the opening chorus. It is most likely that the opening verse from Psalm 8 was alluded to in that chorus to foreshadow John's presentation of Jesus as the glorious Messiah who entered a world of darkness and was rejected by humankind. One triggering factor in Bach's design might have been that John is the only one of the four evangelists to specify the full name "Jesus of Nazareth" on the royal inscription. Many commentators brought out the fact that the words "from Nazareth" bore demeaning associations that John brought out in the first chapter of his Gospel; it therefore seemed to point to Jesus's *Niedrigkeit*, whereas both that chapter and the narrative that surrounded the introduction of Jesus's name in the Passion made clear that the name

---

[46] For Luther's view of law and gospel, or destruction and restoration, as the "summary" of scripture see ch. 2, 85–6.

[47] Arndt, *Auslegung*, fol. 47v.:

> Dieser Zeit Leiden ist nicht werth der Herrligkeit / die an uns soll geoffenbaret werden / und durchs Creutz und Schmach müssen wir auch in Christo zu dieser Herrligkeit erhöhet werden. Weil nu Christus uns zu gute erhöhet ist / sollen wir allezeit uns dieser Herrligkeit trösten und frewen / denn der erhöhete und herrliche Christus ist so wol unser als der gedemütigte / erniedrigte / gekreutzigte Christus / . . . Diß ist der Glaube der die Welt uberwindet / wer ist der die Welt uberwindet / ohn der da gleubet / daß Jesus Gottes Sohn ist / dieser Glaube ist der Sieg / der die Welt uberwindet. Herr unser Herrscher / wie herrlich ist dein Name in allen Landen.

"Jesus of Nazareth" identified the Messiah.[48] In this detail many commentators over the centuries have perceived a connection between the inscription and the name "Jesus of Nazareth" as given by the arresting party in the opening scene of the Passion, sometimes linking one or both to the words "Ich bin's" spoken by Jesus in the opening scene as well as the "I am" sayings of God in the Hebrew Bible and Jesus in the NT.[49]

In the Passion the opening scene centers entirely on Jesus's divinity, manifested first in his foreknowledge of the coming events: "Als nun Jesus wußte alles, was ihm begegnen sollte, ging er hinaus und sprach zu ihnen: 'Wen suchet ihr?' (Since Jesus know everything that would happen to him, he went forth and said to them, "Whom do you seek?"). And after the arresting party answers "Jesus of Nazareth," Jesus's response, "Ich bin's," has the extraordinary outcome that the arresting party "drew back and fell to the ground," a detail that was widely understood for centuries as an expression of messianic self-revelation; the soldiers' failure to recognize Jesus, even after the first of his self-identifications, was understood as a form of spiritual (or even literal) blindness, a symbolic encounter of the darkness of the world and the light of divinity.[50] Thus Jesus's "Ich bin's" was sometimes linked up with the proclamation of his name and identity in the royal inscription.[51] Bach,

---

[48] John's "cosmic" prologue to the Gospel identifies Jesus as the divine logos, with God and as God at the creation, as light and life, then turns to John the Baptist's witness, after which John narrates the calling of the first disciples; then in verses 45–46 he narrates that Philip said to Nathanael, "We have found him, of whom Moses in the law, and the prophets, did write, Jesus of Nazareth, the son of Joseph," to which Nathanael replied "Can there any good thing come out of Nazareth?" (KJV). This passage was interpreted traditionally, including by Luther, as indicating the contrast between Jesus's demeaning earthly origins and his divine origins. Rambach cites it also in his *Betrachtungen über das gantze Leiden Christi*, 145. At the same time, the designation "of Nazareth" was frequently linked up with Jacob's words to his son Joseph in Gen 49: 26, via the expression "Nasir unter seinen Brüdern" (sometimes "crown," "prince" or "ruler" among his brothers). The Latin phrase "Nazareum inter fra res" was thus brought into association with Jesus as "der rechte Nasir, oder Nazarener unter seinen Brüdern den Menschen," as Christian Scriver puts it in *Müßige Land-Stunden* (Königsberg, 1698), 888–89). In his extended discussion of the inscription, Scriver explores the typology behind Jesus as "son of Joseph" under the heading *Die Herrlichkeit Christi*. Many other authors set forth similar interpretations.

[49] For a summary of the "I am" sayings in John, see Brown, *Gospel According to John I-XII*, 533–38.

[50] See, for example, Johann Olearius, *Biblische Erklärung*, 5:777.

[51] In his *Betrachtungen über das gantze Leiden Christi* (1000), Johann Jacob Rambach links up one of the best known instances of God's so referring to himself in the OT (Ex 3:14) to the glorification of Jesus's name in the royal inscription and Pilate's "What I have written I have written" (see ch. 6, n. 37). Likewise, Rambach, in editing Luther's commentary on Jesus's "I am the way, the truth and the life" brought out the fact that John's special concern for Jesus's divinity and the significance of his many "I am" sayings set Jesus apart from ordinary humans, such as John the Baptist, for whom the expression "Ich bin's nicht" was appropriate. Johann Jacob Rambach, "Martini Lutheri Herrliches Zeugniß von Christo dem einigen Wege zur Seligkeit, über Joh. 14, 5–9. Mit einer Vorrede von der genauen Verbinding des Verdienstes und Exempels Christi heraus gegeben von Johann Jacob Rambach," in *D. Martini Lutheri Auserlesene erbauliche Kleine Schriften, aus seinen grossen Tomis genommen . . . . . von D. Johann Jacob Rambach* (1743), 241–94, esp. 241–45. In comparison to the seven "I am" sayings that many modern scholars link up with corresponding signs and discourses, Rambach (ibid., 244) cites twelve of Jesus's sayings that begin with "Ich bin's," indicating that these are only a selection of a still larger number. Rambach sees the "I am" sayings as a manifestation of divine revelation in Jesus, citing the Greek form of the "Ich bin's" and adding (245) a reference to Ex 3:14: "Diese Person [Jesus] aber weiset auf

too, devised symbolic and ingenious means of articulating this connection: first, as we will see, by creating his own internal symmetry to encompass both the worldly and spiritual outcomes of the trial, culminating in the joining of Jesus's name and cross in the chorale "In meines Herzens Grunde," and second, in close conjunction with it, by means of the fivefold repetition of a brief chorus whose first two appearances are sung to the text "Jesus of Nazareth," whereas its other three appearances, all sung to different texts, are bound up with the main theme of the trial: the question of Jesus's identity, particularly as "King of the Jews" (see exx. 4.4, 4.5, 4.6, 4.7) The last of the series of five ("Wir haben keinen König denn den Kaiser") appears at the culminating point of the trial in John, directly preceding the narrative of the judgment of crucifixion. Thus the name "Jesus of Nazareth" and the Christological title debated throughout the trial, and ultimately proclaimed as its ironic decision, come together in these choruses as they do in the royal inscription. And since the texts of the third, fourth, and fifth appearances of the chorus are all antagonistic: "Wir dürfen niemand töten" ("We may not put anyone to death," traditionally understood as a cry from the Jews for the Roman method of execution); "Nicht diesen, sondern Barrabam" ("Not this man, but Barabbas," rejection of Pilate's offer to free Jesus); and "Wir haben keinen König denn den Kaiser" ("We have no king but Caesar," the final rejection of Jesus's spiritual identity, prompting the judgment of crucifixion that ends John's trial); the series as a whole exhibits the character of the Johannine antitheses.

The amazing thing about the five choruses is that their articulation of the fundamental theological meaning of the Passion was entirely Bach's decision. There is nothing about the choruses themselves that would suggest that they alone be based on the same music, especially the music of "Jesus of Nazareth," other than a theological intention. On the average their texts are all short, ranging from three to seven words; but four other of the biblical chorus texts that are of about the same length receive considerably longer musical settings. In the well-known symmetrical structure of the trial length seems to have been an important consideration for Bach. There two choruses stand out for their greater length, "Wir haben ein Gesetz, und nach dem Gesetz soll er sterben; denn er hat sich selbst zu Gottes Sohn gemacht," which has twenty words, and "Lässest du diesen los, so bist du des Kaisers Freund nicht; denn wer sich zum Könige machet, der ist wider den Kaiser," which has twenty-two. In addition, these two longest choruses (33 mm. each) embody the opposition of law and freedom, whereas the two choruses that precede and follow them, "Kreuzige ihn," and "Weg mit dem, Kreuzige ihn," are obviously parallel. The latter choruses have very short texts, but in this instance Bach chose to expand the settings through word repetitions so that they attain the length of twenty-

---

keinen andern, sondern auf sich selbst: Diese führet den Wahlspruch: **Ich bins!** Joh. 8, 24. den keine Creatur ohne Versündigung führen darf. Wer siehet, ja wer greifet nicht, daß dieselbe eben derjenige seyn müsse, welcher zu Mose aus dem brennenden Busch sprach 2 B. Mos. 3, 14. **Ich werde seyn der ich seyn werde:** . . ."

EXAMPLE 4.4 ***St. John Passion*** *no. 2b, chorus "Jesum von Nazareth" I*

two and twenty-four measures, respectively. By repeating the music of the eleven-measure chorus, "Sei gegrüßet, lieber Judenkönig" as "Schreibe nicht: der Juden König, sondern daß er gesaget habe: ich bin der Juden König," Bach brought out the parallel in the repetition of the word[s] "Juden König," even though the one text was relatively short and the other relatively long. The result was a symmetrical arrangement of three choruses that repeated in reverse order, becoming progressively longer as they reached the "center," and progressively shorter in the reversal. But between "Weg mit dem, Kreuzige ihn" and "Schreibe nicht: der Juden König," there is a much greater span of time than appears between any of the other of the

EXAMPLE 4.5 ***St. John Passion*** *no. 16d, chorus "Wir dürfen niemand töten"*

six choruses. The "interruption" that caused "Schreibe nicht, der Juden König" to be substantially delayed was occasioned by the ending of the trial proper with the judgment of crucifixion, directly following the chorus "Wir haben keinen König denn den Kaiser," and the subsequent shift of locale to Golgatha, which Bach marked with the extended dialog with chorus, "Eilt, ihr angefocht'nen Seelen." Had Bach thought only of musical considerations, he could have set "Sei gegrüsset, lieber Judenkönig" and "Wir haben keinen König denn den Kaiser" with the same music, thereby creating a sequence of six choruses that would follow one another more closely in time and culminate with the ending of John's trial. The result of the abovementioned "interruption" was that the brief setting of "Wir haben keinen König denn den Kaiser," prompting the judgment of crucifixion, was not given

EXAMPLE 4.6 ***St. John Passion*** *no. 18b, chorus "Nicht diesen sondern Barrabam"*

anything like the "weight" of the dialog aria with chorus, "Eilt, ihr angefocht'nen Seelen," that follows soon after. That movement leads to the ending of the third *actus*, with the repeat of "Sei gegrüsset" as "Schreibe nicht" and the culminating chorale "In meines Herzens Grunde." In effect "Wir haben keinen König denn den Kaiser" becomes part of the stretching-out of the "symbolic trial" so as to encompass the movements just mentioned; but because it is followed by a modulatory recitative that causes the latter movements to return to the tonality in which the "symbolic trial" began, it is "played down," both theologically and musically. That

EXAMPLE 4.7 ***St. John Passion*** *no. 23f, chorus "Wir haben keinen König denn den Kaiser"*

Bach set it with the music of "Jesus of Nazareth," which had been heard within the trial as "Wir dürfen niemand töten" and "Nicht diesen, sondern Barrabam," projects the fact that these three choruses all represent the crowd's negative reaction to the figure of Jesus, in particular to his being identified with the Messiah, or the "king of the Jews."

In the first and most unusual of those three choruses ("Wir dürfen niemand töten") Bach carried out what is for him the unique procedure of grafting the four measures of the "Jesus of Nazareth" chorus onto the music of an entirely different chorus heard only seconds before: "Wäre dieser nicht ein Übeltäter, wir hätten dir ihn nicht überantwortet worden" (If this man were not an evildoer, we would not have delivered him over to you). The text of "Wäre dieser nicht ein Übeltäter" is twelve words long, and Bach set it as a twenty-eight measure chorus whose first thirteen measures name Jesus an evildoer. These measures comprise a fugue whose initial theme begins with a rising perfect fifth or fourth with reiterated tones, which is identical to Bach's setting of the phrase "dessen Ruhm in allen [Landen herrlich ist]" in "Herr, unser Herrscher." This I believe to be a significant relationship, introduced by Bach in order to bring out the opposition between Jesus's divinity and his rejection by "the world," as announced in John's prologue. In "Herr, unser Herrscher" the theme continues in the chorus with diatonic sixteenth-note roulades for "Landen," the entire passage constructed above circle-of-fifths harmonies similar to those of "Jesus of Nazareth" and featuring a slow interlocking chromatic descent in the oboes, who play tritones on every beat. The dualism of Jesus's *Herrlichkeit* and *Niedrigkeit* seems the obvious interpretation. In "Wäre dieser nicht," however the rising fourths and fifths continue with rising, then falling, chromatic lines for "Übeltäter." And in the descending half of the line Bach introduces unexpected whole tones, thereby flattening the harmony so that the bass reaches a cadential pattern in C minor in the eighth measure of the chorus (in modern terms, the subdominant of the subdominant [IV of IV]: the chorus is in d). After that, a new set of thematic entries leads to a pronounced arrival on the dominant (A) in the thirteenth measure. This completes the music that is carried over into "Wir dürfen niemand töten," where the music of "Jesus of Nazareth" reenters. At this point in "Wäre dieser nicht ein Übeltäter" Bach introduces two new musical ideas that combine with the first, for the remainder of the text, "wir hätten dir ihn nicht überantwortet worden." One of these new ideas introduces the rhythm of an eighth note followed by two sixteenths (on "überantwortet") that will reappear later in the choruses "Kreuzige ihn" and "Weg, weg mit dem, kreuzige ihn." The other is a reiterated punctuation of the word "nicht" that emerges most forcefully at the end of the chorus as all the voices move into rhythmic unison—"nicht, nicht, nicht, nicht"—in what seems obviously a denial of Jesus's messianic identity. In preparation for this second part of the "Wäre dieser nicht ein Übeltäter" chorus, Bach led the first part toward a climactic articulation of the dominant (A), over a two-and-a-half-measure pedal, the bass, tenor, and soprano leading the chromatically rising "Wäre dieser nicht ein Übeltäter" theme to a, a′ and a″ (the highest tone of the chorus), in turn. In relation to this gesture, the second segment of the chorus (whose music is *not* repeated in "Wir dürfen niemand töten") leads back to the tonic, creating the sense of a quasi antecedent/consequent relationship, in which the description of Jesus as an evildoer is given as the reason for his being delivered to Pilate. For the last appearance of the "Wäre dieser nicht" theme, Bach merges it with the repeated negative—"wir hätten dir ihn nicht, nicht, nicht überantwortet"—just before the fourfold repetition of the word "nicht," which suggests (perhaps incidentally) a further "cross" motive (the pitches b♭′, a′, d″, c♯″) as all the voices move into rhythmic unison above the descending tetrachord bass line. Following immediately after the movement's first tonic cadence, in the twenty-fifth of its twenty-eight measures, this gesture powerfully affirms the tonic, D minor, in which the movement closes.

In "Wir dürfen niemand töten," in A minor, Bach omits the fifteen-measure second segment of "Wäre dieser nicht" altogether, beginning the chorus with the first measure of the "Jesus of Nazareth" music, then reintroducing the initial thirteen-measure segment of "Wäre dieser nicht." As it reaches the dominant pedal (now E), he leads it directly into a reappearance of the second, third, and fourth measures of "Jesus of Nazareth," which end the chorus (the entire chorus is transposed from d to a and set, of course, to the text "Wir dürfen niemand töten"). Since at the beginning of the chorus Bach adjusts the initial measure of the "Jesus of Nazareth" music slightly, so as to articulate the dominant (E) followed by the tonic (a), when it continues, after the music of "Wäre dieser nicht," its resolution of the E pedal to A minor lends the return of the "Jesus of Nazareth" music a culminating quality. When the intervening measures (those carried forward from "Wäre dieser nicht") are omitted, the first measure joins up perfectly with mm. 16–18 (as in ex. 4.5), including the flute part, which Bach has extended throughout the entire chorus. Now, instead of the forceful tonic ending for the reiterated negative, the "Jesus of Nazareth" music reintroduces the circle-of-fifths harmony, closing with the dominant sound of the Phrygian cadence. And that dominant leads directly into John's announcement of the meaning of the chorus: that it fulfilled Jesus's prediction of his death as a "lifting up" (Jn 12:32–33). An additional detail of significance in this regard is that the recitative lead-in to the chorus is the same Phrygian cadence harmony as that which ends the chorus; and its melody (sung by the Evangelist) reappears at the end of the soprano part of the chorus as well.

In all these details Bach ensures that in "Wir dürfen niemand töten" the music associated with the identification of Jesus as an evildoer in "Wäre dieser nicht" seems to be embedded within, or enclosed by, "Jesus of Nazareth," an occurrence that has been explained in purely pragmatic terms as the result of Bach's having changed his mind regarding the length of the chorus, originally writing only the four measures of "Jesus of Nazareth," then adding the remainder to correct an imbalance with "Wäre dieser nicht ein Übeltäter."[52] Although this is possible as a sequence of events, it is in my opinion a lame explanation, since "Wir dürfen niemand töten" draws upon only thirteen of the twenty-eight measures of "Wäre dieser nicht"; and no source evidence for such a revision exists. In any case it does not address the question of why Bach, in that view, originally intended to set "Wir dürfen niemand töten" to the music of "Jesus of Nazareth," despite the imbalance, which would have been obvious from the start. I would suggest, rather, that Bach had a particular reason for combining the music of two different choruses into one

[52] See Werner Breig, "Zu den Turba-Chören von Bachs Johannes-Passion," in *Geistliche Musik: Studien zu ihrer Geschichte und Funktion im 18. und 19. Jahrhundert*, ed. Constantin Floros, Hans Joachim Marx, and Peter Petersen, 65–96. Hamburger Jahrbuch für Musikwissenschaft, vol. 8 (Laaber: Laaber-Verlag, 1985).

at this point, a reason related to John's employment of antithesis, irony, and double meaning to project his main points.[53] Regardless of the compositional history of the chorus, the nature of its pairing with "Wäre dieser nicht ein Übeltäter" creates a culmination in the "Jesus of Nazareth" music that is of immense theological significance from a Johannine perspective.

For virtually all Lutheran commentators, including August Hermann Francke, it was Jesus's prediction of his death as a "lifting up" that gave the verse its meaning. In Bach's setting the narrative that follows from the E Phrygian ending of "Wir dürfen niemand töten" continues in A minor ("Auf daß erfüllet würde das Wort Jesus, welches er sagte") until it details Jesus's prediction, at which point it briefly introduces a turn toward C minor ("da er deutete, welches Todes er *sterben würde*"). Although the local effect is the primary one, the C-minor inflection can also be understood as relating back to the flat modulations in both "Wäre dieser nicht" and "Wir dürfen niemand töten" (particularly the former, which had moved to C minor). Continuing, however, the recitative moves further sharp, setting up, for the first time in the scene, the dominant of A minor for the beginning of Jesus's concluding solo, in which he pronounces that his kingdom is not of this world. This then leads to a substantial cadence in A minor for the Christological chorale, "Ach, großer König." It is Bach's leading the scene forward to this point, marking a point of closure, that most brings out the intent behind "Wir dürfen niemand töten": a summary of the meaning of the scene in terms of an emphatic proclamation of Jesus's divinity in the midst of his rejection by the crowd. This caesura in the middle of John's trial has, of course, nothing to do with the traditional division of the Passion into *actus*, which it contradicts rather than affirms. The tonal relationship between "Wir dürfen niemand töten" and "Ach, großer König" can be said to project an antecedent-consequent character culminating in the two verses of the chorale. Bach's incorporating the "Jesus of Nazareth" music into "Wir dürfen niemand töten," like many other of Bach's decisions in the *St. John Passion*, cries out for musico-theological interpretation and attests to an extraordinary degree of theological intent on his part.

In this light, the interrelatedness of the "Jesus of Nazareth" choruses (by which I mean the entire sequence of five choruses) constitutes one of a large array of musico-symbolic devices in the *St. John Passion*, devices that extend ultimately to the structure of the entire work. I argue, thus, that on the largest scale the Passion comprises a symmetrically ordered sequence of nine key areas according to whether

[53] In discussing the "circular" harmony of the "Jesus of Nazareth" choruses in the following chapter, I suggest an association with Jesus as "Alpha" and "Omega," which was bound up with the frequent abbreviation of those terms to "A" and "O," the first and last letters of the Greek alphabet, and the first and fourteenth of the Latin alphabet, a feature that caused the number fourteen to have the same associations. It may be significant, therefore, that in "Wir dürfen niemand töten" thirteen measures of "Wäre dieser nicht ein Übeltäter" are cited. And, since the chorus begins with an incomplete measure followed by the thirteen of "Wäre dieser nicht," the "Jesus of Nazareth" music picks up again in the fourteenth measure.

their key signatures involve the sharp, flat, or natural signs: flat, sharp, natural, flat, sharp, flat, natural, sharp, flat. This pattern can be seen in figures 4.1 and 4.2 (see 183), which I refer to here in advance of the more detailed discussions in which it is rooted (see chs. 5–7). Since this arrangement has been misunderstood by some scholars, and since it is, in fact, supported by a great amount of evidence within the Passion itself, as well as in the theory of the time, I examine it closely in the following chapters in relation to the concept on which it is based, that of the tonal *ambitus* as set forth by Johann David Heinichen in 1711, a concept discussed also, although less interestingly, by other music theorists of the time.[54] Before considering this aspect of Bach's setting, however, I outline the design of Part 1 of the Passion with the aid of August Hermann Francke's lectures on John's Passion account. Although Bach might never have encountered Francke's lectures, they indicate the kind of interpretation that was possible at the time when, as is rare, only a single account (rather than a harmonization of all four evangelists) was the object of study.

August Hermann Francke's *St. John Passion* lectures and Bach's setting, Part 1

If we compare the passages from the Gospel that correspond to August Hermann Francke's ten lectures on John's Passion account (fig. 4.3) with the nine key areas of Bach's setting and the more complex, but related, three-division pattern of Raymond Brown (see figs. 4.1 and 4.2), it is immediately clear that very close, though not exact, correspondences exist among all three. Francke, like Bach, divides the part of the Passion that corresponds to Bach's Part 1 (Jn 18:1–27, Brown's "Division One") into two units (lectures), the first described in his table of contents in very general terms as Christ arrested and brought before Hannas/Annas, and the second as his appearance before Caiphas, along with Peter's denial. The content of these and the remaining eight lectures, however, always goes far beyond what is given in the titles. Francke's third and fourth lectures, taken together, correspond closely to the opening scene of Bach's Part 2, in which Jesus is brought before Pilate, initially questioned by him, and condemned by the crowd, who cry for the release of Barrabas instead. It ends with John's terse remark that Barrabas was a murderer. Francke's fifth lecture then begins with the scourging (the beginning of John 19), which corresponds in Raymond Brown's scheme to the central fourth episode of the chiastic seven-episode trial before Pilate and, in Bach's design, to the event that precipitates the beginning of what I call Bach's "symbolic trial." In Francke's division this segment concludes with the "Ecce homo," that is, the pre-

---

[54] Johann David Heinichen, *Neu erfundene und gründliche Anweisung zu vollkommener Erlernung des General-Basses* (Hamburg, 1711); repr. in *Documenta Musicologica, Erste Reihe*. vol. 40, ed. Wolfgang Horn, 260–67 (Kassel: Bärenreiter, 2000).

The first lecture: on John XVIII, 1–14.
Christ taken captive and at first led to Annas.

The second lecture: on John XVIII, 15–27.
Christ presented before Caiphas and denied by Peter.

The third lecture: on John XVIII, 28–32.
Christ brought before the palace of judgment and to Pilate.

The fourth lecture: on John XVIII, 33–40
Christ heard by Pilate, recognized as innocent, and presented to the people along with Barabbas.

The fifth lecture: on John XIX, 1–5.
Christ scourged and crowned with thorns.

The sixth lecture: on John XIX, 6–16.
Christ rejected by the Jews with a loud cry and delivered over by Pilate for crucifixion.

The seventh lecture: on John XIX, 17–22.
Christ crucified.

The eighth lecture: on John XIX, 23–27.
Christ's clothes divided und lost cast over his robe. His mother commended by him to John.

The ninth lecture: on John XIX, 28–37.
Christ given vinegar to drink, and his side opened with a spear.

The tenth lecture: on John XIX, 38–42.
Christ taken down from the cross and buried.

FIGURE 4.3 **August Hermann Francke** *table of contents for his published lectures on John's Passion account*

sentation of Jesus before the crowd as a mock king, with crown of thorns and purple robe. His next lecture (the sixth) then begins with the demand from the crowd for crucifixion and extends to the end of the trial, as Jesus is delivered over for crucifixion.

Thus Francke's third, fourth, fifth, and sixth lectures correspond to the trial proper (Brown's Division Two), whereas Bach conflates the part of the Passion that corresponds to Francke's third and fourth lectures into one segment, his third (including the transition into the fourth), which can be viewed as an introductory unit within Part 2. Taken together, Bach's fourth and fifth segments correspond to Francke's fifth and sixth divisions, both ending with the judgment of crucifixion; but the internal division between the two units is very different. Francke makes a caesura with the "Ecce homo," which precedes the cry "Kreuzige ihn" from the crowd, whereas Bach continues on, making the first major shift of key in the dialog between Jesus and Pilate that comes between the *turba* choruses, "Wir haben ein Gesetz" and "Lässest du diesen los." It is here that Bach's design departs most radically from the sequence of Francke's lectures and from traditional divisions in general, since it is built around an array of symmetrically ordered *turba* choruses.[55]

[55] Rambach culminates the third of his five divisions of the Passion, Jesus's trial, which is further subdivided into fifteen meditations, with four units (meditations) that correspond very closely to divisions in Bach's trial, and of which the last three are all drawn from John. Rambach's twelfth meditation

After the exhortation to meditate on Jesus's sufferings, in "Betrachte, meine Seele" and "Erwäge, wie sein blutgefärbter Rücken," the sequence of choruses whose music will be repeated in reverse order begins with "Sei gegrüßet, lieber Judenkönig," which precedes the "Ecce homo," and continues through the next two choruses, "Kreuzige ihn," which directly follows the "Ecco homo," and "Wir haben ein Gesetz." After this, Bach uses the subsequent recitative dialog to modulate from F to E, setting up the key of the chorale "Durch dein Gefängnis." In the segment that follows the chorale the three choruses are heard in reverse order, with new texts, as "Lässest du diesen los" (= "Wir haben ein Gesetz," transposed from F to E); "Weg, weg mit dem, kreuzige ihn" (= "Kreuzige ihn," transposed from g to f♯); and "Schreibe nicht: der Juden König" (= "Sei gegrüßet, lieber Judenkönig," now untransposed from its original B♭). The turba choruses form a kind of "backbone" for the symbolic trial, affirming points of tonal arrival that follow a distinctive pattern (one that is nearly identical to Johann David Heinichen's pattern for the very first presentation of the circle of keys, in 1711; see ch. 6). Bach's structure for this segment of the Passion has no equivalent in any division of the Passion; hence its "symbolic" character. Owing partly to the transposition of the first and second of the repeated choruses from flats to sharps (i.e., down a semitone) and the return to the original key for the repeat of the third, Bach's design makes a threefold flat/sharp/flat division out of the part of the Passion corresponding to Francke's fifth, sixth, and seventh lectures (see fig. 4.4).

Viewed in terms of the key areas, Bach's fifth segment, like Francke's sixth lecture, concludes with the delivery of Jesus over for crucifixion, corresponding to the end of the trial proper (and of Brown's sevenfold chiastic symmetry). Bach's sixth begins, as does Francke's seventh, and Brown's Division Three, with the shift of locale to Golgotha for the crucifixion. Bach marks this point with the hortatory G-minor dialog "Eilt ihr angefocht'nen Seelen," returning to flat keys for the third segment of his symbolic trial (the sixth overall). This segment culminates in the immensely symbolic narrative of the royal inscription, ending, as does Francke's seventh lecture, with Pilate's refusal to change it, which Bach follows by the chorale "In meines Herzens Grunde." This chorale is one of the major caesuras of the Passion, following which Bach places another sudden tonal shift.

After this, Francke's eighth lecture comprises two separate narratives: that of the soldiers' casting lots for Jesus's robe, and that of Jesus's words from the cross to his mother and John, the Beloved Disciple. The former episode corresponds to Bach's seventh key area, whereas the latter is the transition to the eighth. Bach sets the chorus of the soldiers in C, and makes the shift of focus to Mary and the Be-

begins with the scourging, his thirteenth begins with Pilate's leading Jesus's forth (the "Ecce homo") and culminates with "Wir haben ein Gesetz," his fourteenth comprises most of the recitative that follows, ending with Jesus's final words in the subsequent recitative (leaving Pilate's words, which close Bach's recitative, for the next meditation), and his fifteenth ends with the judgment of crucifixion. See Rambach, *Betrachtungen über das gantze Leiden Christi*, 826–88.

NO.	KEYS	*TURBA* CHORUSES	RECITATIVES	MEDITATIVE MOVEMENTS
19	E♭			"Betrachte, meine Seele"
20	c			"Erwäge"
21a	g/B♭		"Und die Kriegsknechte"	
21b	B♭	"Sei gegrüßet, lieber Judenkönig"		
21c	g, d, f, g		"Und gaben ihm Bakkenstreiche"	
21d	g	"Kreuzige"		
21e	g, a		"Pilatus sprach zu ihnen"	
21f	F	"Wir haben ein Gesetz"		
21g	g, d, b, c♯, E		"Da Pilatus das Wort hörete"	
22	E			"Durch dein Gefängnis"
23a	V of E		"Die Juden aber"	
23b	E	"Lässest du diesen los"		
23c	f♯, A, b		"Da Pilatus das Wort hörete"	
23d	f♯	"Weg, weg mit dem, kreuzige ihn"		
23e	b		"Spricht Pilatus zu ihnen"	
23f	b	"Wir haben keinen König"		
23g	D, g		"Da überantwortete er ihn"	
24	g			"Eilt, ihr angefocht'nen Seelen"
25a	b♭, E♭, b♭, B♭		"Allda kreuzigten sie ihn"	
25b	B♭	"Schreibe nicht: der Juden König"		
25c	B♭		"Pilatus antwortet"	
26	E♭			"In meines Herzens Grunde"

FIGURE 4.4 ***St. John Passion*** Bach's *"symbolic trial." Flat and sharp* ambitus *within boxes; modulatory recitatives outside*

loved Disciple into a modulation to the penultimate tonal region of the Passion, in sharps, which extends through "Es ist vollbracht" and "Mein teurer Heiland," ending with the "borrowed" narrative of the outbreaks of natural events and the rending of the veil of the Temple. Owing to the scope of the two arias, this segment contains less narrative from John than it does in Francke. Francke's ninth lecture then continues until the piercing of Jesus's side and the narrative of the fulfillment of scripture, which Bach draws into his final burial scene, corresponding to Francke's tenth lecture.

From this comparison outline it is clear that several of Francke's and Bach's divisions of the narrative are the same or very similar, in particular that within Part 1, the division between Parts 1 and 2, the articulation of divisions between the cry for Barrabas's release and the scourging, between the delivery of Jesus over for crucifixion and the shift to Golgotha for the narrative of the crucifixion and royal inscription, then between that scene and the narrative of the soldiers casting lots over Jesus's robe. And when we look at the actual contents of the lectures, the correspondences are closer still. There is an important difference, however. Francke's lectures have of necessity clear-cut points of division, whereas Bach's key areas most often do not. In the remainder of this chapter we consider those comparisons involving Francke's first two lectures and Part 1 of the *St. John Passion*, both of which articulate the traditional sequence of ideas associated with God's plan of redemption.

Beginning with Francke's first lecture, which exhibits much of the character of an introduction to the sequence as a whole, we find that he gives emphasis to four themes that run throughout his ten lectures:

1. Jesus's *Herrlichkeit*: his divinity, manifested in his foreknowledge of and voluntary undertaking of the events of the Passion.
2. Love as the motive for the Passion.
3. The Passion as God's *Rath*, foreordained in heaven, predicted both in scripture and by Jesus himself, and accepted as such by Jesus.
4. The benefit of the Passion for a sinful humanity.

The most relevant of Francke's marginal headings read as follows: "Jesus hat für uns gelitten willig" / "und aus Liebe" / "und aus vorbedachtem Rath GOttes." / "Herrlichkeit Christi." / "Vorspiel des jüngsten Gerichts" / "Beweis der zarten Liebe Jesu" / "welche weiter gehet, als auf seine eilf Jünger." / "Worte Christi müssen erfüllet werden." / "Petri unzeitige Eifer" / "wird bestrafet." / "Warum Christi den Creutzes-Kelch getruncken," / "und sich hat binden und gefangen nehmen lassen." These themes correspond to those of the initial G-minor/D-minor segment of the *St. John Passion*, Part 1. "Herr, unser Herrscher" brings out the theme of Jesus's *Herrlichkeit*, reiterating the words "Herr," "Herrscher," "herrlich" and "verherrlicht." Its principal affect is awe. In his discussion of Jesus's "Ich bin's," Francke says the following:

> Verse 6. *As soon as Jesus said to them, "I am," they drew back and fell to the ground.* Certainly, this is a quite noteworthy circumstance in the description of the suffering of Christ. It was [because of] his splendor that he *NB knew everything that would happen to him*; it was also his splendor that he, setting aside his all-knowing nature, gave himself into suffering out of overflowing great love. But here we have also a glimpse of his splendor, into his all-powerful nature, which he manifested through this word as he said to them "I am." What majesty must have shone in the eyes with these words? What kind of terror must have fallen upon them that they drew back and fell to the ground. Certainly, this was a prefiguration of the last judgment, when as a judge of the living and the dead he will strike terror into the godless with his look.[56]

At the point where Francke emphasizes Jesus's love (Jesus's demanding the release of the disciples), Bach places the chorale "O große Lieb." And at exactly the place associated by Francke with God's foreordained will for the Passion accepted by Jesus, Bach inserts the chorale "Dein Will g'scheh." Finally, at the point corresponding to Francke's discussion of the benefit of the Passion for humanity, Bach places the aria "Von den Stricken," which describes Jesus's being bound setting humanity free from sin, exactly as Francke says.[57]

The first of the four themes just described (Jesus's *Herrlichkeit*) is one of John's best-known emphases, manifested in the character and meaning of Jesus's "Ich bin's." Those words are preceded by the statement "Da nun Jesus wusste alles, was ihm begegnen sollte" (Since Jesus know everything that would happen to him) and followed by the statement that upon Jesus's words the arresting party "drew back and fell to the ground." Francke amplifies the ideas of Jesus's *Herrlichkeit* and foreknowledge by interpreting the initial words of John's account "Da Jesus solches geredet hatte" (which are not included in Bach's text) as referring back to Jesus's predictions in the Farewell Discourse, and by linking Jesus's crossing the brook Cedron (Kidron) to David's crossing the same brook in 2 Samuel 15:23. Since David's crossing the brook was in flight from Absalom, upon which the entire

---

[56] Francke, *Öffentliche Reden*, 10:

v. 6. **Als nun JESUS zu ihnen sprach : Ich bins / wichen sie zurücke / und fielen zu Boden.** Gewiß dieses ist ein gar mercklicher Umstand in der Beschreibung des Leidens Christi. Seine Herrlichkeit war es, daß er **NB. Alles wußte / was ihm begegnen solte;** auch war es seine Herrlichkeit, daß er, seiner Allwissenheit ohnerachtet, sich aus überschwenglich grosser Liebe ins Leiden dahin gab; aber hier ist nun auch ein Blick seiner Herrlichkeit in seiner Allmacht, welche er durch diß Wort beweiset, da er zu ihnen saget: **Ich bins.** Welche Majestät mußte mit diesen Worten ihnen in die Augen leuchten? Was für ein Schrecken mußte sie dabey überfallen, daß sie zurücke wichen, und zu Boden fielen. Gewiß, diß war ein Vorspiel des jüngsten Gerichts, da er als ein Richter der Lebendigen und der Todten mit seinem Anblick die Gottlosen erschrecken, . . ."

[57] Here Francke, like Bach's librettist, introduces the word *Stricken*, which does not appear in John.

country wept, for Francke it prefigured Jesus's sufferings. Francke likewise explains the choice of the garden locale that was known to the disciples, including Judas, in terms of Jesus's foreknowledge and voluntary undergoing of the Passion, as well as of his taking on the burden of Adam's sin in the garden of Eden. And in the above-mentioned paragraph devoted to Jesus's "Ich bin's" Francke interprets the falling of the arresting party to the ground as their seeing in Jesus's glance the all-powerful Jesus of the last judgment.

Jesus's *Herrlichkeit* is a continuing theme in Francke's lectures, one that he emphasizes at key points along with its opposite, Jesus's *Erniedrigung*, as in "Herr, unser Herrscher," and links explicitly with Jesus's foreknowledge and love.[58] In his lecture on the beginning segment of the Passion, Francke follows his discussion of Jesus's foreknowledge ("Als nun Jesus wusste alles was ihm begegnen sollte . . . ": "Since Jesus knew everything that would happen to him., . . ."), with the marginal remark, "Jesus hat für uns gelitten willig / und aus Liebe" (Jesus suffered for us voluntarily and out of love). And in his marginal comments for Jesus's demanding release of the disciples, he adds "Beweiß der zarten Liebe Jesu" and "welche weiter gehet, als auf seine eilf Jünger" (demonstration of the tender love of Jesus, which goes further than for his eleven disciples). The discussion itself makes clear that Jesus's love for the Father and for humanity was the motive for his voluntarily undergoing the Passion. In the discussion as a whole Jesus's *Herrlichkeit* and his love are inseparable, as Bach also recognizes in his placement of "O große Lieb" directly following Jesus's demanding the release of the disciples: "Ich hab's euch gesagt, dass ich's sei, suchet ihr denn mich, so lasset diese gehen!" In this way, the initial G-minor segment of Bach's setting articulates the Johannine themes that are given a comparable degree of emphasis by Francke. They are also the point of departure for the discussion of God's *Rath* or *oikonomia*, as discussed by many Lutheran authors of the sixteenth through the eighteenth centuries (see ch. 2).

At this point John announces that Jesus's protecting the disciples fulfilled a prophecy made by him earlier in the Gospel, juxtaposing it to the narrative of Peter's drawing his sword and cutting off the ear of the high priest's servant. And Francke, too, after emphasizing that Jesus must be recognized as a "great prophet" even in the midst of his sufferings, poses the question, "Was geschahe aber, als der Herr Jesus solches gesaget hatte?" (What happened, however, as the Lord Jesus had just said this?), raising the opposition between Jesus's words and Peter's action. As Francke points out, the fulfillment of Jesus's prediction relates to the theme of his foreknowledge and willing acceptance of God's will. Jesus, who could have exhibited his majesty and power, orders Peter to put away his sword, rebuking him for hindering the events of the Passion, and accepts the "cup" of suffering as God's will

---

[58] I do not wish to imply that Francke is in any way unique in emphasizing the antithesis of Jesus's *Herrlichkeit* and his *Erniedrigung*, which is very prominent in many other commentaries, even those of the "harmonizing" kind, such as Rambach's.

out of love for the Father—"Soll ich den Kelch nicht trinken, den mir mein Vater gegeben hat, den mir mein Vater gegeben hat?"—so that we might do likewise.[59]

With "O große Lieb" Bach meditates on the motive for Jesus's demand for the release of the disciples, thereby separating the recitative on which it contemplates ("Jesus antwortete") from the next one, and thereby delaying John's announcement that it fulfilled a prediction of Jesus. For Bach, as for Francke and many others, the fulfillment of Jesus's predictions and of scripture belongs to the theme of God's plan for the salvation of humanity, which Jesus's subsequent words bring up.[60] Bach therefore allows "O grosse Lieb" to culminate the G minor that has held to this point, then begins the subsequent recitative with John's announcement of the fulfillment of Jesus's prediction, leading it to a cadence in C minor. He then shifts immediately to D minor for the narrative of Peter and the sword. In relation to the g that went before, the two keys can be viewed as the subdominant and dominant; yet, at the same time, they mark a shift in the narrative that Bach confirms by remaining in d for Jesus's accepting the cup (ending of recitative no. 4), the chorale "Dein Will g'scheh" (no. 5) a second recitative ("Die Schaar . . .": no. 6) and the aria "Von den Stricken" (no. 7). Francke's marginal titles for this part of the narrative comprise one continuous sentence, "Warum Christus den Creuzes-Kelch getrunken, / und sich hat binden und gefangen nehmen lassen," an indication that for him they cannot be separated from one another, as would be the case, conceptually at least, by our viewing "Dein Will g'scheh' as the culmination of a "cantata" or *actus*

---

[59] Rambach, *Betrachtungen über das gantze Leiden Christi*, 180–81:

> Er stellet ihm 2. vor, daß es sündlich und unanständig sey, dieweil er ihn verhindern wolle an den Gehorsam gegen seinen Vater, und an der Erlösung des menschlichen Geschlechts: **Soll ich den Kelch nicht trincken, den mir mein Vater gegeben hat?** Er nennet sein Leiden hier einen Kelch, wie Matth. 20, 22. damit er nach einiger Meynung zielet auf die Todes-Strafe der Alten, da sie dem Ubeltäter einen Becher, mit Gift gemischt, auszutrincken geben: Dieses Leiden betrachtet er als zugeschickt von seinem Vater, der es nach seinem vorbedachten Rath ihm bestimmet und abgemessen, Apost. 2, 23. Und fragt daher: Solt ichs nicht übernehmen, solt ich mich demselben entziehen, da ich doch im Rath des Vaters mich dazu erboten habe? Schäme dich Petre, daß du mich mit Gewalt gleichsam zum Lügner machen wilst."

The passage from Acts to which Rambach refers is one that was widely associated with the concept of the history of salvation: "Him [Jesus of Nazareth, as specified in the preceding verse], *being delivered by the determinate counsel and foreknowledge of God,* ye have taken, and by wicked hands have crucified and slain" (KJV).

[60] This can be clearly seen from Francke's marginal remark, one single sentence, which is divided into three separate parts, spanning Francke's commentary on Jesus's foreknowledge ("Jesus hat für uns gelitten willig": Jesus suffered for us willingly), the motive behind the Passion, God's love, ("und aus Liebe": and out of love), and the blindness of the arresting party as the outcome of God's plan of salvation ("und aus vorbedachtem Rath Gottes": and out of God's predetermined plan). See Francke, *Öffentliche Reden*, 8–9. In his discussion of the fulfillment of Jesus's words Francke leads over into the narrative of Peter's taking up the sword, which would have prevented both that fulfillment and the unfolding events of the passion (13–15); and for the narrative of Jesus's accepting the "cup," he refers to Jesus's obedience to the Father, extending the acceptance of God's *Rath* to the contemporary believer (15–16). On the concept of God's *Rath,* see the discussion of Rambach's *Betrachtungen über den Rath Gottes von der Seeligkeit der Menschen* in ch. 2.

within the Passion, as Alfred Dürr suggests.[61] "Dein Will g'scheh" does not culminate what went before, but rather articulates and confirms the initial shift to the dominant region of the original key, where is it is associated with the beginning of a new theme, not a point of completion. The key of d continues through the narrative that Caiphas states that it is good that one man should be put to death for the people (D-minor cadence). It culminates in the aria "Von den Stricken," which summarizes the meaning of the entire D-minor passage as that of the benefit of the Passion for humanity. After the aria, Bach sets the narrative of Peter's following Jesus, along with the aria "Ich folge dir gleichfalls," in B♭ and begins the subsequent recitative in g, thereby linking it up tonally with the opening scene of the Passion before making a large-scale shift of key. That shift, as we will see, is initiated by the narrative of Peter's denial, and culminates in A major, in association with the theme of repentance.

"Von den Stricken" corresponds to the ending of Francke's first lecture, articulating what he calls a "rechte Haupt-Stück der Paßion Christi," the first of a series of such *Hauptstücke* (principal themes) that run throughout the entire series of lectures: the benefit of Jesus's sufferings for humankind. The Brockes text on which it was based served as the introductory chorus to Brockes's poem, setting forth the overall salvific meaning of the Passion. Francke's comments on this part of the narrative make clear that the Passion must be viewed not according to its literal meaning but in light of the knowledge that Jesus's sufferings were voluntarily undergone on behalf of a sinful humanity, in obedience to God's plan for the redemption of the faithful. Here, and again in his discussion of the royal inscription, Francke distinguishes the literal, worldly meaning of the narrative from the spiritual, in this instance by associating the one with Caiphas—"Caiphas meynte es böse zu machen"—and the other with God's intention—"Gott aber gedachte es gut zu machen." That opposition involves a type of antithesis that runs throughout the meditative movements of the *St. John Passion*.[62]

It is now clear that the boundaries between what were the traditional units or divisions of the Passion narrative are seldom treated by Bach as points of closure, marking musical divisions as well. The closest ones to such an arrangement are the point of culmination that comes with "In meines Herzens Gründe" and of course the endings of the two parts of the Passion. Otherwise, the sense is much more one of overlap and continuity, even interlocking, with numerous references back and forth. Even though we may well wish to separate out particular points of demarcation (e.g., the "symbolic trial") for the purpose of indicating a substantial degree of internal construction, they cannot be separated from one another, even in purely conceptual terms, without doing violence to the musical structure.

---

[61] See n. 25.

[62] Francke, *Öffentliche Reden*, 17, The words in question are a paraphrase of the words of Joseph in Exodus and were cited with the same meaning by many other authors of the time. See ch. 1, n. 15.

Bach's treatment of the division between the two principal key areas of Part 1 provides an excellent illustration of this point. Whereas Francke begins his second lecture with the shift to Peter (already a division that does not coincide with that between the traditional *actus*), Bach's design has no unequivocal point of division. Francke's second sermon begins with the words "Simon Petrus aber folgete Jesum nach, und ein and'rer Jünger" (Simon Peter, however, followed Jesus, and another disciple), and centers primarily on the question of Peter's following Jesus and its meaning. For Francke, the shift from Caiphas to Peter takes precedence over the shift of locale. It is presumably why Bach, after setting the words just cited as a three-measure recitative closing in B♭ after the D minor of the preceding movements, follows them immediately by the B♭ aria "Ich folge dir gleichfalls," basing its melody on that of the preceding recitative. Presumably, he intended that the contemporary believer's avowal of loyalty, which is modeled after Peter's, and is set in the first major-key movement of the Passion, project a positive tone that looks backward (in terms of its close relationship to the G-minor tonality) and marks the beginning of a new theme in the Passion. But, as we will see in chapter 5, the continuing narrative of Peter's denials and repentance makes a complete and highly symbolic break with the flat keys that have held to this point in the Passion.

The new theme is, of course, Peter's confrontation with temptation; as Francke explains, Peter, in following the "other disciple" into the high priest's palace, failed to heed Jesus's predictions of his denial.[63] Francke here, as always throughout his lectures, stresses the theme of Jesus's foreknowledge and predictions and their fulfillment, often at the outset of his discussions, as if to present Jesus's *Herrlichkeit* as the background for all that follows. Their exact fulfillment was a necessary outcome of God's plan and its purpose:

> Just as everything that our savior said beforehand matched so precisely that it did not lack in any detail, so through it the disciples were powerfully strengthened in faith, and the evangelists, through the impulse of the Holy Spirit, had to carefully record the said predictions of Christ, so that in meditation on his suffering we also might recognize him in his deep humiliation for the great prophet who came into the world, or for the Christ and savior of the world, believe in him, and be powerfully strengthened in faith.[64]

---

[63] In the concluding recitative ("Er leugnete aber . . .") of Part 1 the insertion from Matthew ("Da gedachte Petrus an die Worte Jesus, und ging hinaus und weinete bitterlich") makes the point that Peter *did* hear Jesus's words, even though their impact came only later, prompting his repentance. In Chafe, *Tonal Allegory*, 329–35, I have suggested that melodic similarities between "Da gedachte Petrus an die Worte Jesu" and earlier points in the narrative may have been intended to reinforce this point.

[64] Francke, *Öffentliche Reden*, 24–25:

> Wie nun das alles was unser Heyland vorher gesagt, so genau eingetroffen, daß er nicht an einem fehlet, so sind dadurch die Jünger im Glauben gewaltig gestärcket worden, und haben die Evangelisten durch Antrieb des Heil. Geistes die Erfüllung gedachter Weissagungen Christi sorgfältig aufzeichnen müssen, auf daß auch wir in der Betrachtung seines Leidens ihn bey seiner tieffen Erniedrigung für den grossen Propheten, der in die Welt kommen sollen, oder für

In this instance, Peter, now feeling secure in the safety of the palace and taken by surprise by the question put to him by the maid guarding the door, fails to remember Jesus's prediction and denies being his disciple, which Francke, like most theologians of the time, calls his "fall." In this light, the directly positive tone of "Ich folge dir gleichfalls" suggests something of the state of mind that leads Peter to follow the "other" disciple without anticipating the outcome, and which Francke warns against repeatedly (his marginal indications "Gott ist mehr als guten Freunden zu folgen," "Den Führern ist nicht allezeit zu folgen," and "Wie weit guten Freunden zu folgen" all give the flavor of his discussions). The aria does not depict Peter's voice but that of the contemporary believer. It projects a state of mind that has not yet been confronted with the kind of trial and temptation that Peter undergoes in the scene that follows.[65] That is, "Ich folge dir gleichfalls" precedes the story of Peter's guilt and penitence, which is the main theme of the sharp-key *ambitus* in which Part 1 ends. Neither the shift of locale from that of the garden to the high priest's palace nor Peter's following Jesus determines that tonal division. The shift begins symbolically with Peter's first denial and is completed with the two chorale verses "Wer hat dich so geschlagen" and "Ich, ich und meine Sünden," both in A. Significantly, "Ich folge dir gleichfalls" is virtually the only movement in the *St. John Passion* whose text does not depend on antithesis. Bach derives its principal melody from the immediately preceding recitative narrative of Peter's following Jesus (see exx. 4.8a and 4.8b). At the beginning of Peter's story it projects a hopeful tone that provides the frame of reference for the subsequent narrative of Peter's denial and repentance. That narrative takes up Peter's "fall," which pivots on his "Ich bin's nicht" (see ch. 5). It is in the ensuing passages leading to Peter's tortured repentance in the next aria, "Ach, mein Sinn," that we must look for Bach's deepest message, that of repentance and ultimate redemption. The tonal motion from B♭ to f♯/A over the course of Peter's story is its analog.

After his initial discussions of Peter's entrance to the high priest's palace, Francke turns to a second theme arising now from Jesus's questioning by Caiphas, his being struck by a servant, and his response "Was schlägest du mich?" That theme is Jesus's innocence, which Francke identifies as his second principal theme, remarking, "Und eben dieses ist auch ein rechtes Haupt-Stück in der Beschreibung des Leidens Christi" (And this also is a true principal theme in the description of Christ's sufferings). Meditation upon Jesus's innocence, which shines forth throughout his sufferings and made special impact on Peter, leads the faithful to recognize the opposite in themselves:

> So look now, O humankind, not only upon the innocence of the Lord Jesu, but also when you see that he suffered innocently, look upon yourself. I and

---

den Christum und Heyland der Welt erkennen, an ihn glauben, und im Glauben kräfftig gestärket werden möchten.

[65] In the middle section, however, for the word *schieben*, Bach introduces a chromatic ascent in the line, as the soloist/believer envisages Jesus's urging (literally "pushing") her to follow.

EXAMPLE 4.8a *St. John Passion no. 8, recitative*

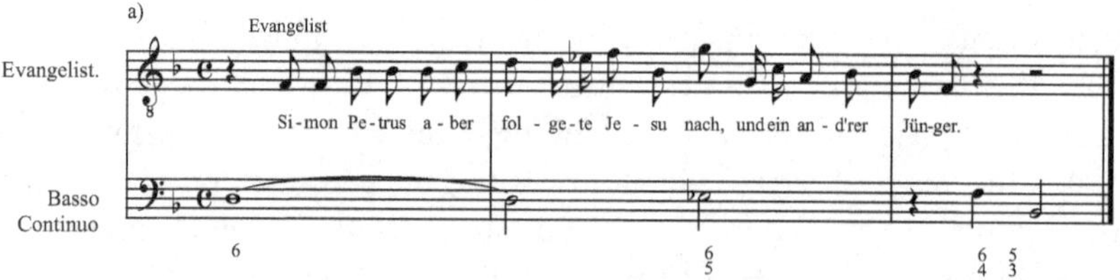

EXAMPLE 4.8b *St. John Passion no. 9, aria "Ich folge dir gleichfalls," beginning*

you, and we all should have suffered eternal shame and disgrace. Thus the innocent lamb of God was beaten and suffered for us according to scripture, so that he would bring us, instead of to eternal shame, to eternal *glory* and majesty. That should cast us down to the ground and teach us to place our mouth in the dust, and with the innermost humiliation of our hearts, thank him for his inexpressible love, but also move us strongly to follow most meticulously after the holy innocence of our Lord Jesus in our entire lives. Lord, help us in that![66]

At the corresponding point in the narrative, Bach places the A-major chorale, "Wer hat dich so geschlagen," indicating two verses, the first of which, after posing the question of who struck Jesus, proclaims his innocence—"Du bist ja nicht ein Sünder, wie wir und unsre Kinder, von Missethaten weisst du nicht" (You are certainly not a sinner, as are we and our children, of misdeeds you know nothing)—and the second verse that gives the answer: "Ich, ich und meine Sünden, die sich wie Körnlein finden des Sandes an dem Meer, die haben dir erreget das Elend, das

[66] Francke, *Öffentliche Reden*, 39–40:

So siehe nun, o Mensch, nicht allein auf die Unschuld des Herren Jesu, sondern wenn du siehest, daß er unschuldig gelitten so siehe dich selbst an. Ich und du, und wir allen hätten ewige Schmach und Schande leiden sollen. Da hat sich das unschuldige Lamm Gottes ins Mittel geschlagen, und für uns gelitten nach der Schrift, damit er uns an statt der ewigen Schmach zur ewigen *Glorie* und Herrlichkeit brächte. Das soll uns auf den Boden dahin werfen, uns lehren, unsern Mund in den Staub legen, und ihm mit der allerinnigsten Demüthigung unsers Herzens dancken für seine unausprechliche Liebe, aber uns kräftliglich bewegen, der heiligen Unschuld des Herren Jesu in unserm ganzen Leben aufs allersorgfältigste nachzufolgen. Herr hilf uns dazu!

dich schläget, und das betrübte Marterheer" (I, I and my sins, which are as numerous as seeds, as the sand by the ocean, they have brought about the suffering that strikes you, and the tormented hoard of martyrs).

When Francke urges that contemporary believers recognize Jesus's innocence and think on their own guilt, that they be cast to the ground (like the arresting party), thanking Jesus humbly for his love, yet at the same time be moved to model themselves after Jesus in his innocence (using the verb "nachfolgen" to indicate that process), he is indicating stages in the process of discipleship or the following of Jesus, referred to frequently as the "Nachfolgung Christi" in Lutheran treatises or what I call the "dynamic" of faith.[67] Meditation on Jesus's innocent sufferings brings out the process of *Sündenerkenntnis*, acknowledgment of sin, that is, of *Erniedrigung* in the believer, leading to repentance and the response of love, after which the believer can model himself more actively after Jesus. This is, of course, the sequence that Luther described in his widely published Passion sermon of 1519, the basis for most later Lutheran writings on the Passion. In that sermon, as in Luther's later writings, the precipitating element in the process of *Sündenerkenntnis* is the law, especially when the satisfaction theory is invoked; here it is the image of Jesus himself in his innocent sufferings and love that brings about the necessary conversion, a descent/ascent process.

After his discussion of Jesus's innocence, Francke returns to Peter and his second and third denials. The thrust of his discussion is that Peter's denials are progressively more serious, since he has had time to think on Jesus's prediction and repent. Francke observes that John ends his narrative merely with the words "und alsobald krähete der Hahn," with no mention of Peter's repentance, but only the symbolic reminder of Jesus's prediction of his fall.[68] This leads Francke to warn the reader regarding what he calls "the most shameful misuse of Peter's case": namely [in light of Peter's ultimate redemption], to excuse one's past sins and to seek the freedom to commit new ones. After condemning this misuse, Francke concludes the lecture with the following summary:

> The essence is this: Do not sin, and if anyone sins, may he hasten with Peter, to turn with burning tears of penitence to the innocent Lamb of God, who

---

[67] The following of Christ was widely associated with the idea of "conformity" to Christ in his sufferings. Two pre-Lutheran works that were of great influence on Lutheran theologians in this respect were Johann Tauler's *Das Buch von geistlicher Armuth*, which made a strong impact on Luther and was translated under the title *Nachfolgung des armen Lebens Christi*, and the *Imitatio Christi* of Thomas à Kempis, translated as *Von der Nachfolge Christi*. See *Zwey alte und edle Büchlein. Das Erste. Die Deutsche Theologia / Das ist: Ein edles Büchlein vom rechten verstande / was Adam und Christus sey / und wie Adam in uns sterben / Christus aber in uns leben soll. Das Ander. Die Nachfolgung Christi / Wie man alle Eitelkeit dieser Welt verschmehen soll. Durch D. Thomam ä Kempis Anno 1441. gantz geistreich beschreieben. . . . / Durch Johannem Arndten* . . . Magdeburg, 1605. See also Tauler, *Das Buch von geistlicher Armuth*, ed. P. Fr. Heinrich Seuse Denifle (Munich, 1877). For an English translation, see John Tauler, *The Following of Christ*, trans. by J. K. Morell (London, n.d.).

[68] The cock's crow was traditionally viewed as the call from the law to the sinner to awaken to repentance. See ch. 5, n. 52.

EXAMPLE 4.8c *St. John Passion no. 21b, chorus "Sei gegrüsset, lieber Jüdenkönig," beginning*

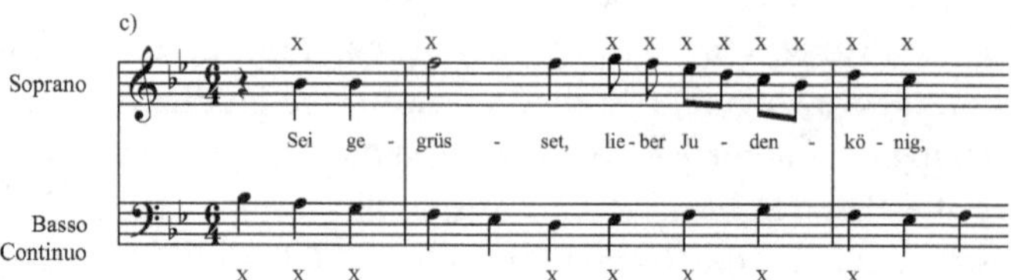

suffered for our sins, and from then on so much more faithfully to follow after this Lamb of God, wherever it leads, as Peter also did.[69]

This excerpt and the one cited earlier urge the believer to model his or her following of Jesus in terms of both Jesus's innocence, which should become an inner part of his or her life, and of turning to Jesus in penitent search for forgiveness. Together, they circumscribe the meaning of Peter's fall and repentance in a manner suggestive of the two arias, "Ich folge dir gleichfalls" (whose affective sphere suggests innocence) and "Ach, mein Sinn," whose tortured expression of penitence is among the most remarkable instances of this affect in Bach's work.[70] Francke's closing words—"desto treulicher nachzufolgen, wo es hingehet, wie es Petrus auch gemacht hat"—remind the reader that Peter did ultimately follow Jesus "wherever it led," a detail that Bach seems to capture in the musical relationship between the beginning of "Ich folge dir gleichfalls" and the first and last of the symmetrical array of choruses in the trial (see ex. 4.8c).

From this standpoint "Ich folge dir gleichfalls" embodies much of the character of Francke's discussions of following Jesus. In its prayer for Jesus, addressed as "mein Leben, mein Licht," to "befördre den Lauf und höre nicht auf, selbst an mir zu ziehen, zu schieben, zu bitten," the aria introduces three well-known Johannine expressions: John presents Jesus as "life" and "light" at many points, whereas "ziehen" is the expression the Johannine Jesus uses in predicting the impact of the crucifixion: "when I am lifted up I will *draw* all men to me." Other expressions are shared with Francke, who uses the verb "schieben" (to push) repeatedly in his discussion of this part of the Passion ("*Schiebet* das Gebet nicht auf . . . "; "Doch wenn ihr auf diß in Acht genommen, sondern eure Wiederkehr *aufgeschoben* hättet, so *schiebets* nur nicht länger auf, . . . "). The reference to the stirring of the

---

[69] Francke, *Öffentliche Reden*, 40: "Die Summa ist diese: Sündiget nicht, und ob jemand sündiget, so eile er mit Petro, in heissen Buß-Thränen sich zu dem unschuldigen Lamm Gottes zu wenden, daß für seine Sünden gelitten hat, und hinfort diesem Lamme Gottes desto treulicher nachzufolgen, wo es hingehet, wie es Petrus auch gemacht hat."

[70] For an interesting discussion of this aria (and "Es ist vollbracht") see Laurence Dreyfus, "The Triumph of 'Instrumental Melody': Aspects of Musical Poetics in Bach's *St. John Passion*," in *Bach Perspectives 8: J. S. Bach and the Oratorio Tradition*, ed. Daniel R. Melamed, 96–121 (Urbana: University of Illinois Press, 2011).

believer's conscience in the *Schluß-Gebet* that ends Francke's second sermon seems, likewise, to find an echo in the chorale that closes Part 1 of the *St. John Passion*: "Wen du aber ietzo in seinem *Gewissen* von seiner vorigen Sünde / oder daß er noch ietzo darin stecket überzeugest / den laßt durch dein Wort und Geist auch kräftig *gerühret* werden . . . " (Francke); "wenn ich böses hab' gethan, *rühre* mein *Gewissen*" (*St. John Passion*).

We now see that the sequence of themes that appears in the meditative movements of the *St. John Passion*, Part 1, corresponds exactly to those presented by August Hermann Francke in his first two lectures:

Francke: themes of sermons 1 and 2	St. John Passion: meditative movements in Part 1
1. Jesus's *Herrlichkeit*, his foreknowledge of all that would take place in the Passion. The Passion as fulfillment of Jesus's and the scriptures' predictions	"Herr, unser Herrscher" and the opening scene
2. Love as the motive for the Passion	"O große Lieb"
3. Jesus's acceptance of God's will, as manifested in the Passion	"Dein Will g'scheh'"
4. The benefit of Jesus's sufferings for humankind	"Von den Stricken"
5. The necessity of following Jesus (*Nachfolgung Christi*)	"Ich folge dir gleichfalls"
6. Jesus's innocence and human guilt	"Wer hat dich so geschlagen?"/ "Ich, ich und meine Sünden"
7. Penitence	"Ach, mein Sinn"/"Petrus, der nicht denkt zurück"

From Jesus himself, his divine nature, love for humanity, and voluntary undergoing the Passion in fulfillment of God's will as reflected in scripture, the direction of Part 1 is toward that of the benefit of the Passion for humanity. That is, it follows a course that is basically that of God's *Rath* as outlined by Rambach and others: from the divine being, his love and will for human salvation, to Jesus's work as *Mittel* (means), and the *Ordnung* (penitance) that involves humanity's response and participation as mirrored in the story of Peter's denial and repentance. Up to the aria "Von den Stricken" the meditative movements all center on Jesus, as the divine being who out of love for humanity voluntarily undertakes the Passion as crux of the work of redemption. From "Ich folge dir gleichfalls" to the end of Part 1 they center on the believer and the means by which Jesus's work becomes efficacious for him. After only minor-key meditative movements, from this point on all meditative movements except "Ach, mein Sinn" are in major. In the theme of the *Nachfolgung Christi* associated with Peter in "Ich folge dir gleichfalls" Bach perhaps intended to anticipate the trial via the melodic resemblance between the aria and the two choruses in Part 2, “Sei gegrüßet, lieber Judenkönig,” and “Schreibe nicht: der Juden König,” and their common B♭ tonality. The connection suggests that the believer must follow “wherever it may lead,” as in Francke’s description of Peter’s following Jesus. In John’s view, however, it is Jesus who draws the believer on through his word and suffering on behalf of humanity. Understanding how Bach represents this “drawing” depends on our understanding the tonal and modulatory character of Bach’s Part 1. And in order to take up that subject, we need to turn now to the practical and theoretical bases of Bach’s tonal design in chapter 5.

{5}

The Concept of *Ambitus* in the *St. John Passion*

Introduction: The need for historical music theory

In Bach's time, the most significant advances in German music theory were those that surrounded the emergence of the twenty-four major and minor keys: the *Musicalischer Circul*, or circle of keys, that served as the new paradigm of tonal relationships, the well-tempered tuning that made their use possible, and the concept of the tonal *ambitus* by means of which the narrower tonal-transpositional range of earlier music expanded to the scope of the closed circle. Theories of modulation and key relationships were a lasting outcome of this situation. For some theorists these concepts rendered the ancient ones—such as solmization and the modes—obsolete, while for others the older conceptions remained the key to musical meaning.[1] As the first composer to produce complete cycles of preludes and fugues according to the new paradigm, Bach was squarely in the modern camp. Yet, at the same time, he produced an array of "allegorical" canons that, along with his cultivation of modal composition, attest to the fact that he had no intention of throwing out the baby with the bathwater as some of his contemporaries did.[2]

---

[1] The principal players in the controversy over mode, solmization, and a variety of other issues were Johann Mattheson, who advocated the abolishment of mode and solmization, principally in his so-called *orchestre* treatises, and Johann Heinrich Buttstett, whose treatise *Ut, Mi, Sol, Re, Fa, La, tota musica* (Erfurt, 1715), held tenaciously to tradition. See Beekman Cannon, *Johann Mattheson: Spectator in Music* (New Haven, CT: Yale University Press, 1947; Cannon, "Johann Mattheson's 'Inquiring Composer,' in *New Mattheson Studies*, ed. George J. Buelow and Hans Joachim Marx, 125–68 (Cambridge: Cambridge University Press, 1983). Also, Joel Lester, "The Fux-Mattheson Correspondence: An Annotated Translation," *Current Musicology* 24 (1977): 37–62.

[2] Eric Chafe, "Allegorical Music: The 'Symbolism' of Tonality in the Bach Canons," *Journal of Musicology* 3 (Fall 1984): 340–62. Many of the Bach canons refer to concepts that were central to the Lutheran "metaphysical" tradition in music theory; one of them—"Mi Fa et Fa Mi est tota musica"—refers to the same widely known catchphrase as the title of Buttstett's treatise (see n. 1). Two canons are headed with the word "Symbolum," indicating the resonance of their allegorical catchphrases with theological concepts.

What follows here is an attempt to describe how the balance of historical and "modern" in Bach's tonal language informs our understanding of the merging of musical and theological intentions in the design of the *St. John Passion*, with particular reference to Part 1.

In this context it is necessary to raise the question of the role of historical music theory in our analysis of Bach's tonal practices. For, paradoxically, the most "advanced" aspects of Bach's tonal writing are often not at all separate from others that derive from concepts and practices—such as solmization and cultivation of the modes—which were soon to disappear entirely from the scene of Western music. In earlier studies I have attempted to show that the circle of keys, as it was initially presented by Johann David Heinichen, retained elements of archaic thought and practice that, although Heinichen expunged them from his updated discussion of the circle seventeen years later, had the capacity of translation into modern terms.[3] Bach's music sometimes exhibits close parallels with Heinichen in its featuring the interaction of ancient and modern concepts. Rooted in the principles that Heinichen expressed in his discussions of modulation and key relationships, it nevertheless introduces "advanced" practices that can be described conceptually in archaic terms. Tritone-related keys, for example, embody elements of the idea of antithesis and contradiction behind the old "mi contra fa" idea, and are therefore meaningful when presented as components of a higher order.[4]

Bach devises various kinds of ordering principles involving movement keys throughout his music. Among them are the "encyclopedic" or indexical ordering of the separate preludes and fugues of the *Well-Tempered Clavier*, one that implies no tonal relationship between adjacent keys. That of the *Art of Fugue*, on the other hand, is just the opposite, involving a single key, but, like the *Well-Tempered Clavier*, with no implication of performance of the set as a whole. The third part of the *Clavierübung*, however, seems to involve multiple kinds of ordering, once again

[3] For example, Heinichen's assigning the names "chromatic" and "enharmonic" to the sharp and flat keys, his describing the keys of B major and B-flat minor as the chromatic and enharmonic "extremes" of the circle, marking the boundaries beyond which the remaining keys were "difficult," even "unusable," represent a residue of older tonal thought, which was conditioned by the narrower range of transpositional practice in the sixteenth and early to mid-seventeenth centuries and its regulation by means of the concepts of solmization, the hexachords, and the modes.

[4] See, for example, the ordering of the keys of the first and second parts of the *Clavierübung* (see Chafe, *Tonal Allegory*, 82). The six partitas outline in a progressively widening zigzag interval pattern—B♭–c–a–D–G–e—the distance of a tritone between the first and last keys, after which the tritone relationship between the keys of the *Italian Concerto* (F) and *French Overture* (b) completes the pattern of the tones of the old *cantus mollis* (F hexachord) and *cantus durus* (or C hexachord). Within the symbolic "circle" of the older paradigm (the gamut), the semitone and tritone or *mi/fa* relationships represent points of antithesis and closure, in the case of the concerto and overture perhaps as a symbol of the national styles that were frequently viewed both as polarized and as subsumed within the larger framework of reconciliation within modern German style. For a highly symbolic tritone relationship as part of the key scheme of a single work, see the discussion of Cantata 121 in Chafe, *Analyzing Bach Cantatas*, 139–49 (briefly summarized on p. 188, below).

with no implication of a cyclic performance.[5] And in smaller collections, and in the movement keys of cantatas and passions, we may or may not find such relationships and patterns. In them, the presence of relatively abstract (or inaudible) patterns such as we find in the ordering of collections of individual pieces, always involves interaction with the necessity of immediate musical continuity. In all cases, therefore, when we do find them, or suspect their existence, we must determine how plausible they are in the terms of Bach's time. And sometimes there appear to be multiple, even overlapping patterns, or partial patterns, no one of which can be considered to represent the "structure" of the work. In the case of the *St. Matthew Passion*, for example, we observe a transposition pattern involving the verses of the chorale "O Haupt voll Blut und Wunden," in that the first that we hear, "Erkenne mich, mein Hüter" is in E and is followed very soon after by "Ich will hier bei dir stehen," not only in E♭ but in the identical harmonization (transposed). When, much later, we hear the verse "Befiehl du deine Wege," sung in D to the same melody, we suspect a pattern (even though that verse comes from a different chorale). But when, later still, we hear two further verses of "O Haupt voll Blut und Wunden," one at its highest pitch, in F major, and the other at its lowest, in E Phrygian (sounding like A minor ending on the dominant), we suspect that Bach intended a sequence of verses sung to the same melody but we may not be able to fully rationalize their keys. And, among the three verses of another chorale in the *St. Matthew Passion*, "Herzliebster Jesu, was hast du gebrochen?" we find an entirely different pattern, that of the tritone-related keys of B minor (its first and third appearances) and F minor (its second appearance), one that likewise seems meaningful for other "structural" and theological reasons as well.[6]

It appears, then, that Bach seeks out patterns in the ordering of his works, and when overall patterns are not forthcoming, is content with partial or multiple overlapping ordering principles. Since such principles may not relate to what we call musical structure, we should, in my view, stick as closely as possible to concepts that belong to Bach's time, and never disregard the question of musical continuity. In the Passions, where a continuous narrative dominates the design, this is essential. In the case of the *St. John Passion* there is good reason to believe that an overall ordering principle—the *ambitus* of the six most closely related keys within any single tonal framework—determines much of the design; and it is one that, whether identified by name or not, remained in force until, and sometimes beyond, the Romantic period. In addition, it is not only historically rich, embodying principles of long pedigree in Western music, but in the *St. John Passion* it can be

[5] In this collection tritone relationships play a prominent role. Within the "framing" relationship provided by the E♭ prelude and fugue, the initial set of Kyrie and Gloria chorale preludes moves from that framework to culminate in the three Gloria settings in F, G, and A, the last of which can be viewed in relation to the initial E♭. Then, toward the end of the collection the four duets—in e, F, G, and a—describe a similar progression in which A minor is now followed by E♭.

[6] See Chafe, *Tonal Allegory*, 372–79 for a discussion of possible explanations for these patterns.

shown to relate to Bach's articulating the structural and thematic qualities of the Gospel itself. And it has the capacity to regulate overlapping patterns on both large and small scales. Nevertheless, despite its functioning, overwhelmingly, as the ubiquitous principle behind the ordering of key relationships in Bach's music, there remains a considerable lack of awareness among musical scholars regarding both its validity and its implementation, a situation that is largely the result of an overreliance on highly abstract schemes, sometimes ones involving the ahistorical bleed-through of tonal principles that came into widespread use only in later times. Such practices intensify issues of various kinds surrounding the perennial questions of audibility and musical logic, in some cases introducing "problems" that can be readily resolved when we think in terms of the music theory of Bach's time. In addition, insufficient attention to detail, the lifeblood of Bach's work, in the areas of both music itself and music in relation to historical theology, leads all too frequently to generalizations of questionable validity. As background to more detailed discussion, what follows is a framework that, although it is highly patterned and intriguing to consider, and dovetails in certain respects with important aspects of the theological character of the work, has for me insurmountable problems, largely in the area of what is historically plausible.

In a recently re-published study of the key ordering of the *St. John Passion*, Klaus Hofmann has set forth a scheme of the keys of the "arias" that follows a pattern of descending thirds from the D minor of "Von den Stricken" in Part 1 to the C minor of "Erwäge, wie sein blutgefärbter Rücken" in Part 2—thereby making that movement its "center"—then of ascending thirds from "Erwäge" to the f of "Zerfließe, mein Herze."[7] The focus on "Erwäge," the longest meditative movement of the Passion, is theologically sound, in my view, since along with the arioso "Betrachte," with which it is coupled, it urges the faithful to meditate on the events of Jesus's suffering, which embody the central meaning of the Passion. In Raymond Brown's chiastic diagram of the structure of John's Passion narrative, for example, the scourging, on which it meditates, is the center of the Roman trial (see fig. 4.2). Hofmann's scheme, however, involves special pleading for the chosen sequence of movements, which are not all arias. The key of E♭ is represented by the arioso, "Betrachte, meine Seel," whereas the arioso "Mein Herz," which begins in G and ends on a C that becomes, by hindsight, the dominant of the f of "Zerfließe," is not included. And the key of E is supplied by a chorale, "Durch dein Gefängnis, Gottes Sohn" (albeit, as Hofmann remarks, a chorale whose text was originally that of an

[7] Klaus Hofmann, "Zur Tonartenordnung der Johannes-Passion," in *Bachs Passionen, Oratorien und Motetten: Das Handbuch*, ed. Reinmar Emans and Sven Hiemke, 179–91 (Laaber: Laaber-Verlag, 2009). Hofmann's ordering is as follows: d ("Von den Stricken"); B♭ ("Ich folge dir gleichfalls"); g♭ (recte f♯: "Ach, mein Sinn"); E♭ ("Betrachte, meine Seele"); c ("Erwäge"); E ("Durch dein Gefängnis"); g ("Eilt, ihr angefochtenen Seelen"); b ("Es ist vollbracht"); D ("Mein teurer Heiland"); f ("Zerfließe"). As Hofmann presents them the pattern is of descent from "Von den Stricken" to "Erwäge," then ascent from "Erwäge" to "Zerfließe." As Hofmann notes, this study, which was originally published in *Musik und Kirche* 61 (1991): 78–86, was slightly reworked for the republished version. Here I refer only to the new version.

aria). Hofmann's explanations for these anomalies are insufficiently convincing; his remark that "it is clear that with this third scheme we are not dealing with an accidental constellation but with a compositional plan" (183) seems inflated.

The greatest problem with Hofmann's scheme is less the pattern of thirds per se than his assigning it priority in the "planning" of the work, as if it could somehow represent the structure of the Passion. Describing the supposed aria pattern as providing "tonal gravitational fields whose power of attraction determines the tonal course of the segments that lie between them," Hofmann outlines tonal motion that also involves the intervening movements according to relative sharpness or flatness—that is, the circle of fifths. But while this is certainly correct, it does not dovetail with the pattern of thirds, since that pattern involves third relations of various kinds that are not compatible with circle-of-fifths–based harmonic motion unless the two are discussed closely in relation to one another. And in that case the need for a large-scale paradigm encompassing both the short- and long-range relationships is needed. The great majority of Hofmann's third relationships are not diatonic, but ones involving distantly related key signatures, such as c and E, E and g, g and b, D and f, and in one instance an enharmonic relation involving interpretation of the key of f♯ as g♭ so as to connect it to B♭ and E♭. In fact, the various problems and exceptions to circle-of-fifths motion as described by Hofmann disappear entirely when we think first not of separate movement types and sequences within the work (the chorales and *turba* choruses as patterns subordinate to the supposed aria sequence) but of the successive *ambitus* within which the various movement types function together to create a large-scale design. Viewed that way, the third relationships between E♭ and c, D and b, which involve movements that are adjacent, or nearly so, are entirely different from those between E and g, D and f, which are widely separated (and, of course, the supposed f♯ (g♭)/E♭ relationship between "Ach, mein Sinn" and "Betrachte" spans the division between the two parts of the work). Circle-of-fifths relationships are very prominent in the Passion, fundamental in fact, but are of entirely different "weight," according to whether they appear in (1) recitatives of highly modulatory character, (2) between closed movements connected by recitatives that do not modulate widely, or (3) between movements in entirely different *ambitus*, which are often widely separated in the work. If we accept such a wide-ranging scheme, no matter how abstract, we are obligated to show how it relates to the question of audibility.

In addition, it is necessary to view the key changes in close relation to the text, and especially a text that features numerous symbolic events of Johannine character, such as the G cadence for Peter's "Ich bin's nicht" and its relation to the g of Jesus's "Ich bin's," the suddenness of the shift to sharp keys within the recitative that precedes "Durch dein Gefängnis," and the like. Hofmann describes an increasingly sharp tonal direction (from "Erwäge" to "Durch dein Gefängnis" and the reverse from the latter movement to "Eilt, ihr angefochtenen Seelen," which is correct; but he does not account for the sudden manner in which the flat/sharp shift that is highlighted in the recitative between the choruses "Wir haben ein Gesetz," in F and "Durch dein Gefängnis"/"Lässest du diesen los" (both in E) is made, or the significant fact that the text of that recitative brings out pointedly the Johannine theme of worlds "above" and "below." Similarly, how the two B♭ choruses, "Sei gegrüßet, lieber Judenkönig" and "Schreibe nicht: der Juden König" relate to the E♭ tonalities of "Betrachte, meine Seele" and "In meines Herzens Grunde" is not discussed. Indeed, Hofmann's speculating that Bach might have thought of a B♭ chorale instead of "In meines Herzens Grunde" (because the recitative that follows "Schreibe nicht" ends in B♭) introduces a completely unnecessary "problem," as does his finding the E major of the chorus "Bist du nicht seiner Jünger einer" a digression from the "direct modulatory course" that leads from the B♭ of "Ich folge dir gleichfalls" to the f♯ of "Ach, mein Sinn."

Viewed independently, Hofmann's aria scheme has little or no relationship to anything corresponding to musical structure. The time distances between the various movements vary greatly, some adjacent or nearly so, and others separated by extended time spans and substantial successions of intervening keys. In other words, it is almost purely abstract, much more so than Smend's *Herzstück*, but nevertheless without the kind of clear symbolic role in the design that would aid us in accepting it as an inaudible but meaningful element from an "allegorical" standpoint. The key areas of the Passion follow a principle—the *ambitus* of closely related keys—that holds for the vast majority of Bach's compositional oeuvre. A telling confirmation of its centrality in this regard is that in revising the Passion in 1725, Bach made sure that although the keys of some of the substitute movements were different from their counterparts, in all instances, without exception, they adhered to this principle. In 1725 the choruses that begin and end the second version of the *St. John Passion*, "O Mensch, bewein" and "Christe, du Lamm Gottes" are in E♭ and c, respectively, rather than the g and E♭ of the corresponding movements of the 1724 version; that is, they remain within their respective *ambitus* despite the changes of key. Likewise, the inserted aria with chorale, "Himmel reiße, Welt erbebe," is in f♯ within the *ambitus* of f♯/A (as is "Ach, mein Sinn"), but the aria "Zerschmettert mich" that Bach introduced to replace "Ach, mein Sinn" is in A, consistent with the *ambitus*, but not with the pattern of thirds. And "Ach, windet euch nicht so," introduced to replace both "Betrachte, meine Seele" and "Erwäge" is in C minor, so that in the 1725 version, the key of E♭ is missing from the design of thirds. Hofmann, noting the key substitutions, but not the correspondences of *ambitus*, nevertheless views the scheme of thirds as having priority in the design and the 1725 key modifications as a deviation. In light of the care with which Bach keeps each of the successive *ambitus* intact, even in the 1725 version, we must conclude that it is the ruling principle behind the succession of key areas, taking precedence even over the precise keys in some instances and forming the basis of the large-scale design. I view that design as an overarching symmetry of key areas, within which the transposition patterns underlying the various subsequences—such as the "Jesus of Nazareth" choruses and the *turba* choruses of the trial—are regulated. Whereas the symmetry itself is certainly an abstract design, the means by which it is generated are easily and entirely audible, not only in terms of the continuity within each individual *ambitus* but also at those points where shift between *ambitus* takes place. And the symmetry has a theological purpose that derives from one of the major concerns of John's Gospel—the meaning of the cross, with all its adversarial and salvific associations. Within this design the possibility of a pattern involving third relationships between some (but certainly not all) the arias might be considered, but as a decidedly secondary phenomenon to the succession of key areas. Although Bach's 1725 version cannot be considered as successful as that of the first/last versions, it offers considerable confirmation of the large-scale role of a symmetrical order in the correspondences pointed out by Dürr many years ago between the four movements that introduce verses of "Jesu, deine Passion" (two arias with chorales and two simple chorales) in 1725.[8]

Hofmann's scheme pays insufficient attention to the fact that the Passion unfolds by means of blocks of closely related keys that are not only unified in themselves but widely separated from those directly preceding and following, and linked by recitatives whose theological interpretation provides the reason for the tonal shifting. From this standpoint Hofmann's enharmonic reinterpretation of the f♯ of "Ach, mein Sinn" as g♭ in order to enable two third progressions between the B♭ of "Ich folge dir gleichfalls" and the E♭ of "Betrachte" (not an aria, we remember) is an insurmountable problem. Since the key that Bach chose, f♯, is not only vastly more practical than g♭ (which appears nowhere else as a movement key, or even a recitative modulation, in Bach's vocal music), but also the key that relates to all the surrounding movements, the question of practicality is irrelevant unless we believe that Bach meant us to understand an enharmonic relationship that he could not notate as such. If he did, it would have to be considered a unique departure from his practice in general, just as would the key of g♭ in any context whatsoever. In Bach's work as a whole we do not find instances of recitatives ending in the enharmonic equivalents of the keys that follow. To postulate g♭ as the "real" key on the basis of an abstract and substantially ahistorical pattern is a serious failing. This is an entirely different situation from Bach's notating the eighth prelude and fugue of the *Well-Tempered Clavier*, Book 1, in e♭ and d♯, respectively (or his indicating the key of the chorale "Ich will hier bei dir stehen" of the *St. Matthew Passion* as D♯ rather than E♭).[9] Whereas the key of G-flat *major* would be difficult to accept in a scene that is otherwise centered mostly around A (and would constitute the only instance of such a key among the hundreds of closed movements of the

[8] That is, the keys of "Himmel reiße" (f♯) and "Petrus, der nicht denkt zurück" (A) do not exactly correspond with those of their counterparts, "Er nahm alles wohl in acht" (A) and "Mein teurer Heiland" (D), whereas the *ambitus* remains the same in both instances.

[9] The former instance can be considered to make the very point of enharmonic equivalence in terms of keys involving five flats and six sharps, respectively. That is, both keys are beyond the four-flat and four-sharp limits of the keys of the closed movements of Bach's cantatas and passions, both "difficult" keys in Heinichen's terms. In the case of "Ich will hier bei dir stehen" designating E♭ as d♯ was a convention that is retained in some of Heinichen's keys, for example.

cantatas and passions) the key of G-flat *minor* flies in the face of all but Wagnerian and post-Wagnerian tonal thought. As the relative minor of the key of B-double-flat major (not A), its scale would involve five flats and two double flats, something unheard of as the key of a movement. Arguing for its existence within any kind of patterned scheme is staggeringly abstract.

Enharmonicism certainly has a role in Bach's music, of course. But when it appears in texted compositions—and even in untexted music such as the *Chromatic Fantasy* or unnotated, as in the canon "per tonos" of the *Musical Offering*—it always has a special meaning, embodying opposition that in some cases may be overcome by a sense of transformation or of a "higher" order.[10] This is the case, for example, in the first recitative of Cantata 121 (*Christum, wir sollen loben schon*) where a sudden shift from the dominant of f♯ to C major (through reinterpretation of e♯ as f) is associated with the "wundervoller Art" by which, in the incarnation of Jesus, God became human.[11] And in that cantata the enharmonic modulation is part of an overall tonal design that derives from a chorale melody that—as in the Gregorian chant in which it originated—shifts from Dorian to Phrygian (usually d to e). Bach transposes the melody so that the first and last movements begin in e and end with highly provocative F-sharp major harmonies, whereas the aria that follows the enharmonic modulation just described is in C major. Bach's overall design incorporates tritone-related keys as symbols of the disparity between the divine and the human that is bridged by the incarnation.[12] And, too, there are tritone relationships in the *St. John Passion* as well, although there they are bridged by recitatives that follow the modulatory principles of the circle of keys (what Heinichen calls *toni intermedii*, a vital concept throughout Bach's music). Other instances of enharmonicism can be similarly explained in terms of an "allegorical" motivation. In the case of "Ach, mein Sinn," however, nothing of the kind exists.[13]

---

[10] In the first recitative of Cantata 48 (*Ich elender Mensch, wer wird mich erlösen*), for example, Bach makes an enharmonic shift involving the reinterpretation of A♭ as G♯ for the opposition of "Leib" and "Seele" in the text. In the *Musical Offering*'s canon "per tonos" the enharmonicism is not notated. The version of the "royal theme" that Bach uses in this canon modulates upward by a whole tone for each successive presentation, outlining the keys c–d–e–f♯–a♭ (or g♯)–b♭–c. Bach does not specify where the changes from flat to sharp notation (and back) take place, but it is important to note that in the canonic parts, which imitate at the fifth, the whole-tone relationships between the adjacent keys are "bridged," so that the shifting is "mediated," so to speak: c–g–d–a–e–b–f♯, and so on. At some point enharmonic notation must still be introduced, but the intent behind the canon seems to be to outline circle-of-fifths motion through the minor keys, so that it remains a stage-by-stage harmonic progression.

[11] See Chafe, *Analyzing Bach Cantatas*, 139–49 for a discussion of this modulation in the context of an analysis of Cantata 121.

[12] That is, the F-sharp major on which the first and last movements of the cantata end is associated with Jesus's divinity, expressed in the medieval hymn on which Luther's chorale is based in terms of an alphabetical acrostic design (an "abecedarius") that outlines the letters of the Greek alphabet, the Alpha and Omega (or "A" and "O" in German and Latin) of Revelation. The C major that the enharmonic modulation sets up is, however, associated with John the Baptist leaping in his mother's womb in response to Mary's relating the incarnation: that is, as a response of the flesh (human).

[13] The only explanation I can think of would be that Peter's (implied) avowal of discipleship, meditated on in the B♭ aria "Ich folge dir gleichfalls" and denied by his "Ich bin's nicht" (which symbolizes

I know of no instances in the Bach cantatas and passions where Bach crosses the line between sharp and flat notation in the manner demanded by Hofmann's reinterpreting the f♯ of "Ach, mein Sinn" as g♭. In them, enharmonicism (which is rare) is entirely confined to recitatives. The keys of the closed movements remain within the limits of four flats and four sharps so consistently that we must conclude that "enharmonic" keys—that is, keys of five or more sharps or flats, in which enharmonically equivalent notation is possible—are purposefully excluded. And Bach sometimes goes to extreme lengths to keep to the correct notation. As an instance of Bach's introducing what I would call *implied* (or *potential*) enharmonicism, that is, modulation to a distant point that would be much more conveniently represented by enharmonic notation, we may consider the C-sharp major fugue of the first book of the *Well-tempered Clavier.* There, following the C♯ in which the exposition ends (m. 7), Bach presents us with a sequence (mm. 7–10) in which the bass notes move down the scale to reach G♯ for an entry in that key (mm. 10–12). The next cadence (m. 15) is to d♯, in which there is another entry, this time in minor, following the pattern of the answer, which means that it arrives on a♭ on the downbeat of m. 16. Here Bach reintroduces the sequence pattern of mm. 7–10, so that the bass reaches the pitch E♯ on the downbeat of m. 19. And in this measure he begins an entry in the alto on b♯ that cadences two measures later in the extremely unusual key of E-sharp minor. When this fugue is re-notated in D♭ rather than the C♯ of Bach's autograph, this entry articulates the key of F minor, not at all difficult conceptually. But as E-sharp minor it involves a plethora of "enharmonic" accidentals—double sharps—that must have evoked associations of what Johann David Heinichen called "difficult," even "unusable" keys. That is, it moves into the extreme regions of the musical circle, suggesting the old idea of the musical "labyrinth" within which one could get lost, the association that underlies Johann Caspar Ferdinand Fischer's *Ariadne Musica*, which Bach could have had in mind. In other words, in a collection whose title evokes the tuning that went hand in hand with the new system of keys, Bach might well have chosen one of the sharpest keys of the collection to demonstrate the advanced possibilities of modulation within the framework of a single movement, pushing the player into uncharted regions, as it were, but nevertheless in a manner that preserves how it was understood historically. Moving to the mediant of C♯, the sharpest key of its *ambitus*, that modulation, although provocative, nevertheless follows the basic principle behind the measuring of modulatory distance in Bach's time, the circle of fifths, now moving in the sharp direction through five of the six keys (or cadence degrees): C♯, G♯, d♯, a♯, e♯. It does not involve enharmonic reinterpretation that crosses the line between sharps and flats, whereas Bach's notating the eighth prelude in d♯ and its companion

the change of *ambitus*; see the discussion of the modulation on 213–20 below), leads him so far from Jesus that the f♯ tonality of "Ach, mein Sinn" also embodies an entirely different meaning, that is, that as g♭ it relates to B♭ in a manner that is "hidden" by its notation. This I consider farfetched, but in the absence of some such explanation for the anomalous enharmonicism the pattern of thirds is entirely abstract.

fugue in e♭ proclaims the equivalence of the two keys within a framework that, significantly, does not constitute part of an ongoing musical structure.

My point is that if we introduce enharmonic equivalents for Bach's keys in a casual manner—that is, without explicitly notated modulatory preparation, or in anything other than recitatives and other kinds of "free" movements such as the *Chromatic Fantasy* (or movements, such as canons, in which some sort of clever demonstration is the point)—we automatically remove all sense of the kinds of associations he might have intended for his key relationships. The *conceptualizing* of key relationships is essential; and no conceptual relationship exists between G-flat minor and A major. In Bach's music the diminished fourth (B♭–f♯) is conceptually separate (a form of "cross" relationship) from the major third (B♭–g♭), whether as a tonal or an interval relationship, whereas diatonic or linear chromatic relationships have different meaning.

That is not to say that within any given *ambitus* expressive modulations to keys outside the normal range cannot occur. But, first of all, such events *do* involve modulation, not enharmonic reinterpretation after the fact and out of local context. Most often they involve major/minor shifting, which occurs in various different ways in the *St. John Passion* recitatives. And there is usually a particular relationship between the "distant" key and a counterpart within the *ambitus*, so that the modulatory event is heard in relation to the primary key, a practice that runs throughout all of Bach's music. In the *St. John Passion* Bach introduces the interplay of C major and C minor briefly within the *ambitus* of A minor when John relates Jesus's having predicted his own death; Bach introduces F minor for the "ecce homo" within the context of B♭/g, and contrasts B-flat major and minor in the scenes that narrate the crucifixion and the events following Jesus's death. Likewise, he presents the two successive arias of Cantata 127 in C minor and C major, respectively, within a cantata in F, and modulates similarly to the dominant minor in the Ascension Oratorio. All such instances, extending beyond the framework of the *ambitus*, are easily explained and perfectly logical and audible within the musical and theological contexts of the works in question.[14]

Large-scale tonal relationships that involve more than a single *ambitus*, and are therefore not as immediately audible, are not at all uncommon. If, for example, we were to consider the key relationships of the chorales of the *St. John Passion* independently of their local functioning, those of Part 1 could be said to fulfill a logical progression: from G minor ("O groß Lieb") to D minor ("Dein Will gescheh") and A major ("Wer hat dich so geschlagen" and "Petrus, der nicht denkt zurück"), as Hofmann suggests. The fifth relationships reflect that Part 1 moves progressively sharp, with a division between the *ambitus* of g/B♭ and A/f♯. After that, in Part 2,

[14] I have discussed Cantata 127 (*Herr Jesu Christ, wahr' Mensch und Gott*) in *Tonal Allegory*, 165–66, and in *Analyzing Bach Cantatas*, 158–59; and the Ascension Oratorio in "Bach's *Ascension Oratorio:* God's Kingdoms and Their Representation,"in *Bach Perspectives 8: J. S. Bach and the Oratorio Tradition*, ed. Daniel R. Melamed (Urbana: University of Illinois Press, 2011), 122–46).

the first three chorales—"Christus, der uns selig macht" (E Phrygian) "Ach, großer König" (A minor), and "Durch dein Gefängnis" (E major)—could be considered to outline motion further sharp according to the circle of fifths, reaching with "Durch dein Gefängnis" the sharpest movement key of the Passion. In the latter sequence as a whole points of comparison exist: between the A major ending of Part 1 and the E Phrygian/A minor beginning of Part 2 (contrasting Peter and Jesus), then between E Phrygian and E major (Jesus's sufferings in themselves versus their salvific meaning). This would certainly reflect much of what the modulatory character of the Passion describes on a large scale. But it would be difficult to reconcile it with the keys of "In meines Herzens Grunde" (E♭) "Mein teurer Heiland"/"Jesu, der du warest tot" (D), "Er nahm alles wohl in Acht" (A), "O hilf Christe" (F Phrygian), and "Ach Herr, laß dein lieb Engelein" (E♭), apart from consideration of the extent to which Bach has dovetailed the various seemingly independent patterns of the design as a whole. Within the context of a succession of differentiated *ambitus*, however, all such "problems" disappear, so that details such as the transposition pattern of the "Jesus of Nazareth" choruses may be considered meaningful within a larger framework. Whereas Hofmann's pattern of thirds breaks down in its "descending" half—between the B♭ of "Ich folge dir gleichfalls" and the f♯ of "Ach, mein Sinn" in Part 1, then between that f♯ and the E♭ of "Betrachte, meine Seele"—the initial part of the "ascending" half forms part of a larger design of motion in the sharp direction within the flat keys that comprise the *ambitus* of B♭/g: that is, from its "subdominant" (E♭/c) to its "dominant" (F/d) region (but see ch. 6). Then, following a complete shift of *ambitus* (to that of A/f♯), the modulatory direction reverses, a pattern that dovetails with the transposed repetition of the choruses in reverse order. And it makes the final dialog between Jesus and Pilate into a pivot in the structure of the work—between spiritual and worldly perspectives on law and freedom—leading to the judgment of crucifixion, now a semitone lower (D) than the beginning of the "ascent" pattern with E♭. After that, Bach returns to the *ambitus* of B♭/g, now with a modulation that mirrors the shift of location to Golgotha and making a profoundly symbolic culmination of the return with the E♭ that began the "ascent." In that respect, the tonal motion from E♭ to E and back to E♭ contributes to a design that places the enormous conflicts and oppositions of John's narrative in the context of their overall theological meaning: the internalizing of the name and cross of Jesus, in the E♭ chorale "In meines Herzens Grunde." It might, perhaps, be argued that the pattern of thirds from "Erwäge" to "Durch dein Gefängnis" is a product of an overarching pattern of "ascent" that subsumes the point of division between the flat and sharp *ambitus*, whereas, after the sudden shift to sharp keys, the pattern is one of "descent," no longer by thirds but through the sharp *ambitus* that culminates in the b/D of "Wir haben keinen König" and is then followed by further "descent" to "In meines Herzens Grunde." Such a design would not involve either enharmonic relationships or the selection of a particular group of movement types. And it would not be strictly that of a pattern of thirds but of reversed circle-of-fifths motion within two highly contrasted *ambitus* that Bach has made components of an immensely symbolic sequence of events. In such a design Hofmann's third sequence would be a product or facet of the modulatory design, not the reverse.

In chapter 6 we will see that Bach's arrangement of tonal centers within the segments that embody the aforementioned tonal "reversal," exhibits a high degree of correspondence with the pattern of Heinichen's presentation of the circle.[15] It is not necessary to argue, however, that this correspondence be understood as a direct reference to that pattern, if only for the reason that the tonal relationships it embodies are entirely comprehensible in the more general terms of the time.[16] That is, the specific arrangement of Heinichen's *ambitus*, although particular to him, reflects widely accepted tonal principles of the early eighteenth century, ones rooted in fifth relationships that bridge the gap between the several "levels" involving (1) harmonic progressions in individual movements, (2) key relationships within and between single movements, and (3) the organization of key successions in multimovement works. Although it is distinctly possible that the considerable correspondence between Bach's design and Heinichen's *ambitus* is coincidental, it seems clear that Bach recognizes the need for an overall structural design (or at least an "allegorical" one, representing a higher order) to overcome what are otherwise disparities and irreconcilable events. Briefly put, Bach's symbolic trial involves two highly contrasted *ambitus* that are reversed in terms of their internal circle-of-fifths–based motion—their modulatory directions—the second (transposed and reversed) one culminating in the judgment of crucifixion as the outcome of the conflict they symbolize. After that, the return to the original *ambitus*, "explains" and resolves that conflict in the chorale that meditates on John's highly symbolic and ironic royal inscription. The difference between the two points is that between the *judgment* of crucifixion, pronounced by a worldly authority, and the crucifixion *itself*, the central component of God's plan for the salvation of humanity. For some, this culminating point represents Bach's following the pattern of the fivefold division of the Passion into separate *actus*, or scenes, which is rooted in what I have just described. But, while this reflection of tradition is true to some

[15] This correspondence to the pattern of Heinichen's circle may not mean that Bach deliberately followed Heinichen in this respect. Nor does it mean that Heinichen's is the classic presentation of the circle. Johann Mattheson's follows a different pattern. Note, however, that Bach himself was the Leipzig agent for the revised 1728 edition of Heinichen's treatise (David, Mendel, Wolff, *New Bach Reader*, 139–40). While that edition was published after the composition of the *St. John Passion*, it is reasonable to conclude that Bach might have known the first edition as well.

[16] Johann Mattheson's circle of keys, for example, follows a different pattern from that of Heinichen, and Mattheson argues for the priority of his on account of its utilizing only third and fifth (i.e., consonant) relationships between adjacent keys, whereas Heinichen's introduces the major second between each "relative major/minor" pairing. In Mattheson's circle the pattern of the C/a *ambitus* is F–d–a–C–G–e, as opposed to Heinichen's F–d–C–a–G–e. Behind them both, however, lies the circle-of-fifths principle. Mattheson describes his circle as an "improved" one in which one can pass "more conveniently through all the keys than the one discovered up to now." See Mattheson, *Kleine Generalbaß-Schule*, facsimile edition with an introduction by Sven Hiemke (Laaber: Laaber-Verlag, 2003), 131.

extent, it does not begin to explain Bach's design. For that we need to understand the basics of Bach's modulatory practices.

Johann David Heinichen and the *ambitus*

In what follows I will adhere as closely as possible to the concepts of the time. The most useful in this endeavor is that of the tonal *ambitus*, named by Johann David Heinichen as both the key to the musical circle and also the means by which the circle solved the problem of key relationships once and for all.[17] As Heinichen presents it, the *ambitus* comprises the six keys and three key-signature levels of our modern subdominant (and supertonic), tonic (and submediant or relative minor), and dominant (and mediant), speaking in terms of the major key. In minor keys the supertonic is replaced by the flat seventh, thereby keeping the six keys the same for relative major/minor pairings. Thus the *ambitus* of both C major and A minor comprises the keys of C–d–e–F–G–a. The *ambitus* was the descendant of the medieval-renaissance hexachord, which was originally a melodic concept but became later, in practice at least, a harmonic one (as in Monteverdi, for example), and by Bach's time was a *tonal* one.[18] Whereas the hexachord is usually described in purely melodic terms as a six-note scale (C–D–E–F–G–A, in the case of the natural hexachord or *cantus naturalis, durus* in a two-hexachord framework) it was in reality much broader in scope, forming a closed circle rooted in the perfect fifth: F–C–G–D–A–E, with the flat/sharp boundaries, F and E, the *fa* and *mi* degrees of solmization, defining its tonal limits. Hexachord shift, or mutation, brought this

---

[17] Johann David Heinichen, *Neu erfundene und Gründliche Anweisung zu vollkommener Erlernung des General-Basses* (Hamburg, 1711). Facsimile reprint, ed. Wolfgang Horn, in Documenta Musicologica, Erste Reihe (Kassel: Bärenreiter, 2000), 261–67.

[18] See Chafe, *Monteverdi's Tonal Language* (New York: Schirmer, 1992), 45–47. Heinichen was not, of course, the only theorist to use the term. In relation to earlier usages, however, his is the most relevant for the understanding of tonal music because his is the only treatment that systematically sets the *ambitus* within the framework of the full circle of keys. It is possible to see a kind of "evolution" not only in the development of the harmonic language it represents from Monteverdi to Bach but also in the meaning of the term from the late seventeenth-century to Heinichen. Thus Andreas Werckmeister discusses the concept frequently, and always to mean octave species (see, e.g., his *Harmonologia Musica* (Frankfurt and Leipzig, 1702), 57ff.; *Musicalische Paradoxal-Discourse* (Quedlinburg, 1707), 56–60. 68–70. 86–88). This view of the *ambitus* already marks a significant change from the meaning of *ambitus* as the range of a mode or melody—a change that reflects its association with tonality. Friedrich Erhard Niedt (*Musicalische Handleitung*, pt. 1, ch. 12 [Hamburg, 1710]) discusses the concept in terms of key signatures, naming the *ambitus* of C minor, for example, as "most of the time, A flat or G sharp," by which he means the last accidental in the key signature (the "meistentheils" refers to the fact that C minor was sometimes written with a two-flat signature; similarly, the *ambitus* of A major is "meistentheils" G sharp). Johann Mattheson calls the *ambitus* the "Umfang" or "Sprengel" of the key, meaning, like Heinichen, the spectrum of closely related keys; but his treatment of the concept is not as comprehensive as Heinichen's, either in terms of its presentation as a theoretical concept or in terms of the keys it encompasses. See, for example, Mattheson's *Grosse General-Bass Schule* (Hamburg, 1731), 49, 229, 233, 339.

out clearly in the shift of the central *mi/fa* semitone at the fourth or fifth—from E/F to A/B♭, for example. The *mi/fa* was, therefore, not only a designation for the placement of the only semitone, dividing the hexachord into two fifth-based scale beginnings—C–D–E, and F–G–A in the case of the natural hexachord—but also the means and symbol of tonal shift.[19] In the circle-of-fifths model of the hexachord the *fa/mi* semitone became the point of closure of the circle, which, when the circle was interpreted in terms of the expanded harmonic content of seventeenth-century music, became the Phrygian cadence, the meeting point of the flattest and sharpest harmonies of the hexachord.[20] Grouped in the key sequence F–d–C–a–G–e (in the case of the C major/A minor *ambitus*), the concept, as Heinichen defined it, expanded the paradigm of medieval and Renaissance music, the *gamut* with its overlapping hexachords, to the new paradigm of the eighteenth-century circle of keys, encompassing, in theory at least, twelve overlapping *ambitus* (fig. 5.1).

In the *St. John Passion* the concept of *ambitus* and the fifth relationships in which it is rooted can hardly be overrated in terms of its defining the tonal "units" of the Passion. In the *St. John Passion* fifth relationships underlie the harmonic and tonal motion at all levels. In Part One the "Jesus of Nazareth" choruses perfectly illustrate the harmonic model of the forerunner of Heinichen's *ambitus*, the harmonically interpreted hexachord of the early seventeenth century. Comprising just the harmonies associated with the six degrees of the hexachord, each chorus outlines a circle of fifths that ends with the Phrygian cadence: g–D–g–c–F–B♭–E♭ [c^6]–D, in the case of the first one (see ex. 4.4, ch. 4), and transposed in that of the others.[21] The word *ambitus* means circle; and each of the "Jesus of Nazareth" choruses is potentially a circle, the final chord of which could lead directly back to the beginning to repeat the pattern ad infinitum (with the necessary adjustments). In associating it with the name "Jesus of Nazareth," Bach perhaps intended that the circular aspect of the harmony symbolize Jesus's divinity, which was a widespread association for the circle in Lutheran theology, mirroring John's presentation of Jesus as Alpha and Omega, beginning and ending (since a circle has no beginning and ending).[22] We find this idea represented musically in Cantata 41, *Jesu, nun sei*

---

19 Lorenzo Penna, for example, describes increasing flats or sharps in the key signatures as changing *mi* into *fa* or vice versa. Penna, *Li Primi Albori Musicali (*Bologna, 1672), 34–35). And Johann Kuhnau describes modulation in terms of *fa/mi* transformation in his preface to *Texte zur Leipziger Kirchen-Musik*, repr. in B. F. Richter, "Eine Abhandlung Joh. Kuhnau's," *Monatshefte für Musik-Geschichte* 34 (1902): 148–54.

20 See Carl Dahlhaus, *Untersuchungen über die Entstehung der harmonischen Tonalität* (Kassel: Bärenreiter, 1968), 260.

21 This statement must be qualified slightly in the case of "Wir dürfen niemand töten" in which the music of "Jesus of Nazareth" appears in part at the beginning and in part at the ending of the music of a different chorus. The difference is that, whereas the other four instances of the chorus begin with articulation of the tonic, then move to the dominant to begin the circle-of-fifths progression, "Wir dürfen niemand töten" begins with the dominant.

22 Johann Olearius, commenting on Rev 2:10 in his *Biblische Erklärung* 5:1910, describes the circle as symbol of "infinite perfection" (*unendliche Vollkommenheit*).

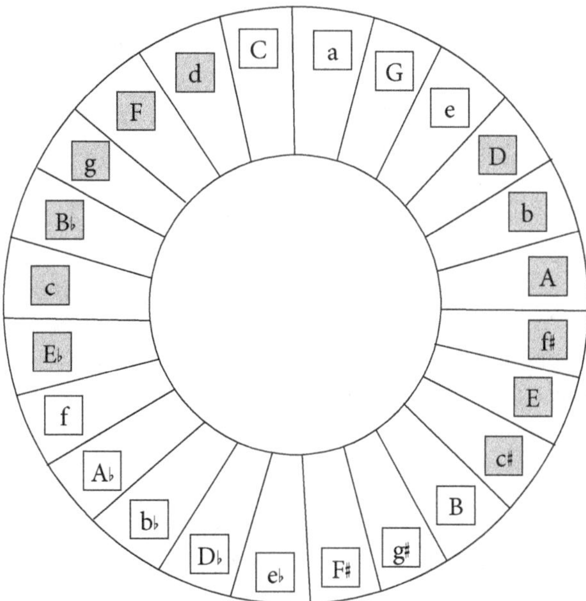

FIGURE 5.1 **Johann David Heinichen's circle-of-keys from the *Neu erfundene und gründliche Anweisung* (1711), 261** *One obvious error corrected. Shaded areas refer to the* ambitus *of the first and second divisions of Bach's "symbolic trial" (see the discussion in ch. 6)*

gepreiset, in which Jesus is described as "A" and "O"—the Alpha and Omega of Revelation—and as beginning and ending (*Anfang und Ende*), a trope associated with New Year's Day, for which the cantata was composed. Bach begins and ends the cantata with the same emblematically conceived music; and the cantata as a whole makes particular associations between the circle of fifths and the idea of cyclic return.[23] In this light, the circular pattern of the "Jesus of Nazareth" choruses is perhaps a representation of the self-contained aspect of God that is projected by the association of Jesus's "Ich bin's" to similar statements of God in the Hebrew Bible: that is, those statements in which the predicate nominative construction is used.[24]

But, whatever the particular association, the patterned character of the movement renders it easily recognizable on its later appearances, when its original association with "Jesus of Nazareth" will be remembered. The harmonies of the first of the choruses correspond to the keys in the initial B♭/g *ambitus* of the Passion,

[23] I have taken up these questions in "*Anfang und Ende:* Cyclic Recurrence in Bach's Cantata *Jesu, nun sei gepreiset,* BWV 41," in *Bach Perspectives* I, ed. Russell Stinson, 103–34 (Lincoln: University of Nebraska Press, 1995). Olearius (see n. 22) describes the circle in the same manner that he does the Alpha and Omega of Rev 1:8 (*höchste Vollkommenheit*).

[24] For Rambach's association of the royal inscription and such sayings, see ch. 6, n. 54.

whose principal subject is Jesus's divine identity: *g*, *c*, F, *B♭*, E♭, *d* (note that the italicized keys are those of the closed movements; F and E♭ appear only in recitatives). It mirrors extraordinarily closely the normal tonal range and the principles of fifth-based tonal organization that we find in the great majority of the Bach cantatas, and that is the principle behind the organization of individual segments of the larger works, such as the passions. In certain extended works, such as the *Mass in B minor* and the *Christmas Oratorio*, adjacent or even contrasted *ambitus* may expand the tonal range significantly, usually according to the degree of dramatic contrast or transformation involved in their texts. Those two works, and certain others that modulate outside the normal range of the *ambitus* (usually relatively briefly), generally identify a single key or *ambitus* as the center (b/D for the *Mass in B minor*, the *Christmas Oratorio*, the *Ascension Oratorio*, and so on). In the case of the passions, however, where the degree of dramatic conflict is at its greatest, the tonal range generally expands to that of all or most of the full circle of keys, and the sense of a single central key or *ambitus* is considerably lessened.[25]

In the *St. John Passion* the nine successive key regions are easily distinguished from one another, most of them featuring no keys that are common to the adjacent *ambitus* (fig. 5.2), a very significant feature in itself. The *ambitus* in question is usually unambiguous, the only real questions arising when the relatively small number of keys admits interpretation in terms of two *ambitus*. In such cases any doubt can normally be resolved by interpreting the most prominent key[s] as the "center" (i.e., as the "tonic" or relative major/minor, rather than as either the subdominant-supertonic or dominant-mediant "side") of the *ambitus*.

Two important qualifications must be introduced here. The first is that the tonal boundaries that correspond to those of a single *ambitus* do not necessarily coincide with anything that might be taken to comprise a self-contained "scene" in the Passion narrative. As we have seen, the B♭ of "Ich folge dir gleichfalls" looks back to the g and d of the preceding segment of the Passion; its role in the unfolding narrative of the scene that ends Part 1 (which centers largely but not exclusively on that of Peter's denial and repentance) necessitates that we view the flat/sharp motion that leads to A as an ongoing process that cuts across the boundaries. We cannot always identify change of *ambitus* with change of location, for example (although we can in the case of the shift to Golgotha after the trial). The recitative that follows the D-minor chorale "Dein Will gescheh" narrates Jesus's being bound and taken to Annas; but, like the aria "Von den Stricken" that follows, it remains in D minor. Change of key, but not of *ambitus*, comes with the recitative and aria that follow "Von den Stricken," both of which are in B♭ and seem to mark another kind of beginning, in that the narrative turns directly to Peter's story. Yet, the following recitative, beginning with the remark that Peter and another disciple followed

---

[25] In practical terms the full spectrum is hardly ever used (unless we consider modulations within recitatives as well as those of the closed movements). Bach's normal range for closed movements in the passions and cantatas is four flats to four sharps.

SEGMENT	MOVEMENTS	KEYS	AMBITUS
1	*"Herr, unser Herrscher"*	g	g/B♭ (♭♭)
	"Jesum von Nazareth" I	g	
	"Jesum von Nazareth" II	c	
	"O große Lieb"	g	
	"Dein Will' gescheh'"	d	
	"Von den Stricken"	d	
	"Ich folge dir gleichfalls"	B♭	
2	1) **"Wer hat dich so geschlagen"**	A	A/f♯ (♯♯♯)
	2) **"Ich, ich und meine Sünden"**		
	"Bist du nicht seiner Jünger einer?"	E	
	"Ach mein Sinn"	f♯	
	"Petrus, der nicht denkt zurück"	A	
3	**"Christus, der uns selig macht"**	E Phrygian (a)	a/C (♮)
	"Wäre dieser nicht ein Übeltater"	d	
	"Wir dürfen niemand töten"	a	
	"Ach, großer König"	a	
	"Nicht diesen, sondern Barrabam"	d	
4	*"Betrachte, meine Seele"*	E♭	B♭/g (♭♭)
	"Erwäge"	c	
	"Sei gegrüßet, lieber Jüdenkönig"	B♭	
	"Kreuzige"	g	
	"Wir haben ein Gesetz"	F	
5	**"Durch dein Gefängnis, Gottessohn"**	E	A/f♯ (♯♯♯)
	"Lässest du diesen loß"	E	
	"Weg, weg mit dem, kreuzige ihn"	f♯	
	"Wir haben keinen König"	b	
6	*"Eilt, ihr angefocht'nen Seelen"*	g	B♭/g (♭♭)
	"Schreibe nicht: der Juden König"	B♭	
	"In meines Herzens Grunde"	E♭	
7	"Lasset uns der nicht zerteilen"	C	C/a (♮)
8	**"Er nahm Alles wohl in Acht"**	A	D/b (♯♯)
	"Es ist vollbracht"	b	
	"Mein teurer Heiland"/**"Jesu, der du warest tot"**	D	
9	*"Zerfließe, mein Herze"*	f	E♭/c or f/A♭ (♭♭♭ or ♭♭♭♭)
	"O hilf, Christe, Gottessohn"	F Phrygian (b♭)	
	"Ruht wohl, ihr heiligen Gebeine"	c	
	"Ach Herr, laß dein lieb' Engelein"	E♭	

FIGURE 5.2 **The keys of the closed movements of the *St. John Passion,* organized by ambitus (chorales in bold, poetic texts in italics, biblical texts in roman type)**

Jesus, returns to G minor before effecting what must be viewed as the most significant tonal shift in Part 1, to A major at the end of the recitative. The *ambitus* of A/f♯ then holds for the remainder of Part 1. In this light, it is clear that the shift from the two-flat to the three-sharp *ambitus* is itself an allegory not so much of the shift of location that is expressed between the first and second of the traditional five divisions of the Passion (*hortus* and *Pontifex*) as it is of the meaning behind Peter's story—his "fall" and "conversion" through repentance. Identifying a single point of division would be arbitrary, especially in light of Bach's not confirming the point of flat/sharp shift with any kind of meditative interpolation. The narrative surrounding Peter's first denial can nevertheless be considered as what I would call the "focal point" for the shift, one whose motivation is primarily theological. In this light, the *ambitus* has somewhat of an abstract character, at least insofar as its exact boundaries are concerned. Its purpose is not to define completely self-contained units, that is, substructures comparable to cantatas, as some scholars have suggested.

And the second qualification is the necessity of recognizing that recitatives and closed movements (the latter interpreted strictly as non-recitative movements that begin and end in the same key) have different roles in the tonal design. Failure to recognize this fact, which is an extension of the relative roles of recitatives and closed movements in the cantatas, has led to considerable misunderstanding.[26] In the *St. John Passion* the successive *ambitus* are normally distant from one another along the circle of keys, and they involve tonal "units" whose sharp, flat, and natural key signatures can be viewed as "descendents" of the old hexachords. The points of shift between these *ambitus* sometimes involve what I would call "crossover" modulations, those in which the change from flat to sharp pitches (or the reverse) is prominent (and usually very pointedly aligned with the meaning of the text). As in the cantatas, whereas the closed movements do not extend beyond the keys represented by signatures of four sharps and flats, the recitatives often do so. At the same time, however, these more wide-ranging, transitional, coloristic, or even incidental-sounding key relationships have nothing like the structural stability of the keys of the closed movements. Yet they certainly inform us concerning the associative qualities of the various keys and *ambitus* in general. In the *St. John Passion* they feature very pronounced qualities of "tonal allegory," in that those points where the modulations between adjacent *ambitus* are most clearly defined are always singled out by Bach with great care.

Between the first and second *ambitus* (B♭/g and A/f♯, respectively), for example, the recitative that accomplishes the shift begins in g, principal key of the first *ambitus*, and ends on E, dominant of the A major chorale that confirms the beginning of the second *ambitus*. The new *ambitus* is bounded by two A-major chorales, the first of which comprises two successive verses, "Wer hat dich so geschlagen?" and "Ich, ich und meine Sünden," sung to the same music in an obvious question/answer relationship, while the second, "Petrus, der nicht denkt zurück," ending Part I, comes from a different chorale. In broad terms, the shift of *ambitus* reflects

---

[26] Alfred Dürr, in a criticism of my initial (1981) presentation of the symmetrical key arrangement of the Passion, remarks that my key arrangement "presupposes that the composer chose to ignore natural relationships, preferring instead to interpret a modulation from G to C as a shift to a new key, and one from G to C♯ as evidence of a single key" (Dürr, *Johann Sebastian Bach's "St. John Passion,"* 100). The latter part of this sentence is, apparently, a reference to the modulation contained in ex. 6.2, ch. 6, although the description is inaccurate and bears no relation to my diagram in which the passage is clearly labeled "modulatory." The full diagram, essentially the same as that given here as figure 4.2, makes clear that the modulation in question is transitional, that it represents a change of *ambitus*, not in any sense "evidence of a single key."

that whereas the beginning of the Passion centers on Jesus, the concluding segment of Part 1 deals with the subject of Peter's denial and repentance as the model for human guilt and repentance. Bach's setting what many would consider the logical beginning point of the episode in John—"Simon Petrus aber folgete Jesum nach, und ein and'rer Jünger"—in B♭ and following it immediately by the B♭ aria "Ich folge dir gleichfalls," underscores the meaning of the flat/sharp shift that is associated with Peter's denial in the transitional recitative that follows. That shift does not represent division of the Passion into discrete cantata-like segments or units but involves, rather, a strong sense of both change and overlap between the adjacent tonal regions. To understand this fully we now consider Part 1 again, from the standpoint of the shift of *ambitus* and its meaning.

The *St. John Passion,* Part 1: The tonal design and its symbolism

The initial *ambitus* of the Passion centers unmistakably on the figure of Jesus: first in majesty ("Herr, unser Herrscher"), then as the self-revealing, foreknowing, and all-powerful Messiah (the two "Jesus of Nazareth" choruses and the words "Ich bin's" associated with them), the loving protector of the disciples (the chorale "O große Lieb'," and the recitative that precedes it), the obedient agent of God's will (the chorale "Dein Will' gescheh'" and the recitative that precedes it), the being who suffers so that humanity may go free (aria "Von den Stricken"), and the Messiah who "draws" his disciples and ultimately the contemporary believer to follow him (aria "Ich folge dir gleichfalls"). With this aria an important shift takes place; for the first time the contemporary believer identifies with a "character" of the narrative, Peter, who embodies the question of discipleship, or the "following" of Jesus ("Nachfolgung Christi"), a theme that dictated the subject matter and titles of numerous treatises in the centuries before Bach.[27]

Within this first *ambitus* all the closed movements except the final one, the B♭ aria "Ich folge dir gleichfalls," are in minor (g, c, or d), which may seem surprising in light of the themes just summarized. Since John is famous for his portrayal of Jesus as the all-powerful divine being who undergoes the Passion voluntarily, with foreknowledge of the coming events and the power to direct everything according to his will, why then does Bach set some of John's most characteristic expressions of Jesus's divinity in minor? And, having done so, why does he turn to A major for the chorale verses "Wer hat dich so geschlagen?"/"Ich, ich und meine Sünden" and "Petrus der nicht denkt zurück," all of which express human guilt? Most of all, why does he set Jesus's expressions of divine self-identification ("Ich bin's"), and the "Jesus of Nazareth" choruses to which they respond, in minor, and Peter's denials ("Ich bin's nicht") in major?

[27] Two of the most influential were those of Thomas à Kempis (especially as translated by Johann Arndt) and Johannes Tauler. See ch. 4, n. 67.

The passages just mentioned are, in fact, a key not only to the two *ambitus* of Part 1 and the points of shift between the two parts, but also to the theological meaning of the Passion as a whole, which, put in its simplest terms, centers on the opposition between the voluntary, loving suffering of Jesus according to God's plan for the salvation of a sinful humanity and the benefit of that work for humanity. Peter is the Passion's foremost representative of humanity. The most obvious point of contradiction between keys is that between G minor and major, the former concerned with Jesus's identity and symbolized very pointedly in his referring to himself with the expression "Ich bin's" ("*ego eimi*" in John's Greek), and the latter with Peter's denial of his discipleship, "Ich bin's nicht" ("*ouk eimi*"). In the third "version" of the Passion, these two keys began and ended Part 1. We need no complex theological demonstrations for the meaning of a verbal parallel that stands forth so clearly on the surface of the narrative. But such demonstrations lie ready to hand, nevertheless. Jesus's "Ich bin's" is one of several "*ego eimi*" sayings in John's Gospel, by which Jesus reveals his divine nature in an expression that had that particular association in the OT.[28] And Peter's twice responding with "Ich bin's nicht" to questions regarding his identity have been widely recognized by theologians as the "negative counterparts" of Jesus's words, the "contrast of Jesus's confession of who He is in defense of the disciples and Peter's denial that he is a disciple."[29] August Hermann Francke does not discuss this theme directly in his Passion lectures, but we find exactly this parallel in the Lutheran chorale "Ich bin's, darf nur Jesus sagen," all four verses (and half-verses) of which begin with "Ich bin's." (Here I cite the text as it appears in the second part of the Freylinghausen *Gesangbuch*, first published in 1713, by Francke's friend and student, Johann Anastasius Freylinghausen.)[30] Note the distinct emphasis on the *Christus victor* portrayal of Jesus in the second and third lines of the first verse, which refer to John's Passion narrative; Freylinghausen indicates John 18:4–8 as the source):

Ich bin's, darf nur Jesus sagen,	I am (he), Jesus only needed say,
so kann er zu Boden schlagen,	in order to strike to the ground
Sünde, Teufel, Höll und Tod:	sin, devil, hell and death.
Ich bin's, lasst die Menschen gehen,	I am (he), let these people go,
Ich will selber für sie stehen,	I will stand for them myself,

[28] See Brown, *Gospel According to John*, I–XII, 533–38. See also ch. 4, n. 51 (Rambach).

[29] Brown, *Gospel According to John*, XIII–XXI, 824, citing W. Grundmann in *Novum Testamentum* 3 (1959): 65.

[30] Freylinghausen, *Neues / Geist—reiches / Gesang-Buch*, 99. I have retained Freylinghausen's boldface script, which appears only for the initial "Ich bins's" and the "Ich bin's nicht" in strophe four, but updated the capitalization of nouns (used by Freylinghausen only for proper names and references ("Heiland" and "Ich") to God. Although Francke does not take up the contrast of Peter's and Jesus's words, it should be mentioned (for those who prefer direct correspondences and influences) that Francke and Freylinghausen were colleagues and friends in Halle at the time of the publication of the *Geistreiches Gesang-Buch* and Francke's lectures. Freylinghausen's second volume was published three years before Francke's lectures were given.

Ich, der wahre Mensch und Gott.	I, the true man and God.
Ich bin's, sagt er zu uns allen,	I am (he), he says to us all,
wenn die Sünden uns anfallen,	when sins assail us,
wenn der Satan uns verklagt:	when Satan works against us.
Ich bin's, sehet meine Wunden,	I am (he), see my wounds,
Ich hab eine Hülfe funden,	I have found a source of help,
glaubet und seyd unverzagt.	believe and be free from despair.
Ich bin's, spricht er, wenn wir fragen,	I am (he), he speaks, when we ask
ob er unsre Sünd getragen,	whether he bears our sins,
ob er unser Heiland sey?	Whether he is our savior?
Ich bin's, der euch vom Gesetze,	I am (He), who makes you free,
von des Teufels Strick und Netze	from the law, from Hell,
von der Hölle machet frey.	from the devil's bonds and nets.
Ich bin's, der da treu verbleibet,	I am (he) who remains faithful,
obgleich Furcht den Petrum treibet,	although fear drives Peter,
daß er schweret: **Ich bin's nicht!**	So that he swears: 'I am not!'
Ich bin's; wohl dem, der nun glaubet,	I am (he); blessed is the one who now believes,
und, wenn auch gleich Saulus schnaubet,	and, even if Saul rails,
Ich bin's, dennoch allzeit spricht!	nevertheless always speaks I am!

From this chorale we see just how Jesus's "Ich bin's" and Peter's "Ich bin's nicht" were understood in the Lutheran tradition. The first verse makes clear that Jesus's response in the *St. John Passion* to the demand for "Jesus of Nazareth" is an expression of messianic self-revelation that strikes not just the arresting party but the familiar forces of evil as identified in Aulén's "classic" view of the atonement—sin, the devil, hell, and death—to the ground.[31] Jesus's identity as "der wahre Mensch und Gott" is crucial. The second identifies faith as the means of avoiding sin, the devil, and despair. The third answers the believer's questions regarding Jesus's identity as savior, his bearing human sin, and his freeing humanity from the law, the

[31] The character of messianic self-revelation behind Jesus's "Ich bin's" was recognized in every Lutheran commentary on the Passion during the seventeenth and eighteenth centuries. Francke, for example, remarks (*Oeffentliche Reden,* 10), "What majesty must have shone in his eyes with these words. What kind of shock must have overcome them with it that they drew back and fell to the ground. Certainly, this was a foreshadowing of the last judgment, where he as a judge of the living and the dead will strike the godless with terror and will say to them, 'Depart from me, you evildoers' (Mt 7:23)." Similarly, on Jesus's remark "Du sagest's: Ich bin ein König," in the trial scene, Francke cites Paul's remarks on Jesus's majesty (cited in ch 6, n. 8), adding "Not only that, however; but he [Paul] also teaches us that from this manifestation of the deep humiliation ("tieffen Erniedrigung") of Christ we may look into the manifestation of his majesty ("Herrlichkeit") and await him as the king of all kings and lord of all lords in his appearance, or second coming ("Erscheinung oder Zukunft")." Francke further refers to Rev 14, 16, and 19:16 (descriptions of the apocalyptic coming of the Lamb) to characterize what underlies Jesus's "Ich bin ein König" (*Oeffentliche Reden,* 63)

devil, and hell. It links up with the text of the dialog with aria and chorale, "Mein teurer Heiland"/"Jesu, der du warest todt," which poses the same questions. And finally, the fourth verse interprets Jesus's "Ich bin's" as his standing by the believer in times when the crisis of faith is greatest, such as when Peter denies Jesus and when Saul (that is, Paul, before his conversion) rails ("schnaubet," lit. snorts) against Jesus. Peter's denial, then, is the product of his fear, his weakness in seeking self-preservation, not his lack of faith. The line "wohl dem, der nun glaubet" makes clear that faith in Jesus overcomes even such profound contradictions.

In fact, the primary messages of Bach's *St. John Passion* are, first, Jesus's identity, the subject of the trial and the catalyst (or stumbling block) to faith, and second, the benefit of his sufferings and death for the believer (the *pro nobis* that dominates Luther's writings on the Passion). The biblical-texted movements of the *St. John Passion* center on the former, whereas the nonbiblical texts are permeated by oppositions rooted in the latter. Bach unfolds this meaning in the initial *ambitus* of the Passion, which involves a shift in its tonal center from g, culminating in the chorale "O grosse Lieb;" to d, which is set up in the following recitative and confirmed in a second chorale, "Dein Will gescheh." In the initial G minor narrative Bach creates a very compact introductory "scene" around the signposts of Jesus's divinity before proceeding with the unfolding events of the Passion. That "scene," bounded by "Herr, unser Herrscher" and "O große Lieb," has the purpose of proclaiming Jesus as the Messiah and God's love for humanity as the motive for the Passion as cornerstone of the work of redemption. Since God's *Herrlichkeit* and his love are inseparably bound up with one another in the Lutheran commentaries, especially those that emphasize God's *Rath*, a closer look at this initial scene is essential to understanding how Bach sets up the modulatory design of Part One.

"Herr, unser Herrscher" to "O große Lieb": the G-minor introductory scene

"Herr, unser Herrscher" announces Jesus's majesty in no uncertain terms. The first line of its text draws from Psalm 8, making a direct link between Jesus and the God of the OT, affirming both the Trinity (more prominent in John than in the other Gospels) and the unity of scripture, as did many of the new cantatas of the 1723–24 cycle. Its primary affect is that of awe, a quality that is mirrored in the motoric, almost inevitable sounding, character of the rising sixteenth-notes on "Herrscher," the off-the-beat cries of "Herr, Herr," and the sequential character of the circle-of-fifths patterns of the main section. At the same time, chromatic writing in the oboes above the "throbbing" pedal tones, brings out the theme of suffering. The first texted appearance of the circle-of-fifths pattern, set to "dessen Ruhm in allen Landen herrlich ist," begins imitatively with a rising fifth followed by a fivefold repetition of the uppermost tone that seems to anticipate the theme of "Wäre dieser nicht ein Übeltäter" and "Wir dürfen niemand töten," whereas the circles of fifths perhaps anticipate those of "Jesus of Nazareth" (including the reappearance of that music in "Wir dürfen niemand töten"). In "Herr, unser Herrscher" these circles mark the principal structural points. In the main "A" section, the first one takes over from the extended tonic pedal point with which the movement begins. At the end of the opening ritornello (mm. 10–18: basically dominant harmonies on D, G, C, F, B♭ circling back to D), it prepares for the initial entrance of the chorus, in g over the G pedal. The second (mm. 37–40, moving at a faster rate, begins on C and circles through the B♭/g *ambitus*, then returns to g for the reprise of the principal music of the "A" section, now with chorus and ritornello together, closing in G minor. The third (mm. 49–58) is equivalent to the first, as the full ensemble completes the reprise of the ritornello with the text "dessen Ruhm in allen Landen herrlich ist" in the chorus. The fourth (mm. 86–95) then closes the "B" section in the dominant, reiterating the music of 10–18 and 49–58 at the fifth to the text "verherrlicht worden bist" (with slight changes to the "dessen Ruhm" theme necessitated by the different text).

Thus the circle-of-fifths passages associate the main points of structural emphasis in the movement with expressions of Jesus's majesty and the process of his glorification, suggesting a link to those of the "Jesus of Nazareth" choruses. When the music first arrives on the dominant in the principal section (m. 33), Bach introduces a new theme, beginning from an octave leap down (with "Herr" as the uppermost tone, "unser" as the lower, a reflection of John's worlds "above" and "below") then rising again through a diminished fourth that has seemed to some commentators a symbol of the cross. This theme will become prominent in the middle section, in association with the first explicit reference to the Passion. When it first enters, Bach transfers the original sixteenth-note "unser Herrscher" figure to the *basso continuo,* treating it as a pedal rather than a rising line, first on D, then G, so that it sets up the circle-of-fifths pattern of mm. 37–40. Against it he assigns the oboes overlapping diatonic lines in quarter notes, the slower rhythmic motion suggestive, perhaps, of an "iconic" element in the depiction of Jesus. In the "A" section this music works its way back to the original material and tonality, completing the symmetrical design of the segment as a whole. In their layered and melodic-directional qualities many of the musical gestures suggest an above/below quality, which reflects John's approach to the interaction of the divine and the human.

In the middle section, which petitions Jesus to "show" the faithful the process of his glorification through the adverse events to follow, Bach reintroduces the "new" theme of the principal section, for "Zeig' uns durch deine Passion" (this time with "Zeig" as the uppermost tone and "uns" as the lower octave), beginning in E♭, then moving toward f, as if to suggest the character of the first reference to the Passion. In light of its original association we are reminded of the kind of meaning that Rambach, in his commentary on the Passion described as Jesus's majesty being revealed behind the curtain of his sufferings ("Dem nun wird auch in einem Thal die Herrlichkeit GOttes, ob wol hinter dem Vorhange des Leidens, offenbahret").[32]

As the text moves on to "daß du, der wahre Gottessohn," however, the tonality moves away from f, seemingly toward g again; but, in fact, when the G pedal reappears ("zu aller Zeit, auch in der grössten Niedrigkeit") it becomes the bass of the dominant of d (on "Niedrigkeit"): that is, an A^4_2 chord. From the point where this harmony is introduced, the melodic direction reverses from the pronouncedly downward motion of "Niedrigkeit," now leading back upward, in d, for "verherrlicht worden bist" (mm. 67–69). And Bach holds a D pedal for seven and a half measures (mm. 71–78). Nevertheless, the D remains largely in the context of g throughout those measures. At their close, however, Bach increasingly introduces the dominant of d, finally reaching *its* dominant (that is, the diminished-seventh chord on G♯) as the span now arrives on A (m. 78). And from this point he begins the "Zeig' uns" music again, this time from A, above the sixteenth-note bass pattern (whether Bach thought of the A in terms of the tritone relationship to the E♭ in which the middle section began is an open question; if so, it would indicate a tonal allegory of the process of glorification in terms of flat/sharp motion). This A is, of course, the dominant of d, which now remains until the end of the middle section (another eighteen measures).

And, to render the d all the more secure, eight measures after the arrival on A in measure 78, Bach moves yet again toward A, this time stretching out the G♯ diminished seventh chord for a full measure, as the soprano describes a descending arpeggio line on "größten Niedrigkeit," landing on the A pedal once again (m. 86). Now the d is as secure as can possibly be; and, accompanied by the circle-of-fifths harmonies, we hear only the words "verherrlicht worden bist" for the final ten measures of the section, which close emphatically and with great dramatic power, in d.

The reader will have noticed that the three arrivals on A, of progressively greater structural significance, all come on "Niedrigkeit," making the point that it is in Jesus's sufferings and humiliations, mirrored in the striking descent of the soprano line at all three points, that the process of his glorification takes place (the increasing emphasis on d). A modulation to the dominant for the close of a middle section is certainly no very unusual event, for Bach or any other tonal composer; but in this case Bach has taken the utmost care to give it the power of a great event. Anyone listening to the movement will respond not only to the force of the successive arrivals and the final culmination in d, but will be aware at a musical level of the coincidence of the downward melodic motion on "Niedrigkeit" and what can only be called the stages of a tonal "ascent" to the dominant, after which return of the opening section following the d cadence lends the movement a powerful sense of symmetry.

I have given this much attention to the opening chorus because, in fact, it embodies a foreshadowing of the message of the Passion in musical as well as textual

---

[32] Rambach, *Betrachtungen über das gantze Leiden Christi*, 5.

terms. On the largest scale of Bach's design (and in countless small scale details as well), fifth motion in the sharp (dominant) direction leads to points associated with Jesus's *Verherrlichung*, the process of "lifting up" that he announced throughout the Gospel and its benefit for the faithful. This principle operates on the scale of extended movement sequences as well. Later in the Passion tonal motion from flat keys (the E♭ and c of "Betrachte" and "Erwäge") toward the E-major chorale, "Durch dein Gefängnis" and, later still, from the G minor of "Eilt, ihr angefocht'nen Seelen" to the D major of the paired arias "Es ist vollbracht" (b/D/b) and "Mein teurer Heiland" (D) will serve as the foremost manifestations of that quality. In Part 1 the A-major second *ambitus* fulfills a similar role in the design: Jesus's "drawing" the faithful, alluded to in "Ich folge dir gleichfalls," leads humanity's sinful but penitent representative, Peter, to the A-major close of Part 1. And the reverse is also true of fifth motion in the flat direction, although it is never as extended and purposive-seeming in its patterning. The move toward E♭ and C minor for the scourging, including the "ecce homo" of the recitative (F minor) and, later, the narratives of the crucifixion (B-flat minor) and the piercing of Jesus's side (also B-flat minor) provide good instances. In "Herr, unser Herrscher" the fifth motion cannot lead to A or D *major*, as it will later in the Passion; for that we need to consider tonal shift on a larger scale, beginning with the shift of *ambitus* in Part 1.

The recitative following "Herr, unser Herrscher" begins in c and cadences first in that key, then in f, as it moves toward the first indication of Jesus's *Erniedrigung*, the arrival of Judas and the arresting party. From that point it turns back, without cadencing, toward c, g, and, finally B♭, as it describes the arrival of the arresting party and leads toward the all-important narrative of Jesus's foreknowledge of the coming events. That narrative was crafted by Bach in a carefully detailed manner, beginning entirely in B♭, and moving, as it appears, toward a decisive cadence in that key, as John sets up Jesus's words: "Als nun Jesus wußte Alles, was ihm begegnen sollte, ging er hinaus, und sprach to ihnen." (See ex. 5.1) The evangelist's line first outlines the B♭ triad on "Als nun Jesus wußte alles," then for "was ihm begegnen sollte," turns to the subdominant E♭, via its dominant, placing the expressive pitch a♭ on "ihm" and leading it down to g on "sollte." This immediately suggests the *Niedrigkeit* that Jesus foresees, after which, for "ging er hinaus," Bach directs the line upwards through the E♭ triad to the g′ an octave higher, beneath which the bass shifts from e♭ to e♮, as the harmony changes to the dominant of the dominant. The upward surge of the line now mirrors the acceptance of the divine will that underlies both Jesus's foreknowledge and his going forth to meet his adversaries. At the same time, the bass line has been moving upward chromatically from the d of the first measure, reaching the dominant (f) for the evangelist's "und sprach zu ihnen." Having outlined an expanded I–IV–V harmonic pattern, Bach completes the line melodically with the most decisive cadence formula of the recitative. In the bass and the harmony the dominant (F) sounds as if preparing the confirming tonic cadence. But, as Jesus speaks, "Wen suchet ihr?" the upward chromatic motion of the bass line continues up to f# instead, deflecting the cadence away from B♭ and

EXAMPLE 5.1 ***St. John Passion*** *nos. 2a, mm. 13–17, 2b, and 2c, beginning*

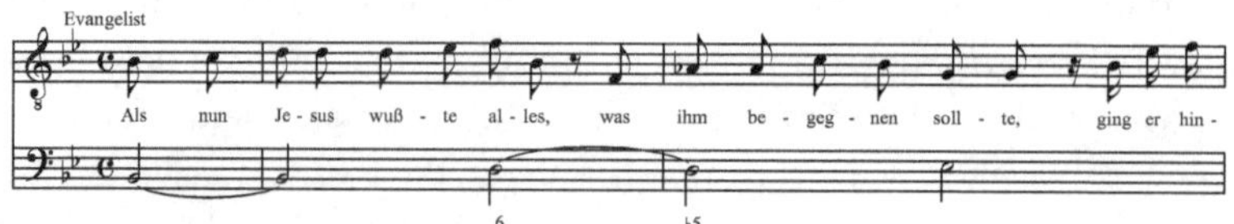

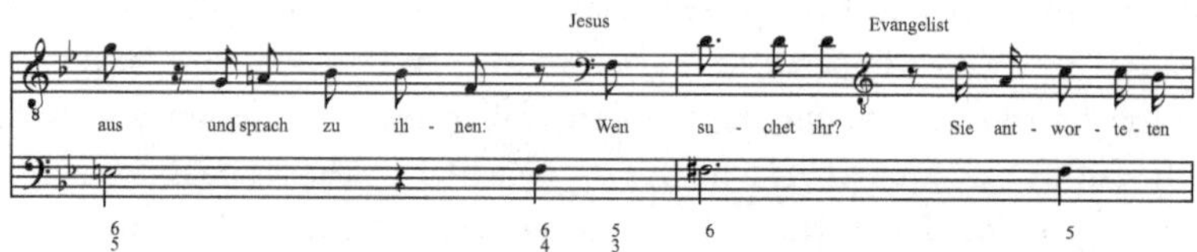

setting up the dominant of g for the response "Jesus of Nazareth." Jesus's very pointed direction of the harmony toward G minor, completes the ascending chromatic tetrachord of the bass line, after which the chorus, as we know, simply circles around the harmonies of G minor, returning to the dominant of g. At this point the dotted rhythm of the word "Nazareth" is the same as that of Jesus's "[Wen] suchet ihr?" upon which Jesus completes the process with the G minor cadence of "Ich bin's."

The recitative just described provides a good example of just how carefully and expertly Bach crafted all the recitatives in the Passion. In this instance the modulatory details mirror very closely the initial sense of Jesus's divinity and foreknowledge (the B♭ beginning), the *Niedrigkeit* that is the object of that foreknowledge (the subdominant and corresponding downward motion of the line), the resolve that is associated with his acceptance of God's will (the dominant and rising motion of the line), his directing the events of the Passion according to that will (the redirecting of the cadence to g), and the underlying theme of Jesus's suffering (the chromatic bass line). As August Hermann Francke and many other commentators have brought out, Jesus's question to the arresting party is unnecessary in light of his foreknowledge, its purpose being to bring out the voluntary nature of his actions, and the revelatory character of his words all the more. After Jesus's "Ich bin's" and John's narrative of how the arresting party was struck to the ground, Jesus puts the question "Wen suchet ihr?" a second time, now shifting from E♭ to the dominant of c for the second "Jesus of Nazareth" chorus. The fifth transposition seems to underscore the continuing theme of Jesus's *Niedrigkeit*. But this time, Jesus's response, "Ich hab's euch gesagt, dass ich's sei, suchet ihr denn mich, so lasset diese gehen" (I have said that I am he; if therefore you seek me then let these ones go) effects a tonal turnaround. The line as a whole expands on the perfect fourth of his "Ich bin's" (now "ich's sei"), cadencing decisively in B♭, a symbolic completion, perhaps, of the earlier, interrupted B♭ cadence. The traditional interpretation of this passage is that Jesus here exhibits divine power in demanding the release of the disciples, as he did in causing the arresting party to draw back and fall to the ground. Both points project Jesus's foreknowledge and divine power. But in this instance the object of Jesus's words is the disciples rather than the arresting party. Here Bach places the G-minor chorale "O große Lieb," making a caesura that links the theme of Jesus's *Herrlichkeit* with the theme of love, the second of the themes cited at the end of chapter 4.

The shift to D minor and its meaning

In John's Gospel, Jesus's demand for the release of the disciples is followed directly by the remark that it was said in fulfillment of what Jesus had predicted earlier in the Gospel, "Ich habe der Keine verloren, die du mir gegeben hast" (Jn 18:9, "I have lost none of those whom you gave to me"). That Bach separates it from the preceding recitative narrative of Jesus's demand for the release of the disciples by the chorale "O große Lieb," leading it to a C-minor cadence, then begins a modulation to D minor with the immediately following narrative of Peter's violent intervention on Jesus's behalf, is a very meaningful sequence of events when we understand the Lutheran interpretation of the passage and its context. That context centers on the meaning of Jesus's references to what God "gave" him, which appear at the beginning and ending of the recitative. The following discussion addresses the question of the shift to D minor, drawing primarily on one theological source from Bach's time, by August Hermann Francke's student and colleague, Johann Anastasius Freylinghausen, author of a number of important theological works in addition to one of the most famous hymnals of the time. In his commentary Freylinghausen draws copiously on earlier exegeses, especially Luther's.[33]

The citation in John 18:9 refers back to John 17:12, one of the most celebrated passages in John, Jesus's extended prayer to the Father (26 verses total), which immediately follows the Farewell Discourse (of which it is sometimes considered a part) and directly precedes the Passion narrative. In that prayer Jesus begins by looking upward to heaven, announcing that his "hour" has come and calling for God to glorify his Son. And over the course of the verses that follow, Jesus refers many times to God's having "sent" him and to what God "gave" him, namely, dominion over all flesh, the power of redemption and eternal life, and especially the disciples, who are themselves sent by Jesus with the mission of continuing his work and extending it to all humanity after Jesus's return to the Father.

Jesus's prayer in John 17 is the fulfillment of the many references to the "hour" of his glorification throughout the Gospel. In the Lutheran tradition, it was commonly divided into three parts: the first (vv. 1–5) culminating in Jesus's announcement of his completion of the work that the Father sent him to do and a prayer for his transfiguration to the "clarity" he had with the Father before the creation of the world; the second (vv. 6–19) dealing with the disciples as those given him by God and now "sent" by Jesus into the world; and the third (vv. 20–26) extending the work of salvation through faith to the entire world.[34] Jesus's prayer, therefore, and related passages in John, were often cited in connection with John's projecting the meaning of God's *Rath* or plan for the salvation of humanity; nowadays these passages are sometimes associated with the theme of determinism. Jesus's proclaiming, in advance of the Passion, his completion of the work given him by God, links the Passion to the resurrection and ascension as the glorious "lifting up" that will begin the process of his return to the Father (bridging to what is commonly called the "book of glory"). In two verses Jesus refers to himself as no longer in the world

---

[33] Freylinghausen, *Das Hohepriesterliche Gebeth.* Freylinghausen cites frequently from Luther's commentary on the chapter in question in the Altenburg edition of Luther's works (of which Bach owned a copy); in addition, he prints as an appendix (677–93) Sebastian Schmidt's commentary, *PARAPHRASIS oder Kurtze Erklärung des XVII Capitels Johannis* (n.d.).

[34] Freylinghausen, *Das Hohepriesterliche Gebeth,* 10–11, 677.

(and the disciples as *in* but not *of* the world). Jesus's prayer has sometimes been understood as John's "spiritual" equivalent of an ascension narrative, taking place paradoxically before the Passion, a thoroughly Johannine characteristic.

In his first chapter Freylinghausen emphasizes both the uniqueness of John's account in relation to those of the Synoptics and the meaning of Jesus's "hour" as that determined by God and predicted by the prophets in scripture:

> Of this, then, he says *It is here*: the hour that you from eternity to now have determined for my suffering in your plan; the hour and time which the Spirit foretold through the prophets (1 Pet 1:11) and in which everything that stands written of the Son of Man should be fulfilled in me (Lk 18:31). . . . the hour now comes, indeed, it is already here and *has come*.[35]

And in his commentary on v. 4 (Jesus's announcement of the completion of the work he was given by God to do), Freylinghausen considers "in what sense Christ could name the work of redemption complete at that time," concluding that

> *since the hour of the Passion had already come* (v. 1), and according to the will, spirit and plan (*Vorsatz*) of the Lord Jesus everything was already complete (for he did not intend to leave anything undone), he could certainly speak with his Father before its completion as if it had already taken place, and say, "I have glorified you on earth; I have completed the work that you gave me to do.[36]

Comparing Jesus to Boaz, husband of Ruth, who "out of love for his poor bride, could not rest until he had brought this great work to its end and completed it (Ruth 3:18)," Freylinghausen links up Jesus's announcement, in John 17:4, of his completed work even before his death, with his "Es ist vollbracht," directly before his death. And in his commentary on v. 7 ("Now they [the disciples] know that

---

[35] Ibid., 8–9, 18–19. The extended discussion of the uniqueness of John's account appears with the marginal remark, "Unterscheid Johannis und der andern Evangelisten in Beschreibung der Paßions-Historie." After expanding on it for several pages, Freylinghausen links it with God's *Rath*: "Davon sagt er denn, **sie ist hie:** Die Stunde, die du von Ewigkeit her in deinem Rath zu meinem Leiden bestimmet hast; die Stunde und Zeit, darauf der Geist in den Propheten gedeutet hat, (1. Pet. I, 11.) und darin alles, was geschreieben stehet von des Menschen Sohn, an mir erfüllet werden soll: Luc. XVIII. 31. . . . die Stunde, rücket nun herbey, ja sie ist schon da, und **ist gekommen**." Over the course of his commentary Freylinghausen makes many further references to God's *Rath* as underlying Jesus's prayer.

[36] Ibid., 102–3. Freylinghausen includes the marginal remark "In welchem Verstande Christus damals das Werck der Erlösung vollendet nennen können." The entire paragraph, from which I have cited the latter part, reads as follows: "Nun ists zwar an dem, daß damals, als der HErr JEsus sagte: **Ich habe vollendet das Werck / das du mir gegeben hast /** er sein grössestes Leiden noch vor sich hatte. Weil aber doch **die Stunde dazu schon da war** (v. 1.) und nach dem Geist, Willen und Vorsatz des Herrn Jesu schon alles vollbracht war, (denn er wolte nichts zurücke lassen,) sihe, so mochte er ja wohl von dieser Vollendung, so, als ob sie schon geschehen wäre, mit seinem Vater reden und sagen: **Ich habe dich verkläret auf Erden; ich habe vollendet das Werck, das du mir gegeben hast / daß ich thun soll.**"

everything that you have given me is from you"), Freylinghausen considers "why the Lord Jesus describes this work as given him by the Father":

> Only, because our savior himself, in this most difficult work for his human nature, looked upon it in no other way than as pure infinite love of the Father toward him, and the entire human race, and because he, in return, loved the Father with his entire heart and soul, and from such love was ready and willing to carry out his will and commands, he did not speak of it as a charge with which he was burdened, but as a gift, of which he, before all in heaven and on earth, was considered worthy, as he also said to Peter in the garden of olives: "Shall I not drink the cup that my father has given me?" (Jn 18:2)[37]

The passages just cited make explicit links among Jesus's announcements of his completed work, Jesus's foreknowledge and the planned nature of that work as given to him by God, and love as the motive behind God's plan, as do many others in Freylinghausen's commentary. In the placement of "O große Lieb," Bach simultaneously links Jesus's protection of the disciples to God's love for humankind and delays John's announcement of the fulfillment of Jesus's prediction until the following recitative, where it links up with the theme of God's plan for the redemption of humanity. In this arrangement the recitative begins and ends with references to what God "gave" Jesus, in the first instance the disciples as transmitters of Jesus's work to the faithful among humanity, and in the latter the "cup" of the Passion itself, undertaken willingly and with complete foreknowledge by Jesus. At the beginning of the recitative Bach, as mentioned earlier, leads John's explanation of the meaning of Jesus's words to a C-minor cadence, after which the subsequent narrative of Peter's violent action shifts the tonality dramatically toward D minor. Bach emphasizes the shift with prominent tritones both within Peter's line and between it and the *basso continuo*. And the D-minor tonality holds without any deviation through the chorale "Dein Will gescheh," the subsequent recitative, and the aria "Von den Stricken."

Bach takes pains to make the meaning of the g/d shift clear. Within the *ambitus* of g, the suddenness of Peter's shift from the subdominant to the dominant of the preceding G minor marks his action as locally disruptive. Jesus's protection of the disciples from arrest is in accordance with God's plan; but Peter's attempt to pro-

---

[37] Ibid., 166–67

Warum der HErr JEsus diß Werck beschreibet als vom Vater ihm gegeben" [margin] "Allein, weil unser Heiland selbst in diesem an sich der menschlichen Natur höchstbeschwerlichen Werke doch nicht anders, als lauter unendliche Liebe des Vaters gegen sich, und das gantze menschliche Geschlecht erblickete, und er hinwiederum den Vater vom gantzen Hertzen und von gantzer Seele liebte, und auß solche Liebe bereitwillig war, dessen Willen und Gebot zu vollbringen; so redet er davon nicht als von einer Last, damit er beschweret sey, sondern als einer Gabe, dero er von seinem Vater vor allen im Himmel und auf Erden würdig geachtet worden, wie er auch zu Petro im Oel-Garten sagte: **Soll ich den Kelch nicht trincken / den mir mein Vater gegeben hat?** Joh. XVIII. II.

tect Jesus from arrest is nevertheless misguided. Jesus's response to Peter affirms that the events of the Passion must go forward; and Bach's confirmation of the shift to d with his words makes that point. Even Peter's impetuous action is part of God's plan, not an accidental response. John has no great scene in Gethsemane, as Matthew does, and Jesus's words, which Bach emphasizes through repetition—"soll ich den Kelch nicht trinken, den mir mein Vater gegeben hat, den mir mein Vater gegeben hat?"—are his equivalent, making the main point, that of Jesus's submission to the Father's will, but without any hint of the suffering and struggle as narrated by Matthew. Jesus's Phrygian cadence to what sounds as the dominant of d, projects, as Phrygian cadences very frequently do for Bach, the meaning of the rhetorical question, upon which Bach brings in the chorale, "Dein Will gescheh," in d, confirming the first substantial shift of tonal center away from g in the Passion. This is not, of course, a shift of *ambitus*. But it prepares for the shift in that the two chorales mark the tonic and the dominant regions of the original *ambitus*, amplifying the meaning behind the move to the dominant in the middle section of "Herr, unser Herrscher," the process of Jesus's glorification through the Passion. The unfolding events of the Passion, which Francke, like the text of "Herr, unser Herrscher," speaks of as a "showing," is the consequence of God's foreordained *Rath*. Commenting on Jesus's reference to his accepting the "cup," Francke remarks: "Thus it had to be shown in every way that he suffered on account of the foreordained will (*Rath*) of God, was not forced to do it, but gave himself willingly to it."[38]

Bach's placing his first and second chorales in close proximity, bringing out first that Jesus's protection of the disciples was brought about by God's love for humanity, then that it followed God's plan, carried out by Jesus, has the effect of overlapping the meaning of the two references to what God "gave" Jesus. Bach's boundaries indicate his understanding this passage as centering on the fulfillment of God's plan or will. One could imagine that the particular chorales to be included were determined by an outside agency, Bach's Leipzig superiors (or, more generally, the influence of the theological tradition as expressed in many treatises of Bach's time and earlier). But the subtle details of their placement are bound up closely with the music in ways that suggest decisions of the composer.

I have mentioned that "Herr, unser Herrscher" introduces the first type of antithesis in the *St. John Passion* text, that between Jesus's sufferings on behalf of humanity on the one hand, and his divine majesty and glorification on the other. "O große Lieb'" introduces the second type, that between Jesus's sufferings and the condition of humanity, whether of guilt or worldliness (the last two lines of the chorale are "Ich lebte mit der Welt in Lust und Freuden, und du mußt leiden"—"I lived with the world in joy and happiness, and you had to suffer"). The shift to

[38] Francke, *Oeffentliche Reden*, 9: "So mußte sichs auf alle Weyse zeigen, daß er aus vorbedachtem Rath Gottes lidte, nicht dazu gezwungen ward, sondern sich freywillig dahin gab."

D minor that is confirmed by "Dein Will gescheh," now continues through the following recitative, culminating in "Von den Stricken" and bringing out the third and most important type of antithesis: that between Jesus's voluntary sufferings and their spiritual benefit for the believer. "Von den Stricken" is the outcome of Jesus's acceptance of God's will in "Dein Will gescheh." The D-minor recitative that comes between "Dein Will gescheh," and "Von den Stricken" ends with the statement that Caiphas had said that it would be good that one man be put to death for the people. This passage was widely cited in the Lutheran tradition to mean that, unwittingly, Caiphas had announced the purpose behind Jesus's death for the people, that is, for humankind, as the outcome of God's plan. In modifying Joseph's words to his brothers, as told in Genesis 50:20—"Ihr gedachtet es böse mit mir zu machen, aber Gott gedachte es gut zu machen" (You thought to do evil unto me, but God intended to make it good)—so as to refer to Caiphas, Francke brought out the fact that God's *Rath* often ran contrary to human intentions and expectations. And it is on this meaning that "Von den Stricken" meditates, introducing the theme of freedom from sin into the Passion. As is the case with several other arias of the *St. John Passion*—most notably "Ich folge dir gleichfalls," "Ach, mein Sinn," and "Es ist vollbracht"—"Von den Stricken" seems to take its initial melodic idea from the ending of the recitative. In this instance, that idea, a simple falling fifth from a″ to d″ in the first oboe, echoes the falling fifth from a to d at the cadence of the recitative. In the aria Bach accompanies the falling fifth by a sequentially rising line in the *basso continuo,* suggesting the dualism of Jesus's suffering and its benefit for humanity.[39]

In his 1928 study of the Passion, Friedrich Smend saw a link between the melodically decorated form of the falling fifth as it appears in the vocal line of "Von den Stricken" and the decorated form of the melody of Jesus's final words, "Es ist vollbracht," that appears in the vocal line of the aria "Es ist vollbracht."[40] Smend's explanation is limited to viewing the similarity as a "framing" element in the structure, with no mention of a possible theological connection. As a purely musical relationship, the resemblance is most likely incidental, especially since the melodic pattern in question can be found in other Bach works.[41] If we are to think of a connection, then a theological association makes the most sense. Not only Freylinghausen but also Rambach made explicit connections between Jesus's "Es ist vollbracht" and his "Soll ich den Kelch nicht trinken, den mir mein Vater gegeben hat" in Part 1, citing also Jesus's "Nicht mein, sondern dein Wille geschehe" (whereas Bach introduces "Dein Will gescheh,"), and linking it up with Jesus's announcement of the fulfillment of God's will in John 17. Rambach concludes:

---

[39] In the *St. Matthew Passion* Bach creates a similar simultaneity to depict the meaning behind the text "Der Heiland fällt vor seinem Vater nieder, dadurch er hebt uns alle zu Gottes Gnade wieder."

[40] Smend, *Bach-Studien*, 54.

[41] See, for example, Bach's setting of the words "Gute Nacht" in the aria "Gute Nacht, du Weltgetümmel" from Cantata 27 (*Wer weiss, wie nah mir meine Ende*).

> Thus we may add: Everything is now fulfilled that the prophets have written of the Son of Man and of the condition of his abasement. In John 17:4 the Son speaks to his Father: "I have completed the work that you have given me to do." Thus we might add "It is fulfilled ["Es ist vollbracht"], the work that my Father gave unto me to do."[42]

It may be that Bach perceived a connection between the D minor segment of Part 1, which centers on Jesus's acceptance of what he was given by God to carry out, and the D major of its fulfillment in the middle section of "Es ist vollbracht" and "Mein teurer Heiland," one that draws the melodic resemblance between "Von den Stricken" and "Es ist vollbracht" into its folds. Whether or not this was the case, "Von den Stricken" introduces for the first time the theme of freedom that is picked up in "Durch dein Gefängnis" and completed after "Es ist vollbracht" in the D major of "Mein teurer Heiland."

Peter's following Jesus, his "fall" and repentance: the transitional recitative

After the culmination of the D minor music in "Von den Stricken," the brief recitative narrative, "Simon Petrus aber folgete Jesu nach, und ein and'rer Jünger" (Simon Peter, however, and another disciple, followed after Jesus), shifts to B♭, returning closer to the center of the *ambitus* for the B♭ aria, "Ich folge dir gleichfalls," whose main melody echoes that of the recitative (see ch. 4, exx. 4.8a and 4.8b). Whether or not this B♭ can be considered to relate to the B♭ of Jesus's foreknowledge and protection of the disciples, the aria certainly has the character of an address to Jesus as protector, taking up the question of discipleship (i.e., the contemporary believer's following Jesus), addressing him, in characteristic Johannine language, as "Mein Leben, mein Licht," and praying for him not to cease "drawing onward, urging and beseeching" the believer. Along with the reference back to g at the beginning of the subsequent recitative (see the following narrative), the B♭ of "Ich folge dir gleichfalls" provides the frame of reference for the large-scale tonal shift to sharp keys that follows, suggesting at the same time, perhaps, the model of Peter's remaining within the ambit of Jesus's discipleship.

In all this, Bach's setting very carefully projects the meaning and johannine character of the narrative, which take precedence over the division of the Passion into discrete units. Instead, it gives emphasis to Jesus's identity, linking it with his divine power and foreknowledge, and also his love, which in John is the motive for

---

[42] Rambach, *Betrachtungen über die Sieben Letzten Worte*, 145: "So mögen wir denn hinzusetzen: Es ist alles vollendet, was die Propheten von des Menschen Sohn, und von dem Stande seiner Erniedrigung, geschrieben haben. Joh. 17, 4. Spricht der Sohn zu seinem Vater: **Ich habe vollendet das Werck, das du mir gegeben hast, daß ichs thun soll.** So mögen wir denn hinzusetzen: Es ist vollbracht das Werck, das mir mein Vater gegeben hat, daß ichs thun soll." See also ibid., 153.

the incarnation. In Bach's design Jesus makes the modulations, pointedly setting up the keys of the two "Jesus of Nazareth" choruses and supplying the meaning of the shift to d, first precipitated by the narrative of Peter's impulsive and worldly action. Up to this point, the recitatives have all been relatively brief. The longest, the introductory first one ("Jesus ging mit"), is seventeen measures while two are under five measures. The narrative is, in fact, dominated by closed movements (among which I consider the "Jesus of Nazareth" choruses, although they are, of course, biblical in origin, within the recitatives).[43]

Now, with John's narrative of Peter and the "other disciple" following Jesus to the high priest's palace, Bach gives us a recitative of forty-six measures in length, effecting the shift of *ambitus* away from G minor and marking a more decided shift toward Peter, who is viewed in immediate terms as the representative of human weakness and sin, but also—and more importantly—of the possibility of human redemption through faith, acknowledgment of sin and repentance. After the B♭ of "Ich folge dir gleichfalls," the first major-key movement in the Passion, the beginning of the transitional recitative refers again to Peter and the other disciple, remaining at first within the original *ambitus* but not articulating a point of closure to the *ambitus* with a chorale, or even a full cadence to g.[44] Nor can "Ich folge dir gleichfalls" be taken as closing the first *ambitus*; there is, in fact, no unequivocal point of division. Bach's procedure is more complex and subtle, concerned with the interconnected, overlapping meaning of the narrative as a whole rather than with discrete boundaries and divisions. The meaning of the narrative demands this. Peter is both a disciple of Jesus and, through his denial, a sinful human being; yet he is redeemed by his penitance. The shift of *ambitus* brings all this out.

Beginning on the dominant of g, the modulatory recitative pauses on g at midphrase, then continues on, making its first full cadence to F. Then, with the narrative of the other disciple's bringing Peter within the high priest's palace ("Derselbige Jünger war dem Hohenpriester bekannt. . . "), it settles in similar fashion on g once more, before moving on to the next full cadence, which is to a. Gradually we sense the shift away from the original frame of reference. As the servant guarding the door questions Peter, "Bist du nicht dieses Menschen Jünger einer?" (Are you not one of this man's disciples?), the tonality moves toward d and G, whereupon Bach, in the autograph portion of the only surviving original score, shifts the key signature from two flats to one, exactly as shown in example 5.2. And with Peter's answer, cadencing on G—"Ich bin's nicht!"—he shifts it again, canceling the one remaining flat. After the g beginning of the recitative, the only full cadences to this point move progressively in the sharp direction, to F, a, and G. And even though the recitative later moves much further sharp, ending on E, there are no more key

---

[43] If we include the two "Jesus of Nazareth" choruses with a single long recitative (nos. 2a–2e), then it extends to thirty-nine measures.

[44] By "full cadence" I mean one in which the bass motion is that of the perfect fifth of the root-position dominant and tonic harmonies, which is usually accompanied by a familiar cadence formula in the vocal part and often followed by a rest.

EXAMPLE 5.2 ***St. John Passion*** *no. 10, recitative, mm. 11–15. Editorial additions in brackets*

signature changes until the A-major chorale that follows. The all-important shift is that symbolized by the question put to Peter and his answer, which *identifies* but does not *confirm* G as the crossover point between the flat and sharp key areas (in historical terms the *cantus mollis* and *cantus durus*). This then becomes the focal point for, but not the completion of, the shift of *ambitus* from B♭/g to A/f#.

In what I have described, and in example 5.2 as I have transcribed Bach's notation from the autograph score of around 1740 (see illustration 5.1), we have a test case for the role of *ambitus* shifting within the *St. John Passion.* Modern editions have differed in important ways in their presentation of what Bach notated. Virtually any edition that is not actually a facsimile will introduce changes that may alter the composer's intention, sometimes substantially. In the case depicted in example 5.2, the score prepared for the New Bach Edition by Arthur Mendel does not follow at all the sequence of Bach's key signature changes. Instead, after the two-flat beginning of the recitative, Mendel has only one further change (as opposed to Bach's two)—to the signature with no flats or sharps—and it does not correspond to either of Bach's, coming instead several measures earlier than the point of Bach's first key-signature shift. Mendel places his single key-signature shift at the end of a system that divides between mm. 8 and 9, some three-and-a-half measures before Bach's first key-signature shift and six measures before Bach's second. Mendel's key-signature shift was apparently determined by two factors: first, from m. 6 on, Bach's vocal lines and harmony have no E♭'s and from m. 7 on, no B♭'s; and second, the convenience of a system division, according to which measure nine is the first to begin a new system. A secondary factor might have been that between mm. 8 and 9 the harmony articulates a progression from the dominant of

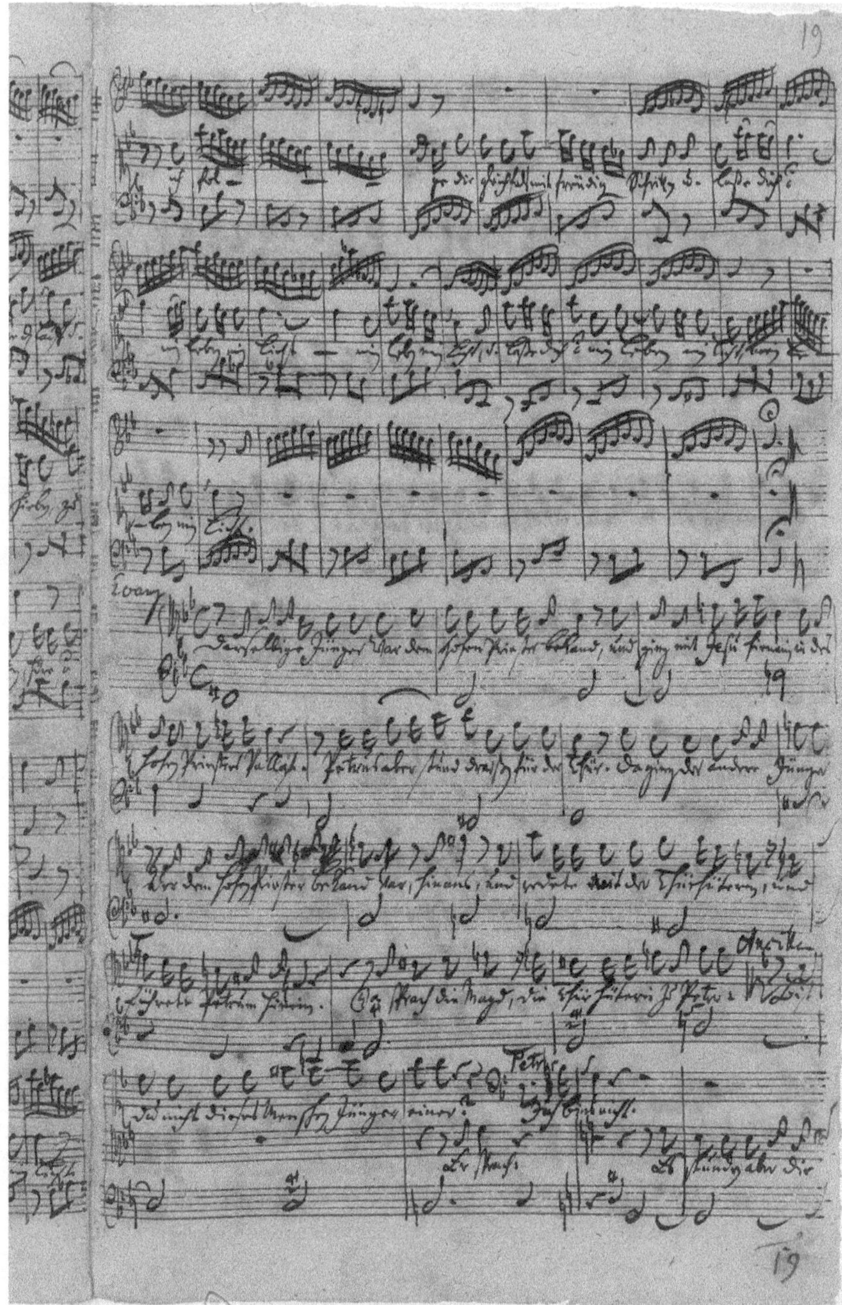

ILLUSTRATION 5.1 ***St. John Passion*** *excerpt from recitative no. 10 (mm. 10–16a) in Bach's hand, from the score of around 1739.*

G (in third inversion) to G (in first inversion), that coincides with a motion of the vocal line up to the high g′. This progression, however, comes in the middle of a sentence that continues on to a cadence to A minor in mm. 10–11. From the standpoint of pitch content alone, Mendel's placement of the key-signature shift is not inaccurate, whereas from a "modern" practical standpoint Bach's retaining the two-flat signature until m. 12 may seem strange. And, indeed, it leads, in m. 10, to the clumsy appearance of a natural sign before the first note of the measure (e♮′) immediately following the e♭′ of the key signature, on which it impinges (and which, in Mendel's view, has been unnecessarily notated for six measures). The difference is that Mendel's key signature is a purely pragmatic device, ignoring what seems particularly clear in Bach's notation: namely, that the key-signature shifting is primarily symbolic, marking out the stages of what I would call the modern equivalent of a *mollis/durus* shift in ancient "hexachordal" terms. That is, the g/G shift that takes place from the beginning of the recitative to the point of Peter's denial (G *moll* to G *dur*) is the symbolic focal point for the larger flat/sharp shift that takes place in the recitative as a whole, and indeed over the course of Part 1. Its meaning centers on Peter's "Ich bin's nicht" as a symbolic denial of the G-minor tonality associated with Jesus's "Ich bin's" (as in ex. 5.1).

Several factors support this conclusion. First of all, Bach's normal practice is not to notate key signature shifts within recitatives, which are not conceived as closed movements, but as transitions between closed movements; when he does notate such shifts they generally have a special purpose, such as a shift to arioso style. This one is exceptional in that regard. And Bach's signatures do not normally appear in mid-phrase as Mendel's does. In the present instance the tonality shifts over the course of the recitative from G minor to A major (even, some might say, to a "tonicized" E as the final chord), but there are only two key-signature changes: first from the initial two flats to one flat, then from one flat to none. The two changes are clustered very closely together, within little more than two measures (mm. 12–14), and placed not only several measures after the flats have been removed from the harmony but long before the shift to sharps (G in m. 37; e in m. 42; A–f♯–E over mm. 43–46). And since Bach does not indicate any new key signature for the stages of the shift to sharps, which is more substantial than the move away from the flat tonalities in which the recitative began, it seems clear that the purpose of the shifting is not merely to specify the correct accidentals.

Second, Bach's scores (as opposed to the sets of parts copied from them) seldom contain much in the way of figured-bass symbols, except at points of unusual harmonic shifting or complexity. In the autograph pages of the *St. John Passion* score, we find very few indeed; this recitative contains six, considerably more than the average; and five of the six are clustered around this particular passage (the sixth introduces the sudden shift to Jesus's words in the final measures of the recitative).[45]

[45] Example 5.2 follows the autograph exactly in this respect; published scores of the Passion always include the figures that appear in the parts as well (as do the other examples in this book).

Yet the harmonies themselves are not unusually complex and should not necessitate such detailed specifying of the chords.

Third, Bach's placement of the new key signatures is irregular, though in a revealing fashion. The first appears normally as the "maid" (*Ancilla*) questions Peter (m. 12); Bach introduces the new clef and one-flat signature together in the vocal part.[46] In the *basso continuo*, however, he indicates the shift one beat earlier, with a natural sign on the "e" space, but placed directly before the half-note d on the third beat (which is tied to another half-note d in the following measure). In the next measure (13) he repeats the natural sign on the "e" space, before the d, where it looks the same as in m. 12 but is now clearly a component of the new key signature, corresponding to that of the system directly above it.

Fourth, the cancellation of both flats in m. 15 is notated differently in the three staves (Bach adds a third staff for the first time at this point in order to aid in differentiating the evangelist, the maid, and Peter). It appears *after* the bar line in the middle staff (the maid), and *before* the bar line in the *basso continuo* staff, both times without the normal repeated clef indication; but there is no clear change at all in Peter's part. Instead, Bach introduces the new clef for Peter and notates the one-flat signature, even though it will remain valid for less than one quarter note: Peter sings only "Ich bin's nicht," introducing the pitch b♮ on the word "bin's." There is, however, an ink smudge directly below Peter's b♮ that might have been a natural sign on the e space or b line; and, if so, it might mean that Bach intended to place the key signature shift here, although it would be highly irregular to do so directly before the last sixteenth note of the measure. In example 5.2 I have introduced a bracketed natural sign at this point as a possible interpretation. Since Bach does not notate the shift to the natural key signature in the next measure to correspond to the two other staves, it appears that he understood it to have come into effect before that point, which could only have been for Peter's "bin's nicht." Two measures later there is a page turn, and the continuing absence of the flat in the signature (with no natural indication) makes clear that the shift has taken place before that.

From all these details we are justified in concluding that Bach intended his key-signature shifting in this recitative to bear primarily symbolic import. On the other hand, I would not go so far as to suggest that the absence of a natural key signature in the vocal part for the measure in which Peter sings the word "nicht" is more than an oversight: that is, that Bach intended Peter to willfully contradict the key signature with his "bin's nicht." But that Bach introduces the one-flat signature for his entrance (before Peter's "ich"), then immediately contradicts it with Peter's high b♮ (on "bin's") I believe to be a deliberate gesture. By far the most important point, however, is the fact that the G of Peter's "ich bin's nicht" as a whole contra-

---

[46] A significant difference between Bach's usage and that of whoever copied the remaining parts of the score is that the copyist does not specify the key signature along with the change of clef that occurs with change of character, whereas Bach does.

dicts the g of Jesus's earlier "Ich bin's" and the central tonality of the original *ambitus*. The irregularities in Bach's notation might well have been the result of uncertainty as to exactly how and at which precise point to convey the symbolism visually. Wilhelm Rust, the editor of the old Bach edition (1863), recognized the symbolic nature of Bach's notation by placing double bar lines around the measures that circumscribe the two key-signature changes and by indicating the first key-signature shift with a b♭ and an e♮ in the middle of the *basso continuo* staff below that of the beginning of the maid's solo. And Arnold Schering, who reworked it for the Eulenberg Edition version (1925) retained this notation. Mendel eliminates it altogether.

In fact, Bach's notation points up the pivotal character of Peter's "Ich bin's nicht" in relation to the overall flat-to-sharp tonal motion of Part 1. Despite this, however, Peter's G, while symbolically initiating the move away from the flat keys, does not prove decisive for the shift of *ambitus*. Instead, after the motion from g through F and a, to G, that leads to his denial, Bach turns back in the flat direction (phrase cadences to e, a, and d, none of them, however, decisive) as the narrative shifts to Peter's standing by the high priest's servants, warming himself at their fire, followed by the questioning of Jesus by the high priest (d). These "modulations" do not turn the tonality back to flat keys, of course; what they bring out is the "weak" character of Peter's G. What *does* prove decisive for the shift to sharps is Jesus's initial response to the questioning of the high priest, his most extended solo to this point (12 mm.). It begins in C and includes a reference to every key of the C/a *ambitus* except d, which serves as its lead-in (in order the keys are [d]–C–a–F–a–e–G), ending securely in G with "siehe, dieselbigen wissen, was ich gesaget habe" (see ex. 5.3). The "dieselbigen" in question—those who know what Jesus has taught—refers above all to the two disciples, who are standing by but nevertheless fail to bear witness. The emphatic character of the cadence in which Jesus refers to his own words, the key to John's importance for Luther, comprises the central issue. From this point on, there is no turning back: the striking of Jesus and Jesus's response shift the tonality toward the aforementioned E cadence. Ending the recitative on the dominant of A, Jesus's question—"hab' ich übel geredt, was schlägest du mich?"—sets up the chorale's extension of the question to the contemporary believer—"Wer hat dich so geschlagen?"—and the answer given by its second verse, "Ich, ich und meine Sünden." As in the E major ending of Part 1 of the *St. Matthew Passion* (cul-

EXAMPLE 5.3 ***St. John Passion*** *no. 10, recitative, mm. 35–36*

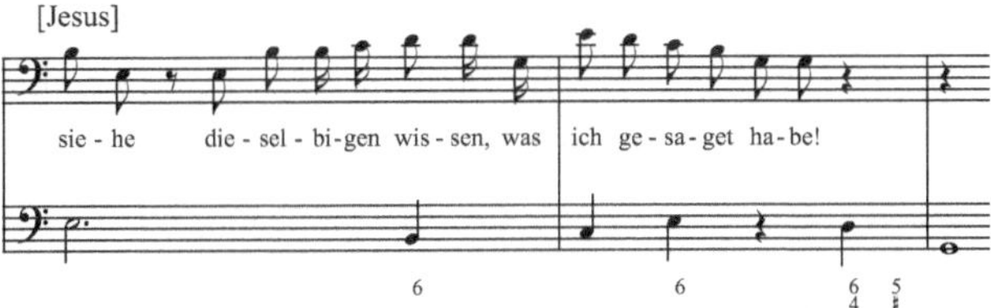

EXAMPLE 5.4 ***St. John Passion*** *no. 10, recitative, closing measures*

minating in "O Mensch, bewein dein Sünde groß"), the motion to sharps describes the positive outcome of acknowledgment of sin for the believer (see ex. 5.4).[47]

An interesting, and telling detail in Bach's interpretation of Peter's "fall" in this scene is that within the circle-of-fifths motion that lapses back toward the flat keys following Peter's denial, Bach introduces a decorative figure on the cadential words "wärmeten sich," which narrates the servants' having made a fire at which they warmed themselves. For the narrative in question the harmony turns from Peter's G to E minor, and the E minor turns immediately into the dominant of a as the narrative turns to Peter, then cadences to a for Peter's standing by them and warming himself. After that it moves on to d for the narrative of the high priest's questioning of Jesus. The flat motion seems to describe a falling off from the G of Peter's denial, locating his cadence within the tonal framework of Jesus's persecutors, making clear that, although Peter's G marks a symbolic point on the way to his ultimate repentance, it is a contradiction of Jesus's earlier "Ich bin's," the product of human weakness ("wärmeten sich"). Like the appoggiatura on Peter's "Ich bin's *nicht*," it adds a subtle element of decoration that points to the lie. As we have seen, it is Jesus who turns the harmony around, making the secure cadence to G that establishes the sharp keys of the remainder of the recitative.

After the confirmation of the flat/sharp shift in the A major of "Wer hat dich so geschlagen," the next recitative begins with the narrative of Jesus's being sent bound to the high priest Caiphas, now reiterating the fact that Peter stood by and warmed himself (no. 12a). And commentators from Bach's time were very clear about what this meant. August Hermann Francke points up the parallel between the two passages as an instance of John's making clear the increasing seriousness of Peter's failing to repent after the first and second denials. The culminating point

---

[47] We may note that the final *ambitus* of the Passion is also a response to a question, "Was willst du deines Ortes tun?" (See ch. 8, 319–320)

in this "fall" of Peter was the word "abermal" (once again) in the narrative of Peter's third denial; and the narrative of the cock's crow sealed it immediately:

> V. 27: *Peter then denied again: and immediately the cock crowed.* When John spoke of the first denial of Peter, in v. 17, he said only of it *"He said: I am not."* As if John wanted to say, he [Peter] was caught by surprise by the maid, had no time to take hold of himself, that these words were certainly not defensible, but might, however, be excused to some extent. However, as he spoke of the second denial, in verse 25, he spoke thus *"He denied however, and said, I am not."* For then Peter had had time to consider and to repent his prior sin. Therefore, this deed was now more atrocious than the previous one. When, however, in v. 27 mention of the third denial takes place, it says *"Then Peter denied once again."* This word *"once again"* (*abermal*) indicates that this third deed was the most atrocious of all, just as, according to the testimony of Mark (14:71) he cursed and swore in addition. Since, however, the evangelist adds to this *"and immediately the cock crowed,"* with which he points only to the foregoing prediction of Christ, which was now fulfilled, and also adds nothing of the conversion of Peter to it, he thereby sets aside what the other evangelists related of it.[48]

It is interesting that Francke attributes to John a deliberate intention of *not* relating Peter's repentance. In his recitative Bach observes the parallel indicated by Francke first by setting the second narrative of Peter's warming himself once again as a descending circle-of-fifths progression, this time beginning on the dominant of f♯ and passing through the dominant of b, before settling on b for "wärmete sich." And he reintroduces the decorative figure of the earlier recitative for John's second reference to Peter's warming himself. Subtle though it is, this parallel underscores Peter's continuing to seek physical comfort along with Jesus's adversaries; the circle-of-fifths tonal motion lends both narratives the character of his "fall."

And in the latter instance the fact that the cadence is to B minor is perhaps significant. For the ensuing narrative of Peter's second and third denials (no. 12c)

---

[48] Francke, *Oeffentliche Reden*, 37–38:

> v. 27. **Da verleugnete Petrus abermal / und alsobald krehete der Hahn.** Da Johannes von der ersten Verleugnung Petri redete v. 17. sagte er nur davon: **er sprach: Ich bins nicht**. Als wolte Johannes sagen: er ward von der Magd übereilet, hatte nicht Zeit sich zu fassen, daß diese Worte zwar nicht vertheidiget, aber doch einiger massen entschuldiget werden mögen. Da er aber von der andern Verleugnung redet v. 25. da redet er so davon: **Er verleugnete aber / und sprach: Ich bins nicht.** Denn da hatte Petrus Zeig gehabt, sich zu bedencken, und seine begangene Sünde zu bereuen; darum war diese That nun greulicher, als die vorige. Da aber v. 27. der dritten Verleugnung Erwehnung geschiehet, heißt es: **Da verleugnete Petrus abermal.** Diß Wort **abermal** zeiget an, daß diese dritte That am allergreulichsten gewesen, wie er sich denn auch dabey nach dem Zeugniß Marc. c. 14, 71. verfluchet und verschworen. Daß aber der Evangelist hinzu setzet: **und alsobald krähete der Hahn** / damit weiset er uns nur auf die vorhergehende Weissagung Christi, die hiermit erfüllet sey; setzet auch von der Bekehrung Petri nichts hinzu, es hierin bey dem lassend, was die übrigen Evangelisten davon gemeldet.

culminates in B minor for John's narrative of the third denial and the cock's crow. This is the ending of the narrative proper in John; the remainder of the recitative comprises an insertion from Matthew narrating Peter's repentance (that is, in the autograph score, representing the fourth version; in the first version of 1724 Mark's shorter narrative of Peter's repentance was apparently inserted). Before Peter's second and third denials, however, the bystanders who are warming themselves beside the fire, put the question to Peter, "Bist du nicht seiner Jünger einer?" (Are you not one of his disciples?), for which Bach shifts quickly from the b of Peter's warming himself to E as if to offer Peter the opportunity to bear witness to the truth by affirming the E. Bach extends the question put to Peter to the scope of a seventeen-measure chorus based on a rising melodic phrase that has recurred several times in the recitatives, in particular when Peter was confronted by the maid and when Jesus was upbraided for his response to the high priest.[49] Punctuated by insistent repetition of the words "Bist du nicht?" this phrase expands the questioning character of the chorus into a fugue-like design that begins with entries on A and E, reiterating the phrase many times in various forms and moving increasingly toward E major as it proceeds. The effect of this setting is to formalize, and perhaps to universalize for humanity, the question put to Peter regarding his discipleship. At the end the tonality turns decisively to E, ending with an "entry" on the dominant, B, in the bass that leads to an E cadence on the fourth beat of the final measure (see ex. 5.5). The leap up from f♯′ to d♯″ in the penultimate measure of the soprano seems particularly significant in articulating the dominant of E. When, directly following the chorus, the *basso continuo* sounds the E-major harmony on the downbeat of the next measure, it appears that Peter has been offered the opportunity to confirm the E with a cadence in that key, as Jesus's "Ich bin's" had confirmed the keys of the "Jesus of Nazareth" choruses.[50] With John's narrative of Peter's second denial, however—"Er leugnete aber und sprach: Ich bin's nicht!"—the line leaps up the minor seventh from e to d♮′, on "leugnete," recalling the upward leap to d♯″ in the chorus, but now denying the E by pointedly flattening the leading tone and causing Peter to cadence in A instead. Just as "Wer hat dich so geschlagen" and "Ich, ich und meine Sünden" had responded with A major to the E of Jesus's "Was schlägest du mich?" so Peter's second denial turns away from E.

To set up Peter's third denial Bach first shifts to F-sharp minor, drawing out the E♯ diminished-seventh chord, whose pitches d′ and g♯ (or g♯′) reinforce Peter's denial. Then as the servant puts the question to Peter—"Sahe ich dich nicht im Garten bei ihm?" (Did I not see you in the garden with him?)—the harmony offers the opportunity for E major once again. This time Peter does not speak, but the

---

[49] See Chafe, *Tonal Allegory*, 330–35 for my discussion of these passages with musical examples (including the entire chorus "Bist du nicht seiner Jünger einer."

[50] That is, if the bass G♯ that begins the recitative in example 5.5 had continued up to A and B, cadencing to E instead, the melodic line could easily have confirmed the E cadence with a transposition of the ending of example 5.1. I am not suggesting that we hear a musical relationship (of denial) between the two cadences, merely that Bach chose to set the second one in a very different manner.

EXAMPLE 5.5 ***St. John Passion*** *no. 12b, chorus "Bist du nicht" (ending) and no. 12c, recitative (beginning)*

evangelist's narrative of his lying yet again—"Da verleugnete Petrus abermal"—is a very striking one: now the *basso continuo* G♯ slips down to G as the evangelist moves to a♯′ (on "leugnete"), eliminating any possibility of E major and initiating the shift to B minor. After that the minor-ninth leap from f♯ to g♮′in the vocal line ("abermal") very dramatically emphasizes, just as Francke did, the atrocity of Peter's lying yet again. Continuing downward from the easily remembered high g♯′ of the evangelist's preceding phrase (a reference, now ironic, back to Peter's cutting off the ear of the high priest's servant), the high g′sets up the linear descent to b′ for the cadential phrase—"und alsobald krähete der Hahn" (and immediately the cock crowed)—after which the *basso continuo* dramatically seals Peter's lie with a graphic "crowing" arpeggio.

In what I have described to this point it is clear that for Bach the detailed crafting of recitatives is a means of conveying the often very subtle and always detailed theological and psychological meanings embodied in them. In this he stands apart from the prevailing tendencies of his time with respect to recitative composition, whether secco or accompanied. Bach's melodic lines, often jagged, even distorted-sounding at times, do not permit the sense that they go down like a raw oyster, that they might just as well be disregarded from the musical standpoint, or that projecting a sense of "naturalism" is of foremost importance. They arise from the harmony, of course, and that harmony is often considerably more complex and original than that of any of his contemporaries. It might be going too far to say that this quality is primarily a response to the fact that the recitative texts are either biblical or centered largely on the interpretation of scripture. Rather, the complexity of Bach's harmonic thought converges with that of the theological ideas; he must have welcomed the opportunities they afforded to unpack the astonishing array of text-musical correspondences we find in virtually every work. They would never have suited the composition of opera, because opera libretti do not demand searching out the "sensus, scopus and pondus," as Johann Kuhnau put it. This does not mean that we always have to listen to Bach for intellectual devices in the matching of word and music; but we do have to hear the importance of how the harmonic motion carries the countless melodic events on its shoulders. The Bach chorales have long been viewed as paradigmatic in this regard, even though, paradoxically, their melodies came first. They show how controlled, imaginative, and detailed the harmony can be, even within such constraints. In the recitatives Bach molds the harmony to the verbal narratives in a manner that relishes constraints of another—theological—kind. Whether the initial impulse is theological or artistic can probably never be determined; the end result lends itself to our viewing them analytically as a fusion.

In John, Peter's story ends with the narrative of his "fall." As we know now, John does not narrate his repentance. In the first, second, and fourth versions of the *St. John Passion*, however, the narrative of his repentance is added from Matthew (or Mark in the lost original version), whereas in the third (only) it is removed (along with the insertion from Mark/Matthew that appears in the first, second, and fourth versions after Jesus death).[51] One would think that around 1730 some external agency might have insisted that the narrative be exactly faithful to John's account. This might in fact have been one of the objections to the text referred to by Bach in 1739. (Or the situation could have been the reverse: that Bach himself "experimented" with setting John's text without the introduction of Peter's repentance, whose omission might then have been objected to). August Hermann Francke takes pointed note of the fact that John does *not* narrate Peter's repentance; and he seems to appreciate John's meaning in that he uses the abrupt ending of the narrative as the springboard to a warning for those who are too secure in not questioning their sins, past and present. In his view Peter's example should lead them to fear and terror, so that they be constantly on the watch against sin and not make the seriousness of their fall even greater, as Peter did over the course of his three denials. Nevertheless, Francke ends his sermon with the positive outcome of repentance, referring to Peter as an example of that as well. Other authors drew a parallel between Peter's denial and repentance and the "dynamic" of faith that was

---

[51] Mendel, *Kritischer Bericht*, 84, 103. In the case of the latter passage, the original insertion is lost but is known to have been shorter than that of the second and fourth versions, corresponding to the relative lengths of the narratives in Mark and Matthew, respectively.

associated with the roles of law and Gospel in faith, a dynamic that Bach sometimes mirrors with descent/ascent patterns, including those involving the flat and sharp modulatory directions. Johann Heermann, for example, describes the cock's crow as God's call to sinners, a "geistliche Hahnen-Geschrey" that God has entrusted to preachers "through the resounding voice of the law," to awaken from the sleep of sin, as Peter himself later preached the law to the Jews in Jerusalem, in Acts 2:14.[52]

In light of the centrality of penitence to Lutheran thought, it is difficult to imagine Peter's repentance not being taken into account (as, in fact, it was in both "Ach, mein Sinn" and "Zerschmettert mich," as well as in the final chorale of Part 1). Bach's original conception of the passage clearly makes the same point. The B-minor cadence of the cock's crow is turned immediately into the dominant of e for Peter's remembering Jesus's words, the triggering event for his repentance. The phrase "Da gedachte Petrus an die Worte Jesu," echoes the recurrent rising phrase mentioned earlier, settling on E minor, so that from the E major offered Peter by "Bist du nicht" to this point the modulatory course of the recitative outlines a major/minor tonal motion, a perfect analog of Peter's "fall."[53] And the ensuing narrative ("Er leugnete aber und sprach") of his weeping bitterly is an extended melisma above a chromatic rising then falling bass whose key does not become clear until, on the final "bitterlich," it turns to f♯. Full of tritones and suspended dissonances, it mirrors the seriousness and pain of the consciousness of sin; yet, when it finally turns to f♯, the key of "Ach, mein Sinn," we may well conclude that Bach intended the reversal of modulatory direction to point to the positive outcome of repentance. Then, after the extraordinarily passionate expression of penitence in the aria "Ach, mein Sinn," the chorale "Petrus, der nicht denkt zurück" begins as if in f♯ (its first phrase), before turning to its true key, A. In the second version the substitute aria, "Zerschmettert mich," was also in A. Bach's point, which emerges in the text of the chorale, is surely that Peter, despite his denials, his lapses or falls from true discipleship, is ultimately redeemed by his turning to Jesus in repentance and the search for forgiveness, that is, his faith.

In the third version of around 1730, however, the removal of the narrative of Peter's repentance caused a significant alteration in the tonal design at this point.

---

[52] Johann Heermann, *Crux Christi, Das ist: Die schmertzliche und traurige Marter-Woche, unsers hochverdienten Heylandes JEsu Christi, ...* (Braunschweig, 1668), 183–85.

[53] For a conceptually parallel instance of an E/e juxtaposition among the cantatas, I invite the reader to consider the E-major chorale cantata, *Es ist das Heil uns kommen hier* (BWV 9). In that work the "Heil" (salvation) announced in the initial E-major chorale fantasia gives way, in the first recitative, to a narrative of humanity's "fall" from God's grace, which prompted the giving of the law. The recitative, taking its tonal cue from the d♮ of the Mixolydian chorale melody, moves in the flat (subdominant) direction setting up the key of the first aria, E minor, which describes the condition of a sinful humanity under the law. That aria, "Wir waren schon zu tief gesunken," brings out that humanity had sunk too far to be able to fulfill the demands of the law, after which the subsequent recitative reverses the modulatory direction, in analogy to the narrative of the work of salvation brought about by Jesus, and the necessity of faith. Ultimately, the tonality returns to E. See my discussion on this in *Analyzing Bach Cantatas*, 149–60.

As Mendel has shown, the recitative now ended with the B-minor narrative of the cock's crow; and the final chorale was transposed down a tone, so as to begin (presumably) in e and turn to G as its counterpart in the other versions had begun in f♯, then turned to A. Of the aria that intervened, however, nothing is known, except that it had a string accompaniment and was probably for either tenor or soprano and in either e or G, which would fit with the e–G of the chorale as the arias of the first and second versions do with the f♯–A version.[54]

Thus in the only version of the Passion that, like John himself, omits the narrative of Peter's repentance, the modulatory character of the music does not turn around to end in A major but instead continues the direction associated with Peter's "fall," perhaps as far as E minor, which we could then interpret as opposite to the E-major chorus that offers him the opportunity of avowing his discipleship. The subsequent G-major ending would alter our precise identification of the *ambitus* in which Part 1 ends; but it would not alter the "abstract" plan of sharp/natural/flat key areas given in chapter 4, figures 4.1 and 4.2. It might lead us to conclude, however, that Bach intended the G-major ending as a counterpart of Peter's first, G-major "Ich bin's nicht," itself an opposite to the G minor of Jesus's "Ich bin's." In that case, the fact that Part 1 would begin in g and end in G might be thought to project an association comparable to that of the *St. Matthew Passion*, Part 1, which begins in e and ends in E. The most important point might be that, in the original version, whereas Peter's "fall" is the result of his own failings, his repentance and restoration are the outcome of Jesus's "glance," as Francke affirms (as does the chorale that concludes Part I). Thus, whereas Jesus's two "Ich bin's" are set with dominant–tonic cadences in g and c, respectively, Peter's two denials are set as pronounced dominant–tonic cadences, first to G (the potential crossover between flats and sharps, symbolized visually in Bach's notation), then to A (the principal key of the new *ambitus*). In both instances, however, the keys are established in the transitional recitative by Jesus, not Peter. The direct simplicity of the cadential fifth progressions of Jesus's earlier "Ich bin's" versus the decorated overemphatic character of the fifth progressions on Peter's denials, is decisive, the latter giving added weight to the word "nicht."

It is this sense that Jesus, through his suffering and obedience to God's will, is the agency of Peter's redemption or, in more general terms, the route to the world above, that caused Francke to issue his warnings against taking the forgiveness of sin for granted. Bach mirrors it perfectly in his making Jesus the agency of the modulations to sharps. From this standpoint, the striking motion from the *ambitus* of g to that of A in Part 1 has a twofold meaning: in terms of the literal meaning of the Gospel, Jesus divinity is manifested in his human suffering and death, the

---

[54] Mendel, *Kritischer Bericht*, 84–88. As Mendel remarks, the possibility that this lost aria was "Zerschmettert mich" transposed down a tone cannot be excluded (87). Dürr, however (*Johann Sebastian Bach's "St. John Passion,"* 8), inclines toward the view that the aria was probably in E minor, taking the position, without offering any concrete evidence, that the aria could not have been "Zerschmettert mich."

condition over which he will triumph, in John's view, in the crucifixion. In the spiritual (i.e., tropological or eschatological) sense, the Passion centers on its benefit, whether immediate (tropological) or ultimate (eschatological) for the believer (the two are closely intertwined in John). The two-flat *ambitus* and minor keys of the first segment of Part 1 project the necessary focus on the adverse events of the narrative, while the shift to sharps for the second *ambitus* proclaims their benefit—effected by Jesus—for a sinful but redeemable humanity, represented by Peter. The A-major chorale ending Part 1, "Petrus, der nicht denkt zurück," is an opposite number to the chorale that begins Part 2, "Christus, der uns selig macht," which, with its juxtaposition of "Christus" to "Petrus," its identity of meter and rhyme scheme with the earlier chorale, and its E Phrygian tonality (sounding, however, like an ending on the dominant of A *minor*), returns the perspective to Jesus's sufferings, extending the meaning of the Peter/Jesus juxtaposition to the trial of Jesus.

In summary, the minor keys (primarily g and d) that dominate the opening "scene" of the *St. John Passion* mirror the fact that Jesus's *Herrlichkeit* is veiled beneath its opposite, his *Erniedrigung* (as Rambach said), whereas the shift to the A-major *ambitus* with which Part 1 ends is primarily associated with Peter's story, symbolizing in a larger sense the beneficial character of faith and repentance for the believer. Modulatory direction is of immense significance in the delineation of such meaning. At the close of the g/B♭ *ambitus* the recitative "Simon Petrus aber folgete Jesu nach und ein ander Jünger" and aria "Ich folge dir gleichfalls," both in B♭, mirror, in their major tonality and upward melodic beginnings, the positive character of the *Nachfolgung Christi*, establishing a frame of reference for the overall flat/sharp motion of Part 1 (see exx. 4.8a and 4.8b, ch. 4). The B♭ tonality harks back to the narratives of Jesus's foreknowledge and his protection of the disciples, points where Jesus's divine nature emerged from behind the veil, although at the former of those points the B♭ was deflected to the dominant of g at its cadence, setting up the first of the "Jesus of Nazareth" choruses. That in Bach's design Jesus himself effects that shift, and in a particularly pointed manner (see ex. 5.1), is an indication of the voluntary character of his suffering, the meaning behind the minor key of the scene as a whole. Bach brings out that meaning in the opposition of the flat and sharp key areas of the Passion as a whole, associating the deep flat *ambitus* with Jesus's sufferings, and the motion toward sharp-major keys with their salvific meaning for humankind.

It seems clear that the organization of the Passion text into a succession of clearly differentiated *ambitus* was Bach's means of bringing out the basic oppositions of its Johannine theology. Close attention to modulatory direction is therefore crucial to understanding that theology. Throughout the trial the threefold reappearances of the music associated with "Jesus of Nazareth," set now to negative pronouncements—"Wir dürfen *niemand* töten," "*Nicht* diesen sondern Barrabam," and "Wir haben *keinen* König denn den Kaiser"—place the denial of Jesus's identity in the foreground. At the same time, the meaning understood by the Christian congregation is the opposite. On the local level the second of each pair of choruses transposes down the fifth, mirroring the adverse events of the narrative: from g to c in the case of "Jesus of Nazareth," from a to d between "Wir dürfen niemand töten" and "Nicht diesen, sondern Barabbam." On a larger scale, however, the choruses move along an upward trajectory of alternating rising fourths and falling thirds (g–c–a–d–b) from a flat to a natural and finally a sharp *ambitus*, the last one immediately prompting Pilate's handing over Jesus for crucifixion (the ending of John's trial) and, along with Bach's subsequent D cadence, completing the central, and sharpest, *ambitus* of the Passion.

Bach's design affirms that the shifting *ambitus* of the circle of keys represent extension of the harmonically conceived hexachords of seventeenth-century practice to a higher tonal level. As a response to the perfect fifths of Jesus's "Ich bin's," the "Jesus of Nazareth" choruses define the harmonic *ambitus* of the keys in question according to the circle-of-fifths pattern that underlies the medieval-renaissance hexachords and their interpretation in harmonic terms from the seventeenth-century on.[55] Ultimately, the centrality of the perfect fifth to tonal music, and to the eighteenth-century circle of keys, underlies Bach's assigning the simplest and most direct of cadences to Jesus's affirmative "Ich bin's." In this sense the underlying meaning of Jesus's words for Bach is their proclamation of the fundamental meaning of the Passion; and his musical setting draws an analogy between that meaning and the extension of the interval that was the underlying basis of music—the perfect fifth—to the melodic hexachord that sounds to Jesus's words "[siehe, dieselbigen wissen] was ich gesaget habe!" completing the shift to sharps in Part 1. At the next level it extends farther, to the harmonically conceived hexachords of the "Jesus of Nazareth" choruses, and ultimately to the *ambitus* and the circle of keys that are the primary tonal-allegorical components of the Passion as a whole.

Thus the most fundamental musical interval, the perfect fifth, is the measure of human response to the central theme of the trial and the Passion, Jesus's identity as the pivot between faith and unbelief. In this respect Bach's design for the *St. John Passion* expands out from the perfect fifth in a manner analogous to the way that Andreas Werckmeister, the foremost representative of the Lutheran "metaphysical" tradition in music theory, described the entire system of well-tempered tuning as extending from the perfect intervals, whose nearness to unity mirrored God and the Trinity to the sphere of human imperfection, mirrored in the necessity of temperament.[56] Beginning with a symbolic expression of Jesus's divine identity, the "Ich bin's," it extends to the conflict in the trial over the title "King of the Jews," where Jesus's identity is cast in worldly terms. At the center of Bach's symbolic trial, however, we hear a still more important title, "Son of God," in the chorale "Durch dein Gefängnis, Gottessohn." The key of this chorale, E major, sharpest key of the

---

[55] Chafe, *Monteverdi's Tonal Language*, 21–31, 38–55; Chafe, *Analyzing Bach Cantatas*, 72–100.

[56] Werckmeister, *Musicae mathematicae*, 145. Bach embodies these principles in his canons, which extend from the harmonic triad through the *Mi/Fa* (diatonicism), the "Christus Coronabit Crucigeros" (chromaticism), the "In Fine videbitur cuius toni" (modulation), to the enharmonic "circle-of-fifths" canon of the *Musical Offering*. See Chafe, "Allegorical Music," 340–62.

Passion, is reserved for the central segment of Bach's "symbolic trial," and is distanced by a tritone from the key of the outermost choruses of the symmetrical array that make up Bach's symbolic trial, B♭. The disparity between "Durch dein Gefängnis" and those choruses, which express mocking of Jesus and objection to his kingship—"Sei gegrüsset, lieber Judenkönig" and "Schreibe nicht: der Juden König"—is one of the means with which Bach differentiates John's worldly and spiritual perspectives on Jesus's identity. In Part 1 Jesus's question to humankind, "Was schlägest du mich?" also sets up the possibility of E major, to which the A-major chorale acknowledgment of human guilt responds. And Peter's failure to affirm the E offered him by "Bist du nicht" may also be viewed in this light. Through such means the entire Passion becomes a kind of "symbolic trial," as is often said of John's Gospel.

In all such details the *St. John Passion* creates the sense of an astonishing degree of interrelatedness and order, a quality that probably arose from the extraordinary character of John's narrative, with its endless circling or spiraling, its reiterations and double or ironic meanings, all introduced in the attempt to convey the nature of "spiritual" meaning and timeless truth. Bach must have interacted very closely and personally as an artist of allegorical bent with John's Passion account, searching for means to create an order that would project its principal themes and their interrelated qualities while conveying its special qualities of opposition, hidden meaning, and the like—all usually associated with its designation as the spiritual Gospel. Needless to say, this could have been the product of a deep intuition conditioned by the thought of the time and not of detailed study or pre-planning.[57] Many of Bach's solutions are, in fact, highly abstract in nature, while others are of the utmost immediacy and drama, just as they are in John. To those who value only the latter, I would respond that the boundary between the "audible" and the "inaudible" is not a certain one, that the whole person is a compound of intellectual and affective qualities whose separation does violence to the whole. In this respect, what Bach achieved in the design of the *St. John Passion* is what most sets him apart from his many lesser contemporaries.

[57] The question of pre-planning, which in the case of the *St. John Passion* is closely bound up with symmetry, has been resisted by Alfred Dürr in his book on the Passion. Dürr views it as a "problem" in interpretation of the work. See Dürr, *Johann Sebastian Bach's "St. John Passion,"* 99–107, 124–27. I view the question of whether Bach "pre-planned" the design of thePassion a red herring, thus dealing only with *when* the design was conceived; the structure itself, however, and its theological correlates are, as this study attempts to demonstrate, solidly grounded.

{6}

Jesus's Trial: John, Francke, Bach

The first segment of the trial: a Christological "scene"

In Part 2, the segment that I have called Bach's "symbolic trial" is the focal point for the oppositions described in the preceding chapters, which it regulates by means of the symmetries of the repeated choruses and keys. By virtue of its very high degree of internal organization, which extends beyond the trial proper to conclude with meditation on the crucifixion and the royal inscription, the symbolic trial comprises a "unit" that does not correspond to either the traditional *actus* (at its beginning point) or to the more modern threefold division (at its ending point). Instead, it takes the scourging of Jesus as its point of departure, articulating that point (the beginning of Jn 19) with the longest meditative focal point of the Passion: the arioso "Betrachte, meine Seele" and aria "Erwäge." Since the scourging is at the center of John's trial, this means that in Bach's design the earlier part of the trial is separated from the symbolic trial. That separation is clearly evident from the fact that the opening scene of Part 2 is in A minor, whereas the symbolic trial begins and ends in E♭. The latter comprises a threefold segment that can be considered the center of the Passion as a whole, whereas the A minor opening scene of Part 2 has an introductory role that parallels to a degree that of the opening scene of Part 1.

The central issue of the trial in John is Jesus's identity, with particular reference to the title "King [of the Jews]." As if to set this up, Bach uses the relatively self-contained unit that begins Part 2 (the beginning of John's trial scene) to introduce the question of Jesus's kingship in preparation for the intense contradictions and oppositions of the symbolic trial. The opening scene culminates in the chorale "Ach, großer König," after which those oppositions are focused in the call for release of Barabbas and the scourging, the events that culminate the intervening recitative, which thereby functions as a transition between the opening segment and the symbolic trial. The introductory opening segment is unified in its articulation of the *ambitus* of A minor and bounded by two chorales of a Christological nature. The first, "Christus, der uns selig macht," reminds us, in its poetic and musical phrase structure, meter, and rhyme scheme, of the chorale that ended Part 1, "Petrus, der nicht denkt zurück." Its first lines, in particular, invite comparison of Peter and Jesus.

"PETRUS, DER NICHT DENKT ZURÜCK"	"CHRISTUS, DER UNS SELIG MACHT"
Petrus, der nicht denkt zurück, seinen Gott verneinet, der doch auf ein' ernsten Blick bitterlichen weinet. Jesu, blicke mich auch an, wenn ich nicht will büßen; wenn ich Böses hab getan, rühre mein Gewissen.	Christus, der uns selig macht, kein Bös' hat begangen, der ward für uns in der Nacht als ein Dieb gefangen, geführt für gottlose Leut und falschlich verklaget, verlacht, verhöhnt und verspeit, wie denn der Schrift saget.
Peter, who did not think back, denies his God, who, however, on a serious look weeps bitterly. Jesus, look upon me if I do not want to repent, if I have done evil, stir my conscience.	Christ, who makes us blessed, and did no evil, who, for us, was in the night taken like a thief, led before godless people, and falsely accused, ridiculed, mocked and spit on, just as scripture now relates.

Concluding Part 1, "Petrus, der nicht denkt zurück" begins with reference to Peter's denial, then alludes to his repentance, which leads to a prayer from the believer for Jesus's "glance" as the stimulus to penitence. Beginning as if in f♯, the key of the narrative of Peter's repentance and the aria "Ach, mein Sinn," it shifts to A major for its second phrase, but continues to suggest f♯ up to the beginning of its fifth phrase (the beginning of the aforementioned prayer). In its wavering and delaying the full affirmation of A, Bach's harmonization seems to mirror consciousness of sin and repentance on the one hand, and the ultimate benefit of repentance for the believer on the other. In contrast to its allusion to the believer's guilt ("wenn ich Böses hab getan"), "Christus, der uns selig macht," reaffirms Jesus's innocence at the outset ("kein Bös' hat begangen") After that the latter chorale centers entirely on Jesus's sufferings on behalf of humanity. And, in contrast to the A major of "Petrus, der nicht denkt zurück," "Christus, der uns selig macht" is in E Phrygian, sounding like A minor. The relationship between the two chorales therefore suggests an extension of the Petrus/Christus opposition in Part 1: between the g of Jesus "Ich bin's" and the G (and A) of Peter's "Ich bin's nicht." As Johann Mattheson pointed out, "Christus, der uns selig macht" narrates Jesus's sufferings up to the point of the scourging, ending with the line "wie denn die Schrift saget," a quality that made it particularly appropriate to begin a setting of the Postel Passion text, which began with the scourging (see ch. 4).[1] This aspect of the chorale also makes it appropriate to introduce the part of the trial that precedes the narrative of the scourging, a possible factor in Bach's placing it at the beginning of Part 2 and reserving the most extended point of meditation in the entire Passion for the beginning of the segment that follows the narrative of the scourging. The Phrygian setting of "Christus, der uns selig macht" underscores the meaning of the Petrus/Christus shift between the ending of Part 1 and the beginning of Part 2—namely, that of setting Jesus's sufferings apart as the only route to salvation for the contemporary believer (a meaning that echoes and intensifies later in the Passion in the chorale "O hilf, Christe, Gottessohn," set to a modified transposition to F Phrygian of the music of "Christus, der uns selig macht").[2]

In relation to "Christus, der uns selig macht," the chorale that Bach chose to culminate his opening scene in Part 2, "Ach großer König, groß zu allen Zeiten," responds to the initial dialog between Jesus and Pilate regarding Jesus's kingship. Its placement, directly following Jesus's proclaiming that his kingdom is not of this world, and its culminating the A-minor tonality of the scene as a whole, make the point that Jesus's sufferings and his kingship are intertwined. Whereas, by virtue of its Phrygian tonality, "Christus, der uns selig macht" can be considered open-ended, as its final line suggests, "Ach großer König" completes the theological purpose of the scene with two A minor strophes. The "zu allen Zeiten" of its second line reminds us of the "zu aller Zeit" of "Herr, unser Herrscher." In its two successive verses (from the same chorale as "O große Lieb'") it not only reaffirms Jesus's *Herrlichkeit*, the theme of "Herr, unser Herrscher," but it also reiterates the theme of Jesus's love for humankind. Thus this segment, which is entirely in the a/C *ambitus*, focuses, like the first scene of Part 1, on the figure of Jesus, culminating in affirmation of his divine nature.

In this part of the narrative, August Hermann Francke, like Bach, sees a parallel to the beginning of the Passion. Near the beginning of Francke's third lecture, he cites once again John's initial announcement of Jesus's foreknowledge, "Als nun Jesus wusste alles, was ihm begegnen sollte," using it to explain why Jesus was brought to Pilate—namely, because he had predicted that he would be delivered over to both the Jews and the gentiles, and would be condemned to death by both. The purpose of the prediction, as Francke explains, was to ensure that the disci-

[1] Johann Mattheson, *Criticae Musicae, Tomus Secundus* (1725), 12.

[2] The relationship between "Christus, der uns selig macht" and "O hilf, Christe, Gottes Sohn" is not one of identical transposition, but it is an exceptionally close one, in which Bach adjusted the harmony and voice leading so as to mirror the different tone of the two verses, as necessary. At some points the differences are relatively small: thus, in the second phrase of "Christus," the second word, "Bös'" receives the emphasis, whereas in the corresponding phrase of "O hilf, Christe," the *third* word, "bitter" (one beat later) is singled out. But at others, such as phrases 5–7, they are very considerable. The final phrase is identical in both settings (except for the transposition).

ples recognized him as the Messiah and, further, that the contemporary faithful would not take offense at his sufferings and would, likewise, recognize him as the Messiah:

> So then we see from this once more that the Lord Jesus knew everything that would happen to him, as John spoke of this in the foregoing fourth verse. And because he knew everything, he therefore also revealed it all to disciples in advance, so that when it then took place they knew from it that he was the one, namely, the promised Messiah or Christ, for which he had made himself known, and they also recognized and accepted him as such. . . . On this account then we also should reflect diligently on this, through and through, in the account of the suffering of Christ, so that it is impossible for us to take offence at the suffering of the Lord Jesus, that we much more just take strong and irrefutable arguments from it so that in his person, since we recognize him for the Messiah, we do not err in the least.[3]

The themes that follow directly are ones we have encountered already in Francke's first lecture: Jesus's innocence, human guilt, the Passion as *Trost*, and a model to follow. And when he comes to the outcry "Wir dürfen niemand töten," Francke returns to his initial theme of Jesus's foreknowledge, explaining that the words of the chorus were in fulfillment of Jesus's prediction of the manner of his death, that is, crucifixion by the Romans, and giving its meaning as follows:

> See how much the Holy Spirit is concerned in this that we recognize as a certainty that in the Lord Jesus the scripture and his own words, which he gave forth before his Passion, are fulfilled in their entirety and completeness, and that all circumstances of his suffering are on that account especially narrated and brought out, so that with it faith in the Lord Jesus, through the word of God and through diligent reflection and comparison on it, might be planted deeply in our hearts.[4]

---

[3] Francke, *Oeffentliche Reden*, 45:

"So sehen wir denn hieraus abermal, daß der HErr JEsus alles gewußt, was ihm begegnen solte, wie Johannes davon im vorhergehenden v. 4. geredtet. Und weil ers alles wußte, so verkündigte ers auch alles seinen Jüngern vorher, auf daß, wenn es nun geschähe, sie daraus erkenneten, daß er es sey, nemlich der verheissene Meßias oder Christus, für welchen er sich bekannt, und sie ihn auch erkannt und aufgenommen hätten. . . . Weswegen denn auch wir dieses durch und durch in der historie des Leidens Christi mit Fleiß erwegen sollen, damit es so ferne von uns sey, uns an dem Leiden des HErrn JEsu zu ärgern, daß wir vielmehr eben daraus starke und unwiderlegliche Beweiß-Gründe nehmen, daß wir an seiner Person, da wir ihn für den Meßiam erkennen, im geringsten nicht irren.

[4] Ibid.,55:

Sehet, wie viel dem Heil. Geist daran gelegen ist, daß wir erkennen und gewiß sein, daß an dem Herrn JESU die Schrift und seine eigene Worte, die er von seinem Leiden vorher geführet, ganz vollkommentlich erfüllet sind, und daß alle Umstände seines Leidens, sonderlich um deßwillen erzählet u. angeführet werden, damit doch ja der Glaube an den HErrn JEsum durchs Wort

Thus, for Francke, the meaning of "Wir dürfen niemand töten" is that by virtue of its fulfilling Jesus's prediction regarding his death, it is a catalyst to faith. In this, Francke lifts its meaning entirely out of its literal frame of reference, viewing it as an affirmation of Jesus's divine identity.

Similarly, Johann Jacob Rambach views John's announcement of the fulfillment of scripture as a reference to God's *Rath*:

> The plan of God may be noted in this event, in that v. 32 [Jn 18] goes: "So that the saying of Jesus might be fulfilled, which he spake, signifying what death he should die." Namely, God in the eternal decisions of his will ordained the crucifixion for the redemption of the world. . . . John makes this remark for the strengthening of our faith, and shows, how under such confused circumstances the will of God directed everything so wisely. . . . God's foreseeing, which had power over the nature of the death of Jesus, is also that which rules over the circumstances of our lives and deaths. The enemies dared go not a single step further than divine foreseeing permitted them. They dared not do what they willed; instead, the entire trial of Christ was directed by the preconceived decision (*Rathschluß*) of God . . . in vain did Pilate say "Judge him according to your law." The manner of his death had to coincide precisely with the predictions of the prophets and the prior predictions of the Lord Jesus himself. For over the sufferings of this person ruled a quite special foreseeing of God, and even the smallest circumstances of it were ordered according to the predetermined plan (*Rath*) of the heavenly Father.[5]

In Francke's and Rambach's remarks we have a ready explanation for Bach's unique setting of "Wir dürfen niemand töten." That is, in its combining the music of two different choruses heard earlier in the Passion, that of "Jesus of Nazareth," and that of the chorus heard only seconds before, "Wäre dieser nicht ein Übeltäter," it brings the same issue to the fore. In response to Pilate's "So nehmet ihr ihn hin

---

Gottes und dessen fleissige Betrachtung und Gegeneinanderhaltung tief in unsere Herzen gepflanzet werden möchte.

[5] Rambach, *Betrachtungen über das gantze Leiden Christi*, 632, 636:

> Der Rath GOttes in dieser Sache bemercket wird, indem es v. 32. heißt: Auf daß erfüllet würde das Wort JEsu, welches er sagte, da er deutete, welches Todes er sterben würde. GOtt hatte nemlich in seinen ewigen Rathschlüssen den Creuzes-Tod zur Erlösung der Welt verordnet. . . . Diese Anmerckung macht Johannes zur Stärkung unsers Glaubens, und zeiget, wie der Rath GOttes unter so verwirrten Umständen alles so weislich regieret habe. . . . Die Vorsehung GOttes, welche über der Art des Todes Jesu gewaltet hat, ist es auch, welche über unsern Lebens- und Todes-Umständen waltet. Die Feinde durften keinen Schritt weiter gehen, als die göttliche Vorsehung ihnen verwilligte. Sie durften nicht thun, was sie wolten; sondern der gantze Proceß Christi wurde dirigiret von dem vorbedachten Rathschluß GOttes. . . . vergeblich sagte Pilatus: Richtet ihn nach eurem Gesetz. Die Art seines Todes muste genau übereintreffen, mit den Weissagungen der Propheten und Vorherverkündigungen des HErren JEsu selbst. Denn über dem Leiden dieser Person waltete eine ganz besondere Vorsehung GOttes, und auch die kleinsten Umstände desselben wurden nach dem vorbedachten Rath des himmlischen Vaters eingerichtet.

und richtet ihn nach eurem Gesetze" (Then take him away and judge him according to your laws), it makes the point, that in the person of Jesus (the "Jesus of Nazareth" music) we must recognize the Messiah who undertook the Passion voluntarily according to the will of God, and not take offense at his being judged and punished as a criminal (the music of "Wäre dieser nicht ein Übeltäter"). In other words we must "see through" the adverse events to the truth that lies behind them. In this light, we may interpret this first instance of the repetition of the "Jesus of Nazareth" music with a text of antagonistic character, in terms of Luther's remark that Jesus is the "yes" behind the "no" of the law.[6]

Bach, however, does not make John's announcement of the fulfillment of Jesus's prophesy into a point of closure as Francke does (although he does set it apart with a full cadence within the recitative). Instead, he continues on with the recitative, which contains most of the first dialog between Jesus and Pilate, introducing the question of Jesus's identity as king of the Jews. The recitative picks up initially from the A minor of "Wir dürfen niemand töten," and its first cadence, completing John's narrative of Jesus's prediction, is to C, but colored with the minor third (on "sterben"), as if to look ahead to the key of the burial chorus. After that, the recitative touches on or articulates most of the keys of the a/C *ambitus*, then returns to end in A minor. Bach makes his caesura after Jesus's response that his kingdom was not of this world, at which point he places the A minor chorale "Ach, grosser König," creating the distinct sense of a "scene" or unit bounded by the chorales "Christus, der uns selig macht" and "Ach, grosser König."

Thus Bach's scene is very logically designed. "Christus, der uns selig macht" reminds us, in its meter, rhyme scheme, and initial line, of "Petrus, der nicht denkt zurück" at the close of Part 1, but in relation to the A major of the latter chorale, its E Phrygian tonality restores the focus on Jesus's sufferings. The recitative ("Da führten sie Jesum") that follows "Christus, der uns selig macht" narrates Jesus's being brought before Pilate, and Pilate's questioning the Jews concerning the charge against him, prompting the parallel choruses, "Wäre dieser nicht ein Übeltäter" (in d) and "Wir dürfen niemand töten" (in a). By adding the *music* of "Jesus of Nazareth" to the beginning and ending of the latter chorus (which otherwise repeats, transposed, the main section of "Wäre dieser nicht ein Übeltäter"), Bach suggests that it has a double function: as the response to Pilate's "so nehmet ihr ihn hin und richtet ihn nach eurem Gesetze," it continues the demand for Jesus's death; but as the fulfillment of Jesus's prediction regarding his death—"Auf dass erfüllet würde das Wort Jesu, welches er sagte, da er deutete, welches Todes er sterben würde"—it affirms his identity as the Messiah.

It might well be argued that in ending with discussion of the words just cited, Francke's third lecture makes a more logical dividing point than Bach does in his setting, since it leaves the extended dialog in which Pilate introduces the question of Jesus's kingship for the fourth lecture. Bach divides that exchange with the two

[6] See Chafe, *Tonal Allegory*, 297.

verses of "Ach großer König," including the initial part of the discussion of Jesus's kingship within the opening scene, thereby making a point of division after a scene that links the theme of Jesus's *Herrlichkeit* and messianic identity with the Christological title that is debated throughout the trial, "King of the Jews." Directly following the C/c cadence that tells of Jesus's having predicted the manner of his death, Bach marks a kind of beginning within the "Auf dass erfüllet" recitative for the words "Da ging Pilatus wieder hinein in das Richthaus und rief Jesu und sprach zu ihm: Bist du der Jüden König?" (Then Pilate went into the house of judgment again and said to him, "Are you the king of the Jews?"). It was presumably for this reason that Smend took this phrase as the beginning of his *Herzstück*. The phrase quickly rises to the pitch e♮″, contradicting the e♭″ heard just before ("sterben"), and it moves toward D, which then turns into the dominant of G, as if offering Jesus the opportunity to affirm his identity in that key. And Jesus's response—"Redest du das von dir selbst, oder habens dir andere von mir gesagt?" (Do you say that of your own accord, or have others said that to you about me?)—begins with the fourth from d to g that Jesus will introduce in the next recitative to answer Pilate's question directly and that echoes the "ich bin's" and "ich bin's nicht" of Part 1. At the point under discussion, however, Jesus answers Pilate with that question of his own. And Bach mirrors this turn by deflecting the tonality of the phrase from G to A minor. For the Evangelist's "Pilatus aber antwortete," Bach mimics the earlier G-major recitative phrase "Jesus antwortete," setting it now in A minor. Pilate's further questioning leads to the dominant of E minor; and as the Evangelist again sets up Jesus's answer ("Jesus antwortete"), the recitative moves to the first and only cadence to the dominant, E minor, in the entire scene. Jesus's answer, "Mein Reich ist nicht von dieser Welt; wäre mein Reich von dieser Welt, meine Diener würden darob kämpfen, daß ich den Jüden nicht überantwortet würde; aber nun ist mein Reich nicht von dannen" (My kingdom is not of this world; if my kingdom were of this world, my followers would fight for it, so that I would not be delivered over to the Jews; however, my kingdom is not from thence), has very much a culminating character. Beginning from the Evangelist's E minor, it quickly turns the harmony into the dominant of a, then, as it refers to Jesus's followers fighting on his behalf, introduces an animated figure ("meiner Diener würden darob kämpfen") that Bach reiterates in the Easter cantata of 1725, where it is associated with the joy of the resurrection (see ch. 9, ex 9.1). Continuing, the phrase leads to D minor ("überantwortet würde"), then turns back to A minor for the closing words (I will discuss it further after considering August Hermann Francke's interpretation of the passage). At this point, though, it is important to note that Jesus's answer, in incorporating the dominant and subdominant, for the first time in the scene, outlines a strongly tonal A-minor ending, in preparation for "Ach, großer König," which thereby seems to function as the goal of the entire scene.

Bach's including two successive verses of "Ach, großer König" and setting it apart from all the others in the Passion by means of a continuously moving eighth-note bass makes much the same point that Francke does in his discussion of the meaning of the recitative in his *fourth* lecture (the beginning of which corresponds to the ending of Bach's recitative). In that lecture Francke extends the emphasis on Jesus's *Herrlichkeit*, identifying Jesus's affirmation of his kingship as another "rechtes Haupt-Stück" of the Passion.[7] To underscore the meaning of the latter passage, Francke refers to Paul's comments on the same event near the end of 1 Timothy 6:15–16), where the apostle names Jesus as "the blessed and only Potentate, the King of kings and Lord of lords (v. 15); who only hath immortality, dwelling in the light which no man can approach unto; whom no man hath seen, nor can see: to whom be power and honour everlasting. Amen (v. 16)" (KJV). For Francke, Paul here "teaches us also that from this condition of Jesus's deep *Erniedrigung* we must look into that of his *Herrlichkeit* and await his future coming as the King of Kings and Lord of Lords, and through this all the more powerfully strengthen and direct ourselves in faith in times of suffering and temptation."[8]

In his discussion of the phrase that culminates Bach's recitative, Francke notes that Jesus, in speaking of his kingdom and servants, makes a "special answer," referring to his kingdom three times, and casting Pilate into a state of wonderment (*Verwunderung*).[9] What Pilate would have understood as a conditional usage ("*if* my kingdom were of this world . . . my servants *would*. . . ") was, in light of other scriptural passages (such as Mt 26:53), not at all conditional. And the wonderment it caused Pilate led him to ask Jesus, now directly and seriously, if he was a king. Bach reserves that question for the next recitative, in which Jesus answers Pilate directly. His placing "Ach, grosser König" after Jesus's initial reference to his kingdom enables the meaning brought out by Francke to culminate a scene whose text otherwise centers on Jesus's sufferings. Like the excerpts from Paul, the two verses of the chorale refer to Jesus's *Herrlichkeit* and its incomprehensibility by humanity, but at the same time it emphasizes Jesus's love, paralleling to a degree the culminating role of "O grosse Lieb" (a verse of the same chorale) in the opening scene of the Passion. Thus, like Francke, Bach seems to see in this segment a parallel to the initial scene of Part 1. The two parallel choruses, "Wäre dieser nicht ein Übeltäter"

---

[7] Francke's marginal note at this point (*Oeffentliche Reden*, 61) is "Bekäntniß Jesu vor Pilato, ein Haupt-Stück seines Leidens."

[8] Ibid., 62–63:

> Nicht allein aber das; sondern er lehret uns auch, daß wir von diesem Stande der tieffen Erniedrigung Christi in den Stand seiner Herrlichkeit hinein schauen, und ihn als **den König aller Könige, und HErrn aller Herren** in seiner Erscheinung oder Zukunft erwarten, und uns hiedurch desto kräftiger unter allen Leiden und Verfolgung im Glauben stärcken und aufrichten sollen. Daß aber der HErr JEsus selbst, der sich hier für einen König vor Pilato bekennet hat, **der König aller Könige, und HERR aller Herren sey**, auch von der Schrift so genennet werde, ist Sonnen-klar aus Offenb. Joh. 14, 17. C. 19, 16. Ach Herr Jesu, gib du uns Weisheit, daß wir diß Stück deines Leidens uns auch also, wie Paulus gethan, und uns angewiesen hat, zu Nutz machen mögen.

[9] Ibid., 65–66.

and "Wir dürfen niemand töten," are in the equivalent tonalities in relation to a as the two "Jesum von Nazareth" choruses are in relation to g in the opening segment of Part 1 (in reverse), that parallel further strengthened by the repetition of the "Jesus of Nazareth" music within "Wir dürfen niemand töten." In both scenes Jesus acknowledges his messianic identity.

As I argued in chapter 4, the A-minor culmination of this "scene" with "Ach großer König" is the point toward which the meaning of the composite chorus "Wir dürfen niemand töten" is directed. The A minor of "Wir dürfen niemand töten" is bound up with the Phrygian tonality of "Christus, der uns selig macht," one of the hallmarks of which (as of Bach's conception of Phrygian harmonizations in general) is its introduction of flat accidentals and harmonies, usually for expressive purposes. Thus in Bach's harmonization of the chorale the pitches B♭ and E♭ color words such as "Bös," "Dieb gefangen," and "und fälsch[lich verklaget]." Ultimately, this quality is an outcome of the "subdominant" quality of the Phrygian mode, its lack of a true dominant (owing to the semitone rather than the whole tone above the final). Bach sometimes builds large structures around this aspect of the Phrygian mode. It underlies the character of such magnificent choruses as those that begin Cantatas 2, 38, 135, and others, not to mention the extraordinary beginning and ending of the second movement of the first Brandenburg Concerto. In the scene under discussion flat accidentals and gestures are particularly associated with Jesus's mistreatment. Directly following the opening chorale Bach inflects the name "Kaiphas" with a B flat, leading the half phrase to an articulation of D minor. The D minor of "Wäre dieser nicht ein Übeltäter" is a response to Pilate's A minor, itself preceded by the Phrygian cadence to E (or half close in a) of the Evangelist. Flat motion is conspicuous in "Wäre dieser nicht," which cadences to C minor in its eighth measure. And following its D-minor close, the recitative lead-in to "Wir dürfen niemand töten" articulates the Phrygian cadence to E, with which the "Jesum von Nazareth" music then enters to begin (and ultimately to end) the chorus. "Wir dürfen niemand töten" cadences to G minor in its eighth measure as "Wäre dieser nicht" had cadenced in c. In this context, the abovementioned C-minor inflection of the cadence of the phrase that follows, narrating Jesus's prediction of the manner of his death, supplies the overall meaning of the subdominant (flat) element of the scene. It represents a tonal quality that can be said to undermine the tonic, as if a symbol of antagonism to Jesus's claims to divinity. In this light, the lone appearance of E minor for Jesus's closing statement on his kingdom is all the more significant. After the E-minor dominant beginning of that phrase, Bach moves by the circle of fifths to the subdominant, d, in which the melodic b♭ on the word "Jüden" ("daß ich den *Jüden* nicht überantwortet würde") seems significant. The final phrase, however, in pointedly leaping the tritone to b♮ on the adversitive conjunction "aber" ("*aber* nun ist mein Reich nicht von dannen"), affirms the A-minor tonality, suggesting at the same time the division implied by the text: that the tendency in the flat (subdominant) direction, points to the ongoing association of flat keys with Jesus's *Niedrigkeit*.

The transitional recitative

In the part of his fourth lecture whose text corresponds to the recitative ("Da sprach Pilatus zu ihm") following "Ach großer König," Francke's initial emphasis remains on Jesus's *Herrlichkeit*, but toward the end it shifts to his *Erniedrigung*, which is exactly what occurs in the transitional recitative that leads to Bach's symbolic trial, marking a complete shift of *ambitus*. Francke first interprets Jesus's "Du sagest's, Ich bin ein König" as an affirmation of his divine identity, another "rechtes Hauptstück," referring again to Paul's remarks on Jesus's *Herrlichkeit*, and linking up Jesus's response to Pilate with his reply "Du sagest's" in Matthew and his "Ich bin's" at the corresponding point in Mark (a reminder of his words to the arresting party in John as well).[10] And Francke adds that Jesus's reference to being *born* a king connects up with the question of the Magi, in search of the Messiah in Matthew: "Wo ist der neugebornen König der Juden," a passage that Bach set, in the *Christmas Oratorio*, in a manner that suggests a direct relationship to the "Jesus of Nazareth" choruses of the *St. John Passion*, in particular the last one, "Wir haben keinen König denn den Kaiser."[11] When Jesus speaks of truth, Pilate, according to Francke, recognizes Jesus's innocence, but instead of "hearing Jesus's voice" (i.e., the truth), takes the view that truth is not within his domain but a matter for the schoolroom, not the court. Pilate could have taken the right way and set Jesus free, but he did not; instead, he attempted to attain that end by "worldly cleverness," in offering the choice of Jesus or Barabbas to the crowd, thinking that the great love of the people for Jesus would ensure his release. "The outcome, however, was entirely different," leading to Jesus's abovementioned *Erniedrigung*, according to God's plan.[12] Bringing his fourth lecture to a close, Francke discusses what must be observed ("was dabey zu betrachten") in the episode of Barabbas:

> This belongs to the deep humiliation of the Lord Jesus, that he, in comparison to Barabbas [Ger: Barrabas], a murderer, was judged, and Barabbas set free, and he [Jesus] on the contrary, as though he were more objectionable

[10] Francke (66) first describes this passage as a "*locus confessionis*, der Ort, da der HERR JEsus ein gut Bekäntniß thun muste." See also 68: "So finden wir, daß der Hohe-Priester Matth. 26, 63. JEsum fraget, ob er Christus der Sohn GOttes sey, und daß JEsus ihm antwortet: **Du sagests.** Welches denn Marcus c. 14, 62. also ausleget, daß JEsus gesagt habe: **Ich bins.** Wenn aber der HErr JEsus in unserm Text nicht nur antwortet: **Du sagests**; sondern auch hinzusetzet: **Ich bin ein König;** ists eben so viel, als ob er gesagt hätte: **Ja ich bins / ich bin ein König.**"

[11] Francke, *Oeffentliche Reden*, 68: "Wenn aber der Herr Jesus in unserm Text nicht nur antwortet: **Du sagests;** sondern auch hinzusetzet: **Ich bin ein König;** ist eben so viel, als ob er gesagt hätte: **Ja ich bins / ich bin ein König.** Und da er noch weiter dabey füget: **Ich bin dazu geboren;** so ist diß nicht allein ein dreyfaches Bekänntniß, sondern es ist auch zugleich eine Beantwortung der wider ihn vorgebrachten Klage. Ich werfe mich nicht, wil er sagen, für einen König auf, wie sie mich beschuldigen, sondern **ich bin dazu geboren** / bin **ein gebohrner König** (wie die Weisen aus Morgen-Land Matth. 2, 2. nach einem solchen **gebohrnen König** gefraget.)." See Chafe, *Tonal Allegory*, 297–99 for the connection between "Wir haben keinen König" and "Wo ist der neugebornen König der Juden."

[12] Francke, *Oeffentliche Reden*, 73.

> than this murderer, was sentenced to crucifixion. This was a symbol that we should be free and Christ must be given over for us according to God's plan. For in Barabbas everyone has to seek himself. And that is again the most prominent thing that we have to extract from the description of the suffering of Christ, namely, that Christ suffered in our place, the just for the unjust. This we should always hold forth before all other teachings, so that we correctly recognize the purpose as well as the fruit of the sufferings of Christ, and seek to ground them ever deeper in such faith. For this meditation is at its most powerful a working in our souls of true conversion from sin, a humble thankfulness for the sufferings of Jesus on our behalf, and a living hope of our eternal salvation.[13]

Bach's making a culminating point out of "Ach, großer König," must have been bound up with the fact that the continuation of the dialog that it interrupts (the culminating point of Francke's *fourth* lecture) leads to the demand for Barabbas from the crowd and the terse remark that Barabbas was a murderer. That is, the recitative that follows "Ach, großer König," which contains the chorus "Nicht diesen, sondern Barrabam" (i.e., the fourth of the "Jesus of Nazareth" choruses) within it, is transitional, describing, like the ending of Francke's fourth lecture, a motion from the theme of Jesus's *Herrlichkeit* to that of his *Erniedrigung*. That shift is symbolized by the transposition of the "Jesus of Nazareth" *music* (now "Nicht diesen, sondern Barrabam") from the a of "Wir dürfen niemand töten" to d, followed by the move toward g with which the recitative ends (the narrative of the scourging, the beginning of John 19, which now becomes the impetus for the symbolic trial).

The recitative in question exemplifies the distinction made earlier (ch. 5), between recitatives and closed movements in defining the key areas. Beginning with Pilate's reiterating the question to Jesus that had prompted Bach's insertion of "Ach, großer König"—"So bist du dennoch ein König?"—it immediately sets up the key of G major, to which Jesus responds "Du sagest's," with virtually the same cadential progression as his earlier "Ich bin's," only now to G major instead of minor (since Jesus now affirms his divine identity without the former "veiling"). (See ex. 6.1)

---

[13] Ibid., 73–74:

> Diß gehöret zu der tieffen Erniedrigung des HERRN JEsu, daß er in eine Vergleichung mit Barraba, ein Mörder, gesetzet, und Barrabas los gegeben, und er hingegen, als ob er ärger wäre als dieser Mörder, zum Creuzes-Tode gefordert wird. Diß war ein Bild, daß wir los seyn sollten, und CHristus für uns nach dem Rath GOttes dahin gegeben werden müsste. Denn in dem Barraba hat ein ieglicher sich selbst zu suchen. Und das ist abermal die allervornehmste Sache, die wir aus der Beschreibung des Leidens CHristi zu nehmen haben, nemlich daß Christus an unserer Statt, der Gerechte für uns Ungerechte gelitten hat. Diß sollen wir immer vor allen andern Lehren daraus behalten, damit wir so wol die Ursache / als die Frucht des Leidens Christi recht erkennen, und im solchem Glauben immer tieffer zu gründen suchen. Denn diese Betrachtung ist am kräftigsten, eine wahre Bekehrung von Sünden, eine demüthige Danckbarkeit gegen den für uns leidenden JESUM, und eine lebendige Hoffnung unsers ewigen Heyls in unsern Seelen zu wircken.

EXAMPLE 6.1 ***St. John Passion*** *no 18a, recitative, mm. 1–11*

Continuing, Jesus's response, "Ich bin ein König. Ich bin dazu geboren und in die Welt kommen, daß ich die Wahrheit zeugen soll" (I am a king. I was born and came into the world, so that I might bear witness to the truth), takes up one of the principal characteristics of John's world "above," that of truth, whose analog is that Jesus moves further sharp, cadencing solidly in D major. The modulation recalls Jesus's effecting the shift to the sharp *ambitus* that closes Part 1, where the disciples fail to bear witness to the truth, but where, as we have seen, Peter's response of penitence attests to his faith (the A-major ending). Jesus's next words, "Wer aus der Wahrheit ist, der höret meine Stimme" (Whoever is of the truth, he hears my voice) move to B minor, perhaps a reflection that as Francke points out, Jesus knows Pilate *not* to be of the truth. Pilate's response, "Was ist Wahrheit?" is not one of faith; and Bach (after hinting at that fact in Jesus's B-minor cadence) has Pilate's solo reverse the modulatory direction with a circle-of-fifths motion (passing through D, e, a, and d) that sets up the d of "Nicht diesen . . . sondern Barrabam," in his question to the crowd, "wollt ihr nun, daß ich euch der Juden König losgebe?" (Do you want now that I set free to you the king of the Jews?). "Nicht diesen sondern Barrabam" (Not this man, but Barabbas) and the first phrase of the subsequent recitative, "Barrabas aber war ein Mörder" (Barabbas, however, was a murderer), effect closure in d, after which the terse narrative of Jesus's scourging completes the shift of *ambitus* with an extravagantly melismatic turn to G minor (on *geisselte*). The recitative therefore outlines a motion from G major (Jesus's affirming his kingship) to G minor (the scourging, symbol of his *Erniedrigung*). In this it corresponds exactly to Francke's description.

In fact, Bach's transitional recitative outlines two levels of major/minor shift, setting Jesus's affirmation of his messianic identity (G) in opposition to the scourging (g), and his D-major reference to truth in opposition to the D minor that is the outcome of Pilate's questioning of truth (on D) and the cry for release of Barabbas (D minor). More significant for subsequent events is the fact that the recitative moves in the flat direction to culminate in G minor. And, in addition to these major/minor, sharp/flat shifts, the movements that precede and follow the recitative, "Ach, großer König," and "Betrachte, meine Seele," describe with a tritone shift the transition from emphasis on Jesus's *Herrlichkeit* in "Ach, großer König" (a) to meditation on his *Erniedrigung* in "Betrachte, meine Seele" (E♭). These G/g, D/d, and a/E♭ symbols of antithesis, particularly of the qualities associated in John with "above" and "below," anticipate the theological oppositions that permeate Bach's symbolic trial and that emerge in its flat/sharp/flat tonal design. "Betrachte, meine Seele," with its "special" instrumentation of lute and two violas d'amore, and the C-minor aria, "Erwäge" (also with two violas d'amore), now meditate on the meaning of Jesus's sufferings in terms of the message of the Passion as a whole.[14]

Bach's "Symbolic Trial"

John's Passion narrative occupies two chapters of approximately equal length (ch. 18, which has 40 verses, and 19, which has 42). Jesus's trial spans the two chapters, extending from the point where he is delivered over to Pilate (18:28) until the judgment of crucifixion (19:16). Thus the twenty-nine verses of the trial are approximately centered between the twenty-seven that precede them and the twenty-six that follow. Likewise, the traditional dividing point between chapters 18 and 19 apportions the trial so that it encompasses the last thirteen verses of chapter 18 and the first sixteen of chapter 19. The chapter division coincides with the release of Barabbas (18:40) and the scourging (19:1), followed by the crown of thorns and mocking of Jesus by the Roman soldiers as "King of the Jews" (19:2–3). (As we have seen, the Postel Passion text begins with chapter nineteen; see ch. 4.)

---

[14] The instrumentation described is that of the first (1724) version; the version of the late 1740s has a different, but still special instrumentation of harpsichord and muted violins. See Mendel, *Kritischer Bericht*, 110.

Francke makes the same point into the division between his fourth and fifth lectures. Nevertheless, he takes pains to bring out continuity between the two. His fourth lecture ends by urging the Christian community to meditate on Jesus's sufferings as the source of eternal benefit, praying God in his mercy to grant the faithful recognition of their sins as the cause of Jesus's sufferings, to give from the unfathomable richness of his grace the "sweet fruit" of those sufferings, which fruits are "righteousness and life and eternal blessedness." And the fifth begins with another prayer for the faithful, in meditating on Jesus's scourging, to gather the "fruits" of Jesus's sufferings.[15] In urging such "Betrachtung" and "Erwägung" at this point, and in emphasizing their "fruits" ("Frucht," "segnete Frucht," and "süsse Frucht") for the believer, Francke seems to understand Jesus's scourging as the beginning of a new meditation-centered phase in the trial, as is the case with Bach's placing the arioso "Betrachte, meine Seele" and the aria "Erwäge" at the same point, the former of which summarizes the meaning of antithesis in the line "du kannst viel süsse Frucht von seiner Wermut brechen."

As John's Passion account is often interpreted today, Jesus's trial is the center of a three-division design, itself forming a sevenfold chiastic symmetry in which the scourging of Jesus by the Roman soldiers, including the narrative of the crown of thorns and the purple clothes, is the center, surrounded by scenes that alternate between dialogs of Jesus and Pilate inside the governor's palace and Pilate's confronting the crowd outside. I have incorporated one such interpretation, that of Raymond Brown, into chapter 4, figures 4.1 and 4.2. In Brown's view, the trial is a model of careful structural design, in which John altered the ordering of certain events—the scourging and even the date of the crucifixion—in relation to that of the Synoptic Gospels, primarily for symbolic purposes to which the pronounced sense of structure gave additional emphasis.[16] The chiastic design seems particularly symbolic: running throughout the trial is the theme of Jesus's *identity*, particularly as it relates to the Christological title "king" or "king of the Jews." Culminating in the outcry "We have no king but Caesar," followed immediately by the judgment of crucifixion, John's trial mirrors in microcosm the fact that his entire Gospel, which features much forensic language, is very much like a symbolic trial over the question of Jesus's identity.

In the traditional fivefold division of the Passion narrative, however, especially in Lutheranism, the segment or *actus* known as "Pilatus" was the central one and

---

[15] Francke, *Oeffentliche Reden*, 74–76.

[16] Brown, *Gospel According to John* XIII–XXI, 785. 857–59; Brown, *The Death of the Messiah*. 2 vols. (New York: Doubleday Anchor Books, 1994), 1:757–59. The best-known instance of John's altering the order of events in relation to the Synoptic Gospels is the date of the crucifixion itself, which John moves forward in time so as to make Jesus's death coincide with the sacrifice of the Passover lambs. Another is that in John the scourging and freeing of Barabbas take place much earlier than in the Synoptics. Remarking that "many exegetes agree in recognizing seven episodes in John in a chiastic arrangement," Brown comments "there can be no doubt that this is deliberate artistry, expanding and arranging what came down in the tradition" (*Death of the Messiah*, 758).

by far the longest of the five: not only did it extend beyond the trial to encompass the narrative of the royal inscription, but also the preceding and following narratives were each divided into two *actus*. It is not unusual, therefore, that the Postel Passion text—set by several composers before Bach and which influenced the *St. John Passion* text—begins with the scourging. Traditionally, the image of Jesus crowned with thorns and bleeding from the scourging (the *Ecce homo*, as Jesus is brought forth and displayed to the crowd) was second only to the crucifixion itself as stimulation to meditation on Jesus's sufferings and their salvific meaning (they appear on facing pages of Rambach's *Betrachtungen über das gantze Leiden Christi*, the one as frontispiece and the other on the title page). This was, presumably, a factor in Bach's assigning the scourging and the royal inscription a special degree of meditative emphasis as the beginning and ending of his "symbolic trial."

A theme that runs through the trial and that might have determined the placement of the division between John's chapters 18 and 19, is whether Jesus should be freed. All the Lutheran theologians treat this theme in terms of Pilate's various pronouncements on Jesus's innocence. John makes much out of this question in his design for the trial, in which the freeing of Barabbas and scourging of Jesus mark the center, and in which, after Jesus speaks to Pilate regarding power from "above" as determining Pilate's actions, John narrates that Pilate sought to free Jesus. In Bach's setting the dialog just mentioned comes between the choruses "Wir haben ein Gesetz, und nach dem Gesetz soll er sterben, denn er hat sich selbst zu Gottes Sohn gemacht" (We have a law, and according to the law he must die, for he has made himself out to be the Son of God) and "Durch dein Gefängnis," which gives the salvific meaning of freedom in advance of the worldly objection given in "Lässest du diesen los." As discussed in chapter 4, this sequence marks a turning point between two interpretations of the law, the spiritual one, according to which Jesus has blasphemed against Jehovah in naming himself Son of God, and the worldly one, in which Jesus's naming himself "king," transgresses against the Roman emperor. Before this turning point, Pilate's questions to Jesus regarding his kingship can be thought to embody a genuine interest in Jesus's true identity. Afterwards, Jesus is silent throughout the trial; and in the absence of dialogs the adverse events move more swiftly. Pilate's continuing references to Jesus as king inflame the crowd further, bringing forth a second demand for crucifixion. Following "Wir haben keinen König denn den Kaiser" (We have no king but Caesar), Pilate passes the judgment of death, ending the trial.[17]

[17] Brown (*Death of the Messiah*, 1:759), characterizing the difference between the scenes that alternate inside and outside locations, remarks "the dialogue inside reveals Pilate's inability to recognize the truth standing incarnate before him; the dialogue outside reveals the true motive behind the hostility of 'the Jews': not Jesus's claim to be 'the King of the Jews' but his claim to be God's Son." In this sense "Wir haben ein Gesetz" is a climactic point, bringing out the real motive for the demand of death. The dialog that follows "Wir haben ein Gesetz" is the last, and most truly climactic of the inside dialogs, the one in which Jesus specifies the world "above" as the source of true power. This is reflected in the modu-

The judgment of crucifixion is a direct response to the outcry "Wir haben keinen König denn den Kaiser." In the royal inscription, however, John proclaims the opposite, although some commentaries, from long before Bach's time to the present day, favor the view that Pilate intended it mockingly. Most, however, including the highly influential *Die Harmonie derer Heiligen vier Evangelisten* of Martin Chemnitz, Polykarp Leyser, and Johann Gerhard, see it as the culmination of Pilate's "Sehet, das ist eure König" and "Soll ich eure König kreuzigen" before the ending of the trial. The high priests, however, in demanding that the wording be changed, point up the possibility of misinterpretation: that the inscription will be read as the truth. That is, of course, the meaning John intends, the culmination of all the literary devices that run through the Gospel and that all serve the purpose of separating the response of the listeners to Jesus's discourses into two categories: believers and nonbelievers. For John this division is a fateful one; for, as he says elsewhere, those with faith, who perceive the truth beyond appearances, the spiritual meaning, are not judged, while those who do not perceive such meaning, the unbelievers, are judged already, a view suggesting both a high degree of determinism and an inversion of meaning regarding who is on trial.

In this framework the meaning of the trial is embodied in the words of Jesus in his dialogs with Pilate, where he proclaims his kingship and spiritual realm—John's world "above"—as the source of power and truth, not in the worldly outcome with which the trial ends. In characteristically Johannine fashion, therefore, the larger trial that spreads throughout the Gospel provides a second answer to the question of Jesus's identity, a spiritual answer for those who believe. The spiritual answer is embodied in the inscription above the cross in multiple languages. Thus telling the truth under the guise of its opposite, the royal inscription has always been viewed as John's means of supplanting the judgment of the trial by shifting the truth to a later point, a second "spiritual" decision, capable of being understood only by those who believe. In John's division of the world into above and below, the contemporary believer allies herself, through faith or lack of faith, with one or the other "world." The truth, apprehended through faith, is centered on

---

lation to sharp keys in that dialog and in the substantial sense that it articulates a tritone opposition (from the G of Pilate's "Weissest du nicht das Macht habe, . . . " to the c♯ that culminates Jesus's speech, beginning "Du hättest keine Macht über mich, wenn sie dir nicht wäre von oben herab gegeben"). The absence of dialogs from this point on causes events to move much more swiftly than before to their final outcome, the judgment of crucifixion. Brown (*Death of the Messiah*, 759, n. 58) speaks of the "double Johannine clarification" of the motives of the Jews in bringing Jesus to Pilate: "the theological motive described above, and the practical motive that it was not permitted them to put anyone to death—a motive that paradoxically has the result of fulfilling Jesus's word signifying what death he was going to die (18:32)." Brown links the two references to the law ("Wir dürfen niemand töten," sung in response to Pilate's "So nehmet ihr ihn hin und richtet ihm nach eurem Gesetze," and "Wir haben ein Gesetz") in terms of "practical" and "theological" motivations. After the latter outcry, the "practical" (worldly) motive returns for the remainder of the (now dialog-less) trial, culminating in "Wir haben keinen König."

Jesus's words and identity, which may even be proclaimed by the antagonistic forces against their will.[18]

Viewed as boundaries of Bach's symbolic trial, the E♭ movements, "Betrachte, meine Seele" and "In meines Herzens Grunde," suggest a long-range connection, especially when we consider that the first and last of the set of symmetrically arranged parallel choruses, "Sei gegrüsset, lieber Judenkönig" and "Schreibe nicht: der Juden König," both in B♭, also appear near the beginning and ending respectively. In the former instance the B♭ tonality forms part of a purposive, even systematic motion in the sharp or dominant direction, whereas in the latter it affirms the return to flats. At the beginning of the symbolic trial "Betrachte" directly follows the G-minor narrative of the scourging, urging the faithful to meditate on Jesus's sufferings, after which its companion aria, "Erwäge," invokes the visual image of the rainbow, formed on Jesus's back from the blood of the scourging mixed with the water of human sinfulness: that is, the water of the flood (*Sintflut* = *Sündflut*). The reference to blood and water looks ahead to the issuing forth of blood and water from the piercing of Jesus's side after his death. As traditional sacramental symbols, blood (the Eucharist) and water (baptism) signify the sphere of the flesh, the world below, which Bach links up, both here and in the narrative of the piercing of Jesus's side, with the deeper flat keys of the Passion. In making the first segment of Part 2 serve as a kind of introduction to the symbolic trial, and in beginning it with the chorale "Christus, der uns selig macht," Bach looked ahead beyond the trial to the final scene of the Passion, in which the Phrygian harmonization of the chorale was heard again, modified, and transposed up a semitone, as "O hilf, Christe, Gottes Sohn." With such means (including the references to freedom discussed in ch. 4) Bach created a scale of correspondences within the Passion within which his "symbolic trial" is "enclosed" as it were, forming a focal point for the meaning of the whole.

The redemptive meaning of Jesus's blood is, of course, the central theme in both "Betrachte"/"Erwäge" and the chorale that culminates Bach's symbolic trial, "In meines Herzens Grunde." And at both points it involves an image of Jesus's sufferings: in the first instance the believer is urged "drum sieh' ohn' Unterlass auf ihn" (therefore look without interruption upon him), and in the second the believer cries "Erschein mir in dem Bilde zu Trost in meiner Not, wie du, Herr Christ, so milde dich hat geblut't zu Tod" (appear to me in the image—for consolation in my need—of how you, Lord Christ, bled so mildly to death). In the former instance Bach draws out the closing words of the arioso, the only phrase to be repeated in the movement, as follows: "drum sieh ohn Unterlaß auf ihn, auf ihn, drum sieh ohn Unterlaß auf ihn, ohn Unterlaß, drum sich ohn Unterlaß auf ihn!" This remarkable and highly expressive emphasis on the image of Jesus's sufferings identifies "Betrachte" as a renewal of the prayer, "Zeig uns durch deine Passion," of the

[18] Francke, for example, so describes it; see 273. Heermann, Rambach, and Heinrich Müller make very similar comments.

very first chorus "Herr, unser Herrscher." Perhaps, therefore, its responding to the G minor of the scourging (even though it meditates on the crown of thorns) links up with the beginning tonality of the Passion. As we have seen, the return to flats with "Eilt, ihr angefocht'nen Seelen" culminates in the E♭ of "In meines Herzens Grunde." Also, at the beginning and ending of the symbolic trial the texts introduce what were understood at the time as equivalent symbols of reconciliation with God: in the first instance the rainbow as sign of God's covenant with humanity after the flood, in the second the cross as sign of the new covenant brought about by Jesus's Passion.

In meines Herzens Grunde	In the depths of my heart
dein Nam' und Kreuz allein	your name and cross alone
funkelt allzeit und Stunde	shines every moment and hour
drauf kann ich fröhlich sein.	so that I can be happy.
Erschein mir in dem Bilde,	Appear to me in the image,
zu Trost in meiner Not,	for comfort in my need,
wie du, Herr Christ, so milde	how you, Lord Christ,
dich hast geblut't zur Tod.	so mildly bled to death.

In keeping with the reminder of God's covenant with Noah, the instrumentation of "Betrachte" (lute and violas d'amore) and "Erwäge" (violas d'amore and perhaps viola da gamba) might have been intended by Bach to invoke an archaizing atmosphere, as Mendel suggests, and as the viola da gamba was perhaps intended to symbolize in the outermost segments of "Es ist vollbracht."[19] Whether or not this was so, the story of Noah and the flood was widely cited as representing the end of the first "era" of salvation history, often the first of three (or four) such eras; and the colors of the rainbow were widely interpreted in this light. Luther saw three colors, a watery blue below, yellow in the middle, and a band of red above, symbols, respectively, of the three judgments on the world pronounced by God in its three eras. The first ended with the flood, the second, which was under the law, ended with the destruction of the Temple by the Romans, and the third, the present era would see the ultimate destruction of the world by fire.[20] Valerius Herberger, writing around the turn of the seventeenth century, remarks that the "old teachers of the church" saw two colors, red, representing Jesus's divinity and a "watery" color, representing his humanity; but Herberger also cites those two colors as signs of the destruction of the world by water and fire, giving the preferred scholarly interpretation as a threefold one: the color of blood, signifying Jesus's suffering and work of redemption, yellow, signifying the crown of Jesus's kingship, and green, signifying the green tree of life, spreading its arms above the earth, as Jesus's

[19] Ibid., 97.

[20] Luther, *Lectures on Genesis, Chapters 1–5*, in *Luther's Works*, vol. 1, 358–59. We may remember that Jesus's death and resurrection were traditionally viewed (on the basis of his words in John) as prefiguring the destruction and rebuilding of the Temple, corresponding to Luther's second era.

spread his arms on the cross to gather in the faithful to God.[21] For Herberger, Jesus himself was the meaning of the rainbow; his chapter is titled "Jesus der schöne Regenbogen, der wahrhaftige Zeuge der Gnaden Gottes." Rambach and others viewed the colors somewhat differently as red and green, corresponding to God's judgment and his mercy, the two joined in Christ as the mediator of the new covenant.[22] And the story of Noah was sometimes cited, without reference to the rainbow, as symbol of parallelism between the oldest parts of the story of Israel in the OT and the NT events they prefigured, as in the arioso "Am Abend, da es kühle war" from the *St. Matthew Passion*.[23] Above all, of course, the rainbow was a symbol of God's grace, embodied in Jesus. As Rambach put it, the rainbow signified the extension of God's "kingdom of nature" into his "kingdom of grace which was ruled by Christ."[24]

In chapter 8 I address the imagery behind the meditative movements of Bach's symbolic trial in greater detail, with a view toward revealing the logic behind their choice and placement. And as figure 4.4 shows, the meditative movements are very carefully placed and few in number. In their emphasis on visual imagery, "Betrachte"/"Erwäge" and "In meines Herzens Grunde" relate back to the petition, "Zeig' uns," in the opening chorus. Their thrust is that Jesus's sufferings, since they are voluntary, are veiled manifestations of his glorification. At the midpoint of the symbolic trial, however, the veiling is removed in the E-major chorale "Durch dein Gefängnis," which, addressing Jesus as "Gottes Sohn," voices the salvific meaning of Jesus's sufferings particularly clearly and in the context not of his scourging or death but of his proclaiming to Pilate (in the preceding recitative) that true power comes only from "above." Further descriptions of Jesus as the refuge of the pious ("der Freistadt aller Frommen"), his imprisonment as the source of the believer's freedom, and his prison as the "throne of grace" (*Gnadenthron*), an obvious opposite number to the "judgment seat" (*Richtstuhl*) on which Pilate sits throughout this segment of John's trial, make clear that meditation on Jesus's sufferings here is less conspicuous than the Johannine counterimage of Jesus in glory. The preceding recitative ("Da Pilatus das Wort hörete, fürchtet' er sich noch mehr"), in which Jesus sets up the shift to sharp keys that now form the tonal "apex," as it were, of the trial, is the culmination of the dialogs between Jesus and Pilate, in which Jesus,

---

[21] Herberger, *De Jesu . . . Magnalia Dei*, 109–12.

[22] Rambach, *Christus in Mose*, 1108.

[23] See Pelikan, *Bach Among the Theologians*, 3.

[24] Rambach, *Christus in Mose*, 1106–7:

> Daß dieser Bund, den GOtt im Reiche der Natur zwischen sich selbsten und allem lebendigen Fleisch aufgerichtet, und den er durch des Bundes Zeichen, den Regen-Bogen versiegelt, daß, sage ich, dieser Bund sein Absehen habe auf das Reich der Gnaden, dessen Verwaltung JEsu Christo anvertrauet ist. . . . Diese Betrachtung nöthiget uns also die Bedeutung des Regen-Bogens nicht nur auf das Reich der Natur einzuschrencken, sondern dieselbe auch auf das Reich der Gnaden zu *extendiren*, welches von Christo verwaltet wird. . . . Wir werden dabey zu bemercken haben, daß dieses Bundes-Zeichen, nemlich der Regen-Bogen, ein sehr bequemes *Symbolum* und Bild sey, die Gnade JESU Christi vorzustellen.

having identified his kingdom as not of this world in the preceding dialog, refers directly to the world "above" as determining events in the one below. From this standpoint, Bach might have considered the E-major tonality of "Durch dein Gefängnis" as a kind of opposite to the two B♭ choruses that come near the beginning and ending of the symbolic trial and whose denial of Jesus's identity represents the world "below."[25]

Bach's symbolic trial is constructed as a threefold design of flat–sharp–flat key areas (or *ambitus*) with conspicuous symmetrical elements, beginning in E♭ and moving sharpward, reaching E at its symbolic midpoint and returning to flat keys, ending in E♭ once again. It can be considered to outline an ascent/descent "shape" that mirrors the rainbow patterns that permeate "Erwäge, wie sein blutgefärbten Rücken," and is echoed in turn in the melodic phrase shapes of "Durch dein Gefängnis" and "In meines Herzens Grunde." The move to sharps is placed so as to mirror the dialog between Jesus and Pilate on power; Jesus's proclamation that power comes only from above establishes the new *ambitus* with a cadence to c♯. Then, following the E-major chorale "Durch dein Gefängnis," and chorus "Lässest du diesen los" (the central pivot between law and freedom), the sequence of keys reverses its direction, reaching B minor for the chorus "We have no king but Caesar," and a D-major cadence for the narrative of the judgment of crucifixion. After that, the music turns immediately back in the flat direction, leading on to g for the shift to Golgotha, and the hortatory bass dialog with chorus, "Eilt, ihr angefocht'nen Seelen," thereby beginning the third segment of Bach's trial and the third division of John's Passion narrative with the key in which the Passion began. The third and final segment of the symbolic trial—corresponding to the shift of locale to Golgotha, the narratives of the crucifixion, and the royal inscription—begins and ends with the keys that begin and end the Passion as a whole.

This third segment of the symbolic trial, beginning with "Eilt, ihr angefocht'nen Seelen" and ending with "In meines Herzens Grunde," has a double, even overlapping role in Bach's design, since it completes the symmetry of the symbolic trial as well as marking a new beginning in the Passion narrative. Within it Bach modulates to "deep" flats (especially b♭) for the narrative of the crucifixion and royal inscription, whose multiple languages fulfill the proclamation "dessen Ruhm in allen

[25] That such a tritone relationship was conceived in antithetical terms is attested to by the theoretical writings of the time as well as by the ordering of the keys of the first and second parts of the *Clavierübung*, which highlight such relationships (see the diagram in Chafe, *Tonal Allegory*, 82). Other Bach works make an association between tritone shifts and theological ideas; one such is Cantata 121, *Christum wir sollen loben schon*, for the second day of Christmas, 1724. In Cantata 121 (see Chafe, *Analyzing Bach Cantatas*, 139–49), the Gregorian melody on which Luther based his chorale paraphrase, in its shifting from the Dorian to the Phrygian mode, stimulated Bach to end the first and last movements of the cantata on F♯, whereas the second aria, based on John the Baptist's leaping in his mother's womb at the news of the incarnation, is in C major. In the recitative that sets up this aria, Bach makes a tritone shift (from the dominant of f♯ to the dominant of C) in association with the miracle of the incarnation. The "above/below" associations of this modulation might be thought to underlie the sharp/flat design of the *St. John Passion*'s "symbolic trial," with its associations of power from above at the center.

Landen herrlich ist" in the opening chorus. At the same time, the modulatory design suggests that the royal inscription fulfills the exhortation in the middle section of "Herr, unser Herrscher" for Jesus to show the faithful the process of his glorification through the *Niedrigkeit* of the Passion (the deep flat keys). In this light the line "Erschein mir in dem Bilde" from "In meines Herzens Grunde" seems significant. Following the reiteration of the music of "Sei gegrüsset, lieber Judenkönig," to the words "Schreibe nicht: der Juden König," Pilate's "Was ich geschrieben habe, dass habe ich geschrieben" (a B♭ cadence) and the E♭ chorale, "In meines Herzens Grunde, dein Nam' und Kreuz allein," complete what is in Bach's design the structural and symbolic equivalent of John's chiastic trial scene (but displaced, as mentioned), a threefold flat–sharp–flat segment that begins in E♭ with the arioso "Betrachte, meine Seele," moves to E for the chorale "Durch dein Gefängnis, Gottes Sohn," then returns to E♭ for "In meines Herzens Grunde." The meditation on Jesus's sufferings that is urged in "Betrachte" and "Erwäge," and whose salvific meaning is given in "Durch dein Gefängnis," is internalized in "In meines Herzens Grunde." The beginning images the rainbow, symbol of God's covenant of grace with Noah, and the ending the cross of its renewal through Jesus, whereas the equivalence of name and cross at the end culminates the symmetrical design.

In Bach's design the trial comes to two decisions, as in John. The first one, embodied in Pilate's succumbing to the demands of the crowd, immediately follows the chorus "Wir haben keinen König denn den Kaiser," which marks the end of the central sharp-key segment of the Passion (see fig. 4.1). This is the end of the trial proper. The second decision, ending the spiritual or symbolic trial, is, of course, the royal inscription, which, like the narrative of the crucifixion itself, is in "deep" flats (mostly b♭), to correspond with the fact that Jesus's glorification coincides with his *Niedrigkeit*. As in Luther's *theologia crucis*, the cross, from the worldly perspective a symbol of degradation, is the means by which God reveals Jesus's divinity, his glorification. After "In meines Herzens Grunde," therefore, the tonality leads upward again to the b/D of "Es ist vollbracht" and "Mein teurer Heiland." In returning to the keys that ended the trial proper (b/D), and in echoing the reference to tormented souls in "Eilt, ihr angefocht'nen Seelen" ("angefocht'nen Seelen"/ "gekränkten Seelen"), "Es ist vollbracht" responds to the dialog's urging flight to the cross to seek fulfillment of the "pilgrimage" of faith: "Nehmet an des Glaubens Flügel, flieht zum Kreuzes Hügel, eure Wohlfahrt blüht allda" (Take up the wings of faith, fly to the hill of the cross, your pilgrimage blooms there). "Eilt, ihr angefocht'nen Seelen" makes Golgotha into the pilgrimage of faith, renewing the tonality of "Herr, unser Herrscher" for what Raymond Brown views as the beginning of John's division three, whereas the D of the middle section of "Es ist vollbracht" and of the Passion's second bass dialog with chorus, "Mein teurer Heiland," affirms the positive outcome of Jesus's death for the believer. The meaning is now that of the world and the cross transformed by faith and Jesus's victory—the message of Easter—which, as in the melodic motion of "Eilt, ihr angefocht'nen Seelen" and the middle section of "Es ist vollbracht," are directed entirely upward. Ultimately, the character of the symbolic trial, with its motion between flat and sharp *ambitus*, extends to the design of the Passion as a whole (see fig. 4.2).

The symbolic trial forms a closed design—or at least the image of a closed design—beginning and ending in E♭. It is not, of course, separate from what precedes and follows it, but it can be said to have its own "shape" and purpose within the Passion. In this light, a very interesting fact concerning Bach's modulatory design is that the tonal motion from "Betrachte, meine Seele" to the beginning of the recitative that effects the shift to sharps at the center of Bach's trial follows *exactly* the pattern of Heinichen's B♭/g *ambitus* in the keys of the closed movements: E♭ ("Betrachte, meine Seele"), c ("Erwäge"), B♭ ("Sei gegrüsset, lieber Judenkönig"), g ("Kreuzige ihn") and F ("Wir haben ein Gesetz"). The one remaining key of the *ambitus*, D minor, completes the first full cadence of the subsequent recitative (the narrative of Pilate's returning within the *Richthaus* to speak to Jesus). (See fig. 5.1 where I have indicated the keys in question.) Whereas the tonal motion from "Betrachte" and "Erwäge" to the D-minor cadence is gradual, what follows in the brief dialog between Jesus and Pilate effects a sudden and highly symbolic shift to sharps, at first without a definitive cadence. After the D-minor cadence of the first phrase of the recitative, the next full cadence in the recitative is a semitone lower, to c♯, effected by Jesus and marking the tonal shift around which the symbolic trial pivots. (This pattern can be clearly seen in fig. 4.4 and the modulation itself in ex. 6.2.) Bach underscores the significance of the shift within the recitative by assigning the cadences to d and c♯ identical melodic, harmonic, and rhythmic structures (with the added detail that a rising major sixth leads into the tonic in both cases). They are the true focal points for the semitone transposition pattern of the choruses that precede and follow. The suddenness and tonal distance involved in the modulation suggests the division between worlds above and below to which Jesus refers.

And from the point just described to the close of the central sharp-key segment of the symbolic trial (the narrative of Pilate's delivering Jesus for crucifixion, which ends the trial proper), Bach's sequence of keys outlines very nearly the exact pattern of Heinichen's A/f♯ *ambitus* in the keys of the closed movements and recitative cadences together, now in reverse, that is, moving from the dominant (E/c♯) to the subdominant (D/b) region of the A/f♯ *ambitus* (the keys in question are also indicated in fig. 5.1). This time the more rapid presentation of the pattern reflects that after the shift to sharp keys, there are no more dialogs between Jesus and Pilate. The sequence is the following: c♯ (Jesus's response to Pilate regarding power from above); E (the narrative of Pilate's seeking to free Jesus, the chorale "Durch dein Gefängnis" [see ex. 6.3] and the chorus "Lässest du diesen los"); f♯ (the first cadence in the subsequent recitative, narrating Pilate's seating himself on the judgment seat in "auf Ebraisch aber: Gabbatha"); A (Pilate's "Sehet, das ist eure König," proclaimed from the judgment seat); f♯ ("Weg, weg mit dem, Kreuzige ihn"); b ("Wir haben keinen König"); and D ("Da überantwortete er ihn, dass er gekreuziget würde," the ending of John's trial). After the A of "Sehet, das ist eure König," to present the

EXAMPLE 6.2 ***St. John Passion*** *no. 21g, recitative (ending)*

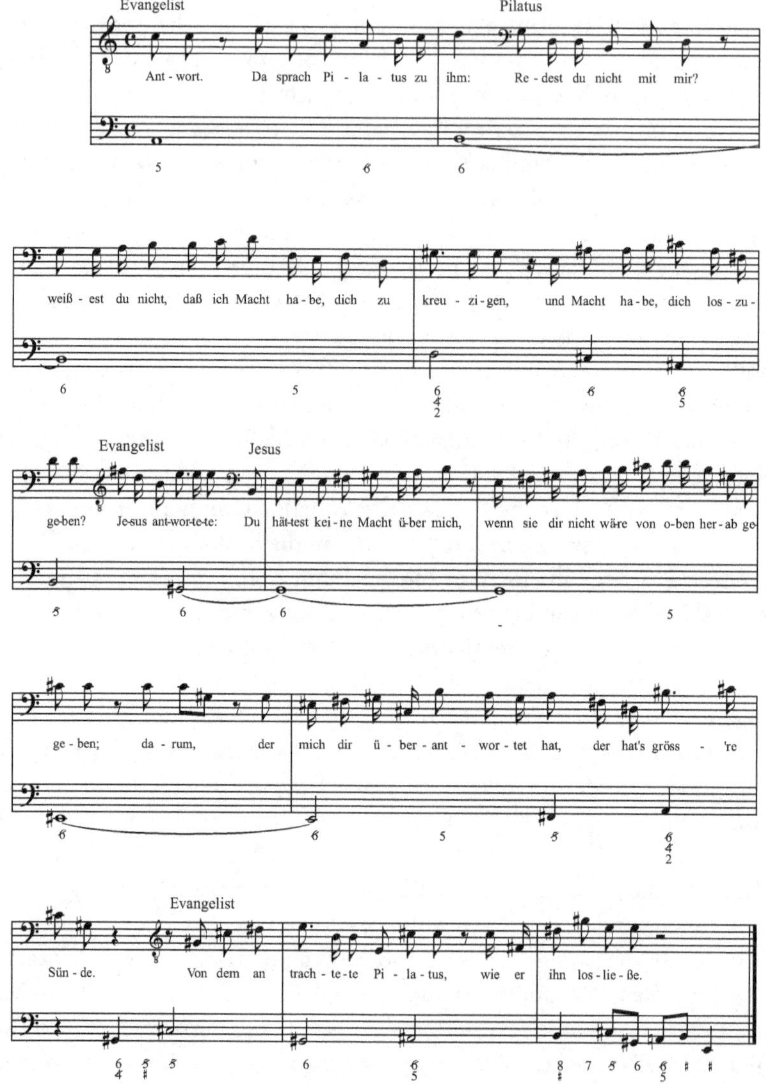

pattern of Heinichen's *ambitus* a semitone lower than the earlier "ascending" one and in reverse (i.e., c♯–E–f♯–A–b–D), would require the keys of b and D in that order, whereas Bach's pattern is the very similar one of c♯–E–f♯–A–[f♯]–b–D. The slight irregularity in the ordering of the keys of the *ambitus* in this instance (the double appearance of f♯), shows that after the first four keys (c♯, E, f♯, and A) had been sounded, Bach had to return to f♯ for the chorus, "Weg, weg mit dem, Kreuzige ihn" because of the pattern of semitone transposition in the parallel choruses (the earlier "Kreuzige ihn" is in g). Pilate's "Sehet, das ist euer König" recalls his earlier

EXAMPLE 6.3 ***St. John Passion*** *no. 22, chorale "Durch dein Gefängnis"*

mocking presentation "Sehet, welch ein Mensch" (the *Ecce homo*) but now, significantly, in major; it leads, as the earlier one had done ("Kreuzige ihn"), to the demand for crucifixion: "Weg, weg mit dem, kreuzige ihn."

Nevertheless, although "Weg, weg mit dem, kreuzige ihn" is in f♯, a semitone lower than its counterpart, "Kreuzige ihn," Bach, for the additional words, "Weg, weg mit dem," begins the chorus in B minor, the correct key in terms of Heinichen's A/f♯ *ambitus,* making reference in the sequential bass pattern to that of the "Jesus of Nazareth" choruses (but with the harmonic direction reversed) and extending the chorus by three measures in relation to "kreuzige ihn." As the chorus ends, on the dominant of f♯, for the final "kreuzige ihn," Bach leads the tonality back to the dominant of b, as he had at the beginning of the chorus. From that point the harmony moves with great tonal logic to the B-minor cadence that ushers in "Wir haben keinen König denn den Kaiser," the last of the "Jesus of Nazareth" choruses, in direct response to Pilate's last reference to Jesus's kingship (apart from the royal inscription): "Soll ich euren König kreuzigen?" The narrative of Pilate's succumbing to the demands of the crowd then completes the *ambitus* with the D-major cadence.

This point marks the ending of the trial proper in John. In Bach's design we hear the judgment of crucifixion not merely as Pilate's response to the rejection of Jesus's kingship but also as a hidden reminder of his true identity: the chorus "Wir haben keinen König denn den Kaiser" completes the series of five choruses set to the "Jesus of Nazareth" music, a sequence that alternately falls a fifth and rises a sixth (or rises a fourth and falls a third: g–c–a–d–b). Bach's treatment of the D-major cadence that follows (the judgment of crucifixion) suggests a double meaning: as D major, it links up with the key of the central segment of "Es ist vollbracht," where the cross is depicted as John's "lifting up," and of "Mein teurer Heiland," which proclaims its meaning for the believer. In his harmonization of the cadence, Bach introduces the diminished-seventh chord on F♯ followed by a C-minor chord, both of which harmonies feature the pitch e♭ as their melody tone, a clear foreshadowing of the move to g that follows with the shift of locale to Golgatha ("Und er trug sein Kreuz und ging hinaus zur Stätte, die da heißet Schädelstätt, welche heißet auf Ebraisch: Golgatha"). (See exx. 6.4 and 6.5.) After the D cadence, Bach returns to the e♭ on "Schädelstätt" (the meaning of "Golgotha as "place of the skull") and again on "Golgatha," where it forms a component of the symbolic return to flat keys for "Eilt, ihr angefocht'nen Seelen." In other words, Bach very pointedly reinterprets the D of the cadence as the dominant of g, returning the tonal perspective to the *ambitus* of g/B♭ and eventually culminating it in the E♭ with which the symbolic trial began. In this he subordinates the ending of the trial to the shift to Golgotha and the hortatory, tropological meaning of "Eilt, ihr angefocht'nen Seelen." The return to E♭, completing Bach's symbolic trial, takes precedence over the D of Pilate's judgment, as the culminating character of "In meines Herzens Grunde" does over "Wir haben keinen König denn den Kaiser." The D of the *judgment* of crucifixion is "contained" within the E♭ of meditation on the crucifixion itself. It will be further reinterpreted in "Es ist vollbracht" and "Mein teurer Heiland."

In contrast to the prolonged "upward" motion through the B♭/g *ambitus* that takes place between "Betrachte"/"Erwäge" and the beginning of the recitative fol-

EXAMPLE 6.4 ***St. John Passion*** *no. 23g, recitative*

EXAMPLE 6.5 ***St. John Passion*** *no. 24, aria with chorus, "Eilt, ihr angefocht'nen Seelen," beginning*

lowing "Wir haben ein Gesetz," the shift to the A/f♯ *ambitus* that Jesus introduces in the recitative dialog with Pilate, and that is confirmed by "Durch dein Gefängnis," takes place quickly. Similarly, following the completion of the directionally reversed A/f♯ *ambitus*, the shift to flats, now that the trial proper is over, occupies a mere seven measures. Those measures, however, create a remarkable sense of resolution and return, because of their brevity, because the D that ends John's trial becomes immediately the dominant of the g of "Eilt, ihr angefocht'nen Seelen," and because the measures in question outline a consistent circle-of-fifths progression. That sense of resolution is amplified, in the segment that follows, by the return of the *turba* chorus "Schreibe nicht: der Juden König" to its original B♭, and above all by the culminating character of the chorale "In meines Herzens Grunde," which, as mentioned earlier, features an ascent/descent melodic shape. The urgent upward motion of "Eilt, ihr angefocht'nen Seelen" comes to rest in this chorale, whose tonal stability and message of the internalizing of Jesus's name and cross create the effect of resolving the antitheses of the trial.

Bach articulates the ascent/descent shape of his symbolic trial by means of the careful placement of the three basic types of movement within the trial: interpolated meditative movements (chorales, arias, etc.), recitatives, and *turba* choruses (within the recitatives). The meditative movements mark the boundaries between the *ambitus*, confirming or culminating the modulations. Thus "Betrachte, meine Seele" (E♭) and "Erwäge, wie sein blutgefärbter Rücken" (C minor), respond to the shift to flats that is completed in the narrative of the scourging (g). After that the initial segment of Bach's symbolic trial moves sharpward, as I have described, culminating the shift to sharp keys in the next of the meditative movements, "Durch dein Gefängnis" (E). "Durch dein Gefängnis" does not culminate anything resembling an *actus*, however, since its E major is picked up again in the chorus ("Lässest du diesen los") that follows. By virtue of its placement between the choruses that articulate the symmetrical reversal, the chorale also serves as a symbolic midpoint, taking up the "central" questions of freedom versus the law, worldly power versus power from above, Jesus as Son of God, belonging to that world (above), and the salvific meaning of his imprisonment.

After the reversal of the modulatory direction and the culmination of the sharp keys in the judgment of crucifixion, the third meditative movement, the aria-dialog with chorus, "Eilt, ihr angefocht'nen Seelen" (g), completes a shift back to flat keys that both symbolizes the change of location to Golgotha and projects its meaning as a tropologically oriented new beginning within the Passion: the way of the cross for the believer. And the chorale "In meines Herzens Grunde dein Nam' und Kreuz allein" (E♭) voices the believer's internalizing the meaning of the crucifixion and the royal inscription. These movements are the tonal and meditative "pillars" of the symbolic trial, in relation to which the *turba* choruses mark out stages in the direction of the tonal motion within each of the three *ambitus*; in addition they lend a strong sense of coherence to the trial as a whole by virtue of their musical and textual interrelatedness (including, in the case of "Sei gegrüßet, lieber Judenkönig" and "Schreibe nicht: der Juden König," tonal equivalence as well).

As we see, *within* each *ambitus* of the symbolic trial (and throughout the Passion) the tonal motion is gradual, whereas *between* the shifting sharp/flat *ambitus* it is often compressed, or elliptical, a quality that mirrors the Gospel text and is owing to the fact that in keeping with the antithetical nature of the trial, the chosen *ambitus* are not adjacent but distant from one another along the circle of keys. In this view, the trial is composed of strong antitheses, regulated by means of the interrelatedness of the *turba* choruses and the logic of the tonal design, with its pronounced sense of "Betrachte" and "Erwäge" as a beginning and "In meines Herzens Grunde" as a point of culmination. Its beginning is meditation on the image of the *Ecce homo*; its ending is the believer's desire to internalize the image of the crucifixion (with the royal inscription). Both appear as symbols of the Passion in countless paintings throughout the centuries.

A slight but interesting inconsistency in the chronological ordering of events in the *St. John Passion* is that in John's narrative the scourging is narrated *before* the crown of thorns, whereas "Betrachte" and "Erwäge" meditate on those two events in reverse order. In the Brockes Passion poem, from which the texts of both movements were derived, the two movements appear in the correct order, the scourging before the crown of thorns. Bach's deviant ordering might well have been intended so that the "rainbow" symbolism of "Erwäge" (response to the scourging) would receive the emphasis of the much greater duration of the aria in relation to the arioso. The rainbow is an image of the ascent/descent "shape" of the symbolic trial as a whole, completed in the chorale "In meines Herzens Gründe." In this view the "apex", the central, sharpest point of the symbolic trial in the chorale "Durch dein Gefängnis," describes Jesus's captivity as the "throne of grace" (*Gnadenthron*) for humanity, an expression often associated with iconographic presentation of him seated on the rainbow.[26] It is important to note, however, that the gradual sharpward tonal motion (i.e., circle-of-fifths–based motion) from the E♭/c of "Betrachte" and "Erwäge" is broken with the sudden shift to sharps in the Jesus/Pilate dialog, thereby preserving the necessary division between worlds "below" and "above." From the image of God's covenant with humanity in the time of Noah to the image of Jesus's crucifixion as sign of the renewal of that covenant, the symbolic trial also invokes the eras of God's revelation.[27]

Put in its simplest terms, the "shape" of Bach's symbolic trial is one of ascent from E♭ ("Betrachte, meine Seele") to E ("Durch dein Gefängnis"), followed by a return descent to E♭ ("In meines Herzens Grunde"). The key sequence first outlines the *ambitus* of g/B♭ from its flattest to its sharpest keys (E♭ and d) before the sudden modulation to sharps; then, after the arrival on c♯ and sustained articulation of E, it reverses, transposing the *ambitus* down a semitone (i.e., that of f♯/A), presenting its keys more quickly and in reverse order, now culminating with the judgment of crucifixion (D), a semitone lower than the key in which it began. Whereas the turning point to the sharp keys is Jesus's cadence to c♯, proclaiming that true power comes only from above, the return to flat keys coincides with Golgotha as the symbol of his *Niedrigkeit*. In this sense Golgotha becomes a symbol of the world below, in opposition to the world above as the source of the "power" mentioned by Jesus, the world in which the believer internalizes Jesus's name and cross. In this design Bach might not have had anything so systematic as the pattern of Heinichen's circle directly in mind; but the arrangement of keys, underscored by the repetition and transposition of choruses, gives the sense of an ascent/descent motion to and from the "center": the chorale "Durch dein Gefängnis." Jesus's setting up its key with reference to the world above as the controlling element in the events of the Passion suggests as much (see ex. 6.2).

Nevertheless, we cannot speak of the stage-by-stage flat/sharp motion of the initial segment of the symbolic trial as mirroring a sequence of events that is increasingly positive. Rather than mirroring the affective character of the events, the key scheme has another purpose altogether, one that was bound up with the overall "shape" and ultimate meaning of the symbolic trial. That is, although the musical

---

[26] Exactly such an image can be seen in Lucia Haselböck, *Bach Textlexikon: Ein Wörterbuch der religiösen Sprachbilder im Vokalwerk von Johann Sebastian Bach* (Kassel: Bärenreiter 2004), 91; see also the accompanying discussion on 90–91. Roland Bainton (*Here I Stand: A Life of Martin Luther* [New York: Mentor Books 1950], 21–23), reproduces and describes an image from 1493 showing Jesus as judge, seated on the rainbow with the earth below as his footstool. Bainton comments (22), "The Christ upon the rainbow with the lily and the sword was a most familiar figure in the illustrated books of the period. Luther had seen pictures such as these and testified that he was utterly terror-stricken at the sight of Christ the Judge." See my discussion on the symbolisim of the rainbow in the *St. John Passion* in ch. 8.

[27] In the arioso "Am Abend, da es kühle war" of the *St. Matthew Passion* the story of Noah is interpreted as a prefiguration of the crucifixion in just this way. Although the rainbow is not introduced, the return of the dove to the ark with an olive branch, after the flood has subsided, (another symbol of reconciliation with God) is expressed as an OT prefiguration of Jesus's crucifixion, expressed in the lines "Der Friedeschluss ist mit Gott gemacht, denn Jesus hat sein Kreuz vollbracht."

affect may mirror the adverse character of the physical events at many individual points, on the largest scale the ascent/descent tonal design of the substitute trial, and the symmetrical array of nine *ambitus* for the Passion as a whole, mirror the redemptive purpose of God's *Rath*, according to the widely cited words of Joseph to his brothers: "Ye thought to do evil unto me, but God turned it to good." God's *Rath* is symbolized by the ascent/descent tonal design of the entire symbolic trial. Since it is Jesus's c♯ cadence, affirming that power comes only from above, that establishes the sharp keys of the central segment, contradicting Pilate's claiming the power to crucify or to free Jesus, it appears plausible to conclude that Bach intended Jesus's words as an indication that the reverse symmetry of the *turba* chouses is primarily an allegory of God's predetermining the events of the trial and reversing their meaning.

Despite the reductive character of its overall tonal "shape," the symbolic trial still permits individual expressive moments within the recitatives, such as the brief cadence to F minor for Pilate's "Sehet welch ein Mensch" (i.e., the *Ecce homo*) in the first segment and the brief excursions to "deeper" flat keys, such as b♭ for the narratives of the crucifixion and royal inscription. They are, of course, symbols of Jesus's *Erniedrigung*, elaborating on the contradiction between the physical events and their meaning that is set forth so strikingly at the outset in "Betrachte, meine Seele." In this introductory movement expressions such as "ängstlichem Vergnügen" (anxious pleasure) and "bitt'rer Lust" (bitter joy) make clear that the greatest benefit ("höchstes Gut") for the believer is the outcome of Jesus's sufferings ("Jesu Schmerzen"), the primrose ("Himmelsschlüsselblume") blossoming forth from the crown of thorns, and sweet fruit ("süße Frucht") from his wormwood ("Wermut").

Jesus's Trial and Crucifixion: Francke and Bach

The antitheses just described are central to August Hermann Francke's interpretation of Jesus's trial in John. For Francke, Jesus's sufferings and physical degradations crystallize in the image that forms the culminating point of his fifth lecture: the presentation of Jesus before the crowd as a spurious king: the *Ecce homo*. Among the sequence of inner/outer shifts of John's trial, this lecture begins with the central and most violent one: Jesus is scourged, crowned with thorns, and dressed in a purple robe by the soldiers inside; then, after being pronounced innocent by Pilate, he is brought outside for the crowd to see. For Francke this brief episode places special focus on Jesus's sufferings as source of benefit for the believer, primarily of *Trost* in sufferings of the present life but also of freedom from God's judgment and, ultimately, of reconciliation with God.[28] Francke begins his fifth lecture with a

[28] Francke, *Oeffentliche Reden*, 80:

Da Christus für mich, der Gerechte für mich Ungerechten, eben das an seinem Fleisch erlitten, so weiß ich nun, daß ich vor dem gestrengen Gerichte GOttes frey ausgehen werde. Nun ich

prayer that announces the special value of meditation (*Betrachtung*) on the scourging and mocking. Such meditation has a visual quality that emerges both here and elsewhere in the lecture where Francke makes reference to the "image" (*Bild*) of Jesus in his *Erniedrigung*, which the believer must keep before his eyes as the counterimage to his own sins and sufferings.[29] In this Francke articulates the message that Bach's librettist chose for "Betrachte, meine Seele," in which the believer is urged to look at Jesus without interruption ("Drum sieh ohn Unterlaß auf ihn"), to recognize in Jesus's sufferings ones own "greatest good," the blooming of the "Himmelsschlüsselblume" from the crown of thorns. In this manner Bach's librettist introduced a striking element of the visual into the Passion, mirroring the "zeig' uns" of the opening chorus. That quality emerges again at the end of the symbolic trial, in the lines "Erschein mir in dem Bilde, zu Trost in meiner Not" from the chorale "In meines Herzens Grunde."

As outlined in chapter 5, three points in Bach's symbolic trial correspond to August Hermann Francke's divisions:

1. its beginning, which follows from the narrative of the scourging, the center of John's trial ("Betrachte"/"Erwäge")
2. the completion of its sharp-key middle section (the ending of John's trial), which narrates that Jesus was handed over for crucifixion
3. the ending, which follows Pilate's refusal to change the inscription over the cross.

The only other division within this part of Francke's trial is that between the "Ecce homo" and the initial demand for crucifixion. The unusually extended meditative focus on the image of the suffering Jesus in "Betrachte, meine Seele" and "Erwäge, wie sein blutgefärbten Rücken" is, of course, the equivalent of the "Ecce homo." Following "Erwäge" the narrative of the crown of thorns and purple robe begins in g and moves to B♭ for "Sei gegrüßet"; after the chorus it moves on to d for Pilate's finding Jesus innocent. After that, the "Ecce homo" is in f and "Kreuzige ihn" in g, following which the next recitative moves on to reach an A-minor cadence

---

denn das weiß, daß mich der Herr JEsus mit GOtt versöhnet, und zu einem lieben Kinde GOttes gemacht hat, so nehme ich alle Streiche an, nicht als ein Knecht von meinem leiblichen Herrn, sondern als ein Sohn von der Hand meines lieben himmlischen Vaters, der mich nicht strafet als einen Knecht, sondern züchtiget als ein Kind, welches er lieb hat.

[29] Ibid., 75:

HERR JESU / du getreuer Heiland / wir kommen ietzt zur Betrachtung eines solchen Stücks deines Leidens / dafür sich alle Creatur entsetzen sollte / nemlich deiner Geisselung und der damit verknüpfften höchstschmahligen Verspöttung. . . . so bitten wir eben . . . daß du . . . uns darreichen wollest / dich unter diesem deinen besondern Leiden recht anzuschauen / und das darin zu finden und zu erkennen / was uns nach unserm Zustand / darin wir uns befinden / zu unserer wahren und gründlichen Besserung das allernöthigste und heylsamste ist / welches du denn auch in unsern Hertzen bewahren / und zu einer gesegneten Frucht bringen wollest. Amen!

On Francke's references to the "image" of Jesus's sufferings, see 86–89.

as Pilate again finds Jesus innocent. The F major of "Wir haben ein Gesetz" and the move to d in the "central" recitative then complete the initial *ambitus* of the symbolic trial. Within the recitatives, therefore, the flatter keys are associated with Jesus's sufferings and the sharper ones with Pilate's proclamations of Jesus's innocence. The overall direction is that of the latter; and after Jesus effects the modulation to sharps with his remarks on power from above, the narrative of Pilate's seeking to free Jesus confirms E major. Bach's design makes no caesura with a meditative movement until this point, at which the E of "Durch dein Gefängnis" proclaims freedom for humanity instead. The transposition and reversal of the choruses after that central point are the Passion's most conspicuous convergence of musical structure and theological meaning; although it does not correspond directly to any of the theological writings of the time, the resultant symmetrical design fulfills a role analogous to Johann Jacob Rambach's discussions of the interrelatedness of scriptural ideas in those terms. Bach not only drew upon the felicitous correspondences between pairs of outcries from the crowd ("Sei gegrüßet, lieber *Judenkönig*" / "Schreibe nicht: der *Juden König*"; "*Kreuzige ihn*" / "Weg, weg mit dem, *Kreuzige ihn*") to lend structural prominence to the symbolic trial, but he also seized on the opportunity of making the opposition of law and freedom into a pivot or turning point (the repetition and transposition of the music of "Wir haben ein Gesetz" as "Lässest du diesen los" and the confirmation of the shift of *ambitus* with "Durch dein Gefängnis ist uns die Freiheit kommen"). The resultant convergence of musical and theological qualities may well be the most striking in all his music.

Within this framework the central modulation to sharps and the point where the now-transposed *ambitus* reverses its direction take on special symbolic significance (see ex. 6.2). And Bach has carefully crafted the recitative so as to bring out its meaning. Directly following the F of "Wir haben ein Gesetz," John tells us that upon hearing these words (given here in the singular—"Da Pilatus das Wort hörete"—as if to suggest that Pilate hears *a* "word," perhaps a veiled reference to Jesus as the divine "Word" or *Logos*, that goes beyond the literal cry from the mob), Pilate was still more afraid, and went inside the "Richthaus" (judgment hall) and spoke to Jesus, "Where are you from?" Bach cadences to D minor on "und sprach zu ihnen," completing the pattern of Heinichen's B♭/g *ambitus* that began with "Betrachte, meine Seele" (E♭–c–B♭–g–F–d), as described earlier. Pilate's fear, as Francke and many others explain, was twofold: first, that Jesus might be a god, as his words in the preceding dialog (that his kingdom was not of this world) suggested, and second, the more worldly fear that he (Pilate) might seem to go against the emperor.[30] Bach subtly suggests a wavering quality by leading the initial narrative of his fear toward g, then potentially toward E♭, or even f, as the Evangelist's line sinks

[30] Ibid, 69–73. Johann Jacob Rambach, Heinrich Müller, Johann Arndt, and the Chemnitz, Leyser, and Gerhard commentary all present similar interpretations.

more than an octave to a diminished-seventh chord and ending with a diminished fourth on "Richthaus." Bach seems carefully to make a point out of the inefficacy of the worldly seat of judgement. For "und sprach zu Jesus" Bach then turns it around by having it leap up a sixth to the leading tone of the d cadence. After that, the music moves to the dominant of a for Pilate's question to Jesus, "Von wannen bist du?" (Where are you from?), and the narrative of Jesus's giving no response makes a secondary cadence to a (the beginning point of ex. 6.2).

The meaning of this passage is discussed in detail in the massive harmony of the gospels that was begun in the sixteenth century by the "other Martin," Martin Chemnitz (1522–86), continued after Chemnitz's death by Polykarp Leyser (1552–1610), and finally completed in the seventeenth century by Johann Gerhard (1582–1637). In this work, which is heavily indebted to early Christian and medieval writings, and which greatly influenced the Lutheran writings that followed, Pilate's question "Von wannen bist du?" is rooted in his fear that Jesus was indeed a god as the Romans understood the concept of deity; and the words "von oben herab" in Jesus's answer affirmed his divinity. At the same time Jesus's response linked up with his earlier confession of his messianic identity and kingdom and attested to the fact that the entire proceeding was controlled in every particular by God's *Rath*:

> . . . to the expression "from whence" in Pilate's question, Christ answers with his "from above." Pilate has asked Christ "from whence he was" and Christ answers that whatever Pilate might do against him was given to Pilate from above. Now he leaves him to understand from it that He is come from above (Jn 3: 31): that he is the Son of God, sent into the world by the heavenly Father, in order to atone for the sins of humanity through his suffering and death. Just as he had said before that he was born and came into the world to bear witness to the truth (Jn 18:37). For, not only does Christ say this in general—that nothing happens in the world without divine permission, and that Pilate, who proclaims the authority to do everything, can do no more, however, than God permits (as many interpret these words of Christ)—but he also indicates God's particular ordering in the sending of his son and the work of redemption to be carried out by him, or, as the apostles say (Acts 4:28), according to the hand and counsel (*Rath*) of God, which can excellently be observed in this entire proceeding. Christ therefore means to say: I am the beloved Son of God, sent down from above ("von oben herab") into the world, therefore you may do nothing against me without divine permission, which comes down from above. Everything that is permitted, however, takes place through special ordering and miraculous counsel (*Rath*), . . . Here, therefore, is not only the general doctrine of divine foreseeing set forth for us, that everything in the world is directed by the wisest decision (*Rathschluß*) of God, so that human beings, even the pious, cannot come to the slightest harm without divine permission (Mt 10:29; Lk 12:7, etc.), but also

that particular plan (*Rath*) of God that is to be observed in Christ's suffering and death, that namely the scribes and elders, Herod and Pilate, by means of a special power given from above acted against Christ, did what they did according to the content of the Passion narrative. As Acts 2:23 says "according to which he was given over out of the deliberate plan and foreseeing of God."[31]

And when we examine Bach's "Da Pilatus das Wort hörete, fürchtet' er sich . . . " recitative closely, its indebtedness to this interpretation stands forth clearly. Pilate's next question is crucial: His "Redest du nicht mit mir? Weißest du nicht, daß ich Macht habe, dich zu kreuzigen, und Macht habe dich loszugeben?" (Do you not speak to me? Do you not know that I have power to crucify you and power to set you free) begins on G and moves into sharps, with tritones on "kreuzigen" (d–g♯) and "Macht" (e–a♯) as seen in ex. 6.2. The latter tritone resolves to B minor on "loszugeben." Significantly, Pilate's reference to his power to crucify Jesus initiates the shift, whereas his claiming the power to free Jesus does not contradict but rather affirms it. However, Pilate's words again do not cadence decisively; his b minor is immediately turned, by Jesus's introducing an E-major harmony, into what sounds like the start of a modulation to A. Jesus's "[Du] hättest keine Macht über mich" (You could have no power over me) begins with the same melodic pattern as Pilate's "Weißest du nicht, daß ich Macht," on E instead of G; and his "wenn sie dir

---

[31] See Chemnitz et al., *Echt evangelische Auslegung der Sonn- und Festtags-Evangelien des Kirchenjahrs*, "übersetzt und ausgezogen aus der Evangelien-Harmonie der lutherischen Theologen M. Chemnitz, Polyk. Leyser und Joh. Gerhard," vol. 6, 2nd ed. (St. Louis, 1878). On 243–44 we read

> . . . auf die Partikel "von wannen" in Pilati Frage antwortet Christus mit dem "von oben herab." Pilatus hatte Christum gefragt "won wannen Er sei?" Christus antwortet, es sei dem Pilato von oben herab gegeben, was er gegen Ihn vermöge; nun überläßt Er es ihm daraus zu erkennen, daß er "von oben herab" gekommen sei, Joh. 3, 31.: daß Er der Sohn Gottes sei, vom himmlischen Vater dazu in die Welt gesandt, daß Er für die Sünden der Menschen durch Sein Leiden und Sterben genug thäte; sowie Er vorher gesagt hatte, daß Er dazu geboren und in die Welt gekommen sei, daß Er von der Wahrheit zeuge', Joh. 28, 37. Denn nicht nur im Allgemeinen sagt dieses Christus, daß Nichts ohne göttlicht Zulassung in der Welt geschehe, und daß Pilatus, der sich rühme, Alles zu vermögen, doch nicht mehr thun könne, als Gott zulasse (wie Etliche diese Worte Christi auslegen); sondern Er weist insonderheit hin auf die besondere göttliche Zuordnung in der Sendung des Sohnes und in dem durch diesen zu leistenden Erlösungswerke, oder, wie die Apostel reden A. Gesch. 4, 28. "Auf die Hand und den Rath Gottes," der bei diesem ganzen Handel vorzüglich zu beachten sei. Das also will Christus sagen: Ich bin der geliebte Sohn Gottes, "von oben herab" in die Welt gesandt, daher vermagst du Nichts wider mich außer durch göttliche Zulassung, die "von oben herab" geschehen ist; jene Zulassung ist aber geschehen aus besonderer Anordnung und wunderbarem Rath, . . . Es wird uns also hier nicht nur die allgemeine Lehre von der göttlichen Vorsehung vorgelegt, daß Alles in der Welt nach dem weisesten Rathschluß Gottes regiert wird, daß den Menschen, zumal den Frommen, auch nicht das geringste Uebel ohne göttliche Zulassung begegnet, Matth. 10, 29., Luc. 12, 7. u. s. w.; sondern auch jener besondere Rath Gottes der bei Christi Leiden und Sterben zu beachten ist, daß nämlich die Schriftgelehrten und Aeltesten, Herodes und Pilatus durch eine von oben herab gegebene Gewalt gegen Christum thaten, was sie nach Inhalt der Passionsgeschichte gethan haben. Ap. Gesch. 2, 23.: "Nachdem Er aus bedachtem Rath und Vorsehung Gottes ergeben war."

nicht wäre von oben" (if it were not [given] to you from above) resembles it, taking the line upward a seventh through the dominant of A to where it can descend again for "oben herab ge[geben]" (given from above). At the end of the phrase Jesus's rising sixth on "gegeben" responds to Pilate's rising sixth on "[los]zugeben," ending a semitone lower. And the harmony, instead of resolving the dominant-seventh chord of "oben herab" to A, moves to what now sounds like the dominant of f♯, the *basso continuo*'s e♯ juxtaposed to the e at the end of the preceding measure. Thus, after the marked descent on "oben herab," Bach singles out "gegeben" for a surprising turn in the harmony to accompany the upward leap, a suggestion that the decision "given from above" runs contrary to human expectations. (Remember that in Part 1, Bach had paid close attention to this quality and its association with Jesus's carrying out what God had "given" him to do.) The awaited f♯ harmony does not appear, however; instead, Bach introduces diminished-chord harmony (first of d♯ above the bass f♯, then of the closely related b♯ diminished-seventh, above the bass a). The goal now is modulation to c♯, expressing a tritone opposition to Pilate's G-major claim to power. The pitch c♯′ that Jesus introduced on "gegeben" continues to resound throughout his phrase until at the end it articulates the key of the cadence, where Jesus's line leaps up another sixth, this time decisively confirming the new key, with "darum, der mich dir überantwortet hat, der *hat's größ're Sünde*." As mentioned earlier, this cadence closely mimics the Evangelist's turning upward to cadence on d at "und spricht zu Jesus," but now a semitone lower. The significance of the shift is underscored by the fact that there are no decisive cadences between these two points.

Jesus's phrase, "the one who has delivered me over to you, that one has greater sin," although in the singular, seems to place the primary responsibility on the Jews, which is the most common interpretation of the passage (although Caiphas and Judas have also been suggested). Francke does not comment on this at the point in question; but at the point where Jesus is delivered over to Pilate, the beginning of the trial (sermon no. 3), he argues that it was not only the Jews who were responsible but Jews and gentiles equally.[32] And ultimately each individual was responsible:

> Blame yourself, O humankind, whether of the Jews or the Gentiles, and consider that your sins have brought Christ to the cross, and say penitently: not only Caiphas and Pilate, but I myself am the murderer. For my sins have

---

[32] Francke, *Oeffentliche Reden*, 41–42:

> Diß ist es aber nicht allein, so wir hiebey zu bemercken haben; sondern hier ist auch dieses als eine Haupt-Sache anzusehen, daß der Herr Jesus, wie von den Jüden, also auch von den Heyden zum Tode verurtheilet werden sollen nach der Schrift. Darum ists Thorheit, so wir, die wir von den Heyden herkommen, den Jüden vorwerfen wolten, daß sie den Herrn Jesum getödtet, wenn wir, sage ich, in der Meynung sie dessen beschuldigten, als wenn die Heyden dißfalls einen Ruhm vor den Jüden hätten. Denn ja Heyden und Jüden ihn zum Tode verdammet, und da diese ihn ungerechter Weyse überantwortet, haben ihn jede mit gleicher Ungerechtigkeit zum Tode gebracht.

> killed God's son. The mob would not have led you to Annas or Caiphas, nor the entire company to Pilate, O you lamb of God. Mine as all other human sins lay on your back.[33]

Whether Bach held a similar view—namely, that the individual meditating on the Passion was the one whose sin was referred to—Jesus's c♯ cadence makes the crucial pivot in the tonality, after which the evangelist narrates Pilate's seeking to free Jesus in "Von nun an trachtete Pilatus, wie er ihn losließe" (from now on Pilate sought how he could set him free) with two further upward leaps of a sixth on "Pilatus" and "[wie] er ihm [losließe]," the latter then leaping further up to g♯′, the highest tone in the recitative, which then descends the third to the tonic, E, in which the recitative closes (ex. 6.2) In other words, this time Bach does *not* utilize the recitative cadence formula we have heard in d and c♯, but he creates an ending that seems to express something very special in its rising above the tonic to approach it from above rather than below. Since both Jesus and Pilate are basses, the high register of the Evangelist's tenor voice singing "losliesse" stands out all the more; and the additional melodic turn in the *basso continuo,* perhaps a suggestion of the response of the world "below" to the message from "above," likewise invites us to consider this a point of special significance.

Many years ago Friedrich Smend noted the special character of this cadence, interpreting it as a "mood of spiritual intensity" ("Stimmung seelischer Sammlung") in preparation for "Durch dein Gefängnis."[34] However, this view, although accurate, is too general. Johann Jacob Rambach viewed John's words at this point and his emphasis on Pilate's desire to free Jesus in general as a reference to Pilate's fear, awakened by his perception that "beneath all the shame in which the Lord Jesus found himself there always radiated forth some majestic rays of a hidden splendor."[35] This accords with Francke's interpretation of the reference to Pilate's fear with which the recitative began, and with his interpretation of Pilate's three pronouncements of Jesus's innocence as an unwitting three-fold "O Lamm Gottes unschuldig."[36] In this view, Pilate's desire to free Jesus articulated the truth of Jesus's innocence, in opposition to the intentions of the crowd, who had just condemned Jesus for making himself into the Son of God. And this, for Rambach, exemplified God's turning evil intentions into the opposite outcomes; Rambach cites here the

---

[33] Ibid., 46:

> Falle auf dich selbst, o Mensch, du seyst von den Jüden oder von den Heyden, und bedencke, daß deine Sünden Christum ans Creutz gebracht haben, und sprich bußfertiglich: Nicht Caiphas und Pilatus allein, sondern ich bin selbst der Mörder; Denn meine Sünden haben GOtt seinen Sohn erwürget. Die Schaar würde dich, du Lamm GOTTes, nicht zu Hannas und Caiphas, noch der gantze Haufe zu Pilatus geführet haben. Meine, wie aller andern Menschen Sünde lagen dir auf deinem Rücken.

[34] Smend, "Bachs Matthäus-Passion," in *Bach-Studien*, 31.

[35] Rambach, *Betrachtungen über das gantze Leiden Christi*, 847; a similar statement appears also on 855–56.

[36] Francke, *Oeffentliche Reden*, 96.

passage from Exodus 50:20 that Francke had cited with regard to Caiphas to indicate the opposition within the trial: "Ihr gedachtets böse mit mir zu machen: aber Gott gedachts gut zu machen."[37] Continuing through "Lässest du diesen los," the E-major tonality can be considered Bach's symbol of how the world above controls events below, of God's plan (*Rath* or *vorbedachter Rath*) for the redemption of humanity. As Rambach adds, "the entire trial of Christ was directed by God's fore-ordained decision" ("der gantze Process Christi wurde dirigiret von dem vorbedachten Rathschluss GOttes").[38]

In this interpretation, Jesus's words supply the overall meaning that there are two levels of "power," from above and below, the former determining the overall course of events no matter what happens at the level of "local" details. In Francke's discussion of this passage, Jesus's initial silence was because he knew his response, like that in the preceding dialog concerning his kingdom—that he came from above—would not be understood. His answer to Pilate's second question, embodying Pilate's claim to power, was necessary because otherwise the "honor of his heavenly Father" would suffer (Pilate's claiming the power of life and death over Jesus would deny God's *Rath* as the true controlling force); and, additionally, it was time to lead Pilate to the point of feeling his sins, as if acknowledging the truth from above.[39] Although in this instance Francke does not refer directly to God's *Rath*, it is clearly implied in his commentary. Other writers were more specific. Thus Johann Heermann, in his *Crux Christi*, paraphrases Jesus's response to Pilate's claim to power:

> "O my lord judge," speaks Christ with great patience and restraint, "you would have no power over me, must certainly leave me un-executed, if God did not give me into your hands according to a determinate plan, and if I myself did not willingly undertake death by crucifixion."[40]

And Rambach, as we might expect, is still more emphatic in explaining the meaning behind Jesus's response:

> Thus with these words the Lord Jesus wanted to lead Pilate according to God's will (*Rath*), and direct him according to a higher hand, through which he (Jesus) was given unto death. Namely, God had decided, before the creation of the world, that his son, having assumed human nature, would die a bloody and violent death, in atonement for the sins of the world. He did not want to execute this judgment directly on the mediator, but rather he wanted to employ, in the execution of the same, the sword of authority, to whom he

[37] Rambach, *Betrachtungen*, 869. See p. 212.

[38] Ibid., 636.

[39] Francke, *Oeffentliche Reden*, 102.

[40] Heermann, *Crux Christi*, 294: "O mein Herr Richter, spricht Christus mit grosser Geduldt und Bescheidenheit, du hettest keine Gewalt über mich, müstest mich wol ungewürget lassen, wenn mich Gott nicht aus beschlossenem Rath in deine Hand gegeben, und ich mich nicht willig dem Creutztode unterwürffe."

> gave the power to judge those to death who through serious crimes made themselves unworthy of life, and whom he in his word had condemned to death. Now since at that time Pilate bore the sword of authority in Judea, God exceptionally ordained that he would be used to execute the judgment of death, which in the eternal plan of God had already fallen for a very long time upon our state. In this, however, one must carefully distinguish the work of God and the work of Pilate from one another. God, the omnipotent judge, used Pilate's power of judgment as a divine power, in order to punish our sins in Christ.[41]

There is more than a hint of the satisfaction theory here, as in other of Rambach's writings. In accordance with Paul Althaus's critique of Gustav Aulén's work, Rambach is saying that Pilate, like the law (brought up in the preceding chorus), is used by God as one of the powers from which Jesus brings freedom. In keeping with this plan, the chorale "Durch dein Gefängnis, Gottessohn" confirms the E-major close of the recitative, formally articulating the center of the symmetrical design of the symbolic trial and the beginning of its sharp-key segment, and supplying its primary theological meaning, which involves two kinds of freedom, physical and spiritual (see ex. 6.3) Bach's choice of chorale melody for his setting of Postel's aria text was an inspired one. Postel's poem responds to the fact that the final word of the recitative, "losließe," has a meaning that goes beyond the literal freeing of Jesus. That is, like Pilate's "loszugeben," it relates to the root of the word "Erlösung" (salvation), and Postel brings this out in the antitheses of "Gefängnis"/ "Freiheit" and "Kerker"/"Freistadt" in the two *Stollen* of his poem. The threefold antitheses of the Passion (see ch. 4) are embodied in Postel's poem: (1) Jesus as divine being *(Gottes Sohn, Gnadenthron)* in contrast to his human punishments (*Gefängnis, Kerker*); (2) those punishments as unique to Jesus's work of redemption (the opposition of "dein" and "uns"); and (3) their benefit (freedom) for humankind (*Freiheit, Freistatt*). The *Abgesang* then goes a step farther, in that it envisions the outcome if Jesus did *not* accept his imprisonment: "Denn gingst du nicht die Knechtschaft ein, müßt unsre Knechtschaft ewig sein." It, therefore, alludes to

---

[41] Rambach, *Betrachtungen über das gantze Leiden Christi*, 852–53:

> So wolte denn der Herr Jesus mit diesen Worten Pilatus auf den Rath Gottes führen, und ihn auf eine höhere Hand leiten, durch welche er in den Tod gegeben worden. Gott hatte nemlich vor Grundlegung der Welt beschlossen, daß sein Sohn in angenommener Menschheit zur Versöhnung der Sünden der Welt eines blutigen und gewaltsamen Todes sterben solte. Dieses Urtheil wolte er nicht unmittelbar an dem Mittler vollstrecken: sondern er wolte zur Execution desselben das Schwerdt der Obrigkeit gebrauchen, welcher er die Macht gegeben, diejenigen am Leben zu strafen, die sich durch schwere Verbrechen des Lebens unwürdig gemacht haben, und die er in seinem Wort zum Tode verdammet hat. Da nun Pilatus damals das obrigkeitliche Schwerdt in Judäa führte: so ließ Gott ausserordentlich zu, daß dasselbe gebrauchet würde, das Todes-Urtheil zu vollstrecken, welches schon längst in dem ewigen Rathschluß Gottes über unsern Bürgen gefället war. Doch muß man hierbey das Werck Gottes und das Werck Pilati wohl von einander unterscheiden. Gott, als der allerhöchste Richter, hat die richterliche Gewalt Pilati, als eine göttliche Gewalt, gebrauchet, unsre Sünden an Christo abzustrafen.

the fact that Pilate's endeavor to free Jesus is, like Peter's drawing the sword in Part 1, in opposition to God's will. At the same time, the formulation "gingst du" points to the voluntary nature of Jesus's sufferings. Bach had, of course, to choose a melody that would fit the metric scheme of Postel's poem, which happens, however, to be a very common one (lines of 8, 7, 8, 7, 8, 7 syllables). In choosing Johann Hermann Schein's melody, "Mach's mit mir, Gott, nach deinem Gut," Bach surely knew that its text, usually associated with death and resurrection, was a very positive one, emphasizing the believer's trusting in God's will. This quality is even more prominent in another poem that was sung to the same melody, "Mein Geist frolocket und mein Sinn," each of whose eleven verses ends with "O grosse Freud und Frölichkeit ob Jesu grosser Herrlichkeit." Whether Bach had anything of the kind in mind, Schein's melody is particularly well suited to Postel's poem, in that it separates the phrases of its two *Stollen* into one that remains within the lower fifth (e′–b′) and one that articulates the upper fourth (b′–e″). The rise from the lowest to the highest tone (e′–e″) from the beginning of the melody to the word "Freiheit" in the second line, is particularly meaningful, and although "Freistadt" could not be quite so precisely aligned in the fourth line, the same meaning obtains. The *Abgesang* then describes a very pointed descent to the final e′ over the course of its two phrases, mirroring the pessimistic outcome of worldly "Knechtschaft" (to which Bach gives a momentarily tortured chromatic twist), should God's will not be fulfilled.

"Durch dein Gefängnis" projects an overall positive meaning, however. And the modulation to sharps can be considered to lead to the "highest" key of the Passion for the image of Jesus on the *Gnadenthron*, bringing freedom to humanity. After that, the immediate response of the crowd, opposing Jesus's freedom in the chorus "Lässest du diesen los," is set to a transposition of the music of "Wir haben ein Gesetz" down a semitone from F to E, thereby pointing up the pivot within the trial in relation to the theme of law versus freedom (and, perhaps, picking up on the meaning behind the reference to "Knechtschaft" in the chorale). In immediate terms, the repetition of music heard shortly before, but to a text that contradicts the meaning of the chorale, even while its key is the same, points up the fact that Pilate, while he can aid in articulating the meaning of freedom, cannot bring about Jesus's freedom because it would go against God's plan, the spiritual meaning of the trial. In literal terms, his fear is increased by the crowd's introducing political issues into "Lässest du diesen los: so bist du des Kaisers Freund nicht; denn wer sich zum Könige machet, der ist wider den Kaiser" (If you set this man free, you are no friend of Caesar. For whoever makes himself into a king is against the emperor).[42] After repeating the music of "Wir haben ein Gesetz," transposed down a semitone, as "Lässest du diesen los," Bach also transposes the beginning of the next recitative "Da Pilatus das Wort hörete führete er Jesum heraus" down a semitone in relation to its earlier counterpart. This time, though, instead of narrating Pilate's

[42] Ibid., 867–71.

fear and his reentering the *Richthaus* to question Jesus further, the recitative tells that Pilate led Jesus forth and sat on the judgment seat (*Richtstuhl*). After the dialog on power from above and the chorale reference to Jesus's *Gnadenthron*, this symbol of Pilate's power is divested of its authority; indeed, even in John some commentators have preferred the interpretation that Pilate has *Jesus* sit on the judgment seat.[43] In Francke's interpretation Pilate, despite his fear of being taken for an enemy of the emperor, which caused him to sit on the judgment seat, was urged by his conscience to seek Jesus's freedom, the root of the parallel between the *Ecce homo*, "Sehet, welch ein Mensch" and his "Sehet, das ist eure König!" Neither this nor his further reference to Jesus as king—"Soll ich euren König kreuzigen?"—could change the outcome. Francke explains the meaning of the high priest's response, "We have no king but Caesar," with the aid of a parable from Luke 19:14, in which a nobleman's citizens hated him and refused to have him rule over them.[44] This, in Francke's view, meant the resistance of the flesh to God, which would be better than subjecting itself to God's word; so the high priests, despite their hatred of the emperor, preferred that to accepting the word of Christ. Likewise, Pilate's "natural justice" could not hold up, and he passed the judgment of crucifixion.

In Bach's design, the reversal of modulatory direction after the E of "Durch dein Gefängnis" and "Lässest du diesen los" is aligned with Pilate's sitting on the judgment seat (f♯), his two references to Jesus's kingship (on A and the dominant of b, respectively, with the second "kreuzige" chorus, in f♯, between them), the chorus of the high priests (b) and judgment of crucifixion (D). The pivot, then, and the reversal of modulatory direction articulate not only the opposition of law and freedom but also a shift from spiritual to worldly interpretation of power and thus the meaning of Jesus's kingship. In that light, the final reappearance of the "Jesus of Nazareth" music for "Wir haben keinen König denn den Kaiser," can be said to embody the kind of double meaning suggested in Francke's interpretation of the word of God, bound up with Jesus's identity, as well as the refusal to accept it. Although, therefore, as Francke says, Pilate passed the judgment of blood on Jesus, "we know from the word of God that the just one suffered this for us unjust ones." Thus, to close out his sixth sermon as a whole, Francke cites the passage from Paul's Epistle to the Galatians (3:13) that was for Luther a key to the meaning of the Passion: "Denn Christus hat uns erlöset von dem Fluch des Gesetzes / da er ward ein Fluch für uns' denn es stehet geschrieben: Verflucht ist jedermann / der am Holz hänget" (Christ hath redeemed us from the curse of the law, being made a

---

[43] For a summary of the issues involved in this interpretation see Brown, *Gospel According to John XIII–XXI*, 880–81.

[44] Francke, *Oeffentliche Reden*, 105–6. In the parable, the nobleman journeys to receive a kingdom, giving ten pounds each to his ten servants to invest until his return. his citizens, however, sent a message after him, refusing to be ruled by him. And three of the servants, having earned ten pounds, five pounds and nothing, respectively, were rewarded accordingly, whereas those who refused to be ruled by him were put to death. This parable was cited in the same context by many authors.

curse for us; for it is written, Cursed *is* every one that hangeth on a tree).[45] Francke interprets the judgment of crucifixion in terms of freedom from the law, the meaning behind the juxtaposition of "Wir haben ein Gesetz" and "Durch dein Gefängnis." In light of the Christological associations of Jesus's kingship throughout the trial, "Wir haben keinen König denn den Kaiser" in b is apt to suggest a rejection of the first commandment, after which the D major of the judgment of crucifixion, a key that had appeared at only one earlier point in the Passion (Jesus's reference to truth), was perhaps intended to look ahead to the freedom associated with "Es ist vollbracht" and "Mein teurer Heiland."

The discussion of the ending of John's trial that appears in the influential commentary of Chemnitz, Leyser, and Gerhard refers to the view of some interpretations that Pilate's twice proclaiming Jesus a king in "Sehet, das ist eure König" and "Soll ich eure König kreuzigen" was intended ironically, as a mocking of the high priests' claim that Jesus was a threat to the emperor. Rejecting this interpretation, their discussion argues that the passage expressed a contradiction between the high priests' outcry of rejection, which the *Evangelienharmonie* presents as two conjoined sentences: "Weg, weg mit dem, kreuzige ihn! Wir haben keinen König denn den Kaiser" and the fact that "four days earlier" the Jews had greeted Jesus as king when he entered Jerusalem:

> The sense [of Pilate's words] was thus: you have already awaited the king promised to you for a very long time; now that he has appeared you want his death: Consider however your honor, so that one need not say of you that you have furiously persecuted the one to whom you yourselves attribute the honor of a king. . . . Thus in this way Pilate, from a secret impulse of God, recognized that Jesus was a king, before he judged him to death by crucifixion; as he also later gave the royal name and honor to Christ through the inscription over the cross, so that we know that Christ therefore died because he is our king.[46]

And when we consider how Bach sets the corresponding passages of the trial, with its reversal of the choruses and the keys of the now-transposed *ambitus* and its setting "Wir haben keinen König" to the "Jesus of Nazareth" music, it seems likely that he intended something of the same kind. From the Phrygian half close to G♯ with which "Lässest du diesen los" ends through much of the recitative that

---

[45] Ibid., 106.

[46] Chemnitz et al., *Echt evangelische Auslegung* . . . , 6:253:

> Der Sinn war hiernach: Schon längst habt ihr den euch verheißenen König erwartet; jetzt, nun er erschienen ist, wünscht ihr seinen Tod? Bedenkt doch eure Ehre, daß man nicht von euch sagen müsse, ihr hättet den wüthend verfolgt, dem ihr selbst die königliche Ehre zuertheiltet. . . . So bekennt also Pilatus auf heimlichen Antrieb Gottes, daß Jesus ein König sei, bevor er Ihn zum Kreuzestode verurtheilt; wie er auch dernach durch die Ueberschrift des Kreuzes Christo den königlichen Namen und Ehre gibt, damit wir wissen, daß Christus deshalb starb, weil Er unser König ist, . . .

follows, we perceive that the harmony has turned in the flat direction. The dominant of c♯ gives way to that of f♯, then to f♯ itself, which holds for one measure before moving to the dominant of E, and the E major harmony. The f♯ of "Gabbatha" marks the first cadence, after which "Sehet, das ist euer König" settles on A, as mentioned earlier. After this point the turn to B minor for the beginning of "Weg, weg mit dem, kreuzige ihn" seems to identify that key as an allegory of the goal of Jesus's persecution. And immediately following the ending of the chorus on the dominant of f♯, the three-and-a-half-measure recitative moves directly to the B minor of "Wir haben keinen König." Not only is the flat motion spelled out in the G♯, C♯, and F♯ dominant harmonies on which the three choruses end, but the harmonic motion in the recitatives affirms it. The tonality gravitates toward B minor throughout the entire sequence. And because the second of those recitatives is very brief (three-and-a-half measures) the two last choruses of the trial almost seem joined (as Chemnitz et al had said). In this way the B-minor introduction of "Weg, weg mit dem," which introduces the bass pattern of the "Jesus of Nazareth" music with rising instead of falling fifths, can be viewed as a device to prepare the reappearance of that music as "Wir haben keinen König." The absence of internal cadences in "Weg, weg mit dem, kreuzige ihn" permits the dominant ending to pass over into the recitative and the B minor of "Wir haben keinen König" as if they formed a continuity. The latter chorus suggests the kind of meaning that underlies the appearance of the "Jesus of Nazareth" music in "Wir dürfen niemand töten." That is, the positive and negative meanings of that music are combined at the ending of the trial. And, as the interpretation of Chemnitz, Leyser and Gerhard makes clear, the meaning looks ahead to the royal inscription.

After the D close of the narrative of Jesus's delivery over for crucifixion, the return to flats that leads to "Eilt, ihr angefocht'nen Seelen" is accomplished by a circle-of-fifths motion to g that gives an immediate sense of the shift of locale for the third division of the Passion. (See exx. 6.4 and 6.5). Since the subsequent flat-key *ambitus* contains the narrative of the crucifixion and the royal inscription, which are set apart by means of their deep flat tonality, it does not exactly follow the pattern of Heinichen's *ambitus*. The reversal that leads to the judgment of crucifixion has taken place; the final segment has another purpose, the symbolic resolution of the antitheses of the trial. After the g of "Eilt, ihr angefocht'nen Seelen," Bach begins the narrative of the crucifixion in b♭ (ex. 6.6), articulating f for the murderers who were crucified with Jesus and cadencing in E♭ for the description of Jesus between them. As in the beginning segment of the symbolic trial, the deeper flat keys align with Jesus's sufferings. The narrative of the royal inscription moves in very slow harmonies, mostly above a single sustained F in the bass, through f, D♭, and A♭ harmonies, after which Bach closes the narrative of the crucifixion and royal inscription in b♭. The narrative of the multiple languages of the inscription leads to c, after which the B♭ of "Schreibe nicht: der Juden König" (counterpart of "Sei gegrüßet, lieber Judenkönig," near the beginning of the symbolic trial) suggests the intrusion of the worldly viewpoint once more. At the same time, it

EXAMPLE 6.6 ***St. John Passion*** *no. 25a, recitative, mm. 1–14*

prepares for the B♭ of Pilate's response, "Was ich geschrieben habe, dass habe ich geschrieben," and the closure of the segment with the E♭ chorale "In meines Herzens Grunde." In all this the return to B♭ and E♭, corresponding to the tonality of the beginning segment of the symbolic trial, mirrors how the ironic truth of the royal inscription resolves the meaning of the antitheses within the trial (see ex. 6.7).

The boundaries of this segment of Bach's setting correspond exactly to those of Francke's seventh lecture. And Francke seems to view its beginning in a manner similar to Bach as marking both a new beginning and a return; here he reintroduces at the outset of his lecture the themes he had brought out in his first lecture: Jesus's divine identity, which is revealed in his greatest shame (the theme of the

EXAMPLE 6.7 ***St. John Passion*** *no. 25c, recitative and no. 26, chorale "In meines Herzens Grunde"*

middle section of "Herr, under Herrscher"); his foreknowledge and prediction of the events of the Passion; his voluntarily undergoing those events; and love as the motive for his doing so:

> *"And they took Jesus and led him away."* . . . Thus was now also this word fulfilled, in which the Lord Jesus had said (Mt 20:19), that he would be delivered over to the gentiles, not only to be mocked and scourged, but also to be crucified. Thus he had said beforehand everything as it would follow in succession, so that even amidst his greatest shame he would nevertheless be recognized as a true prophet, yes even as the promised *Messiah* or Christ, as which he had made himself known. Also it had to be revealed in this way that he was not forced, but according to the predetermined plan of God, and out of heartfelt love for us, was obedient to his Father, unto death, yes even unto death on the cross.[47]

[47] Francke, *Oeffentliche Reden,* 109–10: "**Sie nahmen aber Jesum / und führeten ihn hin.** . . . So ist nun auch diß Wort erfüllet, das der HErr JESUS gesagt hatte Matth. 20, 19. daß er würde überantwortet werden den Heyden / nicht nur zu verspotten und zu geisseln / sondern auch zu creutzigen. Soi hatte er alles vorher gesagt, wie is nach einander gehen würde, auf daß er auch unter seiner grössesten Schmach dennoch erkannt würde als ein wahrhaftiger Prophet, ja als der verheissene *Messias* oder Christus, als für welchen er sich bekannt hatte. Auch mußte auf diese Weise offenbar werden, daß er

If a similar understanding led Bach to return to G minor, the key of "Herr, unser Herrscher," for "Eilt, ihr angefocht'nen Seelen," then the decision to set the last of his symmetrically ordered choruses, "Schreibe nicht: der Juden König," in the original key of its counterpart, B♭, and to end the segment in E♭ with "In meines Herzens Grunde," also shares a community of ideas with Francke. Francke perceives a connection between this segment of the Passion and the one that begins Bach's symbolic trial, in that together they fulfill Jesus's prediction that he would be both mocked and crucified by the *Kriegs-Knechte* who, as Francke informs us (referring to the Synoptic Gospels), now take away the purple robe and restore Jesus's own clothes. In this light, Pilate's two actions involving his delivering Jesus over to the *Kriegs-Knechte*—the scourging and the crucifixion—bring the *Ecce homo* and the royal inscription into a form of symbolic relationship that is amplified by Bach's musical design. The return to the starting keys of the symbolic trial lends a dimension of unity to the question of the ironic truth behind Jesus's kingship at its beginning and ending.[48]

Francke's discussion of the royal inscription brings out the fact that the title "King of the Jews," spoke the truth, owing to the "hand of God," even though Pilate did not intend or will it:

> We observe much more in all this the hand of God, which knows how to rule the hearts even of the godless so that they, without their *intention* and against their will and thought must serve its purpose, that the divine truth is confirmed and made known. For the Lord Jesus was truly the king of the Jews or the King of Israel, whom the prophets had predicted beforehand.[49]

Among the Lutheran theologians of the seventeenth and eighteenth centuries the royal inscription was viewed, implicitly or explicitly, as a response to the question of kingship that culminated in "Wir haben keinen König denn den Kaiser," the outcry that prompted the judgment of crucifixion (and in Bach's design the last of the choruses that sound the music associated with "Jesus of Nazareth"). We have seen this already in the Chemnitz, Leyser, Gerhard commentary. Johannes Heermann, after alluding to this view, brings out the character of the inscription as God's turning around the meaning of physical events and the evil intentions behind them:

---

nicht gezwungen, sondern aus vorbedachtem Rath Gottes, und aus herzlicher Liebe zu uns, seinem Vater bis zum Tode, ja bis zum Tode am Creuz gehorsam worden."

[48] Rambach, too (*Betrachtungen über das ganze Leiden Christi*, 986), made a particular connection between the events that occur at the beginning and ending of Bach's "symbolic trial," the scourging, and the royal inscription, both of which were ordered by Pilate.

[49] Francke, *Oeffentliche Reden*, 118:

> Wir sehen vielmehr in dem allen auf die Hand GOttes, welche die Hertzen auch der Gottlosen so zu regieren weiß, daß sie ohne ihre *intention* und wider ihren Willen und Danck mit dazu dienen müssen, daß die Göttliche Wahrheit bezeuget und kund gemacht werde. Denn der HErr JEsus war wahrhaftig der König der Juden, oder der König von Israel, den die Propheten vorher verkündigt hatten.

Although, to be sure, Pilate did this thing in order to belittle the Lord Jesus, nevertheless in doing so he had to aid, against his consciousness and his will, in spreading the glory, majesty and honor of Christ, as if with a glorious epitaph and memorial inscription. For, although the high priests insisted that he should not write that he was the king of the Jews, but that he had said "I am the king of the Jews," nevertheless the title had to remain unaltered and what was written remain written. . . . In this take comfort, O my soul, in all adverse circumstances. See, your savior is nailed everywhere to such an extent that he can move neither hand nor foot, and yet through his almighty power he controls and directs Pilate's hand and pen so that he, unknowingly, must make the truth known publicly, and dare write nothing other, as though he (Jesus) were doing it himself. From which you may sufficiently conclude that Christ is the Lord who can make all evil into good and transform Bileam's curse into pure blessing . . . soon God transforms anger into pure heartfelt love. What did Joseph say to his brothers? You thought to do evil unto me, but God turned it into good.[50]

The concluding line was cited by Francke twice in his Passion lectures and by many other theologians of the time (often along with the reference to Bileam's curse [see Num 24:10 and 2 Pet 2:16]) in the same or similar contexts. Such passages are the conceptual background for the two judgments of Bach's symbolic trial, that of crucifixion, in response to the chorus "We have no king but Caesar" (sung to the "Jesus of Nazareth" music), and that of the royal inscription, "Jesus of Nazareth, King of the Jews." Francke concludes his discussion of the inscription with an explanation for why it was written in Hebrew, Greek, and Latin; his words are a distinct reminder of the language and the central theme of "Herr, unser Herrscher":

The gentiles should also read it, but not only for the reason that Pilate had in putting it there, but because he was as much the king, Lord and savior of the

[50] Heermann, *Crux Christi*, 336–37:

Ob nun zwar Pilatus solches / den Herrn JEsum zu verkleinern / gethan hat / so muß er doch dadurch / als mit einem herrlichen *Epitaphio* und Grabschrifft / wider seinen Bewust und Willen die Glory / Majestät und Ehre Christi helffen außbreiten. Dannenhero / ob schon die Hohenpriester anhalten / er solle nicht schreiben / daß er der Jüden König sey / sondern daß er gesagt habe / Ich bin der Jüden König: So muss doch solcher Titul ungeendert / und was geschrieben ist/ geschrieben bleiben.

Dessen tröste dich / O meine Seele / in aller Widerwertigkeit. Siehe / dein Heyland ist allhier dermassen angenagelt / daß Er weder Hand noch Fuß regen kan / und dennoch regieret und führet Er durch seine allmächtige Krafft Pilato seine Hand und Feder / daß er unwissende die Warheit öffentlich bekennen muß / und nicht anders schreiben darff / als wie es an ihm selber ist. Hierauß spürest du ja genugsam / Christus sey der HErr / der alles böse gut machen / und Bileams Fluch in lauter Segen verwaldeln kann. . . . . Aber bald verwaldelt Gott den Zorn in eitel herzliche Liebe. Wie sprach Joseph zu seinen Brüdern? Ihr dachtets Böse mit mir zu machen / aber Gott hats gut gemacht.

gentiles as of the Jews, and to them would soon be announced as such through the gospel. Even the one who now hung there on the cross between heaven and earth in the very deepest shame and contempt, as a criminal before God and humanity, and as a curse, would soon sit at the right hand of the majesty of God and be recognized and prayed to as the esteemed Son of God, for the king of kings and ruler of rulers and for the only Lord of Lords.[51]

Rambach's comments on the royal inscription, more detailed and analytical in character than Francke's, make many of the same points. Rambach, too, understands the inscription as solely the work of God, who controlled Pilate's actions in every particular. For him it is one of the principal instances of how God's predetermined plan (*vorbedachter Rath*) for the salvation of humanity is carried out in the world:

> All circumstances of the inscription over the cross of Christ were ordained according to the predetermined plan and will of God. . . . This directed Pilate so that he had to create the title. This also held him back so that he dared not alter anything in it. . . . The hand of God directed Pilate so that he formed the title to correspond with the intentions of the divine wisdom. Namely, this title had to be partly a witness to the innocence of Jesus Christ; . . . partly a testimony to the greatness and majesty of the person who was crucified. . . . Other kings must lay down their dominion in death and leave it to another; this king, however retained in death the most glorious triumph over his enemies, and stepped after this directly into his rule.[52]

---

[51] Francke, *Oeffentliche Reden*, 119:

> Die Heyden soltens auch lesen, aber nicht aus der Ursache allein, die Pilatus hiebey hatte, sondern, weil er der Heyden sowol, als der Jüden König, HErr und Heyland seyn, und ihnen nun bald als ein solcher durchs Evangelium angekündiget werden solte. Eben derjenige, der jetzt da am Creuze in der allertieffsten Schmach und Verachtung, als ein gestrafter von GOTT und Menschen, und als ein Fluch zwischen himmel und Erden hing, solte nun bald zur Rechten der Majestät Gottes sitzen, und als der hochgelobte Sohn GOttes für den König aller Könige, und HErrn aller Herren, und für den einigen HERRN der Herrlichkeit von der Welt erkannt und angebetet werden.

[52] Rambach, *Betrachtungen über das ganze Leiden Christi*, 991–92:

> Alle Umstände der Uberschrift des Creutzes Christi sind nach vorbedachtem Rath und Willen Gottes also eingerichtet worden. . . . Diese hat Pilatum regieret, daß er den Titul also abfassen müssen. Diese hat ihn auch zurück gehalten, daß er nichts darinnen ändern dürfen. . . . Die Hand Gottes hat Pilatum regieret, daß er den Titul also abgefasset, wie es den Absichten der göttlichen Weisheit gemäs gewesen. Es sollte nemlich dieser Titul seyn theils ein Zeugnis der Unschuld Jesu Christi; . . . theils ein Zeugnis von der Hoheit und Herrlichkeit der gekreutzigten Person. . . . Andere Könige müssen im Tode ihre Herrschaft niederlegen, und einem andern überlassen; dieser König aber erhielt im Tode den herrlichsten Triumph über seine Feinde, und trat nach demselben seine Regierung erst recht an.

Heinrich Müller says the same thing in the commentary that influenced the *St. Matthew Passion* text. Müller, *Evangelischer Herzens-Spiegel und Paßions-Predigten*, . . .(Stade, 1736), 1476.

Also, for Rambach the cross and name of Jesus are inseparable, as they are in "In meines Herzens Grunde, dein Nam' und Kreuz allein," the chorale Bach chose to meditate on the crucifixion and inscription:

> It certainly did not happen for nothing that the name Jesus was placed here on the cross. For what had the hidden Will of God intended to make known here other than this: that the one who wants to experience this Jesus as his saviour and redeemer, must resolve himself to the cross. Jesus and the cross are bound up inseparably with one another. The cross is now sweetened and ennobled since Jesus, the redeemer, hung on it and after his glorious name was placed on it.[53]

Finally, Rambach links the royal inscription to the glorification of Jesus's name at the point of his greatest suffering, making a direct connection to one of the most famous of all God's "I am" sayings in the OT, to which it has always been understood that Jesus's "I am" sayings in John refer:

> When things concerning the situation of Christ appear to stand at their most extreme, God reveals his majesty. The enemies had thought that when Jesus of Nazareth finally hung on the cross he would never recover again. And see, now that he hangs on the cross God begins through the word of Pilate—"What I have written, I have written"—to glorify his name, since he in Exodus 3, verse 14, for the comfort of his downtrodden people named himself: "I am, that I am."[54]

Rambach's remarks attest to the kind of interpretation that runs throughout the *St. John Passion* text and that determined, directly or indirectly, Bach's treatment

---

[53] Rambach, *Betrachtungen über das ganze Leiden Christi*, 997–98:

> Es ist gewiss nicht vergeblich geschehen, daß der Name Jesus hier ans Creuz geheftet worden. Denn was hat hierdurch nach dem geheimen Rath Gottes anders angezeiget werden wollen, als dieses, daß derjenige, der diesen Jesum als seinen Heyland und Seligmacher erfahren wolle, sich zum Creuz resolviren müsse. Jesus und das Creuz sind unzertrennlich mit einander verbunden. . . . Das Creuz ist nun versüsset und ehrlich gemachet, nachdem Jesus, der Seligmacher, daran gehangen, und nachdem sein herrlicher Name daran geheftet gewesen.

For a visual representation of the name and cross within the human heart, see ch. 8, illustration 8.1.

[54] Ibid., 1000:

> Wenn es um die Sache Christi am gefährlichsten zu stehen scheinet, so offenbaret Gott seine Herrlichkeit. Die Feinde hatten gedacht, wenn der Jesus von Nazareth nur erst am Creuz hänge, so solle er nicht wieder aufkommen. Und sehet, da er nun am Creuz hinge, so fing Gott an, durch des Pilati Wort, was ich geschrieben habe, das hab ich geschrieben, seinen Namen zu verherrlichen, da er sich 2. B. Mos. 3, 14. zum Trost seines unterdrückten Volckes nennet: Ich bin, der ich bin.

The passage from Exodus to which Rambach refers is as follows : "And God said unto Moses, I AM THAT I AM: and he said, Thus shalt thou say unto the children of Israel, I AM hath sent me unto you" (Ex 3:14, KJV), On John's "I am" sayings and their OT background, including Ex 3:14, "the all-important text for the meaning of 'Yah-weh,'" see Brown, *Gospel According to John*, I–XII, 533–38.

of the "Jesus of Nazareth" choruses and the closely related settings of Jesus's "Ich bin's" in Part 1, the text of "Herr, unser Herrscher," and many other details, including the design of the symbolic trial and the symmetrical plan of key areas. The unified character of John's Passion account and its particular literary qualities are well recognized in many commentaries of the Lutheran tradition, even when such commentaries are avowedly of the "harmonizing" kind. Thus the celebrated treatise of Chemnitz, Leyser, and Gerhard concludes its one hundred and ninety-ninth chapter with discussion of how the royal inscription embodied four signs of God's rule (*Walten*): as evidence ("Zeugnis") of (1) Jesus's innocence; (2) divine foreseeing ("der göttlichen Vorsehung"); (3) the fulfillment of a prefiguration from Exodus; and (4) the majesty and honor of Christ.[55] Taking its point of departure from the view presented in an earlier chapter of the commentary, that for Pilate the inscription was an extension of his "Soll ich euren König kreuzigen?" the question that had prompted the response "Wir haben keinen König denn den Kaiser" and the judgment of crucifixion, the discussion then turned to what *God* intended. And in the second and fourth of the aforementioned "signs," the commentary made clear that proclaiming and spreading Jesus's *Ruhm* and *Herrlichkeit* in all lands, the qualities announced from the outset in "Herr, unser Herrscher," were foremost in God's plan for human salvation. Under the second heading we read:

> on account of God's marvelous counsel it occurred that through this event Christ's honor was all the more widely spread, since God, who "has the heart of the king in his hand" (Prov 21:1), so controlled the hand and the heart of Pilate, that this title, which served the fame of Christ, was written and thereby proclaimed in those three languages that at the time were the foremost and most widespread on the globe, so that the majesty of Christ would be spread among all peoples, languages and tongues. As Bileam's curse was transformed through divine foreseeing into the blessing of Israel (Num 24:10), so was this inscription, which should have increased Christ's shame, transformed into his praise.[56]

And under the fourth heading,

> 4. *A testimony to the majesty and honor of Christ.* For just as John reports that the high priest Caiphas unconsciously prophesied concerning the fruit and

---

[55] Chemnitz et al., *Echt evangelische Auslegung*, 313–18.

[56] Ibid., 313:

> . . . durch Gottes wunderbaren Rath geschieht es, daß durch diese Gelegenheit Christi Ehre um so weiter ausgebreitet wurde, sintemal Gott, der "das Herz des Königs in Seiner Hand hat," Spr. Sal. 21, 1., das Herz und die Hand Pilati so regiert, daß jener Titel, der dem Ruhm Christi diente, in jenen drei Sprachen, die damals die vorzüglichsten und verbreitetsten auf dem Erdkreis waren, geschrieben und somit angezeigt wurde, daß die Herrlichkeit Christi werde ausgebreitet werden unter allen Völkern, Sprachen und Zungen. Wie Bileams Fluch durch die göttliche Vorsehung zum Segen Israels verwandelt wurde, 4 Mos. 24, 10.: so wurde diese Ueberschrift, die Christi Schmach vergrößern sollte, zu Seinem Lob verwandelt.

efficacy of the death of Christ, in that he said "It is better that one man die for the people than that the entire people go under" (Jn 11: 50–51), so we can also say of Pilate that with this inscription he unconsciously pronounced the majesty and worth, the office and the good deeds of Christ. The Gospel of Christ must be spread among all the peoples, under Hebrews, Greeks, and Romans: this mystery compelled Pilate in this inscription, which was written with Hebrew, Greek and Latin letters. . . . And is this not a divine majesty of Christ? He hangs on the cross naked, despised, as if he were abandoned by God and humankind: meanwhile he nevertheless directs the hand of Pilate in such a manner that he furthers the spread of his honor. This, to be sure, is that "rule thou in the midst of his enemies" (Ps 110:2, KJV).[57]

[57] Ibid., 314:

Ein Zeugniß der Majestät und Ehre Christi. Denn gleichwie Johannes vermeldet, daß der Hohepriester Kaiphas unbewußt von der Frucht und Wirkung des Todes Christi weissagte, indem er sprach: "Es ist besser, es sterbe Ein Mensch für das Volk, denn daß das ganze Volk verderbe," Joh. 11, 50. 51.: so können wir auch von Pilato sagen, daß er mit dieser Ueberschrift die Majestät und Würde, das Amt und die Wohlthaten Christi unbewußt ausgesprochen habe. Das Evangelium von Christo sollte unter alle Völker ausgebreitet werden, unter Hebräer, Griechen und Römer: dieses Geheimniß drückte Pilatus in dieser Inschrift, die mit ebräischen, griechischen und lateinischen Buchstaben geschrieben war, aus, . . . Und ist dieses nicht eine göttliche Majestät Christi? Er hängt am Kreuz, nackt, verachtet, als wäre Er von Gott und den Menschen verlassen: unterdeß lenkt Er dennoch die Hand Pilate so, daß er die Ausbreitung Seiner Ehre befördert. Dieses nämlich ist das "Herrschen unter Seinen Feinden," Ps. 110, 2. . . .

{7}

Jesus's Death and Burial

Jesus's robe and its meaning

The theme of Jesus's glorification in the midst of his lowliness, announced in "Herr, unser Herrscher," and its meaning for the faithful, are, for both Francke and Bach, what the Passion in John is directed toward at all points; this first chorus embodies all that underlies John's describing the cross as Jesus's "lifting up," the beginning of his return to the Father in glory. The point where it emerges directly is in the meditative response to Jesus's final words, "Es ist vollbracht," and the dialog aria "Mein teurer Heiland"/"Jesu, der du warest tot," which meditates on his death. The D-major tonality of Jesus's victory in the former aria and of its meaning for the faithful in the latter is a direct expression of the salvific message of the Passion, associated with victory in "Es ist vollbracht" and with the pastorale-like security and comfort of the assurance of salvation in "Mein teurer Heiland."

It may be significant that the ending of John's trial—the judgment of crucifixion—is also set by Bach in D major, although that D is immediately turned into the dominant of g, key of the hortatory dialog "Eilt, ihr angefocht'nen Seelen." The latter movement, introducing what Raymond Brown designates as Division Three of the Passion, begins the process he calls "the way of the cross." In Bach's design that process is a tropological one—directed toward the meaning of the Passion for the faithful. In Part 1 the overall tonal motion from G minor to A major is associated with bringing out a shift of emphasis from Jesus, his sufferings, and divinity to their salvific meaning with Peter's denial and repentance as the focal point for the redeemed sinner at the close. And so it is with Brown's Division Three where we view the motion from the segment that closes Bach's "symbolic trial" to "Es ist vollbracht" and "Mein teurer Heiland" in similar terms, but now with the message of redemption broadened so as to encompass all of humanity. The upward motion described graphically in "Eilt, ihr angefocht'nen Seelen" as the hastening of the tormented faithful to the "Kreuzes Hügel," where their pilgrimage will bloom forth, is a flat-sharp one.

Within that extended flat-sharp motion, Bach places the "crossover" point between the flat and sharp *ambitus* with the narrative of the soldiers casting lots for Jesus's robe. This "scene" comprises basically a C-major chorus surrounded by harmonies, mostly D minor, that bridge to the flat and sharp regions that precede and follow. In this instance the modulations are not sudden, and were it not for the length and arresting character of the C-major chorus, we might not see this as a separate key area. Treating the chorus in such a manner enabled Bach to provide the abstract plan of key areas—the flat, natural, and sharp *ambitus*—in which this movement, virtually alone, articulates the final "natural" region, corresponding in the overall symmetrical design to the much longer A-minor segment that began Part 2 (see ch. 4, fig. 4.1). The fact that this C *ambitus* is thus confined almost to a single movement is exactly the kind of detail that has caused difficulty for some in accepting the idea of a symmetrical array of key areas in general. Why would Bach, or any composer, create a design rooted in symbolically conceived key-signature areas rather than precise keys, and one, moreover, that demands our assigning correspondence within the overall design to a single chorus on the one hand and an entire scene on the other?

These are legitimate questions—up to a point. And the immediate answer—that the plan of key signatures is an abstract one, mirrors what Manfred Bukofzer viewed as part of the opposition of the audible and the inaudible in Baroque music. While true in part, this answer is insufficient unless we can show that the "inaudible" aspect is somehow an integral part of the work's meaning and not merely a construct of the modern interpreter.[1]

One of Francke's main concerns in interpreting John's Passion account is to affirm the unity of scripture by means of a high degree of emphasis on Jesus's foreknowledge, on the fulfillment of Jesus's predictions and those of scripture, on Jesus's willing undergoing the Passion as the will of God, predetermined in heaven. In this view the protagonists of the narrative sometimes act against their will, such as in the instance of the royal inscription. Jesus's rebuke to Peter for drawing his sword was, in Francke's view, because resistance to Jesus's arrest would have hindered God's will. Physical actions are subordinate to divine purpose. In all such instances, Francke articulates one of the themes sometimes associated with John's Gospel: that of a deterministic worldview.[2] And Luther, too, interpreted John in this manner, devoting two chapters (and many other passages) of *On the Bondage*

---

[1] By "inaudible" I mean that unlike the segment in sharp keys that follows it and which is linked through chorale verses as well as its tonal scope with the segment that concludes Part 1, the scene that deals with the dividing of Jesus's robe has no musical connections other than its general "natural" key area with the first scene of Part 2. Only the abstract plan of key areas lends it meaning in the design of the whole. See Manfred Bukofzer, *Music in the Baroque Era* (New York: W. W. Norton, 1947), 390–93.

[2] See ch. 8 for more on this theme.

of the Will to John's denial of free will and assertion that power comes only from above.[3] This is, of course, the substance of the recitative that effects the modulation to the sharpest keys of the *St. John Passion*, the center of the symbolic trial, in which Jesus brings freedom of the kind described in Luther's *On the Freedom of a Christian*, namely, freedom from bondage to sin and the law. Pilate, however, has no such freedom; although he proclaims Jesus's innocence three times, which Francke interprets in terms of an unwitting threefold "O Lamm Gottes unschuldig," his denial of "truth," seeking to free Jesus by the devices of "worldly cleverness," attests to his remaining in bondage to sin, ultimately revealing his lack of the power he claims to have. Pilate's placing the royal inscription on the cross was not his own decision but the outcome of the "hand of God," as Francke says.

And the episode of the soldiers' casting lots over Jesus's robe is interpreted by Francke in exactly the same way. As Francke argues, the robe itself is of no significance (although the fact that Jesus's clothes were taken away meant that he was crucified naked, thereby taking human shame, which originated with Adam's nakedness in the garden of Eden, to the cross with him). But the fact that the episode fulfilled the prediction of scripture, made in Psalm 22:18, was of paramount importance. Directly following the chorus ("Lasset uns den nicht zertheilen") in which the *Kriegsknechte* state their intention of casting lots for the robe, John makes this point: "Auf daß erfüllet würde die Schrift, die da saget: 'Sie haben meine Kleider unter sich geteilet und haben über meinen Rock das Los geworfen'" (So that the scripture would be fulfilled, where it was said: "They have divided my clothes among themselves and have cast lots over my cloak"). This is the first of three such citations from OT prophesies that appear after the crucifixion, the other two appearing together as commentary on the piercing of Jesus's side and the fact that his legs were not broken (Ex 12:46; Ps. 34:20). Along with John's remark that Jesus's last words, "Mich dürstet" and "Es ist vollbracht," (Ps 69:9, 21) were said as the result of his knowledge that scripture had been fulfilled, these passages link up with John's citing Jesus's foreknowledge and references to his own predictions of the protection of the disciples (in Part 1) and of his death (early in Part 2, in response to the chorus "Wir dürfen niemand töten"). We have seen that Bach went to some pains to bring out the significance of all such passages (with the placement of "O grosse Lieb," the joining of the music of two different choruses in "Wir dürfen niemand töten," the dual styles of "Es ist vollbracht"). Bach sets apart the predictions of the Passion that John cites from the OT with *adagio* tempo markings, explicitly indicating the return to normal recitative style afterward. In the case of the scene just mentioned, John's announcement that the episode of Jesus's clothes ful-

[3] Martin Luther, *On the Bondage of the Will* (*De Servo Arbitrio*), trans. and ed. Philip S. Watson in collaboration with B. Drewery, 281–88, 319–27. Published along with Erasmus, *On the Freedom of the Will* (*De Libero Arbitrio*), in *Luther and Erasmus: Free Will and Salvation*, trans. and ed. E. Gordon Rupp in collaboration with A. N. Marlow (Philadelphia: Westminster Press, 1969).

filled such a prediction is marked by a D-minor cadence that is then followed by the words that close off the narrative, "Solches taten die Kriegsknechte," before the change of key that leads to the next scene, in the new *ambitus* of D/b.

The episode of Jesus's robe involves a "framing" element, in that Bach precedes and follows the chorus of the *Kriegsknechte* by recitatives with distinct parallels in their tonalities (see exx. 7.1 and 7.3). The effect is to isolate the episode from those that precede and follow it, whose tonalities are contrasted in the tritone-related chorales in E flat ("In meines Herzens Grunde") and A ("Er nahm alles wohl in acht"). We have seen that a tritone relationship obtains between the closed movements that begin the symbolic trial as well (the A minor of "Ach großer König" and the E♭ of "Betrachte, meine Seele"). In this respect, and in the highly distinctive musical character of the soldiers' chorus, Bach lends the episode a degree of independence that enables it to function in his symmetrical plan of key areas as a separate unit. This quality accords well with Francke's view of the episode that, owing to the intervention of the Holy Spirit, even as Psalm 22 was being written, David foresaw "in the Spirit" that this particular passage would take on great significance in God's plan for the salvation of humanity. Likewise, as Francke points out, the *Kriegsknechte*, who knew nothing of the scriptures, had of necessity to discover that the robe could not be divided and that they therefore had to cast lots for it. As Francke summarizes the narrative: "Thus they did unknowingly that which the Holy Spirit had so clearly predicted beforehand" (So thäten sie nun unwissend das, was der Heilige Geist so deutlich vorher verkündiget hatte).[4] The fact that the episode was so specific regarding details of the soldiers and the robe attested to the nature of the theology of the cross. In Francke's words:

> With this we should remind ourselves of that which has often been said already, namely, that the Passion of Christ is the greatest stumbling block for reason, and that in it, on this very account, the fulfillment of the holy scriptures is at its most clear and open, so that the offensiveness of the cross is countered in this way and faith is all the more powerfully strengthened.[5]

The episode of the *Kriegsknechte* and Jesus's clothes, therefore, while of no particular significance in itself, was of great significance in terms of its function within God's plan. As Francke points out, the various events of the Passion that were predicted in Psalm 22:18–19, were now fulfilled *in exactly the same order* as they appear in the prediction, culminating in the episode of the robe.[6] Their purpose was

---

[4] Francke, *Oeffentliche Reden*, 127.

[5] Ibid., 129–30: "Wir sollen uns hiebey dessen erinnern, was schon zum öftern gesaget ist, nemlich daß das Leiden Christi der Vernunft am alleranstößigsten ist, und daß eben um deßwillen in demselben die Erfüllung der Heil. Schrift am allerkläresten und offenbaresten ist, damit nemlich dem Aergerniß des Creutzes auf diese Weise begegnet, und der Glaube desto kräftiger gestärket werde."

[6] This view of the ordering of the predictions from Psalm 22 in John (in Francke's view) does not correspond with the wider range of predictions of the crucifixion from that psalm that occur in Matthew, for example, where vv. 1 and 8 are cited, not in the order of the psalm itself; nevertheless, Francke's

EXAMPLE 7.1 ***St. John Passion*** *no. 27a, recitative*

that of revealing the fulfillment of scripture and its goal, to strengthen faith in the truth of events that seem an offense to reason.

If we read the Lutheran commentaries on this episode, we find that, although they may diverge considerably in the particular symbolic meaning assigned to Jesus's robe and the dividing of his clothes into four parts (with the view that it is an allegory of the spread of the church throughout the four parts of the world being an ancient and widely cited one), they are nevertheless remarkably consistent in their basic underlying meaning. That meaning centered on the opposition or inversion of meaning that involved, on the one hand, the "shame" and poverty of Jesus's being crucified naked—his *Niedrigkeit*—and, on the other, the benefit for humanity that came as the outcome of his resurrection. Jesus left the world naked, as he entered it, duplicating the shame of Adam's nakedness, so as to clothe humankind with the "cloak" of righteousness and the riches of eternal life. Johann Jacob Rambach devotes several pages of his commentary to scriptural passages that in-

discussion made an impact on Rambach, who repeats it, citing Francke as his source (*Betrachtungen über das gantze Leiden Christi*, 1005).

EXAMPLE 7.2 ***St. John Passion*** *no. 27b, chorus "Lasset uns den nicht zerteilen," beginning*

troduce the metaphor of clothing with this meaning.[7] Rambach, therefore, discusses the robe in terms of four aspects that bring out the kind of descent/ascent pattern that is prominent in his treatises on God's *Rath* and the *Ordnung des Heils*. The first is that Jesus atones for human sin, which Rambach presents in nine headings; throughout this discussion the verb *büssen* reminds us of the necessary human response, that of penitence. This is the downward aspect of the interpretation, whereas the second, third, and fourth aspects—what Jesus earns for humanity, what Jesus sanctifies, and what he provides as model for human behavior—are all upward tending. Johann Gerhard provides a very similar, though less system-

[7] Rambach, *Betrachtungen über das gantze Leiden Christi*, 1009–13.

EXAMPLE 7.3 ***St. John Passion*** *no. 27c, recitative, beginning*

atic interpretation, summarizing it thus: "through this poverty of Christ we have become rich" ("Durch diese Armuth Christi sind wir reich worden").[8]

The meaning drawn by most authors from this episode is the necessity that believers look beyond the robe itself, a symbol of the flesh, and recognize the spiritual blessedness towards which it points. Some authors, such as Rambach, give great weight to the disparity between God's plan for the salvation of humanity and the adverse nature of the physical events. Without exception they cite Psalm 22 as providing the true meaning of the episode, that Jesus was the Messiah who was foretold by God through the Holy Spirit, sent for the redemption of humanity. In this sense, although Jesus's mother was robbed by the soldiers of the rightful inheritance of his clothes, humankind was the inheritor of Jesus's robe, so that the final "wes er sein soll" ("whose it shall be" or "who shall have it") of the soldiers' decision to cast lots and not to divide it, took on a soteriological meaning. And the

---

[8] Johann Gerhard, *Erklährung der Historien des Leidens unnd Sterbens unsers Herrn Christi Jesu nach den vier Evangelisten* (1611), ed. Johann Anselm Steiger (Stuttgart-Bad Cannstatt: Frommann-holzboorg, 2002), 354.

fact that the preservation of the unity of the robe seemed to be through chance—the casting of lots—and the free will of the soldiers, was exactly the opposite of its true meaning. As Rambach says, David, in composing Psalm 22, could have concluded on his own that the Messiah would be crucified naked and his clothes divided among the soldiers:

> But how could David, through mere rational conclusions, have known that lots would be cast over a particular part of the clothes of the Messiah. This situation appeared entirely to depend on the free will of the soldiers. And yet the Holy Spirit had told of this event many hundreds of years before, so that when the fulfillment took place we would be protected against vexation, since it appears as though everything happened by chance. Who would have thought in the time of the Old Testament that this would be fulfilled to the letter and, to be sure, in the exact order that it is prophesied in Ps 22:17 and 18 [Here Rambach cites Francke's having made this point]? Still less, however, who would have had in mind the object of fulfilling the scripture less than these soldiers, not one of whom knew that it had been prophesied beforehand? That is a true miracle of the wisdom of God, that he directs all circumstances such that people fulfill unknowingly what he has decided, and yet are not forced into it, but retain their full freedom. Therefore also John, who participated as a witness, cried out full of wonderment: *These things the soldiers did!*[9]

We cannot know, of course, just how Bach understood the episode of Jesus's robe, or exactly what he had in mind in setting it to music in the manner that he did. But there are, nevertheless, distinct pointers to his interpretation, especially in the remarkable chorus he assigned to the collective voice of the four *Kriegsknechte*: "Lasset uns den nicht zerteilen, sondern darum losen, wes er sein soll" (Let us not

---

[9] Rambach, *Betrachtungen über das gantze Leiden Christi*, 1004–5:

Uber dieses, da David wuste, daß der Messias gecreutziget werden solle, so konte er leicht daraus schliessen, daß er seine Kleider den Henckern werde überlassen müssen; sintemal Niemand anders, als nackend, gecreutziget wurde: und weil mehrere Personen zur Creutzigung gehöreten, so konte er leicht ferner schliessen, daß eine Theilung seiner Kleider werde geschehen müssen. Allein wie konte David durch blosse Vernunft-Schlüsse errathen, daß über ein gewisses Stück der Kleider des Messiae das Loos geworfen werden würde. Dieser Umstand schien gantz von dem freyen Willen der Krieges-Knechte zu dependiren, und doch hat der heilige Geist denselben viel hundert Jahre vorher sagen lassen, damit, wenn nun die Erfüllung erfolgte, wir gegen das Aergernis verwahret würden, da es scheinet, als wenn alles so von ungefehr sich zutrüge. Wer hätte zur Zeit des alten Testamentes dencken sollen, daß dieses nach dem Buchstaben sollte erfüllet werden, und zwar in eben der Ordnung, wie es Ps. 22, 17. 18. geweissaget stehet. Wer hat aber wol weniger den Zweck gehabt, die Schrift zu erfüllen, als diese Soldaten, die nicht einmal wußten, daß dergleichen vorher geweissaget worden. Das ist ein rechtes Wunder der Weisheit GOttes, wenn er alle Umstände also lencket, daß die Menschen unwissend erfüllen, was er beschlossen hat, und doch nicht dazu gezwungen werden, sondern ihre völlige Freyheit behalten. Daher auch Johannes, der es mit angesehen hat, voller Verwunderung ausrufet: **Solches thaten die Krieges-Knechte!**

divide it, but instead cast lots for whose it shall be). Several striking details make a close examination of this chorus unusually fruitful. First of all, is that the movement is set as a "permutation fugue"—a fugue featuring constant rotation of its theme and counterthemes (or, in this instance, the components of the theme itself) in all parts.[10] Second, Bach assigns the *basso continuo* a broken-chord (arpeggiated) bass line throughout the movement, breaking it off only for the final measures (where the text in the bass is "wes, wes, wes, wes er sein soll"). Third, the movement is in C major, not in itself an unusual feature. However, neither the preceding nor the following recitative is in C, whereas the chorales that precede and follow them in turn are in E♭ and A, respectively. Here Bach seems to have intended the chorus to stand apart in some respects, perhaps to mediate between the tritone-related keys of three flats and sharps. In addition, it is the longest *turba* chorus of the Passion.

One might imagine, first of all, that Bach viewed this episode in a manner comparable to Francke, assigning it a greater symbolic role in his overall design than its intrinsic significance would warrant, by analogy that what it points to is the way that God's plan involves opposition of meaning. The soldiers' casting lots is the perfect symbol of both a chance event and their free will, but the impression created by the permutational elements of the movement is just the opposite. As Neumann brings out, the chorus is constructed from seven sets of entries for all four voices (beginning in mm. 1, 8, 15, 24, 29, 38, 43, when we begin the chorus, rather than the recitative, with m. 1). Except for the sectional cadences in mm. 24, 38, and 55, each set of entries is overlapped with the ending of the preceding one. Of the seven, the last four comprise a huge series of falling-fifth canons (canons rooted in circle-of-fifths harmonic progressions) whereas the first three (mm. 1–24), more directly suggestive of fugal procedure, involve sets of entries that alternate first on C and G, then (transposed) on A and E, and finally on C and G again. The first and second, and the fourth through seventh sets of entries all follow either the ascending voice pattern BTAS (1, 2, 6, 7) or the descending SATB one (4 and 5). Neumann therefore finds the third set puzzling, both on account of its rotated TASB ordering of the entries and its cadencing in E minor.[11] The explanation is not difficult to find, however, and it involves in part a consideration of the text, which

---

[10] Werner Neumann, *J. S. Bachs Chorfuge: Ein Beitrag zur Kompositionstechnik Bachs Bach-Studien*, 3rd ed. (1938; repr. Leipzig: Breitkopf & Härtel, 1953), 3:44–47. In contrast to Neumann, I would question the identification of this movement as a fugue, although the permutation aspect is certainly unquestionable, and the entries involve "tonal" answers at the fifth. Some of the aspects of the chorus that Neumann finds anomalous or inexplicable disappear once the necessity of making a comparison to fugal forms is removed. In this instance it is not, strictly speaking, a theme and four countersubjects that rotate, but the various elements of the theme itself. One might almost speak of a *fuga canonica*, although the movement is not, of course, strictly that. The close answering of the theme after only one measure, even at the beginning, as if in stretto, is a canonic, not a fugal device. One reason for the particular nature of the rotation in this movement is that the phrase that sets the full text has a fifth element that furthers the overlap among the successive sets of theme entries.

[11] Ibid., 44.

Neumann does not address. The E-minor ending of the third set (m. 24) has a particular role in the design of the movement, in that it permits the immediately following fourth set to begin from e/E, the sharpest non-dominant harmony of the piece, which serves as the start of the unusually extended "descending" circle-of-fifth harmonic patterns that dominate the remainder of the movement: downbeat harmonies whose roots are E, A, D, G, C, F, B♭, e°, A, d, g, within the second segment (entry sets 4 and 5), and d, G, C, F, b°, e, a, d, G, C, F, within the third set (entry sets 6 and 7). In the second and third segments these circles lead to cadences—to d and C, respectively—for "wes er sein soll." When we consider that the TASB ordering of the third set is basically that of the ascending pattern (TAS) with the bass entry displaced until the end (or with the four entries rotated), it seems clear that this modification was introduced so that the four-note musical unit that sets the final words of the text, "wes er sein soll," would appear in the bass voice for the first of the movement's three cadences (as it does for the second and third as well).[12]

The theme itself is constructed of five "units" rather than four, with the first through the fourth occupying exactly one measure each and the fourth speeding up to sixteenth notes (on "losen") after the predominating eighth-note motion of the preceding measures. Along with the speeding up, the rising fifth melodic pattern on "losen" suggests the casting of the lots. After that, the fifth unit of the theme, setting "wes er sein soll," is separated from the others by a quarter note rest; and it slows down the rhythm to quarter notes thereby drawing out the words "wes er sein soll" and lending them a certain gravitas. This fifth unit of the theme has distinctly the character of a bass cadence (that is, it is a slow articulation of the scale degrees 6–4–5–1). In pictorial terms, the overall effect is of the casting of the lots (the rapid sixteenth-note figure of the fourth unit of the theme), followed by a momentary awaiting of the outcome (the rest between the fourth and fifth units of the theme), then the result (the cadence pattern of the fifth unit).[13]

As a result of the delaying and slowing down of the fifth unit of the theme, the presentation of the theme in all four voices takes nine measures. And as the successive voices sound the final "wes er sein soll" in turn, Bach progressively modifies its tonal relationship to the theme as a whole, and in a manner that goes beyond the alternation of "real" and "tonal" answers. He transposes the "wes er sein soll" component of the theme in a circle-of-fifths pattern as the successive voices

[12] The pattern of this unit is basically the same as that of the symbolic cadence in octaves that appears in the *St. Matthew Passion* at the end of the *turba* chorus "Andern hat er geholfen," where it sets the words "Ich bin Gottes Sohn," which proclaim the reason for the crucifixion and can be considered to project a considerable degree of irony (especially in light of the symbolic importance Bach assigns them in the structure of the Passion).

[13] Interestingly, the rising pattern of sixteenth notes that sets the word "losen" in the fourth unit is the same as that used by Heinrich Schütz in the duet "Meister, wir haben die ganze Nacht gearbeitet," from the *Kleine geistliche Konzerte*, where it is introduced at the end for the disciples' (really Peter's) reference to casting out the net once again ("aber auf dein Wort will ich das Netz *auswerfen*").

complete the fifth unit of the theme: ending on g in the bass (m. 6), d in the tenor (m. 7), a in the alto (m. 8), and e′ in the soprano (m. 9). Thus the tendency toward the dominant in the theme itself is extended in the set as a whole through the diatonic fifth levels C, G, d, a (and their dominants).

Bach now overlaps the entrance of the second set of entries with the point where the transposition by fifths of the "wes er sein soll" element reaches a and e′in the alto and soprano. The transposition enables the second set to articulate the relative minor. And, although this set returns to C for the start of the third set, the rotation of the entries in the third set so as to end with the "wes er sein soll" pattern in the bass rather than the soprano brings about a full modulation to E minor, in which the "wes er sein soll" pattern articulates the first of the movement's three cadences (m. 24). The new key, e, is thereby heard as the outcome of the rising-fifth pattern of the "wes er sein soll" component of the first set. In the third set the tenor, alto, and soprano entries outline a rising fifth and progressively sharpening pattern in which "wes er sein soll" ends on a, e′ and b″ in turn (mm. 20–22). And for the cadence in m. 24 Bach modifies the final entry in the bass, extending it by one measure so as to lead to a secure E-minor cadence for the end of the first section of the movement, which comprises the first, second, and third of the seven sets of entries. The E that had been attained by the rising-fifth transpositions of "wes er sein soll" in the first set, which had served as the starting pitch and the dominant in the second, now becomes the key of the first sectional cadence. The rotation of the order of the voices in the third set of entries enables Bach to set up the sharpest harmonies of the movement from which to begin the extended circle-of-fifths rotation patterns that dominate the movement after the E minor cadence.

And Bach uses the "wes er seil soll" element to articulate the cadences of the second and third sections of the movement as well. For the second, the "wes er sein soll" unit appears again in the bass, owing simply to the fact that the pattern is now the descending SATB one. And for the final cadence of the third section, in which the pitches of the entries follow an ascending pattern once again, Bach provides an extension, using the "wes er sein soll" pattern in the bass for the third time, but now twice in succession, as the cadential pattern repeats (varied) at the end of the movement. These three cadences—to e (m. 24), d (m. 38), and C (m. 55)—delineate the tri-sectional form of the movement, the second and third of which are entirely occupied with circle-of-fifths harmonic rotation.[14]

---

[14] Quite possibly Bach embedded numerological associations within this movement. The patterns involving four voices, four sets of entries, and four components of the "theme" seem obviously related to the four *Kriegsknechte* and might also have been conceived as an allegory of the "worldly" aspect of the text associated with their actions (four being the number most widely viewed as an allegory of the world, divided into four parts). But the seven sets of entries and the seven-measure distance between the sets of entries in the first section suggest an eschatological association, via the widespread association of that number with the book of Revelation. These are the most likely numerological allegories of the movement, and they go hand in hand with the above/below aspect in John. Whether the three sections and the fifth element of the theme bear such meaning is an open question.

"Lasset uns den nicht zerteilen" is an extraordinarily excogitated movement, its various unusual features all projecting the meaning of its text. Can we really doubt that the uniquely extended circle-of-fifths patterns, beginning at the point where the pattern of voice entries descends for the first time (m. 24), is an allegory of the fact that, as John tells us, Jesus's robe was woven "from the top down?" At the same time, this pictorial element is not the primary one, which is entirely theological. That is, its pictorial qualities, centered primarily on descent/ascent elements, attest to the apparent opposition between God's purpose and that of the Roman soldiers. In this respect, it projects the same kind of meaning as Jesus's remark to Pilate on power from above ("von oben herab") in the trial. In the interpretation of Chemnitz, Leyser, and Gerhard, the poverty of Jesus's incarnation, which culminates in the crucifixion, marks a turnaround, so that the fleshly poverty of his being crucified naked is reinterpreted as his gloriously earning riches for the faithful.[15] In the recitative that precedes "Lasset uns den nicht zerteilen" Bach depicts the words "von oben an gewürket" as a C arpeggio that descends from g′ down a tenth to e. (see mm. 7–8 of ex. 7.1) And in the chorus itself he ingeniously represents John's description of the seamless robe by "weaving" the four voices together with overlapping between its successive sets of entries. This is in keeping with the most ancient interpretations of John's treatment of Jesus's robe: those that distinguish an outer cloak that was divided into four parts and an inner tunic that was completely of one piece. Again, those interpretations associate the four divided parts of the cloak with the four parts of the world and the indivisible tunic with the unity of the church.[16] They link up with the above/below aspect of John's Gospel that the unity of the church came from God and must not be "destroyed or cut up by men."[17] Since this interpretation was very much alive in Lutheran commentary on the Passion, it is conceivable that Bach thought along similar lines, creating a rotation among the four voices of a theme whose fifth part overlaps the seams between the successive sets of entries and serves as the bass of the three principal sectional cadences.

Such an interpretation remains speculative, of course. The separate elements of the subject, which rotate in quadruple counterpoint among the four voices (symbolizing in immediate terms the four *Kriegsknechte*), are built from repeated-tone, triadic, and scalar elements that Bach uses to lend the movement an unusually "harmonic" character. As Neumann emphasizes (without any reference to the text), the alternation of tonic and dominant harmonies in the permutation patterns projects an extraordinary degree of "verticality."[18] In addition, Bach's assigning the *basso continuo* broken-chord patterns throughout the movement reinforces its harmonic character, suggesting that the chords themselves bind the pitches together into a unity (see ex. 7.2). For long stretches the bass moves not only in circle-of-

[15] Chemnitz et al., *Echt evangelische Auslegung*, 321–23.

[16] Gerhard (*Erklährung der Historien*, 356–57) discusses this interpretation, which he designates an allegory, citing the commentaries on John of Cyril and Augustine.

[17] Brown, *Gospel According to John XIII–XXI*, 921.

[18] Neumann, *J. S. Bachs Chorfuge*, 44–45.

fifths patterns articulated by the downbeats of the successive measures but also in scalar ascending or descending patterns that link them (the latter mostly), simply introducing octave displacement when necessary. The combination of all these devices lends the chorus the character of the robe that was indivisibly interwoven. And the fact that it was woven from the top down perhaps underlies the fact that the circle-of-fifths patterns move only in the flat direction. The second section projects this sense of descent graphically in the falling pitch of each group of successive entries: e″–a′–d′–g, followed by a measure of C harmony, then entries on f″–b♭′–e′–a. The "diatonic" circle (with e′ rather than e♭′ after the entry on b♭′) leads to the D-minor close of the section, so that as a whole it can be viewed as an overall "descent" from the E-minor close of the first segment, from which it takes its point of departure (from the e cadence of m. 24, the tonality moves through a to the d of 38). Nevertheless, it is significant from an analytical standpoint that the highest pitches in the soprano throughout the fifteen measures of this segment rise from the initial e″ of the first set, to f″ in the second and, finally, g″ before the cadence, as if to point toward another kind of meaning, one whose ultimate trajectory is upward. And, as if to underscore this point, after the D-minor cadence of the second segment, the first entry of the third begins from d′ in the bass and the succession of voices now *rises* in pitch by fourths through the two sets. The sense of reversal, despite the continuing circle-of-fifths harmonies, causes the third section to suggest what Neumann calls a "mirror" of the second section. Although the circle-of-fifths harmonies run through both sections, the rising pattern in the pitches of the successive sets of entries causes the fourth (soprano) entry to emphasize the pitch f″, and the eighth (soprano) to emphasize g″, before the cadence to C that completes the mirror segment. And in contrast to the preceding section, where the descending entries *began* from the highest pitches, now those pitches appear at the *ends* of the successive ascending sets, as if serving as their goals (a projection of the outcome of the lot-casting in "spiritual" terms). For the last set Bach extends the segment by three measures, dropping the broken-chord accompaniment, as if to suggest that the lots have now been cast. The measures in question are basically a close variant of the endings of the two preceding sections of the piece, in which Bach introduces a non-thematic rising line in eighth notes that culminates in the final "wes er sein soll." Now he reiterates the entire text and, when he reaches the concluding words, has the soprano leap up an octave to the high a″ that has been heard only once before, at the close of the opening section. Coming at the very end of the movement, it sounds as the culmination of the rising sequence of pitches for the third segment. Bach's having the voice leap up to the word "wes" (whose), then drop again for the cadence, has the effect of throwing into high relief the word that was perhaps intended to suggest the individual believer as inheritor of the *Seeligkeit* (blessedness) symbolized by the eschatological interpretation of Jesus's robe that appears in some of the Lutheran authors.

Most of all, however, the "mirror" segment of the movement suggests the quality of inversion symbolized in the theological meaning of the chorus: flesh-spirit, poverty/riches, suffering/glory. In this view we might conclude that Bach's conception of the chorus was that it fulfills much more than a dramatic/pictorial role in the structure, although its dramatic aspect is, of course, its most directly audible quality. It is worth considering that in addition to the unidirectional character of the circle-of-fifths motion that runs through the second and third sections of the movement, Bach has provided, in the rising voice patterns of the third a suggestion of the descent/ascent dynamic that is such a ubiquitous presence in Lutheran thought. The tonal pattern of the first three sets outlines such an arrangement in the transposition of the C/G entries down a third to A/E and back to C/G, before the cadence to e. And the second segment delineates entirely a downward motion, both in the harmonic circle and the sequence of vocal registers, leading to the key of d as a kind of tonal "nadir" for the movement, whereas the reversal of the pitch, but not the tonal, pattern in the third section leads back to C in a manner that suggests a reversal that is bound up with the original descending motion. At the same time, the pattern of entries in the third section extends the aforementioned rising pattern of the soprano high pitches of the preceding section (e″–f″–g″) to the highest pitch of the movement (now f″–g″–a″). Whereas the circle-of-fifths harmonies, descending pitch patterns and concluding d cadence of the second segment may suggest an allegory of control emanating from "above," the rising pitch patterns of the third invite interpretation in terms of the ultimately salvific meaning of the descending elements, just as in Bach's "Christus Coronabit Crucigeros" canon. In this sense, the movement embodies, at least in theological terms, a combination of the dramatic and the salvific, an interaction of "above" and "below," as in God's *Ordnung* and its impact on humankind.

After the chorus in the recitative "Auf dass erfüllet" John closes off the narrative with the words "Solches taten die Kriegsknechte," before turning to the next episode: "Es stund aber bei dem Kreuze Jesu seine Mutter, und seine Mutter Schwester, Maria Cleophas Weib, und Maria Magdalena." Rather than bringing out the kind of wonderment that Rambach found in John's closing words, Bach treats them purely as the point of closure. Earlier I hinted at Bach's "enclosing" the chorus of the *Kriegsknechte* within the recitatives that precede and follow. Bach draws distinct parallels between the two recitatives, in that the primary cadence in both instances is to D minor, making direct reference to Jesus's robe; and even the patterns of harmony and voice-leading are closely related. And after the cadence in both instances, the subsequent phrases outline the D-minor triad melodically, the first time moving on to prepare the chorus and the second closing off the episode (see mm. 4–7 of exx. 7.1 and 7.3).

Jesus's death: the redemption of the world

Francke, as described earlier, discusses the episode comprising Jesus's last words from the cross in John and his death in the same lecture as that of the episode of the robe, making no connection between the two. Bach, however, uses the episode of Jesus's mother and the beloved disciple as the beginning of the Passion's final sharp-key region, which ultimately reaches its climactic point with Jesus's death. He therefore marks the division between the two episodes by cadencing in D minor at the end of John's citing the prediction from Psalm 22 and extending the D-minor triad to an arpeggio in the voice for "Solches taten die Kriegsknechte," then modulating to E minor for the shift of topic, "Es stund aber bei dem Kreuze Jesu seine Mutter." He completes the modulation by echoing the earlier D-minor cadence a tone higher, "und seine Mutter Schwester" (see ex. 7.3). In other words, he separates the actions of the soldiers from Jesus's words to his mother and the beloved disciple with a "crossover" modulation. The question of tonal distance is not the issue; the E minor could, of course, belong to the preceding C *ambitus*. Bach's point now is to make the d/e shift into the focal point of a continuing motion to sharps.[19] From this point he cadences in B minor, completing the phrase "Maria, Kleophas Weib, und Maria Magdalena," and moves on from there to A major for Jesus's words to his mother and the disciple. Jesus's "Weib, siehe, das ist dein Sohn!" is an imperfect authentic cadence to A that is completed with his "Siehe, das ist deine Mutter!" and confirmed by the A-major chorale "Er nahm Alles wohl in Acht." The procedure is very similar to that of the ending of the modulatory recitative in Part 1. The final sentence of the episode—"Und von Stund' an nahm sie die Jünger zu sich" (And from then on the disciple took her unto him)—he defers to the following recitative, where it cadences decisively in D major. The placement of "Er nahm Alles wohl in Acht" makes clear that Jesus's words, traditionally viewed as the sign of his love and divinity, take precedence over the strict boundary of the narrative. Once again Bach emphasizes overlap and continuity rather than the separateness of the various episodes.

Thematically, the text of "Er nahm Alles wohl in Acht" corresponds closely to the ending of Francke's lecture, which brings out Jesus's *Sorgfältigkeit* (caring attention to detail) and love, ending (characteristically for Francke) with love for one's "neighbor." Bach links it and the episode of Jesus's mother and the beloved disciple up, via the sharp keys that follow, with "Es ist vollbracht" and "Mein teurer Heiland," the latter containing a verse of the same chorale within it, "Jesus, der du warest tot," now in D. The latter two movements, projecting the redemptive meaning of Jesus's last words and his death, are in many respects the climax of the message of the Passion. Then, after a recitative ("Und siehe da" describing the outbreak of natural events with Jesus's death (borrowed from Matthew), the movements that follow turn to "deep" flats for the final segment of the Passion.[20]

---

[19] Exactly the same melodic pattern appears in the following recitative, also set to an E minor harmony, for the words "[Darnach, als Jesus wußte, daß schon alles vollbracht war], daß die Schrift erfüllet würde." Perhaps this is a reminder of John's announcement of the fulfillment of scripture in the preceding recitative.

[20] The recitative that follows "Mein teurer Heiland" is in E minor and is, from that standpoint, a part of the preceding *ambitus*. However, through its connection to the accompanied recitative that ensues (as narrative of and meditation on the outbreaks of nature), it can also be considered a part of the transition to the flat-key *ambitus* that is completed in the aria "Zerfließe."

Thus, whereas Francke deals with the episode of Jesus's clothes and that of his words to his mother and the beloved disciple within the same lecture, but without any intrinsic connection, Bach separates out the action of the *Kriegsknechte* from what follows. The reason is not difficult to discern. The action of the soldiers stands apart from the intervention of the Christian community as represented in the chorale meditations on the royal inscription and Jesus's words to his mother that precede and follow. Yet those two "scenes," the one in the *ambitus* of B♭/g, ending in E♭, and the other in the *ambitus* of D/b, confirmed at the beginning with an A-major chorale, are both unified in their musico-theological meaning. "In meines Herzens Grunde" culminates the scene of the crucifixion and royal inscription with the message of the internalizing of the union of Jesus's name and the cross by the believer. The visual aspect of the prayer it contains ("Erschein mir in dem Bilde . . . ") is a prominent quality in many Passion commentaries, where it evokes the believer's response to Jesus's sufferings, crystalized in images of the crucifixion (and the *Ecce homo*). At the same time, behind it lies the meaning that John emphasizes in his various references to Jesus's describing the crucifixion as his "lifting up." Johann Jacob Rambach discusses the latter in detail in three sermons devoted to the typological meaning of Moses's elevating a bronze serpent in the desert at God's command, so that anyone bitten by the fiery serpents God had sent as punishment for Israel's sins might be healed by looking at it. (The elevation of the serpent was, of course, a prefiguration of Jesus's lifting up on the cross.) And Rambach devotes his third and final sermon to the meaning of the looking (*Anschauen*), a metaphor for faith, and its outcome, the healing of the snake bite as metaphor for Jesus's bringing freedom from sin.[21] "In meines Herzens Grunde," however, does not project the sense of victory that belongs to the "lifting up." Its tropological goal is consolation for the faithful ("zu Trost in meiner Not"); the chorale does not proclaim the eschatological character of the certainty of salvation, which Bach reserves for the scene that follows the narrative of Jesus's robe, culminating in "Es ist vollbracht" and "Mein teurer Heiland." In his tonal design Bach makes the actions of the *Kriegsknechte* regarding Jesus's robe into a transitional episode, binding the scene of the crucifixion and royal inscription into a continuity that leads to Jesus's last words and his death. The latter scene is unified in the D/b *ambitus*, projecting the ultimate meaning of the cross in Johannine terms.

In John, Jesus speaks three times from the cross, all in close proximity: first, his words to his mother and the beloved disciple; second, his "I thirst," followed by the narrative of the drink of vinegar; and third, his "Es ist vollbracht." Bach binds them into a single scene not only by means of the D/b *ambitus* but also by having a verse of the same chorale sound near the beginning and ending of the scene: "Er nahm Alles wohl in acht" after Jesus's words to his mother, and "Jesu, der du warest tot, lebtest nun ohn' Ende" in dialog with "Mein teurer Heiland," after Jesus's last words,

---

[21] Johann Jacob Rambach, *Betrachtung des Geheimnisses JEsu Christi in dem Vorbilde der Ehernen Schlange und der Frey-Städte Israels* (Halle, 1726), 61–84.

the aria "Es ist vollbracht" and his death.[22] In culminating the scene with two arias that are both tonally related and in the closest proximity of any closed movements in the Passion (apart from arioso/aria pairings), Bach extended the meaning of Jesus's "Es ist vollbracht." The text of "Mein teurer Heiland" refers back to Jesus's "Es ist vollbracht," making clear that Jesus's death was conceived as another "word" from the cross, now a silent one, given to the believer internally, rather than to the historical characters of the narrative:

Mein teurer Heiland, laß dich fragen,	My dear savior, let me ask you,
da du nunmehr ans Kreuz geschlagen,	since now you are nailed to the cross,
und selbst gesagt: Es ist vollbracht,	and have said yourself: It is accomplished,
bin ich vom Sterben frei gemacht?	am I made free from death?
Kann ich durch deine Pein und sterben	Can I, through your pain and death,
das Himmelreich ererben?	inherit the kingdom of heaven?
Ist aller Welt Erlösung da?	Is there redemption for the world?
Du kannst vor Schmerzen zwar nichts sagen;	To be sure, you can, from pain, say nothing;
doch neigest du das Haupt und sprichst stillschweigend: ja.	yet you bow your head and speak silently: yes.

In the first of his words from the cross in John, Jesus's address to his mother as "Weib" rather than "Mutter" was explained by many commentators as a reference back to the so-called proto-Gospel of Genesis (3:15), where God had announced that the seed of woman ("des Weibes Saamen"), the Messiah, would crush the head of the serpent (Satan). If this interpretation played a part in Bach's setting Jesus's three "words" from the cross within a single *ambitus*, it would indicate that Bach perceived the traditional connection between the prediction of Genesis and its fulfillment in "Es ist vollbracht" (and "Mein teurer Heiland"), which was one of the recurrent interpretations of Jesus's "Es ist vollbracht."[23] The text of the middle section of the "Es ist vollbracht" aria—"der Held aus Juda siegt mit Macht, und schließt den Kampf"—refers to Jesus's descent from the tribe of Judah (as Gen 49:8–10 was

[22] We may remember that, as shown in chapter 4, figure 4.1, in the 1725 version of the Passion, Bach created a parallel between the two settings of the chorale "Jesu, deine Passion" that appear here and the two that resulted in Part 1 from the insertion of the aria with chorale "Himmel reiße, Welt erbebe." This relationship, which involved a dialog aria with chorale and a simple chorale setting in both scenes, was first discussed by Alfred Dürr in 1950 (see the source cited in ch. 1, n. 18, *Luther's Works*, vol. 24: *Sermons on the Gospel of St. John, Chapters 14–16*, ed. Jaroslav Pelikan and Daniel E. Poellot). In light of the inappropriateness of "Himmel reiße" to the earlier scene (since it meditates on Golgotha), it appears that Bach might have intended to draw a parallel of symmetry between the two scenes.

[23] See, for example, Heermann, *Heptalogus Christi*, 33; Rambach, *Betrachtungen über die Sieben Letzten Worte*, 56–57.

widely interpreted), which Luther and many others linked up with Genesis 3:15. Intricate as all this may sound, it represented a widespread pattern of thought for many centuries and is echoed in several Bach cantatas, including the Easter cantata that followed the *St. John Passion* in the 1725 liturgical sequence (see ch. 9).

August Hermann Francke begins his ninth lecture with one of his favorite Johannine themes, the fulfillment of scripture, dividing the lecture into three principal parts (*Hauptstücke*), the first and second of which—the meaning of the drink of vinegar and Jesus's death—are those of Bach's sharp-key segment; the third extends up to the narrative of the soldiers' finding Jesus to be dead, not breaking his legs but piercing his side with a spear, the flowing forth of blood and water, and the announcement of the fulfillment of scripture in those events. Although Bach sets the latter events within a different key region, he marks this point in a manner that brings out the meaning of the passage as Francke describes it. Francke first connects up John's narrative of Jesus's knowledge of the fulfillment of scripture—"Darnach, als Jesus wusste, dass schon alles vollbracht war, dass die Schrift erfüllet würde, spricht er: Mich dürstet" (Thereupon, since Jesus know that everything was already completed, that the scripture had been fulfilled, he spoke, "I thirst")—with his foreknowledge of the coming events as voiced in the opening scene of the Passion, bringing out the themes of Jesus's *Herrlichkeit/Niedrigkeit* and love that were paramount in the earlier scene.[24] He then gives a detailed account of Jesus's thirst and the drink of vinegar as predicted in Psalm 69:21, indicating that the *Kriegsknechte* carried out this action despite their knowing nothing of scripture or the purpose of its fulfillment, which was for the benefit of the faithful who would believe scripture and its predictions, "that Jesus was Christ, the Son of God and through faith have life in his name."[25] As his second *Hauptstück* he takes up Jesus's "Es ist vollbracht" and death, linking them directly to the drink of vinegar by explaining that with the scripture fulfilled, Jesus gave up his life voluntarily. As Francke argues, Jesus's thirst was an indication that physically ("der Natur nach") He was not near death; rather, he willed his own death because "everything that had been said about him in scripture regarding his dealings with humanity before his return to the Father" had been completed.[26] Francke notes that John gives particular emphasis to this theme:

---

[24] Francke, *Oeffentliche Reden*, 142:

> Wie wir nun hieraus sehen, daß Johanni gar viel daran gelegen war, daß er uns dieses einschärfete, wie der HErr JESUS alles sein Leiden vorher gewußt und erkannt habe, so sollen wir denn gar eben mercken, daß wir bey allen Umständen seines Leidens hierauf zu sehen, es dadurch desto tiefer einzuschauen, und es uns auf die Weise, als es schon unterschiedene mal erinnert worden, zu Nutz zu machen haben; sintemal uns eben hiedurch seine Herrlichkeit mitten in seinem Leiden und in seiner grössesten Erniedrigung, samt seiner unausprechlichen Liebe zu uns, durch welche er alles Leiden williglich übernommen offenbar wird.

[25] Ibid., 145.

[26] Ibid., 143.

> With the words *"It is fulfilled,"* John indicates very pointedly that which he had said in the twenty-eighth verse, how the Lord Jesus had known that everything in his Passion had been fulfilled excepting only that he had not yet been given vinegar to drink. Since now this too had taken place, the Lord Jesus wanted to confirm with these words *"It is fulfilled"* that he no longer had to wait for anything else concerning his death to be fulfilled according to scripture, and for that reason he now *bowed his head and departed*. . . . We, however, should recognize in this all the more the nobility and majesty of Christ, after having seen from the previously cited words of John 10:18 that the Lord Jesus predicted this also and at the same time showed us the reason for the event.[27]

A fuller treatment of these words can be found in the commentary of Chemnitz, Leyser, and Gerhard, where Jesus's "Es ist vollbracht" is considered from seven standpoints that, different though they are, are remarkably unified in their portrayal of the same basic meaning as that of Francke.[28] The seven aspects—fulfillment of OT prophesy; fulfillment of the OT "types" (i.e., Isaac, the bronze serpent in the desert, the Passover lamb, and the like); fulfillment of the divine plan and the Father's commands; fulfillment of the sufferings; of the persecutions; of the work of redemption;and of the "spiritual edifice of the church"—outline the story of God's plan in a quasi-chronological sequence, beginning with OT prefigurations and ending with the "spiritual temple" of the church, which is compared with Noah's ark, with Jesus described as "der himmlische Noah." Prominent in them all is the fulfillment of God's *Rath*, which emerges particularly clearly in the closely related third and sixth categories but can easily be found in the statement in the fourth, that Jesus, in descending into hell underwent no further sufferings but "showed himself far more as a victor and glorious *Triumphator* over the demonic powers" and the fifth, that the persecutors of Christ had a "certain boundary" placed by God on their activities, as a "great consolation for us." Also, the twofold character of the scriptural predictions—Jesus's sufferings and his *Herrlichkeit*—was fulfilled in Jesus's words, the quality that underlies the two styles of Bach's "Es

---

[27] Ibid., 146–47:

> Johannes zielet gar deutlich mit dem Wort: **Es ist vollbracht**, auf das, was er im 28. v. gesaget hätte, wie der HErr JEsus gewußt hätte, daß man in seinem Leiden nun alles an ihm vollbracht, was die Schrift von ihm vorher gesaget, nur daß er noch nicht mit Eßig geträncket sey. Da denn nun dieses auch geschehen, habe der HErr JEsus mit diesem Wort: **Es ist vollbracht**, bezeugen wollen, daß er nun auf nichts mehr mit seinem Tode länger zu warten habe, so noch etwa nach der Schrift an ihm erfüllet werden müßte, und um deßwillen habe er nun **das Haupt geneiget / und sey verschieden**. . . . Wir aber sollen noch vielmehr die Herrlichkeit und Mäjestät Christi hierin erkennen, nachdem wir aus dem vorherangezogenen Worten Joh. 10, 18. sehen, daß der HErr JEsus solches auch zuvor gesaget, und zugleich auch den Grund der Sache uns angezeiget habe.

[28] Chemnitz et al., *Echt evangelische Auslegung*, 7:23–26.

ist vollbracht."[29] Most of all, perhaps, it is in the third and sixth aspects that Jesus's words are interpreted as completion of the work of redemption according to God's plan, a work described by Francke as the "preaching of the Gospel followed by the redemption of the world" ("Erlösung der Welt"), as it is in Bach's "Mein teurer Heiland" ("Ist aller Welt Erlösung da?"). And, as in the *St. John Passion*, Jesus's victory is the sole source of *Trost* for humanity:

> Christ is "the A and the O," the "beginning and the end" (Rev 1:8); "the author and the finisher of our faith" (Heb 12:2). Therefore, it is inadmissable to say that, with his merits and satisfying, our merits and our satisfying must be bound up. As he says here, "It is fulfilled," so he speaks in the parallel of Luke 25, 7: "Come, for everything is prepared." Therefore it is not necessary that we bring anything at all of our own, but that we enjoy through faith the blessings that will be offered and set forth before us. Through Christ's suffering and satisfaction everything is prepared. Prepared is the victory over sin, death and hell; prepared is heaven; prepared all heavenly blessings. Whoever continually understands rightly these brief words "It is fulfilled" and grasps them with firm faith, can in all temptations take an unshakable consolation from them.[30]

These words are perfectly in the spirit of the *St. John Passion* and its *Christus victor* theology (see ch. 4), and especially, of course, in the spirit of Bach's "Es ist vollbracht" and "Mein teurer Heiland."

Bach gives the greatest possible emphasis to Jesus's death through the close pairing of "Es ist vollbracht" and "Mein teurer Heiland," which are separated by only two measures of recitative. Together, these two movements embody the goal of the Passion: Jesus's death as the means of salvation for humanity, the fulfillment of God's plan, as reflected in the following chorale verse:[31]

Es ist vollbracht am creutze dort	It is fulfilled there on the cross
gesetz und der Propheten wort,	the law and the word of the prophets,
was wir niemal vollbringen kunten,	what we could never bring to pass,

[29] Ibid., 23.

[30] Ibid., 25 :

> Christus ist "das A und das O," "der Anfang und das Ende," Offb. 1, 8,: "der Anfänger und Vollender des Glaubens," Hebr. 12, 2. Daher ist es unstatthaft, zu sagen, daß mit seinen Verdiensten und Genugthuung unsere Verdienste und unsere Genugthuungen verbunden werden müßten. Wie er hier sagt: "es ist vollbracht," so spricht er in der Parallele, Luc. 14, 7.: "Kommt, denn es ist alles bereit." Daher ist es nicht nöthig, daß wir irgend etwas von dem unsrigen herzubringen, sondern daß wir die Wohlthaten, welche uns dargebracht und vorgelegt werden, durch den Glauben genießen. Durch Christi Leiden und Genugthuung ist alles bereit; bereit ist der Sieg über Sünde, Tod und Hölle; bereit ist der Himmel; bereit alle himmlischen Güter. Wer immer dieses kurze Wort "es ist vollbracht" recht versteht und mit festem Glauben erfaßt, der kann in allen Anfechtungen einen unbeweglichen Trost aus demselben nehmen.

[31] I have cited the verse exactly as it appears in Johann Anastasius Freylinghausen, *Neues Geistreiches Gesang-Buch* (Halle, 1719), 91.

ist nun vollbracht, durch Jesu wunden;	is now fulfilled through Jesus's wounds;
was GOttes rath von ewigkeit bedacht,	what God's will conceived from eternity,
das ist durch seinen tod vollbracht.	that is through his death fulfilled.

Francke's lectures on the *St. John Passion* continually emphasize Jesus's Passion as the fulfillment of scripture and God's will (or plan) of salvation, as do the writings of Rambach and many others of the time. For them, as for John, Jesus's death is its point of completion. Among the various *Hauptstücke* that run throughout his lectures, Francke singles out this one as the most important one; here Francke does not merely say that its importance is that Jesus died for our sins, but (citing Paul), that he died for our sins *according to the scriptures*:

> What, by the way, is said here with a single word—*he departed*, or he died—is something on which we might well speak for many hours. For we know well that the death of Christ is the ground of our salvation and life, and that accordingly among the principal themes of the Passion of Christ this itself is the most prominent principal theme: that he died for our sins according to the scriptures. . . .[32]

The miniscule recitative that follows "Es ist vollbracht" simply says "und neigte das Haupt und verschied" (and bowed his head and departed). Bach now introduces a second meditation on Jesus's death, which brings out that here, in "Mein teurer Heiland," Jesus is addressed, implicitly at least, as the good shepherd, a quality projected musically in the pastorale style of the movement.[33] Rambach associates Jesus's words to his mother with his role as good shepherd caring for "his own," even at the point of his "tieffsten Erniedrigung," a quality that links up with the character of "Mein teurer Heiland."[34] In this sense, the flat-sharp modulatory sequence from the beginning of the third division, "Eilt, ihr angefocht'nen Seelen," to "Es ist vollbracht" and "Mein teurer Heiland," articulates the meaning of the events at Golgotha in terms suggestive of motion from the tropological to the eschatological sense. This sense of a single motion may underlie the fact that both "Eilt" and "Mein teurer Heiland" are dialogs for solo bass and chorus.[35] The actions of the *Kriegsknechte*, although forming a part of that motion (the outcome

---

[32] Francke, *Oeffentliche Reden*, 148: "Was übrigens hier mit einem einigen Worte gesaget wird: **er verschied,** oder er starb, ist eine Sache, davon wir wol viele Stunden reden solten. Denn wir wissen ja, daß der Tod Christi die Ursache unsers Heyls und Lebens ist, und daß demnach unter den Haupt-Stücken des Leidens Christi selbst dieses das vornehmste Haupt-Stück ist, daß er für unsere Sünde gestorben ist nach der Schrift . . . ."

[33] See Renate Steiger, "'Die Welt ist euch ein Himmelreich': Zu J. S. Bachs Deutung der Pastoralen," *Musik und Kirche* 41 (1971): 1–8, 69–79.

[34] Rambach, *Betrachtungen über die Sieben Letzten Worte*, 54, 68–69.

[35] The bass parts of the two dialogs sometimes resemble each other very closely in their melodic material; compare, for example, mm. 49–50 of "Eilt"with m. 27 of "Mein teurer Heiland."

of God's plan) are nevertheless separated from the response of the faithful to those events.

In this light, what Raymond Brown calls "the way of the cross," following the ending of the trial and beginning a new division in the narrative, extends from the hortatory dialog "Eilt, ihr angefochtnen Seelen" to "Es ist vollbracht" and "Mein teurer Heiland." What follows "Mein teurer Heiland" centers on the response of the faithful to Jesus's death. Whereas "Eilt, ihr angefochtnen Seelen" urges the faithful to hasten to the "Kreuzes Hügel," Golgotha, where their pilgrimage will be fulfilled, "Es ist vollbracht" and "Mein teurer Heiland" proclaim the fulfillment of the pilgrimage itself. Over the course of three successive *ambitus,* Bach delineates a spiritual motion from the tropological sense of "Eilt" to the eschatological of "Es ist vollbracht" and "Mein teurer Heiland," making the narrative of the dividing of Jesus's cloak into a symbolic "crossover" between the two, one whose role in the design is analogous to its place in God's plan. The sharp-key *ambitus* that culminates this motion is symbolically "enclosed" by two verses of the same chorale, the first (responding to Jesus's words to his mother and the beloved disciple) addressing Jesus's taking care of earthly matters, and the second bringing out the ultimate meaning of the Passion (responding to the believer's questions regarding the meaning of Jesus's death in "Mein teurer Heiland"). In "Mein teurer Heiland" the "stillschweigend: Ja!" the silent affirmative given by Jesus's bowing his head at the point of death thus becomes the culmination of Jesus's words from the cross.

John's realized eschatology: The four senses of scripture in "Es ist vollbracht" and "Mein teurer Heiland"

As one of the two most extended points of meditation in the *St. John Passion* (the other being the pairing of "Betrachte, meine Seele" and "Erwäge, wie sein blutgefärbter Rücken"), the close conjunction of "Es ist vollbracht" and "Mein teurer Heiland"/"Jesu, der du warest tot" has special significance in the work as a whole. "Es ist vollbracht," like "Betrachte" and "Erwäge," features a unique instrumental complement, viola da gamba solo in its outermost segments, thus suggesting an intention of setting Jesus's last words apart. Like the gamba solo aria "Komm, süsses Kreuz" in the *St. Matthew Passion*, "Es ist vollbracht" deals directly with the meaning of the cross, but now in a manner that, more perhaps than any other movement of the Passion, represents its Johannine character. And "Mein teurer Heiland" also cites Jesus's last words, turning now to their meaning for the faithful: the freedom alluded to earlier. Interestingly, it now features a lively cello part in the continuo, with which it begins. And Bach makes the change in instrumentation into a component of a truly extraordinary meditative sequence, and one that relates closely to the meditative character of the ancient principle of the four senses of scripture that are essential to understanding the character of the final sharp-key segment of the Passion and its relationship to the other two.

"Es ist vollbracht"

In John, Jesus speaks three times from the cross; and in his setting Bach arranges that they all appear within a single "scene," one that is highly unified in terms of its tonality. And all three utterances—Jesus's assigning the care of his mother to the "beloved disciple," his "I thirst," and his "Es ist vollbracht"—exhibit what theologians identify as "Johannine" characteristics:they affirm Jesus's control over the events of the Passion, his voluntary, even triumphant death (as all Lutheran commentaries from Bach's time assert). The second and third of these "words" appear close together and are preceded by John's announcement that Jesus said "I thirst" because he knew that everything was completed ("vollbracht"), that the scriptures had been fulfilled. In the close tonal relationship he assigns to these passages Bach leads the "scene" as a whole toward the two arias in question. And, like others of the time, he divides the recitative narrative after the words "Es ist vollbracht," picking up with the narrative of Jesus's death ("und neigte das Haupt und verschied") after the first of the two arias and without the pronoun that would lend it a degree of independence (i.e., "und *er* neigte. . ."). As a result, the two arias are not separated but linked along a continuum of ideas by a scant two measures of recitative.

"Es ist vollbracht" addresses two layers of meaning behind Jesus's last words. The beginning and ending sections of the aria, in minor, unfold a very slow, highly elegiac melody for viola da gamba solo, whose beginning theme, from which the solo unfolds, is a variation of the melody of Jesus's dying words, "Es ist vollbracht," at the end of the preceding biblical recitative. Whereas the recitative melody is as simple as possible—a straightforward scalar descent from the flat sixth to the minor tonic—the viola da gamba melody is a decorated "commentary," an interpretation that intermingles the positive message that Jesus's death is beneficial for the faithful ("O Trost für die gekränkten Seelen"—O comfort for the diseased souls) with an unmistakable sense of sorrow over the physical event. To deny the latter quality would be to place religious meaning beyond the human sphere altogether. The text, nevertheless, tells us that the last moments of the time of sorrow are being counted out. And upon our hearing those words, the character of the aria is instantly transformed, and its middle section now centers entirely on John's projection of the meaning of Jesus's words, and in a manner that seems to extend beyond the human response to the physical events of the narrative. In major, accompanied by full strings, and in an entirely contrasted, rapid, and triumphant *concitato* style, it brings out the foremost meaning of John's Greek expression: that Jesus's death is to be viewed as a victory over death, as the perspective of Easter in the midst of the Passion. The excitement it projects is almost uncontainable. If we ever needed evidence that Bach was a composer of great dramatic power, this is it. And the word "power" (*Macht*) is a key here. For with the concluding phrase of this middle section, "der Held aus Juda siegt mit Macht und schließt den Kampf" (The hero from Judea conquers with power and ends the battle), Bach builds from the word *Macht* toward the word *Kampf* with the aid of a sustained trill on the highest pitch in the first violin and some highly rhythmic and militaristic-sounding patterns that ascend sequentially in the bass toward the climax: the cry "und schlieβt den Kampf, und schlieβt den Kampf."[36] In the climactic vocal phrases downward stepwise motion on "und schlieβt den" followed by the sudden and progressively higher leap up of a sixth each time, on "[den] Kampf," says it all. At the peak of its upward-surging patterns, however, this music suddenly stops abruptly, on dominant harmony, and after one of music's most pregnant pauses, the voice, now unaccompanied, slowly and quietly sings the words "Es ist vollbracht," as given by Jesus in the recitative. The falling cadential melody projects the character of a consequence, a resolution or completion of the victorious music that preceded it. As if remembering how the aria began, it ushers in the return of the viola da gamba solo music, as before.

The music of the gamba solo now continues alone with the four measures of the initial ritornello. But this time, as it comes to a close in the final cadence of the aria, the voice reenters to sing "Es ist vollbracht" a last time, to the melody of the recitative, the only simultaneous convergence of the phrase as sung by Jesus and the instrumental melodic line derived from it. At the end we are back in minor, back in the suffering world, shorn of Jesus's physical presence. But the meaning of the text of the initial elegiac segment of the aria—that the words "Es ist vollbracht" are to be viewed as comforting for those who are deeply tormented, that the last hours of the "night of sorrow" are being counted out—has been dramatized by the triumphant middle section. Bach does not merely depict the victorious meaning of Jesus's words, he brings out the characteristically Johannine disparity between the spheres of "above" and "below" (markedly evident in the opposite directions of his two melodies), between Jesus's divinity and the world that, at its worst, prefers darkness to light. In this closing segment of the aria we hear only the words "Es ist vollbracht," sung in their original form, and without the explicating text of the opening section. Since the cosmic sense of victory projected in the middle section is Jesus's alone, the aria is entirely in the third person. But the taking over of Jesus's words by the believer is a key to the more personal character of the aria that follows. It is as if we have gone back to the source, which we now understand more fully. That understanding is the point of departure for the next aria.

To this point, the meditative response to Jesus's dying words fulfills Smend's requirement that Jesus's death be elevated in the immensity of its importance above

[36] In emphasizing the words "Macht" and "Kampf," the text and music of "Es ist vollbracht" look back to Jesus's dialogs with Pilate in the trial scene of the Passion, in particular, Jesus's remark that if his kingdom were of the world his servants would fight (*kämpfen*) on his behalf, and his response to Pilate's claiming the power (*Macht*) of crucifying Jesus or setting him free: [Pilate] "weissest du nicht, daβ ich Macht habe, dich zu kreuzigen, und Macht habe, dich loβzugeben?" [Jesus] "Du hättest keine Macht über mich, wenn es dir nicht wäre von oben herab gegeben." In this sense "Es ist vollbracht" is the fulfillment of Jesus's earlier proclamations, namely, that power comes from "above" and is associated with Jesus's divinity.

the concerns of the contemporary believer regarding death.[37] But that is, of course, not the full story. Now that the point of Jesus's triumphant death has been made, the miniature recitative that follows "Es ist vollbracht" does not exhibit the sorrowful falling character of his dying words. Instead, for "und neigte das Haupt" the melody descends at first ("und neigte das"), then leaps up a sixth for the word "Haupt," after which "und verschied" picks up from the initial descent to cadence in the low register. Subtly, the falling and rising contour of "und neigte das Haupt" mirrors that of "und schliesst den Kampf" in "Es ist vollbracht." While at one level this might be considered routine—descent for "neigte," ascent for "Haupt," descent again for "verschied"—it is in fact a sign of the extraordinary care that Bach lavished on all the recitatives of the Passion, which should not be viewed as merely single-word emphases. Here the "Haupt" signifies much more than the fact that it is the highest point in the body; it stands apart from the descending pitches as Jesus, in his divine nature, stands apart from his sufferings. And the words "neigte" and "verschied" were understood, like his "I thirst," as expressions of Jesus's voluntary death in many interpretations of Bach's time. This very subtle, even conventional, difference between the melodic characters of the two recitatives that surround the aria "Es ist vollbracht" is just the kind of detail that we need to be always on the watch for with Bach. In this instance what we are dealing with is not only the sense that the divine Jesus of John's Gospel descended voluntarily to the lowest possible human condition, but also the metaphor of Jesus as "head" of the "body" of the church (indirect and distant as it may seem from the immediacy of the dramatic events). That "body" will be symbolized in the aria that follows.

"MEIN TEURER HEILAND"

Upon the close of the recitative just described, the cello enters to begin the second aria, which combines a bass solo, "Mein teurer Heiland" (My dear savior), with an intertwined chorale for the choir, "Jesus, der du warest tot, lebtest nun ohn' Ende" (Jesus, you who were dead, now live eternally). The chorale refers not only to the resurrected but to the ascended Jesus. The two arias must be considered to be paired, since the bass solo is also a meditation on the meaning of "Es ist vollbracht," but one that is rooted in an unusual conceit. Now we hear a first-person dialog with Jesus who, from the literal standpoint of the narrative, has just died (but who, as the chorale proclaims, lives eternally); and the believer's questions

[37] Smend set forth this view in his 1928 study of the *St. Matthew Passion*, in which he argued for the inappropriateness of the final chorale of the Passion, "Wenn ich einmal soll scheiden," on account of its meditating on the believer's death rather than that of Jesus. He then built a theory of the origin of the Passion around that interpretation, maintaining that the chorale was carried over from the 1728 funeral music for Leopold of Anhalt-Cöthen. See Smend, "Bachs Matthäus-Passion: Untersuchungen zur Geschichte des Werkes bis 1750," in *Bach-Studien*, ed. Christoph Wolff (Kassel/Basel: Bärenreiter, 1969), 62–63.

regarding his/her freedom from death, inheriting God's kingdom and the redemption of the world, are answered only by the silent falling of Jesus's head at the point of death, which is interpreted as an affirmative, "Yes." As in the *St. Matthew Passion's* "Wenn ich einmal soll scheiden," the focus on the individual contemporary believer takes over. With the events of the narrative frozen momentarily, at the point of his death Jesus dialogs internally with the believer.

While both the aria and chorale texts move back and forth between the literal and spiritual perspectives on Jesus's death, the chorale in "Mein teurer Heiland" also functions as a symbol of the support and comfort of the church (the "body" alluded to earlier). So the key of the aria is that of the triumphant middle section of the preceding one. The style, however, is very different and is highlighted by the change from viola da gamba to cello. This time, the ritornello features wide leaps and a bouncy spiccato articulation rather than the mostly stepwise legato melody of "Es ist vollbracht." Its affect is one of joy, peace, and security. "Mein teurer Heiland" is a comforting pastorale, and its bringing back the major key of the middle section of "Es ist vollbracht," provides another level of reinterpretation. Whereas "Es ist vollbracht" returns to the unadorned word of scripture at its close, "Mein teurer Heiland" symbolizes the internalizing of the word of promise, the inner hearing of Jesus's affirmative "Yes," a quality usually associated with the Holy Spirit; hence the chorale as symbol of the church's sustaining the believer.

By no means, however, do these qualities suggest that the meaning associated with the viola da gamba solo is to be thought of as *passé*, replaced, or updated, any more than is scripture itself by its interpretation. Just the opposite: as its text makes clear, this second meditation on Jesus's last words and his death brings out the fact that the meaning of the two arias, both very beautiful in entirely different ways, lies along a continuum with a purpose, a goal that is directed toward the contemporary believer. The comfort for the tormented faithful, announced in minor in the former aria, then offset by the sudden and elemental flash of light in the middle section, is projected more openly in the latter. The succession of events and styles has to be the way it is; first, the sorrow, then the victory, followed by the perspective of the world, now transformed by understanding the benefit of the momentous event. The two arias, taken together, reveal the indebtedness of Bach's text, direct or indirect, to one of the "patterns" alluded to earlier: that of the traditional "four senses" of scripture, which outline a progression from direct, literal, or historical meaning through the three "spiritual" stages that culminate in the eschatological perspective. In arranging the meditative movements in relation to the biblical narrative, Bach and his librettist separated Jesus's "Es ist vollbracht" from the narrative of his death so as to bring out its multiple meanings. The "night of sorrow" (*Trauernacht*) in "Es ist vollbracht" conveys much more than the darkness that came with Jesus's death (which John does not relate): its primary meaning is of a time that is about to pass, an era in the history of salvation that the appearance of Jesus brought to an end. This is clearly stated in a great deal of sixteenth- and seventeenth-century Lutheran commentary. There are, of course, dramatic changes from one era to the next, but they all belong together in the succession that comprises what many Lutherans and their predecessors called God's "economy" of salvation.

In Bach's two meditations we can say that the one aria continues and expands the meaning behind the other, eliminating the sharp contrast between darkness and light, suffering and peace, and providing a form of inner light by moving the discourse forward to ultimate things, even as it makes clear that those final—eschatological—hopes are all to be understood within the framework of the present, and a present that meditates on the meaning of the past. The texts of the arias and the traditional patterns of interpretation associated with them express how the past—in this case the past of scripture narrative viewed as God's design for humanity—elicited a treatment from Bach that is at once metaphoric and direct, drawing on background meanings that could hardly be suspected if we take a "simple" approach to the texts. Nevertheless, the latter approach was more the norm in musical settings of the time: although the two aria texts were derived from a Passion poem that was set by several other prominent composers, none of those other settings exhibits the layered approach to their meaning that Bach's does. In its projecting the certainty of salvation for the faithful in the present, Bach's "Mein teurer Heiland" is a perfect representation of the "realized" eschatology associated with John.

What I have described is also a metaphor for Bach's music in general. In his approach to the past—modal chorale melodies, for example—Bach never adopts a condescending or purely "historical" tone: instead, as if aware of his own place in history, he seeks out kinds of meaning that belong to the older style but at the same time "explains" that meaning to his own audiences (of which, three centuries farther on, we are a part). That is, he does not accept unquestioningly the terms of the past as it might be understood according to stereotypes but thinks them through thoroughly and, in the process, he leads them to new and surprising solutions. It is tempting to suggest that the change from an instrument of normally restrained character, prominent in Renaissance music, the viola da gamba, to the *concitato* style that emerged in Monteverdi's *Madrigali Guerrieri* has a "historical" dimension in "Es ist vollbracht." After the dramatic opposition in that aria the cello emerges in the next one as a symbol of a new era, the contemporary world. But Bach probably knew little of that history. Some aspects of history, however, are recoverable through meditation, through intuition rather than study. Bach does not take an overtly historical approach to modal writing, for example. The categorization of modes, their names, and traditional attributes are vastly less interesting to him than what might be called their underlying meaning and relevance for successive generations. This quality set him apart from the great majority of his contemporaries. Paradoxically, therefore, what might be viewed as a conservative trait, is perhaps his most advanced quality. Modal writing is the springboard to harmonic writing so much beyond the norms of its time that it has served for generations as a model for compositional study. What Theodor Adorno called Bach's "genius of

EXAMPLE 7.4 ***St. John Passion** no. 33, recitative*

meditation" still leads us onward.[38] And some of its deepest, most interesting and enduring manifestations are in the musical interpretation of scriptural texts.

The outbreaks of nature: transition to flats

After "Mein teurer Heiland," for the culmination of the sharp keys of his penultimate scene, Bach placed a recitative insertion from Matthew narrating the rending of the veil of the temple, the earthquakes, splitting of rocks and opening of the graves of holy men at the point of Jesus's death, and ending in e (ex. 7.4). The return to flat keys for the part of the Passion that corresponds to the third "Hauptstück" of Francke's ninth lecture and his tenth in its entirety is then accomplished in the arioso "Mein Herz" for tenor with flutes, oboes da caccia, and strings, which begins on G and wavers between sharp and flat harmonies, ending on C (ex. 7.5). The C then becomes, by hindsight, the dominant of the F-minor aria, "Zerfließe, mein Herz, in Fluthen der Zähren," for soprano with flutes and oboes da caccia.

Bach's introducing the excerpt from Matthew has sometimes been viewed as a purely descriptive and dramatic device: he took the opportunity here of introducing music of a highly excited nature to shock or impress the congregation. I would

[38] Theodor Adorno, "Bach Defended Against His Devotees," in *Prisms*, trans. Samuel Weber and Shierry Weber, 133–46 (Cambridge, MA: MIT Press, 1981).

EXAMPLE 7.5 ***St. John Passion*** *no 34, arioso "Mein Herz," ending*

argue that this is a very unlikely explanation; on the contrary, there is a distinct theological message in this sequence of movements that is vital to our understanding the concluding segment of the Passion. John has no such description, and Francke sticks closely to his narrative, without introducing anything from the Synoptic Gospels at this point (although his description of Jesus as "Eingang in der ewige Herrlichkeit"—entrance into the eternal glory—is rooted in eschatological interpretation of the rending of the veil of the temple).[39] However, in the lectures on Mark whose later editions were printed along with those on John, Francke has a great deal to say on this subject, devoting a considerable discussion to Mark's narrating that darkness came over the land from the sixth to the ninth hour. The opposition of light and darkness is, of course, one of John's principal themes, and one that is alluded to in "Es ist vollbracht," then reappears in Bach's arioso "Mein Herz," with the words "Die Sonne sich in Trauer kleidet" (although darkness is not mentioned in the recitative excerpt from Matthew).

In all the Synoptic Gospels the description of the darkness that came over the land from the sixth to the ninth hour precedes Jesus's death (Mt 27:45; Mk 15:33; Lk 23:44); the other events took place after his death and were recounted a few verses later. Only Luke links the darkness to anything else, the rending of the veil of the Temple (v. 45), which in his narrative (only) takes place *before* Jesus's death.

[39] In the third version of the Passion (around 1730), the recitative insertion from Matthew (apparently Mark in the first version) was removed, along with the arioso and aria that followed. They were replaced by a now-lost *Sinfonia*.

That John does not mention the darkness—which was linked in Matthew and Mark with Jesus's words "My God, my God, why hast thou forsaken me?" directly before his death—was presumably because he conceived of Jesus's final moments as a victory, with which the expression of forsakenness would not fit. I have mentioned that "Es ist vollbracht" contains the line "die Trauernacht läßt sich die letzte Stunde zählen," which directly precedes the shift to major and the narrative of Jesus's victory, "Der Held aus Juda siegt mit Macht, uns schließt den Kampf." As a reference to the darkness that preceded Jesus's death, the "letzte Stunde" would mean, of course, the ninth hour, which is when the Synoptic Gospels narrate that Jesus's forsaken cry and his death took place. After the meditation on Jesus's death in "Mein teurer Heiland" and the narrative of supernatural events borrowed from Matthew, the arioso "Mein Herz" then reflects back on all the events, including the darkness, seeming to recall the line from "Es ist vollbracht" in its reference to the sun "clothing itself in mourning." Its ending, however—"was willst du deines Ortes tun?"—is directed toward the contemporary believer, the word "Ort" (location) following from the reference to the "entire world" that was covered in darkness. That is, if the entire world responded to Jesus's death, what could the individual believer do in his more resticted locale? In the arioso Bach marks this phrase *adagio* and also causes it to stand apart from the preceding ones by entirely altering the character of the string accompaniment, from the *stile concitato* that has held to this point to slurred duplets, at first oscillating slowly between two chords, then settling on repeated tones. And he places the modulation from sharps to flats at this point, thereby suggesting that the question is one of great significance. The movements that follow, comprising the final segment of the Passion, provide the answer.

In his lecture on the darkness as described in Mark, Francke explains that it could not have been a naturally occurring event (i.e., an eclipse), adducing testimony from as far away as China and Egypt to show that it was, in fact, worldwide, as Bach's arioso affirms ("in dem *die ganze Welt* bei Jesu Leiden gleichfalls leidet"). In his discussion Francke draws, as did many other theologians of his time, on ancient references to the darkness that were cited as far back as the church fathers and by countless authors that followed. One citation that was never overlooked was that Dionysius the Areopagite had said, commenting on the same events in Heliopolis (city of the sun), that "Es müsse entweder der Schöpfer der Natur selber leiden, oder die Natur zu Grunde gehen" (Either the creator of nature itself must suffer, or nature be destroyed) a statement that reminds us of the explanation for the outbreak of nature in Bach's arioso, "weil sie den Schöpfer sehn erkalten!" (Because they see the creator die).[40] These ideas are especially relevant for John's Gos-

[40] Rambach makes a very similar statement (*Betrachtungen über das gantze Leiden Christi*, 1134): "Nun aber mußte die gantze Natur durch ausserordentliche Bewegungen bezeugen, daß der Schöpfer der Natur verschieden, daß Gott, geoffenbahret im Fleisch, gestorben, daß der Fürst des Lebens getödtet, und der HErr der Herrlichkeit gecreutziget worden."

pel, in light of the way its prologue presents Jesus as both the creator and the light itself. Francke, like other authors, likewise discusses how three days of darkness preceded the release of the Israelites from bondage, whereas now the three hours of darkness presage the redemption of the faithful.

The imagery of the sun clothing itself in mourning was also quite widespread. Johannes Heermann compares it to David and the people covering their heads in mourning over the conflict with Absalom (2 Sam 15:30) and to the mourning clothes worn by the members of a household whose head had died.[41] Allegorically, the darkness was a prefiguration of the darkness of the Jews who were blinded to the acceptance of Christ. It was sometimes linked up with the arresting party's "blindness" in not recognizing Jesus even after his "Ich bin's," while tropologically it was a warning to Christians who did not accept the "sun of righteousness, Jesus Christ and disregarded him and the brilliance of his holy Gospel." Heermann therefore urged his contemporaries as follows:

> O therefore, since your savior lets also the rays of his grace and the light of his word shine in and with you, O, therefore, walk in the light, while you have the light, so that the darkness will not fall upon you. O believe in the light, while you have the light, so that you are a child of light, and that you may be suitable there for the splendor of the eternal glory. Sigh and pray: "Ah, abide with us Lord, for it is toward evening and the day is far spent" (Lk 24:29).[42]

Heermann's quotation from Luke is the motto that begins Cantata 6, "Bleib' bei uns, denn es will Abend werden," for the second day of Easter 1725, where it seems to make the same connection to the ending of the *St. John Passion* (see part 3 of this book, chs. 9–14). But in discussion of the darkness that occurred before Jesus's death, it was the insistence that it covered the *entire world* that was of the greatest significance, since it meant that Jesus's death was the fulfillment of God's plan for the salvation of all humanity, Jews and gentiles alike, as in the last and most mo-

---

[41] Heermann, *Crux Christi*, 348:

> Ists nicht also? Wann der Hausherr Todes verblichen ist / so trauret alles Hausgesind / die Angehörigen verhüllen ihren Leib mit schwartzen Trauer-Kleidern / die Wände werden mit Leich-Tuche bekleidet? Nun sihe / die stirbet der grosse Haus-HErr JEsus Christus / was ists denn Wunder / daß die Sonne ihren klaren Glanz verbirget / und das Welthaus mit schwarzem Trauer Gewand / das ist/ mit Finsternüß bedecket wird?

[42] Ibid., 347:

> Sihe / du Christliche Seele / also gehts / wann man die Sonne der Gerechtigkeit Christum JEsum nicht leyden wil / und ihn mit dem Glantz seines heiligen Evangelii verachtet. O darum weil dein Heyland auch die Stralen seiner Gnaden / und das Liecht seines Worts in und bey dir scheinen lest / O so wandele im Liecht / weil du das Liecht hast / auff daß dich die Finsternüß nicht überfallen. O gläube an das Liecht / weil du das Liecht hast / auff daß du ein Kind des Liechtes seyn / und dort mit dem Glantz der ewigen Herrligkeit angethan werden mögest. Seufftze und bete: **Ach bleib bey uns HERR denn es wil Abend werden / und der Tag hat sich geneiget.**

mentous question put to the dying Jesus in “Mein teurer Heiland”: “Ist aller Welt Erlösung da?”[43]

In the various versions of the Passion that we know about (summarized in ch. 1), the miraculous events that followed Jesus's death (immediately after “Mein teurer Heiland” in Bach's setting) were the most subject to alteration, added as they were from the Synoptic Gospels. In the final version, which is the only one we have in its entirety, the two movements that are occupied with those events and their meaning are the recitative “Und siehe da,” for the evangelist and *basso continuo,* and the arioso “Mein Herz,” for tenor, strings, *basso continuo,* and a pair each of flutes and oboes da caccia (or oboes d'amore). These are the movements that accomplish the shift to flat keys for the final *ambitus* of the Passion. “Und siehe da,” in setting the descriptive Gospel account, begins on the dominant of e and ends with a full close in that key (see ex. 7.4), whereas “Mein Herz” places the previously narrated events in a meditative context that leads to the question, “was willst du deines Ortes tun?” In the following aria, “Zerfließe, mein Herz, in Fluten der Zähren,” Bach treats the cadence to C on which this question and the arioso ends as the dominant of F minor, And this sequence, in effecting the final such modulation of the Passion, takes on a meaning that derives from the Lutheran interpretative tradition.

Although all the miraculous events were interpreted in light of other scriptural references to rocks, earthquakes, and the like, after the darkness that came over the world the event that was most subject to interpretation was the rending of the veil of the Temple. The Chemnitz, Leyser, and Gerhard commentary divides the various events into categories according to whether they involved Jesus (the flowing of blood and water from his side), created beings (the conversion of the centurian), or inanimate nature (the sun above and the rocks, earthquakes, and opening up of graves below). The rending of the veil, however, was considered not to belong to any of these categories because of its multiplicity of meanings, all of which were symbolic of Jesus's death as the completion of his work on earth. Among them was a parallel to the soldiers' taking Jesus's clothes, whereas now the Temple itself had its clothing taken away (the implicit parallel to the undivided cloak, symbolizing the church, and the divided veil of the synagogue, as well as that of the inner and outer clothes and veils is not developed). Most of all, however, the rending of the veil signified that the Holy of Holies was now visible to all, the world of Jews and gentiles alike, as the result of Jesus's office as priest. Now the tables of the law, the ark of the covenant in which they were housed, the *Gnadenstuhl* that was placed on the ark and that was interpreted as Jesus himself, were all open to the entire world through faith. That this event was a miraculous one, reflecting the plan of

---

[43] In some discussions of the seven last words, “Es ist vollbracht,” usually given as the sixth, was described as the only one spoken to the world as a whole. See, for example, Heermann, “Die Allerholdseligsten Sieben Worte unsers treuen und hochverdienten Heylandes JEsu Christi, mit welchen er am Creutze sein heiliges Leben geendet, betrachtet von J. M. D.,” in *Crux Christi* (1618), published together with Heermann's *Labores Sacri, Geistliche Kirch-Arbeit, In Erklärung aller gewöhnlichen Sonntags- und vornehmsten Fest-Evangelien* (Leipzig, 1726), 142.

God, like the flowing forth of blood and water from Jesus's side, was carefully argued. And, while we may not know exactly what Bach intended in the movements that take them up, his assigning them the role of the final modulation between the various *ambitus* of the Passion is worth considering in some detail. In what follows I argue that the question "was willst du deines Ortes tun?" which symbolizes the shift, is an important key to the meaning of the Passion.

Within the "borrowed" narrative of the outbreaks of nature Bach gives the greatest attention to the rending of the veil. The recitative "Und sieha da"(ex. 7.4) begins on the dominant of E minor (intensifying progressively to the dominant seventh and minor dominant ninth), which holds for most of the first three (of seven) measures. In the third measure, which narrates the rending of the veil, the vocal line plummets downward more than an octave, from a′ to g, for the words "[von] oben an bis unten aus." Then, after a precipitous downward-rushing E-minor scale of two octaves in the *basso continuo*, the harmony shifts suddenly to the first-inversion B♭ harmony for "[und die] Erde erbebete." The tonal "functionality" of this event is perfectly clear by hindsight, of course: the B♭ harmony is soon interpreted as the Neapolitan sixth chord of the subdominant, A minor. Nevertheless, the downward motion in pitch from "oben" to "Erde" is aligned with the shift from B to B♭ harmonies. After the low pitch on the word "Erde," however, the line is occupied with ascent first to a high g♯′ on "zerrissen," then to the high a′ heard before on "Vorhang" and "oben." The twofold appearance of the word "auf" ("und die Gräber thäten sich *auf*, und stunden *auf* viele Leiber der Heiligen!"—and the graves opened up and there arose many bodies of the saints), are set in both instances with dramatic rising lines, first to e′, then to the high a′. Their harmonies rivet the E minor in place (in the first instance the harmony is the subdominant of e and in the second a d♯ diminished-seventh chord over the bass C, functioning as a preparation for the dominant of the cadence). As a result the recitative as a whole outlines a descent/ascent shape that can also be described as a motion in the flat direction culminating on "Erde" and a return ascent (see ex. 7.4). The meaning as Francke explains, is that Jesus's death enabled the resurrection of holy men who had died at much earlier times, one of the central tenets of Luther's eschatology.

The movement just described can be considered the completion of the sharp-key *ambitus* that began with the shift from the end of the narrative of Jesus's robe. At the same time, directly following the very positive D major of "Mein teurer Heiland," it seems also a part of the transition to the concluding flat-key *ambitus*, at least by hindsight. The arioso "Mein Herz!" that follows begins in G; but, in meditating on and therefore recalling the outbreaks of nature, it brings back the *stile concitato* effects of the preceding narrative and the character of its shifting harmonies. Now the held initial pedal tone is G (this time for five and a half of the total nine measures); and the considerably more dissonant harmonies that sound above it point first to C minor (with a sudden e♭′ for "Jesu" in the phrase "indem die ganze Welt bei Jesu Leiden gleichfalls leidet"), which is emphasized for more than two measures, then to D minor, as the text refers back to the veil, the rocks, the earthquake, and the graves. For the penultimate phrase the tonality settles on D minor; then, with a sudden shift to *Adagio*, we hear the final question "was willst du deines Ortes tun?" turn to the dominant of C/c (the e♮'s suggest C major, but we remember the prominence of C minor earlier on). This is the signal event in the final modulation between *ambitus*; and it is a highly symbolic one, as the next section will argue. The final segment of the Passion is, in fact, the answer to the question posed by the shift of key area.

Jesus's Burial: the final *ambitus* of the Passion

In keeping with the announcement in "Herr, unser Herrscher" that God's *Ruhm* (praise) is "glorious in all lands," the royal inscription had proclaimed Jesus's kingship in the principal languages of the world; and behind the dividing of Jesus's cloak into four parts lay the widespread allegory of the four parts of the world. After Jesus's affirmation of the redemption of the "whole world" in "Mein teurer Heiland," and the symbolic opening up of the Holy of Holies in the recitative narrative, the turn to flat keys for the final segment of the Passion begins with the phrase "in dem die ganze Welt bei Jesu Leiden gleichfalls leidet, die Sonne sich in Trauer kleidet" (since the entire world suffers along with Jesus's suffering, the sun clothes itself in mourning), which turns the initial G of the arioso "Mein Herz" into the dominant of C minor. Whether Bach might have thought so precisely about his key references as to remember the C major of Jesus's clothing, or to look ahead to the C minor of "Ruht wohl," is an open question. But surely, after the recitative and arioso itemize the responses of inanimate nature to Jesus's death, when the final phrase of the arioso turns to a C major that is immediately made the dominant of F minor by the aria "Zerfließe," framing that phrase as a question to the believer in his own locale ("was willst du *deines Ortes* tun?"), we are justified in viewing the final return to flat keys as symbolizing the world as the place where the answer must be given, by each and every individual. There is an unmistakable similarity in contour between the melody that sets the question and the beginning flute melody of "Zerfließe"; the circle-of-fifths harmonies that end the arioso—from the dominant of d (mm. 5–7), to d, G and C (mm. 8–9)—are continued in the f of "Zerfließe." The "Trauernacht" alluded to in "Es ist vollbracht" spreads throughout the world in the very daytime with the sun's clothing itself in mourning, which is, in "Zerfließe," the first stage—a predominantly physical one—of the response to that question.

We perhaps at this point have an explanation for why Bach does not center the final flat-key segment of the Passion simply on the narrative of Jesus's burial, as it was in the fifth *actus* according to the traditional fivefold view of the Passion. In drawing on the Synoptic Gospels' narratives of the outbreaks of nature that followed Jesus's death (including the darkness that preceded it), Bach and his librettist[s] introduced reference to the meditative tradition surrounding those events—the response of nature (the physical world) to Jesus's death—in order to project the initial response of the faithful. There are four meditative movements in this final segment: the aria "Zerfließe, mein Herze, in Fluten der Zähren"; the chorale "O hilf, Christe, Gottes Sohn"; the chorus "Ruht wohl, ihr heiligen Gebeine"; and the chorale "Ach Herr, laß dein lieb Engelein." If we understand them as a response to the question "was willst du deines Ortes tun?" then we observe that running through them is a progression of ideas that leads from the natural and physical to the eschatological understanding of death. The initial human response, in the aria "Zerfließe, mein Herze, in Fluten der Zähren," is one of mourning—floods of tears—the natural response of humankind to the death of a loved one. In "Zerfließe" Bach's reinterpretation of the C of "was willst du deines Ortes tun?" as the dominant of F minor brings about a sudden shift to deep flats, specifically to the key that was most widely associated with lamentation, tears, and sorrow. We have only to think of the F-minor aria, "Bäche von gesalz'nen Zähren, Fluthen rauschen stets einher," of Cantata 21, *Ich hatte viel Bekümnernis,* where the floods of tears, the outcome of the believer's tribulation and sorrow over feelings of desertion by God, have the effect of emotional release, turning him toward God. There are many other instances in which F minor is associated with like emotional states in Bach's work.[44] Yet, even here, in keeping with the character of John's Gospel, "Zerfließe" emphasizes that the believer's tears are a means of *honoring* God: "dem Höchsten zu Ehren," a theme (honor) that Francke brings up in the context of Jesus's burial, and to which we will return.

The third *Haupt-Stück* of Francke's ninth lecture turns from the death of Jesus to the events immediately following—the piercing of his side and the flow of blood and water—and their fulfilling scripture prophesy. Francke explains that the *Kriegsknechte*, in intending to break Jesus's legs, wanted to torture him further; also, out of malice and evil they wanted his death. Francke adds, "However, be this as it may, there was among them all a higher hand, which John recognized very well, who interpreted it for us also very deeply from the Holy Scripture through the Holy Spirit."[45]

Thus Francke begins and ends his ninth lecture with emphasis on God's control of the events of the Passion and the fulfillment of scripture, which was for him vital to the strengthening of faith. In this particular instance, even John himself had made that statement, with the words "Und der das gesehen hat, der hat es bezeuget, und sein Zeugnis ist wahr, und derselbige weiss, dass er die Wahrheit saget, auf das ihr glaubet" ("And he that saw it attested to it, and his witness is true; and he knows

[44] Among the many such instances, perhaps the first to come to mind are the opening chorus of Cantata 12, *Weinen, Klagen, Sorgen, Zagen* and the arioso "O Schmerz" from the *St. Matthew Passion.* But even instrumental pieces fit in their musical styles with this association: the tortured F minor Sinfonia for harpsichord and the *Lamento* of the *Capriccio on the departure of a beloved brother,* for example.

[45] Francke, *Oeffentliche Reden,* 150: "Dem sey aber wie ihm wolle, so war unter dem allen eine höhere Hand, welches demnach Johannes gar wohl erkannte, der uns auch durch den Heil. Geist solches aus der H. Schrift gar tief ausgeleget hat."

that he speaks the truth, so that you might believe"). Francke links these words up, as did many others, with John's remark regarding the resurrection, at the end of John 20:31: "but these things are written, that you might believe in Christ; and that believing you might have life through his name" ("daß solches alles zu dem Ende aufgeschrieben sey, auf daß man an Christum gläubete und selig würde"). For Francke, John's "quite special emphasis" mirrored the fact that John, who, as Francke believed, was witness to the events in question and whose "heart was bound to Jesus in such tender love" was himself wounded to the heart by the piercing of Jesus's side; it is therefore "believable" that the Gospel writer himself did not understand these events fully at the time but only later, after Jesus's glorification, as he had said in 12:16 ("These things understood not his disciples at the first: but when Jesus was glorified, then remembered they that these things were written of him, and that they had done these things unto him").[46] Francke's remark points, like "Zerfließe," to the opposition between response to the sorrowful events themselves and understanding their meaning according to God's plan, fully manifested in Jesus's glorification. Bach mirrors this quality in the tonal character of the recitative ("Die Juden aber") following "Zerfließe," which, to the point of John's remark on the purpose of his witness to the events (faith), is twenty-three measures in length, touching on the keys of c and g, and cadencing in E♭ and B♭. The latter key lends a very positive character to the cadence at "auf das ihr glaubet." With the record of the fulfillment of scriptural predictions that follows, however, comprising an additional seven measures of recitative, Bach moves steadily back into deeper flat keys, principally f and A♭ for the first prediction and b♭ (in which the recitative closes) for the second. As Francke described the meaning of the predictions, it was necessary that Jesus's death be certain, so that faith in the resurrection would be firm. The fact that Jesus's bones were not broken was to fulfill the description (Ex 12:46) of him as the "true Passover lamb," symbolizing his sacrifice for the redemption of humanity, while the piercing of his side fulfilled a prediction in Zechariah 12:10).[47] Bach's shift from B-flat major to B-flat minor highlights—like the g/G of Part 1, the A/a between Parts 1 and 2, and the sharp/flat, major/minor modulations in the recitative that leads into the "symbolic trial"—the opposition between the *Niedrigkeit* of Christ and the benefit for the faithful.

The flowing forth of blood and water from Jesus's side is, as we might expect, given a very detailed treatment in Chemnitz, Leyser, and Gerhard.[48] The interpretation given there is a wide-ranging one, but its core derives, as those authors make clear, from Augustine, who emphasized the sacramental meaning of the blood and water.[49] In their commentary Chemnitz et al. view this particular "wonder" as the culminating and most symbolic of all those that followed Jesus's death. After a

---

[46] Ibid., 150–51.

[47] Ibid., 151–52.

[48] Chemnitz et al., *Echt evangelische Auslegung*, 58–70.

[49] Ibid., 65.

string of citations from the Johannine Gospel reading for Quasimodogeniti (the Sunday after Easter; but see ch. 9), all of which treat of God's "witnesses" of the blood, water, and Spirit, the commentary continues:

> John means to say this: the heavenly Father has shown the innocence and divinity of his Son, suffering on the cross, not only through miracles that involved lifeless creatures, such as the darkening of the sun, through the rending of the veil, through the earthquakes, through the splitting of the rocks, through the opening of the graves, etc., but also through an especially majestic miracle, which happened with the body of Christ itself, namely, that after his death blood and water flowed from him. This miracle the Holy Spirit wanted to have recorded by me [John], as writer and eyewitness, so that in this manner there were three constant signs of the divinity of Christ, namely the Spirit, the water and the blood. For it was not only once that these signs, the flowing of blood and water from his side, bore witness to Christ, but even today they determine this commemorating authority, since the Holy Spirit in the words of the evangelist, which is called "an office of the Spirit" (2 Cor 3:6), bears witness to Christ (Jn 16:27). The water of baptism and the blood of the Holy Eucharist testify just as much to Christ, because these two sacraments are seals that confirm, seal and strengthen the richness of grace of the forgiveness of sins in Christ. To this living fountain, which broke forth from the side of Christ, various figures of the Old Testament can properly be applied. In Genesis 9:13 the rainbow is set forth as a sign of God's grace. This, however, has a watery and a purple color. From the side of Christ streams a bow ("Bogen") of water and purple color as the most certain sign of the majestic, divine grace.[50]

---

[50] Ibid., 66:

> Johannes will dieses sagen: Der himmlische Vater hat von der Unschund und Gottheit seines am Kreuze leidenden Sohnes nicht allein durch Wunder gezeugt, die an leblosen Creaturen geschahen, wie durch die Sonnenfinsterniß, durch das Zerreiß en des Vorhangs, durch das Sichbeween der Erde, durch die Spaltung der Felsen, durch die Oeffnung der Gräber u. s. w., sondern auch durch ein besonderes herrliches Wunder, welches am Leibe Christi selbst geschah, daß nämlich nach dem Tode aus ihm herausfloß Blut und Wasser. Dieses Wunder wollte der heilige Geist durch mich, als den Schreiber und den Augenzeugen, in der evangelischen Geschichte aufzeichnen lassen, damit auf diese Weise drei beständige Zeugen von der Gottheit Christi seien, nämlich der Geist, das Wasser und das Blut. Denn nicht Einmal nur haben diese Zeugen von Christo gezeugt, als Blut und Wasser aus seiner Seite floß, sondern noch heute verwalten sie dieses Zeugenamt, weil der heilige Geist im Worte des Evangelii, welches genannt wird "ein Amt des Geistes," 2 Cor. 3, 6., von Christo zeuget, Joh. 16, 27. Das Wasser der Taufe und das Blut im heiligen Abendmahl zeugen ebenfalls von Christo, weil diese beiden Sacraments Siegel sind, die da bezeugen, versiegeln und bekräftigen die gnadenreiche Bergebung der Sünden in Christo. Auf diesen Lebensquell, der aus der Seite Christi hervorbrach, können verschiedene Figuren des alten Testamentes recht wohl angewandt werden. 1 Mos. 9, 13. Wird der Regenbogen als Zeuge der göttlichen Gnade hingestellt. Dieser aber hat eine wässerige und purpurne Farbe. Aus Christi Seite strahlt ein Bogen von Wasser- und Purpurfarbe, als der gewisseste Zeuge der herrlichen, göttlichen Gnade.

In this passage we see clearly that the rainbow imagery of "Erwäge, wie sein blutgefärbter Rücken" links up with the interpretation of John's narrative of the blood and water; and, indeed, an excerpt from Augustine cited earlier in the commentary made this explicit. Many other commentaries made the same point. Bach's moving into deep flats for that narrative, and for "O hilf, Christe," therefore seems to give special attention to the point that concludes the fourth *actus* with references back to earlier points in the trial. In this light, the flats seem to associate the sacramental interpretation with the "flesh" (in its more positive sense), that is of the church and the faithful in the world. Bach, however, does not make "O hilf Christe" into a point of closure but instead links its deep-flat tonality with the final flat-key region of the Passion, which began with response to the question "was willst du deines Ortes tun?" It therefore forms part of a continuity rather than a point of division (the ensuing narrative of the burial begins in the same key that had preceded the chorale, B-flat minor). At the same time, the chorale, one of the most widely cited in Lutheran Passion commentaries, observes the ending of the fourth *actus* with a summary of the purpose of the Passion, "deinen Tod und sein Ursach fruchtbarlich bedenken." It, therefore, seems also to allude to the imagery of the faithful picking "sweet fruit" from Jesus's "wormwood" in "Betrachte." The F Phrygian tonality, within the same *ambitus* as the B-flat minor of the recitative ending, links up with the B-flat minor narrative of the crucifixion and royal inscription and the beginning of the burial narrative that follows. The points of Jesus's greatest *Niedrigkeit* (or *Erniedrigung*, as Francke puts it) become springboards to the cry from the faithful. At this point the Phrygian harmonization mirrors the believer's state of mind, not Jesus's sufferings; the chorale is a prayer for Jesus's aid from the "poor" and "weak" believer.[51] It marks the second meditative response to the question put to the believer at the end of "Mein Herz."

Francke's tenth and last lecture takes up Jesus's burial, whereas Bach, although he emphasizes the fulfillment of scripture as a kind of reference backward to "O hilf, Christe" at the beginning of Part 2, begins the "Darnach bat Pilatum" recitative that follows with the narrative of Joseph of Arimathea's asking Pilate for Jesus's body in the same tonal region, B-flat minor, shifting toward the dominant of F minor for "der ein Jünger Jesu war" (who was a disciple of Jesus), to f, for the parenthetical remark "doch heimlich, aus Furcht vor den Juden" (although secretly, from fear of the Jews), and on to a full close in c, for the narrative of Joseph's taking the body away. Bach indicates, exceptionally, that the parenthetical remark be sung *piano*, after which he marks the return to the normal *forte*. And in a sense the deepest flat keys in this segment of the Passion can be considered, if not "parenthetical," then at least secondary in relation to the primary *ambitus* of c/E♭. That is, they mirror the understanding of Jesus's *Niedrigkeit* in the way Francke described John's remarks on the purpose of the piercing of Jesus's side: as ultimately to be illuminated by

---

[51] Heinrich Müller cites this verse in the first, second, and third of his nine sermons on the Passion, with the same basic association. See *Evangelischer Herzens-Spiegel*, 1405, 1414, 1425.

Jesus's glorification. Bach's modulatory sequence is very carefully outlined, leading from the B-flat minor tonality of the preceding narrative to the key of the burial chorus, c, in which the recitative ends, after further narrative concerning Nicodemus, cadencing in f and c. We might consider that Bach's returning to the *ambitus* in which the Passion began mirrors the scene of Jesus's burial in a garden (the final return to c) as was the beginning of the Passion narrative (see the first recitative, also in c), a point brought out by some commentators, who also related it to the fall of humanity in the garden of Eden. The more direct meaning, however, relates to Francke's perception of Joseph and Nicodemus as representatives of humanity as a whole.

Francke begins his tenth lecture by considering why Joseph of Arimathea and Nicodemus should have been the ones to look after Jesus's body, remarking that among the four evangelists Nicodemus's presence was mentioned only by John (20:39). In the episode of Jesus's burial, Francke finds it particularly significant that Joseph and Nicodemus, who held high positions among the Jews, were "hidden" disciples of Jesus, that is, disciples who were afraid to come forth openly, "from fear of the Jews." Nicodemus, in particular, came forth only by night. It is interesting, therefore, to note that Francke, in 1701, published a short treatise on human fear titled *Nicodemus*, which was later translated into English.[52] In Francke's view, John's telling of Nicodemus's participation in Jesus's burial continued his treatment of Nicodemus in chapters 3 and 7 of his Gospel. In the third chapter Nicodemus came forth only by night; in the seventh, while reminding the reader of that fact, John has him reveal what Francke calls "einen rechten Helden-Muth" (a true hero's spirit), in that he went against his colleagues in questioning that Jesus be judged by the law without being heard; now, with the burial of Jesus, he came fully into the open.[53] As believers whose faith was weak, Joseph and Nicodemus provided a good model for the contemporary believer, illustrating the fact that faith was the work of God, who might choose to give new strength according to his will: "So then the finger of God should be recognized in this above all, and everyone should take note that this was his work, who '*giveth power to the faint; and to them that have no might he increaseth strength.' Isaiah 40:29.*"[54]

After speculating that "perhaps God held back from those upright souls who were possessed with a greater measure of faith and of strength, so that on an especially important occasion his divine power would be revealed in those others [i.e., persons of weaker faith] for their greater conviction and edification, and for the

---

[52] August Hermann Francke, *Nicodemus / Oder / Tractätlein / von der Menschen-Furcht,* 3rd ed. (Halle, 1727).

[53] Francke, *Oeffentliche Reden,* 159. See ch. 13, in Cantata 176, "Es ist ein trotzig und verzagt Ding um aller Menschen Herzen" (There is a stubbornness and fearfulness to all human hearts), Nicodemus is again taken as a representative of human weakness.

[54] Ibid., 161: "So solte denn nun der Finger Gottes hierin so viel mehr von allen erkannt werden, und iederman solte mercken, daß es sein Werck sey, der **den Müden Kraft / und Stärcke genug den Unvermögenden geben könne. Jes. 40, 29.**"

greater glorification of his name, such as happened here with Joseph and Nicodemus," Francke raises the question of reason contra faith, in particular, whether through cross and persecution God's work might be laid low ("zu Grunde gehen"). On the contrary, he concludes, this text shows us how the cross and death of Christ have an effect that is completely opposite to what reason might think, for "God works in his most powerful manner in those weak and ignorant hearts where the need and the danger are greatest."[55] We, therefore, can "learn from the example of Joseph and Nicodemus that if we only remain in constant battle with our own weakness of faith, and continue on calling to him to strengthen our faith, at the right time God will give the strength so that we will not deny but freely acknowledge him and glorify his name."

As we might expect, Francke's interpretation of Jesus's burial takes up the theme of Lutheran eschatology that underlies the final choruses of both Bach Passions as well as many other movements and passages throughout the cantatas: the sleep of death. Francke prepares for this theme by reminding the reader that Joseph and Nicodemus "loved the Lord Jesus so much and were so faithful to him, even in death, that, although they did not expect, believe or understand his resurrection at the time (otherwise they would not have thought of balsam), nevertheless honored him in death to the highest degree that they were capable of, and thereby denied all their honor before their own people."[56] "However," Francke continues, "it is the Lord Jesus on whom we principally have to look." Since Jesus handed over his spirit to his Father, "what we have now is his dead body, the temple and hut in which the spirit dwelt; the same temple that mankind destroyed and that, as told in advance (Jn 2:19), he would rebuild himself on the third day. His death was a true death in light of his resurrection, but it was for God only a sleep. . . . His rest was honor, which was not at all disturbed by the last loving service these two men showed him."

In this passage Francke makes clear that Jesus's foreknowledge and voluntary acceptance of God's will comprise the principal meaning of his death and burial. Joseph and Nicodemus honored him as much as they could, but his honor went beyond even such loving deeds, since his death was a death in light of the resurrection to come. Francke continues:

> Here we see now the "first fruits of them that slept," *primirias dormientium*, 1 Cor 15:20, who on the third day shall be the *first born* from the *dead. Rev 1:5*. For he alone is the one through whom our rest in the grave has become a true rest, even an honor. And also those who previously had died in faith, for example Abraham, Isaac and Jacob, are only *fallen asleep* through the power of his death. Therefore God also after their death named himself their God *who is not a God of the dead, but of the living: for all live unto him.*

[55] Ibid., 161–62.
[56] Ibid., 163–64.

> Lk 20:38. So we should look upon the dead body of Jesus with living faith. Thus we will gain the power from his death to fear death and the grave as little as though a child is carried to bed by its dear mother and placed in it for a gentle sleep; since neither mother nor child fear that they will lose one another, but know already that they will soon see and embrace one another with joy. And to be sure in his sleep a child has to enjoy the true love of his mother in no way other than unconsciously [*unwissend*]. But if one of the faithful dies [*entschläft*, falls asleep] then to be sure the body is dead, but the soul is with Christ.[57]

In all this Francke removes Jesus's death and burial from the sphere of Joseph and Nicodemus, whose acts of love, praiseworthy though they were, were apart from the honor of Jesus's death. It was Jesus alone who made it possible for death to be a sleep, awaiting the resurrection, even for those who had died long before, such as Abraham, Isaac, and Jacob.[58] Francke thus describes a shift from the perspective of human actions to those of Jesus's completed work, the former rooted in the physical (which the expression "Liebes-Dienst" evokes) and in Jesus's *Erniedrigung*, whereas the latter belong to his glorification and honor.

A similar progression can be seen in Bach's *St. John Passion*, providing an explanation for why Bach binds the events that followed Jesus's death into one long flat-key closing region of the Passion. We have considered that the recitative narrative of the opening up of graves and resurrection of saints that took place at the point of Jesus's death had symbolic significance, like the opening up of the Holy of Holies. As the response to the question "was willst du deines Ortes thun?" at the close of the ariso "Mein Herz," the aria "Zerfließe, mein Herz in Fluthen der Zähren," which begins the final segment, represents the natural sorrow over the death of a loved one. The "Ort" is the believer's place in the world "below"; yet, at the same time, the aria describes the believer's tears as *honoring* the "most high," as if looking ahead to the interpretation of the believer's tears as burial spices, both in

---

[57] Ibid., 165–66:

> Hier sehen wir nun den **Erstling under denen / die da schlafen** / *primirias dormientium*, **1. Cor. 15, 20.** der am dritten Tage der **Erstgebohrne** seyn soll von den **Todten, Offenb. 1, 5.** Denn er ist es allein, durch welchen der Tod zu einem Schlaf worden, und Er ist es allein, durch welchen unsere Ruhe im Grabe eine rechte Ruhe, ja Ehre worden ist. Und auch die vorhin im Glauben gestorben sind, zum Exempel Abraham, Isaac und Jacob, sind nur **entschlafen** durch die Kraft seines Todes. Darum sich GOtt auch nach ihrem Tode ihren GOtt genennet / **der nicht der Todten / sondern der Lebendigen GOtt ist. Denn sie leben ihm alle.** Luc. 20, 38. So sollen wir den todten Leichnam Jesu mit lebendigem Glauben anschauen. Dem so werden wir aus seinem Tode die Kraft gewinnen, uns so wenig vor dem Tode und Grabe zu fürchten, als wenn ein Kind von seiner lieben Mutter ins Bett getragen, und zum sanften Schlaf hinein geleget wird; da weder Mutter noch Kind fürchten, daß sie einander verlieren, sondern schon wissen, daß sie einander bald mit Freuden wieder sehen und umarmen werden. Und zwar ein Kind hat in seinem Schlaf der treuen Liebe seiner Mutter anders nicht als unwissend, zu geniessen. Aber wenn ein Gläubiger entschläft, so ist der Leib zwar todt, aber die Seele ist bey Christo.

[58] See Althaus, *Theology of Martin Luther*, 408–17.

EXAMPLE 7.6 ***St. John Passion*** *no. 38, recitative, excerpt*

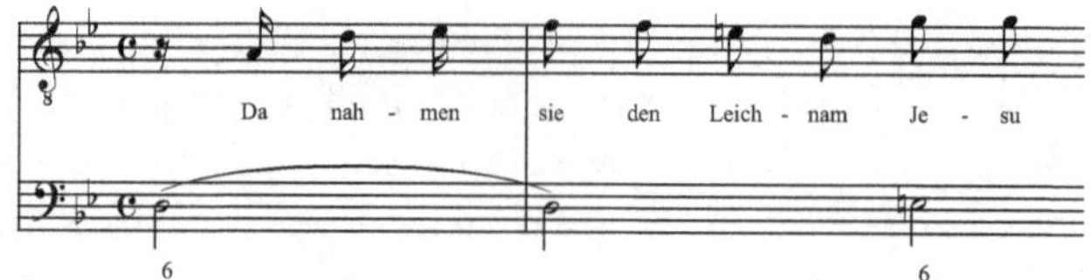

vain, in the *Easter Oratorio* of 1725. That is, it mirrors the actions of Joseph and Nicodemus in looking after Jesus's burial. Despite the fact that the middle section of "Zerfließe"—"Erzähle der Welt und dem Himmel die Noth, dein Jesus ist todt"—emphasizes the sorrowful impact of Jesus's death on the believer, mourning is not the final or most important message of the Passion. The chorale "O hilf, Christe" prays for "fruitful" meditation on Jesus's death, acknowledging the more important theme of its benefit for the believer: "deinen Tod und sein' Ursach' fruchtbarlich bedenken, dafür, wiewohl arm und schwach, dir Dank opfer schenken." The response of understanding the meaning of the Passion and thanking God rather than mourning his death arises directly from recognition of Jesus's work in light of the fulfillment of scripture. With the narrative of Joseph and Nicodemus, Bach seems to cast back to "Mein Herz," and the fear that arose from the outbreak of nature, in that he brings back the melody that ended the arioso—"was willst du deines Ortes tun?" (see ex. 7.6)—as the recitative turns to the burial, "Da nahmen sie den Leichnam Jesu"—which leads to f, as the original question had (see ex. 7.6 and 7.5). The relationship suggests that Joseph's and Nicodemus's looking after Jesus's burial is their response to the earlier question.[59] Then, in the burial chorus, "Ruht, wohl, ihr heiligen Gebeine," the lullaby-like sarabande character establishes a sonorous equivalent to the sleep of death, while the text makes clear that the weeping of "Zerfließe" is over: "die ich nun weiter *nicht* beweine." Likewise, whereas "Zerfließe" had urged the faithful to proclaim to the world and to heaven the "Noth," of Jesus's death, the middle section of "Ruht wohl" counters with "Das Grab, so euch bestimmet ist, und ferne *keine Noth umschliesst* macht mir den Himmel auf, und schliesst die Hölle zu" (The grave, which was appointed for you, and in addition encompasses no distress, opens up heaven for me and closes off hell). The expression "bestimmet ist" makes clear that Jesus's burial was part of God's plan for the salvation of humanity. Nowhere in the text of this movement is there the slightest indication of sorrow, which was also the thrust of Francke's discussion of the burial.

---

[59] Francke, *Nicodemus*, 243, 250. At the close of his treatise on fear, Francke provides lists of biblical figures who exhibited fear and those who either did not or "put down their fear and came to the joy of faith." Interestingly, Joseph of Arimathea and Nicodemus appear in both lists, the first time for their coming forth only by night and the second for their carrying out the burial of Jesus.

The progression of Francke's tenth lecture is a threefold one. After the story of Joseph and Nicodemus, then the discussion of the sleep of death, Francke turns to another aspect of Jesus's death for the contemporary believer: the theme of baptism as a symbolic reenactment of Jesus's death and resurrection. This theme was perfectly understood by Bach, of course, since it underlies the great enharmonic transformation that appears in the Credo of the *Mass in B minor* as the music of the Confiteor (I acknowledge one baptisim for the remission of sin) gives way to the "Et exspecto resurrectionem mortuorum" (and I look for the resurrection of the dead), which introduces a mirroring of the shift that takes place at the end of the Crucifixus (passus et sepultus est) and the Et resurrexit.[60] Francke's concluding pages, like the passages just cited from Bach's Credo, take their inspiration from 1 Corinthians:15, where, as Francke points out, Paul links the theme of Jesus's burial and resurrection to the message of the Gospel as a whole.[61]

As Francke narrates, just as in baptism (as described in scripture) the believer descends into the water, experiences a moment of stillness, then emerges in a new state, so eventually he/she dies, enters the peace of the sleep of death, and is resurrected into a new life. Behind Francke's description lie the multiple senses of scripture: Jesus's death and resurrection are the true subject of scripture, prefigured in many OT stories such as Daniel in the lion's den, the three men in the fiery furnace, and the like (the literal-historical and allegorical senses), while the believer's own death and resurrection are the eschatological sense, prefigured in her baptism. The tropological sense of Jesus's burial and the sleep of death, then, is the peace that comes to the believer through faith:

> Here in the quiet spirit of faith should the noble fruit of the death of Christ be enjoyed. Blessed are we, that we consider ourselves through the death of Christ to have died to sin, that it has no right to cause us restlessness in the conscience, to seek more from us, or to dare to presume its former rule over us; but instead that we, as those who are buried with Christ have now become free from the wrath of God and companions in his love, and now along with Christ may rise again through the power of the Holy Spirit, and change into a new life, just as he is awakened through the glory of the Father, and what he brings to life God brings to life.[62]

---

[60] See ch. 8 for more on the *Mass in B minor*.

[61] Francke, *Oeffentliche Reden*, 167.

[62] Ibid., 169–70:

> Hier soll in dem stillen Geiste des Glaubens die edle Frucht des Todes CHristi genossen werden. Wohl uns, so wir uns durch den Tod Christi der Sünden abgestorben zu seyn achten, daß sie kein Recht, uns im Gewissen zu beunruhigen, mehr an uns suchen, noch die vorige Herrschaft ihr über uns anmassen dürfe; sondern daß wir als die Begrabenen mit CHristo nun vom Zorn GOttes los und Genossen seiner Liebe worden sind, und nun samt CHristo auferstehen mögen in der Kraft des Heiligen Geistes, und in einem neuen Leben wandeln, gleichwie er auferwecket ist durch die Herrlichkeit des Vaters, und was er lebet, GOtte lebet.

Francke ends by describing the proper use ("rechten Gebrauch") of "what has been said and heard regarding the sufferings of Christ," namely,

> . . . that you beseech God humbly that he remind you of all that which you have heard through the Holy Spirit, at his time, and where you have need of it, and that it will instill in you a divine seed of life, through which you will be born again, and will bring the fruits of the new life to the Lord in abundance. If you take unto yourselves, according to the instruction given to you, the story of the Passion death and burial of Jesus Christ, to meditate and to reflect on it in the fear of the Lord, with heartfelt prayer and beseeching of God, then you will become within that which one finds for wisdom and power in the cross of Christ and the kind of great treasure of blessedness and of divine peace that meditation on the same obtains.[63]

Note that in this passage as well as in the *Schluß-Gebet* (final prayer) that completes his entire series of lectures, Francke reiterates the words "betrachte," and "erwege" and the "fruit" they bring to those who meditate on Jesus's sufferings, death and burial.

When, therefore, we turn to the ending of Bach's *St. John Passion*, we can hardly fail to observe that, while "Ruht wohl" prayed for Jesus to bring the believer to rest in the sleep of death, the chorale "Ach Herr, laß dein lieb Engelein," after reiterating that prayer in its *Stollen*, turns in its *Abgesang* to a prayer for the believer's resurrection:

Alsdenn vom Tod erwecke mich,	So then from death awaken me,
daß meine Augen sehen dich	that my eyes see you
in aller Freud, o Gottes Sohn,	in all joy, Oh Son of God,
mein Heiland und Genadenthron!	my savior and throne of grace!
Herr Jesu Christ,	Lord Jesus Christ,
erhöre mich, erhöre mich,	hear me, hear me,
ich will dich preisen ewiglich!	I long to praise you eternally!

Between "Ruht wohl" and "Ach Herr, laß dein lieb Engelein" the keys of "Betrachte" and "Erwäge," E♭ and c, appear now in reverse order, perhaps as a reminder of the "rechten Gebrauch" of the Passion, and the "Frucht" it brings to the faithful on earth.

---

[63] Ibid., 171:

> . . . daß ihr GOTT demüthiglich bittet, daß er euch doch alles dessen, so ihr gehöret habet, durch den Heiligen Geist, zu seiner Zeit, und da es euch noth thut, erinnere, und es in euch werden lasse einen göttlichen Samen des Lebens, dadurch ihr neugebohren werdet, und dem HERRN die Früchte des neuen Lebens reichlich bringet. Nehmet nun selbst, nach der euch gegebenen Anleitung, die Historie des Leidens, Sterbens und Begräbnisses JEsu CHristi vor, sie in der Furcht des HErrn zu betrachten und zu erwegen, unter hertzlichem Gebet und Flehen zu GOTT, so werdet ihr inne werden, was für Weisheit und Kraft man in dem Creutze CHristi finde, und was für einen grossen Schatz der Seligkeit und des göttlichen Friedes man in der Betrachtung desselben erlange.

"Ach Herr, laß dein lieb Engelein" is a remarkably positive-sounding, tonally emphatic setting, its thirteen-phrase cadences settling only on the three degrees of the E♭ triad, mostly the tonic and dominant. This is in keeping with the eschatological anticipation with which it ends. It is worth mentioning, nevertheless, that in its first phrase Bach, exceptionally for all his harmonizations of this melody, gives special emphasis to the word "lieb" in the harmonic coloring. That is, above the bass tone b♭ he assigns the tenor a d♭′ above which the soprano and alto sing a♭′ and f′ on the beat, resolving them immediately to g′ and e♭′ respectively—that is as a double appoggiatura effect. Nevertheless, very briefly we hear a B-flat-minor seventh chord as a reminder of the importance of love in the Johannine conception of the Passion and of God's plan. In the second of the two *Stollen* this detail sounds to the believer's reference to the body in the grave ("den Leib in sein *Schlaf*kämmerlein"), the momentary very expressive darkening of the harmony lending the phrase a clear reminder of the physical framework in which the believer's eschatological hopes are voiced.

{8}

The *Theologia Crucis* and the Passion's Symbolic Structure

Like other great religious artworks, such as Leonardo's *Last Supper*, Bach's *St. John Passion* is embedded in a dense web of historical, theological, and artistic intentions, impossible, perhaps, to fully disentangle, and extending far beyond the "design" that can be attributed to the composer and seen to reflect his immediate surroundings. It demands, as does Leonardo's *Il Cenacolo*, investigation in terms of what Leo Steinberg calls a "duplex" meaning, that is, as an artwork centered on theological (even abstract) as well as on affective, structural, and dramatic-psychological qualities.[1] In the *St. John Passion* this duplex quality reflects the interaction of theological and artistic sides to John's Gospel, which are not, of course, separate from one another. Like Leonardo's masterpiece, the *St. John Passion* is an enormously excogitated work, projecting simultaneously elements of great dramatic intensity and affective power along with others that are highly ordered, as if imposed from without, or "above," in what many would consider to be "inaudible" ways. The symmetrical key scheme outlined in figures 4.1 and 4.2 in chapter 4 is the most outstanding, and for some the most controversial, of the latter qualities. In the structural and theological overlapping and dovetailing, the design of the Passion perfectly illustrates the qualities of *nexus, ordo,* and *relatio* that Bach's contemporary, the theologian Johann Jacob Rambach, associated with the analogy of faith, the foremost concept in the unity and interrelatedness of scripture, and whose highest level, in Rambach's view, was the concept of symmetry. In fact, the themes to be taken up in this chapter are interwoven particularly closely in the case of the *St. John Passion*. From the theological standpoint their center is the theology of the cross, or *theologia crucis*.

In Lutheran discussions of the cross one of the most commonly encountered themes is the *Äergernis* (vexation, hostility, opposition) that it provokes in nonbelievers. Usually coupled with reason, which is nearly always viewed very pejora-

---

[1] Leo Steinberg, *Leonardo's Incessant Last Supper* (New York: Zone Books, 2001), 38ff.

tively, *Äergernis* may be presented as something that believers themselves have always to be on the watch for, as in Cantata 186, *Ärgre dich, o Seele, nicht*; but it is much more likely to be associated with the perceived opponents of Lutheran Christianity, most often the Jews, particularly in the Passion. Its thrust—hostility toward those who hold different beliefs from ours—is often the opposite of the values we hope to embody in our own lives. Nowadays the Gospel of John, and by extension Bach's *St. John Passion*, are considered to embody qualities of antagonism that run decidedly contrary to our aspirations toward global harmony, and that have, we hope, lessened substantially since Bach's time, owing in part to the much higher degree of interaction among diverse peoples and beliefs in our own age. In the introduction I cited Woodrow Wilson to the effect that investigation of the past should not hold up a yardstick to the past, should not view it in a condescending manner. This is more difficult than the mere words indicate, for in many aspects of our lives, including moral and religious ones, we have no desire or capacity to return to the beliefs of past ages. That is not entirely the issue, however; and it might be argued that we have our own versions of *Ärgernis*, which extend to a far wider range of ideas than religious ones. The meaning of the cross in Lutheranism is hardly likely to be thought of at all in such contexts. Nevertheless, this does not mean that what it meant for many believers of Bach's time has been overcome by our belief in the greater "reasonableness" of our own time, with respect to religious tolerance. As historians we have an obligation to understand the past as accurately as possible, which means treating it on its own terms, no matter how much they conflict with our own, and not, paradoxically, to get stuck on the slippery slope of Wilson's "condescension," itself a form of *Ärgernis*. The reader will encounter, perhaps more than in the foregoing discussions, ideas that may render the suspension of disbelief difficult or impossible. I advance them as the closest I can come to historical accuracy (including, of course, speculative theories).

Determinism, Descent, and Ascent

It is clear that the interpretation of John's Passion narrative by the foremost Lutheran theologians of Bach's time and before was an immensely deterministic one. This determinism, however, was not that of automatic natural processes, of a universe in which God set the clock, then removed himself from the picture. Rather, God's presence and intervention in history were ubiquitous, his controlling hand always at work, although no one in the physical world but Jesus could know the intent and purpose, the plan behind actions and events in the world. Rambach's remark that the entire trial of Jesus was controlled by God's foreordained decision applies to the Passion as a whole.

John's Gospel affords many opportunities to bring out this theme, especially in his emphasizing at the outset of the narrative, and again before Jesus's "Es ist vollbracht," that Jesus knew what would take place beforehand and carried it out to the letter. John's various references to what God gave Jesus directly allude to it as well. This quality runs throughout that Gospel, and August Hermann Francke seizes every possible opportunity to bring it out, emphasizing and even amplifying what he perceives as John's particular concerns: Jesus's foreknowledge of events to come, those events as the fulfillment either of his predictions earlier in the Gospel, or of OT foretellings, and the broader theme of God's foreordaining the events of the Passion and the presence of his "hand" (or "finger") in those events. The protagonists in the narrative not only carry out actions unwittingly but even, in some instances, against their true intentions. Thus, the soldiers' casting lots for Jesus's robe, giving him vinegar to drink, placing the inscription over the cross, and piercing his side were all carried out in complete ignorance of scripture, solely to realize God's plan, foreordained in heaven. David, in writing Psalm 22, prefigured the events of Jesus's Passion, because the Holy Spirit caused him to see "in the Spirit" far into the future. Pilate was unable to act according to either his conscience or his inclinations because of God's higher power. Joseph and Nicodemus looked after Jesus's burial, rather than Peter or John, because God ordained that in this instance men whose faith was weak rather than strong should now come forth openly and glorify his name. Not only did Jesus voluntarily undergo the events of the Passion, even though he could at any point bring them to a halt or turn them in an entirely different direction, but also his death and resurrection were the *means of resurrection* for those who had died centuries earlier. Thus even time had no single inevitable or absolute direction, no "arrow"; God, who existed outside of time, controlled it as well.

In Lutheran thought determinism of this kind was rooted, of course, in the belief that scripture, as the record of God's dealings with humanity, above all his plan for its salvation was a unity, dictated to its various human authors in diverse circumstances and across eons of human history by the Holy Spirit. As history, scripture could be interpreted according to the methods used for other historical texts; but as God's plan for salvation, it transcended such an approach, since its purpose was to instill faith. Interpreted according to the analogy of faith, scripture, therefore, in Luther's view, possessed external and internal "clarity," the former objective and the latter subjective, in the sense that it was given by the Holy Spirit. All scripture, both Old and New Testaments, pointed to Christ, its true subject matter, either as prophecy (OT) or fulfillment of prophecy (NT). And it was its own interpreter, self-contained and understandable according to the "signs" or "types" of "literal-prophetic" interpretation, Luther's substitute for the four senses of traditional hermeneutics.[2]

The concept of the unity of scripture involved an enormous degree of antithesis and resolution, the principle according to which even the most adverse physical

---

[2] See Althaus, *Theology of Martin Luther*, 72–102; Heinrich Bornkamm, *Luther and the Old Testament*, trans. Eric W. Gritsch and Ruth C. Gritsch, ed. Victor I. Gruhn, 87–101 (Philadelphia: Fortress Press, 1974).

events came to serve God's larger purposes, which transcended human understanding. And in pointing to Christ as its sole subject, scripture led directly to the cross as both the instrument of the fulfillment of God's plan for the redemption of humanity and also the symbol of antithesis and reversal of meaning between physical events and their salvific meaning. The cross was therefore a symbol for the disparity between God's all-determining will and human expectations, embodying the twofold meaning of adversity in this world and the hope of salvation in the next. All the principal ideas of Lutheranism—patience in adversity through the willing acceptance of suffering, justification through faith rather than works, "conformity" to Christ, the roles of law and gospel as instruments of God's "alien" and "proper" work, and the like—are expressions of what Luther called the only true theology, the *theologia crucis*, which was not to be contained within the limits of human reason, centered as it was on the false *theologia gloriae*.

The reader may well ask to what extent we may relate such beliefs to Bach, given the age in which he lived. And the answer is inevitably a complex one, since the Enlightenment had by his time spread throughout Europe, including even such bastions of Lutheran orthodoxy as Leipzig. And Bach's music, while retaining countless aspects of the past, was in other respects the most advanced of its time (though not the most progressive, in the sense of the most up-to-date styles). This very sense of dualism may well be its most advanced quality. The surface/depth metaphor that ruled much of nineteenth-century thought, and that continues to dominate much of our own, hardly permits us, however, to conclude that one particular aspect of Bach's work—his adherence to Lutheran orthodoxy—constitutes either its "appearance" or its "essence," in the language of a later time. It is not obvious that as a musician Bach was one thing, and as a servant of the beliefs of his employers another. Nevertheless, that view, which draws greatly from the nineteenth-century idea of "absolute" music, is probably a widespread one. I once participated in a seriously conducted doctoral oral examination on the first movement of Cantata 77 (*Du sollt Gott, deinen Herren lieben*), in which its treatment of the chorale melody in an augmentation canon, its numerological features, its modal qualities, and its text setting were all set aside for the purpose of limiting discussion to "the piece *itself*—how the notes work." Although an extreme instance, it is not isolated or entirely untypical of much contemporary analysis. Where exactly to draw the line between what is essential and what merely superficial is not at all self-evident.

In considering Bach's relationship to Lutheran orthodoxy, we may have the lingering feeling that, if his music is truly universal (if we can say that), then it must be closer to our own beliefs than it appears. Beneath its obeisance must lie an enormous degree of self-determination, at least where musical notes are concerned. When we witness Bach underlining passages in his "Calov Bible" that advocate leaving worldly matters in God's hand, we cannot be certain whether to interpret them as the direct expression of religious belief or the record of his struggles in Leipzig, the frustrated dealings of a man of great ability with his unappreciative contemporaries. That the latter was real enough is evident from other documents.

The two are not, of course, necessarily mutually exclusive. For the sake of indicating the resonance between such passages and the theological views that underlie much of the design of works such as the *St. John Passion*, I will cite a few of a much larger number:

> God prescribes, carves out, calculates, and arranges everything for us and thus explains his will, how He wants to be respected by us; therefore in matters of religion we should presume and do nothing without his revealed word.
>
> Even if all men on earth should tear themselves apart, God will not let them set the clock–the kings, princes, and masters on earth. He will set the clock himself. We should not tell him what occurs, he will tell us.
>
> [N]o one can carry out plans how and when they want, unless the hour has come that they intend to place before God's timing. . . . Just as no man can be certain at what hour a child will be born or die, thus should we say: Lord God, the highest governance is with you, my life and death are in your hands.
>
> The Lord God has given every man his hour and his measure for our lives and our deaths, all our endeavors, all our labor and work that we perform from our first breath to our last. . . . It is already decided in God what shall become of each man—his name, his entire being on earth—from the first moment to the last. . . . Since the book and register of our lives is already written and closed in God, what good is it for us to fly about with our thoughts and for anyone to aim higher than what God has given him, . . . Why do we torment ourselves with our thoughts when future matters are not for a moment in our power? Thus we should be content with the manifest gifts which God has provided and we should commend everything to God, who alone knows and governs both the present and future.
>
> God however has everything firmly before his eyes, the present is ever before him and the future is equally certain with him. . . . all this happens because we do not know the time that God determines, and we can neither impede nor alter it. [3]

Among Bach's vocal works the most outstanding instance of his mirroring such ideas is probably the *Actus Tragicus* (Cantata 106, *Gottes Zeit ist die allerbeste Zeit*), in which the concept of "God's time" is expressed at the outset in terms of God's control over life, history and death ("in ihm leben weben und sind wir, so lange er will. In ihm sterben wir zu rechter Zeit, wenn er will" [God's time is the very best time; in him we live, move and have our being, so long as he wills it. In him we die at the appropriate time, if he wills it]). After that the cantata mirrors the structure

[3] All excerpts are cited from *The Calov Bible of J. S. Bach*, ed. Howard H. Cox, with translations by Ellis Finger (Ann Arbor: UMI Research Press, 1985), 418, 424–45, 427, 430, 435–36.

of scripture in all its dimensions, historico-chronological, external/internal, and above all as a unity centered on Christ. At the center it allegorizes the faith experience as the coming of Christ to the individual via the working of scripture and the believer's acceptance of God's will, symbolized in the word from the cross; and at the end it refers to God's time in terms of the central concept of Lutheran eschatology, the "sleep of death." The *Actus Tragicus* projects the same sense of God's control of human events that we have found in Francke's lectures. Despite their differences, behind Francke's lectures, the structure of the *Actus Tragicus* and the design of the *St. John Passion*, lies a single set of ideas.

Quite often, in Francke's commentaries, we perceive several different interpretative processes at work simultaneously. In the opening scene of the Passion, for example, he notes that the arresting party had to seek out and ask for Jesus, despite the fact that his identity must have been known to them, and that John took pains to record Judas's standing by him. His explanation—that they were struck blind by God, as were the men of Sodom at Lot's door (Gen 19:11) and the Syrians who warred against Israel in the time of Elisha (2 Kings 6:18)—covers not only scriptural prefiguration and God's intervention, Jesus's *Herrlichkeit* and voluntary acceptance of the Passion (the main theme in his view), but also the well-known Johannine oppositions of light and darkness and worlds "above" and "below."[4] The latter theme emerged from the fact that the arresting party drew back and fell to the ground, which Francke interpreted as their recognizing in Jesus the judge of his Second Coming.[5] These themes belong, of course, to the considerable array of interrelated "symbolic" themes that run through John's Gospel, characterizing its unique and unified literary style. And among them the one that for many modern scholars is foremost and that underlies the opposition of Jesus's *Herrlichkeit* and *Erniedrigung* is what Rudolph Bultmann described as Jesus's "descent/ascent" character. Bultmann identified this theme as the necessary starting point for investigation of the Gospel in general, emphasizing its relation to gnostic descending/ascending redeemer myths as a pattern used, and in the process demythologized, by the evangelist to set Jesus apart from all others.[6] That is, it had a Christological

---

[4] Francke, *Oeffentliche Reden*, 9; Rambach (*Betrachtungen über das gantze Leiden Christi*, 144) gives exactly the same explanation of the arresting party's being struck with blindness, perhaps taking it over directly from Francke, but adding (145) that Jesus, rather than using his adversaries' blindness to take flight, restored their sight, so that the situation was "ganz anders" than with Elisha.

[5] Francke, *Oeffentliche Reden*, 10:

> aber hier ist nun auch ein Blick seiner Herrlichkeit in seiner Allmacht, welche er durch dies Wort beweiset, da er zu ihnen saget: **Ich bin's.** Welche Majestät müßte mit diesen Worten ihnen in die Augen leuchten? Was für ein Schrecken mußte sie dabey überfallen, daß sie zurücke wichen, und zu Boden fielen. Gewiß, diß war ein Vorspiel des jüngsten Gerichts, da er als ein Richter der Lebendigen und der Todten mit seinem Anblick die Gottlosen erschrecken, . . .

[6] Rudolf Bultmann, "Die Bedeutung der neuerschlossenen mandäischen und manichäischen Quellen für das Verständnis des Johannesevangeliums," *ZNW* 24 (1925): 100–146; Bultmann, "Johanneische Schriften und Gnosis," *OLZ* 43 (1940): 150–75. Both articles are reprinted in Bultmann, *Exegetica*

purpose, which in comparison to gnostic descent/ascent redeemer myths was not concerned so much with *what* was revealed by the "hero" but rather with that it was to him alone that the pattern applied. It, therefore, belonged with the other symbolic devices in John, such as Jesus's signs and "I am" sayings, and the literary devices of the discourses, as confirmation of his divine identity.

Many other scholars have taken up this theme in various forms, usually identifying it as that of worlds "above" and "below" (as described by Jesus in Jn 8:23: "Ye are from beneath; I am from above: ye are of this world; I am not of this world"), a division that is used to support a wide variety of Johannine antitheses (light/darkness; truth/falsehood; good/evil, and the like). It gives John's realized eschatology its particular force: that salvation and judgment take place in the present as the result of the response of either faith or unbelief in the encounter with Jesus. Jesus's identity is therefore the crucial point. Thus Wayne A. Meeks in a study devoted to the meaning of *anabasis/katabasis* patterns in John, points out that "the references to descent and ascent are introduced into the middle of things in John as explanations of something else. *The motif belongs exclusively to discourse, not to narrative.* [italics original] In John . . . it is used exclusively to identify Jesus . . . as the stranger *par excellence*."[7] Similarly, Stephen S. Smalley remarks:

> In the Fourth Gospel Jesus not only "descends" to earth and "ascends" to heaven; he is also represented as ascending "where he was before." In other words, the ascension is "built in" to every part of John's theological line. The earthly life and life-giving ministry of Jesus presuppose, in John's view, both his divine origin (before the incarnation) and his exalted destiny (after the resurrection); and with all three—the origin, life and destiny of Christ—John is deeply concerned. This is the reason for the theological "overlapping" in the Fourth Gospel. . . . For John the act of revelation in Christ shades inevitably into his glorification. There is no mention in this Gospel of the transfiguration as a separate event because the "glory," the transfigured nature, of Jesus is to be seen—by the eye of faith—at all times. Likewise the cross and indeed every part of the self-giving ministry of Jesus constantly imply his exaltation as well as pointing towards it.[8]

That Jesus ascends to "where he was before," and that his earthly existence is to be viewed in that light, is, of course, a highly deterministic outlook, one that is expressed in Bach's *St. John Passion* right from the beginning. The last two sentences of the passage just cited correspond to the prayer of the middle section of "Herr,

---

(Tübingen: Mohr, 1967), 55–104 and 230–54. Raymond Brown discusses the qualities in question as the "vertical" and "horizontal" views of God's salvific action, pointing out the many instances of the former along with those of the latter and concluding that "the Johannine view of salvation is both vertical and horizontal." See Brown, *Gospel According to John* I–XII, cxv–cxvi.

[7] Wayne A. Meeks, "The Man from Heaven in Johannine Sectarianism." *Journal of Biblical Literature* 91, no. 1 (March 1972): 44–72; see esp. 50.

[8] Stephen S. Smalley, *John Evangelist and Interpreter*, 237.

unser Herrscher": that Jesus's "transfigured nature" be perceived through faith *at all times*, including the crucifixion. This is the meaning behind Bach's treatment of the "Jesus of Nazareth" choruses. The unusually symbolic character of John's Gospel, which extends to the structure and meaning of the Gospel as a whole, is directed toward the cross as the instrument of Jesus's "exaltation"—his "lifting up" or *Verherrlichung*—the greatest of Jesus's symbolic "signs." This is the root of the connection between "Herr, unser Herrscher" and "Es ist vollbracht"; it is bound up with Jesus's descent/ascent character, his coming from above and oneness with the Father, to whom he ultimately returns.[9]

It is necessary to point out that in speaking of themes such as light and darkness, worlds above and below, we are following tendencies in the literary analysis of biblical texts that emerged along with Enlightenment hermeneutics after Bach's time. In the second half of the eighteenth century the focus of biblical scholarship shifted, gradually at first, but decisively, away from belief in the unity of scripture as God's word dictated to its writers (not truly authors) by the Holy Spirit and toward literary and historical themes, the legacy of present-day biblical interpretation.[10] It is rare to find, in pre-Enlightenment hermeneutics, themes such as those just mentioned discussed as characteristics of the evangelist's literary style, *Sitz im Leben*, and the like. The obverse of this focus, is that nowhere in the modern commentaries on John just cited or in many others, do we find reference to what was the greatest concern of the Passion in seventeenth- and eighteenth-century Lutheranism: the meaning, or "use" of the Passion for the contemporary believer. The older Lutheran theologians preferred to treat scripture in very concrete terms and always in terms of its unity as the word of God and its significance in the present. The themes in question were recognized not primarily as literary tropes but as oppositions whose force resided *in their concrete immediate manifestations* and their spiritual impact on the contemporary believer. The descent/ascent character of Jesus's life and work was, in fact, a central expression of the aforementioned "use" of the Passion in that tradition. That it was widely viewed as the counterpart to the fall of humanity in the garden of Eden and its restoration through the cross hardly needs any comment. That story underlies countless interpretations, such as Francke's reminder that the soldiers' dividing Jesus's clothes was because Jesus was crucified naked, thereby taking Adam's shame to the cross with him. Thus Johann Jacob Rambach emphasizes Jesus's "lifting up" along with the opposition of "high" and "low" places as the symbols of Jesus's divinity and *Erniedrigung*, interpreting them tropologically in terms of the believer's journey through the "valleys" of hu-

[9] All this is crystal clear in Francke's lectures on the Passion. In his discussion of Jesus's voluntary death, predicted by him in John 10:18 and completed with his "Es ist vollbracht," Francke remarks (*Oeffentliche Reden*, 148), "Wir aber sollen noch vielmehr die Herrlichkeit und Majestät Christi hierin erkennen, nach dem wir aus dem vorangezogenen Worten Joh. 10, 18. sehen, daß der Herr Jesu solches auch zuvor gesaget, und zugleich auch den Grund der Sache uns angezeiget habe." Here we see the fulfillment of the *Zeig' uns* of "Herr, unser Herrscher."

[10] See Hans W. Frei, *The Eclipse of Biblical Narrative* (New Haven, CT: Yale University Press, 1974).

mility and of tears along the "way to eternity."[11] Heinrich Müller likewise described the understanding of the Gospels as a "mirror" within the heart (*Herzensspiegel*) of how knowledge of Jesus and of ourselves is the foundation of the whole of Christianity. The purpose of such self-knowledge was to strike the believer down, bringing awareness of his nothingness, which led to humility and penitence, then to the knowledge of how the image of God, lost in the garden of Eden, was renewed through the cross.[12] And Francke's discussion of Peter's "fall" and repentance as the model for the believer's following Jesus, and his ending his lecture series with a discussion of how immersion in and reemergence from water in baptism mirrors the pattern of Jesus's burial and resurrection, indicate that for him, as for many others, the descent/ascent pattern of Jesus's life and work must become operative for the believer, the "shape" of his life.

The Credo of the *Mass in B minor*

Perhaps the most direct instance of the descent/ascent character of Jesus's work, and one that is widely interpreted as the central grouping within a larger symmetrical design, is the sequence Et incarnatus/Crucifixus/Et resurrexit in the Credo of the *Mass in B minor*. As Friedrich Smend outlined the structure of the Credo, it comprises a nine-movement complex (3 + 3 + 3), in which the three movements just mentioned are preceded and followed directly by solos (Et in unum Dominum, Jesum Christum and Et in Spiritum Sanctam), and those in turn by two pairings of two movements each, the first of each pair (Credo in unum Deum and Confiteor unum baptisma, respectively) making use of a Gregorian chant cantus firmus, and the second (Patrem omnipotentem and Et exspecto resurrectionem mortuorum) set in modern style and scored for full orchestra.[13] Smend's view is compelling, especially in the centralizing of the Crucifixus, and has been widely cited in the literature. Nevertheless, as Smend recognized, it runs contrary to the grouping of the sections of the Credo as Luther outlined them in his large and small catechisms, which, instead of a 3 + 3 + 3 design, is clearly a 2 + 4 + 3 one (in terms of Bach's movement sequence). And that Bach respects this latter grouping, which expresses the Father, Son, Spirit (or creation, redemption, sanctification) sequence that was fundamental to Luther's understanding, is clear from the music. Bach builds three times toward a climax for chorus and full orchestration with trumpets and kettledrums for the *second*, sixth, and ninth movements, the completion of each of Luther's divisions (Patrem omnipotentem, Et resurrexit, and Et exspecto resurrectionem mortuorum).

---

[11] Rambach, *Betrachtungen über das gantze Leiden Christi*, 5.

[12] Müller, *Evangelischer Herzens-Spiegel*, 2–3.

[13] Smend, "Luther und Bach," in Smend, *Bach-Studien*, 166–73.

This design was firmly in place even in the oldest layer of the autograph score, at which point Bach had not intended to include the Et incarnatus as a separate movement. In that version, the text of the Et incarnatus came at the end of the G-major Domine Deus; and at that point Bach began a turn toward the tonic minor that was completed with the words "et homo factus est." Thus Bach amplified the idea of descent by using the major/minor mode juxtaposition to point up Jesus's divine and human natures. The Crucifixus then began in e and, likewise, featured flat coloring at its final cadence. The return to D for Et resurrexit had, of course, the same triumphant character in all versions. In the older one, the Credo would have encompassed eight movements (2 + 3 + 3) instead of the final nine. Adding the separate Et incarnatus and altering the Domine Deus to take account of that change, Bach made the shift toward the tonic minor coincide with "et propter nos homines et propter nostram salutem," thereby retaining the association of divine versus human in the harmonic coloring. When we look beyond the tonal aspects of the movements to their thematic and figurational characters, the idea of descent/ascent abounds to a degree that requires little comment. From all this it appears that Bach might have revised the movement in order to create the centralized Et incarnatus/Crucifixus/Et resurrexit of Smend's symmetrical interpretation.

Certainly the most dramatic moment in the Credo, however, is the succession of the Confiteor unum baptisma and the Ex exspecto resurrectionem mortuorum, leading to the climactic ending of the Credo. Perhaps to balance the subdominant motion of the G, b, and e of the Domine Deus, Et incarnatus, Crucifixus sequence, Bach turns to the dominant, A, for Et in Spiritum Sanctam, after which he shifts to f♯ for the Confiteor, then to D for the Et exspecto resurrectionem, so that as a whole the keynotes of the final three-movement grouping outline the tones of the tonic triad. Structurally, the return to D is rock solid, completing a pattern of tonal motion for the Credo as a whole (in simplified terms tonic, subdominant, dominant, tonic) that appears in many large-scale works of his (including several of the cantatas for spring 1725; see part 3 of this book).[14] But within this large-scale design, in m. 120 of the Confiteor, on the word "peccatorum" (of *sins*), Bach changes the tempo to *Adagio*, altering the bass motion and moving toward the sound of flat-minor keys again. Leading this to the dominant of D, on "mortuorum," in m. 137, Bach introduces the famous enharmonic passage that forms a transition to the "et exspecto." By presenting the complete text "et exspecto resurrectionem mortuorum" in two forms, Bach first emphasizes the idea of death ("mortuorum"), then, with the return to D, that of resurrection. The transformational tonally shifting character of the enharmonic passage suggests the disintegration of the physical

[14] In this context I intend "subdominant" to include the relative minor and supertonic keys as well. In the Bach cantatas tonal "descent" from the tonic through the relative minor and subdominant to the supertonic is a fairly common device, underlying even the entire tonal plans of some cantatas (e.g., 136 and 179) and a significant part of others (e.g., 94).

body in the grave, after which the music suddenly snaps back into sharp tonal focus by introducing a low-register augmented-sixth chord (suggestive of D minor) to set up the final return to D major and the electrifying entrance of the trumpets, as if from above.

This passage has been described elsewhere by many authors. The point of the transition, that baptism (Confiteor unum baptisma) reenacts symbolically the death and resurrection of Christ, gives this moment a special, cumulative meaning in terms of the three-division interpretation of the Credo. That is, the final return of D for "et exspecto resurrectionem mortuorum et vitam venturi saeculi, Amen" expresses the believer's own death and resurrection in the terms of those of Jesus. The death/resurrection sequence of the middle segment of the Credo is now mirrored in the immersion/reemergence act of baptism. August Hermann Francke's comments on this theme in the last of his *St. John Passion* lectures are worth citing in full; Francke begins with Paul:

> On this Paul speaks quite emphatically (Rom 6:3--4): "*Know ye not that so many of us as were baptized into Jesus Christ were baptized into his death? / Therefore we are buried with him by baptism into death: that like as Christ was raised up from the dead by the glory of the Father, even so we also should walk in newness of life.*"

And, continuing, he describes the basis of the analogy and its meaning:

> Those who were baptized by John in the Jordan, or also afterwards in other rivers, they stepped down into the water (see Acts 8:38). And were then like the dead, who are placed in the earth and buried. Thus Paul says now that it is not only a fact that in baptism there is an external image of the burial of the dead; but also that through baptism, which Christ instituted, and ordained as the entry into his kingdom, we are buried with Christ, in this, namely, that we are baptized into his death, or that for us there, the fruit and power of his death are dedicated, so that it is just as if we ourselves had satisfied the righteousness of God regarding our sins, as a result of which it has no more claims on us, as it now demands nothing more from Christ, since he sacrificed himself to God for us on the cross, and now is laid in the grave. Here was now a complete stillness, pure rest, nothing but Sabbath, a peaceful awaiting of the resurrection. In the same way in baptism, whose power remains for us as long as we remain in faith, we are received into the peace of God, where there is forgiveness of sin, justification and blessedness, and we, as we believe, enter into, according to Hebrews 4:2, the same rest. Christ, our head is buried, and we, the members, are all buried with him. He has brought his members to rest and peace with him. Here in the still spirit of peace the noble fruit of the death of Christ will be enjoyed. Blessed are we that we regard ourselves to have died to sin through the death of Christ, that it has no power to make us restless in the conscience, to seek anything further from

> us, nor to dare assert its former dominion over us, but that we who are buried with Christ have now become freed from the wrath of God and now may awaken with Christ through the power of the Holy Spirit and change into a new life just as he is awakened through the glory of the Father, and what he brings to life God brings to life.[15]

Behind Francke's discussion lies exactly the same idea as that behind Luther's tropological explanation of the destruction and restoration of Jerusalem. The descent/ascent pattern of baptism is the literal-historical or physical meaning, whereas its allegorical dimension is as a symbolic reenactment of the death, burial, and resurrection of Christ. Its tropological aspect is expressed in the affective (or spiritual) character of the progression from meditation on death to what Francke calls the "stillen Geist des Glaubens"—the outcome of the believer's understanding death as the outcome of God's wrath against sin (embodied in the law) and the comfort (*Trost*, the "edle Frucht" mentioned by Francke) that arises from acceptance of the Gospel. It passes over into the eschatological sense, which is embodied in the believer's understanding of Jesus's resurrection as the source of the believer's new life of faith and the anticipation of the ultimate fulfillment of her hopes for life with God after death.

---

[15] Francke, *Öeffentliche Reden*, 168–170: "

Hiervon redet Paulus gar nachdrücklich Rom. 6, 3.4. **Wisset ihr nicht / daß alle / die wir in JEsum CHrist getauft sind / die sind in seinen Tod getauft. So sind wir je mit ihm begraben durch die Taufe in den Tod / auf daß / gleich wie Christus ist auferwecket von den Todten / durch die Herrlichkeit des Vaters / also sollen auch wir in einem neuen Leben wandeln. . . .** Die von Johanne im Jordan, oder auch nachhero in andern Flüssen getaufet wurden, die stiegen hinab in das Wasser (siehe Apost. Gesch. 8, 38.) Und waren darin gleich einem Todten, der hinab in die Erde gelassen und begraben wird. So saget denn nun Paulus, das sey nicht allein die Sache, daß in der Taufe ein solch äusserlich Bild der Begrabung eines Todten sey, sondern durch die Taufe, die Christus eingesetzet, und sie zum Eingang in sein Gnaden-Reich geordnet, werden wir mit Christo beygraben, in dem nemlich, daß wir auf seinen Tod getaufet werden, oder daß uns da die Frucht und Kraft seines Todes zugeeignet wird, so, daß es eben so viel ist, als wenn wir selbst für unsere Sünden der Gerechtigkeit GOttes ein Genügen gethan hätten, folglich dieselbe nun keine Beforderung mehr an uns hat, wie sie an Christo nun nichts mehr gefordert, nachdem er sich am Creutze für uns GOtte geopfert, und nun ins Grab geleget ward. Hier war nun eine lautere Stille, eitel Ruhe, nichts denn Sabbath, ein friedsames Erwarten der Auferstehung. Auf gleiche Weise sind wir in der Taufe, deren Kraft uns bleibet, so lange wir im Glauben bleiben, in der Frieden GOttes eingenommen. Da ist Vergebung der Sünde, Gerechtigkeit und Seligkeit, und wir, die wir glauben, gehen ein, nach Ebr. 4, 2. in dieselbige Ruhe. CHristus unser Haupt ist begraben, und wir, die Glieder, sind samt ihm begraben. Er hat seine Glieder mit zur Ruhe und zum Frieden gebracht. Hier soll in dem stillen Geiste des Glaubens die edle Frucht des Todes CHristi genossen werden. Wohl uns, so wir uns durch den Tod Christi der Sünden abgestorben zu seyn achten, daß sie kein Recht, uns im Gewissen zu beunruhigen, mehr an uns suchen, noch die vorige Herrschaft ihr über uns anmassen dürfe; sondern daß wir als die Begrabenen mit CHristo nun vom Zorn GOttes los und Genossen seiner Liebe worden sind, und nun samt CHristo auferstehen mögen in der Kraft des Heiligen Geistes, und in einem neuen Leben wandeln, gleichwie er auferwecket ist durch die Herrlichkeit des Vaters, und was er lebet, GOtte lebet."

Underlying Bach's division of the Credo into three large movement groupings is the concept of God's *Rath*, as embodied in the image of Jesus as the descending/ascending redeemer that John presents so forcefully. The first grouping, Credo in unum Deum and Patrem omnipotentem, since it deals with God the Father, remains in D major.[16] The second turns to the subdominant, G, for Et in unum Dominum Jesum Christum, then to b for the Et incarnatus and to e for the Crucifixus. It moves in the subdominant key region, an analog of Jesus's descent, which reaches its lowest point in the Crucifixus. It then returns to D for the Et resurrexit, after which the next division moves "up" to the dominant, A, as if to describe the tropological character of the ending of the Credo in terms of the descent of the Spirit (Et in Spiritum Sanctam), mirrored in the descending major triad. At the same time, the return to D through the f♯ of the Confiteor, involves within it a descent/ascent motion that mirrors the pattern of Jesus's death and resurrection. The divine/human, descent/ascent character of Jesus's work is mirrored in the minor triad G–b–e, formed by the movement keys of the part of the Credo that deals with the historical narrative of Jesus's incarnation, death, and burial, whereas, after the D of his resurrection, the major triad, A–f♯–D, mirrors the impact of those events on the believer, beginning with the coming of the Holy Spirit, then turning to baptism, which leads to an expression of the believer's eschatological hopes (Et exspecto resurrectionem mortuorum in D). The close relationship of this chronological, trinitarian design with the eras of salvation history and the senses of hermeneutics needs no further comment.

The motion to the three D-major climaxes, all for full orchestra with trumpets and kettledrums, is so outstanding in the auditory experience of the Credo that it threatens to render the symmetrical view—the image of God's plan—into a mere paper design. However, it is not necessary to make a decision in favor of either interpretation, because, as the *Actus Tragicus* clearly indicates, Bach was perfectly capable of distinguishing between two different aspects of structure, the one (symmetry) forming an image of God's order, the Trinity, the eras of salvation history, the principles of scripture interpretation, and the like, while the other mirrored the faith experience of the believer in affective terms that involved a greater sense of the temporal aspect, of directed forward motion, climactic points, and so forth. The mirroring of the believer's faith experience (the tropological sense) of necessity follows the mirroring of the objective dimension of scripture.[17]

---

[16] Bach's setting of the Gregorian intonation, Credo in unum Deum, begins and ends as if in A, but, as the sevenfold sequence of entries, all on A and D, indicate, the tonality is predominantly D; the Patrem omnipotentem is entirely in D.

[17] That is, the central movement complex of the *Actus Tragicus*—beginning with the fugue "Es ist der alte Bund: Mensch du musst sterben" and continuing with the soprano solo "Ja komm, Herr Jesu" and the untexted instrumental chorale—ends with reduction of the instruments and voices to the unaccompanied soprano solo: "Ja komm, Herr Jesu." This is then followed by an empty measure with a pause, marking the division between the chronologically presented message of death of the preceding movements and the believer's acceptance of death as God's will in the alto solo "In deine Hände befehl' ich meinen Geist."

Thus, after the centralized "historical" or "objective" depiction of the eras of scripture in the *Actus Tragicus*, the believer, in "In deine Hände," expresses her faith in words spoken by Jesus from the cross, where they were a quotation from Psalm 31 (a unifying of the three eras of "salvation history," directly following their separate presentations in the fugue-solo-chorale complex). In the Credo the duplication of Jesus's historical death/resurrection dynamic in the spiritual, symbolic shape of baptism forms a second descent/ascent motion in the structure. At such points the shape of the believer's life converges with what Luther called the "summary" of scripture. In the *Actus Tragicus* the biblical "stages" depicted in the OT movement sequence, are experienced "according to our own history, internally and spiritually." And in the Credo the history is Jesus's incarnation, death, and resurrection, which is mirrored allegorically in the descent/ascent pattern of baptism, and tropologically as the "shape" of the believer's faith experience, his "conformity" (*Gleichförmigkeit*) to Christ in his suffering and resurrection. In the Credo the symmetrical and the descent/ascent dimensions, although distinguishable, are not mutually exclusive, nor do they have to exactly coincide; rather, they exist in a kind of contrapuntal interaction of the audible and the inaudible, of worlds below and above, the human and divine. The former sphere is more closely mirrored in the tonal design or shape, the latter in the plan of symmetry.[18]

What I have just described briefly runs throughout much of Bach's music. In a forthcoming study of the four *Missae Breves* I demonstrate that the descent/ascent (or flat/sharp) dynamic underlies the Gloria in all four instances and derives from very similar designs in the cantatas from which they were parodied. The association is of the "shape" of the Gloria as descent from the sphere of God (Gloria in excelsis Deo contrasted with Et in terra pax in the opening movement), to that of sinful humanity in need of God's mercy (the Qui tollis peccata mundi, miserere nobis), and back (the Cum Sancto Spirito in Gloria Dei Patris, Amen). As in the Credo, the descent is from God above, through Jesus and the incarnation to his work on earth, then back to God in glory.[19] It is mirrored in the *Soli Deo Gloria* (*SDG*) and *Jesu Juva* (*JJ*) inscriptions that Bach placed on many of his manuscripts. The conceptual relationship of such designs to the "shape" of the *Actus Tragicus* is expressed in the latter work as the idea that the believer lives, moves, and has being *in* God (the E♭ of the opening chorus). Then, after internalizing the message of the law, the inevitability of death as judgment for sin, the believer consigns herself to God in the alto solo "In deine Hände," which is then the beginning of his "ascent" to God (and back to E♭).

[18] In using the terms "audible" and "inaudible," I do not imply that they are absolutely distinct from one another. The terns *sensus* and *ratio*, used by Baroque authors are in many respects better ones.

[19] An extract from this study (Chafe, "Bach and Hypocrisy: Truth and Appearance in Cantatas 136 and 179") appears in *The Century of Bach and Mozart: Perspectives on Historiography, Composition, Theory and Performance*, ed. Sean Gallagher and Thomas Forrest Kelly, 121–43 (Cambridge, MA: Harvard University Press, 2008). As in the Credo the tonal motion in all three of the major-key masses is from the tonic major to the supertonic minor (the Qui tollis) and back.

The choruses of Bach's symbolic trial

To return to the *St. John Passion*: In light of the association of highly ordered designs, especially symmetrical ones, with God's *Rath*, it seems very possible that the complex of ideas that surrounds the opposition of law and gospel in Lutheranism suggested to Bach not only that the trial of Jesus pivot around law and freedom but also that the choruses of Jesus's persecutors, the Romans and the Jews (associated with secular and religious law, respectively), form a reverse symmetry that would in the end articulate something of the predetermined quality of God's plan that Rambach had emphasized in his commentary.[20] For Francke and Rambach, as perhaps for Bach as well, two sources above all lent support for such a view. The first was, of course, John himself; Francke's lectures make clear that these traits are particularly brought out by John.[21] And the second was Luther, who, in many writings, but particularly in *The Bondage of the Will*, argued that human "free" will could only turn to evil; it was therefore not free at all but enslaved by sin. Only by submitting completely to the will of God could human beings attain freedom from sin, death, the devil, and the law. The view of God's *Rath* that runs throughout later Lutheran writings is indebted to Luther in this respect.

In the Part 2 chorus "Wir haben ein Gesetz, und nach dem Gesetz soll er sterben," therefore, Bach has the crowd extol its own bondage to sin, death, and the law, symbolized in a "strict" form, the fugue, and with a theme that perhaps embodies an echo of the initial phrase of the "ten-commandments" chorale, as Friedrich Smend argued. Although that reference is not a close one and might well be called into question, Smend's view that the chorus symbolizes the law by means of its ten fugal entries is convincing, especially in light of other similar instances of Bach's "counting" procedures.[22] And, in fact, not only "Wir haben ein Gesetz" and

---

[20] Werner Breig ("Zu den Turba-Chören von Bachs Johannes-Passion," 88–91) makes a very similar assessment of the role of symmetry in the *turba* choruses. Dürr (*Johann Sebastian Bach's "St. John Passion,"* 104) paraphrases Breig's conclusions: "He construes the order of the turba choruses as an image of St. John's theological position, according to which Jesus arranged his return to the Father in a both systematic and prescient manner, so that his 'enemies, without knowing or wishing it, contribute to the realization of the divine plan of salvation.'" That plan of salvation is, of course, the impetus behind the design of the *Actus Tragicus* and the Credo as well.

[21] And determinism remains a theme of some modern commentaries on John, one that is often resisted. See, for example, Rudolf Bultmann, *Theology of the New Testament*, trans. Kandrick Grobel (New York: Charles Scribner's Sons, 1955), 2:21–26; Robert Kysar, *John, the Maverick Gospel* (Atlanta: John Knox Press, 1976), 58–62. It is sometimes linked to the emphasis on Jesus as pre-existent Logos in the prologue to the gospel, and to the character of the first chapter as summarizing "the entire sweep of salvation history with which it is concerned" (Smalley, *John, Evangelist and Interpreter* [Exeter: Paternoster Press, 1978], 93). Oscar Cullmann (*Christ and Time*, xxii–xxiv) brings out the latter association in response to the belief of some that Luke, not John, is the principal NT source for the idea of salvation history. Cullmann notes that it is "*particularly* in John," not "*even* in John," where redemptive history is to be seen (italics added).

[22] Among those works in which the number 10 figures prominently are Cantata 77, *Du sollt Gott* (first movement), the *Goldberg Variations*, the canons of the *Musical Offering*, the organ *Canonic Varia-*

"Lässest du diesen los" but also the two boundary choruses of the symbolic trial, "Sei gegrüßet, lieber Judenkönig," and "Schreibe nicht: der Juden König, feature ten entries of their themes, even though "Sei gegrüßet" represents the voice of the *Kriegsknechte*, not of the Jews, while "Schreibe nicht" is outside the trial proper and is sung by the high priests. In the case of the other set of paired choruses within the symbolic trial, "Kreuzige ihn" and "Weg, weg mit dem! Kreuzige ihn," "Kreuzige ihn" is sung by the high priests and servants in response to the *Ecce homo* ("Sehet! Welch ein Mensch"), and "Weg, weg" by "the Jews" in response to Pilate's "Sehet! Das ist eurer König." The parallel between the two situations is clear: Pilate brings out Jesus, now dressed in the crown of thorns and purple robe, and presents him to the crowd, first as a man, then as king. Jesus does not speak, but the choruses depicting the crowd are the most rabid of those in the symbolic trial. This time Bach does not set them as fugues, but rather in an unusual manner that also appears to utilize symbolic devices, possibly even numerological ones.[23]

The main body of these two choruses is the twenty-three-and-a-half measures of the first one, which is expanded in the second by the addition of three measures at the beginning. Those three measures, which bear some resemblance to the "Jesus of Nazareth" music, especially in their bass patterns, introduce the words "Weg, weg mit dem" before we hear the "kreuzige ihn" that is shared by both choruses. Otherwise, those measures are formed from two musical ideas that repeat insistently throughout them, especially in the instruments. The first is associated entirely with the rhythm of the word "kreuzige"—an eighth note followed by two sixteenths sounding on every beat. The second idea is a series of slow-moving two-voice suspension-resolution patterns for either soprano and alto or tenor and bass in invertible counterpoint (ex. 8.1). In this form it is reiterated twelve times in immediate succession, after which it appears twice more in voice pairs doubled at the third or sixth. This pairing provides the contrapuntal basis for the entire movement. The suspended dissonances with which it begins may be minor or major sevenths or seconds (the most characteristic form is the major seventh/minor second); and the material that presents the pattern is a descending tetrachord in one voice and a motive often associated with the cross in the other (its contour is that of the theme of the "Lass ihn kreuzigen" choruses of the *St. Matthew Passion*). This pattern is heard throughout the entire movement in both cases, usually with slight overlapping. Against it the rapid "kreuzige" figures sound continually in the instruments and frequently also in the voices of the first of the pair of choruses. In the second of pair the "Weg, weg mit dem" figure sounds in the voices at first and

---

tions on "Vom Himmel hoch," and the organ chorale prelude *Dies sind die heiligen zehn Gebot* from Clavier-übung III.

[23] In both the "Kreuzige ihn" and "Weg, weg mit dem, Kreuzige ihn" choruses the theme (along with its countertheme) appears fourteen times, possibly a reference to the association of the number 14 with Jesus as "Alpha" and "Omega," in response to his being presented both times to the crowd as a mock king.

EXAMPLE 8.1 ***St. John Passion*** *no. 23d, chorus "Weg, weg mit dem," beginning*

EXAMPLE 8.1 (*continued*)

the "kreuzige" figure is limited to the instruments until the fifteenth measure; and some of the rapid "kreuzige" figures are replaced by "Weg, weg mit dem," a relatively easy matter, in light of their relative freedom and more mobile character.

In these details Bach might have had in mind a particular pictorial idea such as that of the depiction of the high priests as more grave and thoughtful, the servants as more impulsive and thoughtless. Or he might have wanted to project a "duplex" meaning, such as that behind the "Jesus of Nazareth" choruses. The slow-moving dissonance-resolution counterpoint exhibits another aspect: it resembles somewhat the pattern of the slow-moving flutes and oboes of "Herr, unser Herrscher," which sound over the sixteenth notes of the choral parts. If Bach meant this to be a meaningful connection, it would have to be that behind "Herr, unser Herrscher" lies the image of the crucified Jesus, and, conversely, behind the "kreuzige" choruses lies the image of Jesus's *Herrlichkeit*. But, like the insistently reiterated patterns of the "kreuzige" choruses, "Herr, unser Herrscher" also has an almost motoric sense of inevitability in the sixteenth-note patterns in particular, a quality that I view as a projection not only of Jesus's majesty but also of God's *vorbedachter Rath*. If this applies to the "Kreuzige" choruses as well, then it must mean that Bach intended that the continual permutation of the contrapuntal idea, its appearing in invertible counterpoint and even in four parts with doubling of the two lines at the third and sixth (twice, and also in invertible counterpoint at the end of the movement) as an allegory of the lack of freedom of Jesus's antagonists, whether Roman soldiers or Jews. As is the case with "Lasset uns den nicht zerteilen," Bach projects a striking sense that events "below" are controlled by God.

That all the choruses of the trial feature music that repeats to different texts suggests that like Pilate, the Jews, the high priests and servants, and the *Kriegsknechte* are all entirely subject to God's predetermining. True freedom, in the Lutheran view, was submission to God's will. Heinrich Müller describes it with the analogy of God as a fisherman who casts out a line with *Himmels-Trost* as the bait.[24] Once this bait is taken by the believer, he is free to move as the fish on the line does through the water. The only freedom of choice is whether to take the bait of God's love. Müller concludes by citing John to the effect that the "highest freedom is the loving service of God." That involves, of course, whether God is understood to be manifested in Jesus. In this light, the kind of freedom exercised by those who deny Jesus's kingship in the trial—Pilate, the Jews, and the *Kriegsknechte*—is freedom from God's love but not from his all-determining will, that is, bondage to sin. Thus the *turba* choruses of the trial articulate a twofold meaning corresponding to John's worlds "below" and "above": the sinful nature of Christ's persecutors, and the redemptive character of God's *Rath*. Locally, events may depict Jesus's *Erniedrigung*, but overall their meaning is just the opposite. An analog of this opposition, perhaps, is that within the central sharp-key segment of Bach's symbolic trial, "Wir haben keinen König denn den Kaiser" is the outcome of tonal motion in the flat direction from the E of "Durch dein Gefängnis"; but within the sequence of five "Jesus of Nazareth" choruses that extend over the much wider course of events that began in the initial scene of the Passion, it represents the completion of a sharpward overall motion. And this is exactly how the relationship of the physical events and their spiritual meaning is described by the major Lutheran theologians of Bach's time. Luther emphasizes this double approach to the understanding of scripture in his well-known and widely published sermons on the Farewell Discourse, especially in his discussion of Jesus's "I am the way, the truth, and the life."[25]

Thus, from one standpoint, the trial of Jesus in Bach's *St. John Passion* pivots around questions of power and agency, worldly or divine, which is indeed the way it has been understood according to post-Enlightenment hermeneutics, and the question of Jesus's identity. Regarding the former, the crucial point for John is that true power comes from above. In his typical either/or fashion, John demands that we resolve the opposition of whether Jesus is the Messiah, king of the Jews, and the Son of God, or a common criminal. If the former, which is of course what John intends us to believe, then his power and kingdom are of the world above, the world of truth, of those who hear Jesus's voice and believe; and the crucifixion is the beginning of his triumphant return to the Father, his "lifting up," predicted at various points throughout the Gospel. In the *St. John Passion* this question begins with Jesus's messianic self-revelatory pronouncement, "Ich bin's." It echoes in his response to Pilate, "Du sagest's. Ich bin ein König," is affirmed in the chorale "O großer König," and is given as the reason for his death in "Wir haben ein Gesetz, und nach

[24] Heinrich Müller, *Geistliche Erquick-Stunden, oder Dreyhundert Hauß- und Tisch-Andachten*. I have used the edition published in Hamburg in 1736. See 28–29.

[25] *Luther's Works*, vol. 24, *Sermons on the Gospel of St. John*, 33–35.

dem Gesetz soll er sterben, *denn er hat sich selbst zu Gottes Sohn gemacht*" and "Schreibe nicht: der Juden König, sondern *daß er gesaget hatte 'Ich bin der Juden König.'*" These and other affirmations or denials of Jesus's identity parallel those of the *St. Matthew Passion*, in particular the abovementioned cadence "denn er hat gesagt: Ich bin Gottes Sohn" and the later avowal "Wahrlich dieser ist Gottes Sohn gewesen." In the *St. John Passion*, the crowd, in insisting on the negative, can have no more real freedom or agency than Pilate; their music has all been heard before, most of it in reverse order, and in something like the opposite key areas. Crying out a worldly interpretation of the law, they are enslaved by sin, their freedom less truly free than Jesus's imprisonment. Francke's remark on Caiphas's seeking the imprisonment and ultimate death of Jesus—"Caiphas meynte es böse zu machen"/ "Gott aber gedachte es gut zu machen"—applies here as well.[26]

In its return to the flat keys in which it began, the final segment of Bach's symbolic trial resolves the antitheses associated with the cross in its middle part (the judgment of crucifixion, especially), meditating on the event (the royal inscription) that expresses, in ironic terms, the opposition between the worldly and salvific meanings of the cross. In contrast, the ongoing motion toward the sharps of "Es ist vollbracht" and "Mein teurer Heiland," in the segment that follows the trial, depicts the meaning of the cross as the instrument of Jesus's "lifting up," fulfilling God's "proper work," the salvation of humanity (the "aller Welt Erlösung" of the dialog). The return to flats reaffirms the framework of the world (below), in which Jesus is crucified and his identity proclaimed ironically via the multiple languages of the inscription. The sharpward motion that follows and leads to "Es ist vollbracht" points to the world above, the direct manifestation of truth.

Bach seems, therefore, to polarize the sharp and flat keys within the design of the symbolic trial and the Passion as a whole (see figs. 4.1 and 4.2, ch. 4), bringing his symbolic trial, and the third of the traditional five *actus* to a powerful point of culmination and closure in the chorale "In meines Herzens Grunde." The event on which "In meines Herzens Grunde" meditates, the royal inscription, is the most outstanding instance of God's reversal of meaning in the Passion. As such, it is the perfect symbol for the *theologia crucis*. I have described the "Nam'" and "Kreuz" of "In meines Herzens Grunde" as a symbolic expression of the correlates for symmetry, chiastic structure (derived from the Greek letter chi (*X*), which begins the name Christ), and cruciform design (derived from the cross), an interpretation that Smend's study implies but does not explicitly state.

---

[26] In the 279th meditation of his *Geistliche Erquick-Stunden* (599) Heinrich Müller cites the scriptural passage on which Francke's remark is based, Joseph's words to his brothers (in Ex 50:20): "Ihr gedachts böse mit mir zu machen / aber Gott gedachts gut zu machen." The context of this and the following meditation 279: "Von der Liebe Gottes im Creutz. Alles gut/ was GOtt thut" and 280: "Von GOttes wunderbahrer Regierung im Creutz. Wunderlich/Weißlich") is that of God's unfathomable working through the cross, for the salvation of humankind.

The meditative movements of Bach's symbolic trial

The segment of the Passion that I see as a symbolic trial, and which is related but not identical to what Friedrich Smend called the *Herzstück*, is indeed a kind of symbolic "core" of the work, a focal point for the antitheses for which John's Gospel is famous, and a design that exhibits a considerable degree of musical unification. It begins and ends in E♭, taking as its point of departure the pronounced shift from Jesus's *Herrlichkeit*, as proclaimed in Jesus's words to Pilate and affirmed in "Ach großer König," to his *Niedrigkeit*, as articulated in Pilate's denial of truth, the release of Barabbas and the scourging, and meditated on in "Betrachte, meine Seele." The beginning A-minor segment of Part 2, while belonging to the trial proper, is separated from the symbolic trial by the tritone span between "Ach großer König" and "Betrachte, meine Seele," so that after the avowal of Jesus's divine identity, the modulation to flat keys rivets the shift of focus in place. Following the violent G-minor narrative of the scourging, the E♭ of "Betrachte, meine Seele" lends the beginning of the symbolic trial the necessary character of meditation on adverse events that are ultimately positive, salvific, in nature. The meditative focus of "Betrachte" and "Erwäge" is entirely on the figure of the suffering Jesus, often associated with the *Ecce homo*. And that visual quality reappears at the end of the symbolic trial in the *Abgesang* of "In meines Herzens Grunde," with the believer's petition for Jesus to appear in the consoling image of the crucifixion ("Erschein mir in dem Bilde, zu Trost in meiner Not, wie du, Herr Christ, so milde dich hast geblüh't zu Tod"). In musical terms, the E♭ movements that form the "boundaries" of the symbolic trial create a sense of enclosure, in which the image of Jesus is central, as it is in "Herr, unser Herrscher."

The tonal motion away from and back to that E♭ is given much of its meaning by the pattern of the repeated *turba* choruses and the point where their reversal and transposition from flat to sharp keys take place. This aspect of Bach's design fairly bristles with theological intent, especially when considered in relation to the role of the meditative movements in confirming the major shifts of tonal region. This is particularly evident in the centralizing of the chorale "Durch dein Gefängnis" directly following the shift to sharps, which it confirms. Likewise, the movement that articulates the return to flat keys in association with the shift of locale to Golgotha, the dialog "Eilt, ihr angefocht'nen Seelen," has enormous significance in its articulating the way of the cross, which is then crystalized in "In meines Herzens Grunde."

I have suggested that the flat/sharp/flat (or ascent/descent) shape of the symbolic trial as a whole might relate to that of the rainbow described in the patterns of Jesus's blood in "Erwäge," a view that may well seem fanciful to many. Whether Bach intended it as such (and we cannot know for sure), there is ample evidence for an underlying set of ideas that renders it plausible. And in my view there is one very striking instance elsewhere in Bach's music of his creating a set of musical patterns

EXAMPLE 8.2 **Clavierübung** *Part 3, duet in E minor, beginning*

that suggest the same set of ideas: the first of the four duets that come toward the end of the third part of the *Clavierübung*, whose first theme describes the most pronounced set of ascent/descent melodic patterns in Bach's music, a perfect image of the rainbow, while its second is the one most widely associated with the cross, as in the Crucifixus of the *Mass in B minor* (ex. 8.2)[27] In themselves and in their contrapuntal combinations the two patterns invite the kinds of associations that were described by Lutheran writers in connection with the rainbow and the cross as signs of God's covenant with humanity at the time of Noah and its fulfillment in the cross of Christ. The placement of textual references to the images of the rainbow and the cross at the beginning and ending of the *St. John Passion*'s symbolic trial suggests that its design might indeed have been conceived in relation to this idea.[28]

---

[27] And, of course, Bach associates rising and falling shapes with God's majesty in themes such as that of Cantata 71, *Gott ist mein König*, and even with worldly glory, such as in the well-known rising whole-tone modulations of the canon of the *Musical Offering*, to which Bach added the inscription in his dedicatory copy "Ascendenteque Modulatione ascendat Gloria Regis" (and as the modulation ascends so may the king's glory). Ascending whole-tone modulations are, of course, increasingly sharp (i.e., C minor, D minor, E minor, etc.), although at some point, presumably with G-sharp minor or A-flat minor, an enharmonic shift to flats must be made.

[28] In my view, the four duets mirror in their styles and key sequence—e, F, G, a—a set of ideas that involve an "eschatological" progression such as appears frequently toward the end of treatises: the highly symmetrical F-major duet deals with the antitheses of the cross, around which its center pivots; the G-major duet mirrors the beatific aspect of the afterlife, the positive eschatological character associated with the pastorale; and the A-minor duet suggests the judgment that is often discussed along with it. The tritone a/E♭ relationship between the last of the duets and the concluding fugue renders the latter, along with the prelude to the collection, a "framing" element. Rambach, for example, calls the rainbow a *Symbolum Christi* (see ch. 6, n. 26), viewing its form as a "half circle" or a "bow without an arrow," because in Christ God put down the arrows of his wrath; its blood-red color was the "image of divine justice, according to which no sins could be forgiven without the pouring forth of [Christ's]

Within Lutheran thought God's salvific activity reaches its point of fulfillment in the Passion of Jesus, and God's greatest "sign" is therefore the cross (named the "Zeichen Jesu" in the first movement of Cantata 12, *Weinen, Klagen, Sorgen, Zagen*), the agency, in John's account of Jesus's ignominious death and his triumphant ascent, or lifting up (*Erhöhung* or *Verherrlichung*). The double meaning of the cross underlies all the aforementioned oppositions that run throughout the poetic texts of the *St. John Passion*, especially those that articulate the benefit of Jesus's sufferings for the contemporary believer. In the theology of Bach's time (and the texts of some Bach cantatas) the cross was described as a scandal or an "offense" (*Ärgernis*) to human reason, especially for the Jews, who had contrary expectations of how the Messiah would be revealed. The cross was, therefore, a symbol of reversal, both of the immediate meaning of events (simultaneous reversal) and in the temporal (successive) sense of its creating a new life for the believer. Many Bach cantatas depict this progression, often by means of the pattern of ascending keys, such as that of Cantata 12, and sometimes with highly provocative musical gestures that describe the role of the cross in the life of faith. In Cantata 60, *O Ewigkeit, du Donnerwort*, for example, the anomalous D♯ that causes the initial phrase of the chorale "Es ist genung" to move strikingly in the sharp direction and thereby to bring about the shift of the tonal center of the cantata from D to A is such a gesture, enabling what the preceding recitative describes as a "glance" into the joy of eternal life.[29]

The idea of reversal that permeated the meaning of the cross was, as Friedrich Smend showed convincingly, perfectly expressed in the kind of symmetrical reversal associated with chiastic or cruciform structure.[30] In order to pursue its meaning, consider the imagery of the meditative movements of Bach's symbolic trial: the arioso "Betrachte" and aria "Erwäge" with which it begins, the chorale "Durch dein Gefängnis," at its center, the dialog, "Eilt, ihr angefocht'nen Seelen," which introduces its final division, and the chorale "In meines Herzens Gründe," with which it ends. "Betrachte, meine Seele" occupies a special place in the Passion by virtue of its urging the believer to meditation on Jesus's physical sufferings, which begin with the scourging. The arioso, however, meditates on the crown of thorns, after which the aria "Erwäge" meditates on the scourging, an ordering that deviates

blood . . . the green color, however, is an image of divine grace," whereas the mixing of the two colors in the central circle represented how, through Christ's mediating between divine justice and goodness, the two were placed in the "angenehmste *Temperament.*" Hence, in Rambach's view, depictions that sometimes encircled Christ's throne, sometimes his head, with the rainbow. See his *COLLEGIUM HISTORIAE ECCLESIASTICAE VETERIS* TESTAMENTI, *oder Ausführlicher und gründlicher Discurs über die Kirchen-Historie des alten Testaments von Erschaffung der Welt bis auf die Geburt Christi. . . Franckfurth, 1736–37,* 1:182–84; 2:954 (index). Likewise, Johann Arndt (*Postille*, [*Passions-Predigten*] 2:134) draws a parallel between Noah's ark and the cross: "Noah ist im Wasser des Zorns Gottes der Sündfluth erhalten worden durch die Arche / wir werden durchs Holz des Creutzes für dem Fluch und Zorn Gottes erhalten." And in 1:306, he draws extensive parallels between the entire story of Noah and Jesus's baptism as signs of the old and new covenants, making reference to the antiquity of those views.

[29] Chafe, *Analyzing Bach Cantatas*, 223–40.

[30] Smend, "Luther und Bach," in *Bach-Studien*, 166–73.

from John, but is logical from the standpoint of the musical depiction, which expands the rainbow imagery behind "Erwäge" at far greater length than that of the thorns of "Betrachte."

Bach sets these two movements apart within the Passion by virtue of their length, the viola d'amore sonority in both, and the lute accompaniment in "Betrachte," which suggests (as does the alternate harpsichord accompaniment) the pricking quality of the thorns. "Betrachte" crystallizes the opposition of meaning that pervades the *St. John Passion* text by means of its striking image of the *Himmelsschlüsselblume* blooming from the crown of thorns: "Betrachte, . . . dein höchstes Gut in Jesu Schmerzen, wie dir auf Dornen, so ihn stechen, die Himmelsschlüsselblume blühn. Du kannst viel süße Frucht von seiner Wermut brechen," (Consider, . . . your greatest benefit in Jesus's sufferings, how for you the primrose blooms from the thorns that prick him. You can pick much sweet fruit from his wormwood). The texts of "Betrachte" and its companion aria "Erwäge" had their origins, as Alfred Dürr points out, in the 1713 edition of the Passion poem of Barthold Heinrich Brockes, *Der Für die Sünde der Welt Gemarterte und Sterbende Jesus.*[31] In the case of "Betrachte," the first six of its seven lines correspond closely to those of the Brockes poem (whose remaining lines were not used), whereas the seventh, "drum sieh ohn Unterlaß auf ihn," which is repeated several times at the end of the movement, does not appear in Brockes (although the words "drum sieh" were presumably derived from Brockes's opening line, "Drum, Seele, schau mit ängstlichem Vergnügen"). The repetitions of the final line have the obvious function of intensifying the visual quality of meditation that is associated with the *Ecce homo* and the crucifixion, and might well have been introduced so as to connect up with the rainbow imagery in the movement that follows.

The central image of "Betrachte," the *Himmelsschlüsselblume*, as the Grimm brothers tell us (with historical examples going back well before Bach's time), is the primrose, or cowslip (*primula veris*), given its name because of its early blooming (in April), which, "opens up the mild spring heaven," and, interpreted symbolically, "represents a prayer of faith that opens up heaven," that "brings us the dear spring, and thus brings a prayer of faith for the foretaste of the heavenly spring."[32] This quality of opening up a new life for the believer analogous to the coming of spring underlies the placement of reference to the *Himmelsschlüsselblume* at the point of meditation that initiates Bach's symbolic trial, the point where meditation on the image of the suffering Jesus is most pronounced. In the third and fifth lines of Brockes's poem the expressions "Dein Himmelreich in deinen Schmertzen" and "des Himmels Schlüssel-Blumen" make clear the parallel between the physical and spiritual firmaments. And in a poem from the fourth part of his *Irdisches Vergnügen in Gott*, titled "Primulae veris und Aurickeln," Brockes expands on the associations of the two flowers that were associated with the coming of spring as the

---

[31] Dürr, *Johann Sebastian Bach's "St. John Passion,"* 43.

[32] Jacob and Wilhelm Grimm, *Deutsches Wörterbuch*, revised by Moriz Heyne (Leipzig, 1877), 1352.

"foretaste" of "eternal bliss," speaking of the fivefold heart-shaped leaf of the *primula veris* and its yellow center as a metaphor for the poet's desire that a ray from the eternal sun (i.e., Jesus) sink into his heart, providing thereby a foretaste of eternal bliss already in the present life.[33]

Brockes places this poem directly following the introductory poem to the segment of his book *Betrachtung der Veränderung der Zeiten, samt dem Nutzen und der Lustbarkeit derselben* (Meditation on the changing of the seasons along with the use and joyful pleasure of the same). His poem on the two flowers transfers the changing of the seasons to the inner change that comes through faith. In his description of the flower Brockes seems to allude to the symbolism that was widely associated with Martin Luther's signet ring, which featured a black cross within a red heart within a white rose of five heart-shaped petals. Luther's description of the symbolism he intended does not specify the primrose, but the associations of the primrose, as prime or first rose, and the rose that bloomed later in the season were very closely related, the principal differences being the time of blooming and the wider associations of the rose, which, unlike the primrose, brought forth thorns as well as flowers. In "Betrachte" the imagery of the thorns of Jesus's crown bringing forth the "flowers that are the key to heaven" combines the associations of the primrose and the normal rose. The design of Luther's ring itself corresponds to Brockes's description of the primrose, and Luther makes clear the association of the firmament: "Such a rose is set in a sky-blue field, because such joy in the Spirit and in faith is the beginning of future joy in heaven. It is already here in part, and is grasped by hope, even though it has not been revealed."[34] Engravings in a 1667 edition of Valerius Herberger's *Evangelische Herz-Postille* make an association between the design of Luther's ring and the imagery of Jesus's name and cross within the heart that appears in Herberger's chorale "In meines Herzens Grunde," thereby pointing up a background textual connection between the beginning and ending movements of Bach's symbolic trial.[35] In this sense the *Himmelsschlüsselblume* sug-

[33] Brockes, *Irdisches Vergnügen in GOTT, bestehend in Physicalisch- und Moralischen Gedichten, Vierter Theil*, . . . (Tubingen, 1753), 26–30.

[34] *Luther's Works*, ed. Jaroslav Pelikan and Helmut T. Lehmann, vol. 49 (1972), ed. Gottfried G. Krodel, 356–59. Johann Michael Dilherr included a full-page image of the "Passion rose" as frontispiece to his sermons on the *Ecce homo* and the Seven Last Words of pt. 4 from his *Weg zu der Seligkeit* (Nuremberg, 1655; see the illustration facing 601). And the illustration very closely resembles Luther's ring, both in the shape of its five petals and the cross and sun that appear in the center. In Dilherr's engraving each petal is associated with one of Jesus's five wounds, with that to the heart placed at the top.

[35] Herberger, *Herz-Postille*. The first of these images, "Bildnis deß Hertzens S. Ignatii," simply represents the name "Jesus" within a heart; the second, "Bildnis deß Hertzens S. Clarae," places the image of the crucified Jesus with the royal inscription within a heart; the third, headed "Desz seligen Herrn D. Martini Lutheri Signet," shows Luther's signet ring as a cross within a heart that is itself within a double-layered flower, each layer with five heart-shaped petals. In his *Paradies Blümlein*, Herberger associates the "Himmelsschlüsselblume" with Psalm 17, describing the various forms of "Himmelsschlüsseln" (prayer, the cross, etc.) that culminate in what Herberger calls the *primulas veris aeterni*, the awakening after the "sleep of death" to eternal life. The ending is remarkably evocative of the final chorale of the *St. John Passion*.

gests the kind of upward looking that emerges more directly in the rainbow imagery of "Erwäge." It is an ideal image with which to heighten meditation on the Passion's central opposition, between the physical events and their salvific meaning.

The imagery of the "rose [or lily, which is the more correct translation, but was seldom used at the time] among thorns," as invoked by the text of "Betrachte, meine Seele," is one that appears sometimes in emblem books or descriptions of Jesus's sufferings, where it usually signifies exactly what the text of "Betrachte" brings out: their ultimate benefit for the believer.[36] In a set of Gospel sermons with emblems for the Sundays and feast days of the church year by Johann Michael Dilherr, for example, the final emblem, for the feast day of the apostles Simon and Judas (October 28), features three crowns, the first full of thorns along with a representation of the rod of the scourging, the second with buds and beginning growth intermingled with the thorns, and the third in full bloom, covered with roses and completely without thorns.[37] The accompanying verses "Was ich getragen," "Wird euch auch plagen," and "Zu letzt behagen" (What I [i.e., Jesus] have borne, / will also torment you / [and] finally content you), mark out three stages. And in a separate publication of the emblems with additional commentary, a corresponding explanatory paragraph makes clear that in order to be a disciple of Christ the believer will have to expect nothing better than suffering (the first image), whereas the second image shows that "the Lord Jesus in his cross did not want to leave us without *Trost und Linderung* (consolation and alleviation)"; the third image showed that "after the suffering of this temporal life would follow an eternal unmixed joy" ("Die dritte ist von Rosen / ohne Dornen: anzuzeigen; daß / auf das zeitliche Leiden / eine ewige unvermengte Freude folgen werde. 2. Cor. 4/17").[38]

Also, behind the imagery lies a tradition in the visual arts that was fairly widespread in representations of Jesus's face since ancient times: that of the "floriated" nimbus that was primarily associated with images of Christ as *salvator mundi*, Christ in glory. Always presented in tripartite form—articulating the left, right, and top of the head—and often highly stylized, the floriated nimbus, like its counterpart, the "radiant" nimbus, was a form of cross, which was, of course, the most common type. As early as the fifteenth century, however, this pattern was combined with the crown of thorns in images of Christ as "man of sorrows" or the *Ecce homo*; and in some instances, the floral elements, now less stylized, emerge from

---

[36] Luther translated the flower mentioned in the Song of Songs as the rose, but already in the sixteenth century it was noted that the Hebrew original referred to the lily. In subsequent Lutheran writings the rose was by far the one most referred to.

[37] Johann Michael Dilherr, *Heilige Sabbaths Arbeit*, 2nd ed. (Nuremberg, 1674), 1117. See also Johann Michael Dilherr and Georg Philipp Harsdörffer, *Drei-ständige Sonn- und Festtag-Emblemata, oder Sinne-bilder* (ca. 1660), facsimile ed. (Hildesheim: Georg Olms, 1994), n.p.

[38] All the images in the Dilherr/Harsdörffer collection feature three stages, with close affinities to the pattern of traditional hermeneutics, usually moving from a state of suffering or worldliness to an eschatological perspective.

the crown of thorns itself. Such is the case in some of Albrecht Dürer's Passion woodcuts. In other instances the radiant and cross forms of the nimbus may be combined with the crown of thorns and floriated forms. The meaning of such depictions is, of course, the dual nature of Jesus's sufferings and their salvific meaning for the believer.[39] Jesus's divinity radiates forth despite its being clothed by his human sufferings; by extension, the believer responds in a twofold manner: sorrow for Jesus's sufferings, and joy in the salvation they bring for humanity. In some sophisticated representations of Jesus's face, such as those of Jan van Eyck and Petrus Christus, the lifelike quality of the depiction, enclosed in a *trompe-l'oeil* frame, not only established a "unity between the holy figure and the believer," but it also achieved "direct eye contact between the portrait and the viewer. When the viewer moves, the eyes of the painted Christ follow him. The idea was to 'see through' the depiction to the actual physical presence of the figure represented."[40] This process is similar to the believer's seeing through the adverse events of the Passion to the redemptive meaning it embodied, the most pronounced quality of the meditative movements of the *St. John Passion*. As expressed, for example, by Heinrich Müller in his *Evangelischer Herzens Spiegel*, such recognition (*Erkenntnis*) of Jesus led to a mirroring within the heart of the meaning of the Passion, bringing about the internalized, tropological, or faith understanding that was described in the concept of "conformity" to Christ.

The *Himmelsschlüsselblume*, like the rainbow, was associated with Jesus; but a secondary association was to St. Peter, who carried the keys to heaven (*Himmelsschlüssel*). When, therefore, Bach alludes to the melody and key of "Ich folge dir gleichfalls" in the first and last choruses of his symbolic trial (see exx. 4.8b and 4.8c, ch. 4), he perhaps intended to remind the listener that the following of Jesus, widely associated with Peter's "fall" and subsequent "conversion," is the way of the cross, focused in Jesus's trial and crucifixion. If so, then we have another instance of his projecting the sense that beneath the adversarial text lies a salvific meaning. At the beginning of Bach's symbolic trial, the image of the *Himmelsschlüsselblume* sprouting from the crown of thorns is an allegorical expression of Jesus's sufferings as the entranceway to eternal life, the way of the cross that the believer, like Peter, must follow. In the modulatory design of the symbolic trial (in particular, the tonal motion from E♭ and c at the beginning to E at the center) the simultaneous antithesis in the imagery of "Betrachte, meine Seele" becomes a temporal span, a symbolic motion from the world below to the source of spiritual meaning (and, as Jesus says, of power), the world above. In "Durch dein Gefängnis," as we will see, the depiction of Jesus is directly as the *salvator mundi*. The keys of the intervening

[39] Christian Scriver in his *Müssige Land-Stunden* (897–921) discusses the crown of thorns in terms of its double meaning as "two kinds of crowns," that of suffering in the world, and that of the eschatological hopes of the faithful.

[40] Maryan W. Ainsworth, with Maximiliaan J. Martens, *Petrus Christus: Renaissance Master of Bruges* (New York: Metropolitan Museum of Art, 1994), 86–88.

choruses are made to conform to this directed upward motion, an allegory of God's *Rath*.

Interestingly, in "Betrachte, meine Seele," for the lines "in Jesu Schmerzen, wie dir auf Dornen, so ihn stechen, die Himmelsschlüsselblume blühn," Bach makes a tritone leap in the voice from c′ to f♯ on "Schmerzen" (the first sharp accidental in the movement), using the resultant diminished-seventh chord as springboard to a brief introduction of sharpened harmonies, whose raised pitches and tritones depict the thorns, after which he leads the tonality back to flats (G minor) on "blühn." This easily audible effect places the thorns, symbol of Jesus's sufferings, in the context of their benefit for the faithful, a quality akin to the *Trost und Linderung* of Dilherr's second crown of thorns emblem. But it is the key of E-flat major with which "Betrachte" begins and ends that most suggests that benefit, directly following the violent G-minor narrative of the scourging. The third relationship has a blissful, even "romantic" quality that is underscored by the calm of the prelude-like figuration (decorated immediately in m. 2) and, of course, the "special" instrumentation. For the repeated urging of the believer to "sieh" at the end of the movement, the tormented harmonies that first entered in m. 3 ("mit ängstlichem Vergnügen"), reappear, then give way to the rise in the vocal line toward the high e♭′ that affirms the return to E♭ (and the opening measures) at the end.

The rainbow imagery of the following movement, "Erwäge, wie sein blutgefärbter Rükken," is vastly more widespread and of greater theological import than the *Himmelsschlüsselblume* of "Betrachte, meine Seele." Perhaps the most detailed consideration of its meaning from within the Lutheran tradition is that of Johann Mathesius's treatise, *Diluvium*, of 1587 (originally given as a series of sermons in 1557–58), an examination of the meaning of the story of Noah and the flood consisting of nearly 1,000 pages, divided into fifty-seven chapters.[41] Mathesius's study draws upon countless earlier sources of interpretation of the flood and served as a source for many later ones. As such, it embodies the astonishing degree to which Lutheran writers articulated a network of interconnected ideas that span the relationship between the Old and New Testaments and that reflect many of the same concerns in the NT authors themselves. The flood offered a perfect story since it brought up the entire question of God's "old" and "new" covenants (or testaments, as Mathesius emphasizes at many points), and the unity of scripture itself:

> On this, however, the Lord placed a most blessed consolation, of the covenant of grace that he wanted to set up with Noah, which is the covenant of the New Testament, and consists in the incarnation of the eternal son of God, and in his sacrifice, blood and death, through which we are redeemed from God's wrath, from sin, death, the devil and hell, come once again to grace and

---

[41] Johann Mathesius, *DILVVIUM, das ist, Historia von der Sündflut, dadurch Gott der Herr zum schrecklichen exempel seines zorns wider die sünde, zu Noah zeiten, die erste unbußfertige Welt erseufft, und nicht allein die menschen, sondern alles was odem gehabt, vertilget hat* (Nuremberg, 1587), hereafter Mathesius, *Diluvium*.

become God's children and heirs. . . . "With you," God said to Noah, "I will set up, confirm and reinforce my covenant, which earlier I made with Adam . . . " Here this [i.e., the promise "I will set up and confirm my covenant"] means that God after the flood will once again think on this very covenant, and with a particular sign or sacrament, namely with the rainbow, will strengthen it. . . . This is the new and eternal covenant of God, which he at first made with Adam after the fall, and now repeats and renews, and afterwards confirms many more times and in the fullness of time achieved through the incarnation, birth, blood and death of his son, and will fulfill on the day of judgment. . . . For the old covenant was the promise of the entire sphere of the earth, when God spoke to Adam and Eve before the fall (Gen 1). . . If Adam had not fallen, God would also have carried out this old covenant with him and granted him dominion over the entire earth until the number of fallen angels had been restored and God had translated him into the blessed divine state, with his entire race. . . Nevertheless, the covenant of eternal life, which God had set up with Adam after the fall, and confirmed in Christ's blood and death (as the old covenant was bolstered only with the blood of cattle, the slaughtering of lambs, goats and the like), the same is the new and eternal covenant, as the master quite nicely speaks of in the ninth chapter of the epistle to the Hebrews. . . . Therefore take note, that this covenant, of which God speaks here with Noah, in contrast to the old and antiquated covenant, is the new and eternal covenant, and that God calls it his covenant, which he himself made with Adam in the blood of his only begotten son.[42]

---

[42] Mathesius, *Diluvium*, 89–92:

Daran henget aber der Herr einen holdseligen trost / von dem Gnadenbunde / den er mit Noah wolle auffrichten / welcher ist der bund des neuen Testaments / und stehet in der menschwerdung des ewigen Sone Gottes / und inn seinem opffer / blut und tod / dadurch wir von Gottes zorn / sünd / todt / teufel und höll erlöset / widerumb zu gnaden kommen / unnd Gottes kinder und erben werden. . . . Mit dir / spricht Gott zu Noah / will ich auffrichten / bestettigen und befestigen (*constabiliam*) meinen Bund / den ich zuvor mit Adam gemacht hab. . . . Das heist hie / Ich will auffrichten unnd bestettigen meinen Bund: wie Gott eben dises Bundes nach der Sündflut widerumb gedencken wird / und mit einem sonderlichen zeichen oder Sacrament / nemlich mit dem Regenbogen bekrefftigen. . . . Diß ist der neu und ewige Bund Gottes / welchen er erstlich mit Adam nach dem fall gemacht / und allhie widerholet und verneuet / und hernach zum öffternmal bestettiget / und inn der fülle der zeit / durch die Menschwerdung / Geburt / Blut und Tod seines Sones geleistet hat / und am Jüngsten tage vollenden wird. . . . Denn der alte bund war die verheissung des gantzen Erdenkreises / da Gott zu Adam und Eva für dem fall sprach / Gen. 1. . . . Wenn Adam nicht gefallen were / so hette ihm Gott disen alten Bund auch geleistet / unnd die herrschafft über den gantzen Erdboden geliehen / biß die zahl der gefallenen Engel were erstattet worden / und Gott in inn das Himlische selige wesen versatzt hette / mit seinem gantzen geschlecht. . . . Aber der bund des ewigen lebens / welchen Gott mit Adam nach dem fall hat auffgericht / und mit Christi blut und todt bestettigt / wie der alte bund nur mit vihischen blut / schlachtung der lemblein und böcklkein u. besteiffet wurde / derselb ist der neue und ewige bund / wie der Meister in der Epistel an die Ebreer far fein hievon redet / im 9. . . . . Darumb mercket / daß diser bund / von dem hie Gott mit Noah redet / gegen dem alten und antiquirten Bund / der neue und ewige bund ist / unnd das ihn Gott seinen Bund heisset / welchen er selbst in seines eingebornen Sons blut mit Adam gemacht hat.

As Mathesius explains repeatedly, the covenant with Noah was the covenant to which Adam had failed to adhere, which was renewed in the time of the flood with a sign or sacrament, the rainbow, but that was merely observed throughout the history of Israel, by means of sacrificial offerings, until it was finally renewed once again and fulfilled in the sacrificial death of Christ. This view was the source of numerous references to Noah and the flood whenever the ideas of salvation history and the unity of scripture were invoked. The arioso "Am Abend, da es kühle war" from toward the end of Bach's *St. Matthew Passion* makes reference to the flood to describe the fullness of the soteriological meaning of the Passion as a whole. Reaching back to the story of the fall of humanity in Genesis and comparing it with Jesus's subduing Adam (i.e., the trope of the "old man," now to be replaced by the new), the text of "Am Abend" invokes scriptural references to evening to unite the return of the dove to Noah in the ark with the olive branch as sign of humankind's reconciliation with God. The profound sense of fulfillment that appears in Bach's music for the phrase "Der Friedeschluß ist nun mit Gott gemacht, denn Jesus hat sein Kreuz vollbracht" (reconciliation with God is now complete, for Jesus has fulfilled his cross) reflects all that the Lutherans believed concerning the meaning of the cross and the fulfillment of scripture, as Paul Minear has shown.[43]

However, in neither of the Bach Passions does reference to the story of Noah and the flood appear more than once, and then only briefly. Moreover, in both instances the references are poeticized (the images of the rainbow and the evening) in a manner that may appear to play down the seriousness of the underlying theological meaning. This should not lead us astray from the fact that the underlying meaning itself is all-determining. The unity of scripture and its meaning as the Lutherans saw it is not limited to a single story that needs to be emphasized repeatedly in order for its meaning to be understood. Just the opposite, as the numerous references to parallel biblical stories in Mathesius's treatise on the flood demonstrate. The meaning is a single one that is embodied in many stories, among which the flood was central because of its centering on the covenant of grace with humankind. It is not necessary to insist that the modulatory patterns of Bach's symbolic trial are specifically illustrative of the rainbow or some other single image. They represent a range of ideas, such as John's above/below dualism, the reconciliation associated with the cross, and the opposition of law and freedom, that belong to the meaning of scripture as a whole, and were focused particularly clearly in the interpretation of certain stories such as the flood. The concept of the "analogy of faith" brought out the fact that such parallels ran throughout the whole of scripture.

[43] Paul Minear, "J. S. Bach and J. A. Ernesti: A Case Study in Exegetical and Theological Conflict," in *Our Common History as Christians: Essays in Honor of Alberg C. Ousler*, ed. John Deschner, L. T. Howe, and K. Penzel, 131–55 (New York: Oxford University Press, 1975. Minear, "Matthew, Evangelist, and Johann, Composer," *Theology Today* 30 (1973): 243–55. Minear's arguments locate Bach within the pre-critical exegetical tradition according to which scripture, both Old and New Testaments, represented a unity of meaning. See also R. Steiger, "O schöne Zeit, O Abendstunde." See also ch. 2, n. 21 of the present study.

To return to "Erwäge": Bach's text makes clear that the image of the rainbow that forms on Jesus's back from the blood and water of the scourging (and which looks ahead to John's narrative of the blood and water that flowed from the piercing of his side on the cross, in both instances sacramental symbols) is described as outlining a pattern similar to that of the firmament: "Erwäge, wie sein blutgefärbter Rücken in allen Stücken dem Himmel gleiche geht" (Consider, how his bloodspattered back resembles the heavens at all points). The text then goes on to compare the multiplicity of rainbow patterns as signs of God's grace ("Gottes Gnadenzeichen)," while in the music the multiplicity of symmetrical, ascent/descent figures mirror the shape of the firmament and the trial, reinforcing the message of Jesus's sufferings as sign of God's grace, his unearned favor, coming from above.

The rainbow was discussed in this manner for centuries before Bach or Luther, and it appears in many pictorial representations with the same or similar associations. Since it embodied the twofold aspect of Jesus as bringing grace and judgment, it was also associated with the interpretation of Jesus as the *Gnadenstuhl* (or *Gnadenthron*) of Israel, the image that appears in Bach's next meditative movement, the chorale "Durch dein Gefängnis" (see the discussion of that chorale on 361ff). Rooted in passages from the apocalyptic books of Ezekiel (1:26–28) and Revelation (4:3; 10:1) in which the rainbow and the throne of God ("Stuhl") are described, the imagery of the rainbow as *Gnadenstuhl* embodied both the most common association of God's grace and mercy (the "mercy seat") and that of Jesus's second coming "in the clouds of heaven" as described in Matthew (24:30).[44] Although the texts of Bach's meditative movements were drawn from divergent sources (Brockes and Postel), in the *St. John Passion* text they reflect the same set of underlying ideas. In the chapter of his *Magnalia Dei* in which Jesus himself is described as the rainbow, Valerius Herberger makes these and many other points, including special links between the rainbow and Jesus's "Es ist vollbracht" in John and the Johannine imagery of Jesus's "lifting up" drawing all humanity to him.[45] Most of all, perhaps, is the link that Herberger and others (including Rambach) saw between the rainbow as spanning the heavens and the salvific meaning of the cross. Thus Herberger also associates the rainbow with the imagery of Jesus on the cross spreading out his arms to gather in humanity, as we find in the dialog aria "Sehet, Jesus hat die Hand uns zu fassen ausgespannt" in the *St. Matthew Passion*:

> The rainbow spreads its arms down from the heights, and acts as though it wanted to grasp the earth and draw it upwards. You, Lord Jesus, touch heaven

---

[44] See Herberger, *De Jesu . . . Magnalia Dei*, 109–12; Rambach, *Christus in Mose*, 1105–9; Mathesius, *Diluvium*, 349.

[45] Herberger, *De Jesu . . . Magnalia Dei*, 109: "Nachdem der Regenbogen am Himmel geleuchtet hat, kommt keine Sündflut mehr. Nachdem du, Herr Jesu, dich unser angenommen hast, verdirbt kein gläubiges Herz in der Welt mehr. Die Zornfluth deines Vaters wird uns bußfertige Sünder nicht ersäufen; du hast mit deinem Triumphlied: 'Es ist vollbracht!' uns ein ewiges, helles, schönes Wetter über Leib und Seel erworben." See also n. 46.

> and earth; you are true God and man: God from heaven; man of the earth. The heavens are your throne; the earth is your footstool. You step also into the elevation of the cross and spread your arms out wide. You grasp after our soul; you reach after the earthly sphere of our hearts. For you say (Jn 12:32), "When I am lifted up from the earth, I will draw all men unto me." You want to draw humanity upwards into heaven and bring it to your Father. You spread these arms even today in the holy Gospel and entice us as a fortunate hen her little chickens beneath her wings. Whoever follows you, hears your voice and comes to you, you draw into eternal life.[46]

Behind such passages lies the meaning of the trial and crucifixion as embodying a "higher" meaning than that told by the physical events, a meaning given, like the rainbow, from above, as God's sign.

The meaning, as described by Mathesius, is above all that of God's old and new covenants, to which Mathesius devotes two chapters and numerous subsidiary discussions. Behind them is a complex network of associations throughout scripture, involving especially that between the flood and baptism, the rainbow as embodying the colors of water and blood, symbols not only of the sacraments of baptism and the eucharist, but of Jesus divine and human natures and the eras of salvation history. In three extended chapters on the rainbow itself Mathesius explores these and other meanings. The following excerpt is typical of a large number throughout the treatise:

> The rainbow is the miraculous bow of the eternal son of God, of two principal colors and placed from above down into the clouds, and ordered according to the future incarnation, suffering and death of the Messiah and the atonement for the human race, so that it would be, for Noah and all his descendants until the day of judgment, a sign of the covenant of grace or of the covenant of good conscience, and a truly certain sign in the heavens that the faithful have forgiveness of sins, [which would be] in vain unless it is according to the will of the eternal mediator, and that it also be a memorial to the Son of God himself, with which he reminds himself of his promise and us of the greater mystery of the two natures of the eternal mediator, of the sacra-

---

[46] Ibid., 111:

> Der Regenbogen breitet seine Arme herab von der Höhe, und thut, als wollte er die Erde fassen und hinauf ziehen: Du, Herr Jesu, rührest Himmel und Erde an; du bist wahrer Gott und Mensch: Gott vom Himmel, Mensch von der Erde; der Himmel ist dein Stuhl, die Erde ist dein Fußschemel, du trittst auch in die Höhe des Kreuzes, und breitest dein Arme weit aus: du greifest nach unserer Seele; du greifest nach der Erdkugel unsers Herzens. Denn du sagst, Joh. 12, 32: 'Wenn ich erhöhet werde von der Erde, will ich sie alle zu mir ziehen.' Du willst die Menschen hinauf in den Himmel ziehen und sie zu deinem Vater bringen. Du breitest noch heute deine Arme aus im heiligen Evangelio, und lockest uns wie eine Gluckhenne ihre Küchlein unter ihre Flügel; wer dir folgt, deiner Stimme gehorcht und zu dir kommt, den ziehst du ins ewige Leben.

ments of the new testament and of the waters of the old flood and the fire of the last judgment.[47]

In Herberger's description of the rainbow spreading its arms "herab von der Höhe" and Mathesius's "von oben herab" we may be reminded of the above/below character of Jesus's remark to Pilate that true power comes only from above ("von oben herab gegeben"). Needless to say, neither Bach nor his librettist needed to consult a theological treatise in order to introduce this turn of phrase, or that it necessarily refers to the rainbow. The above/below idea is built into the theological ideas that control the "shape" of the trial and its modulation to the sharpest keys of the Passion at the point where this reference is made. And, of course, Mathesius, like many other Lutheran authors, provides extensive treatment of the theme of God's *Rath*, utilizing most of the terminology we have encountered on that subject to this point and expanding on the list of synonoms and related expressions with discussion of God's *Beschluß*, *Decret*, *Vorsatz*, *Rathschluß*, *Oeconomie*, *Ordnung*, *legatum*, *Policey*, *Bund*, *Testament*, and the like, all of which refer in one way or another to, or form components of, God's plan of salvation.[48]

Thus both "Betrachte" and "Erwäge" center on imagery of the firmament, presenting the suffering Christ with overtones of the *salvator mundi*, and heaven as the goal of the believer's pilgrimage through the trial of life. The continuing sharpward tonal motion that leads on to the beginning of the recitative dialog on power between Jesus and Pilate might have been introduced by Bach so as to enable the modulation to the sharpest keys of the Passion for the central segment of the symbolic trial. Pilate initiates the modulation in his claim of the power to crucify or to set free, whereas Jesus completes it with the assertion that real power comes only from above, words that, as John tells us, caused Pilate from then on to seek to free Jesus. The power from above, as Bach's contemporary Johann Jacob Rambach interpreted it, is bound up with God's *vorbedachter Rath*, which Jesus followed willingly and according to which he could not be freed, since the events of the Passion were decided before the creation. Directly following the E-major cadence narrating

---

[47] Mathesius, *Diluvium*, 342r.:

> Der Regenbogen ist des ewigen Sohne Gottes Wunderbogen / von zweyen hauptfarben / und von oben herab in die wolken gesetzt / und dem Bunde oder verheissung von Messie künfftigen Menschwerdung / leiden und sterben / unnd von der versühnung des menschlichen geschlechts zugeordnet / daß er Noah und allen seinen nachkommen / biß an Jüngsten tage / ein zeichen sey des Gnadenbundes / oder des Bunds des guten gewissens / unnd ein warhafftiger gewisser zeuge am Himel / daß die glaubigen haben vergebung der sünden / umb sonst / allein umb des ewigen Mittlers willen / unnd daß er auch dem Sone Gottes selbst ein memorial sey / darbey er sich seiner verheissung unnd uns grosser geheimnuß erinnere / von zweyen naturen des ewigen Mittlers / von den Sacramenten des neuen Testaments / unnd von den wassern der alten Sündflut / und feuer des Jüngsten tages.

[48] Ibid., 327–33. This discussion, ch. 40 of Mathesius's treatise, directly precedes the three chapters in which he discusses the rainbow directly and in detail. Mathesius sees the concept of God's plan as the background for the meaning of the rainbow as encompassing the two covenants as well as the distant past, the time of Christ, and the coming judgment.

Pilate's seeking to free Jesus, we hear the chorale "Durch dein Gefängnis," borrowing its text from Postel, who had placed it at exactly the same point in the narrative. No earlier composer, however, had made it into a chorale, or the recitative just mentioned into anything like the "center" of a symmetrically conceived substructure within the work. And no one had introduced such a striking modulatory design. In doing so, Bach must have seen the potential of expanding Postel's arrangement, presumably on the basis, at least in part, of his grasp of the meaning behind the biblical allusions within the aria text.

Within "Durch dein Gefängnis" the line "Dein Kerker ist der Gnadenthron, die Freistatt aller Frommen" makes two OT references that were understood in Bach's time, and long before, as prefigurations of Jesus: the words *Gnadenthron* and "*Freistatt* (or *Freistadt*). In his *Christus in Mose*, devoted to such prefigurations, Rambach discusses them at some length, and in a treatise devoted to the bronze serpent lifted up by Moses in the desert and the *Frey-Städte Israels*, he makes clear that "under both prefigurations is represented in very lovely and expressive terms the rescue from God's wrath and eternal death for which we have to thank the crucified Jesus."[49]

The word *Gnadenthron* derives from the mercy seat (usually *Gnadenstuhl*) that God ordered Moses to place on the ark of the covenant (Ex 25:17–22), which, as Johann Arndt, for example, tells us, was a type of Jesus's cross, whereas *Freistatt* refers to the six cities of refuge for the guilty Levites as discussed in Numbers 35 and elsewhere.[50] The *Gnadenstuhl* was the place chosen by God for communication of his commandments to Moses and his successors, the place where, as Rambach says, he revealed his *Herrlichkeit*. In Luther's translation of Romans 3:24–25, and Hebrews 4:16, as cited by Rambach, Jesus was identified directly as the *Gnadenstuhl*; the latter passage—"Let us therefore come boldly unto the throne of grace, that we may obtain mercy, and find grace to help in time of need (KJV)"—was widely cited between the time of Luther and Bach. The difference between "Thron" and "Stuhl" (God's footstool) was sometimes associated with the above/below com-

[49] Johann Jacob Rambach, *Christus in Mose, oder Betrachtungen über die vornehmsten Weissagungen und Vorbilder in den fünf Büchern Mosis auf Christum . . . zum Druck ausgefertigt . . . von Johannes Philipp Fresenius* (Frankfurt and Leipzig, 1736–37). See also Rambach's treatise, *Betrachtung / des Geheimnisses / JEsu CHristi*, (Halle, 1726), 4: "weil unter beyderley Vorbildern die Errettung von dem Zorn Gottes und ewigen Tode, welche wir dem gecreutzigten Jesu zu dancken haben, gar lieblich und nachdrücklich vorgestellet wird."

[50] Arndt, *Postilla*, (*Passions-Predigten*), 2:134, 148. Scriver (*Müssige Land-Stunden*, 1030–32), referring to five *Freistädte*, sees them as prefiguring the salvific meaning of Jesus's five wounds in the Passion. Each city seemed to say "Hieher zu mir / hier könnet ihr euer Leben *salviren*," which Scriver calls the "way of the cross" (Creutz-Weg). Rambach (*Betrachtung des Geheimnisses* . . . 104–5) cites Valerius Herberger's *De Jesu . . . Magnalia Dei* on the association between the six *Freistädte* and Jesus's wounds, adding as the sixth the crown of thorns: "Dein heiliges Haupt, das von der Dornen-Crone zerrissen ist, ist meine erste Frey-Stadt, da werde ich los der Dornen meines bösen Gewissens, und erlange Hoffnung zur Crone des ewigen Lebens." Perhaps Bach perceived such a connection between the thorns meditated on in "Betrachte" (indebted to Brockes) and the *Freistatt* of "Durch dein Gefängnis" (Postel). Such a connection would arise naturally within the understanding of the Passion at the time.

ponent of Jesus as mediator, the two colors of the rainbow symbolizing his two aspects, judgmental and merciful, and the rainbow as the floor of heaven and the ceiling of earth. The meaning of Jesus as *Gnadenstuhl* was then further extended to passages, such as Matthew 11:26 and John 1:18, in which the identity of Jesus as the only one to know and see God was affirmed. Thus the Calov Bible comments (on Ex 25:22), "also offenbahret GOtt seinen Willen durch Christum den rechten Gnadenstuhl" (thus God revealed his will through Christ, the true throne of grace).[51]

Behind the symbolism of Jesus as *Gnadenstuhl/Gnadenthron* lay, of course, the opposition between, on the one hand, the *Gnadenstuhl* as *locus* of God's commandments to Israel, placed upon the ark of the covenant, which contained the two tables of the law, and on the other, the interpretation of Jesus as "mercy seat," rooted, of course, in the Gospel.[52] In Jesus the believer found refuge from God's strict demands; yet Jesus was also the judge of the Second Coming, for which reason it was necessary for the faithful to step up to the *Gnadenthron* (now interpreted as the resurrected Jesus) before it was too late. God's grace and mercy, manifested in Jesus as *Gnadenthron*, were viewed by Valerius Herberger as a covenant of peace similar to that with Noah, after the flood:

> Thus it is clear that he [Jesus] is the true throne of grace who protects his people, and can hold up the water of the flood (*Süntfluth)* of God's wrath, so that it does not drown us, and can give us a secure passage through the deep Jordan of death to the true promised land of the eternal blessedness, where milk and honey flow [Ex 3:8] and there will be the fullness of joy.[53]

Five of Bach's cantatas refer to either the *Gnadenstuhl* (BWV 83, 194) or the *Gnadenthron* (BWV 55, 76, 248/4), all with the associations of God's dispensing mercy and justice according to his will, and three urging the faithful to step up to, hasten to, or stand before the throne of grace.

Johann Jacob Rambach discusses seven means by which the *Gnadenstuhl* prefigured Jesus, at least four of which were exactly the kind of interpretation that might have prompted Postel's placing "Durch dein Gefängnis" where he does as well as stimulating Bach in the structure of his symbolic trial. The first, for Ram-

---

[51] Abraham Calov, *Die Heilige Bibel nach D. MARTINI LUTHERI Deutscher Dolmetschung und Erklärung* . . . 3 vols. (Wittenberg, 1681–82), 1:542.

[52] Thus John 1:17 proclaims that "the law was given by Moses, but grace and truth came by Jesus Christ," after which v. 18, associated with Jesus as *Gnadenstuhl*, brought out that only Jesus, "the only begotten Son, which is in the bosom of the Father, he hath declared *him*."

[53] Herberger, *De Jesu . . . Magnalia Dei*, 434: "Da wird klar / daß er sey der rechte Gnaden-Thron / welcher sein Volck decken / und die Wasser der Sündfluth des Zorns GOttes auffhalten kan / daß sie uns nicht ersäuffen / und uns einen sicheren Durchzug geben kan durch den tieffen Jordan des Todes zu dem rechten gelobten Lande der ewigen Seligkeit / da Milch und Honig fliessen / 2 Buch Mos. 3 / v.8 / und Freude die Fülle seyn wird."

bach, is that God himself ordered the building of the *Gnadenstuhl* as well as its exact size, proportions and other features. For Rambach this signified the fulfillment of God's *Rathschluß*:

> . . . thus in his eternal plan God himself prescribed Jesus Christ and in the fullness of time sent him on that account into the world, so that he should found the reconciliation between God and humankind. Therefore it is said expressly in Romans 3:25: "God has ordained Christ for a throne of grace."[54]

Mathesius and other authors went much farther, linking up the proportions of the ark, the *Gnadenstuhl*, Solomon's Temple, the heavenly Jerusalem, and the like, with the idea that, as Mathesius put it, God was a God of order (*Ordnung)* a "Mathematicus, and has made everything according to measure, analogy and proportion."[55] Such ideas were sometimes carried over into music theory. Thus the idea that the proportions of the *Gnadenstuhl* prefigured the major triad that was associated with Christ and the Trinity was, for Andreas Werckmeister, a symbol of God's *Ordnung*.[56] The extent to which Bach adopted such numerological devices has often been debated and, as we know, sometimes carried to extremes. Nevertheless it does not seem farfetched to imagine that the reference to Jesus as *Gnadenthron* in "Durch dein Gefängnis" was a felicitous occurrence for Bach as he formed the idea for his own symbol of God's *Ordnung* with the chorale as its central pivot.

Additionally, Rambach, following long-standing tradition, emphasizes the fact that the *Gnadenstuhl*, which he calls a *Versöhn-Deckel* (lid of reconciliation),

> covered the stone tables of the law, which were in the ark of the covenant, and on which those conditions were written that God the Lord commanded in the setting up of the covenant and which also the people of Israel had accepted. Therefore, this cover was, on the one hand, for the purpose of protecting the monument of the divine covenant, and keeping it in safety, and on the other to push down and block the accusations of disobedience that continually arose up from the tables of the law, so that they did not come before God's countenance. Through this important condition was prefigured the fact that Jesus Christ, through his perfect obedience covered our transgressions and freed us from the accusations of the law, but also through his

[54] Rambach, *Christus in Mose*, 742: "also hat auch GOtt selbst JEsum Christum in seinem ewigen Rath-Schluß dazu verordnet / und in der Fülle der Zeit dazu in die Welt sendet / daß er die Versöhnung zwischen GOtt und den Menschen stiften solte. Daher es Röm. III, 25. ausdrücklich heiset: **GOtt hat JEsum Christum vorgestellet zu einem Gnaden-Stuhl.**"

[55] Mathesius, *Diluvium*, 83–85: "Denn Gott ist ein Mathematicus / und hat alles nach dem Maß, Analogi und Proportion gemacht. . . . Darauß wir zu lernen haben / das Gott nicht der unordnung / sondern der ordnung unnd proportion ist . . ."

[56] Werckmeister refers to the *Gnadenstuhl* in this way in several of his treatises. See, for example, his *Musicae mathematicae hodegus curiosus*, 149–50.

Spirit made us capable of achieving the demands of the law in an evangelical manner ("evangelische Weise") through love of God and our neighbor.[57]

Not only the above/below imagery behind the *Gnadenstuhl* and Christ as mediator, but the opposition of God's judgment and mercy render "Durch dein Gefängnis" particularly appropriate to follow the affirmation of the law in the chorus "Wir haben ein Gesetz" and the reference to power from above in the recitative that followed it, setting up the key of the chorale.

In the placement of "Durch dein Gefängnis" there is also a background connection to the idea of the "keys" of heaven as poeticized in the *Himmelsschlüsselblume* of "Betrachte, meine Selele." As Johann Anastasius Freylinghausen tells us, the "keys of the kingdom of God" ("Schlüssel des Himmelreichs") are of two kinds (as described in Mt 16:19 and elsewhere in scripture): the *Bindeschlüssel* that are associated with sin, and the *Löseschlüssel* that represent freedom from sin. Freylinghausen discusses the entire doctrine of the keys of heaven as inseparably bound up with that of law and gospel, which appears to underlie the relationship of "Wir haben ein Gesetz" to "Durch dein Gefängnis," with "Lässest du diesen los" serving as a symbolic denial or distortion of the *Löseschlüssel.*[58] The opposition of God's wrath and his mercy is the meaning Bach's audience was intended to glean from the meditative movements to this point.

In woodcuts and engravings depicting God and the firmament from the Reformation era, God (or Jesus) was sometimes seated on the rainbow, sometimes on the *Gnadenstuhl* of the ark.[59] Luther described how he was terrified in his youth by such images, which embodied the dualism of God's judgment and mercy.[60] Mathesius, emphasizing the redemptive quality of the image of Jesus seated on the rain-

---

[57] Rambach, *Christus in Mose*, 743:

Diese güldene Platte, und dieser güldene Versöhn–Deckel bedeckte die steinerne Tafeln des Gesetzes, welche in der Lade des Bundes waren, und auf welche diejenige Bedingungen geschrieben waren, welche GOtt der HErr bey der Aufrichtung des Bundes vorgetragen, den das Israelitische Volck aber auch angenommen hatte; daher denn dieser Deckel der Lade theils dieses Denckmahl des göttlichen Bundes verwahrete und in Sicherheit setzte, theils auch die Anklage des Ungehorsams welche gleichsam immer von den Gesetz-Tafeln aufstiege, wiederum niederdruckte und verhinderte, daß sie nicht vor das Angesicht Gottes kämen, welcher oben über der Lade des Bundes auf den Flügeln der Chreubinnen wohnete. Hiedurch wurde denn angezeiget, daß Jesus Christus mit seinem vollkommenen Gehorsam unsern Ungehorsam zudecken, und uns von der Anklage des Gesetzes befreyen, aber auch durch seinen Geist uns tüchtig machen solte, der Forderung des Gesetzes auf eine Evangelische Art, durch eine aufrichtige Liebe Gottes und des Nächsten ein Genüge zu thun.

[58] Johann Anastasius Freylinghausen, *COMPENDIUM, oder Kurtzer Begriff der gantzen Christlichen Lehre in* XXXIV. *Articuln nebst einer Summarischen Vorstellung der Göttlichen Ordnung des Heyls* . . . 4th ed. (Halle, 1719), 85–88 ("Der XII. Articul Von den Schlüsseln des Himmelreichs"); Freylinghausen, *DEFINITIONES THEOLOGICAE, oder Theologische Beschreibungen der Christlichen Glaubens-Articul* . . . (Halle, 1717), 46–48 ("Von den Schlüsseln des Himmelreichs").

[59] See ch. 6, notes 24 and 26.

[60] See Roland Bainton, *Here I Stand: A Life of Martin Luther* (Nashville, TN: Abingdon Press 1950), 22–25.

bow, described Noah's ark as his *Gnadenthron* or *Gnadenkasten* (thereby making the association, more evident in English than in German, between Noah's ark and the ark of the covenant), associating the rainbow as *Gnadenzeichen* or *Gnadenbund* with the water of the flood as a *Gnadentaufe*.[61] If such connections were invoked for Bach by Postel's text, they might have played a part in the modulatory sequence that leads from "Betrachte" and "Erwäge" to "Durch dein Gefängnis." In "Erwäge" Bach's rainbow images suggest the upward curve from the world in which Jesus's sufferings take place to what in "Durch dein Gefängnis" is the image of him seated on the *Gnadenthron*, the source of the power from above, as the *Gnadenstuhl* was for Moses. The eschatological character of the identification of the rainbow and the *Gnadenthron* in the passages from Ezekiel and Revelation (mentioned earlier) was perhaps instrumental in Bach's culminating the modulation to E major first with Pilate's seeking to free Jesus, then with "Durch dein Gefängnis." In setting Postel's aria text to a chorale melody of Johann Hermann Schein, Bach created a chorale of unique symbolic significance, marking the "apex" of an upward curve from flat to sharp keys, which is mirrored in the overall shape of the chorale melody as a whole, as well as of several of its individual phrases. The *Gnadenthron* of the chorale thereby becomes the symbol of divine power, in contrast with the worldly *Richtstuhl* on which Pilate seats himself. The sharpward tonal motion that culminates in "Durch dein Gefängnis" might then be thought to fulfill the meaning of the rainbow patterns as God's *Gnadenzeichen* in "Erwäge," whereas at the end of Bach's symbolic trial the cross, which Arndt equates to the *Gnadenstuhl*, describing it as the "Schlüssel zum Paradies," is another of God's *Gnadenzeichen*.[62] At the very least, we must recognize that in the movements that mark out the three main points in its ascent/descent curve, Bach's symbolic trial alludes to the primrose, the rainbow, the mercy seat, and the cross as God's signs of grace.

To return to "Durch dein Gefängnis": the word *Freistatt* also embodies a biblical reference that was understood in Bach's time as a prefiguration of Christ. The *Freistädte* of the OT were described in various places (principally Num 35) as cities of refuge for those who had killed someone accidentally and without premeditation. Judged innocent of true murder, the killer could remain in the *Freistadt* safely until the death of the current high priest, after which he could return to his home. As Rambach, for example, interpreted the prefiguration, Jesus was a "refuge for awakened consciences in which those who believe in him can abide in sufficient security from God's strict judgment and punishment."[63] One who had committed an acci-

---

[61] Matthesius, *Diluvium*, 94–95, 348.

[62] Arndt, *Postilla*, *(Passions-Predigten)*, 2:148, 150. August Pfeiffer, for example, so describes the cross ("Gottes Gnadenzeichen") in his *Evangelische Erquickstunden* (Leipzig, 1753), see the index reference to 279.

[63] Rambach, *Betrachtung des Geheimnisses* 92:

> Wie aber in **CHristo** die Wahrheit von allen Schatten-Bildern des alten Testaments anzutreffen ist, so haben auch die Frey-Städte auf Niemand anders, als auf ihn, ihr Absehen gehabt, **so fern**

dental or unpremeditated killing had through weakness transgressed against the law of Moses.[64] Such a person could escape the punishment of death by seeking refuge in the *Freistadt*, which "represented the promised redeemer of Israel, Jesus Christ, who for those Israelites, who in their tormented consciences took their refuge in him through faith, and their protection against God's strict judgment, spread his bloody wings of grace over them and procured security for them beneath the same."[65]

For the Jews the *Freistädte*, although a blessing, were tempered by the constraints of the law:

> The cities of refuge were to be sure a great blessing, but at the same time they also represented a tolerable prison. In the same way the Jews were through faith in the promised Messiah protected from the wrath of God, but at the same time they were also under the law as if in a prison, which brought many burdens with it.[66]

No one committing murder intentionally could be protected by the *Freistädte*:

> *The cities of refuge could not protect any deliberate murderer.* If he took his refuge within, he was nevertheless extradited to the courts and delivered up, so that the prescribed punishment for the murder was carried out on him. . . . This depicts again the condition of Israel under the Old Testament.[67]

---

er die einige Zuflucht aufgewachter Gewissen ist, und diejenigen, die an ihn glauben, gegen die Straf-Gerechtigkeit GOttes in gnugsame Sicherheit setzen kan.

[64] Ibid., 97:

> Ein unvorsichtiger **Todschläger** war also ein Bild eines Israeliten, der aus Schwachheit und Ubereilung das Gesetz Mosis übertreten, und dadurch sein eigen Gewissen gefährlich verwundet und verletzet hatte.

[65] Ibid., 97:

> Die **Frey-Stadt** aber, dahin ein solcher von der Gerechtigkeit GOttes verfolgter Israelit stehen muste, bildete ab den versprochenen Erlöser Israels, JEum CHristum, welcher diejenigen Israeliten, die in ihrer Gewissens–Angst im Glauben ihre Zuflucht zu ihm nahmen, gegen die Straf–Gerechtigkeit Gottes in Schutz nahm, seine blutigen Gnaden–Flügel über sie ausbreitete, und ihnen unter denselben Sicherheit verschaffte.

[66] Ibid, 98:

> Waren die Freistädte zwar an und vor sich selbst eine große **Wohlthat**, weil ein unvorsichtiger Todschläger sein Leben darinnen retten konte; aber sie waren doch auch zugleich **einem erträglichen Gefängniß ähnlich;** indem ein solcher Israelit daselbst als im Elend leben, und von seinem Vaterlande und Freundschaft entfernet seyn muste. . . . Sie wurden zwar durch den Glauben an den zukünftigen Meßiam vor dem Zorn Gottes bewahret, und ihre Sünden blieben unter göttlichen Geduld Röm. 3, 25. aber, sie waren auch dabey mancherley Beschwerungen unterworfen, und wurden in dem Gesetz als in einem Gefängniß verwahret und verschlossen, . . ."

[67] Ibid., 99:

> **Es konten diese Frey–Städte keinen muthwilligen Todschläger schützen.** Wenn er gleich seine Zuflucht dahin nahm, so wurde er doch den Gerichten *extradiret* und ausgeliefert, damit die auf den Todschlag gesetzte Strafe an ihm vollzogen wurde. . . Diß bildet wiederum ab die Beschaffenheit Israels unter dem alten Testament.

And freedom from the *Freistädte* was possible only with the death of the high priest. Therefore, as Rambach explains:

> Release from the cities of refuge was grounded in the death of the high priest. . . . That shows clearly that the freeing of the faithful Israelites from the imprisonment of the law depended utterly on the death of Jesus Christ, the true high priest.[68]

Rambach therefore urges the tropological seeking out of the *Freistadt* by the faithful in search of freedom from God's judgment and of rescue for their souls. Hastening to the *Freistadt*, a metaphor for faith in Jesus that for him was "proven" by many scriptural passages, was fulfilled in the recognition of Jesus's outstretched arms as an invitation.[69]

From Rambach we learn that, like the *Gnadenstuhl* (or *Gnadenthron*), the *Freistadt* prefigured Jesus as place of refuge for the sinner, from God's wrath as manifested in the law. Behind "Durch dein Gefängnis," therefore, lies a complex of ideas that respond to the invocation of the law in "Wir haben ein Gesetz, und nach dem Gesetz soll er sterben," that allude to the old and new covenants and to God's *Rath* as the power from above manifested in Jesus as *Gnadenstuhl*, and that identify the freedom that comes to all through Jesus's death. Like the rainbow, sign of the new covenant that prefigured the cross, Jesus is, as Rambach states, the "*Freistadt* of the new covenant." In this view the choruses, "Wir haben ein Gesetz," and "Lässest du diesen los" cry out the "Gesetzesgefangenschaft" of the Jews of John's trial, whose willful (*muthwillig*) demand for Jesus's death both identifies them as inadmissible to the *Freistadt* and creates the situation (the death of Jesus, the high priest) that enables the freedom of the faithful. Their actions, determined by God's *vorbedachtem Rath*, cannot be altered, any more than Pilate's; hence Bach's symmetrical array of repeated *turba* choruses of the Jews and Romans.

In this context, the interpretation of the *Freistädte* in the Lutheran theology of the sixteenth through the eighteenth centuries addresses an issue that was, and still is, a traditional interpretation of the meaning of Jesus's words to Pilate regarding the greater sin of those who had handed him over for trial, namely, the question of intentionality. As Johann Arndt explains:

---

[68] Ibid., 100:

> Das zeigete klärlich an, daß die Befreyung der gläubigen Israeliten von der Gefangenschaft des Gesetzes schlechterdings von dem Tode JEsu CHristi des wahren Hohenpriesters *dependire*, und als eine Frucht und Folge desselben anzusehen sey.

[69] Ibid., 94, 114:

> Es läßt sich dieses erweisen aus denselben Stellen der Schrift, **da der Glaube an den Herrn Jesum als ein fliehen und kommen zu Christo** beschrieben wird. . . . . Ach! darum eile, und errette deine Seele. Hörest du nicht, wie dein Heyland dich so beweglich einladet? Siehest du nicht, wie er seine blutigen Arme nach dir ausstrecket?

> Here the Lord makes a distinction among sins and wants to say so much: 'Those who have antagonistic, envious, poisonous, bloodthirsty and murderous hearts against me have much more to answer for; they are true murderers. God judges according to the heart, and not according to the deed. Those who in their hearts are murderers and evil, poisonous and envious people are more dreadful than those who spill blood, and greater sinners. Pilate is not so evil in his deed as the Jews with their intention and evil hearts; therefore God will judge each one according to his heart and his conscience.[70]

In such passages we have quintessential instances of the anti-Judaism (as opposed to anti-Semitism) that is associated with John and forms a considerable part of Lutheran discussions of the Passion. Depending on the particular commentaries we read, that quality will be more or less prominent. As described in chapter 6, August Hermann Francke broadens the guilt of those who delivered Jesus up for crucifixion to include *both* Jews and gentiles, and it is more common in the eighteenth century to hear that view as an alternative to the one that centers guilt on the Jews alone. We cannot know what Bach intended; but it is certainly possible that in creating a "higher level" symmetrical design that pivoted around the opposition of law and freedom, he was giving priority to theological issues over the conflicts and antagonisms that set the styles of the *turba* choruses apart from those of the meditative movements. The juxtaposition of the old and new covenants that Rambach brings out in his discussions of the *Gnadenstuhl* and the *Freistädte* is the root of the connection between the symmetrical designs of the *Actus Tragicus* (BWV 106) and the *St. John Passion*. In the *Actus Tragicus* the central complex begins with reference to the old covenant and death under the law "Es ist der alte Bund: Mensch, du musst sterben" and in the *St. John Passion* "Wir haben ein Gesetz, und nach dem Gesetz soll er sterben" is an equivalent, both movements set as fugues that appear to symbolize the strictness of the law. In the *Actus Tragicus* the freedom that is set in opposition to it is given forth by the soprano solo and its "free" melody, seeming to paraphrase the first phrase of the chorale "Herzlich tut mich verlangen." At the same time the instrumental chorale, "Ich hab' mein Sach' Gott

---

[70] Arndt, *Postilla*, (*Passions-Predigten*), 2:120:

> **Darum / der mich dir überantwortet hat / der hats größere Sünde.** Hier machet der HErr einen Unterschied unter den Sünden / und wil so viel sagen: Die / so feindselige / neidische / gifftige / blutdürstige und mörderische Hertzen haben wider mich / habens schwerer zu verantworten / das sind rechte Mörder. GOtt richtet nach dem Hertzen / und nicht nach der That. Die im Hertzen Mörder / und böse / gifftige / neidische Leute sind / sind ärger / dann die Blut vergiessen / und grössere Sünder. Pilatus ist nicht so böse mit der That / als die Juden mit ihrem Rath und bösen Hertzen / darum wird auch GOtt einen jeden nach seinem Hertzen und nach seinem Gewissen richten.

Or, as Raymond Brown states, "The implication seems to be that, since Pilate has been given a role in the passion by God, he is acting against Jesus unwittingly, but the one who handed Jesus over is acting deliberately." See *Gospel According to John (XIII–XXI)*, 29:879.

heimgestellt," adds a symbolic representation of the church. In "Durch dein Gefängnis," for reasons both theological and musical, Bach's chorale setting unifies the two.

Thus, contrary to Werner Breig's view that symmetry has entirely different meanings in the *St. John Passion* and the Credo of the *Mass in B minor* (and the motet *Jesu, meine Freude*), it is clear that the same complex of ideas underlies the designs of the *Actus Tragicus*, the Credo, and the symbolic trial of the *St. John Passion* (and, although it is beyond the scope of this discussion, the motet as well).[71] The theology of the cross is not separate in the Lutheran theology of Bach's time from God's plan of salvation or the idea of death under the law/gospel. What unifies them all is primarily the story of God's plan of redemption as told in scripture, its culmination in the work of Jesus and its meaning for present-day believers.

In his discussions of both the *Gnadenstuhl* and the *Freistadt* Rambach emphasizes the necessity of the believer's hastening to receive the benefits of her faith (a nineteenth-century edition of *Christus in Mose* even includes an engraving of a sinner running to the *Freistadt*).[72] And this hortatory character, which echoes, for example, in the line "Eilt zu seinen Gnadenthron" in Cantata 76 (*Die Himmel erzählen die Ehre Gottes*), underlies the imagery of the next meditative movement of the *St. John Passion*, the dialog for bass and chorus, "Eilt, ihr angefocht'nen Seelen." Bach's placing it at the point where, directly following John's trial, the scene shifts to Golgotha, marking the beginning of John's "Division Three" (the "way of the cross," in Raymond Brown's view). The span from "Eilt, ihr angefocht'nen Seelen" to "In meines Herzens Grunde" completes Bach's symbolic trial, articulating what Rambach called the believer's reconciling himself to the cross.

Like "Durch dein Gefängnis," "Eilt, ihr angefocht'nen Seelen" also articulates ideas of imprisonment and freedom, the former in the line "geht aus ihren Marterhöhlen" (go forth from your caves of martyrdom) and the latter in "nehmet an des Glaubens Flügel" (take up the wings of faith). Johann Mathesius, interpreting Peter's reference to the flood (1 Pet 3:10ff) in terms of the distinction between flesh and spirit in Jesus's death and resurrection, draws a parallel between those in prison ("gefengnuß") to whom Jesus preached "through the mouth of Noah" and those who were "ensnared, sitting in their bodies as though captured in prison" ("unnd sitzen im leib wie in einem Kercker gefangen"), "meaning a prison or hole, therefore that the soul in the body is ensnared as if in a prison of sin."[73] Mathesius's language makes the background connection between "Durch dein Gefängnis" and "Eilt, ihr angefocht'nen Seelen" clear. The hastening to the *Gnadenthron* that Rambach describes is the same as that urged in Bach's dialog, from the prison (*Gefängnis, Kerker*) or hole (*Höhle*) of sin and the flesh, associated with the law, to the freedom

---

[71] Breig, "Zu den Turba-Chören von Bachs Johannes-Passion," 94.

[72] Rambach, *Christus in Mose* . . . frei bearbeitet von J. Rächele (Cleveland: Lauer & Yost 1886), 457.

[73] Mathesius, *Diluvium*, fol. 98v.: "das heist ein Kercker oder Hüle / darumb daß die Seele im Leibe / wie in einem Sündekercker verstrickt ist." Mathesius refers to Isa 42:22 ("Dennoch ist es ein beraubtes und geplündertes Volk; sie sind alle gebunden in Gefängnissen und verschlossen in Kerkern."), which is alluded to in "Durch dein Gefängnis."

of the spirit. In "Eilt" the motion is rapid and upward, to the "hill of the cross" (*Kreuzeshügel*), Golgotha, which Rambach discusses as one of the sublime "high" places of scripture. Interestingly Rambach makes exactly the same association to the *Freistädte*, most of which which he describes as located on "sublime high mountains," explaining that in scripture the verbs to flee ("fliehen") and to come ("kommen") are metaphors for faith.[74]

I have described the sense of a new beginning in this movement, and its return to the key of "Herr, unser Herrscher" as a mirroring of the way of the cross in tropological terms, indicating that this idea also underlay Bach's placing a "Golgotha" dialog ("Kommt, ihr Töchter") at the head of the *St. Matthew Passion*. In this light, "Eilt, ihr angefocht'nen Seelen" fulfills the necessary hastening of the believer to the *Gnadenstuhl* and the *Freistadt*. Thus the dialog has a double function: it initiates meditation on the crucifixion itself, and it allegorizes the internalizing of its meaning. That Bach returned to the flat key *ambitus* with which the symbolic trial (and the Passion) began, presenting the last of the symmetrical *turba* choruses in its original B♭, marks this segment as one of resolution, completed with "In meines Herzens Grunde." Yet at the same time the "upward" motion continues on to the point of Jesus's death, in "Es ist vollbracht" and "Mein teurer Heiland," the latter of which, once again a dialog for bass solo with chorus, voices the question of freedom for the faithful in its most comforting form, that of the pastorale.

"In meines Herzens Grunde" is both an affirmation of the believer's commitment to the name and cross of Christ as key to his salvation and a prayer for Jesus to appear to the believer in the image of his suffering, source of *Trost*. This link back to "Betrachte, meine Seele" and "Erwäge" is amplified by the ancient association between God's new covenant with Noah after the flood (the rainbow imagery of "Erwäge") and the fulfillment of that covenant, through Jesus's cross, a traditional parallel that is drawn in many of the theological books of the seventeenth and eighteenth centuries.

Some of the imagery underlying "In meines Herzens Gründe" and its role in Bach's symbolic trial can be seen in the double-paged frontispiece to the edition of Heinrich Müller's *Evangelischer Herzens-Spiegel* that was published in 1705 together with Joachim Lütkemann's *Apostolischer Herzens-Wecker*, as well as with the Müller Passion sermons that influenced Picander's poetry for the *St. Matthew Passion* (Ill. 8.1).[75] As we see, the two pages are entirely symmetrical in layout, and the concept of symmetry is itself reinforced by the mirror imagery that occupies the upper half of the first page. There we see the principal image of "In meines Herzens Grunde" in the center: two cherubs hold a heart within which the cross

[74] Rambach, *Betrachtung des Geheimnisses*, 94–95. See also n. 75.

[75] Müller, *D. Henrici Müllers, . . . Evangelischer Herzens-Spiegel; Imgleichen D. Joachimi Lütkemanns, . . . Apostolischer Herzens-Wecker, . . . Wiederum aufgelegt mit der Vorrede D. Johannis Diekmanns* (Stade, 1705). I have used the edition of 1736. Lütkemann (1608–55) and Müller (1631–75) have been described, along with Christian Scriver (1629–93), as the "trio of outstanding Arndtian Pietists"; see also F. Ernest Stoeffler, *The Rise of Evangelical Pietism* (Leiden: E. J. Brill, 1973), 224.

appears with the name "Jesus" in both horizontal and vertical forms ("dein Nam' und Kreuz allein"). The connection to Luther's signet ring, which also seems to allude to the *Himmsleschlüsselblume* of "Betrachte, meine Seele," is apparent. On the top of the heart, flames and sparks issue forth ("funkelt allzeit und Stunde"). Müller's introductory remarks explain the mirror imagery as representing a double process according to which the understanding of Jesus ("Erkänntniß Christi") fans the "little sparks" ("Fünklein") of love for Christ.[76] In this book the concept of scripture as a mirror is central to Müller's interpretations of the Gospels of the liturgical year, each of which he discusses in terms of what he calls a "tröstliches Jesus-Spiegel" (comforting Jesus-mirror) on the one hand, and an "erbauliches Herzens-Spiegel" (edifying mirror of the heart), on the other. In keeping with this twofold meaning, with their other hands the cherubs (ill. 8.1) hold two mirrors in which the central image is reflected out to the viewer. The idea that the image of Jesus in scripture produces a comforting image in the heart suggests the line "erschein mir in dem Bild zu Trost in meiner Not" of "In meines Herzens Grunde." In this view the believer's understanding (*Erkenntnis*) of Jesus through scripture leads to self-understanding, a process that is very close to the descent/ascent character of Luther's "summary" meaning of scripture. As Müller presents it, the "Erkenntnis Christi" embodied in recognition of Jesus's love is made firm through the cross, the supreme manifestation of Jesus's love. The impact of this first stage on the believer leads to the second one, knowledge of ourselves ("Erkänntniß unser selbst"), that is, of our unworthiness and condemned nature, which "strikes us down" (*schlägt uns nieder*), after which the third stage "shows what we should be" (*was wir seyn sollen*), effecting the more positive work of revealing "how the image of God in us is restored through the cross" (*wie das Bild Gottes durchs Creutz in uns solle erneuert werden*). Thus Müller usually divides the aspect he calls the "erbauliches Herzens-Spiegel" into three stages—a threefold "showing"—that describe how the meaning of scripture is internalized by the believer.[77] And the theology of the cross is, as we might expect, central to the entire process. In the first of the Passion sermons that appear directly following the cycle of Gospel and epistle sermons, Müller returns to the idea of the mirror. The life of faith is, of course, a pilgrimage toward the heavenly Jerusalem; and, as Müller explains, analogous to the images of the Passion that were placed along the pilgrimage routes for the consolation of pilgrims in their need, the image of the crucified Jesus impressed itself "within the heart of the faithful as a living *Trost-Spiegel*, from which full revival comes for the burdened and troubled hearts."[78] This is, of course, the substance of the lines "Erschein mir in dem Bilde, zu Trost in meiner Not, wie du, Herr Christ, so milde dich hast geblut' zu Tod" of "In meines Herzens Grunde." In this the span from "Eilt, ihr angefocht'nen Seelen," whose text describes the be-

---

[76] Müller, *Evangelischer Herzens-Spiegel*, 2.

[77] Ibid., 2–3.

[78] Ibid., 1405.

ILLUSTRATION 8.1a and b **Frontispiece and title page of Heinrich Müller's *Evangelischer Herzens-Spiegel* and Joachim Lütkemann's *Apostolischer Herzens-Wecker,* from the edition of Stade 1736.**

liever's hastening to Golgotha as a pilgrimage ("euer Wohlfahrt blüht allda"), to "In meines Herzens Grunde," whose text calls for the image of the Jesus of the Passion to appear within the believer's heart, mirrors the tropological sense as Müller presents it.

The mirrored engravings of the name and cross of Jesus within the heart on Müller's frontispiece serve as a symbol of the entire process according to which Jesus's life and work become operative in the believer. The reversal of the name

ILLUSTRATION 8.1a and b (*continued*)

"Jesus," as the cross within the heart is reflected out toward the viewer, makes a conceptual correlation between symmetrical reversal and the meaning of the cross. And the symmetry of the mirror images extends to the images of Müller and Lütkemann below (Müller holding out the motto "Crux Christi nostra Gloria") and the medallions that flank a central image of their call as preachers (Müller's medallion has several further heart images containing crosses). The righthand page then extends the symmetry to images of the Last Supper, the crucifixion, resurrection, ascension, and descent of the Holy Spirit on the top, with figures right and left below, beneath whom appear a pair of crossed keys on the left pedestal and the cross itself on the right, an obvious projection of equivalence. The figures may have been intended as the apostles Peter and John, with the *Himmelsschlüssel* as Peter's emblem and the cross as John's (as well as the book in his right hand). In his introductory first sermon, Müller speaks of Peter and John according to their traditional character types, Peter as "fiery and zealous," John as "gentle and soft of mood," Peter as flesh and John as spirit, adding that both must be contained within the believer and that both must struggle within the believer, but in such a manner that John must be the victor.[79]

In illustration 8.1 we see some of the correlates for the symmetrical design of the symbolic trial of the *St. John Passion* as it is reflected in the imagery of the *Himmelsschlüssel* of "Betrachte, meine Seele" and the cross and name of Jesus within "In meines Herzens Grunde." Clearly, "In meines Herzens Grunde" is to be thought of as a symbol of how meditation on the Passion is internalized by the believer, mirrored within the heart, as it were. Its prayer for the image of the crucified Jesus as one of *Trost* for the believer ("Erschein' mir in dem Bilde, zu Trost in meiner Not, wie du, Herr Christ, so milde, dich hast geblüt't zu Tod") is a culminating point in the "showing" of the meaning of the Passion that is prayed for in "Herr, unser Herrscher." That meaning is, of course, one that encompasses "inversion" or reversal, in the sense that the literal, adverse events of Jesus's Passion are understood in terms of their salvific meaning. In this way the expression of Jesus's identity by means of the irony of the royal inscription extends to the meaning of the Passion (and beyond the Passion) as a whole.

The "Nam'" and "Kreuz" of "In meines Herzens Grunde" link up with the rainbow of "Erwäge" and the *Gnadenthron* of "Durch dein Gefängnis" as God's *Gnadenzeichen*, embodying a double reference to the symmetrical design of the symbolic trial (i.e., cruciform design and chiastic structure), so that with "In meines Herzens Grunde" Bach can be said to summarize the elevated meaning of his symbolic trial as that of a sign from above within the suffering world below. The power from above that prevents Pilate's freeing Jesus—God's *Rath*—causes him to place the inscription. The flat/sharp curve from "Betrachte" and "Erwäge" to "Durch dein Gefängnis" is a motion from Jesus's sufferings to the message of their meaning for humanity, from meditation on Jesus's *Niedrigkeit* to the image of him seated on the *Gnadenthron*; it anticipates his glorification via the "lifting up" of the cross, expressed ironically in the royal inscription and meditated on in "In meines Herzens Grunde," then openly proclaimed in "Es ist vollbracht." The es-

[79] Ibid., 3 (sermon on the gospel for the first Sunday in Advent, questioning whether the two disciples sent by Jesus to fetch a donkey for his entry into Jerusalem were Peter and John):

> Obs Petrus und Johannes gewesen, stehet eigentlich nicht zu wissen. Es ist aber wol glaublich. Denn Petrus war hitzig und eiferig, Johannes aber sanfftmühtig und gelinde. Beydes, mein Herz, ist in dir zusammen, der hitzige Petrus, dein Fleisch, und der sanfftmühtige Johannes, dein Geist. Beydes muß in dir seyn, beydes muß zusammen streiten, aber Johannes muß den Sieg behalten.

sence of the cross is that it express two contrary extremes, of worldly suffering and eternal glory (as in the *symbola* of Müller's "Crux Christi Nostra Gloria" and Bach's "Christus Coronabit Crucigeros"); hence the narrative of the crucifixion in deep flats and the projection of its meaning in the triumphant D of "Es ist vollbracht" and the pastorale security of "Mein teurer Heiland." The symbolic trial (Smend's *Herzstück*) is an image of these extremes. In its flat/sharp antitheses it mirrors the provocative character of the cross in the world—all that the Lutheranism of Bach's time understood as the meaning of *Ärgernis*. In its return to the flat keys in which it began it allegorizes the believer's resolving him or herself to the cross.

Bach's most common means of depicting the double meaning of the cross, however, are not concerned with large-scale symmetry, such as we find in the *St. John Passion*, where the "problem" of finding a logical design for the diverse movement types was paramount. As Smend pointed out, in a number of Bach's autograph scores he utilizes the sign *X* as abbreviation for the word "Kreuz."[80] Smend, oddly, does not mention the fact that the same sign was widely associated with the sharp sign, as was the word "Kreuz" in the music treatises of the seventeenth and eighteenth centuries. And, of course, it was even more widely used as an abbreviation for all or part of the word "Christus." Thus in the emblem book of Dilherr/Harsdörffer, mentioned earlier, we find fairly frequent use of a sign (called "Zeichen" by the authors) that embodies the letters *CHRS* surmounted by a cross (usually placed between the letters *H* and *R* and rising above them, in one instance mounted on the letter *H*).[81] In two instances this sign, unifying the name and cross, is placed within a heart, in another within a heart-shaped shield. And Bach uses the *X* as abbreviation for "Kreuz" in movements where the meaning of the cross is the subject matter, such as the arias "Durchs Feuer wird das Silber rein" from Cantata 2 (*Ach Gott, vom Himmel sieh darein*) and "Kreuz und Krone sind verbunden" from Cantata 12 (*Weinen, Klagen, Sorgen, Zagen*), and the first movement of the "Kreuzstab" cantata (BWV 56, I*ch will den Kreuzstab gerne tragen*).[82] Likewise he uses the *X* sign for the beginning of the word "Christus" several times in the autograph score of the *Christmas Oratorio*, for example, whereas in the autograph score of the *St. Matthew Passion* we find the *X* appearing not only as an abbreviation for the words "Kreuz" and the first four letters of the name "*Chr*istus" (i.e., as substitute for the Greek letter *chi*), but also, as in the "Kreuzstab" cantata, in association with sharpened, provocative pitches.[83] In addition the sign also appears for expressions

---

[80] Smend, "Luther und Bach," in *Bach-Studien*, 168. Smend does not make the connection to the sharp sign as "Kreuz" either here or in his later study of Cantata 56 (*Joh. Seb. Bach: Kirchen-Kantaten, Heft* 6. [Berlin: Der Christliche Zeitschriftenverlag, 1947], 25–27).

[81] See n. 37.

[82] In the aria from Cantata 2 the abbreviation appears for the lines "Durchs X [Kreuz] das Wort bewährt erfunden" and "Drum soll ein Xst [Christ] zu allen Stunden im X [Kreuz] und Not geduldig sein."

[83] These and many more instances of the *X* as abbreviation for "Kreuz" appear in the Altnikol copy of the earlier version of the *St. Matthew Passion* (In "Andern hat er geholfen," Ja, freilich will das Fleisch und Blut" and "Komm, süsses Kreuz," for example), and were presumably carried over from an earlier (now lost) score of Bach's.

of the softening, or "sweetening," of the cross for the believer. The last mentioned association has a long pedigree in medieval hermeneutics. As Henri de Lubac indicates, in the culminating segment of his chapter on the tropological sense, the internalizing of God's word was widely described in exactly such terms throughout the Middle Ages and associated with the tropological sense as "interiorized allegory."[84] We have encountered this double meaning of the cross in Rambach's view of the cross and the royal inscription mentioned in chapter 7. The most significant appearances of this last-mentioned association in the *St. Matthew Passion* are the arias "Gerne will ich mich bequemen" and "Komm, süsses Kreuz," in the latter of which the instances of the "sharp" association of the cross sign are outnumbered by others that suggest resolution instead; indeed, the manner in which Bach's opening theme places the sharpened pitch on the word "süsses," rather than "Kreuz," points out that, coming late in the Passion, "Komm, süsses Kreuz" is occupied entirely with the positive, tropological meaning of the cross.

Conclusion: The "duplex" meaning of the St. John Passion

The "symbolic" aspect of the *St. John Passion* structure, with which this study has dealt extensively, is only one view of the work, one corresponding to a vision or image of God's divine control over human events. And this view is quite similar in concept to the design of the *Actus Tragicus*, where it mirrors the understanding of God's time and word, or of the Credo of the *Mass in B minor*, where it depicts the summary meaning of scripture. As in those and many other works, it can be understood only in relation to those aspects of the works that are more directly concerned with the sphere of human affect: that of expression. In the musical tradition most closely bound up with the religious character of such works (what I have called the Lutheran metaphysical tradition, exemplified above all by Andreas Werckmeister), the separation of the two aspects in question was conceived as that of *ratio* and *sensus*, the former concerned with proportion, *Ordnung*, eternal verities, and all else that pointed to God the omnipotent creator, and the latter to the imperfect sphere of the human senses. Mathematically, God's sphere was simpler and more perfect, centered on the first six whole numbers, their multiples and ratios, whereas the human world was one clouded by ambiguities, uncertainties, doubts, and faulty perceptions, all mirrored in the irrational ratios of the tempered scale, which Werckmeister, its foremost advocate, called "a nice moral [i.e., an allegory] of our mortality and imperfection in this life."[85]

---

[84] de Lubac, *Medieval Exegesis*, 2:162–77.

[85] Werckmeister, *Musicae mathematicae hodegus curiosus*, 145. As in the title of the appendix in which this phrase appears, "Anhang von der allegorischen und moralischen Music," Werckmeister is here using the term "moralischen" to signify the tropological sense. Similar associations appear in Werckmeister's *Harmonologia Musica* and *Musicalische Paradoxal-Discourse*.

In Bach's time the force of these ideas was substantially lessened under the influence of both pietism and the enlightenment; and the change was mirrored in music theory by Johann Mattheson's proclaiming *sensus* unequivocally the victor in the conflict with *ratio*.[86] For him, and for most musicians, the ear was virtually the sole judge of such matters as consonance and dissonance, the relevance of the modes, and of older music theory in general for the understanding of music and the like. From one standpoint the outcome of this new view was a substantial lightening of the texture and loosening-up of the rhythmic character of music, changes that often suggest simplification and transitoriness, which Bach himself perhaps recognized and resisted in his remark about the music of his son Carl Phillip Emmanuel, that "it's like Prussian blue, it fades." (This remark should probably not be taken too seriously as a value judgment on his son's music, which is still very much alive, and still vivid.) While it became simpler in some respects, the new music also turned to a more complex view of human psychology, at least in terms of its capacity to mirror rapidly changing moods in closed movements (rather than just the recitatives). A new sense of dramatic individualism was the outcome, a fluidity in the conception of "character" that went far beyond the concerns of seventeenth- and early-eighteenth-century styles. Immediacy of affect became paramount while traditional, hierarchical systems of thought declined. And this emphasis on psychological motivations, our legacy, had a very powerful influence on the interpretation of artworks, above all in a lessening of interest in and understanding of theological meaning, also our legacy.

At the outset of this chapter I referred to Leo Steinberg's book on Leonardo Da Vinci's *Last Supper*, a painting that, in recent years has come again, with a vengeance, into the public eye, and for all the wrong reasons. Nevertheless, as Steinberg presents it, Leonardo's masterpiece has enormous parallels to the *St. John Passion* in the simultaneity of its symmetrical and its dynamic aspects, its two themes: (1) the drama of the announcement of Judas's betrayal, with all its immediate psychological ramifications, and (2) the institution of the sacrament, timeless in its impact for future generations. In a situation parallel to musical interpretation after Bach's time, the dramatic, psychological aspect dominated for a long time in the interpretation of Leonardo's painting, especially after the tremendous influence of its advocacy by Goethe. From the one perspective the painting exhibits an astonishing degree of predeterminism: the grouping of the figures, the contours of their bodies, direction of their arms, placement of the hands, all align with the geometry of the wall tapestries, floor tiles, and ceiling coffers. Jesus is centralized as an equilateral triangle, symbol of the Trinity, while countless correspondences and antitheses in the interactions of the disciples lend the picture its profound sense of predetermined order, all suggestive of the theological subject and the plan of God that

[86] This view of the priority of *sensus* over *ratio* is proclaimed immediately on the title page to Mattheson's, *Das forschende Orchestre* (Hamburg, 1713) "darinn *SENSUS VINDICIAE* . . ."

gave it being.[87] Geometrically, the picture's symmetrical dimension delineates the cross, the last judgment, and the Trinity, while the many traditional gestures Leonardo carried over from earlier artworks introduce sets of signific correlates that reach well beyond the literal narrative. At the same time, the disciples can be viewed as individuals, reacting in their various ways to a dramatic moment and contributing, with many of the same gestures and geometries, to a more subjective-seeming left/right, dark/light, descending/ascending direction, that is both symmetrical and subverting of symmetry. In Werckmeister's terms, *sensus* and *ratio* come into congruence but do not resolve into one another.

The comparison to Bach's design for the *St. John Passion* seems obvious. From a dramatic-psychological standpoint, the choruses of the Jews exhibit at times a frenzied character, above all "Wäre dieser nicht ein Übeltäter" and "Wir dürfen niemand töten" with their rising and falling chromatic lines, and the two "kreuzige ihn" choruses with their fast-galloping "kreuzige" rhythmic figures. The former pair, which I have placed outside the symbolic trial, can be thought to "frame" the first reference to the law (Pilate's "So nehmet ihr ihn hin und richtet ihn nach eurem Gesetze"), while the appearance of the "Jesus of Nazareth" music in the second of the two provides an alternative meaning that, soon afterwards, echoes in "Nicht diesen, sondern Barrabam." The "kreuzige ihn" choruses form part of a larger array that pivots around the issue of law versus freedom; again, soon after the second of the pair ("Weg, weg mit dem, kreuzige ihn") we hear the last appearance of the "Jesus of Nazareth" music (as "Wir haben keinen König denn den Kaiser"), where it seems almost to be joined to "Weg, weg mit dem," (see ch. 7). It appears that the "Jesus of Nazareth" music is at least in part a response to the frenzy of the mob, a hidden meaning that emerges, still in partial disguise, to give voice to the principle of meaning reversal. That the repetitions of music are components of a higher order, from which the meaning reversal comes, is just what Leonardo accomplished in the "duplex" character of Leonardo's *Last Supper*, in which "in severe symmetry the Apostles exhibit every conceivable emotional reflex."[88]

---

[87] In the *Last Supper* St. John leans passively away from Jesus on his right side, forming a descending triangle in opposition to the ascending triangle of Jesus's figure, whereas on Jesus's left St. Thomas presses forward aggressively, intruding himself into the space between Jesus and James Major (another "descending" triangle, less articulated than that between John and Jesus). Among the welter of activity involving the disciples' hands, John's are restful, placed on the table folded, a virtually unique occurrence. One might imagine that Leonardo set the two disciples in a kind of opposition that mirrors the fact that Thomas is the arch skeptic, demanding physical evidence for belief, whereas John is the evangelist who most emphasizes faith and in whose gospel Jesus says to Thomas: "Thomas, because thou hast seen me, thou hast believed: blessed are they that have not seen, and yet have believed" (20:29, KJV). And surely the well-known convergence of the perspective lines on Jesus's right temple reflects his reference (cited in ch. 2, n. 68) to his body as the Temple that would be destroyed in the Passion and rebuilt in the resurrection. Italian and Latin, like English, make an association between the "temple" of the body and the church.

[88] Max Semrau, *Die Kunst der Renaissance in Italien und im Norden* (Esslingen a. N., 1912), 270; cited in Steinberg, *Leonardo's Incessant Last Supper*, 129. In Bach's *St. John Passion* the closest equivalents to the emotional response of the disciples are those involving Peter: his drawing the sword early

Leonardo, however, as Steinberg shows, "subverts" the symmetry in countless ways, none of which is more compelling than the left/right, darkness/light motion of the picture overall, which seems to indicate the ultimate trajectory of the duplex event. It is also, as Steinberg suggests, a descent/ascent motion, dependent on the outlining of that shape by the architectural elements that—in any culture that reads from left to right—perceives "that which runs in the direction of a left-right diagonal" as "rising, the opposite as falling."[89] Left/right motion is, of course, spatial, not temporal, as are music and scripture. But descent/ascent and darkness/light are powerful Johannine themes that may be mirrored in music. And the privileging of one direction over another is possible in music as well. In the *St. John Passion,* too, Bach very pointedly "subverts" his symmetrical design. And his means are, as we would expect, bound up with the purely temporal quality of music. I have mentioned how the flat/sharp motion from "Betrachte, meine Seele" to "Durch dein Gefängnis" outlines the keys of Heinichen's B♭/g *ambitus* in the keys of the closed movements, a process that lasts some fifteen minutes or longer (depending on the performance). From "Durch dein Gefängnis" to "Eilt, ihr angefocht'nen Seelen," however, lasts less than five minutes and is reflected in the reverse pattern of the A/f♯ *ambitus* that takes us to D for the end of the trial proper and involves recitative cadences as well as the keys of the closed movements. Then, after the quick shift to flats, the span from "Eilt, ihr angefocht'nen Seelen" through "In meines Herzens Grunde" lasts approximately seven minutes. The second "half" is noticeably shorter than the first, largely because "Erwäge" often takes more than eight minutes on its own.[90] The point is not that of balance or imbalance in length or timing, but of the fact that our hearing of the span is affected enormously by the lengths of individual movements and the reasons for those lengths, by the pacing of the modulations. The different kinds and diverse weighting of temporal motion that are contained within this span, the very idea of symmetry seems questionable to some. Yet, in other works in which symmetry is prominent, the second-act love scene of Wagner's *Tristan und Isolde*, and most of the second act of Alban Berg's *Lulu*, for example, the journey "out" is longer than the journey "back," which is probably a necessity because the journey back involves so much repetition (that is, the process of recognizing what was heard be-

---

in the Passion, his denials, and, above all, the aria "Ach, mein Sinn" (which is not actually Peter but the response of the contemporary believer to Peter's denials). "Ach, mein Sinn" is celebrated for its tormented affective character.

[89] Steinberg, 130, n. 6. Steinberg cites a letter from Rudolf Arnheim as the source of the quotation.

[90] In an as yet unpublished study of the *St. John Passion* that he very kindly sent to me, John Eliot Gardiner views "Betrachte" and "Erwäge" as the center of the Passion, its most sustained meditative movements. In their instrumentation, length, pictorial correlates, and expressive depth these two movements certainly stand out. And in their associating the central theme of the urge to meditation with the center of John's trial, they articulate the view of the Lutheranism of Bach's time like no others. That multiple views are possible—that the two movements also mark a beginning (of the "symbolic trial")—attests to the "duplex" character of the Passion, its confronting *sensus* (hearing, affect), and *ratio* (proportion, visual correlates, and the like) at all levels of its design.

fore does not require full statement; there are probably other, "psychological" reasons as well).

Suffice it to say, that in the *St. John Passion* Bach produced his *own* complex vision of the trial of Jesus, one whose oppositions and "shape" extended to the layout of the entire work. Whereas other Bach works give great emphasis to the process of descent, the *St. John Passion* emphasizes, like Leonardo's *Last Supper*, the ascent element, represented in the three regions of flat/sharp motion, as described earlier. They can be thought of as comparable to the left/right motion in the *Last Supper*. The "ascending" character of Jesus's identity and work that many theologians have seen in John's Gospel is the dominant one. The E major at the center of the symbolic trial ("Durch dein Gefängnis") is an expression of the "highest good" as anticipated in "Betrachte, meine Seele," the believer's seeing "through" the adverse events of the physical drama below to the vision of Jesus on the throne of grace. The turnaround that follows, as that E is picked up in "Lässest du diesen los" and eventually led back to the flat keys with which the trial began, returns the perspective to the physical world, in both its positive and negative lights. It is in this way that Peter's failure to affirm the E that is offered him in "Bist du nicht seiner Jünger einer?" should be viewed. When we listen to the narrative of the ascending modulations of the Passion we are presented with how, as Stephen S. Smalley remarks, "the ascension is 'built-in' to every aspect of John's theological line" (see n. 8). The framework is the world; the meaning points elsewhere. In the best tradition of religious art, the *St. John Passion* conveys a profound sense of the divine and the human. No serious attempt to grapple with John could do otherwise.

{ PART III }

The Cantatas for Spring 1725

{9}

Easter through Misericordias: Cantatas 249, 6, 42, and 85

Spring 1725: An overview

In the liturgical year as Bach knew it, the fifty-day period from Easter to Pentecost commemorated the climactic fulfillment of Jesus's work on earth—the Passion and resurrection—followed, after a series of Jesus's intermittent appearances to the disciples and others, by his return to the world above (Ascension Day). This was followed in turn by feast days celebrating the coming of the Holy Spirit and the Trinity. Rooted in the Jewish Pentecost, or feast of seven weeks from Passover (*pesach*, pascha), to the feast of first fruits, the Christian fifty-day period was subdivided at the fortieth day, in commemoration of Jesus's ascension, which had its opposite time in the season of Lent, associated with the forty days of Jesus's fasting in the wilderness.

This time period, sometimes known as the "great forty days," was rooted in Acts 1:3, "To whom [i.e., the disciples] also he showed himself alive after his Passion by many infallible proofs, being seen of them forty days, and speaking of the things pertaining to the kingdom of God." As Johann Arndt described the forty days, they served as a preparation for the disciples, providing love and consolation through Jesus's discourses ("Wort und Rede") and providing a "Trost-Spiegel" of the holy Christian church.[1] Johann Jacob Rambach gave special emphasis to Ascension Day and the great forty days in terms of God's *Rath*, even titling an Ascension Day sermon "Der Rath Gottes in der Himmelfahrt Jesu Christi."[2] For August Pfeiffer,

---

[1] Johann Arndt, *Postilla*, 3:164–65.

[2] Rambach, *Evangelische Betrachtungen über die Sonn- und Fest-Tags-Evangelia des gantzen Jahrs*, 635–60. Rambach draws a detailed analogy between the great forty days and the forty days from Christmas to the feast of the Purification (formerly Epiphany), comparing the temple in which the infant Jesus was presented with the heavenly temple of the ascension, the offering prescribed by Jewish law with Jesus's offering himself as an offering on behalf of humanity, and Jesus's *Niedrigkeit* on the Mount of Olives in the Passion with his ascension from the mount of olives.

and many before him, the forty days involved a threefold "scopus," according to which Jesus was a triumphant "Überwinder," an extension of the Easter victory, a "Durchbrecher" (the traditional view of Jesus's opening up heaven for humanity through his ascension) and the giver of life through the Spirit and the sacraments (Pentecost).[3] At the same time, Arndt and many other Lutherans viewed the forty days as a mirror, or prefiguration of the eternal life to come, when Jesus would speak to the faithful "not just forty days, but ever and eternally."[4] Jesus's "Wort und Rede" during the forty days were associated with his last comforting words to the disciples, John's Farewell Discourse, from which the Gospel readings for the three Sundays before and the two following Ascension Day, culminating on Pentecost, were drawn and embedded within the larger framework of readings from elsewhere in John (see fig. 3.2, ch. 3). Through the metaphor of Jesus as "head" (of the church) and the faithful as "members," Jesus's ascension assured the ascension of the faithful, so that, as Arndt put it, "in faith and hope we have already journeyed spiritually to heaven with Him."[5] Thus, although John has no ascension narrative, the character of that feast was indebted to his emphasis on realized eschatology.

From very early times the reading of John's account of the Passion and resurrection was associated with the Passion and Easter, whereas the readings from John during the time after Easter apparently came only later, during the increasing reformulation of the liturgy as a historico-commemorative cycle. It is significant that those readings begin on Quasimodogeniti, the Sunday after Easter, which commemorates the second and third post-resurrection appearances of Jesus as told by John, the first—Jn 20:14–17—having been to Mary Magdalene at the tomb. In the liturgy they follow Luke's narratives of Jesus's post-resurrection appearances (Lk 24:13–35 and 36–47), which took place on the evening of the resurrection and were assigned as the Gospel readings for Easter Monday and Tuesday. John's second and third post-resurrection appearances (Jn 20:19–31) likewise took place on the evening of the resurrection, and as was the case with the three days of Christ-

[3] Pfeiffer, *Evangelisches Schatz-Kammer,* 523–25.

[4] Arndt, *Postilla,* 3:165: "In diese vierzigtäge Beywohnung ist ein Spiegel des ewigen Lebens da wir bey dem Herrn seyn werden allezeit und aus seinem holdselige Munde / als von dem Baum des Lebens essen werden / die höchste Süssigkeit und Lieblichkeit seiner Rede . . . Was für grosse Freude und Holdseligkeit wird im ewigen Leben aus dem Munde JEsu Christi gehen / da er nicht viertzig Tage mit uns reden wird / sondern immer und ewig?"; Martin Moller, *Praxis Evangeliorum,* 269: "Ja meine Seele / wir lesen nicht / daß er diese viertzig Tage uber einigen Anstoß behabt / weder vom Teuffel noch Welt / noch Tode. Denn er hatte alles uberwunden. Darumb / liebe Seele / waren diese viertzig Tage ein schönes Vorbild des ewigen Lebens / darinnen wir bey unserm HErrn weyn werden / nicht nur viertzig Tage lang / sondern immer und ewiglich."

[5] Arndt, *Postilla,* 3:175: "Also sind wir im Glauben und Hoffnung allbereit geistlich mit ihm gen Himmel gefahren. (Many others say the same, often citing Paul in Ephesians 2:6 to the effect that God has already "made us sit together in heavenly places in Christ Jesus.") Arndt views the spiritual ascension of the faithful as one that will be followed at the last judgment by an ascension that is more real or actual (*wirklich*), in that it will also involve our physical bodies. Commenting on the same passage, August Hermann Francke says "daß sie nicht ernst am jüngsten Tage, sondern bereits in dieser Welt in das himmlische Wesen samt und in Christo gesetzet sind." (*Predigten über Sonn- und Fest-Tags Episteln,* Halle, 1724, 863).

mas, his account was arranged so as to follow narratives of the evangelist who is most concerned with history. Luke's recounting of Jesus's appearances presents him as the promised redeemer of Israel who, in both accounts, expounds on scripture from Moses through the prophets with particular reference to their prediction of the events that have now just taken place. Luke's second account relates to those of John in that Jesus appears suddenly in the midst of the troubled disciples, speaking "Peace be with you," and showing his hands and feet.

In John's account Jesus's second appearance to the disciples (Jn 20:19–23) was followed directly by the third (Jn 20:24–31), which related the story of "doubting Thomas," eight days later, when Jesus again appeared in the midst of the disciples who were within, "the doors being shut." In the liturgy both narratives were read as the Gospel for the Sunday after Easter, initiating the series of Johannine readings that continued, with only one exception, through Pentecost and Trinity Sunday. The identification of the sabbath with the first day of the week, Sunday, rather than the last, Saturday, is significant in light of the fact that this oldest part of the Christian liturgy was closely bound up with the change from Judaism to Christianity. Quasimodogeniti has a special role in this process, since in the early church baptism took place on Easter Day, and confirmation (which was not observed at all times and places, and was dropped from the Lutheran liturgy), either immediately followed baptism or took place on the following Sunday, which was called "white Sunday," or *Domenica in Albis*, a reference to the taking off of the white robes worn by the newly baptized and confirmed, a symbol of purity and rebirth.[6]

Thus, on Quasimodogeniti, after celebration of the Passion and resurrection, the liturgy symbolically enacted those events in the immersion/emergence pattern of baptism, as August Hermann Francke described at the end of his lectures on the *St. John Passion*. Quasimodogeniti not only begins the sequence of Johannine post-Easter readings but it is also the only Sunday of that sequence on which both the Gospel and epistle readings come from John. And when we consider those readings the rationale behind their choice is clear. In the Gospel (Jn 20:19–31) Jesus's appearance in the midst of the disciples, who were behind locked doors, is an addition of John's that emphasized the miraculous character of the event more than Luke's account. For many authors throughout the centuries, therefore, it received a tropological interpretation: Jesus's sudden appearance within the heart (a metaphor for faith and rebirth). And this quality was reflected in the fact that both the epistle and Gospel for the day refer to the Holy Spirit. In the part of the Gospel narrative that took place on the evening of Easter Day, Jesus speaks the words "Peace be unto you" (peace encompassing a reference to the sabbath, as in Francke's tropological interpretation of baptism), following it with the words that were traditionally understood as his giving his "mission" to the disciples: "as my Father

[6] Martin Moller (*Praxis Evangeliorum*, 119) so describes Quasimodogeniti, explaining the word, as do August Hermann Francke and Valerius Herberger (*Herz-Postilla*, 402) and many others, as referring to those who were reborn through baptism.

hath sent me, even so send I you (v. 21)." John continues, "And when he had said this, he breathed on them, and said unto them, receive ye the Holy Ghost (v. 22); whoever's sins ye remit, they are remitted unto them; and whose sins you retain, they are retained (v. 23)." This verse, known to Lutherans as the narrative of the "keys" (because of its conferring authority as the keys of the kingdom on the disciples), had been understood by the Roman church to refer to the papacy, an interpretation resisted by the Lutherans, who nevertheless understood it to refer to the establishing of the Christian church. As God had breathed physical life into Adam, now (in the epistle for Quasimodogeniti) Jesus breathed the Holy Spirit into the disciples, giving them their mission. And, as God had promised in the "proto-Gospel" of Genesis, Jesus in his Passion and resurrection had restored humanity to God's grace. The evening time was a symbolic bond between the two, as Johann Gerhard pointed out:

> As in earlier times he came to our first parents in the evening as the day had become cool, and revealed to them the promise regarding the seed of woman, that humanity would tread upon the head of the serpent, so he also comes now toward evening to his disciples, brings them the message that he has now trod upon the head of the serpent of hell through his resurrection, and won the true peace, and has also made everything good again that was lost through the fall.[7]

Then, in the part of the narrative that took place the following week, Jesus speaks the words of faith that reach out to future generations, "Thomas, because you have seen me, you have believed: blessed are they that have not seen, and yet have believed" (v. 29). Together, the two episodes that form the Gospel reading for Quasimodogeniti establish the authority of the disciples in the early church while at the same time indicating faith as the means by which later Christians could attain the victory won by Jesus. The Gospel ends with the famous words regarding other "signs" performed by Jesus with the disciples as witnesses: "But these are written that you might believe that Jesus is the Christ, the Son of God; and that believing you might have life through his name."

The epistle for the day (1 Jn 5:4–10) must have been selected so as to relate directly to the Gospel reading, for it likewise seems to make foundational statements regarding the early church, its sacraments and the power of faith. John begins with

---

[7] Johann Gerhard, *Postille, das ist Auslegung und Erklärung der sonntäglichen und vornehmsten Fest-Evangelien über das ganze Jahr . . . Nach den Original-Ausgaben fon 1613 und 1616. Vermehrt durch die Zusätze der Ausgabe von 1663* (Berlin, 1870), 389: "Wie Er vorzeiten um den Abend, da der Tag kühle war, zu den ersten Eltern kam und ihnen die Verheißung vom Weibessamen offenbarete, daß derselbe der Schlange den Kopf zertreten sollte, also kommt Er auch allhie gegen Abend zu seinen Jüngern, bringet ihnen die Botschaft, daß Er nunmehr durch seine Auferstehung der hölllischen Schlange den Kopf zertreten und den wahren Frieden erworben, auch alles wiederum gemacht habe, was durch den Fall verderbet war." The resonance of this text to that of the arioso "Am Abend, da es kühle war" from the *St. Matthew Passion* is noteworthy. For a broader range of associations for the Genesis passage and evening in general see ch. 2, n. 21.

faith: "For whatsoever is born of God overcomes the world; and this is the victory that overcomes the world, even our faith." John then speaks of "three who bear witness in heaven, the Father, the Word, and the Holy Spirit; and these three are one," then of "three that bear witness in earth, the spirit, and the water, and the blood: and these three agree in one." Water is associated with baptism, of course, whereas blood is associated with the Eucharist, and the Holy Spirit with both. In the choice of this reading, the two major means of induction into the church, baptism and confirmation were brought into a liturgical relationship with Easter and Quasimodogeniti. Taken along with John's remark, in the epistle for Quasimodogeniti, that faith in Jesus was the victory that overcame the world, this bonding through the Spirit of the Trinity above with the institutes of the church below projects a striking sense of purpose regarding the meaning of the great fifty days as both an expression of the church's celebration of union with the kingdom of God, and the transition from Easter to Pentecost.[8] Quasimodogeniti is, in Raymond Brown's words, "this Sunday on which, through the gift of the Spirit, Jesus makes possible his permanent presence among his followers."[9] It seems clear, therefore, that the placement of the narratives of Jesus's post-resurrection appearances was bound up with the manner in which John adds a "spiritual" meaning to those events as told by Luke, one that is uniquely concerned with the shift to the perspective of the church and its sacraments, and that inaugurates the season that leads to Pentecost, celebrating the coming of the Holy Spirit and symbolizing the "birthday of the church." In this sense it looks ahead to Pentecost as the fulfillment of what Jesus announces to the disciples early in the season.

Between Quasimodogeniti and Jubilate, on which the readings from John's Farewell Discourse begin, comes the Sunday that most centers on John's image of Jesus as the good shepherd, one that is directly concerned with linking Jesus to the presentation of the God of Israel as shepherd in such texts as Psalm 23. It therefore embodied a second articulation of the Trinity (after that of Quasimodogeniti). The readings for the first and second Sundays after Easter can be considered a background for the turn to the Farewell Discourse that comes on the following week (Jubilate), introducing an increased emphasis on the preparation of the disciples for Jesus's departure (Ascension Day) and his permanent presence through the Spirit.

---

[8] Everything I have described is expressed in theological treatises from the seventeenth and eighteenth centuries. Johann Arndt (*Postilla*, 3:98) writes about the ancient usage regarding baptism, confirmation, and the Eucharist. Joachim Lütkemann (*Apostolischer Herzens-Wecker*, coupled with Heinrich Müller's *Evangelischer Herzens-Spiegel*, 559) makes the same connection, describing Quasimodogeniti as "the day of the born-again." August Hermann Francke (*Predigten über die Sonn- und Fest-Tags Episteln*, 611–26) emphasizes John's remarks on the victory of faith, the Spirit, and the Trinitarian parallels between heaven above and the church below. Lütkemann (*Apostolischer Herzens-Wecker*, 558–59) speaks of the latter as "Gottes Ordnung," an expression, used widely by Lutheran writers, that seems to echo in Cantata 42.

[9] Brown, *Gospel According to John XIII–XXI*, 1019.

By Luther's time the liturgical cycle was fully set in place, so that he could describe the Farewell Discourse as having been assigned "since time immemorial as Gospel lessons between Pentecost and Easter."[10] And Luther, as we saw, was especially attracted to those lessons, which exemplified for him the foremost quality of the Gospel of John, namely its emphasizing Jesus's words rather than his works. The sermons he preached on the Farewell Discourse between Easter and Pentecost 1537 he considered one of his best books (in 1540 proclaiming it *the* best), remarking in his preface that "nowhere else in Scripture are they [the true, chief high articles of Christian doctrine] to be found side by side in this way. For example, the doctrine of the three distinct Persons in the Holy Trinity, particularly of the divine and human natures in the eternally undivided Person of the Lord Christ; also the doctrine of justification by faith and of the real comfort for consciences."[11] The last of these qualities, *Trost*, was John's special province for Luther; Luther then remarked "now that his battle against death and the devil had reached its highest point, .. [in the Farewell Discourse] Christ richly poured out his great and heartfelt comfort, which is the property of all Christendom and which men should long for in all troubles and afflictions." Thus, Luther's sermons are concerned extensively with the Holy Spirit, the comforter, constituting what has been described as "a transition from Easter to Pentecost both exegetically and liturgically. . . . the presentation of the doctrine of the Holy Spirit in this exposition was appropriate both to the Biblical material Luther was expounding and to the season of the church year."[12] In the Gospel the comfort was, of course, for the disciples who were about to undergo persecution in the world without the protection they had enjoyed from Jesus's physical presence. But, as Luther emphasized, it was also to be understood in terms of contemporary Christian life in the world. It is a key to the Bach cantatas for this time period and their following from the *St. John Passion*, in which Jesus protects the disciples in the opening scene.

Throughout the post-Easter season the theme of *Trost*—encapsulated in the *dictum* from John that Mariane von Ziegler chose for Cantata 87's central movement text, "In der Welt habt ihr Angst, aber seid getrost, ich habe die Welt überwunden"—derives from Jesus's victory in the Passion, whose primary locus in the *St. John Passion* is the middle section of "Es ist vollbracht" ("Der Held aus Juda siegt mit Macht und schliesst den Kampf"). Introducing a sudden surge of the triumph of the resurrection into the framework of the suffering world, it anticipates the sense of victory that resounds in the final words of the 1725 cantata for Easter Day (BWV 249): "Höll und Teufel sind bezwungen . . . Der Löwe von Juda kommt siegend gezogen." The link between the two works is mirrored musically by Bach by means of the D-major fanfare style associated with trumpet music.

---

[10] *Luther's Works*, vol. 24, *Sermons on the Gospel of St. John, Chapters 14–16*, , 8.

[11] Ibid., 8.

[12] Ibid., ix.

In keeping with the ancient character of the great fifty days as a time of unbroken rejoicing, the message of Jesus's victory at Easter and its benefit for humanity runs throughout the season, projected with special emphasis in the reappearance of the D-major trumpet style in arias in Cantatas 103 (Jubilate), 128 (Ascension Day), and 175 (the second day of Pentecost). Likewise, the traditional names for the Sundays after Easter, drawn from the Mass introits (themselves taken from scripture, often the psalms), tend very much to reflect this character; one thinks immediately of Jubilate, Cantate, Vocem Jucunditatis (the alternate name for Rogate) and Exaudi. And they were often viewed as a sequence. Thus Valerius Herberger describes the six Sundays between Easter and Pentecost as an "artistic Easter sermon," reflected in their names:

> Our devout forefathers made an artistic Easter sermon through the names of the Sundays after Easter. For if one wants to know what the resurrection of the Lord Jesus brings of great use to us, then the first two names tell it to us. We believers should all (1) be and be known as new born children of God [i.e., Quasimodogeniti]. (2) The earth and our hearts should be full of the goodness of the Lord [Misericordias]. If one asks further what kind of thankfulness belongs to this then the following two [names] say (1) *Jubilate Deo omnis terra,* "Make a joyful noise unto God, all ye lands: Sing forth the honor of his name: make his praise glorious." (Ps 66:2) *Cantate Dominum Canticum novum,* "Sing unto the Lord a new song, for he does wonders," (Ps 98:1). If anyone says, I would really like to know what kind of pleasure God takes in this, then the last two names give the answer: (1) *Voces jucunditas* [i.e., Rogate]. (2) *Audit ubique Deus* [i.e., Exaudi], God will hear it, for to praise our God, that is a precious thing, such praise is lovely and beautiful (Ps 147:1).[13]

At the same time, however, this very positive tone of rejoicing, the primary message of the post-Easter weeks, is offset by another that arises from Jesus's departure: that of the encroachment of "the world" on the life of faith. Already in the cantata for Easter Monday this quality is present and linked to the evening time at which Jesus appeared to Cleopas and his companion on the road to Emmaus. As

---

[13] Herberger, *Herz-Postilla*, 425–26:

> Unsere andächtige Vorfahren haben durch die Namen der Sontage nach Ostern eine künstliche Oster-Predigt gethan. Denn wenn man will wissen / was uns die Aufferstehung des HErrn Jesu für grossen Nutz bringe / so sagens uns die ersten zwey Namen. Wir Gläubige sollen alle 1. Neugebohrne Kinder Gottes seyn und heissen. 2. Die Erde und unser Hertz soll voll seyn der Güte des Herrn. Wenn man weiter fraget / was für Danckbarkeit darauff gehöre / so sagens die folgenden zweene 1. *Jubilate Deo omnis terra,* **Jauchzet Gott alle Land / Lobsinget zu Ehren seinem Namen / rühmet ihn herrlich / Ps. 66. V.2.** 2. *Cantate Dominum Canticum novum,* **Singet dem HErrn ein neues Lied / denn er thut Wunder** / Psal. 98. V. 1. Saget jemand / ich wollte aber gerne wissen / was Gott für ein Wollgefallen daran trage / so geben die **letzten zweene Namen** Antwort: 1. *Voces jucunditas.* 2, *Audit ubique DEus* **GOtt wirds hören** / denn unsren Gott loben / daß ist ein köstlich Ding / solch Lob ist **lieblich und schöne** Psal. 147. Vers. 1.

Martin Moller explained, in all particulars this story prefigured our "*Osterleben* in this wretched world . . . how it would go with us on earth before we would enter into the true perfection [*rechten Vollkommenheit*]." For Moller the crucial issue was the believer's understanding and acceptance of God's "'dear cross,' for which he must pray, 'open the eyes of my heart, so that I will not take offense at the sorrowful form of the cross, but rather, in patience and consolation believe and say from the heart: although I wander in the dark valley, I will fear no misfortune, for you are with me.'"[14] The "dark valley" of Psalm 23, associated with the second Sunday after Easter, Misericordias Domini, was also linked with the evening time of the Gospel for Easter Monday as a metaphor for the darkness of the world and the believer's struggle for faith in the face of her inability to perceive Jesus's presence.[15] On Misericordias, therefore, Moller returned to the theme of the darkness of the world, citing the Gospel for Easter Monday, now in relation to Jesus the shepherd's protecting "the flock of his Christianity" from the wolf (Satan) who comes by night:

> See, it is the last, evil, restless time: Satan is loose, and rages horribly in his opposition, and arms his Gog and Magog against the little sheep of your pasture. Yes, Lord, toward evening the danger is greatest, when the wolf rages most violently. O Lord, remain with us, for it will soon be evening, the days of the world have declined.[16]

Moller seems to perceive the same kind of relationship between Easter Monday and Misericordias that, as we will see, emerges in Bach's 1725 cantatas for those occasions. That is, although those cantatas, numbers 6 and 85, offer *Trost* for the faithful, behind that message and mirrored in their C-minor tonalities is the metaphor of worldly darkness. And the intervening Sunday, Quasimodogeniti, was linked up with them via the interpretation of the disciples' struggles in the world as prefiguring those of the Christian church. Five of the six chorales that appear in Bach's 1725 cantatas for those three feast days appear in close proximity in the section of the Dresden song book titled "Von der Christlichen Kirche, Gottes Wort und Religion," along with other chorales that center on the same themes.[17] And in

---

[14] Moller, *Praxis Evangeliorum*, 118–19.

[15] Ibid., 123–24 (following discussion of the purpose and necessity of the believer's acceptance of the cross): "Merke das / meine Seele / das ist auch deines Herrn Weisen eine. Und solches treibet er täglich bey seinen Brüdern / daß sie offt meynen / Nu werde es Abend / unnd aus seyn mit all ihrem Glauben unnd Hoffnung / unnd der Herr sey gantz von ihnen gewichen . . . . Mein Heiland / sihe auff mich in diesem meinen Elend: Sihe / es wil Abend werden in meinem Hertzen: Satan setzet mir so hart zu / daß ich offt gedencke / du seyst gar von mir gewichen."

[16] Ibid., 176–77: "Sihe / Es sind die letzten bösen / unruhigen Zeiten: Satan ist loß / und wütet grausam in seinem Widerschrift / und rüstet seinen Gog und Magog wider die Schäfflein deiner Weide. Ja Herr / gegen abends ist die Gefahr am grössesten / da wütet der Wolff am hefftigsten. O Herr / bleib bey uns / denn es wil Abend werden / die Tage der Welt haben sich geneiget."

[17] *Das Privilegirte Ordentliche und Vermehrte Dresdnische Gesang-Buch* (Dresden and Leipzig, 1735), 305–11 (hereafter *Dresdnische Gesang-Buch*). The only chorale in those cantatas that does not appear in this section is the one that concludes Cantata 85; that chorale, however, relates to the others very closely in its thematic content.

the weeks to follow, questions surrounding Jesus's presence or departure, along with the negative perspective on the world, remain, now within the framework of the readings drawn from the Farewell Discourse. In them Jesus's words provide comfort for the disciples regarding his immanent departure and the treatment the disciples can expect from the world. Thus, in his discussion of the Gospel for Jubilate, the Sunday whose traditional name most suggests rejoicing, Moller emphasizes the passage that Mariane von Ziegler chose to begin Cantata 103, *Ihr werdet weinen und heulen* (You will weep and cry out), then, after bringing out the association behind the name Jubilate, characterizes the Gospel as a "Creutzpredigt," posing the question "how does this sermon on the cross rhyme together with the *Jubilate*?" (Wie reimet sich die Predigt vom Creutz und das *Jubilate* zusammen?).[18] Moller's answer, as we might expect, is that whereas worldly suffering, the cross, is brief, it will be turned into a joy that is eternal and beyond all measure, won for humanity by Jesus's "Creutz und Leiden."[19] In the liturgy, the Gospel for the following Sunday, Cantate (which, we remember, Moller considered to complete an octave with Jubilate), responds by announcing the coming of the Spirit as the means by which Jesus will return. And in her cantata text for the following Sunday, Rogate (Cantata 87, *Bisher habt ihr nichts gebeten in meinem Name*), Ziegler introduces as the second *dictum* of the cantata, the final verse of John's Farewell Discourse, not, strictly speaking, a part of the Gospel for the day, which ends three verses earlier. In that *dictum*, the theme of overcoming the world, associated with faith in the epistle for Quasimodogeniti, bridges to Ascension Day, making the point that after the ascension (celebrated on the following Thursday), the disciples will face worldly adversity without Jesus's presence. In the spring cantata sequence this is a reminder of Jesus's extended prayer to the Father that directly follows the Farewell Discourse, a prayer that has been understood by some as John's equivalent of (or substitute for) an ascension narrative. In this sense it anticipates the *Trost* that comes with Jesus's presence through the Holy Spirit as the next "stage" following the triumph of the resurrection and ascension. On Ascension Day, Ziegler's text for the opening movement of Cantata 128, *Auf Christi Himmelfahrt allein,* draws on a chorale verse that proclaims the believer's own overcoming of the world through the joining of the resurrected and ascended Christ as "head" (*Haupt*) and the faithful below as members (*Glieder*) of one body, the church under the direction of the Holy Spirit.

How Bach's cantata designs bring out these themes will be taken up in the chapters to follow. At this point we may note that throughout the spring 1725 cantata sequence the joy and victory of Easter appear in the context of the concerns of the faithful in the world, who, like the disciples hearing the Farewell Discourse, need the reassurance of Jesus's words and the means of reestablishing intimate contact with God. The Holy Spirit provides that means (Pentecost), after which the Gospel

[18] Moller, *Praxis Evangeliorum*, 183.

[19] Ibid., 198–200.

for Trinity Sunday (Jn 3:1–15, Jesus's dialog with Nicodemus) turns to themes heard earlier on in the post-Easter sequence. The story of Nicodemus recalls both the ending of the *St. John Passion* and the darkness/light theme of *Bleib bei uns*, while the subject of the dialog, rebirth through baptism and the Spirit, harks back to Quasimodogeniti. Interestingly, the *dictum* chosen by Ziegler for her Trinity cantata, BWV 176, *Es ist ein trotzig und verzagt Ding um aller Menschen Herzen* (Jer 17:9), was cited by Moller in the *Praxis Evangeliorum* in connection with the Gospels for Easter Monday and Misericordias, on *both* occasions for the purpose of illustrating how the believer must overcome resistance to revealing himself, in sin and weakness, openly to God, a close analog to Nicodemus's coming forth only by night.[20] Bach, very strikingly, sets all three 1725 cantatas for those Sundays in C minor.

Clearly, there is a strong sense of purpose and direction in the themes of the great fifty days, one that is bound up with the Johannine readings and that is often reflected in Ziegler's cantata texts and Bach's music. The joyful, celebratory character of Easter is present but clouded at times by the perspective of the world. This part of the year was viewed in terms of the coming of the Spirit as preparation for the time of the church undergoing crises of faith in the world (the Trinity season). Thus in Bach's post-Easter cantatas for 1725, the message of Easter is often presented in hortatory rather than directly celebratory tones, urging the believer to cling to Jesus's victory in the face of worldly pressures and adversities, present and forthcoming. Human qualities that are viewed as stumbling blocks to faith must arouse themselves from what Lutheranism viewed as the "flesh." In Cantata 103, *Ihr werdet weinen und heulen*, for Jubilate, the climactic second aria—"Erholet euch, betrübte Sinnen," scored for bass, trumpet, and strings in D—addresses the "troubled senses," setting immanent sorrow and adversity up against Jesus's promise of his return, which is viewed in eschatological (future) terms. On Ascension Day, in an aria of the same basic type and key (for bass, trumpet, and strings), "Auf, auf, mit hellem Schall," the believer first proclaims the joy of Jesus's ascension, anticipating joining him in eternity, then castigates his mouth for voicing the desire to build a dwelling place in advance, thereby reducing God to human terms. Subtly, the opposition to reason and works righteousness enters the picture, in advance of Pentecost, when God will be described as coming to dwell in the human heart.[21] In Cantata 175, for the third day of Pentecost, another D-major trumpet aria of decidedly hortatory character, "Öffnet euch, ihr beiden Ohren," renews the

[20] Ibid., 119, 152. In addition, the word "verzagt" in the biblical *dictum* that begins Cantata 176 resonates with the appearance of that word in Cantata 42, for Quasimodogeniti, suggesting a perceived association between Nicodemus's coming forth only by night and the disciples' hiding out of fear behind closed doors on the evening of the Sabbath. Aegidius Hunnius makes this connection explicit in his commentary on the Gospel for Quasimodogeniti, which takes Jeremiah's "Es ist ein trotzig und verzagt Ding . . ." as underlying the disciples' fear. See Aegidius Hunnius, *Postilla* (Frankfurt, 1591), 2:57–58. For further references to the word "verzagt" in association with Nicodemus, see ch. 13, p. 553.

[21] See Prenter, *Spiritus Creator*, 85.

message of the Passion and Easter in response to the Johannine theme of misunderstanding, presented in the preceding recitative in terms of human reliance on reason rather than faith. In militant tones "Öffnet euch" urges the faithful to open their ears to the message of Jesus's defeat of death and the devil, and his promise of eternal life for those who take up the cross and follow ("Jesus hat euch zugeschworen, daß er Teufel, Tod erlegt. Gnade, Gnüge, volles Leben will er allen Christen geben, wer ihm folgt, sein Kreuz nachträgt"). The context now is one in which the message of Easter is "contained" within a view of Pentecost that is in part conditioned by its preparing for the Trinity season. The cantata that follows, on Trinity Sunday, contains another hortatory aria, "Ermuntert euch, furchtsam und schüchterne Sinnen" (now without trumpet); even as it voices anticipation of seeing God in eternity it is dominated by the fact that the cantata as a whole places a pronounced emphasis on human weakness and life in the world.

Running throughout the season is the idea that human attributes, especially reason and the senses, are inadequate to sustain the life of faith, which inevitably succumbs to worldly pressures. Something more is needed—the Holy Spirit—and it is the purpose of the season as a whole to set forth both the need and the solution. The first signs of the shift of perspective to worldly concerns appear in the cantatas that deal with Jesus's post-resurrection appearances, in which Bach's librettist introduces the disciples' need for Jesus's presence and protection, now transferred to the Christian community. Already the cantata for Easter Monday, *Bleib bei uns, denn es will Abend werden*, marks a significant change in tone that Bach emphasizes by turning to a rather darkly colored C minor after the festive D major of *Kommt, gehet und eilet*. (This is the title for the 1725 performance; *Kommt eilet und laufet* is the original title that was altered before 1725.) In contrast to the light of the resurrection morning, *Bleib bei uns* characterizes the world without Jesus's light and physical presence as a place of increasing spiritual darkness, in "these last troubled times" (a reference to the "evening of the world," discussed in ch. 2). Its penultimate movement prays that the faithful may see Jesus again by means of the shining light of his word, after which the final chorale is a cry for the resurrected and all-powerful Jesus to protect his "poor Christianity" (*arme Christenheit*). The Gospel for Easter Monday, Jesus's post-resurrection appearance to two travelers on the road to Emmaus, in telling of Jesus's walking with the disciples and expounding the scriptures "concerning himself," formed a basis for Jesus's spiritual "walk" with the faithful through the trials of worldly life. His presence, as *Bleib bei uns* brings out, will be "seen" through the light of word and sacrament.

On the following Sunday the theme of God's protection carries forward, now in more militant terms, in the next surviving cantata, *Am Abend aber desselbigen Sabbats*, for Quasimodogeniti, which alludes in its introductory D-major sinfonia to something of the character of *Kommt, gehet und eilet*. Now, however, the message of the Easter victory is considerably tempered by the narrative of the disciples' hiding in the evening ("Am Abend . . . im finstern Schatten"), behind closed doors, out of fear of the Jews. The unknown librettist links up this theme with the place of the church in the world, "evening" serving now as a metaphor for its "hiddenness," an echo of the apostolic era that is extended, in didactic tones, to the contemporary church's struggles with worldly adversaries. In contrast to the sense of universality projected by the three-movement "orchestral" concerto that begins *Kommt, gehet und eilet*, the three-section sinfonia of *Am Abend aber desselbigen Sabbats* is scaled down, both in its instrumental complement and its tone, which, although positive, is complicated by adversarial elements that perhaps descend from a parodied instrumental movement. In the context of Cantata 42 its chamber music character seems to announce the intimate setting described in the Gospel, which was associated in the cantata text with Matthew's "two or three" who are gathered in Jesus's name (the first aria), as well as the "small group" of the faithful described in the first chorale, "Verzage nicht, o Häuflein klein." In this cantata Jesus's protection is presented in terms of his bringing peace and freedom from persecution. The expression "verzage nicht" (do not be fainthearted) has considerable biblical resonance, especially in the older parts of the Hebrew Bible, such as Deuteronomy 31:6 and the book of Joshua, where God promises his presence with the Israelites, often in militant tones.[22] Although the penultimate movement (also very much a chamber music conception) describes Jesus's protection as a golden banner with which the sun shines on the faithful, that theme is mediated by the two chorale strophes with which the cantata ends. Whereas the former of these strophes is a prayer to God, who alone fights for his people, the latter is a prayer for God to give peace and good government to temporal rulers ("Fürsten und all'r Obrigkeit"). The shift to the worldly perspective is unmistakable.

As if in response, the next cantata in the sequence, BWV 85, *Ich bin ein guter Hirt*, for Misericordias, shifts the perspective on God's protection once again, now to a more personal context. In the liturgy the reading for this Sunday breaks with the historical narrative of Jesus's post-resurrection appearances to draw instead from John 10, in which Jesus describes himself as the good shepherd who gives his life for the sheep, watching over the faithful while the hired hands sleep. Drawing also on Psalm 23, the librettist paints in less militant tones than in the preceding cantata. And Bach responds by turning back to the C-minor tonality of *Bleib bei uns*, bringing back also the *violoncello piccolo*, which had appeared in the earlier cantata in association with the chorale "Bleib bei uns," the central expression of longing for Jesus's continuing presence. Since after Cantata 85 that instrument does not reappear again until after Ascension Day, when it sounds in three more cantatas, seeming increasingly to symbolize Jesus's presence through the Spirit, there is a sense that in *Ich bin ein guter Hirt* it conveys the equivalence of the resurrected Messiah (*Christus Victor*) and the good shepherd. This time it accompanies the first verse of Cornelius Becker's chorale paraphrase of Psalm 23, which is sung to the Trinitarian melody, "Allein Gott in der Höh' sei Ehr," thereby bringing out the equivalence of Jesus, the shepherd, and the Father. In this respect it continues

[22] See ch. 13, n. 11.

from the Trinitarian element in the epistle for Quasimodogeniti. It is clear that the Gospel reading for Misericordias not only marks a shift away from the narrative character of the Gospels for the preceding feast days, serving as a transition to the character of Jesus's words to the disciples in the Farewell Discourse, but it also looks ahead to the third day of Pentecost (whose Gospel is an adjacent passage from John 10), when the *violoncello piccolo* appears for the fifth and last time in the spring sequence (see fig. 11.1). The latter cantata proclaims the equivalence of three images of God that are prominent in John (where they have been viewed as Trinitarian in nature) and that run throughout the post-Easter season—the good shepherd, the *Christus Victor*, and the Holy Spirit—a theme not yet fully articulated in Cantata 85.

In the next three cantatas after *Ich bin ein guter Hirt*, all based on the Farewell Discourse, the spiritual character that was traditionally associated with John's Gospel takes over in preparation for Pentecost. Beginning with Cantata 103, for Jubilate, Bach set the well-known series of nine texts by Mariane von Ziegler. They, too, exhibit a high degree of consistency in their designs, and they can be divided into subgroups that arise from the large-scale ordering of themes throughout the period as a whole. Ascension Day provides a logical dividing point, since it commemorates Jesus's return to the world above, the end of the great forty days. The three Ziegler cantatas that precede Ascension Day (BWV 103, for Jubilate; 108, for Cantate; and 87, for Rogate) utilize themes from the Farewell Discourse in order to emphasize preparation for life in the world after Jesus's departure: in particular, worldly suffering that will be turned ultimately to joy (103 and 87), Jesus's foretelling his departure and the coming of the Holy Spirit (108), and love and the necessity of prayer (87). A principal subject of the discourse is Jesus's immanent departure, described in the Gospel as his return to the Father, or to the world "above," even as his being "lifted up" (the crucifixion, resurrection, and ascension as a single upward motion). As a result of Jesus's departure, the disciples will suffer persecution in "the world" (meaning the world "below"). Yet Jesus speaks also of his return and of his sending another—described variously as the "Spirit of truth," the comforter, the Advocate, and the like—in his place. Through the presence of Jesus and the Spirit, the disciples' sorrow will be turned into joy.[23]

One outcome of the fact that the Farewell Discourse *precedes* Jesus's death and resurrection in John's Gospel, whereas the Johannine readings of the spring liturgy *follow* the Passion and Easter, is that certain of Jesus's sayings regarding his departure and return that would ordinarily be taken to predict his death and resurrection or his Second Coming (and perhaps the post-resurrection appearances) are applied to his ascension and return through the Holy Spirit. I have referred earlier to Raymond Brown's view that John's Farewell Discourse "transcends time and space," that Jesus's words to the disciples are really directed at "Christians of all times." In bringing out the difference between the "eschatological discourse" of the

[23] Brown, *Gospel According to John XIII–XXI*, 601.

Synoptic Gospels and John's Farewell Discourse, Brown points out that "some of the futuristic eschatological elements found in the farewell speeches of Jewish apocalyptic writings appear in John in an atmosphere of realized eschatology," citing instances of joy as "a reward for those who have died in a state of justice"; in John "this joy seems to be characteristic of Christian life in this world after the resurrection of Jesus."[24] In the case of Cantatas 103 and 108, the sequence of departure/return ideas expresses the continuity between longing for Jesus's physical presence, as articulated in the preceding group of cantatas, longing for eschatological union with him (Cantata 103), and the coming of the Holy Spirit, which is foretold by Jesus in the opening movement of Cantata 108, then anticipated by the believer in the first recitative of that work: "Dein Geist wird mich also regieren . . . Ich frage sorgensvoll: Ach, ist er nicht schon hier?" ("Your Spirit will therefore direct me. . . . I ask, full of cares, 'Ah, is he not already here?'"). Cantata 87 then places the turning of sorrow into joy within the context of prayer and the *Trost* that comes from Jesus's having overcome "the world." The believer holds onto faith in the midst of worldly tribulation, and, in Cantata 128, for Ascension Day, glimpses eternity as his inheritance. As mentioned earlier, owing to the narrative, event-centered character of the Ascension, it is the only feast day between the three days of Easter and Trinity Sunday for which the Gospel reading is *not* drawn from John (who has no narrative of the Ascension per se). Perhaps for this reason, Mariane von Ziegler's cantata for Ascension Day, *Auf Christi Himmelfahrt allein* (BWV 128), does not draw on a motto cited or derived from the Gospel for the day (Mk 16:14–20); her text avoids entirely the narrative character that figures so prominently in the "Ascension Oratorio" (BWV 11), supplying instead a meditation on the meaning of the Ascension for the faithful. This brings the tone of Cantata 128 closer to John. Through faith the world above becomes a palpable reality for the believer, the message of John's "realized eschatology."

Initiating the final subgrouping among the spring 1725 cantatas, the cantata that comes between Ascension Day and Pentecost, *Sie werden euch in den Bann tun* (BWV 183, for Exaudi), echoes the anticipation of Pentecost in Cantata 108, returning to the Farewell Discourse. It begins with a motto from the Gospel reading for Exaudi, which forms a sequence with the readings for the three Sundays before Ascension Day. Cantata 183 reflects on all the themes taken up in the works for those Sundays, placing them more directly in the context of the Holy Spirit. After that, the cantatas for the three feast days of Pentecost, BWV 74, 68, and 175, develop the meaning of Pentecost in terms of themes that have echoed throughout the season. It is as if all that was formerly obscure in Jesus's words is now manifest. Jesus's return, foretold in Cantatas 103 and 108, becomes the indwelling of Jesus and the Father within the believer's heart (Cantata 74), the source of the promised joy, won by Jesus's defeat of the devil. God's love, manifested both in the incarnation, and in Jesus's presence through faith in the believer's heart removes the ne-

[24] Ibid.

cessity of God's judgment (Cantata 68). And intimate communion with Jesus, the shepherd and the *Christus Victor*, is possible through the Spirit and God's word (Cantata 175). As Pentecost comes to an end, the final chorale of Cantata 175 ("Nun, werter Geist, ich folg dir") voices the believer's readiness to follow the Holy Spirit, to seek a "different life," of grace, according to God's word.

After these very positive messages, Cantata 176 for Trinity Sunday bridges to the season that follows. On the one hand, the "new life" in the text of Cantata 175 underlies the Gospel reading for the day, Jesus's dialog with Nicodemus, in which Jesus describes rebirth through water and the Spirit as the requirement for eternal life (thus looking back to Quasimodogeniti). Yet, at the same time, the darkness of the world, articulated at the beginning of the series of post-Easter cantatas, reappears in association with Nicodemus, who represents all that is fearful and despairing in human nature. The message toward which Cantata 176 leads, as if in preparation for the Trinity season, is to hold onto God's promise through faith, in the hope of glorifying the Trinity in the afterlife.

I hope that it is clear from all this that one of the main themes of the cantatas between Easter and Trinity Sunday is the shift from history to spiritual understanding. This is the essence of Luther's view of the Holy Spirit, and the understanding of scripture, as Regin Prenter has shown.[25] Jesus's words as spoken to his original listeners, in particular the disciples, but also to others with and without faith, are understood increasingly in terms of the contemporary Christian community and believing individual, whose encounter with Jesus is wholly through the word of scripture, transmitted and understood by means of the Holy Spirit. His words to the disciples regarding his departure and return, therefore, receive a particular orientation toward Pentecost and his coming again through the Spirit. Pentecost is the axis of the year, affirming the Holy Spirit as the means by which Jesus's words are lifted out of their purely historical context so as to apply directly to the believer. In the sense that the seasons of the liturgical year parallel both the eras of salvation history and the ancient senses of scripture interpretation, Pentecost embodies an increasingly tropological emphasis, commemorating not only the historical first coming of the Holy Spirit to the disciples and the completion of humankind's knowledge of the Trinity but also the centrality of understanding God's word to the church and Christian life in general. Through the Holy Spirit the new life referred to in Cantata 175 is one in which, through faith, the resurrected Christ is a present experience in the believer, making the believer "conformable" to Christ in his suffering and victory.[26]

At no other time of the year is the transition from the historical to the spiritual so directly a part of the liturgical message as during the great fifty days. And in Bach's cantatas for spring 1725 that transition is particularly evident, even in literal terms, since the cantata for Easter Sunday that year retains the dramatic character

---

[25] Prenter, *Spiritus Creator*, 53ff.

[26] Ibid., 27–130, 205–39.

of the Passion in its featuring the historical characters of Peter, John, Mary Magdalene, and Mary the mother of James (Maria Jacobi). At the same time, the anonymous text is not directly drawn from any one single Gospel but rather paraphrases the resurrection story as told by them all. The arias, although assigned to historical persons, voice the concerns and perspective of the contemporary believer, after which the remainder of the post-Easter cantatas of that season are concerned with reinterpreting the last events of Jesus's time on earth and his words to the disciples in terms of their application to contemporary Christian life. Because of the prominence of mottoes from John in most of the cantatas, there is often a considerable focus on the person of Jesus, a feature that is reflected in one of the most remarkable musical aspects of the sequence: the emergence of *violoncello piccolo* as a solo voice in five cantatas (BWV 6, 85, 183, 68, and 175).

Kommt, gehet und eilet (BWV 249)

This cantata, produced on Easter Day 1725, originated as a parody of Bach's "Shepherd" cantata (BWV 249a), composed for the birthday of Duke Christian of Saxe-Weissenfels on February 23 that year. Due in part to its origins, it has a uniquely dramatic character that sets it apart among all the Bach sacred cantatas, bridging between the directly dramatic nature of the *St. John Passion* and the meditative character of the cantatas to follow.[27] Although the Gospel for Easter Day is from Mark, and the text of Bach's composition draws on elements of the resurrection story as told by all the Gospels, only John recounts the presence of Peter and "the disciple whom Jesus loved" at the tomb. Among the four protagonists, John (bass) stands apart in that he sings no aria, having instead the only recitative assigned to a single "character," summarizing the meaning of the cantata before the final chorus. Each of the others sings an aria that in some way refers to a well-known event or attribute associated with that character: Maria Jacobi's aria refers to the anointing of Jesus after his burial, as told by the Synoptic Gospels, whereas Peter's aria (tenor) speaks of his weeping, as well as the folded burial cloth whose significance he is the first to realize in John's narrative. And Mary Magdalene's aria poeticizes

[27] The music of the "Shepherd" cantata (BWV 249a), written for Duke Christian of Sachsen-Weißenfels is lost; but owing to the survival of Picander's printed text, Friedrich Smend was able to show that it was parodied twice by Bach, first in Cantata 249 (1725) then in the birthday cantata (*Dramma musicale*) for Graf Joachim Friedrich von Flemming, *Die Feier des Genius*, which was performed in Leipzig in 1726. Smend published a reconstruction of the former work, with recitatives composed by Hermann Keller (*Entfliehet, verschwindet, entweichet, ihr Sorgen*, BWV 249a [Kassel: Bärenreiter 1943]). See Smend, "Neue Bach Funde," in Smend, *Bach-Studien*, 137–44. The original form of Bach's parodied Easter cantata, that of 1725, differs in certain respects from the version of the work we know as the Easter Oratorio, *Kommt, eilet und laufet* (dated in the 1730s); an intermediate version also existed. Only the first version specifies the four biblical characters. See Dürr, *Cantatas*, 271–74.

love in a religious context. The first and second of these solos, those of Maria Jacobi and Peter, introduce the kind of antithesis that is prominent in many of the *St. John Passion* texts. An event or physical object associated with Jesus's suffering and death is reinterpreted in terms of its spiritual benefit for the believer, as was the case, for example, with the *Himmelsschlüsselblume* that sprung from the crown of thorns in "Betrachte, meine Seele" and the rainbow patterns that were formed from the blood on Jesus's back in "Erwäge." Both the anointing of Jesus for burial and Peter's weeping link up directly with the Passion, but now their meanings are reinterpreted in light of the resurrection. Thus, after narrating Peter's recognizing the significance of the burial cloth ("Hier seh ich mit Vergnügen das Schweißtuch abgewickelt liegen"—Here I see with pleasure the burial cloth lying unwound), the librettist of Bach's cantata assigns Peter an aria in which the burial cloth is associated with wiping the tears "tröstlich" from Peter's cheeks, a familiar image of the time with widespread eschatological associations derived from Revelation 7. And in Maria Jacobi's aria the spice commonly associated with burial is replaced by laurel, emblem of victory.

The theme of love, associated with Mary Magdalene, is central to the meaning of the Passion, especially as told by John; hence the *St. John Passion*'s first chorale, "O große Lieb," which is the response of the faithful to Jesus's protection of the disciples. In *Kommt, gehet und eilet*, though, love is associated particularly with the two female characters. In the first recitative, directly following the opening "concerto" complex, Mary Magdalene pronounces it a "debt" owed to Jesus by the two male disciples, "O kalter Männer Sinn! Wie ist die Liebe hin, die ihr dem Heiland schuldig seid?" (O the cold minds of men! Where has the love gone that you owe to the savior?), to which Maria Jacobi adds "Ein schwaches Weib muss euch beschämen!" (A weak woman must put you to shame!). Then, after the arias of Maria Jacobi and Peter, the two women sing a brief duet recitative, "Indessen seufzen wir mit brennenden Begier" (Meanwhile we sigh with burning longing) that then turns into the cantata's only arioso, drawing out the lines "Ach! Ach! Könnt es bald geschehen, den Heiland selbst zu sehen!" (Alas! Alas! If only it could happen soon that we could see the savior himself!). In historical terms this could refer to the post-resurrection appearances; but in terms of the contemporary believer love here takes on an unmistakably eschatological character directly before Maria Magdalene's aria. With this latter grouping of movements, the tone becomes more directly positive, turning to joy for the final recitative, sung by John. It may be significant, therefore, that at the beginning of John's concluding recitative—"*Wir sind erfreut*, dass unser Jesus wieder lebt" (We rejoice that our Jesus lives again)—Bach seems to quote musically from a passage in the *St. John Passion*, where Jesus, having just referred to his kingdom as not of this world, proclaims that, were it otherwise, his followers would fight (*kämpfen*). This perhaps incidental, though meaningful, connection to the Passion is rooted in the Johannine image of Jesus as *Christus Victor* (ex. 9.1a/b).

EXAMPLE 9.1a *St. John Passion* *no. 16e, recitative excerpt*

EXAMPLE 9.1.b Cantata 249a, *Kommt, gehet und eilet* *final recitative, beginning*

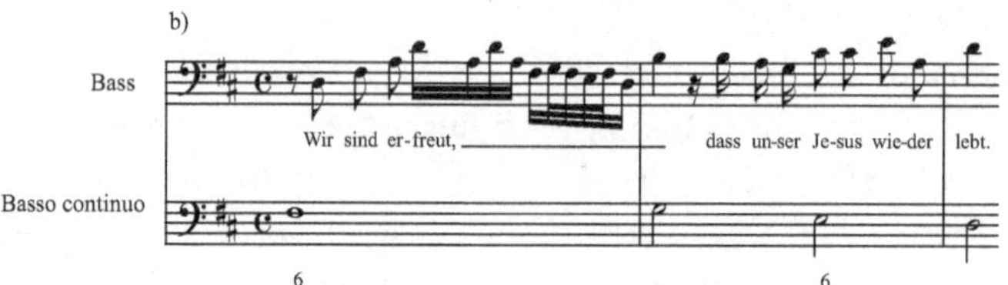

The final chorus, begun by the bass (John), then celebrates Jesus's victory and his return to the world above; its final line recalls the middle section of "Es ist vollbracht":

Preis und Dank	Praise and thanks
bleibe, Herr, dein Lobgesang!	remain, Lord, your song of worship!
Höll' und Teufel sind bezwungen,	Hell and the devil are overcome,
ihre Pforten sind zerstört;	their portals are destroyed;
jauchzet, ihr erlösten Zungen,	rejoice, you loosened tongues,
dass man es im Himmel hört!	so that it is heard in heaven!
Eröffnet, ihr Himmel, die prächtigen Bogen,	Open wide, heaven, your mighty arches,
der Löwe von Juda kommt siegend gezogen!	the lion from Judea comes drawn in victory!

The beginning and ending of *Kommt, gehet und eilet* can be said to project a framework of triumph for the cantata as a whole, one in which the trumpets and their D-major tonality expand on the affective character of the middle section of "Es ist vollbracht," bringing its fanfare qualities into the open. In "Es ist vollbracht" the b/D/b tonal design and the contrasted instrumentation between the central section and the flanking outer sections represent, on the one hand, the literal and spiritual aspects of Jesus's death and, on the other, the double interpretation of his death as *Trost* for the tormented faithful (the outer sections) and the triumphant defeat of the forces of evil (the middle segment). In this scheme the portrayal of Jesus as *Christus Victor* is "contained" within the minor-key framework—that is, the literal-historical sense—which returns at the end of the aria to the musical setting of Jesus's final words as given in the preceding recitative narrative. In contrast, *Kommt, gehet und eilet* begins with a grouping of three concerto-like movements, the voices entering only in the third; their D/b/D tonality both expands and reverses the arrangement of "Es ist vollbracht," giving precedence to Jesus's victory, now an accomplished fact. When the voices enter in the concerto "finale" as a duet for Peter and John, the hortatory character of the text, *Kommt, gehet und eilet*, echoes that of the dialog, "Eilt, ihr angefocht'nen Seelen" in the *St. John Passion.* But whereas the earlier movement is a dialog urging the faithful to leave their *Marterhöhlen* and fly with the wings of faith to Golgotha, where their pilgrimage will be fulfilled, *Kommt, gehet und eilet*, urges flight to the cave (*Höhle*) that no longer encloses Jesus, the tomb of the resurrected Christ. This detail derives from John's narrative of the resurrection, in which, after Mary Magdalene tells Peter and John of the resurrection, the disciples "run" to his tomb. In the Passion, fulfillment of the pilgrimage of faith is indicated first in "Es ist vollbracht," which links *Trost* for the suffering faithful to Jesus's victory, then in a second dialog, "Mein teurer Heiland," now between the believer and the silent Jesus, accompanied by a chorale that provides the perspective of the resurrection, "Jesu, der du warest tot, lebest nun ohn' Ende." "Mein teurer Heiland" confirms the D associated with Jesus's victory in "Es ist vollbracht," lending a striking tone of the assurance of salvation to the entire grouping. In the Passion the framework for the Easter message is that of Jesus's suffering and death, from which it stands apart, in a quasi-antithetical relationship. The final E♭ chorale provides a very positive message of the believer's hope of resurrection after the sleep of death. But, after the D of "Mein teurer Heiland," the return to flat tonalities—especially the f of "Zerfliesse," the F Phrygian of "O hilf, Christe," and the b♭ of the narrative of the piercing of Jesus's side—seems to place the fulfillment of the pilgrimage of faith in the future. However, the final lines of *Kommt, gehet und eilet*—"Lachen und Scherzen begleitet die Herzen, denn unser Heil ist auferweckt" (Laughing and lightheartedness accompany our hearts, for our salvation is awakened)—project a very forceful sense of triumph and the immediacy of Jesus's victory, which carries over into the lives of the faithful, even though their concerns remain.

The tonal design of *Kommt, gehet und eilet* derives from the interaction of the joyful Easter message and the concerns of the faithful in the present. Bach articulates the latter by turning to B minor for the first recitative and aria, directly following the initial concerto-like grouping, then by moving from there to the subdominant, G, for the second aria, a reminder of the eschatological message of

"Ruht wohl," the sleep of death. After the "Lachen und Scherzen" that Peter and John voice in the D-major duet, the gendered statements of the two women in the first recitative—beginning with Mary Magdalene's chiding Peter and John for their "cold masculine minds" and asking "where has the love gone that you owe to the savior?"—introduce the quality that will be the key to joy in the resurrection in the third aria, Mary Magdalene's "Saget mir geschwinde, wo ich Jesum finde, welchen meine Seele liebt" (Tell me quickly where I will find Jesus, whom my soul loves). Maria Jacobi's "a weak woman puts you to shame" cadences in b, to which the male "characters" respond, first Peter, then John, with the lines "Ach! ein betrübtes Grämen und banges Herzeleid hat mit gesalz'nen Thränen, und wehmuthsvollem Sehnen, ihm eine Salbung zugedacht" (Alas! Our tormented grief and the timid suffering of our hearts intended to anoint him with salty tears and sorrowful longing). Although the recitative begins and ends in B minor, this response suddenly introduces the dominant of f♯ ("Ach!"), then moves via the circle of fifths, almost reaching D minor ("wehmuthsvollem Sehnen"—sorrowful longing), which is deflected to e for the reference to the intended annointing. When the female voices return to complete the recitative in b with the addition of "die Ihr, wie sie, umsonst gemacht" (which you, as we, did in vain), it is clear that the response of sorrow over Jesus's death, like that of longing for Jesus to remain on earth in the *Ascension Oratorio*, is inappropriate.

In B minor, Maria Jacobi's aria, "Seele, deine Spezereien sollen nicht mehr Myrrhen sein" (Soul, your precious ointments shall no longer be myrrh), continues the theme with which the recitative ended: the inadequacy of tears as anointment. Juxtaposing the laurel wreath, emblem of victory, to myrrh, emblem of death—"Denn allein, mit dem Lorbeerkranze prangen, stillt dein ängstliches Verlangen" (For only displaying [yourself] with the laurel wreath stills your anxious longing)—the text draws Mark's association of Mary, the mother of James, with anointment spices (Matthew recounts the presence of "the other Mary" at the tomb, and Luke refers to spices brought by "the women who came with him from Galilee"). At the same time, the altered nature of the spices suggests a possible conflation with Mary of Bethany, who had anointed Jesus earlier in John as well as the Synoptic Gospels, and whose story was widely associated with the strength of faith and penitence—that is spiritual strength as opposed to physical weakness.[28]

[28] This was not a common conflation; but that of Mary of Bethany with the sinful woman who anointed Jesus in Luke and even with Mary Magdalene was widespread, leading to the situation, described by Raymond Brown, that the Roman liturgy "came to honor all three women (the sinner of Galilee, Mary of Bethany, Mary of Magdala) as one saint" (see Brown, *Gospel According to John I–XII*, 452). When, in the first recitative, Maria Jacobi echoes Mary Magdalene's words of reproach to Peter and John for their forgotten "debt of love" to Jesus, with the words "Ein schwaches Weib muß euch beschämen" (A weak woman has to shame you), we may well associate the "weakness" in question with the sinful woman of Galilee. Heinrich Müller in an extended treatise inspired by Luke's account of the sinful woman who anointed Jesus's feet (*Thränen- und Trost-Quelle, Bey Erklärung der Geschichte, von der Großen Sünderin, Luc. VII. V. 36. 37. Etc.*, Hanover, 1724), uses very similar language to that of Cantata 249 to describe the sinner of Galilee: "Sonst ist das Weibliche Geschlecht ein schwaches Gefäß,

In its musical style "Seele, deine Spezereien," scored for soprano, flute, and pizzicato *basso continuo*, is of a very delicate and personal tone that shifts the focus from the triumphant character of the opening concerto complex to the perspective of the faithful. A measure of emphasis on A major emerges briefly for the beginning of the B section (the initial reference to the laurel wreath), but the minor keys predominate, and the middle section moves to the subdominant, e, as it dwells on the "ängstliches Verlangen" that remains a real presence, projected throughout by the pizzicato *basso continuo.*

After this aria, the third-descent continues on to G for Peter's aria, which introduces (or *reintroduces*, if we remember the ending of the *St. John Passion*) the central idea of Lutheran eschatology—the transformation of death into a gentle sleep—as the benefit of Jesus's resurrection. The second recitative, for Peter, John, and Mary Magdalene, sets up the change of key with further symbolic instances of shifting tonal direction. The initial phrases, for the two disciples, move via circle-of-fifths harmonies (A–D–G) and progressively lower pitch to the subdominant as Peter and John refer to the grave and stone that sealed it. Then suddenly Bach shifts to the dominant of f♯, as he had in the first recitative, as John asks "wo aber wird mein Heiland sein?" (Where, however, will my savior be?). And Mary Magdalene's narration of the resurrection—"Er ist vom Tode auferweckt: wir trafen einen Engel an, der hat uns solches kund gethan" (He is awakened from death: we encountered an angel who gave us that news)—moves on to an A-major cadence, upon which Peter observes the folded burial cloth, closing in b. Following immediately, the return of the subdominant for Peter's aria, in combination with the pastorale-lullaby style and an even gentler scoring than that of "Seele, deine Spezereien"—for two recorders and muted violins—creates a tone that, within the framework of an entirely festive cantata, represents the opposite affective pole to the trumpet fanfares of the resurrection: "Sanfte soll mein Todeskummer nur ein Schlummer, Jesu, durch dein Schweißtuch sein" (Gently shall my fear of death be only a slumber, Jesus, through your burial cloth). (See ex. 9.2) Now, Jesus's folded burial cloth (*Schweisstuch*), as described in the Gospel, is reinterpreted as the means of wiping the tears from the believer's cheeks. The primary meaning is that the believer identifies with the weeping Peter of the Passion, whose discovery of the significance of the unwound cloth in the resurrection narrative now symbolizes the change from torment regarding death (*Todeskummer*) to *Trost.*[29] Beginning with a tonic pedal, like other movements of the same type in Bach's *oeuvre*—the virgin Mary's lullaby aria "Schlafe, mein Liebster, genieβe der Ruh" from the *Christ-*

---

und das hätte man auch bißher an diesem Weibe gemerket, da sie der Satan nach seimem Willen in seinen Stricken gehalten. Aber siehe, nun, siehe was fur Stärke ist bey diesem schwachen Weibe!" (51–52)

[29] As Moller relates (*Soliloquia de Passione Jesu Christi, Das ist: Heilige Betrachtung deß Leidens und Sterbens unsers HErrn und Heilandes JEsu Christi,* [Lüneburg, 1730, 35]), "Man schreibet von S. Petro / so offt er habe einen Hahn krähen hören / oder an seinen Fall gedacht / habe er sich deß Weinens nicht erhalten können / also daß er täglich ein Schweiß-Tüchlein bey sich getragen / damit er die Thränen von seinen Augen wischte."

EXAMPLE 9.2 **Cantata 249a, *Kommt, gehet und eilet*** *aria, "Sanfte soll mein Todeskummer" (Peter), beginning*

mas Oratorio or "Mache dich, mein Herze, rein" from the *St. Matthew Passion*, for example—it introduces the flat seventh (F) on "*Todes*kummer" in a manner that relates to the circle-of-fifths motion in the two recitatives, and the association of such harmonic-tonal events with death and downward motion in Bach's music generally. But there is a decidedly eschatological dimension as well: Jesus's wiping the tears from the believer's cheeks was an image derived from Revelation 7, which was very commonly cited in the theological books of the time, and even depicted in engravings of the faithful entering the heavenly Jerusalem (in Heinrich Müller's

Himmlischer Liebeskuß, for example).[30] Here it transfers the ultimate goal of the "sleep of death," prominent at the end of the *St. John Passion*, more directly to the believer than does the Passion chorus. In Peter's aria the slowly moving harmonies and slurred duplet eighth and sixteenth notes above unchanging pedal tones in the *basso continuo* are devices that Bach uses in other works to represent the sleep of death in a lullaby-like manner (see, for example, the setting of "der Tod ist mein Schlaf worden" from the *Actus Tragicus*, BWV 106). As a sequence, therefore, the arias of Maria Jacobi and Peter depict the believer's change in attitude toward death—from sorrow and anxiety to *Trost*—as the result of Jesus's resurrection. The subdominant is its analog.

Between the triumph of Jesus's resurrection in the outermost movements of *Kommt, gehet und eilet* and the intimacy of the first and second arias stands the all-important theme of love, associated particularly with Mary Magdalene, who introduced it in the first recitative. There its character was reproachful toward the two disciples. Following Peter's aria, an arioso for the two women and an aria of Mary Magdalene reintroduce it, but in a very different manner. As the only arioso of the cantata, the duet for the two women has a special role in the design. Focused entirely on the desire to see Jesus, it expresses that longing in terms that seem to go beyond the immediate dramatic situation and reach out to the contemporary believer—that is, it suggests an eschatological perspective, now of a different kind from that of Peter's aria.[31] The line "Ach, könnt es doch nur bald geschehen, den Heiland selbst zu sehen!" (Ah, if only it could happen soon that I might see the savior himself) might easily have come from one of Bach's cantatas on death, such as *Komm, du süße Todesstunde* (BWV 161) or *Wer weiss, wie nahe mir mein Ende* (BWV 27). And in the much-reiterated melodic and harmonic material of the movement—especially that of "Ach! ach! könnt' es doch nur bald geschehen"—there is more than a passing reminiscence of the "Jesus of Nazareth" choruses of the *St. John Passion*. The reiterated "Ach, ach" may remind us of "Wir, wir" in "Wir haben keinen König denn den Kaiser" as well as of "Wo, wo" in the closely related chorus "Wo ist der neugebornen König der Juden" in the *Christmas Oratorio*. The *basso continuo* pattern of a rising and falling third (here decorated somewhat) delineates circle-of-fifths harmonic motion here as in the Passion choruses (though not as systematically following the degrees of the scale). Thus the first sequence features the pattern on G♯, C♯, f♯, b, and e harmonies. The "sixth" harmony, A, is not included because Bach does not circle back to G♯ via the Phrygian cadence, as in the Passion. Instead, after an extension, the pattern starts over once again, this time with harmonies on E, A, D, G, c♯, f♯, and b. The tightly enclosed circling structure of the "Jesus of Nazareth" choruses is not present; and in fact the resemblance to the Passion might well have been incidental, although it is certainly audible. If Bach,

---

[30] Heinrich Müller, *Himmlischer Liebeskuß oder Übung des wahren Christenthumbs* (Rostock, 1659, rev. ed., *Göttliche Liebes-Flamme Oder Auffmunterung zur Liebe Gottes* (Frankfurt, 1676, 662).

[31] The theme of seeing Jesus in the cantata sequence as a whole will be taken up in ch. 10.

consciously or unconsciously, made an association to the Passion, it would be that of the female characters' longing to see Jesus. Here it seems to be associated with the necessity of waiting for the time of Jesus's revelation. In more immediate terms, Bach uses the circling to set up the dominant, A major, for Mary Magdalene's aria.

That aria, "Saget, saget mir geschwinde" (Tell, oh tell me quickly), poeticizes longing to embrace Jesus in the intimate language associated in other Bach cantatas, such as *Ich geh und suche mit Verlangen* (BWV 49), with anticipation of eternity: "Saget, wo ich Jesum finde, welchen meine Seele liebt! Komm doch, komm, umfasse mich, denn mein Herz ist ohne dich Ganz verwaiset und betrübt" (Say where I will find Jesus, whom my soul loves! Come now, come, embrace me, for without you my heart is forlorn and troubled). When John begins the final recitative with the message of joy in Jesus's victory, we sense that love bridges between *Trost,* as the quality that enables the believer to overcome worldly tribulation (i.e., *Trost* as the intersecting point for faith and experience), and joy, as the quality associated with anticipation of the future life. Love, more active and mutual than *Trost,* leads to the concrete anticipation of eternity that in the Lutheran tradition was often called the "foretaste" of eternity, akin to the feeling quality of faith.[32] In this aria the key of A major may recall its earlier, very positive appearance in the second recitative, where it is also sung by Mary Magdalene. Now its florid, extravert style moves in another direction altogether from that of the two earlier arias—no longer downward but decidedly anticipatory and actively hopeful in the emphatic diatonicism of its main theme, which anticipates the beginning theme of the final chorus, "Preis und Dank." The dominant tonality, carried forward in the ending of the following recitative, aids in rendering the return to D for the final chorus its aura of unquestioned triumph.

As a whole, *Kommt, gehet und eilet* exhibits a very solid tonal design that can be found in numerous variations throughout the Bach cantatas, and often with similar associations. Rooted in an extended I–IV–V–I tonal progression, its move to the subdominant for Peter's aria is counterbalanced by the turn to the dominant for Mary Magdalene's (ex. 9.3). After the believer's anticipation of death in Peter's aria, this aria and the accompanying arioso leap forward to the perspective of the resurrection, anticipating seeing Jesus in eternity. In contrast to the increasing quiet of "Seele, deine Spezereien" and "Sanfte soll mein Todeskummer," this aria projects a lively extraverted character, an "active" quality that balances the tone of Peter's aria and prepares for the overt rejoicing of John's recitative and the final chorus in D (both of which, as mentioned earlier, echo passages in the *St. John Passion*). The

---

[32] In this regard the most popular Lutheran devotional book after Arndt's *Wahres Christenthum* was Joachim Lütkemann's *Vorschmack der göttlichen Güte* (1643), a work that, along with the *Wahres Christenthum*, influenced the *Himmlischer Liebeskuß* of Lütkemann's pupil, Heinrich Müller. Müller's treatise depicts the kiss of love between Jesus and the soul on the title page and in several other engravings within the book, in one instance supplying a poem that refers to the foretaste of eternity.

EXAMPLE 9.3 **Cantata 249a, *Kommt, gehet und eilet*** *aria "Saget, saget mir geschwinde" (Mary Magdalene), beginning*

sleep of death corresponds to the subdominant "side" of the *ambitus* and the perspective of the resurrection to the dominant side.[33]

Behind the *Trost* that emerges in "Sanfte soll mein Todeskummer" lies, of course, the original association of its counterpart in the pastorale "shepherd" cantata, where it responds to Silvia's concern for the sheep (since the four characters of the drama have decided to search for flowers with which to create a gratulatory wreath for Duke Christian): "Wer aber wird die Schafe pflegen?" (Who, however, will care for the sheep?). The aria is Menalcas's assurance that the satiated sheep will sleep in safety: "Wieget euch, ihr satten Schafe, in dem Schlafe unterdessen

[33] Hindermann (*Die nachösterlichen Kantaten des Bachschen Choralkantaten-Jahrgangs*, Hofheim am Taunus: Friedrich Hofmeister 1975) discusses this and other similar tonal designs in the 1725 cantatas in terms of their exhibiting the I–IV–V–I tonal pattern (or a variant thereof), which is certainly correct. Viewing it in terms of the flat (subdominant) and sharp (dominant) sides of the *ambitus* points up more of the sense that, historically, the emergence of this most familiar of tonal patterns involved reconciliation of what was in earlier times viewed as an opposition, especially in minor keys, where the subdominant was often flat (minor) and the dominant sharp (viewed, of course, as a harmony, not as a key). The bringing together of the subdominant and dominant as a core means of strengthening the sense of a tonic key can be very easily traced in the madrigals of Monteverdi (see Chafe, *Monteverdi's Tonal Language*, esp. ch. 9, on the sixth madrigal book). What in earlier works (such as *Orfeo*) served as the symbol of antithesis and tonal rupture—the g/E juxtapositions of the messenger's arrival and Orfeo's reaction in Act 2—became rationalized musically as the subdominant followed by the dominant of the dominant. The processes by which this took place (what we now call functional harmony) involved the harmonic-tonal interpretation of the hexachord within the framework of the new sense of tonic centricity that was involved in the shift from mode to key. The idea of the *ambitus* of the mode became that of its flat/sharp boundaries; that is, it came to encompass not just melodic but harmonic range. And by the time of Heinichen's circle of keys it was interpreted tonally in terms of the family of tonic and secondary keys, not just of harmonies within the key. Of course, for Bach all this was well in the past. Nevertheless, I would suggest that the residue of modal and hexachordal thinking that remained in the early eighteenth century might have led Bach to polarize the subdominant and dominant regions of the key as a kind of cross symbol, somewhat like the presumed melodic cross symbols that involve the diminished fourth (a sharp/flat juxtaposition, or melodic cross relation), such as the "Lass ihn kreuzigen" theme of the *St. Matthew Passion*. Fanciful as this may sound, it is borne out by the fact that in certain cantatas the flat, or subdominant region (which may involve the dominant minor instead) is associated with death and the dominant with resurrection, that is, the double meaning behind the cross. For an instance see the reference to Cantata 127 in n. 36.

selber ein!" (In the meantime, rock yourselves to sleep, you satiated sheep). The connection to Peter's aria is that of the protective, personal character of Jesus as good shepherd, looking after his own. And, as we will see, the dual portrait of Jesus as *Christus Victor* and good shepherd, the latter linked unmistakably with *Trost* and love, provides an important key to the spring 1725 cantata sequence overall. In this context it links up with the meaning of the arias "Es ist vollbracht" and "Mein teurer Heiland" in the *St. John Passion*.

Bleib bei uns, denn es will Abend werden (BWV 6)

The role of the subdominant and dominant regions of the *ambitus* in articulating divergent but complementary aspects of the theological message of *Kommt, gehet und eilet* is one that appears in many Bach cantatas. In works that are less dominated by a single outlook or affective sphere than *Kommt, gehet und eilet*, in works of greater length, and in recitatives, Bach often expands the tonal range beyond that of the single *ambitus*, introducing modulation to sharp and flat keys in order to amplify the kinds of qualities associated with the dominant (relatively sharp) and subdominant (relatively flat) regions. Thus, in the *Ascension Oratorio* (BWV 11, *Lobet Gott in seinen Reichen*), after the extraordinarily festive D-major chorus, the initial narrative of Jesus's ascension leads from B minor to the dominant, A major.[34] Then, for the sorrowful response of the faithful to his departure, an accompanied recitative moves widely through the circle of fifths, from the dominant of F♯ to A *minor*, in which it closes. In the dominant minor we now hear the aria "Ach, bleibe doch," a tormented cry for Jesus to remain, after which the continuing narrative, which now describes Jesus's ascent, reverses the modulatory direction, leading back from e to f♯. Owing to the measured character of the shift from A major to A minor, those two keys seem to spell out the distance between worlds above and below.[35] In later years Bach parodied either this version of "Ach, bleibe doch" or (more likely perhaps) a lost original on which it was based, as the Agnus Dei of the *Mass in B minor*, transposing it to G minor, the only flat-key movement of the

[34] I have described the tonal design of the *Ascension Oratorio* in "Bach's *Ascension Oratorio*: God's Kingdoms and their Representation," in *Bach Perspectives* 8: *J. S. Bach and the Oratorio Tradition*, ed. Daniel Melamed, 122–45 (Urbana Champaign: University of Illinois Press 2010).

[35] In his discussion of the modulatory uses of the *Musicalischer Circul* Johann David Heinichen (*Neu erfundene und Gründliche Anweisung*, 266) gives examples of shift from A minor to A major to illustrate the concept he calls *toni intermedii* (intervening keys). In the relatively few Bach cantatas in which tonic major/minor shift appears, Bach usually follows similar principles, especially when something like the difference between worlds "below" and "above" is present. Thus, the shift from c to C between parts 1 and 2 of Cantata 21 is achieved by means of the "toni intermedii" of E♭, g, and F. In a single recitative, such as that of Cantata 11, the degrees that come between the two keys are, of course, not keys. Instances of *immediate* shift from minor to major, or vice versa, while rare, do occur; and when they do, such as in the shift from the first aria of Cantata 127, in C minor, to the second, in C major, there is usually a reason (see n. 36).

entire mass, in which it gives striking voice to the final cry for mercy from the sinful world, Qui tollis peccata mundi, miserere nobis, serving, along with the return to D for the Dona nobis pacem, as a kind of symbolic extended plagal cadence to the work. Thus the subdominant region of the *ambitus* (to which the dominant minor belongs) expands to a flat-minor counterpart.

Similar associations carry forward to the cantatas as well, in which Jesus's victory (like other festive or triumphant affects) is often closely associated with D major and the trumpet style, whereas death, especially when conceived as the Lutheran sleep of death, is often linked with c.[36] And even in cantata sequences Bach appears sometimes to choose the varying *ambitus* of individual works for similar purposes. This is the case several times in the post-Easter cantatas of 1725. Thus, on Easter Monday, one day after the first performance of *Kommt, gehet und eilet*, he turned from the festive D major of his Easter cantata to a darkly colored C minor in what seems a very purposive manner, and one that might well seem surprising if we expect that Easter cantatas will always be triumphant in tone. In fact, *Bleib bei uns* marks a substantial shift in theological perspective, one comparable in concept to the shift to A minor for "Ach, bleibe doch" in the *Ascension Oratorio*. If the beginning of *Kommt, gehet und eilet* expands the affective sphere associated with D and b in "Es ist vollbracht," then that of *Bleib bei uns* continues the tone with which the *St. John Passion ended.* Its opening chorus, in C minor, bears a distinct resemblance to the burial chorus of the Passion, "Ruht wohl, ihr heilige Gebeine." (See ex. 9.4a and b)In *Kommt, gehet und eilet* the series of non-chorale cantatas begins with the victory of the resurrection, then shifts on the following day to the more somber concerns of the faithful living in the world. The association of the onset of darkness with Jesus's departure from the world is the reverse of the message of Jesus as the light coming to the world in John's prologue; the pendular upswing of the resurrection is described now from the perspective of the world as a place of darkness in which the faithful long for Jesus's continuing presence.

Movements one to four of *Bleib bei uns* are very telling in this regard. The first three pray for Jesus to remain through the coming darkness; but whereas the onset of darkness is immanent in the chorus and aria and has just taken place in the chorale (a reflection of the shift to present life), it is a well-established fact in the recitative (no. 4), which takes up its metaphoric meaning—the widespread sinful-

---

[36] When the two are presented in a single work, the juxtaposition is more likely to involve trumpets in C, rather than D, so that the kind of opposition we found between the dominant major and minor in the *Ascension Oratorio* is expressed in terms of a c/C juxtaposition. Perhaps the most outstanding instance of this is Cantata 127, in F. In that work the first aria, "Die Seele ruht in Jesu Händen," is a classic depiction of the sleep of death, in C minor, whereas the immediately following recitative/aria complex, "Wenn einstens die Posaunen schallen," in C major, begins with one of the most pronounced depictions of the resurrection in Bach's music. Many passages might be supported in support of the association of C minor to the sleep of death: Cantatas 27, 82, 94, 95, 106, and 127 all have clear instances. In both Passions the "burial" chorus is in c, while in the *St. Matthew Passion* the tenor solo whose message of human weakness was inspired by the disciples' falling asleep in Gethsemane, "Ich will bei meinem Jesu wachen" (with answering chorus "So schlafen uns're Sünden ein") is also in c.

EXAMPLE 9.4a **St. John Passion** *no. 39, final chorus, "Ruht wohl," beginning*

EXAMPLE 9.4b **Cantata 6, *Bleib bei uns,*** *opening chorus, beginning*

ness of the world—in explanatory fashion. As if to oppose the increasing darkness, over the course of the first three movements, the key sequence moves in the sharp (dominant) direction, from c (the opening chorus) through E♭ (the alto aria, "Hochgelobter Gottes Sohn," with oboe da caccia) to B♭ (the chorale "Bleib bei uns" for soprano and *violoncello piccolo*), before returning to c for the beginning of the only recitative (the metaphoric explanation of darkness). The aria is a prayer for Jesus's light to shine through the coming darkness, after which the solo chorale setting prays that the "bright light" of God's word will not be extinguished, that the faithful "in this last troubled time" ("in dieser letzt'n betrübten Zeit") will be able to hold onto God's "word and sacrament" until the end ("dass wir dein Word und Sacrament rein behalt'n bis unser End").

The lines just cited point to another metaphoric interpretation of light and darkness that underlies the placement of *Bleib bei uns* in the liturgical year. As the first cantata after Easter Day, *Bleib bei uns* brings out the theme of Jesus's physical absence from the world and the means—"word and sacrament"—by which the faithful will continue to experience his presence in the time to come. The reference to the faithful in the "last troubled time" coincides with the fact that darkness is now an accomplished fact. In this respect it looks ahead to the Trinity season, in which the "End" anticipated in the text will take place. This metaphoric interpretation of the "evening" of Jesus's post-resurrection appearance as the "evening of the world" is a very old one, according to which, with Jesus's departure the world reverted to the darkness that was its primary characteristic before the advent of Jesus, the light. It was very much alive in the era of Lutheran orthodoxy, as we find in the theological books of the time. August Pfeiffer's *Antimelancholicus*, for example, a copy of which was in Bach's collection, indexes his discussion of "the evening of the world and the last times" under Easter Monday, taking up some of the same themes that we find in *Bleib bei uns.* Pfeiffer views the spread of darkness throughout the world as the result of the setting of the "Evangelische Gnaden-Sonne" (Jesus), which he associates with John's reference in his prologue to those who prefer darkness to light and who reject the "light of truth." The result, as in the recitative of Cantata 6, is that God overturns the lamp of his word for them (a reference to Rev 2:5) where the church of Ephesus is urged to repent or have God remove its golden candlestick from its place.[37] Behind Cantata 6, therefore, lies a warning to the church in the world not to succumb to darkness and sin. Johann Arndt and Heinrich Müller make the same association to Easter Monday, both speaking of the "evening of the world," as a metaphor not only for the prevalence of sin in the world, but also of the "letzte Zeit," that is, what was traditionally viewed as the final era of "salvation history," the era of the church, or the "Gnadenzeit," which would come to an end with Jesus's Second Coming.[38] The connection

[37] Pfeiffer, *Antimelancholicus*, 555–56.

[38] Arndt, *Postilla*, 3:30. Heinrich Müller, *Evangelischer Herzens-Spiegel*, 517–18: "Bleib bey uns. Mein Hertz, der Abend dieser Welt ist vor der Thür. Es ist die letzte Stunde. Das Ende aller Dinge ist

of this "evening of the world" with that described by de Lubac (see ch. 2 in relation to the multiple senses of Advent) is that the onset of the metaphoric evening immediately following the resurrection marks the beginning of the transition to the era of the church, completed at Pentecost and symbolized in the Trinity season. At Advent Jesus's coming put an end to the darkness, which was viewed historically as the time of Israel, tropologically as the dominance of the law, and eschatologically as the Second Coming and the end of the world. Liturgically, however, the association of the coming light was to the end of the Trinity season and the beginning of the New Year.[39] Hence August Pfeiffer's placing his discussion of the "evening of the world and the last times" at the end of the first book of his treatise, in the context of fears for the coming new year, with considerable reference to the last judgment.

It is perhaps no coincidence, therefore, that *Bleib bei uns* shares its C-minor tonality with the cantata for Trinity Sunday 1725, *Es ist ein trotzig und verzagt Ding*, which also develops the metaphor of light and darkness extensively (and whose introductory *dictum* Martin Moller cited in connection with Easter Monday). There the antithesis arises from the Johannine story of Nicodemus, "ein Oberster unter den Juden," who comes to Jesus only by night, a fact that is recalled in the final recitative of the *St. John Passion*, before the choral meditation on Jesus's burial, along with the narrative of Joseph of Arimathea, who also kept his discipleship secret, "out of fear of the Jews."[40] Since no other of Bach's Trinity cantatas makes any reference to Nicodemus or the light/darkness opposition whatsoever, it seems possible that the appearance of this theme in the post-Easter cantatas of 1725 was introduced so as to emphasize continuity with the darkness of the world that marked the final shift to flats at the end of the *St. John Passion*. In *Bleib bei uns* the description of God's word as "light" (which reappears in the cantata for the third day of Pentecost) refers, of course, to the enlightening role of the Holy Spirit, while "word and sacrament" are the mainstays of Christian life in the world after Jesus's

---

nahe herbey kommen. Die Boßheit nimmt zu, die Liebe nimmt ab; Das sind Zeichen der letzten Zeit. Mit dem Abend der Welt dringet herein Jammer und Noth." The passage cited appears under the heading "Evangelium am andern Oster-Tage." Müller then ends his sequence of three Easter sermons on the following day with similar sentiments, now closing his sermon for Easter Tuesday with the verse of "Bleib bei uns" that serves as text for the third movement of Cantata 6 (539–40). And he ends his sermon for the twenty-seventh Sunday after Trinity, and therefore the entire cycle of sermons, with the same verse (1278). See ch. 2, n. 21 for further references to Pfeiffer's and Müller's interpretations of the "evening of the world." Four Bach cantatas (BWV 30, 147a, 162, and 172) introduce the expression "Gnadenzeit" with the meaning I have described.

[39] We find exactly this association in Cantata 61, for Advent Sunday, in which the four senses are presented directly. There the second, or allegorical sense, appears in the first aria, "Komm, Jesu, komm zu deiner Kirche und gib ein selig neues Jahr." *Bleib' bei uns* is not, of course, a new beginning in this sense; rather, it looks ahead to the end, casting the shadow of the world across the light of Easter.

[40] The recitative in question begins "Darnach bat Pilatum Joseph von Arimathia, der ein Junger Jesu war, (doch heimlich aus Furcht vor den Juden) daß er möchte abnehmen den Leichnem Jesu." Later we read "Es kam aber Nicodemus, der vormals in der Nacht zu Jesu kommen war, und brachte Myrrhen und Aloen unter einander bei hundert Pfunden. Da nahmen sie den Leichnam Jesu." Thus two of Jesus's "secret" disciples came out into the open to bury him.

physical departure. Thus *Bleib bei uns* looks ahead to the end of the first half of the year—Pentecost and Trinity—and the shift to the Trinity season, the era of the church, symbolically the "letzte Zeit," even to the end of the Trinity season. The need for Jesus's protective presence, expressed in its final chorale, emerges still more directly in association with the church six days later in the cantata for Quasimodogeniti, *Am Abend aber desselbigen Sabbats*, which again introduces the light/darkness antithesis in association with the disciples' hiding "from fear of the Jews" (and once again it is the only cantata for that Sunday to bring out this theme).

The connection just mentioned traces in part to the chorales that end Cantatas 6 and 42, respectively, the second verse of Luther's three-strophe "Erhalt uns, Herr, bei deinem Wort" (1542), and the single verse of his "Verleih uns Frieden gnädiglich" (1529), whose text is a German version of the antiphon *Da pacem Domine*. Those two chorales had an intertwined relationship throughout their histories, appeared in succession in many chorale books, and were often sung together, particularly at the end of services. Although composed at different times, they have two principal features in common: first, both their melodies are based (as was Luther's other hymn, "Nun komm, der Heiden Heiland") on the plainchant melody of the hymn "Veni redemptor gentium"; and second, they both respond to the threat of the sixteenth-century Turkish invasions of Europe. But whereas "Verleih uns Frieden" is a prayer for peace and good government, "Erhalt uns, Herr," is considerably more militant in tone, calling in its second line, "und steur' des Papsts und Türken Mord" for God's protection from murder by the papists and Turks. It was headed "A Children's Hymn, to Be Sung against the Two Arch-enemies of Christ and his Holy Church, the Pope and the Turk."[41] Understandably, therefore, it was despised and even parodied by Roman Catholics, forbidden to be sung in some places and considered controversial in others. Luther organized its three strophes around the Trinity, and the verse that ends "Bleib bei uns" (the second), although calling for Jesus to manifest his power, is primarily an appeal for protection that, in isolation from the others, is not contentious. In fact, the tone becomes less militant from the first to the third verse, as if reflecting God's wrath at the outset and the comforting character of the Holy Spirit at the end.

Musically, the complex history of the two chorales after Luther's time, including a second verse of "Verleih uns Frieden" that was composed by Johann Walther more than thirty years after Luther's original, is reflected in Bach's settings. Thus, whereas "Erhalt uns, Herr" has four phrases, that closely mirror the plainchant, "Verleih uns Frieden" has five in Luther's original version, the fifth phrase put together from elements of earlier ones and standing apart from them in its breaking the rhyme scheme (ababc). Walther's strophe, however, has seven lines with the

---

[41] The translation is that of Robin Leaver (*Luther's Liturgical Music: Principles and Implications* [Grand Rapids, MI: William B. Eerdmans], 107), who gives an excellent account of both "Erhalt uns, Herr" (107–15) and "Verleih uns Frieden" (200–203). See also Johann Christoph Olearius, *Evangelischer Lieder-Schatz* (Jena, 1706), 87–103. Alfred Dürr outlines the history of later additions to the two chorales in *Cantatas*, 239.

rhyme scheme abcdee followed by a melismatic "Amen" phrase. Its melody is much more loosely related to the plainchant than Luther's version, so that one might just as well speak of a single twelve-phrase strophe. As a result of this complex history, the chorale books of Bach's time and earlier present the two chorales separately, though sometimes in immediate succession. In Bach's 1725 chorale cantata *Erhalt uns, Herr, bei deinem Wort* (BWV 126 for Sexagesima), the first movement features the four phrases of the first verse of the chorale "Erhalt uns, Herr," whereas the movements that follow paraphrase a seven-strophe version, of which verses one through five comprise the expanded version of that chorale, and verses six and seven consist of the two verses of "Verleih uns Frieden." The third movement presents the four-phrase melody of the third strophe (with text) of "Erhalt uns, Herr" in dialog with recitative interpolations; and the cantata ends with the five- and seven-phrase verses (or twelve-phrase verse) of "Verleih uns Frieden," as does *Bleib bei uns*.

In the context of the spring 1725 cantata sequence Bach's ending Cantata 6 with the second verse of "Erhalt uns, Herr" and Cantata 42 with both strophes of "Verleih uns Frieden" (presumably a decision of the librettist) brings out the fact that both chorales center on the need for God's protection of the faithful against their enemies.[42] In this the unknown librettist drew a parallel between the struggles of the Christian church in the world and the struggles of the disciples and early Christians. The theme of light and darkness poeticizes John's division of good and evil in terms of that struggle.

In Bach's cantatas darkness is associated almost exclusively with flat tonalities, but it is no more possible for such an association to bear wholly pejorative import than it is for evening itself to be viewed that way. Darkness often represents the inevitable imperfection of human life, the sphere of the "flesh," which must be acknowledged for there to be any possibility of redemption; in certain works, such as the *St. Matthew Passion*, it is possible for "evening" to be described as a "schöne Zeit," representing the time of reconciliation with God (although the association of "darkness" to Golgotha is not forgotten).[43] Nevertheless, the darkness is something that God will bring to an end in his own time. The idea of the faithful holding onto the vehicles of Jesus's presence—word and sacrament—through the time of increasing darkness—symbolized liturgically in the end of the Trinity season—provides, in fact, a very important key to the most pronounced set of musical symbols in *Bleib bei uns*: those that surround the idea of descent on the one hand and of holding fast on the other. Bach depicts these two ideas very palpably in the ritornello of the opening chorus in which, at the outset, all the strings play long series of repeated pitches—at first twenty-five g's in succession, later thirty-five

[42] This is a prominent theme in the section of the *Das Privilegirte Ordentliche und Vermehrte Dresdnische Gesang-Buch* in which these and other chorale verses in this cantata grouping appear; see n. 17.

[43] See Renate Steiger, "'O schöne Zeit! O Abendstunde!': Affekt und Symbol in J. S. Bachs Matthäus-Passion." *Musik und Kirche* 46 (1976): 1–13.

b♭'s—against which the other parts move (see ex. 9.4b). The second idea of the ritornello, a long descending scalar line from g″ to e♮′, sets up further descending sequences throughout the first and third (last) sections of the movement, always in association with "denn es will Abend werden, und der Tag hat sich geneiget."

In the middle section Bach makes this idea even more clear, associating the words "Bleib bei uns" with three successive half-note iterations of a single pitch that stand apart from the two other chorus themes, both of which describe musical descent patterns in shorter note values. The reiterated pitches give great weight to the idea of something that does not change, while the descent patterns—the one a scalar descent and the other a circle-of-fifths motion in the flat direction—subtly extend the idea of descent, associated, of course, with "denn es will Abend werden" (the scalar-descent theme) and "und der Tag hat sich geneiget" (the circle-of-fifths theme) to its tonal dimension. From an initial suggestion of the subdominant, f, at the beginning of the section, the music eventually works its way through a passage that becomes increasingly flat, articulating the key of F minor much more palpably, until, just before the final return to c, the chorus cries out "Bleib bei uns" in octaves—G, g, g′, and g″—before the abbreviated return of the opening section. It is as if the final cry from the chorus pulls the tonality back to c from its potential drift still further flat.

Nevertheless, the character of the chorus as a whole is a comforting one, rooted in its associations with the Sarabande and with the character of evening as time of rest (as in the final chorus of the *St. John Passion*). And the first through the third movements of Bach's cantata project a positive character. The E♭ aria, "Hochgelobter Gottes Sohn," accompanied by oboe da caccia and pizzicato *basso continuo*, contains the pejorative aspect of darkness within the framework of a major-key piece whose opening section suggests in its thematic material the brightness and splendor associated with "hochgelobter." At the same time, however, the two segments that follow introduce some very conspicuous chromatic-enharmonic accidentals associated with flat-minor keys as the emblem of the darkness whose onset is now under way. The principal thematic idea in these sections comprises a melodic ascent/descent pattern in the voice, against a single held tone in the bass that, owing to the upper parts, becomes a dominant and leads, therefore, to the key a fifth below. Bach passes this idea through circle-of-fifths sequences that lead to the subdominant, A♭, which is preceded by extensive flat/minor coloring suggestive even of the subdominant *minor*. The third section then uses the same idea to reach the dominant minor, b♭, and even e♭, before returning to E♭ for the closing repetition of the opening ritornello. In these two sections the fact that the modulations all lead to cadences in major suggests the hope that the darkness they symbolize will be overcome by Jesus's presence.[44]

[44] After the E♭ ritornello and the close of the aria's A section in B♭, the first of two parallel segments of the B section modulates successively through c and f ("Bleib', ach bleibe unser Licht"), closing in A♭; Bach colors the harmonies of the principal A♭ cadence, prolonging the word "Finsternis" for four mea-

EXAMPLE 9.5 **Cantata 6, *Bleib bei uns*** *no. 3, chorale, "Ach bleib bei uns," beginning*

The instrumentation of "Hochgelobter Gottes Sohn" lends the movement a personal, intimate quality that continues in the B♭ chorale for solo soprano with *violoncello piccolo* (ex. 9.5).The rise in pitch of the voice and the corresponding lowering of the pitch of the instrumental soloist can be understood in terms of the light/darkness opposition, while the *violoncello piccolo* "mediates" between the *basso continuo* and the soprano in a way that may remind us of Forkel's statement that Bach invented the *viola pomposa* (which some believe was in reality the *violoncello piccolo*) for a similar purpose in accompanying the violin (see ch. 11). Like the preceding movements, this one features sequences of unchanging repeated tones (longing for Jesus's continued presence) against which the other lines move. Now we find these are derived from the reiterated tones in the initial phrase of the chorale, "Ach, bleib bei uns." Owing, perhaps, to the tonal stability of the chorale, there are no excursions into flat/minor regions as there were in "Hochgelobter Gottes Sohn."

If the motion from c to E♭, then B♭, over the first three movements of *Bleib bei uns* mirrors the believer's longing for the "light" of Jesus's presence amidst his recognition of the darkness of the world, then the tortured character of the motion back to c in the first recitative is surely associated with its explanation of the meaning of darkness as a metaphor for sin having gained the upper hand throughout the world. Now the bass voice lends the movement a rather more doctrinal tone. Above a chromatically descending bass line, Bach leads the recitative toward a C-minor cadence that, coming as it does in the eighth measure (of a ten-measure solo), sounds like the ending. With the arrival on c, however, the vocal line of the

sures with e♭, $A\flat^{7}$ and d♭ harmonies, the tones g♭ and f♭ appearing in the vocal line on "Finsternis." Then he transposes the beginning of the B section down so as to modulate through b♭ and e♭ (again for "Bleib', ach bleibe unser Licht") but alters the continuation so that the closing cadence, prolonged and colored harmonically on "Finsternis" as before, returns to E♭. It is worth noting that in the *St. Matthew Passion,* flat harmonies such as these appear in association with the darkness of Golgotha, in particular in the arioso "Ach, Golgatha" and for Jesus's last words, "My God, My God, why hast thou forsaken me"; the pitch f♭ (flattest pitch in the Passion) sounds conspicuously on "Finsternis." In "Hochgelobter Gottes Sohn" Bach uses similar tonal devices to offset the darkness of the world by the redemption offered through Jesus.

final phrase plummets down an octave and a sixth, from the highest to the lowest tone of the recitative (e♭ to G), cadencing again, now in g, as it relates that God has extinguished the light for the sinful ("Drum hast du auch den Leuchter umgestossen"). While the drop in pitch suggests God's overturning the lamp, the shift of key at the end has the effect of mirroring God's dividing the light from the darkness, that is, the sinful from the faithful, metaphorically. In relation to the B♭ of the preceding chorale and the c of the preceding cadence, the G minor, which now holds as the key of the remaining two movements of the cantata, is a kind of "inbetween" key, accompanying expressions of the need of the faithful for God's aid in avoiding succumbing to the darkness that is all around.

The second aria, "Jesu, lass uns auf dich sehen," for tenor, prays for Jesus to let himself be seen, so as to aid the faithful in avoiding the path of sin ("dass wir nicht auf den Sündenwegen gehen"), to let the light of his word shine more brightly on them, making them at all times faithful ("lass das Licht deines Worts uns heller scheinen und dich jederzeit treu meinen"). Its initial musical idea is a subtle depiction of the human desire to see Jesus, the first measure circling around the tonic (g) triad ("Jesu, lass uns"), and the second shifting up the fifth to the dominant (D) for "auf dich sehen." Here the prayer for Jesus to let himself be seen is unmistakably linked to the Word of scripture; and in this respect it looks ahead to the coming of the Holy Spirit. The world remains a place of darkness, but Jesus's word brings illumination. Throughout the movement rising and falling patterns suggest, respectively, the petition for Jesus to let himself be seen, and Jesus's response. The cantata ends in g with a chorale prayer for Jesus to manifest his power and to protect his "poor Christianity" ("arme Christenheit") so that they may praise him in eternity. In toto, therefore, *Bleib bei uns* is a vision of the world as a place and a time of darkness and tribulation ("dieser letzt'n betrübten Zeit"), in which the faithful must hold to God's word and depend on his protection.

Am Abend aber desselbigen Sabbats (BWV 42)

John's account of Jesus's second and third post-resurrection appearances to the disciples, the former (20:19–23) taking place on the evening of the resurrection (and followed by the narrative of Thomas's disbelief (20:24–25), and the latter (20:26–31) occurring one week later, were both assigned as the Gospel reading for the Sunday after Easter, Quasimodogeniti, where they echoed in some respects Luke's second account, heard on Easter Tuesday. John, however, intensifies both the miraculous and the faith-centered character of the narrative by telling that Jesus's appearance to the disciples took place behind closed doors, and by developing the story of Thomas, so as to lead to Jesus's remarks on faith. He also specifies the appearances as having taken place on the first day of the week, thereby making clear the change from the Jewish sabbath, a detail that goes hand in hand with his telling that the disciples were in hiding "from fear of the Jews." Most significant of all, perhaps, especially in the associations that Quasimodogeniti had for later generations, was his breathing on the disciples with the words "Receive you the Holy Spirit" in the earlier of the two appearances. However, although Quasimodogeniti was the liturgical occasion associated with Jesus's announcing the Holy Spirit as the means of his "permanent presence" among the disciples, Bach's librettist does not mention the Holy Spirit, either here or in *Bleib bei uns* and *Ich bin ein guter Hirt*. Since, in fact, none of the cantatas for Cantate, Rogate, Exaudi, and Ascension Day 1724 (those whose texts are all presumed to have been produced by the same author as the first three of 1725) mentions the Holy Spirit, it might have been that this particular author meant to leave all reference to the Spirit for the feast day that commemorates his appearance, Pentecost. In contrast, Mariane von Ziegler's texts are more in keeping with the character of the Farewell Discourse, in which Jesus introduces the coming of the Spirit frequently. In Cantata 42 the absence of any reference to the Spirit is particularly surprising, given not only the references to the Spirit in both the Gospel and epistle readings but also the librettist's concern with Jesus's protection of the church. As we will see, Bach might have intended a "hidden" musical reference to the Spirit in Cantata 42.

The need of the faithful for God's protection remains the subject of the next two surviving cantatas of the 1725 sequence, *Am Abend aber desselbigen Sabbats* (BWV 42), for Quasimodogeniti, and *Ich bin ein guter Hirt* (BWV 85), for Misericordias. In presenting Jesus with distinct echoes of the *Christus Victor* (Cantata 42), then in the role of the good shepherd (Cantata 85), those cantatas can be considered to prepare for the union of those aspects of Jesus at Pentecost. In narrating that the disciples hid "from fear of the Jews," John is not only reiterating a theme that runs throughout his Gospel, in which "the Jews" represent all those who in his worldview were antagonistic to Jesus and his circle, but he is echoing the ending of his Passion narrative, where we are told that Joseph of Arimathea kept his discipleship secret "from fear of the Jews," a fact that linked him with Nicodemus, described earlier in the Gospel as a "high official among the Jews" ("ein Oberster unter den Juden"), who was also a "secret" disciple, coming forth only by night.[45] In this context, the darkness of *Am Abend aber desselbigen Sabbats* is refuge from the world that persecutes the disciples, who are now reinterpreted as the Christian church, whereas the light is Jesus's aiding the faithful to overcome worldly persecution (in the aria "Jesus ist ein Schild der Seinen").

Am Abend aber desselbigen Sabbats is the only Bach cantata to mention the Jews explicitly, which it does twice, since the unknown librettist reiterated the opening motto in the recitative fifth movement, adding first the ponderously didactic remark that it provided a good example of the fact that Jesus's protection of the disciples was a sign of his protection of his church, then the concluding phrase, "Drum laßt die Feinde wüten!" (Therefore let your enemies rage). The text does not say

[45] See Brown, *Gospel According to John I–XII*, lxx–lxxiii. Brown, like many other contemporary authors, places John's references to "the Jews" in quotation marks throughout his two-volume study.

that the enemies in question would still be the Jews, even in eighteenth-century Leipzig; and it would be a misinterpretation to so understand it. But they were certainly viewed as among the opponents of Christianity (along with the Turks and papists!). And, following soon after the *St. John Passion* (whose text, like that of *Am Abend*, was presumably written in 1724), it seems likely that the librettist intended as much. The motto in question is one of only two Johannine *dicta* among those that begin the 1725 post-Easter cantatas that does not set the words of Jesus, the other being that of *Er rufet seinen Schafen mit Namen* (Cantata 175), which is of a wholly different character. And Cantata 42 is the only instance among these cantatas of Bach's beginning with an instrumental movement rather than with the *dictum* itself. Whether this indicates his attitude toward the Johannine passage is impossible to say. That the verse was not suitable for a chorus seems obvious; but it could certainly have been set as an opening recitative, as in the case of *Sie werden euch in den Bann tun* (Cantata 183: "They will put you under a ban [or out of the synagogue]"), where the word "sie" referred to the Jews in the Gospel itself, but could only have had a historical meaning in Bach's surroundings. In fact, the passage tended to be interpreted allegorically, that is, transferred to the only modern equivalent for Lutherans, excommunication by the pope. Luther himself did this; and some of his followers extended that meaning to Quasimodogeniti as well.[46] And so the choice of "Verleih uns Frieden gnädlich" to end the cantata resonates with the peace that Jesus brings the disciples in the Gospel for the day.

Bach preceded the opening *dictum* of Cantata 42 with an extended instrumental sinfonia for two oboes, bassoon and strings, and followed it by an even more extended aria with the same instrumentation, both of which movements are generally presumed to have been parodied from a lost instrumental concerto.[47] This decision, which must have been Bach's alone, places a great deal of emphasis on the dramatic situation: of the resurrected Jesus's appearing "in the midst" of the fearful disciples, calming their fear with his "Friede sei mit euch." Those words are not given in the text of Cantata 42, but they would certainly have been understood. They embody the tropological meaning of sabbath in Lutheranism: the rest or peace of faith.[48] And, in this context we may remember that in his magnificent

---

[46] See, for example, Luther's second sermon for Exaudi from the *Kirchenpostille*, vol. 2.1, 259–71, English ed. (Grand Rapids, MI: Baker Book House Company 2000). This is a reprint of *The Precious and Sacred Writings of Martin Luther*, vol. 12, ed. John Nicholas Lenker (Minneapolis: Lutherans in All Lands, 1907). The sermon in question was translated by S. E. Ochsenford. See also Aegidius Hunnius, *Postilla* , 2:60–61 (Quasimodogeniti).

[47] Dürr, *Cantatas,* 296. Joshua Rifkin argues that both movements might have originated in the lost serenata, *Der Himmel dacht auf Anhalts Ruhm und Glück* (BWV 66a), composed in 1718. See Rifkin, "Verlorene Quellen, verlorene Werke" in *Bachs Orchesterwerke: Bericht über das 1. Dortmunder Bach-Symposium 1996*, ed. Martin Geck, 65–67. (Witten, 1997).

[48] See Johann Jacob Rambach's multilayered spiritual interpretation of the word "Sabbath" as cited in ch. 2, n. 3. In a funeral sermon titled "Sabbathum Quadruplex," Johann Heermann explores the meaning of "Sabbath" according to the four senses of scripture. See Heermann, *CHRISTIANAE / Ευθαναβιας [Euthanasias] Statue / Lehr- und Erinnerungs-Seulen.* (Breslau, 1621), 231–57. .

1724 cantata for Quasimodogeniti, *Halt im Gedächtnis Jesum Christ* (BWV 67), Bach and his librettist had emphasized the *Christus Victor* portrayal of Jesus from the outset, introducing the believer's recognition of Jesus's victory through faith in the second movement, then countering it with the theme of worldly struggle: "Mein Glaube kennt des Heilands Sieg, doch fühlt mein Herze Streit und Krieg" (My faith knows the savior's victory, yet my heart feels struggle and combat). A chorale celebration of Jesus's victory in the third movement introduces the theme of the enemies of Jesus and the faithful, after which a recitative prays that now that Jesus has been victorious he will struggle along with his child, the believer, against the latter's enemies, fulfilling his word and work through faith. The sixth movement, arguably the crown of the entire cantata, then depicts in very dramatic fashion Jesus's appearance in the midst of the disciples as his appearing to the faithful. This movement, which Bach took over a decade later as the beginning segment of the Gloria of his *Missa Brevis* in A, makes an eightfold alternation between musical styles depicting first the agitation of the world (the instrumental introduction), followed by Jesus's appearance bringing peace with the words "Friede sei mit euch" (Et in terra pax in the Gloria). The style juxtaposition then continues in choral expressions of Jesus's helping in the struggle against Satan and the enemies of the faithful, his providing peace for the faithful, reviving them physically and spiritually, and finally, his leading them into his *Ehrenreich*, each of these followed by Jesus's "Friede sei mit Euch."

In contrast, Cantata 42 takes a far more doctrinal approach to the subject of Jesus's aiding the faithful in their worldly struggles. Whatever was its original function, Bach seems to have intended the introductory sinfonia to function here, at least in part, as a mirroring of the disciples' unrest, since the movement features elements of the *concitato* (excited) style associated with such states of mind throughout the Baroque period. The D-major tonality links up with the key of *Kommt, gehet und eilet*, in suggesting a very positive, even somewhat militant tone. At the same time, however, the tone of overt rejoicing and triumph that dominated the introductory instrumental movements of *Kommt, gehet und eilet* is replaced by a much more down-to-earth character, the result of the change from the triple-meter triadic sweep of the trumpet-dominated beginning of the Easter cantata to the often sequential concertizing of strings and winds in quadruple-meter sixteenth-note patterns. The atmosphere is no longer that of the elemental character of Jesus's dramatic victory over the forces of evil, but something much closer to the struggle of the faithful against worldly opponents, which involves a dialog element suggestive of rationality, a quality suitable to the didactic tone of the text as a whole. A narrative element may be present, even in the sinfonia, in that twice in the section that immediately follows the introductory ritornello (entirely for strings) Bach drops out the *basso continuo* while the violins and viola play unison repeated eighths, marked *piano*, as an accompaniment to the oboes and bassoon, who play a variant of the ritornello theme. The effect is to set the winds in relief, especially the bassoon, whose entrance is delayed each time by half a measure. In pictorial terms appropriate to the subject matter of the cantata, these two instances of the *bassetchen* texture are suggestive of the appearance of Jesus amid the disciples, as if from the world above. After these two passages, however, Bach presents all appearances of this music with the *basso continuo*. Later the two groups toss short figures back and forth at rapid intervals in an atmosphere that suggests the disciples' restless state of mind. In the middle section, however, there is a sudden change, as each oboe in turn plays with the bassoon a long-drawn-out line that Bach marks *cantabile*, against which the strings play rapid *concitato*-like figures marked *piano*. The effect of such a simultaneous opposition is that of the suppression of excitement or unease beneath the calming tone of the melody in the winds. The passage is short-lived, however, and the former concertizing reappears even before the end of the middle section, after which the opening section is repeated in its entirety.

Following the movement just described, which usually takes between six and seven minutes in performance, the Johannine motto (ex. 9.6) lasts some thirty seconds, its B-minor tonality bridging between the D of the sinfonia and the G of the long aria that follows (often over ten minutes in performance). Thus the motto is virtually swallowed up by two extended movements with the same instrumentation, suggestive of a common concerto origin. The character of the motto is given in the constantly reiterated sixteenth notes of the *basso continuo*, a symbol of the disciples' fear, after which the G-major aria, "Wo zwei und drei versammlet sind," describing Jesus's presence in the midst of the disciples, is an oasis of *Trost* (ex. 9.7), projecting a tone that Alfred Dürr describes as one of "supraterrestrial calm."[49] In it the two instrumental groups sound together throughout the A section (marked *adagio*), the winds carrying all the principal thematic material in eighth- and sixteenth-note rhythms, while the strings provide a sustained *piano sempre* accompaniment, in longer note values. Within its principal section a texture similar to the one just described in the sinfonia—unison repeated eighths in the strings (*piano*) accompanying sixteenth-note figures in the winds (*forte*)—returns to set the words "da stellt sich Jesus mitten ein" (confirming the association to Jesus's appearance as described earlier). The line then continues each time with a florid passage, "und spricht dazu das Amen," for voice and *basso continuo* alone, after which the instruments reenter, the winds marked *forte* and the strings still *piano sempre*. The point of these passages is to suggest Jesus "in the midst" of an agitated world, bringing inner peace to the fearful disciples.[50]

---

[49] Dürr, *Cantatas*, 297.

[50] The repeated eighth notes may be compared to the reiterated tones in several movements of *Bleib bei uns*, the repeated eighth notes in the Sinfonia of Cantata 42 and the rapid repeated sixteenths that form the bass of the biblical motto that follows it. Their associations are well established in Bach's vocal works. For example, the dialog for tenor and chorus, "O Schmerz! wie zittert das gequälte Herz" from the *St. Matthew Passion*, or the most graphic of all Bach's representations of the stilling of *Gewissensangst*, the final chorale of Cantata 105, in which the repeated tones decrease in note values throughout several changes of time signature (the interludes in this movement are, incidentally, also set without *basso continuo*).

EXAMPLE 9.6 **Cantata 42, *Am Abend aber desselbigen Sabbats*** *no. 2, recitative*

After such a convincing sense of the effect of Jesus's presence on the disciples, the middle section of the aria reverts to a more doctrinal tone again, changing to 12/8 from 4/4 and a slightly faster tempo ("un poco andante"). Set simply for voice and *basso continuo*, it concludes that "whatever takes place out of love and necessity does not break the ordinance of the most high" ("des Höchste Ordnung"). The allusion here is, presumably, to passages such as Paul's explanation to the Galatians that there is no law against the "fruits of the Spirit," such as love, joy, peace, patience, and the like, words of comfort to those among the early church who feared the consequences of their break with Judaism.[51] In fact, many Lutheran commentaries

[51] See Melvin P. Unger, *Handbook to Bach's Sacred Cantata Texts: An Interlinear Translation with Reference Guide to Biblical Quotations and Allusions* (Lanham, MD: Scarecrow Press, 1996), 150. Many Lutheran commentaries refer to God's *Ordnung* in connection with Quasimodogeniti. August Her-

EXAMPLE 9.7 **Cantata 42, *Am Abend aber desselbigen Sabbats*** *no. 3, aria, "Wo zwei und drei versammlet sind," beginning*

associate the words Jesus speaks to the disciples directly following his giving them the Holy Spirit—"Whoever's sins you remit, they are remitted unto them; and whoever's sins you retain, they are retained"—with God's *Ordnung*, according to which the disciples now had the power of the so-called *Bindeschlüssel* and *Löseschlüssel*, the keys to the kingdom of heaven. For some Lutherans the Roman church, in associating the "keys" with Peter only, and therefore with the papacy, had arrogated the power of the keys that Jesus had given to all the disciples in the Gospel for Quasimodogeniti.[52] As mentioned earlier (n. 9), one prominent seventeenth-century Lutheran theologian, Joachim Lütkemann, began his commentary on the epistle for Quasimodogeniti with a discussion of God's *Ordnung*, which, in secular judgments, demanded the testimony of two or three witnesses before judgment could be passed (as in Deut 20:15). In keeping with the epistle reference to three witnesses in heaven and three on earth, Lütkemann drew a parallel with the *Ordnung* that was interpreted in tropological terms as the sudden appearance of Jesus in the human heart, the onset of faith. Jesus's appearance in the midst of the disciples was that they had been chosen beforehand by God as witnesses to the resurrection; Jesus did not appear to everyone because of the importance of faith as the evidence of things not seen (as Jesus had said to Thomas in the Gospel for the day). Thus Lütkemann linked the "two or three who are gathered together" (Mt 18:20) with the disciples to whom Jesus appeared on the evening of the sabbath as God's witnesses to the truth of the resurrection. What inspired him was undoubtedly the fact that the word "Zeugnis" appears four times in the epistle for the day. Hence his heading his epistle sermon for Quasimodogeniti "Von Zeugnissen des Glaubens" and his emphasis on John's reference to the idea of being "born" in faith (associated with the meaning of Quasimodogeniti as the day of the "newly born" or "reborn" through baptism). And it appears that Bach's librettist made the same connection, not only in "Wo zwei und drei versammlet sind," but also in his description of Jesus's sudden appearance as a "Zeugnis" of his protection of the church.

In the view of Bach's librettist, God's *Ordnung* was a sign of the authority of the church, a view that underlies his beginning the group of texts that have been assigned to his authorship, with a biblical *dictum* followed by a recitative and chorale, a sequence that usually involves interpretation of the initial motto through successive paraphrases. In this pattern the chorale sums up the theme of the preceding motto and aria. In Cantatas 6 and 85 the mottos in question are famous scriptural passages of highly poetic character, cited often and paraphrased as hymns.

---

mann Francke, for example, discusses the Gospel for the day in terms of how God's word is the means of instilling faith, describing this process as God's *Ordnung* (*Sonn- und Fest-Tags Predigten* [Halle, 1724], 769, 771. And he comments elsewhere on the epistle in a similar fashion, adding that through faith the believer, "in his mortal body, becomes a living dwelling for God's witness (*Zeugnis*), which runs through the entire divine *oeconomie*, that Jesus is the true Christ who works by means of water and blood" (Francke, *Predigten über die Sonn- und Fest-Tags Episteln* [Halle, 1726], 621). For Francke, the word "Zeugnis," which runs throughout the latter commentary, signifies faith.

[52] See Aegidius Hunnius, *Postilla* 2: 60–61.

In Cantata 42, however, the doctrinal, adversarial character of the motto hardly lent itself to such a role. And in this case, the chorale, "Verzage nicht, o Häuflein klein," intensifies the sense of opposition, emphasizing the persecution of the faithful by the world that the preceding aria had seemed to overcome, whereas the summing up comes in the second recitative, *after* the chorale. The librettist's concern to make clear the analogy between the disciples and the church led him to introduce a chorale that is dominated by a tone of warning to the "Häuflein klein" (i.e., lit. "little flock," the small group of the faithful) that Satan is ever present, seeking their downfall.

And Bach, in keeping with the sense of opposition between the world and the faithful, set it in a most unusual manner (ex. 9.8a). The movement is a soprano/tenor duet with an obbligato part for unison bassoon and cello in addition to the *basso continuo*. Instead of presenting the chorale melody openly, however, Bach conceals it in the bassoon and cello lines (and occasionally the voices), which feature ostinato elements that were derived from the chorale melody (ex. 9.8b), five of whose six phrases feature the descending minor tetrachord. The ostinato figure that Bach assigns to every bar of the cello/bassoon line belongs to a type he uses elsewhere to represent falling (the organ chorale *Durch Adams Fall* from the *Orgelbüchlein* being the most famous example); and Bach intensifies that association by introducing pronounced circle-of-fifths ascent and descent patterns in association with the lines "obschon die Feinde willens sein, dich gänzlich zu verstören" (ascent) and "und suchen deinen Untergang" (descent). The obbligato part therefore emerges as a symbol of the antagonistic forces, depicting how those forces seek the downfall of the faithful, whereas the presumed chorale references suggest the "hiddenness" of the church (disciples) in the world.[53] In contrast to the comforting presence of Jesus as symbolized in the *violoncello piccolo* part of *Bleib bei uns* (and, as we will see, of *Ich bin ein guter Hirt*), the cello/bassoon sonority of *Am Abend aber desselbigen Sabbats* can be considered to mirror the dominance of the world.

A perhaps significant fact concerning this chorale setting is that its melody, that of "Komm her zu mir spricht Gottes Sohn," appears in two other cantatas of the spring 1725 sequence and in one of the spring 1724 cantatas whose text is presumed to have been written by the librettist of Cantata 42, but *nowhere else* in Bach's entire cantata oeuvre. And only in the 1724 cantata, *Wahrlich, wahrlich, ich sage euch* (BWV 86, for Rogate), is the melody sung to a verse of "Komm her zu mir." "Verzage nicht, o Häuflein klein" is the first verse of a different chorale, whereas the two other appearances in spring 1725, ending Cantatas 108 and 74, are both

[53] Charles Sanford Terry (*Bach's Orchestra*, 1st ed. [London: Oxford University Press, 1932, 117]) hypothesizes that the obbligato part "was evidently written to accompany a melody *never actually sounded*." Terry includes an example demonstrating that the first line of the melody associated with "Verzage nicht, du Häuflein klein" fits with the ritornello of Bach's setting. The hiddenness of the church in the apostolic era echoes in Luther's concept of the "hidden church," which could well have influenced the chorale setting of Cantata 42, whose text echoes Luther's language. See Althaus, *Theology of Martin Luther*, 291–93.

EXAMPLE 9.8a **Cantata 42, *Am Abend aber desselbigen Sabbats*** *no. 4, chorale, "Verzage nicht, o Häuflein klein," beginning*

EXAMPLE 9.8b **Chorale melody, "Komm her zu mir spricht Gottes Sohn"**

taken from the hymn "Gott Vater, sende deinen Geist," a Pentecost chorale, that is very appropriate to the two cantatas just mentioned. It may be, therefore, that the unusual appearance of three verses sung to this melody in the spring 1725 sequence expresses a link among them. Mariane von Ziegler (and/or Bach), in selecting the verses in question for Cantatas 108 and 74, *might* have done so in conjunction with its appearance in Cantata 42, bringing out the fact that the Holy Spirit is not mentioned in that cantata as it is in both the Gospel and the epistle. That is, the "hidden" character of the melody in Cantata 42 might, perhaps, have been intended as an allegory of what Luther called the "hidden" church, the membership of the faithful, as opposed to the institution.[54] This would fit exactly with Lütkemann's view, and the reference to the "Häuflein klein" in the chorale. In this view the full emergence of the chorale melody in Cantatas 108 and 74 would correspond to the transitional character of the season as a whole, whose goal is the coming of the Holy Spirit. This is admittedly a speculative explanation for the unusual setting in Cantata 42; it is influenced by the fact that Ziegler anticipates the coming of the Holy Spirit in Cantata 108, in which the believer at one point questions whether or not the Spirit is already present (the recitative ending "Ach, ist er nicht schon hier?"). The verse of "Gott Vater, sende deinen Geist" that ends Cantata 108—the tenth, beginning "Dein Geist, den Gott vom Himmel gibt"—is particularly appropriate for the first cantata of the spring sequence to introduce reference to the Holy Spirit.

In Cantata 42 the recitative that follows "Verzage nicht, o Häuflein klein" explains Jesus's appearance to the disciples allegorically as his protecting the church, paraphrasing the earlier *dictum* as part of the analogy. In its final measures the continuo, including bassoon, introduces another descent figure (marked *animoso*) in association with "laßt die Feinde wüten." The aria that follows, "Jesus ist ein Schild der Seinen," then describes Jesus's causing the sun to shine on the faithful with the "goldnen Überschrift: Jesus ist ein Schild der Seinen," a representation not of the inevitability of darkness, as in *Bleib bei uns*, but of the overcoming of darkness by light (ex. 9.9a/b). Bach indicates *divisi* first violins for this aria, presumably meaning two solo violins in an equal-voice trio sonata texture. The solo violins suggest the brightness of the sunshine and the "goldnen Überschrift" of the text, while the principal melody, largely triadic and festive, sometimes resembles that of the *concitato* strings in the middle section of the sinfonia. Throughout the movement the violins concertize with the *basso continuo*, the latter (to which the bassoon lends its characteristic sonority) reintroducing and expanding the *animoso* figure from the recitative, its downward plummeting serving as a reminder of the overthrow of the enemies.

As in *Kommt, gehet und eilet*, the D-major beginning of Cantata 42 links up with the *Christus Victor* portrayal of Jesus, its pictorial imagery centered on the idea of Jesus's protection of the faithful from their enemies in the world. Yet, although the

---

[54] Althaus, *Theology of Martin Luther*, 32, 291–93.

EXAMPLE 9.9a **Cantata 42, *Am Abend aber desselbigen Sabbats*** *no. 5, recitative, ending*

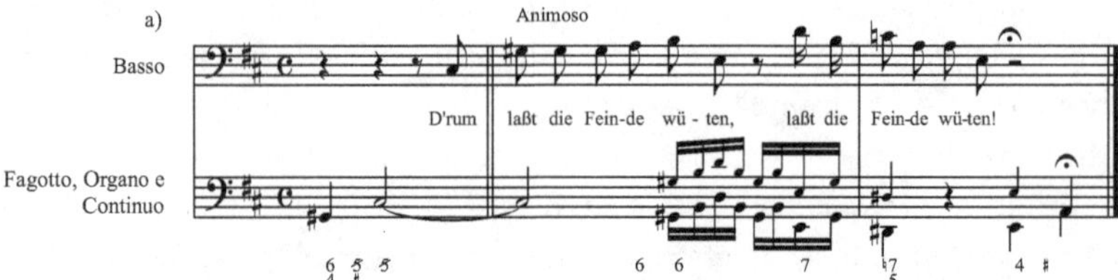

EXAMPLE 9.9b **Cantata 42, *Am Abend aber desselbigen Sabbats*** *no. 6, aria, "Jesus ist ein Schild der Seinen," beginning*

association of D with the triumph of the resurrection is now in the background, the tonal motion over the initial group of movements mirrors that from the beginning of *Kommt, gehet und eilet* to Peter's aria "Sanfte soll mein Todeskummer nur ein Schlummer sein," shifting from D through b (the biblical motto, set as a brief recitative), to the subdominant, G, for the first aria. Again, that aria is an expression of peace, now associated with Jesus's appearance in the midst of the faithful. The first chorale, however, moves back to B minor as it draws the analogy between the disciples, who are hiding in fear, and the faithful ("Häuflein klein,") whom it urges not to despair, despite the persecution of their enemies. In a sense, therefore, this movement might be considered the center of the cantata, preceded and followed by recitative/aria pairings, the former in the subdominant and the latter in the dominant. The two arias describe, in their different ways, the nature of Jesus's protection of the disciples, first by calming their fears (the G-major aria), then, in the A-major aria "Jesus ist ein Schild der Seinen" by shielding them from persecution. As in *Kommt, gehet und eilet*, the subdominant aria projects a peaceful, or passive affect and the dominant aria the reverse.

In Cantata 42 the faithful place their hopes in Jesus's victory over the powers of darkness, compared to the sun's shining on the faithful. Behind it, therefore, is something of John's elemental victory of light (the resurrected Christ) over the darkness of the world. In keeping with the doctrinal tone of the cantata, however, the final chorale, "Verleih uns Frieden gnädiglich, Herr Gott zu unsern Zeiten," seems to retreat from the brightness of the A major of Jesus's protection, the expression "zu unsern Zeiten" suggesting the perspective of present reality. In the initial phrase complex God's protection, described aggressively with the verb "streiten," affirms the f♯ tonality of the setting, while the shift to prayer for good government from the worldly "Fürsten" and "Obrigkeit" who will act as God's representatives turns to A: "gib unsern Fürsten und der Obrigkeit [A] Fried' und gut Regiment [A], daß wir unter ihnen [f♯] ein geruhig und stilles Leben führen mögen" [A]. In the end, the prayer is for a worldly equivalent of God's *Ordnung* as alluded to in the middle section of the first aria. When the final lines—"in aller Gottseligkeit und Ehrbarkeit, Amen!"—return to f♯ for the final drawn-out "Amen," the effect is a sober one.

Ich bin ein guter Hirt (BWV 85)

Since the cantata that came between *Bleib bei uns* and *Am Abend, aber* has not survived, we cannot say how, or even whether, Bach bridged between the musico-theological characters of the two works, which are not only owing to their differing instrumental characteristics but also reflected in their tonal spheres.[55] After the D of *Kommt, gehet und eilet*, the c of *Bleib bei uns* seems associated with the world as "arme Christenheit" in need of illumination and protection. Then, with Cantata 85 Bach once again follows a cantata centered on the *ambitus* of D/b by one centered on that of c/E♭; and once again the D-major cantata features concerto-derived movements at the outset, while the C-minor cantata again features a movement with *violoncello piccolo* solo with associations that follow from those of its counterpart in *Bleib bei uns*. The qualities that underlie this parallel were reflected in the

[55] The parodied cantata that Bach performed on Easter Tuesday 1724 (BWV 134) makes reference to John's imagery of Jesus as "light," in addition to describing the resurrection in terms reminiscent of "Es ist vollbracht" and emphasizing Jesus's protection of the faithful. See, for example, the lines "Euch scheinet ein herrlich verneuetes Licht" in the first aria; "Der Heiland lebt und siegt mit Macht" in the tenor recitative; "Dein großer Sieg macht uns von Feinden los und bringet uns zum Leben" in the final recitative.

link that Martin Moller drew between the two occasions (Easter Monday and Misericordias), as cited earlier.

In *Ich bin ein guter Hirt* the return of the *violoncello piccolo* and the C-minor tonality signal another change in tone. Many of the themes of the preceding two cantatas echo in Cantata 85, especially that of Jesus's protection of the faithful from their enemies, and the implied darkness of a world in which other forms of protection fail (recitative, "Wenn die Mietlinge schlafen"). But now the fear and adversarial character of *Am Abend aber desselbigen Sabbats* are gone, and with it the militant tone and doctrinal character by which the librettist related the Jews of John's Gospel to the enemies of the present-day church (and that sounded particularly unnecessary when reiterated in paraphrase in the fifth movement). After the dramatic character of Jesus's appearance to the disciples on Quasimodogeniti, the Gospel for Misericordias draws from an earlier point in John, Jesus's discourse on his identity as good shepherd (Jn 10:12–16), introducing an image of Jesus that, as Bach's theologian contemporaries were quick to point out, not only linked him with descriptions of God in the OT (foremost among which was Psalm 23), but also brought out the self-sacrificial means by which God effected human salvation.[56] In Cantata 85 the image of Jesus as good shepherd combines the power of the protector with the gentleness and intimacy of the "friend" (the last line of the final chorale is "Ich habe Gott zum Freunde"). The key to their union is Jesus's Passion and the love that motivated it (the second aria, "Seht, was die Liebe tut").

Trust in the good shepherd dominates the tone of *Ich bin ein guter Hirt*, the first three movements of which form a sequence bearing a distinct conceptual resemblance to the corresponding movements of *Bleib bei uns*. A biblical motto from John, set now as bass solo with oboe and strings in arioso style ("Ich bin ein guter Hirt. Ein guter Hirt lässt sein Leben für die Schafe") is followed by an alto aria with *violoncello piccolo* that amplifies its message with direct reference to Jesus ("Jesus ist ein guter Hirt, denn er hat bereits sein Leben für die Schafe hingegeben, die ihm Niemand rauben wird"), after which a decorated chorale strophe for soprano, oboes, and *continuo* summarizes the whole with emphasis on the benefit of *Trost* for the believer ("Der Herr ist mein getreuer Hirt, dem ich mich ganz vertraue," a paraphrase of Psalm 23, "The Lord is my shepherd"). Over the course of these three movements the progression from a scripture-derived text to a solo aria (speaking of Jesus in the third person), then a first-person solo chorale based on the same idea lends an increasingly personal character to the whole (that is mirrored, as in Cantata 6, in the rising vocal ranges). At the same time, the gradual expansion of the idea of the shepherd reaches back into the OT, both to express the identity of Jesus and the Father (Ps 23) and to bring out (via the solo setting of the

[56] Rambach, *Seeligkeit der Gläubigen in der Zeit und in der Ewigkeit. . . . Anhang / einer Predigt von der Seeligen Bekantschaft der Schafe Jesu Christi mit derem guten Hirten; welche in der Schul Kirche in Halle am Sontage* Misericordias Domini Anno 1729 *gehalten worden*, 66–67.

chorale) the personal nature of that identity, anticipating the final line of the cantata, "Ich habe Gott zum Freunde."

Entering immediately after the Johannine motto, the aria with *violoncello piccolo* affirms the identity of Jesus and the good shepherd of the motto, conveying the centrality of the Passion to Jesus's protection; and the chorale paraphrase of Psalm 23 that follows immediately brings out the benefits the shepherd gives the believer "durchs selig Wort der Gnaden." In the aria the *violoncello piccolo* plays in virtually the identical register as in "Ach bleib bei uns" and in a very closely related style featuring harmonic string writing and a sparing use of the lowest register (ex. 9.10). The minor key mirrors the reference to the Passion, after which the major-key chorale takes up God's blessings for the faithful. In this regard, it is significant that the key sequence of movements one through three—c–g–B♭—not only resembles the c–E♭–B♭ of *Bleib bei uns* but describes, like the vocal registers, an ascending motion toward "Der Herr ist mein getreuer Hirt," which appears in all Bach's cantatas for Misericordias set to the melody associated with the chorale paraphrase of the Gloria, "Allein Gott in der Höh' sei Ehr'." This association unmistakably affirms the glory of God, to whom the self-sacrificing shepherd leads his sheep. Behind it lies the Trinitarian emphasis that Luther found most clearly expressed in John (as expressed in the epistle for the preceding Sunday, for example). Subtle thematic connectors between the motto and chorale beginnings further underscore the sense of unity among the opening group of movements, while the return of the oboes in the third movement, now with dotted rhythms, and a highly ornate version of the chorale melody in the vocal line, lends the pastorale tone something of the majestic style. The *violoncello piccolo* symbolizes the believer's naming Jesus as the shepherd in the second movement, while the oboes of the first and third movements represent simultaneously the pastorale and majestic character associated with God as shepherd. The good shepherd of this cantata, equated at first with the Jesus of the Passion, is also the creator God of the Hebrew Bible.

Among Bach's three surviving cantatas for Misericordias (BWV 104, 85, and 112) the first and second feature the first verse from the chorale paraphrase of Psalm 23, "Der Herr ist mein getreuer Hirt," while Cantata 112, a chorale cantata written in 1731, features all five verses. In Cantata 104, *Du Hirte Israel, höre*, first produced one year before *Ich bin ein guter Hirt*, the opening chorus is addressed to the God of Israel (Ps 80:2), who is equated to Jesus as good shepherd in the fifth movement, directly before the final chorale "Der Herr ist mein getreuer Hirt." *Du Hirte Israel, höre* features an ascending key pattern (G–e–b–b–D–D–A), which is associated with a movement sequence that contains a very striking expression of realized eschatology. The design of Cantata 104 emphasizes continuity of the Gospel theme of the good shepherd from the post-resurrection appearances of the preceding feast days, calling in its opening chorus for the shepherd to hear the prayer of the faithful and to appear. Its text, drawn from Psalm 80, forms part of a design that begins by reaching back into the OT to affirm God's protection of the Israelites in Egypt ("Du Hirte Israel, höre, der du Joseph hütest wie der Schafe, erscheine,

EXAMPLE 9.10 **Cantata 85, *Ich bin ein guter Hirt*** *no. 2, aria, "Jesus ist ein guter Hirt," beginning*

EXAMPLE 9.10 (*continued*)

der du sitzest über Cherubim": You shepherd of Israel, you who watch over Joseph like a sheep, appear, you who sit above the cherubim) and moves forward through the Exodus, with references to the desert, God's word as the manna given to the Israelites, the following of the shepherd by the faithful as Moses's leading God's people through the wilderness, the promise of green pastures as the foretaste of eternity. At the end of the second recitative the believer cries out for the journey to end: "Ach laß den Weg nur bald geendet sein und führe uns in deinen Schafstall ein!" (Ah, let the way soon be ended and lead us into your sheepfold). And the D-major aria that follows, a pure pastorale movement, describes the effect of the foretaste: for the faithful the world has become a "Himmelreich," in which Jesus's blessings can already be tasted. The meaning of the biblical reference to the shepherd's sitting above the cherubim is the widespread interpretation of Jesus as the *Gnadenstuhl* (see ch. 8). In this context it brings out the equivalence of Jesus and the Father. And as Renate Steiger has shown, the aria "Beglückte Herde, Jesu Schafe, die Welt ist euch ein Himmelreich" makes an association between the vision of the world as God's kingdom, which is related to John's realized eschatology, and the pastorale style, an association that runs throughout Bach's work.[57] This movement, the first one to mention Jesus, is followed by the concluding A-major chorale, a paraphrase of Psalm 23 (as usual, set to the melody of the Gloria, "Allein Gott in der Höh' sei Ehr'"). In this cantata the "Weg" is unequivocally upward, the believer's anticipation of eternity in the present life. The D-major aria is the fulfillment of the cry for the shepherd to hear and appear in the first movement; and the chorale, making clear the equivalence of Jesus and the shepherd of the time of Israel, is the end of the believer's journey, the outcome of the internalizing of God's "selig Wort der Gnaden." The A-major tonality of "Der Herr ist mein getreuer Hirt" extends the meaning of the anticipation of eternity to the sphere of God, toward which the shepherd leads the faithful.

In similar fashion, in Cantata 85 the third movement, "Der Herr ist mein getreuer Hirt" is the apex of an ascent/descent shape for the work as a whole. After the chorale the remaining three movements all deal with Jesus's protection of his own from the *Höllenwolf* (Satan) who threatens the flock (recitative) and the *Feinde* who cause the believer "Angst und Pein" (chorale). Like *Am Abend aber desselbigen Sab-*

---

[57] See R. Steiger, "'Die Welt ist euch ein Himmelreich,'" *Musik und Kirche* 41 (1971): 1–8, 69–79. In Chafe, *Tonal Allegory*, 190, the rising sequence of tonalities in Cantata 104 mirrors the realized eschatology expressed in the textual reference in the aria "Beglückte Herde." That concept was given wide currency in Lutheran thought by Joachim Lütkemann's book, *Vorschmack der göttlichen Güte* (1643), which, as F. Ernest Stoeffler points out (*Rise of Evangelical Pietism*, 219), "for a time rivalled the popularity of Arndt's *True Christianity*." During the seventeenth and eighteenth centuries Lutheran theological treatises refer frequently to the concept. In his sermon on the Gospel for Misericordias (*Evangelische Betrachtungen über die Sonn- und Fest-Tage-Evangelia*, 538–63), Johann Jacob Rambach takes as his theme "Das Vorspiel des ewigen Lebens auf der guten Weide JEsu Christi," discussing the concept (most often referred to in his text as "Vorschmack") in a manner that resonates very closely with the text of Cantata 104. Rambach makes clear the double eschatological perspective (future/present) by linking up the shepherd of the Gospel for the day with an eschatological interpretation of the shepherd of Psalm 23 and with the lamb of Revelation (548). At the same time, he emphasizes the presentness of the blessings of salvation for the faithful (549ff.): "Aber auch hiervon haben die Schafe Christi bereits in dieses Welt ein liebliches **Vorspiel**." The rising tonal progression in the cantata seems a perfect mirroring of this anticipation of eternity in the present. The idea of a rising tonal sequence leading to "Allein see Gott in der Höh' sei Ehr" is shared with the third part of the *Clavierübung*, in which the three settings of that melody (associated with the Gloria) delineate a progression through the successive keys of F, G, and A.

bats, Ich bin ein guter Hirt is a response to the appeal for Jesus to remain and protect the faithful. Now, however, the light/darkness imagery recedes into the background, alluded to only indirectly in the fourth movement (an accompanied recitative), which describes Jesus's watchfulness over the flock while the "Mietlinge" (hired hands) sleep. The accompanied recitative and aria feature only strings, a softening of the sound that is mirrored in the fact that the lone recitative turns to the subdominant, A♭, as it describes the gentle protectiveness of the shepherd. At the outset the recitative invokes the image, from John, of the hired hands who abandon the sheep and flee when the wolf comes, introducing the idea (not in John) of their sleeping, whereas the shepherd watches over the flock. Bach begins in E♭, with a hint of the subdominant, and leads the initial sentence to a g cadence as it brings out the benefit for the faithful of the shepherd's watchfulness. After that, the tonality turns toward f for the "Höllenwolf," but cadences in A♭ instead for the narrative of Jesus's protection. In this context the E♭ of the pastorale aria, "Seht, was die Liebe thut," with its even eighth-note melodic style, triadic, diatonic lines with parallel thirds and sixths against held tones in the voice, exudes an atmosphere of consolation and security, making clear in its middle section ("Er hat am Kreuzes Stamm vergossen für sie sein theures Blut") that the Passion is the source of the believer's benefit: the good shepherd is at the same time the sacrificial victim, substituting his own life for those of his "sheep." The flowing eighth-note instrumental line in 9/8 meter lends the movement an unmistakable character of gentleness and security, while the homely image of Jesus "holding his own in tender keeping" ("Mein Jesus hält in zarter Hut die Seinen feste eingeschlossen") depicts Jesus's protection as transforming the world from a place of fear to one of security and peace.[58] The final chorale then returns to C minor, affirming Jesus's protection of the believer ("Ist Gott mein Schutz und treuer Hirt, kein Unglück mich berühren wird"). Between its parallel lines "weicht, alle meine *Feinde*" and "Ich habe Gott zur *Freunde*" (the latter repeated for the last two phrases), the ending of Cantata 85 represents, even more than Cantata 42, God's response to the prayer that closed *Bleib bei uns*. The simple device of cadencing "deceptively" to A♭, then to c, for the two versions of the repeated final line, "Ich habe Gott zum Freunde," preserves the aura of security.

Ich bin ein guter Hirt closes the sequence of three textually interrelated cantatas that come between *Kommt, gehet und eilet* and the nine cantatas that are based on Mariane von Ziegler's texts. In them Bach creates parallels between *Bleib bei uns* and *Ich bin ein guter Hirt*, both in the key sequences of their first three movements and their use of *violoncello piccolo*, which utilizes a similar style and register in both

[58] The idea behind this movement is shared with two places in the *St. Matthew Passion*, both of which are focal points for the flat-key regions of the Passion. The first, the C-minor dialogue for tenor and chorus, "Ich will bei meinem Jesu wachen," is a meditation on Jesus's watching and praying while the disciples sleep; the second is the E♭ dialogue for alto and chorus, "Sehet, Jesus hat die Hand uns zu fassen ausgespannt," which describes Jesus on the cross reaching out to embrace the faithful, described as "ihr verlaßnen Küchlein." Both movements project a pastorale character.

cantatas. In *Bleib bei uns* C minor seems to carry forward from the close of the *St. John Passion*, representing the world as a place of darkness and Jesus as the light. In contrast, the more militant, doctrinal tone of *Am Abend aber desselbigen Sabbats* gives voice to the *Christus Victor* depiction of Jesus, while seemingly suggesting the presence of the Holy Spirit only as a hidden aspect of the church (or one that defines the church as the body of the faithful rather than the institution). The return to C minor in *Ich bin ein guter Hirt*, along with the imagery of Jesus watching over the sheep while the hired hands sleep, may well remind us of the C minor of the Mount of Olives scene of the *St. Matthew Passion* (not yet written) with its turn to E♭ and A♭ as Jesus tells the disciples to watch while he prays. The unity of the watchful shepherd with the God of the OT in "Jesus ist ein guter Hirt" and with the self-sacrificing savior in "Seht, was die Liebe tut" aids in the transformation for the faithful of the darkness of the world to a time of peace and security.

{10}

Jubilate to Ascension Day: Cantatas 103, 108, 87, and 128

Introduction: Jesus's departure and return, seeing and hearing

Beginning on Jubilate Sunday the sequence of Johannine Gospel readings turns to the Farewell Discourse for the three weeks preceding Ascension Day and the two that follow it, culminating on Pentecost. Although John has no narrative of the ascension per se, in the Farewell Discourse Jesus returns over and again to the themes of his leaving and the coming of the Holy Spirit. The historical context of those themes—Jesus's preparation of the disciples at the Last Supper for the time after his departure—carries forward in the liturgy to the life of the faithful in the world under the guidance of the Holy Spirit.[1] Ascension Day and Pentecost, ten days apart in the liturgy, are complementary in a sense that derives from John's worlds "above" and "below," the one describing an upward motion (Jesus's ascension, described by writers of Bach's time as the fulfillment of his remarks concerning his "lifting up") and the other a descending one (the coming of the Holy Spirit). As mentioned earlier, John 17, considered by some authors not to belong to the Farewell Discourse since it is addressed to the Father rather than the disciples, has been viewed as John's poeticized equivalent of Jesus's ascension. Bridging the narratives of the Last Supper and the Passion, it sets the stage, so to speak, for John's vision of the Passion as Jesus glorification, his "lifting up" as the fulfillment of God's plan for the salvation of humanity. This is the way that Johann Jacob Rambach interpreted Jesus's ascension. In advance of the Passion, Jesus prays to the Father for his glorification, affirming his completion of the work given him by the Father, describing himself as no longer in the world, and the disciples as not *of* the world (although they are in it), and praying that those who believe the word as preached by the disciples may be one with Jesus and the Father.

[1] Luther says this explicitly in the beginning of his commentary on the Farewell Discourse, *Luther's Works*, vol. 24, 9–17.

Noteworthy in John 17 is the above/below character that permeates that Gospel, with further reference to God's word as the truth that sanctifies, and the world as resistant or opposed to that word. Despite the lack of an ascension narrative in John, the Lutheran view of the ascension very much emphasizes the qualities Jesus brings out in this, his final extended prayer. The "vertical" view of salvation and eschatology is evident in all the Lutheran writers whether or not the context is that of John or the Synoptic Gospels. Even Bach's *Ascension Oratorio*, based entirely on the Synoptics' narratives of the ascension, overtly features this quality.[2]

Mariane von Ziegler's beginning her series of 1725 cantata texts with the Gospel readings of the Farewell Discourse might have been dictated by purely accidental circumstances; nevertheless the close manner in which those texts attend to the Johannine themes of the discourse is noteworthy and suggests that the sequence began with regard for how they related to the cantatas of the preceding weeks. Beginning with a cantata (BWV 103) whose initial *dictum* sets the disciples in opposition to the world, *Ihr werdet weinen und heulen, aber die Welt wird sich freuen* (You will weep and cry out, but the world will rejoice), Ziegler explores the above/below aspect of John in terms of its antithetical and complementary aspects in the cantatas that lead to and culminate on Ascension Day. Among the mottoes from John that she chose for those cantatas, the two that form the cornerstones of Cantata 108 fully embody the complementarity just described. Bach ingeniously projects it in the music as well.

Running through Mariane von Ziegler's texts is a theme complex that closely reflects the eschatological character of the above/below complementarity: that of the *seeing* of Jesus, which is prominent in the cantatas for the earlier part of the season, but which gradually gives way to the theme of *hearing* him in the latter part, a symbolic motion from external to internal that leads to Pentecost and the "indwelling" of God in the faithful. Inspired initially by the resurrection and the post-resurrection appearances, the theme of seeing Jesus is at first a response to the physical absence or presence of Jesus on those occasions. In Cantata 249, *Kommt, gehet und eilet* the seeing is clearly future oriented (since the cantata deals with the resurrection, making no reference to post-resurrection appearances), whereas in no. 6, *Bleib bei uns,* it is introduced first as the disciples' plea for Jesus to remain through the coming darkness, then at the end for him to let himself be seen through the shining light of his word. And this double sense of present/future, physical/spiritual seeing runs throughout the cantatas for the spring sequence. We see it clearly in the first and second cantatas based on the last discourse, *Ihr werdet weinen und heulen*, (BWV 103) for Jubilate, and *Es ist euch gut daß ich hingehe* (BWV 108) for Cantate. At first, largely eschatological—upward-directed—in focus, the theme of seeing Jesus reaches a culminating point in Cantata 128 for Ascension Day, historically a commemoration of Jesus's being seen "externally" for the last time, whereas the theme of hearing Jesus is oriented toward the present life and

[2] See the source cited in ch. 9, n. 34.

centers, as we might expect, on the coming of the Holy Spirit, climaxing in Cantata 175 for the third day of Pentecost. Through its association with the Holy Spirit, the theme of hearing also involves that of being heard by God—prayer—which enters in Cantata 87 almost as a countertheme to the seeing of Jesus in the preceding cantatas and increases in the cantatas after Ascension Day. The intimacy of *hearing* and *being heard* by God is the spiritual context of the various dialogs between Jesus and the soul in the Bach cantatas, no matter what the liturgical occasion.[3] Although Mariane von Ziegler's texts for spring 1725 have no dialog movements, the theme of the inner seeing and hearing of God is prominent and voiced in terms of the coming of the Holy Spirit.

Continuing from the shift to the perspective of the world in Cantatas 6, 42, and 85, the first of Ziegler's cantatas, Cantata 103, *Ihr werdet weinen und heulen,* announces the opposition between the disciples and "the world" in the opening motto (Jn 16:20), and develops it throughout. Jesus's departure brings sorrow and leaves his followers at the mercy of the world, which takes pleasure in their torment. The motto, however, also contains a promise of change—sorrow turned to joy—that, as the cantata makes clear, will be the outcome of Jesus's return. In the Farewell Discourse Jesus does not specify in what context the disciples will see him again. As Raymond Brown points out, in the context of the Last Supper, Jesus's words would seem to indicate his prediction of the post-resurrection appearances, which was the interpretation of most of the Greek fathers. Yet Jesus's remark that after a little while the disciples would experience "a joy that no one can take from you" (Jn 16:22) and, indeed, most of the latter part of that chapter, in Brown's view "anticipates a more permanent union with Jesus than that afforded by transitory post-resurrectional appearances."[4] Brown explains that the liturgy seems to follow Augustine's interpretation, which was that Jesus was speaking of his Second Coming, that the disciples would see him in eternity. Brown himself, however, advances

---

[3] The inner seeing and hearing of God through the "indwelling" (*Einwohnung; Inhabitatio*) of the Holy Spirit is a pronounced feature of the writings of Johann Arndt, for example, who describes it in the third book of his *Wahres Christenthum,* titled "vom Innern Menschen / und von seinem inwendigen Schatz." As Bernhard Lohse remarks (*Martin Luther's Theology: Its Historical and Systematic Development*, trans. and ed. Roy A. Harrisville [Minneapolis: Fortress Press, 1999], 235–36, 238):

> [W]ith [its] constant reference to Christ the Holy Spirit assumed an extraordinarily important place in Luther's theology . . . . For Luther, there was not a single doctrine in all of theology where the activity of the Spirit would not be fundamental. . . . Where Luther is concerned, we may actually establish the principle that a relationship with God is possible only through the Spirit . . . . Luther held to the same idea by taking up the distinction between "outward" and "inward"; Now when God sends forth his holy Gospel, he deals with us in a twofold manner, first outwardly, then inwardly. Outwardly he deals with us through the oral word of the Gospel and through material signs, that is, baptism and the sacrament of the altar. Inwardly he deals with us through the Holy Spirit, faith, and other gifts. But whatever their measure or order the outward factors should and must precede.

In the post-Easter cantatas of 1725 there is a progression from "seeing" Jesus through his word in *Bleib bei uns* to the hearing of Jesus's voice, in Cantata 175, for the third day of Pentecost.

[4] Brown, *Gospel According to John XIII–XXI*, 729.

the interpretation that what is meant by John is the "seeing" of Jesus in terms of the Holy Spirit:

> As we turn from what the saying may have meant if it was uttered at the Last Supper to what it came to mean in the total Gospel context, we find that in Johannine thought "seeing" Jesus and the joy and knowledge that are consequent upon this experience are considered as privileges of Christian existence after the resurrection. Jesus's promises have been fulfilled (at least to a significant extent) in what has been granted to all Christians, for the Last Discourse is addressed to all who believe in Jesus and not only to those who were actually present. "Seeing" Jesus has been reinterpreted to mean the continued experience of his presence in the Christian, and this can only mean the presence of the Paraclete/Spirit.[5]

The seeing of Jesus, as it is presented in Cantatas 249 and 6, tends, in the former instance toward the eschatological (future) frame of reference and in the latter toward the present. Cantatas 103 and 108 now reflect more directly the situation described by Brown; and once again the former cantata presents the seeing in predominantly eschatological terms, whereas the latter effects a shift of focus to the coming of the Holy Spirit. The penultimate movements (arias) of both cantatas refer to the believer's "seeing" Jesus. In that of Cantata 103, it suggests the unique joy of such seeing that appears in verse 22: "Mein Jesus läßt sich wieder sehen, O Freude, der nichts gleichen kann!" (My Jesus will be seen again, O Joy to which nothing can compare). After that, the final chorale makes the eschatological association clear: "Ich hab dich einen Augenblick, o liebes Kind, verlassen; Sieh', aber, sieh', mit großem Glück und Trost ohn alle Maßen will ich dir schon die Freudenkron aufsetzen und verehren; dein kurzes Leid soll sich in Freud und ewig Wohl verkehren" (I have left you for a moment, O dear child; see, however, see with great joy and comfort beyond measure, I will adorn and honor you with the crown of joy; your brief suffering shall be turned into joy and eternal good).

Likewise, on the following week, the second aria of Cantata 108 specifies the believer's seeing Jesus in eternity: "Führe mich auf deinen Wegen, daß ich in der Ewigkeit schaue deine Herrlichkeit!" (Lead me along your paths, so that in eternity I will behold your glory). But now a recitative raises the question of whether or not the Spirit is already present ("Ich frage sorgensvoll: Ach, ist er nicht schon hier?"); and the final chorale associates the "Wege" in question with the Holy Spirit: "Dein Geist, den Gott vom Himmel gibt, der leitet alles, was ihn liebt, auf wohl gebähntem Wege" (Your Spirit, which God gives from heaven, he directs all who love him, on a well laid out path). The expression "*dein* Geist" equates the Holy Spirit with Jesus's spirit. Thus, Cantata 108 mirrors the fact that this part of the liturgical year is a transition to Pentecost and the Trinity season that follows by articulating a shift of perspective from the future to the present.

---

[5] Ibid., 730.

Then, in her cantata for Rogation Sunday, *Bisher habt ihr nicht gebeten in meinem Namen*, Ziegler turns to the *means* by which the Spirit leads the faithful along God's path, so that worldly tribulation can be overcome *in the present*. Cantata 87 takes up the theme of prayer, which, as Cantata 183 tells us one week later, is taught by the Holy Spirit.[6] Directly preceding and following Ascension Day, these two cantatas, taken together, reveal an unfolding understanding of prayer and its close association to the Spirit. In Cantata 87 the first aria, "Vergib, o Vater! Unsre Schuld" (Forgive, O Father, our trespasses), is a response to the seriousness of human sin and the terror of God's (implied) judgment in the recitative ("O Wort! das Geist und Seel erschreckt"). Addressing first God the Father in words reminiscent of the Lord's Prayer, it then refers to Jesus's words in the Gospel for the day ("Und sagen, Herr, auf dein Geheiß: Ach rede nicht mehr sprüchwortsweis"), and then to Paul's widely cited description of the Holy Spirit as intercessor in Romans 8: "Hilf uns vielmehr vertreten." The latter reference will reappear, along with the "vertreten"/ "beten" rhyme in Cantata 183 as "Hilf meine Schwacheit mit vertreten", where the believer will address the Holy Spirit directly for the first time in the cantata sequence. As if to set the stage, so to speak, for the direct appearance of the Holy Spirit in Cantata 183, Cantata 87 introduces for virtually the only time in these cantatas the theme complex of acknowledgment of guilt, penitence, and the need for God's forgiveness, moving from there to *Trost* as the outcome of Jesus's overcoming the world, then to acceptance of suffering, and finally, to love as the key to the transformation of sorrow into joy, ending "Seine Liebe macht zur Freuden auch das bittre Leiden" (His love makes even bitter suffering into joy). Analogous to the disciples in the Farewell Discourse, the community of believers learns to deal with the trials it can expect in the world.

In Cantata 87 the central pivot is the line from John that was a key to the meaning of the Gospel for Luther: "In der Welt ihr habt Angst; aber seid getrost, ich habe die Welt überwunden," which announces Jesus's victory over the world as the source of the believer's comfort. In Cantata 128 for Ascension Day, *Auf Christi Himmelfahrt allein*, Mariane von Ziegler begins with a chorale verse that takes up the believer's *own* overcoming the world, once again bringing out the believer's hopes of seeing Jesus, who now, despite his ascent to the world above, is joined to the faithful below as the head of a body to its members, a traditional metaphor for the church that was widely cited by the Lutheran authors in association with As-

[6] In the penultimate movement of Cantata 183, "Höchster Tröster, Heilger Geist," addressed to the Holy Spirit, the believer prays for help in his weakness, "for on my own I can not pray" (denn von mir selbst kann ich nicht beten), after which the final chorale, still addressed to the Holy Spirit, proclaims "Du bist ein Geist, der lehret, wie man recht beten soll; dein Beten wird erhöret . . . " (You are a Spirit that teaches how one should pray rightly; your prayers will be heard . . .). On prayer as a means by which the Spirit leads humankind to God, see Prenter, *Spiritus Creator*, 3–27, 125–27. On the meaning of prayer in Cantata 87 and its relationship to the Lord's Prayer, see Renate Steiger, "*Bisher habt ihr nichts gebeten in meinem Namen*" Die Kantate BWV 87 und das Vaterunser. Eine Antwort an Ulrich Konrad," in *Gnadengegenwart: Johann Sebastian Bach im Kontext lutherischer Orthodoxie und Frömmigkeit* (Stuttgart-Bad Canstatt: Friedrich Frommann Verlag, 2002), 318–41.

cension Day. In this cantata the theme of seeing Jesus appears in no less than four movements, which ultimately reconcile its future and present eschatological aspects, one of the foremost qualities in the Lutheran interpretation of Jesus's ascension. After Cantata 128 the theme drops out of the cantata sequence until Cantata 175, which completes the message of Pentecost not only by uniting the images of Jesus as *Christus victor,* good shepherd, and Holy Spirit but also by taking up, again, both the seeing and hearing of Jesus.

Among these cantatas there is a sense, though not an absolute one, that the seeing of Jesus is primarily a future-oriented experience and will be manifested externally, whereas hearing him, which takes place through the Holy Spirit, is internal and takes place in the present. In fact, the initial four Ziegler cantatas are concerned with balancing the future and present aspects of their eschatological themes. We might summarize the overall sequence of these four cantatas as proclaiming that whereas Jesus's departure means that the disciples will be persecuted by "the world" (Cantata 103), his return will bring joy; and the Holy Spirit will show the way to the other world (Cantata 108). Prayer will enable one to overcome this world, turning sorrow into joy (Cantata 87), while, through the relationship of Jesus to the faithful as that of head to body, the vision of Jesus in glory in the world above provides the foundation for all future hopes: the certainty of salvation (Cantata 128).

Ihr werdet weinen und heulen (BWV 103)

Drawing on an entire verse from John's Gospel for the day, the opening motto of Cantata 103 announces the themes of worldly persecution and suffering:

> **John 16:20:** Ihr werdet weinen und heulen, aber die Welt wird sich freuen. Ihr aber werdet traurig sein. Doch eure Traurigkeit soll in Freude verkehret werden.
>
> (You will weep and cry out, but the world will rejoice. You, however, will be sorrowful. But your sorrow will be changed to joy.)

In Cantata 103, the "solution" to suffering is primarily eschatological—the believer looks to the future for the transformation of sorrow to joy—whereas, when that theme returns in Cantata 87, two weeks later, we hear that Jesus's love turns sorrow into joy in the present. In Cantata 103 the texts of the first recitative and aria make clear that the disciples' sorrow is the result of Jesus's departure, describing him first as the beloved who is snatched away—"Wer sollte nicht in Klagen untergehn, wenn uns der Liebste wird entrissen?" (Who would not fall into lamenting, when our beloved is torn away?), then as a physician who cannot be found by the one whose "wounds of sin" are in need of healing. In a fashion similar to Cantatas 42 and 85, and possibly modeled after those works (though less doctrinal in tone), Ziegler then introduces a recitative that paraphrases the motto in contemporary terms.

The believer now voices willingness to await Jesus's return: "Du wirst mich nach der Angst auch wiederum erquicken; so will ich mich zu deiner Ankunft schicken, ich traue dem Verheißungswort, daß meine Traurigkeit in Freude soll verkehret werden" (You will revive me once more after my torment; therefore I will direct myself toward your coming; I trust your promise that my sorrow shall be turned into joy). The subsequent aria makes clear that the joy is the result of Jesus's reappearance with the line: "Mein Jesus läßt sich wieder sehen, o Freude, der nichts gleichen kann!" (My Jesus can be seen again; O joy to which nothing can compare). And the final chorale represents Jesus's words to the faithful soul (*Kind*) who has been left alone for a moment but will receive the "crown of joy" after his brief sufferings have been turned into joy and eternal blessings.

This cantata, therefore, contains a turning point, its first recitative/aria pair voicing the state of sorrow, whereas the second, following the pivotal recitative, expresses joy. The aria does not specify whether the joy belongs to the present or the future, but the chorale places the meaning of the whole in an unmistakably eschatological perspective. The theme of sorrow turned to joy, voiced in movements 1, 3, and 6, elaborates on the opening motto, rendering John"s antithesis between the suffering disciples and the rejoicing of "the world" into a foreshadowing of the split between this world and the world to come. From the historical situation of the disciples, the sequence of ideas turns to the present day community of believers ("wenn *uns* der Liebste wird entrissen" and "acht nicht auf *unsre* Schmerzen" in the first recitative), then to the individual in need of healing ("*Ich* suche," "*meiner* Sünden," "so muß *ich* sterben," "*mein* Jesus," and many other first-person constructions in the next three movements), and finally to the anticipation of eternity. Behind it lies the progression from the literal-historical to the eschatological sense that can be found in many Bach cantatas.[7]

The idea of joy "to which nothing can be compared" is of particular significance in Cantata 103; for in the music of the opening chorus the disciples' joy is one to which another kind of joy *can* be compared: that of the world, which rejoices while the disciples suffer: "Ihr werdet weinen und heulen, aber die Welt wird sich freuen" (You will weep and cry out, but the world will rejoice). In that movement the prediction of the disciples' sorrow being turned into joy, announced in the final section ("doch ihr Traurigkeit soll in Freude verkehret werden": however, your sorrow shall be turned to joy), involves reiteration of the same music that was associated earlier with the rejoicing of the world ("aber die Welt wird sich freuen" = "soll in Freude verkehret werden"). It is possible, of course, to take a pragmatic view of this occurrence: since the musical structure of the opening movement demanded a solid reprise, Bach simply adapted the earlier music to the new text for musical reasons. This decision implies the belief that music in itself cannot differentiate

[7] The literal-historical sense is, of course, that of the biblical motto; the allegorical is expressed in the analogy between the disciples and the church; the tropological is reflected in the change from the collective to the personal; and the eschatological emerges in the future "crown of joy" in the final chorale.

between the rejoicing of the world and the joy of the disciples (and the Christian community). Only the text can make such an association. Bach's predecessor in Leipzig, Johann Kuhnau, made this point clear in the preface to his *Biblical Sonatas*.[8] Yet it is also possible over the course of several movements to depict the transformation of suffering into joy in different ways, suggesting that joy becomes increasingly liberated from the worldly perspective as the cantata progresses. This is the case here. In this sense, Cantata 103 is bound up with the intrusion of the world on the life of faith, whose fulfillment is presented as a future one and, in this cantata, was understood as such by Bach.

The first half of Cantata 103 (movements 1–3) is entirely in minor, including both the rejoicing of the world and the promise of the transformation of the disciples' sorrow into joy in the first movement. That movement features a highly active *flauto piccolo* (soprano recorder pitched in A) doubled by solo violin or transverse flute, which is apt to suggest the hope contained in Jesus's prediction, but can also sound shrill, especially when forced into the very high register. The instrument then reappears in the first aria, playing a very active part that seems to offer hope beyond the words of the text. But in neither case is incomparable joy the predominant affect. At the close of the second recitative (no. 4), however, Bach shifts to D as the alto paraphrases the motto of the opening movement, now in personal terms: "Ich traue dem Verheißungswort, daß meine Traurigkeit in Freude soll verkehren werden" (I trust your word of promise that my sorrow will be turned to joy). The second aria, in D major, for tenor, trumpet, and strings, then voices "joy to which nothing can compare" at the believer's thought of seeing Jesus once again. The line "laßt von dem traurigen Beginnen" (depart from your sorrowful beginning) seems to refer back to the preceding movements, the trumpet now replacing the *flauto piccolo*. In light of such a pronounced sense of transformation, why does Bach end the cantata in its original key, B minor, and with a chorale whose final line—"Dein kurzes Leid soll sich in Freud und ewig Wohl verkehren" (Your brief sorrow will be turned into joy and eternal good)—paraphrases the ending of the motto with which the cantata began?

The answer to this question, which is important for the understanding of the design of the work as a whole, may be considered first of all from the standpoint of the fact that only the line just cited speaks of the believer's *eternal* benefit ("*ewig* Wohl"), thereby differentiating joy that takes place in the present from that of the afterlife. From the motto of the first movement through the paraphrase of the fourth to the ending of the sixth we sense the abovementioned progression from the historical to the tropological and eschatological senses of the same basic idea, the final chorale representing Jesus's speaking directly to the believer ("O liebes Kind")

[8] Johann Kuhnau, *Six Biblical Sonatas, for Keyboard, 1700,* with the original preface and introductions in German (facsimile) and English, trans. and ed. Kurt Stone (New York: Broude Brothers, 1953), xii–xiv.

with the assurance of eternal life. That the eschatological sense coincides with return to B minor after the D of the preceding movements mirrors the fulfillment that will take place in the future. The ecstatic "Mein Jesus läßt sich wieder sehen, o Freude, der nichts gleichen kann" with which the second aria ends is, from this standpoint, an expression of the transforming nature of faith and, in the context of the overall cantata sequence, of the anticipation of the coming of the Holy Spirit, which Cantata 108 will explore more directly on the following week, again ending in B minor.

In *Ihr werdet weinen und heulen* the idea of reprise is central, as the symbol of Jesus's return within the contained perspective of present existence. This quality is offset, however, by the fact that none of the individual movements of the cantata features a *textual* reprise, a feature that mirrors the promise of change predicted at the outset. All four closed movements feature *musical* reprises (even the final chorale); and in each case the nature of the reprise is illuminating since it necessarily involves change of text.

The first movement is a three-section fugue with an introductory ritornello and a brief modulating bass solo between the second and third fugal sections. The second and third sections of the fugue are nearly identical, except for changes necessitated by the transposition at the fourth. The introductory ritornello introduces the music that will later reappear for "aber die Welt wird sich freuen," its marchlike rhythmic character suggesting a worldly tone. In contrast, the fugue theme, entering with the chorus, is one of the most tormented sounding in Bach's oeuvre on account of the tortured leaps and dissonant chromatic intervals (*saltus duriusculus* and *passus duriusculus* in the terms of Baroque rhetoric) that Bach introduces to depict "weinen und heulen." Its tritone leap from b to e♯′ on "heulen" introduces a push to the dominant, f♯, that is particularly graphic (ex. 10.1).

Of the three principal choral sections, the first (mm. 27–55) keeps its two themes completely separate, "Ihr werdet weinen und heulen" (27–42) in b and "aber die Welt wird sich freuen" (set to the ritornello material, mm. 43–55) closing in e. After that, the second section of the fugue begins in the subdominant, then combines the two themes, becoming progressively sharper until, at its climax, the theme finally enters on f♯″ in the *flauto piccolo.* Its tritone leap, now from f♯″ to b♯″, sets up the dominant (of the dominant), C♯, from which point both music and text deal only with the rejoicing of the world (mm. 75–101); the section closes in f♯ after a lengthy dominant (c♯) pedal. It is tempting to conclude that Bach intended

EXAMPLE 10.1 **Cantata 103, *Ihr werdet weinen und heulen*** *opening chorus, mm. 27–32, fugue theme*

EXAMPLE 10.2 **Cantata 103, *Ihr werdet weinen und heulen*** *opening chorus, mm. 101–108*

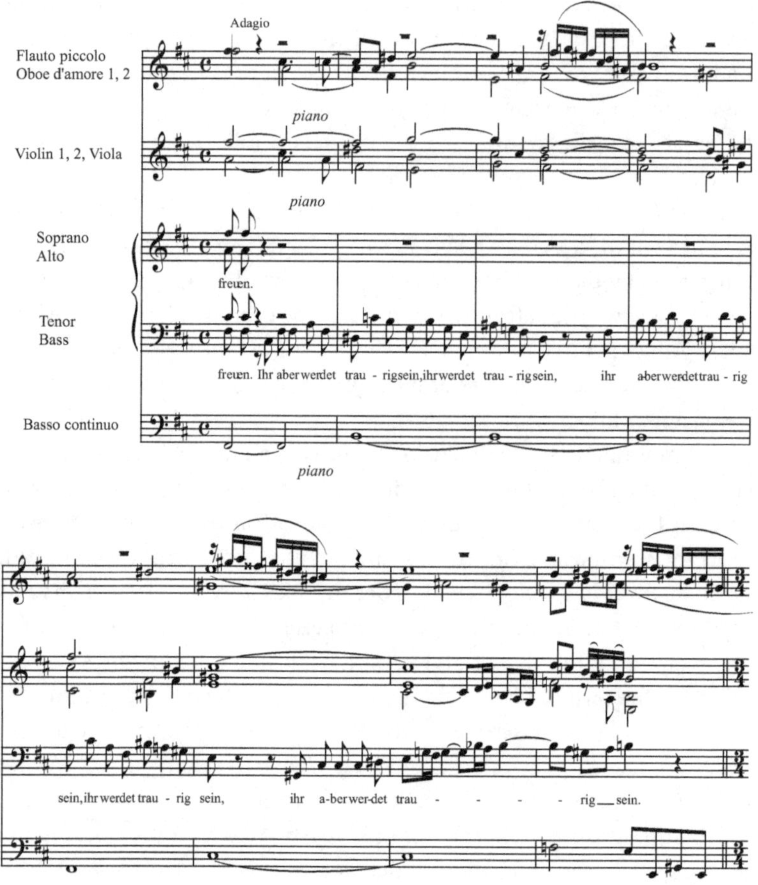

something akin to the archaic association of sharp-minor keys with the term "*durus*" to depict the rejoicing of the world.[9]

Then, after the arrival in the dominant (m. 101), Bach shifts suddenly to an *Adagio* arioso-like style of extraordinarily sorrowful affect, as the bass soloist, accompanied by the instruments in more sustained style, but still closely related to the tortured character of the fugue theme, takes up the text that will eventually lead to the idea of transformation: "Ihr aber werdet traurig sein" (ex. 10.2) This it draws out for several repetitions in a rising-fifth sequence that cadences after a few measures to C♯ minor (m. 106), the furthest point in the sharp direction for the

[9] In the treatises of Andreas Werckmeister we frequently encounter this older usage, which traces back to the hard (*durus*) and soft (*mollis*) hexachords of Renaissance music and theory. Werckmeister, for example, describes the key of A flat as *A moll* and that of A minor as *A dur*.

entire cantata.[10] As it begins the line over again, the voice moves up in a series of minor thirds, outlining a diminished-seventh chord. Although the upward motion might be thought, superficially, to suggest hope, it does not: its g♮ clashes momentarily with the g♯′ of the sustained c♯ triad in the strings and winds, and its b♭ turns around the apparent upward tendency of the second oboe's a♯′. Shifting to F in the bass, Bach introduces an augmented-sixth chord, which, although it appears relatively infrequently in Bach's music, is, when it does, often associated with transformation (as in the transition from the words "Et exspecto resurrectionem mortuorum" to the "Et vitam venturi saeculi" in the *Mass in B minor*, for example). This then moves to the dominant of a in preparation for the third phase of the fugue, which is basically a reiteration of the second at the fourth up, one degree flatter, with a new text. Over the course of the movement the fugue's beginnings are increasingly flattened from B minor to E minor and, finally, A minor. The first of these segments shifts from b to e and deals primarily with the disciples' sorrow; the second moves from e to f♯ and climaxes in the rejoicing of the world; and the third, following the sharpward motion and the transformation to a, moves from a back to b, as it predicts the disciples' sorrow changing to joy. In terms of Bach's frequent practice of associating increasing suffering and tribulation with modulation to flat-minor keys, it suggests that this movement is another version of the destruction/restoration "shape" that appears in many cantatas: in other words, the shift to a is the "nadir" or point of reversal and the motion back to b the restoration.

An additional sign of transformation is that over the course of the three fugal segments the theme is altered, although some of the alteration is owing to adjustments necessitated by the transposition at the fourth in the final section. Nevertheless, the character of the theme becomes somewhat less tortured as Bach first drops the chromaticism on "weinen" that appears at the close of the theme only in the first segment, then transposes the latter part of the theme down an octave in the vocal entries, eliminating the leap up a seventh. In all other respects, however, the music of the second and third segments of the fugue remains basically the same, except for the transposition. At this point the joy predicted for the disciples is entirely conditioned by the perspective of the world.

And the recitative that follows moves once again to c♯, as it narrates sorrow not only over the "dearest one" being "torn away" but also that the "savior of the soul, the refuge of diseased hearts" disregards the pain of the faithful. The f♯ aria, for alto and *flauto piccolo*, "Kein Artzt ist außer dir zu finden" (No physician can be found other than you), then gives sustained expression to the believer's feelings of loss, despite the fact that the often ornate *flauto piccolo* line seems to invite hope. Its first segment moves again to c♯ (now the dominant), as the soloist makes an implicit

---

[10] Johann David Heinichen, in outlining the *ambitus* of his paired major/minor keys, does not include the supertonic within the minor mode—c♯ within B minor, for example—since it would involve two key-signature levels, and as a harmony is often diminished (as in the rising sequences of Bach's recitative). In Bach's music the supertonic is generally much less common in minor than in major keys and is apt to express tormented states of mind.

comparison of her sin to that of Jerusalem before its destruction by the Babylonians in 587 BCE (by invoking Jeremiah's lament that no balsam could be found in Gilead). After an abbreviated version of the ritornello in c♯, the tonality then moves in the flat direction as it voices the believer's tormented anticipation of the outcome of God the physician's "hiddenness": "Verbirgst du dich, so muß ich sterben" (If you conceal yourself I must die). God's self-concealment, or hiddenness is one of the cornerstones of Luther's theology of the cross, appearing in a considerable number of the Bach cantata texts, including several of the spring 1725 sequence.[11] On an immediate level it contributes to the believer's feelings of tribulation and forsakenness, voiced widely in the psalms, for example; but as God's "alien work," it fulfills the purpose of driving the believer to cry out to God for aid, thereby bringing on God's response of faith, his "proper work." In Cantata 103 it seems to make the point that reliance on the senses, or the flesh—the worldly view that seeing is believing—is the greatest obstacle to the believer's salvation.[12] The six measures that voice the believer's fear of the outcome of God's hiddenness progressively flatten the harmony, suggesting, but not actually cadencing in, A minor. Then, in a very characteristic change for Bach, the tonal direction reverses for the believer's prayer for mercy "Erbarme dich, ach höre doch" (Have mercy, ah hear me), emphasizing the dominant of f♯ repeatedly for the believer's initial expression of hope: "Du suchest ja nicht mein Verderben, wohlan, so hofft mein Herze noch" (You certainly do not seek my destruction; well then, my heart hopes still). At these points the *flauto piccolo* plays in its most active, hopeful vein, although its resolution into a repetition of the opening ritornello affirms the initial forlorn affect. The directional opposition is a reminder of the destruction/restoration dynamic of the first movement, but once again the believer's hopes are contained within the predominant affect of sorrow.

The next recitative sets up the primary transformation of the cantata, as hope turns to faith in Jesus's promise. The first five measures outline a consistent motion in the flat or subdominant direction (b–G–e), coinciding with the believer's hope that Jesus's return will bring the awaited revival. Then, for the anticipation of transformation, Bach reinterprets the continuo's initial sustained A♯ as B♭, turning it down to A on "Freude" and completing a shift to D with an extended vocal melisma for the cadence, "soll verkehret werden" (ex. 10.3).

The transformation to D complete, the bass aria with trumpet and strings, "Erholet euch, betrübte Sinnen" (Gather yourselves together, tormented senses), gives expression to the ecstasy that accompanies the believer's anticipating "seeing" Jesus. Within the cantatas of the spring 1725 sequence, this aria is the first of three hortatory trumpet arias in D associated with the senses, the others appearing in

---

[11] For a recent detailed study of this subject, see Jochen Arnold, *Von Gott poetisch-musikalisch reden: Gottes verborgenes und offenbares Handeln in Bachs Kantaten* (Göttingen: Vandenhoeck & Ruprecht, 2012).

[12] See Loewenich, *Luther's Theology of the Cross*, 27–49.

EXAMPLE 10.3 **Cantata 103, *Ihr werdet weinen und heulen*** *no. 4, recitative*

Cantatas 128 and 175. As we might expect, given the through-composed nature of the text, the ecstasy of seeing Jesus comes at the end, and it coincides with the reprise of the music of its opening section. In the opening movement a new, more hopeful, text had accompanied the reprise of the music associated with Jesus's prediction of the disciples sorrow and the rejoicing of the world. Here, however, the trumpet-influenced primary material of the movement marks a great change in the affective character of the text right at the outset (ex. 10.4). Nevertheless, even in the ritornello it gives way to music of contrasted character that, after the voice enters, is developed further for "betrübte Sinnen, ihr tut euch selber allzu weh" (tormented minds, you do yourselves too much injury). This sets up a move to the dominant minor, a, which then turns to major at the last moment for the ritornello that completes the first section. References to the key of A minor, associated with tribulation in the opening chorus and first aria, are now subordinate to and ultimately overcome by its major mode. The beginning of the second segment, "Laß von dem traurigen Beginnen, eh' ich in Tränen untergeh'" (Abandon the sorrow you have had up to now, before I drop in tears), turns to the mediant minor, f♯. After sounding the ritornello in that key, however, the character of the music changes, and we hear the line cited earlier, "Mein Jesus läßt sich wieder sehen, o Freude, der nichts gleichen kann" (ex. 10.5). For this remarkable passage Bach draws out the word "Freude" in several lengthy melismas, presenting the initial trumpet triads in both ascending and descending configurations in all the instruments, passing the harmony through circles of fifths and allusions to secondary

EXAMPLE 10.4 **Cantata 103, *Ihr werdet weinen und heulen*** *no. 5, aria, "Erholet euch, betrübte Sinnen," beginning*

EXAMPLE 10.5 **Cantata 103, *Ihr werdet weinen und heulen*** *no. 5, aria, "Erholet euch, betrübte Sinnen," mm. 46–54*

EXAMPLE 10.5 *(continued)*

keys until, beneath the longest roulades in the voice (six full measures of sixteenth notes), he leads the strings slowly down the scale to the tonic, punctuated all the while by triadic figures in alternation between trumpet and *basso continuo*. The character is entirely anticipatory. While the voice is still occupied with its ecstatic cry on "Freude," the reprise begins *piano* in the instruments in its original D (m. 51). The effect is that the believer's joy in the confidence of faith is confirmed symbolically by the return. This time, to the music formerly associated with "ihr tut euch selber allzu weh," we hear "wie wohl ist mir dadurch geschehen, nimm, nimm mein Herz zum Opfer an" (how well through all this it has turned out for me; take, take my heart as an offering), altered in some of its melodic emphases so as to suggest a leaping, joyful character. The music that had suggested the dominant minor now introduces hints of the tonic minor, but altered at the end so as to subordinate it entirely to D. In its transformed reprise the aria recalls the "traurigen Beginnen" of the movement (and the cantata) as if a memory, its force erased by the circle of fifths, the melismas, and the return of D beneath the voice.

For the concluding chorale verse Mariane von Ziegler, perhaps with Bach's collaboration, chose an elaboration on Jesus's words to the disciples, now directed to the believer personally, "Ich hab' dich einen Augenblick, o liebes Kind verlassen" (I have left you for a moment, O beloved child). Sung to the melody of "Was mein Gott will, dass gescheh' allzeit," this verse is perfectly suited to bridge between D and b, since the first phrase of its *Stollen* is in D and its second in b (both repeated). In addition, these two phrases return to end the chorale, creating an AABA musical form in which the final lines, although reiterating the promise of sorrow turned to joy, end in b. Since the text of this chorale makes clear that Jesus's departure, the source of the believer's suffering, is only for an instant ("Augenblick"), urging him to "see" that Jesus already provides happiness and consolation beyond all measure, promising to honor the believer with the crown of joy ("Sieh aber, sieh, mit großem Glück und Trost ohn' alle Maßen will ich dir schon die Freudenkron aufsetzen und verehren"), it expresses a sense of continuity between the seeing of Jesus in faith, as at the close of the preceding movement, and in eternity. Over the four phrases of the *Abgesang*, including the reprise of the opening phrase, the sequence of cadences delineates a pattern of descent by thirds: A–f♯/F♯ (i.e., V of b)–D–b as the text moves from Jesus's gift of the "crown of joy" to the reminder that "Freud" and "ewig Wohl" will come only after "kurzes Leid." While "Freud" coincides with the penultimate D major cadence, the promise of future transformation ends the cantata in b ("soll . . . verkehren"). In relation to D, then, the return to b is associated with the perspective of present existence, the world "below," which, although transformed by faith, awaits the fullness of joy as a future condition.

Martin Moller, citing the verse from John with which Cantata 103 begins, posed the question of how such a *Creutzpredigt* could "rhyme" with *Jubilate*, answering, as Bach seems to in his design for *Ihr werdet weinen und heulen*, with the juxtaposition of brief suffering in the present to the joy of eternal life. The D/b relationship in Cantata 103 may well remind the reader of what I have said regarding the relationship of those two keys in "Es ist vollbracht," *Kommt, gehet und eilet* (BWV 249), and *Am Abend aber desselbigen Sabbats* (BWV 42). That is, within a single *ambitus*—in this case that of D/b—the arrangement of keys and their associations (when verbal texts are present) often mirror affective qualities that may suggest John's worlds above and below, the divine and the human, or a set of related affections, such as the triumph of (Jesus's) victory versus peace and *Trost* in the world. Such associations are not, of course, absolute, either in terms of particular keys or their position within the *ambitus*. But in many cases Bach creates a sense of tonal direction that aligns closely with qualities in the text: for example, G (along with b and e) for Jesus's incarnation in the Credo of the *Mass in B minor;* for Jesus's bringing peace to the disciples in Cantata 42; for Peter's "Sanfte soll mein Todeskummer nur ein Schlummer" aria in *Kommt, gehet und eilet*; and so forth. Sharp-major keys may exhibit very positive, active or triumphant associations, often of an upward-tending character (Maria Magdalene's A-major aria in *Kommt, gehet und eilet*, "Jesus ist ein Schild der Seinen" in Cantata 42, and the like), whereas sharp-minor keys tend to be clouded by qualities such as I have described for "Wer sollte nicht in Klagen untergehn" from Cantata 103. And the relative major/minor pairing is apt to suggest, when amplified by other musical and textual features, the opposition that underlies John's worlds above and below. But since the world above is presented as an anticipation within the present, the relationship is not one of stark separation.

Viewed this way, it is significant that in *Ihr werdet weinen und heulen* the key of G does not appear (since the text affords no scope for peaceful or comforting worldly associations), whereas the extension of the B-minor tonic in the sharp minor direction (f♯ and c♯, the latter key outside the normal *ambitus* of D/b) projects qualities associated with the rejoicing of the world and sorrow over Jesus's departure. Their counterparts on the flat side of the key, e and most particularly a (again, outside the normal *ambitus*), seem to parallel affective states more closely allied to internal rather than external torment: self-abnegation, penitence, and the like. In contrast, the D/A relationship of the trumpet aria and the final chorale distinguishes Jesus's promise of future reward for the believer from the b of the believer's life in the world. Coincidental or not, the A, f♯, D, and b of the last four phrases of the chorale form the successive keys of the movements of the next cantata in the series, Cantata 108, in which the descent by thirds seems to indicate "the Spirit that God gives from heaven" as the means by which in the present life God leads the faithful along the path to blessedness.

Es ist euch gut, daß ich hingehe (BWV 108)

From the perspective of the contemporary believer, the coming of the Holy Spirit is not fixed in time, as is the feast day celebrating his appearance to the disciples, but belongs to both the era of the church (the time after Jesus was no longer physically present) and the faith experience of the individual believer. In the Farewell Discourse Jesus's speaking of his departure and return may have multiple or overlapping meanings, as Brown describes, but in the liturgy as interpreted by Mariane von Ziegler's cantata texts it leads to Pentecost and the coming of the Holy Spirit.

In several of her cantata texts Ziegler might have adopted the idea of a central movement that "applies" the principal idea of the motto to the contemporary believer from the cantata texts that came earlier in the season. As I mentioned, along with the shift to the first person, this procedure mirrors the stages by which traditional hermeneutics moves from the literal-historical to the spiritual (allegorical, tropological, eschatological) senses. In the remaining two cantatas before Ascension Day, and a few others of the series, Ziegler introduced, in addition to the Johannine motto that appears at the beginning, a second *dictum* from John, usually at or near the midpoint of the cantata. Cantatas 108, 87, 74, and 175 all introduce two such mottoes, one at the beginning and one at approximately the midpoint, while

Cantatas 68 and 176 (and to a lesser extent, Cantata 103) can be considered variants of that procedure.[13] In most cases the second motto (and, in the case of the cantata for Pentecost the third as well) serves as a "turning point" or pivot within the work.

Cantata 103 does not refer to the Spirit directly, but in the Farewell Discourse its theme of sorrow turned to joy directly follows the discussion of the Spirit that forms the Gospel reading for the following Sunday, Cantate. Since, after Ascension Day, the Gospel reading for Exaudi, from a still earlier point in the discourse, speaks even more directly about the Spirit, the abovementioned reverse ordering of the readings seems to form part of a deliberate anticipation of Pentecost. In Cantata 108, *Es ist euch gut, daß ich hingehe*, Mariane von Ziegler brings out this quality by beginning with Jesus's announcement to the disciples that his immanent departure (introduced in Cantata 103) will ultimately be beneficial for them, since the Spirit will replace his physical presence. Then, in the only recitative (no. 3), she raises the question of the believer's anxious uncertainty regarding the experience of the Spirit, using that movement to set up the second *dictum* from John. That *dictum*, further clarifying the work of the Spirit, is a response to the believer's anxiety, which the ending of the second aria seems to overcome.

After such a pronounced sense of opposition in Cantata 103 between the immediacy of suffering and the hope of future transformation, the second Ziegler cantata responds with a sequence of movements that shifts the emphasis more directly to the present. Its means of accomplishing such a shift is given in the two mottos from John, the first announcing that the benefit of Jesus's departure—his death, resurrection, and ascension—is the coming of the Holy Spirit:

> **John 16:7:** "Es ist euch gut, daß ich hingehe; denn so ich nicht hingehe, kömmt der Tröster nicht zu euch. So ich aber gehe, will ich ihn zu euch senden."
>
> (It is good for you that I go away; for if I did not go, the comforter would not come to you. Since I go, however, I will send him to you.)

Set as a representation of the voice of Jesus (*vox Christi*), for bass, oboe d'amore, strings, and *basso continuo*, this movement projects a remarkable sense of the historical situation of the Farewell Discourse, depicting Jesus's assurance to the disciples at the Last Supper that he would be with them in the Spirit, the comforter. And the aria that follows, for tenor, solo violin, and *basso continuo*, continues the

---

[13] In her printed texts for these nine cantatas, Mariane von Ziegler always identifies those movements that cite scriptural passages with the heading *Dictum*. Cantata 128 has, of course, no movement with that designation. Cantatas 68 and 176 have one *Dictum* each, the last and first movements respectively; but Cantata 68 begins with a chorale paraphrase from the Gospel, and a recitative paraphrase from the Gospel appears in the third movement. A recitative paraphrase from John likewise appears in the fourth movement of Cantata 176. Thus Cantatas 68 and 176 contain Gospel paraphrases at points comparable to where Ziegler placed her second *Dictum* in several cantatas. In Cantata 103 there is no second *Dictum*, but the fourth movement, a recitative that serves as a central pivot in the design, paraphrases the *Dictum* of the opening movement.

chamber-music atmosphere, affirming faith in Jesus's words and the understanding of his departure as source of the believer's ultimately attaining the "desired port," which can be understood only in eschatological terms.[14]

So far the emphasis is on the coming of the Holy Spirit as a future event. The turning point to the present is the cantata's only recitative, which now follows, its meaning affirmed in the second *dictum*, now set for chorus with doubling instruments. First, the tenor affirms that the Spirit will direct him along the true path, but ends with the anguished cry, "Ich frage sorgensvoll: Ach, ist er nicht schon hier? Ach, ist er nicht schon hier?" (I ask, full of cares: Ah, is he not already here? Ah, is he not already here?). The answer, set as a tripartite fugue for full chorus and doubling instruments, seems to embody a more universal tone, as if the question of the Holy Spirit is one that goes beyond private experience:

> **John 16:13:** "Wenn aber jener, der Geist der Wahrheit, kommen wird, der wird euch in alle Wahrheit leiten. Denn er wird nicht von ihm selber reden, sondern was er hören wird, das wird er reden; und was zukünftig ist, wird er verkündigen."
>
> (When, however, he, the Spirit of truth comes, he will lead you into the fullness of truth. For he will speak not of himself, but of what he hears, of that will he speak; and what is to come he will reveal.)

Behind the question in the recitative lies the Lutheran doctrine that the presence of the Spirit may not be recognized at first, since his work transcends any idea of mere inner feeling. And in proclaiming that the Holy Spirit will communicate the fullness of truth ("alle Wahrheit"), speaking of what he hears rather than of himself, as well as revealing knowledge of what is to come, the second *dictum*, in Luther's view, represents the Spirit as speaking only of "Christ and his Word," not of any arbitrary additions or fabrications such as the "pope's doctrines":

> In this way Christ sets bounds for the message of the Holy Spirit himself. He is not to preach anything new or anything else than Christ and his Word. Thus we have a sure guide and touchstone for judging the false spirits. We can declare that it surely does not indicate the presence of the Holy Spirit when a person proclaims his own thoughts and notions and begins to teach in Christendom something apart from or in addition to what Christ taught.[15]

Luther, therefore, viewed this verse entirely in a Trinitarian light, unifying and distinguishing the Father as the one who speaks, the Son as the word, and the Spirit as the one who listens and conveys.[16] In Ziegler's cantata sequence the theme of hearing, mentioned earlier, is subtly introduced in the office of the Spirit, in advance

---

[14] This is the substance of Luther's discussion of this passage in his 1537 sermon (*Luther's Works*, vol. 24; see 334–35).

[15] Ibid., 363.

[16] Ibid., 362–65.

of its association with the believer's hearing the Spirit (from Cantata 183 on). Bach's tripartite fugal setting of the second *dictum* of Cantata 108 lends it the character of a pronouncement that goes beyond subjective interpretation of the experience of the Spirit. In conveying what he "hears" to humanity, the Spirit, as Cantata 108 emphasizes, directs the path of the faithful according to God's will, which transcends human expectations, even though the goal of those expectations is told by God. The idea of a journey forward emerges in this cantata in the many references to "going" and the "path" of life ("hingehe," "gehe," "auf rechter Bahn geh," "leiten," "führe mich," "auf wohl gebähntem Wege," "er . . . richtet unsern Fuß," "treten muß"), all of which represent progression to the "gewünschten Port" that constitutes its goal.

Bach sets the opening motto of Cantata 108 in A, then follows it by a "descending" sequence of keys: f♯ (the first aria), b/D (recitative), D (the second Johannine motto), b (the second aria and the final chorale). The two minor-key arias respond to the major keys of the two *dicta*, first with an expression of *Trost* following from belief in Jesus's "word" of promise, then with a prayer that culminates with the believer's anticipation of seeing Jesus in eternity. That the overall motion is a "downward" one, parallels the fact that the second *dictum* (a D/b/D design) describes the work of the Spirit as that of conveying "truth" (from the world above) to the faithful (below) an extension of the b/D relationship of Cantata 103. In this light, the many expressions of motion and direction in Ziegler's text for Cantata 108 are mirrored in the continuous downward direction of its tonal design. Truth as the prerogative of the realm of the Spirit, or the world "above," is, of course, one of John's most characteristic themes, present also in a dialog between Jesus and Pilate in the *St. John Passion*.[17] When, in the second motto of Cantata 108, Jesus describes the Spirit as bringing truth to the disciples, as not speaking of himself (or on his own) but of what he hears (from Jesus and the Father), and as revealing things to come, there is again a strong sense of the "vertical" (above/below) nature of John's eschatology, in response to the present/future character of sorrow turned to joy in Cantata 103. Bach's setting of the second motto of Cantata 108 is built around this issue.

The downward motion of Cantata 108, however, is not simply an allegory of the descent of the Spirit but also an expression of how the Spirit works according to Lutheran thought. Regin Prenter has explored this subject in detail in an influential study of Luther's concept of the Holy Spirit. As Prenter shows, Luther's view of the Spirit was bound up with the theme of the believer's becoming "conformable" to Christ, which meant acceptance of suffering and inner conflict as God's will, his "alien work"—the cross in its most direct meaning, leading to death as the punishment for sin. Without such acceptance the Spirit was reduced to mere subjective feeling.[18] The Spirit, in teaching acceptance of suffering, also taught prayer, the means by which the believer could step onto God's path (as articulated in Bach's

---

[17] See ch. 6, ex. 6.1.

[18] Prenter, *Spiritus Creator*, 3–27. 125–30.

Weimar cantata, *Tritt auf den Glaubensbahn*, BWV 152). And God's path is at first a downward one. Without understanding of this aspect of the Lutheran doctrine of the Spirit, the character of the next cantata (BWV 87) in the spring 1725 sequence, *Bisher habt ihr nichts gebeten in meinem Name*, which takes guilt and acknowledgment of sin as its starting point, is much more difficult to comprehend.[19] Cantata 108, in fact, shares its downward tonal motion with cantatas in which the descent is an expression of the abovementioned "conformity." Cantata 73, *Herr, wie du willt, so schicks mit mir*, is an outstanding example of this quality, its five-movement sequence outlining a descent through the keynotes of the C-minor triad (g–E♭–c–c–c), as its text unfolds the imagery of the believer's "sinking" into God's will, a quality that is mirrored in countless other aspects of the cantata. In two other cantatas with "descending" tonal designs, *Erforsche mich Gott, und erfahre mein Herz* (BWV 136), and *Siehe zu, daß deine Gottesfurcht nicht Heuchelei sei* (BWV 179), the descent is primarily a mirroring of the adoption of God's will by the sinner, whereas in the *Missae Breves* that take over the basis of their tonal designs within their Glorias, it is simultaneously an image of the world above (Gloria in excelsis Deo) and the sinful nature of the world itself, as embodied in the Qui tollis peccata mundi.[20] In the cantatas the descent mirrors God's "alien" rather than his "proper" work, but its outcome is a positive one.

Easily the closest mirroring of the descent of the Spirit by means of a tonally descending design, however, is *Erschallet, ihr Lieder*, composed at Weimar in 1714 for Pentecost. In that cantata Bach begins in C with trumpets and timpani, an instrumentation associated in the first chorus and the first aria ("Heiligste Dreifaltigkeit") with the splendor of the Trinity. The movement succession then turns to the relative minor for a second aria, then the subdominant, F, for a duet between the soul and the Holy Spirit, followed by the fourth strophe of Philip Nicolai's chorale "Wie schön leuchtet der Morgenstern": "Von Gott kömmt mir ein Freudenschein," associated with the Holy Spirit. Completing the triadic descent to the subdominant, the duet modulates strikingly in the flat direction, reaching C minor for the "kiss of grace" (*Gnadenkuss*) that the Spirit gives the soul. In numerous details Bach depicts the coming of the Holy Spirit in increasingly intimate terms that are mirrored in the descending tonal pattern of the cantata.[21]

---

[19] See the study of Cantata 87 by Renate Steiger cited in n. 6.

[20] See the study referred to in ch. 8, n. 19. Cantatas 136 and 179 exhibit very similar tonal designs to that of Cantata 108: descent from A through f♯ to b in the former work, and from G through e to a in the latter. These modulatory designs influenced those of the Glorias of the *Missae Breves* in A and G. Both cantatas involve the theme of the inner truth of the heart as opposed to the outward appearance of piety. Cantata 136, *Erforsche mich, Gott, und erfahre mein Herz*, is a prayer for God to search the heart for that inner truth, whereas in Cantata 179, *Siehe zu, daß deine Gottesfurcht nicht Heuchelei sei*, the subject matter of hypocrisy involves ideas that are shared by Regin Prenter's interpretation of Luther's view of the working of the Holy Spirit, in particular that of *odium sui*, rather than self-love (see Prenter, *Spiritus Creator*, 4–13, 64–100).

[21] I study this cantata in detail in a forthcoming book, *Tears into Wine: Bach's Cantata 21, "Ich hatte viel Bekümmernis" in its Musical and Theological Contexts.*

The first motto of *Es ist euch gut, daß ich hingehe* makes the very important point that Jesus's departure, lamented in Cantata 103, is not only beneficial for the disciples but also necessary for the coming of the Holy Spirit. Jesus's going, however, is not simply his ascension but, as Luther described it, encompasses the Passion, resurrection, and ascension:

> Christ wants to say that it has been proclaimed in Scripture and foretold by all the prophets that Christ will suffer, die, be buried, and rise again, and thus establish a new, eternal kingdom in which mankind has everlasting life and is redeemed from sin, death, and hell. This must be fulfilled; and the hour of its fulfillment has now come. "For the predictions of all the prophets point to this time, and I am the Person who is to carry them out. Therefore your joy and salvation are now beginning; but you must learn to forget about my physical presence for a little while and to look for the Comforter. For my kingdom cannot be ushered in, nor can the Holy Spirit be given, until I have died and departed this life. My death and resurrection will renew everything in heaven and on earth, and will establish a rule in which the Holy Spirit will reign everywhere through the Gospel and your ministry.... That is the treasure and the glory which I will achieve and acquire for you. But this cannot happen to you before I have accomplished that through which it is to come to pass and have paid for and earned it with my death."[22]

Both Ziegler's choice of opening *dictum* and Bach's setting make a point of the equivalence Luther describes, which involves the negative pronouncement that if Jesus does *not* depart, the Spirit will *not* come. In this respect Cantata 108 is a preparation for Ascension Day and Pentecost, reinterpreting Jesus's return as described in Cantata 103 more specifically as his return through the Spirit. The starting point is Bach's setting of the first *dictum*, which in several respects projects a character that seems to transcend the historical circumstances of the discourse, to be more appropriate to the resurrected and ascended Jesus. Owing to a symmetrical quality in the setting, the impression created is of Jesus centered among his disciples and speaking from a state of glorification, such as that seen in John 17.

The first indication of this quality is the head motive of the initial oboe d'amore solo, which, after a perfect-fourth upbeat, ascends in a decorated scalar motion from the tonic to the fifth (ex. 10.6a).On its second appearance, immediately afterwards, it is much more extravagantly decorated with swirling thirty-second-note figures and scales. Nevertheless, the bare melodic pattern on which this theme is based often appears in movements whose texts take up the following of Jesus; well-known examples are the melody of "Ich folge dir gleichfalls" from the *St. John Passion,* "Ich folge Christo nach" from Cantata 12, and "Ich folge dir nach" from Cantata 159, in all of which, although the following in question is the way of the cross, that is, of worldly tribulation, the musical character is determined by the

[22] *Luther's Works*, vol. 24, 334.

EXAMPLE 10.6a and b **Cantata 108, *Es ist euch gut, daß ich hingehe*** *first movement, beginning instrumental and vocal themes*

positive outcome. Within the theme as it appears in Cantata 108, Bach adds dotted rhythms that suggest a majestic quality; this is even more the case when the dotted rhythms are taken over by the punctuating strings in *staccato sempre* style. Against and in dialog with the strings, the oboe d'amore generally plays a highly decorated line, the two coming together with the dotted-rhythm style mostly at cadence points. Perhaps the most interesting indication of the majestic character of the movement is that when the voice enters with the head motive Bach alters the decoration so as to highlight the main notes, and instead of the pure ascent of the instrumental theme, he sets "Es ist euch gut" as an ascent only to the third, after which the motto pivots around the word "daß" and descends through a slightly decorated reversal of the initial tones ("ich hingehe"; see ex. 10.6b). Without any decoration, the theme would be exactly symmetrical (i.e., e–a–b–c♯′–b–c♯′–b–a–e) its pitch sequence (transposed) very close to that of the well-known symmetrical "et resurrexit" theme of the *Mass in B minor*. The point of this is that Jesus's departure, which encompasses his death, resurrection, and ascension, is of benefit for the disciples because of its counterpart: the descent of the Holy Spirit. In itself the symmetry presents the ascending and descending elements as part of a larger whole that is ultimately entirely positive.

Likewise, the theme of the middle section, the abovementioned negative pronouncement, contains within it a kind of retrograde inversion of its first four tones as its last four (with one sharpened pitch). This theme effects a modulation to the relative minor, f♯, in which Bach brings back the beginning of the original theme, now set to the negative part of the motto, leading it into melismas of unusual length on "nicht hin*gehe*." From this we see that except for the shift to minor the negative aspect of the motto is equivalent to the positive. A and f♯ complement each other as "above" (*hingehe*) and "below" (*nicht hingehe*). One interesting, although probably incidental, feature of Bach's beginning the principal vocal motive in minor is that it now resembles the beginning melody of the f♯ aria, "Kein Arzt ist außer dir zu finden" from Cantata 103, which was the earlier cantata's principal expression of loss over Jesus's departure. Now, there is no loss; since Bach's point is the equivalence of Jesus's departure and the coming of the Holy Spirit, the movement offers many symbols of motion and complementarity: in the "walking" bass patterns, the "step" figures in the voice, and the interaction between the highly decorated oboe d'amore line and the punctuating phrases in the strings. In addition, the movement is an ABA′ form in which "Es ist euch gut, daß ich hingehe" modulates from A to the dominant, E, after which "denn so ich nicht hingehe, kömmt der Tröster nicht zu euch," moves to f♯ (from the initial appearance of "kömmt der Tröster nicht zu euch") and "So ich aber gehe, will ich ihn zu euch senden" returns to A. The long vocal melismas on "hingehe" in the first section, "[nicht] hingehe" in the second, and "senden" in the third, underscore the main point.

After the very positive A major of Jesus's words of promise, the aria in f♯ that follows seems immediately to symbolize the human response. It features a one-measure ostinato-like figure of five eighth notes (four repeated tones plus an upbeat) in the *basso continuo* that runs throughout nearly every single measure of the movement, presumably to suggest a framework for the tenor's claim of being free from all doubt: "Mich kann kein Zweifel stören, auf dein Wort, Herr, zu hören." Above it, in the solo violin, is a pattern that resembles the melodic line of a two-part prelude (such as the D-major prelude from *WTC* I, for example). Beginning with a rising minor sixth, often associated with entreaty in Bach's music (the most celebrated instance of which is the beginning of the aria "Erbarme dich" from the *St. Matthew Passion*), its predominant sixteenth-note motion (sometimes reaching upward and pausing on the second eighth note of the measure in a quasi-ostinato rhythm of its own) suggests, along with the *basso continuo*, the supportive quality of Jesus's words in the believer's path through life. An interesting feature is that after the tenor's opening phrase, the tonality moves away from the tonic, f♯, and does not return to it until the voice comes to a close at the "gewünschten Port," directly before the final return of the ritornello. There Bach breaks the quasi-ostinato pattern for the only time, holding the tone f♯″ for four measures in the violin, then bringing voice and violin together in rhythmic unison (and in parallel sixths or thirds) as the violin's initial prelude-like pattern reappears for the final "komm an gewünschten Port." As voice and violin move into rhythmic unison, the main theme of the movement sounds to a falling third sequence (beginning on f♯″, d″, b′ in the voice) before settling on f♯. The ending, which mirrors the overall third descent in the movement keys of the cantata as a whole, suggests that the believer's faith is bound up with accepting Jesus's promise of return through the Spirit as the foundation for his own reaching the desired port, in this context an allegory of the coming of the Spirit to direct the faithful.

Now the lone recitative, also for tenor, summarizes the believer's faith in the coming of the Holy Spirit to direct his/her path as the result of Jesus's departure. Beginning in b, it moves at once to D, as it expresses faith that the Holy Spirit will show the "rechter Bahn." Yet, the understanding of Jesus's words remains uncertain. After the initial expression of faith, Ziegler introduces the anxious question that Bach reiterates to end the solo—"Ach, ist er nicht schon hier? Ach, ist er nicht schon hier?" This concerns, of course, the experience of the Spirit, the inner replacement for Jesus's physical presence. How will the Spirit be experienced and recognized as such? This was a matter of concern for Lutheranism, owing to the necessity of distinguishing between interpretation of the Spirit as mere "feeling," that is, as a psychological quality, and as the real presence of God. Ending on the dominant of D, the recitative sets up the second motto as the answer.

Bach sets the second Johannine *dictum* as a tripartite fugal design for chorus; the third fugue expands the material of the first, whereas the central fugue is based on a different theme. The theme of the first and third fugues features an initial leap upward of a major sixth that changes to a major seventh as the movement progresses, the seventh becoming its predominant form. Since the cantata's initial motto also emphasized the rising major sixth (i.e., a rising fourth that continued on to the major sixth), whereas the two arias begin with rising minor sixths, a pronounced element of continuity accompanies the many expressions of directionality throughout the cantata. The minor form (the two arias) seems associated with the human sphere, whereas the major (the two mottoes) suggests qualities associated with the world "above." This is especially the case when, in the second motto, the sixth expands, provocatively, to a major seventh, the leading-tone character of the uppermost pitch thereby demanding upward resolution.

The expansion of the rising sixth to a seventh in the choral motto is central to its structure and to the above/below idea. In the initial fugue Bach begins with the rising sixth, e′–c♯′, reserving the rising seventh, d′–c♯″, for the third entry; and after all four voices have entered, he transposes it by successive fifths, first to a–g♯′, then e′–d♯″, using the last of these entries to effect a secure move to the dominant, A, in which the fugue closes. The successive rising sevenths and their sharpward motion seem to associate the move to the dominant with the text's describing the Spirit of Truth leading the disciples along the path to "alle Wahrheit" ("Wenn aber jener, der Geist der Wahrheit, kommen wird, der wird euch in alle Wahrheit leiten"), that is, upward, as truth is presented in John's Gospel.

In contrast, the second fugue is based entirely on downward motion, basically a circle-of-fifths pattern in which the descending fifths are filled in by thirds. This means that at many points in the movement one part, usually the lowest, outlines a long sequence of falling thirds, again a foreshadowing of the overall tonal design of the cantata. Since Bach uses this pattern to set Jesus's reference to the Spirit's speaking not of himself but of what he *hears*—"Denn er wird nicht von ihm selber reden, sondern was er hören wird das wird er reden"—it suggests that the Spirit will communicate from the world "above" to that "below." As the movement goes on, the descending lines become more prominent, while the tonality moves to B minor, in which it closes.

The third fugue, based on the first, now has the task of linking the upward motion associated with the truth of the world "above" with the downward one of the Spirit's communicating it to the faithful (ex. 10.7).Bach begins with alto and tenor and expands outward, as if indicating that the voice of the Spirit comes from within, and he introduces the major seventh immediately, from the first entry, widening the distance between entries of the theme in relation to those of the first section. As soon as all four voices have completed their entries, he moves to the dominant, and from that point he brings in the theme in successive entries, beginning from the bass up and now overlapped so as to enter one measure apart. These he transposes upward by fifths: the progressively sharpening sequence of rising major sev-

EXAMPLE 10.7 **Cantata 108, *Es ist euch gut, daß ich hingehe*** *no. 4, chorus, Wenn aber jener," mm. 30–44*

EXAMPLE 10.7 (*continued*)

enths (A–g♯, e–d♯′, b–a♯′, and f♯′–e♯″) produce a tremendous allegory of the world above as the meaning behind "und was zukünftig ist." (See mm. 30–43 of ex. 10.7)

A characteristic of the theme that Bach emphasizes more here than in the first fugue is that each time, after the rising-seventh leap (on "und was zukünftig ist") the melodic line resolves both the raised pitch and the upward motion by moving downward, cancelling the sharpened pitches as it does ("wird er verkündigen"). This is surely an allegory of the initial upward nature of the realm of truth above followed by the Spirit's communication of that truth to the world below. The tonality does not articulate full-fledged modulation through the keys represented by these entries, though very briefly it does suggest f♯; instead, it reverses, though not systematically, returning, mostly via the circle of fifths, to D a few measures later. At this point Bach passes a one-measure sequence downward by step through what is essentially a four-measure circle of fifths, reiterating the line "und was zukünftig ist, wird er verkündigen." In the melodic idea itself a rising scalar fourth suggests the sphere above for "was zukünftig ist" and the downward transposition that below for "wird er verkündigen." A single entry of the fugue theme in the soprano, beginning from the a′–g♯″ seventh (its highest pitch) closes the movement, giving the final association of the rising seventh with "und was zukünftig ist," whereas the descending motion to the tonic, canceling, of course, the g♯″, aligns with "wird er verkündigen."

I have described this magnificent movement in detail because the theological idea on which it is based is fundamental to the spring 1725 cantata sequence: in John's terms the "future" that the Spirit will reveal to the disciples (and the community) is the manifestation of truth from the world above to that below, which Bach's tonal design for the cantata as a whole mirrors in its descent by thirds from A to b. In this chorus the falling thirds of the middle section of the second motto and its B minor tonality anticipate the shift to b for the next two movements. In contrast to the rising pattern of Cantata 104 (see ch. 9), the B-minor ending of Cantata 108 is concerned not now with the foretaste of eternal life but with articulating the role of the Spirit in directing the path of the faithful on earth. The theology is not different, but the affective emphasis is. The second aria makes that clear in its emphasizing not the believer's longing for the "Weg" to end, but her readiness to be led by the Spirit: "Führe mich auf deinen Wegen, daß ich in der Ewigkeit schaue deine Herrlichkeit!" (Lead me along your paths, so that in eternity I look upon your glory). And the final chorale is entirely concerned with the Spirit on earth. In this context, the second aria is a very subtle and carefully crafted expression of hope and longing intermingled with a degree of tentativeness: "Was mein Herz dir begehrt, ach, das wird mir wohl gewährt" (What my heart desires from you, ah, that will surely be granted to me). In this respect the affect seems to carry forward from the "Ach, ist er nicht schon da" of the first recitative. After the second *dictum*, the believer grapples once again with uncertainty regarding the presence of the Spirit, now with increasing hope and confidence.

Bach begins the ritornello with a series of five short units in the strings and *continuo*, each five eighth notes in length, separated by an eighth-note rest from the others, and cadencing to dominant, tonic, dominant, subdominant, dominant in turn. Each unit begins with an upbeat of three eighth notes, all units except the third ending with an appoggiatura on the downbeat and no continuation. Bach varies the melodic patterns of the units, the first leaping up to the appoggiatura, the second rising to it by scalar motion, the third moving downward, the fourth leaping downward, then upward and the fifth moving down the scale then leaping up to the cadence. The effect is that of entreaty and hesitancy in the contradictory directions, but one that as a whole gradually works its way up the scale, despite many downward gestures that suggest slipping back, until the fifth unit reaches the peak, an appoggiatura (b″/a♯″) settling on the dominant. And following that gesture, Bach changes the figuration entirely: now we hear a descending first violin line accompanied by a descending scalar bass line against which the second violin and viola hold the pitch b′ (which is also reiterated in the first violin as an alternating "pedal" tone to the descending scale). As it cadences in b, we finally hear the appoggiatura resolve to the tonic in the lower register (a♯′/b′).

In contrast to the halting character of the five units, the latter part of the ritornello is entirely consistent in rhythm and melodic direction. It is as if the initial uncertainty in the appeal to God is answered in the descent with which the ritornello ends. Bach uses these contrasted ideas to project a sense of the believer's increasing confidence throughout the aria. He limits the brief opening vocal section of the aria (mm. 8–20) to permutations and variations of the short units, setting the first two lines of the text—the believer's tentative "Was mein Herz dir begehrt, das wird mir wohl gewährt"—twice before cadencing in D first with the voice, then with an abbreviated version of the ritornello. Only the latter cadences depart from the patterns of the units, becoming more elaborate and hopeful in character. After that, the remainder of the aria consists of two sections, each setting the believer's hopeful prayer: "Überschütte mich mit Segen, führe mich auf deinen Wegen, daβ ich in der Ewigkeit schaue deine Herrlichkeit" (Cover me with blessings, lead me along your paths, so that in eternity I see your glory). The first of these sections closes in f♯ (m. 28 for voice and continuo, m. 31 for strings and continuo). In this segment Bach departs more noticeably from the short patterns of the units, leading the voice and *basso continuo* to a florid cadence on "schaue deine Herrlichkeit," after which the instruments confirm the cadence with a variant of the closing part of the ritornello. The sense that the soloist/believer has gained confidence is a palpable one.

Then, for the third and longest of the three sections, which returns to b (with the same text as the second section), Bach begins with a variant of the second section, but now, however, assigns the vocal soloist long sixteenth-note roulades (mm. 31–39). As the text reaches "daβ ich in der Ewigkeit" (the beginning of ex. 10.8), Bach brings in the beginning of the ritornello (the melody of the first three units, now with the second and third units compressed into one). This leads to a tonic cadence on "schaue deine Herrlichkeit" (m. 39). At this point a statement of the ritornello would give satisfactory closure to the movement. And, indeed, the instruments do return with the remaining fourth and fifth units, following them by the closing segment of the ritornello, now in b. Along with them, however, the voice continues with the text of the prayer once again, now with a rising scalar sequence that works its way up to the point where the final long descent of the first violin begins (mm. 39–41). Against the descent the voice holds the b′ for "daß ich in der Ewigkeit," after which the instruments move to the ritornello cadence (m. 44), as in m. 8. After the entreating, tentatively ascending character of the short units, the descending violin line seems to depict response from above, while the held tone suggests the believer's *holding on* in faith through the course of present life. Again, the movement might well have ended with a reprise of the ritornello here (m. 44). But Bach has another surprise in store: instead of cadencing at the end of the ritornello along with the instruments, the voice continues through the cadence, with punctuation from the instrumental appoggiatura figures at first, then with *basso continuo* only, drawing out the word "schaue" ("deine Herrlichkeit") in a very purposeful rising line that leads to another cadence, two-and-a-half measures later. Throughout the concluding vocal segment, as presented in example 10.8, the believer's state of mind is projected increasingly by the ascending lines (anticipating the seeing of Jesus in eternity), complemented by the descending line of the second part of the ritornello, which now returns in its entirety to end the movement.

This movement is a remarkable depiction of the believer's longing to see Jesus, as described earlier, and the increasing confidence that comes as the result of his experience of the Spirit. At the close of the aria Bach projects the sense of joy that surrounds the believer's anticipating seeing Jesus, once again in an eschatological context. In the context of all I have said to this point regarding the overall tonal design of the cantata, the return to b after the positive-sounding D of the opening section and Bach's ending the cantata in b, can be considered to indicate acceptance of God's will in the present life in the hope of the future fulfillment. The text of the second and third sections of the aria takes up the believer's prayer for God

EXAMPLE 10.8 **Cantata 108, *Es ist euch gut, daß ich hingehe*** *no. 5, aria "Was mein Herz von dir begehrt," mm. 35–47*

EXAMPLE 10.8 (*continued*)

to lead her along his path, which culminates, of course, in eternity, but which is, while it lasts, that of the Holy Spirit on earth.

The device of suddenly reducing the texture just before a cadence (which normally should have the full weight of the ensemble) is one that Bach uses elsewhere to suggest the intimacy of personal contact with God, especially of an eschatological nature. We may be reminded of the soprano solo that ends the central fugal movement of the *Actus Tragicus*.[23] If, as it seems, the hesitant character of the fragmented first half of the ritornello, and those parts of the aria that are based on it, are related to the believer's uncertainty regarding the presence of the Spirit, as voiced earlier in the lone recitative, then the ending might be considered to depict God's coming to him through faith and the Spirit. The effect of the reprise and the delaying of the ending in this case is to suggest waiting for the end, making a point out of the time on earth when the Spirit will direct the path of the faithful.

That directing is the subject matter of the final chorale, every phrase of which features a walking bass:

Dein Geist, den Gott vom Himmel gibt,	Your Spirit, which God gives from Heaven,
Der leitet alles, was ihn liebt,	Directs all who love him,
Auf wohl gabähntem Wege.	On a well-laid-out path.
Er setzt und richtet unsren Fuß,	He places and directs our feet,
Daß er nicht anders treten muß,	So that they may tread nowhere
Als wo man findt den Segen.	But where blessing is found

In taking over the "Wege[n]"/"Segen" rhyme of this chorale for the second aria, Mariane von Ziegler made the chorale's introduction of the Holy Spirit into a re-

[23] Another instance is the ending of Cantata 35, for obbligato organ, strings and soprano with *basso continuo*. In that work the soprano solo trails off before the end and the organ enters to complete its line, an allegory of the believer's giving himself/herself into God's hands, an effect that relates conceptually to the soprano solo in the *Actus Tragicus*, whose ending on the dominant of B-flat minor is answered by the rising B-flat minor scale of the next movement "In deine Hände befehl' ich meinen Geist."

sponse to the tentative character of the believer's expressions of longing in the aria. It may be significant, therefore, that the chorale melody is the same one that was "hidden" in Cantata 42 (see ex. 9.8b, ch. 9), and in the same key. There the text was a response to the persecution of the faithful in the world; now what emerges is God's solution, the Holy Spirit. As a whole, this cantata moves from Jesus's announcement of his departure and the coming of the Spirit to an exploration of what this means for the believer. In its relationship to Cantata 103—primarily, its directing the future-eschatological perspective of that cantata to the present—we perhaps have an echo of what Martin Moller meant by naming Jubilate and Cantate a "single eight-day feast."

Bisher habt ihr nichts gebeten in meinem Namen (BWV 87)

The third Ziegler cantata, which directly precedes Ascension Day, *Bisher habt ihr nichts gebeten in meinem Namen*, for Rogation Sunday (Rogate), takes up the theme that dominates not only that Sunday but also the three "rogation days" that come between it and Ascension Day: prayer.[24] Although Cantata 87 does not directly anticipate the coming of the Holy Spirit, as does its predecessor, prayer is in fact one of the principal means by which the Spirit directs the faithful on earth. The final aria and chorale of Cantata 183 (heard one week later, on the Sunday after Ascension Day) bring this out directly. In its original context, therefore, the *dictum* that begins Cantata 87 continues the preparation of the disciples for the time after Jesus's departure.

Cantata 87, like Cantata 108, is one of four consecutive Ziegler cantatas (the second) for occasions on which the cantata heard the preceding year had been newly composed. Except for the cantatas for Ascension Day, all those works (for both years) draw on mottoes from John, in most cases ones that are closely related or even identical (the motto that begins the two Cantatas for Exaudi). Usually, however, the texts explore aspects not taken up in the other year. In the case of Cantata 87, Mariane von Ziegler's text takes up another side of the message of prayer from that of Cantata 86 of the preceding year. The anonymous text of the earlier cantata had taken as its opening motto Jesus's words to the disciples on the power of prayer: *Wahrlich, wahrlich, ich sage euch, so ihr den Vater etwas bitten werdet in meinem Namen, so wird er's euch geben* (Truly, truly I say unto you, if you ask the Father for something in my name, he will give it unto you). And the remainder of the work had emphasized both the psychological benefit of this message for the believer and the certainty of God's response, which was given particular focus in

---

[24] In Lutheran theological treatises of the seventeenth and eighteenth centuries this Sunday was often called "Vocem jucunditatis" rather than "Rogate," following the custom of naming the Sunday after the Introit at Mass ("Vocem jucunditatis annuntiate, et audiatur, alleluia . . . "); on this Sunday, exceptionally, the more familiar designation, "Rogate" (pray), refers to the Gospel for the day (Jn 16:23–30). Martin Moller and Heinrich Müller, for example, use the "Vocem jucunditatis" designation.

the aria "Gott hilft gewiß." In contrast, Cantata 87 begins with the negative pronouncement, "Bisher habt ihr nichts gebeten in meinem Namen" (Up to now you have asked for nothing in my name), and the work as a whole projects a far more complex theological character than its predecessor. Its "goal," expressed in the final aria ("Ich will leiden, ich will schweigen"—I will suffer, I will be silent) and chorale ("Muß ich sein betrübet?"—Must I be troubled?), is the willing acceptance of suffering that complements the message of sorrow turned to joy in Cantata 103. That quality enables Cantata 87 to end not merely with the idea that joy will follow sorrow, as in Cantata 103, but that sorrow will *itself* be turned into joy: "So mich Jesus liebet, ist mir aller Schmerz über Honig süße, tausend Zuckerküsse drücket er ans Herz. Wenn die Pein sich stellet ein, seine Liebe macht zur Freuden auch das bittre Leiden" (If Jesus loves me, all my pain is sweeter than honey; a thousand sugar kisses he presses to my heart. When pain comes his love makes even bitter suffering into joy). The theological idea that enables this change, so that pain can become "sweet," is, of course, love, which John emphasizes like no other of the evangelists, and which Mariane von Ziegler adds to the text of Cantata 87 in her choice of chorale.

In Cantata 87 the progression from the negative tone of the opening motto to the positive one of the final chorale pivots on Ziegler's introduction of a second motto from John at approximately the midpoint of the work. That motto, "In der Welt habt ihr Angst; aber sei getrost, ich habe die Welt überwunden" is not, strictly speaking, drawn from the Gospel for the day (Jn 16:23–30), but follows two verses later, ending the Farewell Discourse proper and ushering in the chapter in which Jesus names his "hour" as having come and prays to the Father for his glorification. In this respect, the verse is especially appropriate for the Sunday before Ascension Day and its theme of prayer. In the context of the cantata as a whole the negative pronouncement of the beginning motto has the purpose of bringing about the believer's acknowledgment of guilt, leading to the *Gewissensangst* (qualms of conscience) with which the second motto begins; after that the change of tone in the second motto brings about the positive other side of the acknowledgment of sin, consolation for the troubled conscience, as Luther described it in his *Sermon on the Meditation of Christ's Passion* (1519) and other writings.

Whereas Ziegler's published text comprises a six-movement sequence, the text as set by Bach has *seven* movements, since it features a recitative that is missing from Ziegler's printed text of three years later and might have originated with Bach himself.[25] That recitative is the third movement of the text as Bach set it; it therefore directly precedes the pivotal second motto, which it prepares. At the same

[25] This is Alfred Dürr's conclusion (see *Cantatas*, 323). We do not know the exact version of Ziegler's texts from which Bach worked and hence do not know the extent to which Ziegler herself might have reworked her texts between their composition in 1725 and their publication in 1728. It is conceivable, of course, that this addition came from neither Bach nor Ziegler, but from someone in higher authority over the theological content of the cantata texts. See Neumann, *Sämtliche von Johann Sebastian Bach vertonte Texte*, 359–65. Mark Peters (*A Woman's Voice in Baroque Music*) takes the view that virtually all changes are Ziegler's.

time, it echoes the theme of the preceding aria, a prayer for God's forgiveness on the basis of the believer's acknowledgment of guilt: "Vergib, o Vater! unsre Schuld"—Forgive, O Father, our guilt). The aria in question also includes the believer's request that God no longer "speak in proverbs" ("Ach rede nicht mehr sprüchwortsweis"), an allusion to qualities in Jesus's discourses that are familiar to students of John's literary style: indirect speech, antithesis, double and hidden meanings, contradiction, and the like, all of which lead to misunderstanding on the part of the listeners, and consequently prompt further discourse from Jesus.

The aria just described and the "extra" recitative introduce virtually the only references to human guilt in the entire series of cantatas for this time period. Its presence may even seem out of place after the introduction of the Holy Spirit in Cantata 108. But, in fact, it follows very logically within Luther's thought. As Regin Prenter explains, the work of human guilt and inner conflict is the very "background" on which Luther "proclaims the work of the Holy Spirit" as interceding through prayer and "as the source of the true love to God."[26] Ending with a prayer for *Trost*, the recitative that sets the extra lines—"Wenn unsre Schuld bis an den Himmel steigt, du siehst und kennest ja mein Herz, das nichts vor dir verschweigt; drum suche mich zu trösten" (When our guilt ascends even up to heaven, you see and know my heart, which conceals nothing from you; therefore endeavor to comfort me)—bridges between the first aria and the second motto. Together, these two movements articulate the turning point to the abovementioned transformation of suffering to joy and affirmation of love with which the cantata ends. It is significant, therefore, that the recitative introduces the theme of silence that reappears in the second aria, "Ich will leiden, ich will *schweigen*." Taken in conjunction with the exhortation to pray in the first recitative, the sequence identifies prayer with the acknowledgment of sin, making the point that personal contact with God through prayer enables the individual to remain silent in the face of worldly tribulation.

The second motto, entering with the message of *Trost* as the result of Jesus's overcoming the world,provides a positive framework, which overcomes the negative beginning. Its meaning is not immediately connected with the theme of Rogate but echoes the dualism of the suffering world and Jesus's victory that underlies the aria "Es ist vollbracht" of the *St. John Passion* (as well as the proclamation that faith is the victory that overcomes the world in the epistle for Quasimodogeniti). It is itself echoed in the opening chorus of the next cantata of the series, Cantata 128, which speaks of the *believer's* overcoming the pain and anxiety of the world. Cantata 87 makes the point that the world that rejoices over the disciples' sorrow in Cantata 103 is overcome through faith and prayer. In relation to the turning point in Cantata 103, which began "Du wirst mich nach der Angst auch wiederum erquicken" and ended with the believer's trust in Jesus's promise that sorrow would be turned to joy, that of Cantata 87 places greater emphasis on the *present* benefit of Jesus's victory. The second motto initiates a progression over the last three move-

[26] Prenter, *Spiritus Creator*, 16–17.

ments of Cantata 87, from guilt and *Angst* to Jesus's *Trost* as the source of the individual's ability to accept suffering in silence (the fifth movement, "Ich will leiden, ich will schweigen") and, finally, to the transformed view of suffering that Jesus's love brings about (the final chorale). In this sense victory over the world can be thought of in terms of an upward progression from *Trost* to love and joy, a progression we have already seen in Cantata 249. Cantata 87 therefore serves to complete a subgroup comprising the first three Ziegler cantatas, all of which deal with the understanding of suffering within the context of Jesus's victory and love, increasingly articulating how the tribulation of the world is overcome; it prepares for Ascension Day as well as introducing the theme of love that will be especially prominent at Pentecost.

Until the "extra" recitative, Cantata 87 speaks collectively to the disciples (the opening motto) and their modern counterpart, the community of believers: the "ihr" of the opening motto becomes "Ihr Menschen" in the first recitative; the first aria retains this collective aspect ("*unsre* Schuld," "wenn *wir* in Andacht beten," "hilf *uns* vielmehr vertreten!"), and the added recitative begins with the plural: "*unsre* Schuld." Within that recitative, however, a change to the first-person singular enters with the reference to God's seeing into the heart ("du siehst und kennest ja *mein* Herz") and leads to the prayer for *Trost* ("drum suche *mich* zu trösten"), thereby lending the "ihr" of the second motto a personal cast, which remains (along with the first-person singular) throughout the rest of the cantata.

Most remarkable of all, perhaps, is the fact that from this point on *in the entire cantata sequence* every single cantata centers on the individual believer (represented by the first-person singular) and his or her relationship with Jesus. *Bleib bei uns* and *Am Abend aber desselbigen Sabbats* are completely collective, a feature owing in part to their association with the disciples as a group and in part to the doctrinal tone of their texts; *Ich bin ein guter Hirt* wavers between third and first person, and *Ihr werdet weinen und Heulen* shifts from first-person plural to singular in its third movement. After that, *Es ist euch gut, daß ich hingehe* features the first person exclusively; the reason is not difficult to determine: this is the first cantata in the sequence to introduce the Holy Spirit. That *Bisher habt ihr nichts gebeten in meinem Namen* brings back the collective emphasis at the start then shifts to first-person singular is owing, of course, to the personal nature of prayer. The echoing of its turning point (especially the verb *überwinden* of the second motto) in the first movement of Cantata 128, in the first person ("Auf Christi Himmelfahrt allein ich meine Nachfahrt gründe und allen Zweifel, Angst und Pein hiermit stets überwinde") marks a turning point in the sequence as a whole, since after Jesus's ascension the believer's contact with God will be through prayer and the Holy Spirit—that is, an internal experience.

The impact of the turning point in Cantata 87 can be truly understood only from Bach's setting, which realizes the change in a very convincing manner. The obvious suitability of textual features of certain kinds, such as turning points, to musical designs of a kind that had figured prominently in Bach's work long before his collaboration with Ziegler raises, in fact, the more general question of Bach's input into Ziegler's texts. Although it cannot be definitively answered, we may note that the instance described is not an isolated one. Cantata 128 also contains lines that do not appear in Ziegler's print at the end of its "central" recitative (see p. 478). And Ziegler or Bach supplied a brief paraphrase from John's Gospel for the day in question (Trinity Sunday) at the end of the recitative fourth movement of Cantata 176, setting it in a protracted bass arioso style that, as Dürr points out, is longer than the remainder of the recitative as a whole. Cantata 176 would otherwise have had no *dictum* from John.[27]

After the essentially positive foretelling of the coming of the Holy Spirit to direct the faithful on earth in Cantata 108, Cantata 87 offers a characterization of the world whose first half is once again tinged with pejoratives. For that characterization Bach introduced the key of C minor once again, this time not as the "tonic" key of the cantata but as the tonal nadir and turning point in a D-minor structure, whose straightforward descent/ascent tonal design (d–g–g–c–c–B♭–d) mirrors the two stage process of acknowledgment of guilt followed by the overcoming of anxiety through faith in Jesus's victory over the world.

The opening motto, set as an arioso scored for bass solo and strings doubled by oboes (including oboe da caccia), is based on a theme formed from a rising minor sixth (set always to the word "bisher," but suggesting entreaty) followed by further ascent by decorated stepwise motion to the tone an octave above the starting pitch, the tonic, d, where it cadences conspicuously, on "Namen." The initial rising sixth recalls that of nearly every movement of Cantata 108. Here its continuation with rising motion to the tonic is an indication of the essentially positive context of what seems negative at first. In the introductory ritornello entries of this theme in tonic and dominant suggest a process of attainment that the cadential element seems to symbolize. After reaching the dominant in mm. 5–6, the midpoint of the ritornello, the cadential element of the theme ushers in a falling-third harmonic pattern (a–F–d–B♭–g), which leads to the d cadence of m. 12. Since two successive entries on tonic and dominant describe what is essentially a continuing ascent in the melodic line, the ritornello outlines a curve upwards and back down. And this "shape" is retained in the movement as a whole, culminating in a dominant cadence in m. 25, at which point Bach leads the cadential element of the theme immediately to C, and begins a sequential third descent of the cadential element of the theme, once per measure (C–a–F–d–B♭–g) that ushers in the final cadence. The sustained harmonic descent perhaps represents the humility of "[ge]beten," which is drawn out in a melisma of more than four measures. This gesture and the addition of words to what is essentially a reprise of the initial instrumental ritornello,

[27] Dürr, *Cantatas*, 377. Dürr attributes the extra lines to Bach. See the discussion of Bach's insertion on p. 478. Perhaps Ziegler later removed passages from her 1725 texts that seemed to her (for whatever reason) unrepresentative of her own poetic conceptions. That she originally produced them (which is the most likely scenario) can be viewed as a facet of their fulfilling the theological needs of the cantatas in question and, in that sense, owing in part to Bach.

suggest that prayer, which the cantata for the following Sunday tells us is taught by the Holy Spirit, brings confidence as in Jesus's words of promise and hope to the disciples in the Gospel for the day.

Cantata 87 is a work in which the directional qualities of harmony and tonality are utilized extensively in interpretation of similar qualities in the text. The first recitative outlines a pronounced circle-of-fifths descent extending from the dominant of a to the subdominant and Neapolitan harmonies of g, the key of its final cadence, in conjunction with the need of a transgressing humanity for God's forgiveness. The downward motion, as in the movement keys of the preceding cantata, is associated with the acknowledgment of sin through prayer, the work of the Holy Spirit, although it is not named as such in Cantata 87. As the concluding line of the recitative makes clear, the only means by which humanity can receive forgiveness for having transgressed against law and Gospel is to pray in "Buss' und Andacht."

After this, the first aria, "Vergib, o Vater! unsre Schuld," in g, for alto and a pair of oboes da caccia with *basso continuo*, is an extraordinary expression of penitance, its ascending arpeggio figures in the *basso continuo* and slurred descending duplets in the voice and oboes da caccia suggesting gestures of entreaty and torment simultaneously. The believer petitions God for forgiveness in a manner reminiscent of the Lord's Prayer; the cry for God to have patience suggests that the believer has not truly learned to pray, and this along with the addition, in the middle section, of the line "ach, rede nicht mehr sprüchwortsweise, hilf uns vielmehr vertreten" (Ah, speak no more in proverbs, help us rather by interceding) is indeed suggestive of the passages of scripture that most defined for Luther the role of the Holy Spirit in teaching prayer, Romans 8:26: "Likewise the Spirit also helpeth our infirmities: for we know not what we should pray for as we ought: but the Spirit itself maketh intercession for us with groanings which cannot be uttered" (and the surrounding verses). Together the rising bass figures and sigh figures in the oboes da caccia invite interpretation as the "groanings that cannot be uttered" (*unaussprechliche Seufzen*). The verb "vertreten" is the one Luther uses to translate Paul's speaking of the Spirit's interceding for the faithful with "unaussprechliche Seuffzen." At the beginning of the middle section Bach passes the bass figure of supplication up the scale from D to A, first chromatically then diatonically (D–E♮–F–F♯–G–G♯–A, then D–E–F–G–A) as the tormented believer cries for God to "speak in proverbs" no longer but to help the faithful advance their cause ("Ach rede nicht mehr sprüchwortsweis, hilf uns vielmehr vertreten!"). In the Gospel, Jesus promises the disciples a time when he will speak no longer in proverbs but will speak plainly, on which day the disciples will ask in Jesus's name and Jesus will no longer have to intercede. The merging of this passage with Romans 8 therefore reflects the running theme of the season of how the disciples will function, sustained by prayer and the Holy Spirit, in a hostile world after Jesus's absence.

Between this movement and the second Johannine motto appears the recitative that is not contained in Ziegler's printed text. Within the design of the cantata as a whole it fulfills a culminating role. At two levels—melodic and tonal—it summarizes the meaning of the sequence of events that lead to the second motto as a downward motion, the direction of penitence. The ordering of its keys in yet another descent pattern (d, g, and c) recapitulates the keys of the first three movements of the cantata, as its overall harmonic progression mirrors that of the first recitative, now a fifth flatter. At the same time, the first violin line, from the b♭″ of its first phrase to its final tone, c′, delineates a descent of nearly two octaves (ex. 10.9). The turn to c that comes at its midpoint for "drum suche mich zu trösten" introduces both the turning point to the first-person singular in the text of the cantata and a series of expressive harmonic and melodic gestures (including an even more pronounced Neapolitan harmonic coloring than that on "Buss" in the first recitative) that link the turn to c with the sphere of tormented, pathetic affections that characterize the world.

After this movement, the second bass motto, a C-minor aria with quasi-ostinato bass in $\frac{3}{8}$ meter, represents with its low pitch, its suggestions of the descending chromatic tetrachord in the *basso continuo* pattern, and the melodic character of its two principal lines, both the angst-ridden "fallen" nature of the world and the means by which it is overcome (ex. 10.10).[28] When Bach shifts to E♭ at "aber seid getrost," the sense of a turning point is unmistakable, even though it lasts only nine measures, after which the C-minor music returns.[29]

At this point, the key of c represents the world as a place of tribulation, in which the brief E♭passage indicates the hopeful message of *Trost*. The B♭ Siciliano aria that follows, "Ich will leiden, ich will schweigen," then voices the silent acceptance of suffering as the key to overcoming the world, its major key continuing from the E♭ of the preceding motto. Nevertheless, in its initial rising minor-seventh interval, slow tempo, and hints of minor (including scale segments with the augmented seconds characteristic of the harmonic minor scale), this aria is an extraordinary expression of entreaty (somewhat like that of "Erbarme dich" from the *St. Matthew Passion*) and hope simultaneously. In this solo suffering and consolation go together, and the major key does not dissipate the believer's acceptance of suffering. Bach ends the two principal subdivisions of the middle section of the aria with minor/major juxtapositions. First he inflects the modulation to the dominant (F) with the dominant minor (f), marking a change in dynamics (*piano* to *forte*) for

---

[28] The pattern of the main *basso continuo* melody outlines a descent from g through f♯–f–e–and e♭, while the reiterated figure of mm. 2 and 4 suggests upward striving and falling by turns. Bach sets the word *Angst* with descending chromaticism (e.g., mm. 11–12, 17–18), slurred duplets reminiscent of the first aria (e.g., mm. 17, 22, 27), and a rising line featuring an augmented second (mm. 32–33).

[29] As a parallel instance, in the C-minor solo, "Ach Herr, lehre uns bedenken, dass wir sterben müssen, auf dass wir klug werden" from the *Actus Tragicus*, a ground bass of downward character sounds for the entire movement except for the line "auf dass wir klug werden," which shifts briefly, but very significantly, to E♭, abandoning the ground bass, after which, however, both the ground bass and C-minor tonality return. As in "In der Welt ihr habe Angst," the sense is that the C minor depicts the world and the inevitability of death, while the shift to the relative major signifies the "wisdom" of faith.

EXAMPLE 10.9 **Cantata 87, *Bisher habt ihr nicht gebeten in meinem Namen*** *no. 4, recitative*

EXAMPLE 10.10 **Cantata 87, *Bisher habt ihr nicht gebeten in meinem Namen*** *no. 5, aria "In der Welt habt ihr Angst," beginning*

the subsequent return to F; the text reads "denn er tröst"t mich nach dem Schmerz" (for he comforts me after my pain), virtually paraphrasing the motto of the preceding movement. Then, for the final return to the tonic Bach makes a comparable b♭/B♭ change for "warum sollt' ich verzagen? [b♭] fasse dich, betrübtes Herz! [B♭]" (Why should I despair?/Take hold of yourself, troubled heart!). The final chorale, a verse of "Jesu, meine Freude," in d, begins by echoing the last line of the aria "Muss ich sein betrübet?" after which the remaining chorale lines describe the transformation of sorrow itself into joy through Jesus's love.

In this cantata the world of *Angst* is overcome by means of the Lutheran descent/ascent shape of faith, tribulation, and acknowledgment of sin through prayer (the aria "Vergib, o Vater! unsre Schuld" and the prayer for *Trost* that concludes the extra recitative), acceptance of the message of Jesus's resurrection (the second Johannine motto), and the willing acceptance of suffering through God's love ("Ich will leiden, ich will schweigen" and the final chorale). In the added recitative the line "Du siehst und kennest ja mein Herz, das nichts vor dir *verschweigt*" seems to anticipate "Ich will leiden, ich will *schweigen*," making the point that for the one who prays God knows all that cannot be expressed so that the believer can endure worldly tribulation in silence. Prayer, as Bach's design represents it, is an act of true humility before God, an act that acknowledges human sinfulness and hopes for restoration of the soul on the basis of God's mercy. The "descent" to C minor that coincides with the motto that typified John's value for Luther, and that is anticipated in the "extra" recitative, represents the depth of the human need for contact with God, its principal link to the c of *Bleib bei uns* and *Ich bin ein guter Hirt* (and eventually to the c of *Es ist ein trotzig und verzagt Ding* as well).

Cantata 87 typifies the reception of John's Gospel by the Lutheranism of Bach's time. The text of the final chorale, set to the melody of "Jesu, meine Freude," invokes all the qualities of Jesus-love that became prominent among seventeenth-century authors such as Valerius Herberger and Heinrich Müller.[30] Nevertheless, Bach's design is dominated by its recognition of the intensity of prayer arising out of the sinful human condition. The message of the minor-key descent that leads to the central Johannine motto is not overcome by the brief shift to E♭ that occurs within it or even by the turn to major in "Ich will leiden" and the return to the original key of the cantata at the end. The final d is a reminder of the necessity of suffering in the world and the divine love that ultimately overcomes it. In contrast to Cantata 86 of the preceding year (an E-major cantata that emphasizes the certainty of God's promise, and contains only a single minor-key movement that is, in fact, very optimistic in character), *Bisher habt ihr nichts gebeten in meinem Namen*, at least in its musical design, does not allow the reality of worldly tribulation to dissipate. Exactly what Bach intended by setting the work in d—a contrast to the D major of several earlier cantatas in the series, for example—may not be fully ascertainable, but the descent to and return from c, representing the "directions" associated with the world and its overcoming, is a very palpable underlying shape.

Auf Christi Himmelfahrt allein (BWV 128)

The second *dictum* of Cantata 87, with its theme of Jesus's victory over the world and its benefit for humanity (*Trost*), concludes the Farewell Discourse proper (Jn 16), after which Jesus turns to the theme of his glorification, which in the context of the liturgy can be understood as an anticipation of Ascension Day, four days later. Since John has no narrative of the ascension per se, Mariane von Ziegler would have had to turn to one of the Synoptic Gospels for a beginning motto. Instead, she chose a chorale verse whose initial lines express how Jesus's ascension becomes the foundation for individual human hopes for heaven "Auf Christi Himmelfahrt allein ich meine Nachfahrt gründe" (On Christ's ascension alone do I base my journey hence), while the lines that directly follow—"Und allen Zweifel, Angst und Pein hiermit stets überwinde" (and all doubt, anxiety, and pain thereby continually overcome) link up, through the imagery of a world of *Angst* and the verb *überwinden*, with the pivotal second *dictum* of Cantata 87. After the transformation of suffering into joy at the end of Cantata 87, the believer now "overcomes" the world. As mentioned earlier, many Lutheran commentaries retained the an-

[30] As Elke Axmacher points out with regard to the *St. Matthew Passion*, (*Aus Liebe*, 178–79), the prominence of love in the devotional texts of Bach's time and surroundings brought about a lessening of the reality of suffering, which could be described, as it is at the end of Cantata 87, as "sweet."

cient threefold interpretation of Easter, Ascension Day, and Pentecost as celebrating three aspects of Jesus's work, as "Überwinder" "Durchbrecher," and giver of life to the faithful through the word, the sacraments and the Holy Spirit (*Tröster*).[31] The remaining lines of the chorale represent the divine/human relationship in terms of the image of a body (the church, described traditionally as the body of Christ) whose "Haupt," Jesus, is in heaven, while its "Glieder" (members), still on earth, will be summoned above "at the right time": "Denn weil das Haupt im Himmel ist, wird seine Glieder Jesus Christ zu rechter Zeit nachholen" (For since the head is in heaven, Jesus Christ will fetch up the members at the right time).[32] The idea that the "member" of Christ lives in certainty of his or her future "Nachfahrt," despite living in a world of "Zweifel, Angst, und Pein," and the vertical element projected in the central *Haupt/Glieder* image both lend the eschatological perspective of this cantata a Johannine dimension (even though the Gospel for the day was *not* drawn from John). This clear sense of simultaneously existing worlds above and below colors the meaning of the whole.

The first recitative of *Auf Christi Himmelfahrt allein* carries forward the juxtaposition of worldly *Angst* and triumph over the world from Cantata 87: "Hier in der Welt ist [nichts als] Jammer, Angst und Pein; hingegen dort in Salems Zelt werd ich verkläret sein," linking it up with the believer's hopes of seeing God in eternity. This is the fulfillment of the theme of seeing Jesus throughout the post-Easter cantatas: "Da seh' ich Gott von Angesicht zu Angesicht" (There I will see God face to face). In the next two movements, an aria and recitative, Ziegler begins with the image of Jesus seated at the right hand of God and the believer's anticipation of joining him, ending the aria "Wird er mir gleich weggenommen, werd ich doch dahin auch kommen" (If he is taken away from me, I will nevertheless come there also), and beginning the recitative "Mein Auge wird ihn einst in größter Klarheit schauen" (My eye will ultimately see him in great clarity). Then she turns to an expression of longing—"O! könnt ich schon allda mir eine Hütte bauen" (Oh! If only I could already build myself a dwelling place)—but one that must be rejected

---

[31] Good discussions can be found in Pfeiffer, *Evangelischer Schatz-Kammer*, 1:523–27, and Martin Moller, *Praxis Evangeliorum*, 2:258. Pfeiffer also uses the traditional Latin terms for Jesus's three aspects: *mortis triumphatio, coeli referatio,* and *vitae aeterniae donatio* (523–24). For a still more detailed description of Jesus as *Überwinder* and *Durchbrecher* (the latter based, as are all such characterizations, on Micah 2:13), see Valerius Herberger, *Epistolische Herz-Postilla*, 2:46–54.

[32] The *Haupt/Glieder* metaphor is an ancient one that appears frequently in the writings of Bach's time. August Pfeiffer, for example, uses it to characterize the relationship of Jesus and the faithful in connection with both the resurrection and ascension (*Evangelische Schatz-Kammer*, 1:421, 524). The metaphor also figures prominently in Bach's Easter cantata, *Der Himmel lacht! Die Erde jubilieret* (BWV 31) written in Weimar in 1715 to a text of Salomo Franck, and re-performed by Bach in Leipzig in 1724. Its clearest expression comes in the seventh movement of that work, a recitative: "Weil dann das Haupt sein Glied natürlich nach sich zieht, so kann mich nichts von Jesu scheiden." The verb "ziehen" (to draw) is reminiscent of John's frequent references to Jesus's "drawing" the faithful after him, especially through the "lifting up" (glorification) of the crucifixion and resurrection (see, for example, Jn 12:32: "And when I am lifted up from the earth, I shall draw all men to myself"). On the significance of the metaphor, see Dom Gregory Dix, *Shape of the Liturgy*, 340.

since it implies human aspiration to God's sphere, the church as a human institution or edifice rather than the body of Christ, its head. The recitative warns against the individual's anticipation of eternity as a "place" that can be grasped in physical terms: "Wohin? Vergebner Wunsch! Er wohnet nicht auf Berg und Tal, sein Allmacht zeigt sich überall" (Where? Futile wish! he does not dwell on mountain or in valley; his omnipotence can be seen everywhere). Although this passage denies any foundation for human "ascent" other than that supplied by the relationship to Jesus as poeticized in the opening movement, the word "Hütte" (hut) nevertheless foreshadows the message of Pentecost, that God will come to dwell in the human heart. This is described as the "Herzenshütten" in the cantata heard on the first day of Pentecost the year before, *Erschallet, ihr Lieder* (BWV 172), and "die heilgen Hütten" in Bach's later cantata for that day, *O ewiges Feuer, o Ursprung der Liebe* (BWV 34).

In this movement Bach's own conception is strikingly evident. Bach binds Ziegler's aria and recitative into a single movement of highly interesting and unusual form. It seems likely that even if Ziegler's original division of the text were identical to that of Bach's setting, it must have been influenced by the composer. The final two lines, which do not appear in Ziegler's printed text—"So schweig, verwegner Mund, und suche nicht dieselbe zu ergründen!" (So be silent, presumptuous mouth, and do not attempt to fathom this)—bridge, like the extra recitative of Cantata 87, to what in Ziegler's printed text is the next movement, the second aria: "Sein Allmacht zu ergründen, wird sich kein Mensche finden, mein Mund verstummt und schweigt" (To fathom his omnipotence, will no human be capable; my mouth is speechless and silent), which Bach sets as a duet. In Cantata 87 the idea of silence expresses both intimate contact with God (who knows the unspoken heart of the believer) and the patient enduring of worldly tribulation. In Cantata 128 it affirms the distance between God and humankind, echoing the condemnation of basing the hope of salvation on human aspiration and reason.[33]

In both arias the injunctions against attempting to fathom God's glory ("suche nicht dieselbe zu *ergründen*!" and "Sein Allmacht zu *ergründen*, wird sich kein Mensche finden") expand the message of the opening movement: "Auf Christi Himmelfahrt allein ich meine Nachfahrt *gründe*." Both arias take up the image of Jesus seated at the right hand of the Father in heaven, but the latter now describes it as something that the believer sees from a distance ("Ich sehe durch die Sterne, daß er sich schon von ferne zur Rechten Gottes zeigt"—I see through the stars that he, already from far away, reveals himself at the right hand of God), a sign that although the believer's own "ascent" lies in the future, his relationship to Jesus renders it a certainty. Thus Cantata 128 caps a progression throughout the first four

---

[33] The quintessential expression of that quality is the aria "Schweig' nur, taumelnde Vernunft" from Cantata 178; I have taken it up in the context of reason in the Bach cantatas elsewhere (see Chafe, *Tonal Allegory*, 227–39).

EXAMPLE 10.11 **Cantata 128, *Auf Christi Himmelfahrt allein*** *first movement, first phrase of soprano* cantus firmus *(melody of "Allein sei Gott in der Höh' sei Ehr'")*

Ziegler cantatas that increasingly articulates the positive message of overcoming the world.

Bisher habt ihr nichts gebeten in meinem Namen is the only cantata in the spring sequence to seriously address the question of human guilt. After such a complex work, centered on minor keys and a pronounced descent/ascent shape, *Auf Christi Himmelfahrt allein* makes a virtually unqualified assertion of Jesus's majesty. The opening chorus names Jesus's ascension as the sole "foundation" of the believer's hopes for his/her own ascent, a change in tone from Cantata 87 that Bach mirrors with a solid G-major setting–the first cantata wholly in a major key since Easter Day. Moreover, Cantata 128 is relatively short and of circumscribed tonal range, anchored in the tonic key of the framing chorale fantasia and final four-part chorale setting (both with a pair of obbligato horns).[34] In contrast to the descent/ascent shape of Cantata 87, Bach's overall design for *Auf Christi Himmelfahrt allein* is that of an ascent/descent shape through the tones of the tonic triad, leading from the G of the chorale fantasia through b at the close of the first recitative to D for the first aria, then back through b (the second aria) to G (the final chorale). This shape derives directly from the opening movement, whose chorale melody is that of the Trinitarian chorale "Allein Gott in der Höh' sei Ehr'" (ex.10.12), a tune whose beginning (and several later points) outlines the rising major triad. As Alfred Dürr points out, in his setting Bach bases much of the motivic material on this element (ex. 10.11).[35]

The *Haupt*/*Glieder* metaphor of the chorale verse that begins Cantata 128 provided Ziegler with poetic means of overcoming the disparity between the worlds

[34] Cantatas 6, 85, 103, and 87 begin and end in minor keys, whereas Cantatas 42 and 108 begin in major and end in minor. After Ascension Day Cantatas 183, 68 and 176 begin and end in minor, while Cantata 74 begins in major and ends in minor; only Cantata 175, like Cantata 128 in G, begins and ends in major.

[35] Dürr, *Cantatas*, 330.

EXAMPLE 10.12 **Cantata 128, *Auf Christi Himmelfahrt allein*** *first movement, beginning*

"above" and "below" that Jesus's ascension might seem to increase. At the same time, it provided Bach with a conceptual basis for the inseparable bond between keys whose tonic tones were "members" of a single triad, a suggestion of the Trinitarian associations of the major triad in the music treatises of the Lutheran metaphysical tradition. The pejorative characterization of the world set forth in Cantata 87 is now "contained" within the positive context of the ascension. From its initial E minor, the first recitative moves "down" toward A minor ("Hier in der Welt ist Jammer, Angst und Pein"—Here in the world is sorrow, anxiety and pain) then turns back "up" through e to b ("hingegen dort, in Salems Zelt, werd ich verkläret sei"—up there, however, in Salem's courts, I will be transformed), a conceptual link to the overall descent/ascent shape of the cantata, which juxtaposed worldly *Angst* to the benefits of Jesus's overcoming the world. By leading to the third of the G-major triad this gesture now aids in articulating the ascent/descent shape of Cantata 128.

Ziegler's adoption of "structural" or architectural metaphors derived from the "gründe" of the opening chorale serves the purpose of warning against attempting to "build" knowledge of God. This theme comes to a head in the first aria where it is projected by means of the unusual form that Bach created from Ziegler's aria and recitative texts. "Auf, auf mit hellem Schall" is the penultimate D-major trumpet aria in the spring cantatas (the last being the aria "Öffnet euch, ihr beiden Ohren" in Cantata 175, Bach's other G-major cantata). In both instances the arias with D trumpet are strikingly hortatory movements in the dominant in which the brilliant sound, the "heller Schall" of the instrument associated with the *Christus victor* theme predominates (ex. 10.13).

In the version of "Auf, auf mit hellem Schall" set by Bach, an extra line that does not appear in Ziegler's printed version ("wo mein Erlöser lebt") bridges between the final line of the aria text ("ich werd einst dahin kommen"—I will one day come there) and the beginning of the recitative ("Mein Augen werden ihn in größter Klarheit schauen"—my eyes will see him in the greatest clarity). Whether he had any input into the presence of that line, Bach used it to effect a shift of focus within the aria. After the splendid sixty-measure "A" section, the triadic trumpet music virtually dissolves by stages into a recitative for bass and strings: first the trumpet drops out, and the first violin and voice generate scalar ascent figures against the descent sequences of the bass, while the harmony moves first to the dominant of e ("ist er von mir genommen"), then to that of f♯ ("ich werd einst dahin kommen") (ex. 10.14). Now the dynamic changes to *piano*, the time signature to quadruple meter (from $\frac{3}{4}$), and the strings to sustained chordal accompaniment, as the bass

EXAMPLE 10.13 **Cantata 128, *Auf Christi Himmelfahrt allein*** *no. 3, aria, "Auf, auf, mit hellem Schall," beginning*

completes the sentence ("wo mein Erlöser lebt"), moving on to an A-major cadence for "Mein Augen werden ihn in größter Klarheit schauen." After this, however, the believer voices longing to build a dwelling place ("Hütte") in advance, first moving to b, then rejecting such limited conceptions of the deity: "Wohin? Vergebner Wunsch! Er wohnet nicht auf Berg und Tal, sein Allmacht zeigt sich überall: so schweig, verwegner Mund und suche nicht dieselbe zu ergründen" (Where to? Futile wish! he does not dwell on mountain or valley, his omnipotence reveals itself everywhere; so be silent, presumptuous mouth, and do not seek to fathom this thing). This passage as a whole moves in the sharp-minor direction, finally reaching a c♯ harmony on "[Er] wohnet," after which it curves back to end on b ("ergründen") directly before the final ritornello. Throughout the entire passage the upper register of the bass voice recurs regularly, often with an exaggeratedly dramatic quality that points up the state of mind of the believer in opposing his own impulses and nature. Although building a dwelling place looks ahead to God's "indwelling" at Pentecost, there is a crucial difference here, in that the building in question is a reflection of the attempt to comprehend God through reason. In Bach's music we may be reminded of the almost hysterical tenfold iterations of the word "Schweig!" at the beginning of Cantata 189, "Schweig, taumelnde Vernunft," the most dramatic of all Bach's settings of the rejection of reason.[36] In the recitative segment of "Auf, auf mit hellem Schall," the sudden shift of tone, introducing the sharpest harmonies of the cantata, accompanies the "vergeb'ner Wunsch" of aspiration to the sphere of God, at the end of which the register plummets suddenly at the end for "[und suche nicht] dieselbe zu ergründen." The low pitch of the cadence and the return to b suggest a dissipation of the resistant quality as the believer comes to his senses, so to speak.

Overall, the middle section of the aria marks the sharpest, most unstable region of the work, moving outside the framework defined by the *ambitus* of G and D, as if mirroring the out-of-control aspect of the human failure to grasp divine things.

[36] See n. 33.

EXAMPLE 10.14 **Cantata 128, *Auf Christi Himmelfahrt allein*** *no. 3, aria, "Auf, auf, mit hellem Schall," mm. 57–74*

EXAMPLE 10.14 (*continued*)

Thus, after the lines just cited, the D-major ritornello returns, but the aria contains no further text. The triadic trumpet music, now without the voice, makes the point that glory is God's alone, illustrating the line "so schweig', verweg'ner Mund" of the text, and suggesting that, like the hybrid form, it originated with Bach. And the B-minor aria duetto, for alto, tenor, oboe d'amore, and continuo, "Sein Allmacht zu ergründen, wird sich kein Mensche finden," continues this theme, even reflecting back on the "silence" of the voice at the end of the preceding aria ("mein Mund verstummt und schweigt").[37] Its middle section returns to D as it replaces the futility of attempting to fathom God's omnipotence with the image of Jesus in glory ("Ich sehe durch die Sterne, daß er sich schon von ferne zur Rechten Gottes zeigt"—

[37] In the ritornello of this duet Bach projects the quality of balanced phrase designs with complementary and sequential ascent/descent shapes and a rising sequence toward the end that intensifies the approach to the tonic cadence, then dissipates its energy in a descending scale. Along with the two-part imitation at the beginning (four-part imitation after the voices enter) these musical qualities represent the certainty of the dogma behind the text: that humanity cannot seek to fathom the *Allmacht* of God, Luther's famous *dictum* "Let God be God." These very qualities of balance and solidity, perhaps, led Max Reger to choose the ritornello of this duet as the theme of his *Bach Variations for Piano*, op. 81.

I see through the stars, that he shows himself in the distance on the right hand of God). Along with the horns of the opening movement, the return to G for the final chorale, sung to the melody associated with "Was frag' ich nach der Welt," completes the triadic ascent/descent tonal design, reaffirming the foundation of the believer's hopes in Jesus's ascent. Its last lines place the aria/recitative complex of the preceding aria in perspective, echoing the believer's desire to be with God rather than "seeing" him from a distance: "Alsdenn so wirst du mich zu deiner Rechten stellen . . . mich bringen zu der Lust, wo deine Herrlichkeit ich werde schauen an in alle Ewigkeit" (Therefore you will place me at your right hand . . . bring me to joy, where I will look upon your glory for all eternity).

{ 11 }

Instrumental Characteristics

Introduction

Among Bach's vocal works, taken as a whole, one of the most engaging qualities, and one that lends a sense of immediacy and vividness to what might otherwise seem abstract theological ideas, is their instrumental sonorities and styles. The two Passions provide outstanding instances of instrumental usages, which are associated particularly with meditation on Jesus himself, and in contexts where his standing apart from the adverse physical events of the Passion is most prominent. The aria "Aus Liebe will mein Heiland sterben" in the *St. Matthew Passion*, whose ethereal scoring for soprano and transverse flute accompanied by two oboes da caccia without *basso continuo*, and its placement between the two ponderous "Lass ihn kreuzigen" choruses, lend a special focus to the theme of Jesus's innocent suffering, setting him apart from the world of his persecutors and project the theme of God's love, embodied in the figure of Jesus, as a central key to understanding the message of the Passion.[1]

Likewise, in the original version of the *St. John Passion* Bach created a special point of meditation in the paired arioso "Betrachte, meine Seele" and aria "Erwäge, wie sein blutgefärbter Rücken," the beginning of his "symbolic trial." In response to an unusually graphic and intense recitative ending, projecting the violence of the scourging in the protracted and tortured melisma on "geisselte ihn," the pace suddenly slows enormously in relation to the preceding segment of the trial. And Bach underscores the urging of the faithful to meditation on Jesus's sufferings by means of "special" instrumentation in all the versions of the Passion. Although there is some uncertainty about the exact details of each performance, there is no doubt that Bach intended to set this unique point of meditative focus on Jesus's

[1] Elke Axmacher (*"Aus Liebe will mein Heiland sterben"*) takes "Aus Liebe" as symbol of the understanding of the Passion in Bach's time.

sufferings apart from its dramatic surroundings by means of its instrumentation. The first version, apparently the same as or very close to the version of the score of around 1740, featured two violas d'amore and lute for "Betrachte," and two violas d'amore for "Erwäge" (with viola da gamba instead of violone as well). In later performances the instrumentation was altered, presumably because of the unavailability of lute and viola d'amore players, to muted violins instead of violas d'amore, harpsichord or obbligato organ instead of lute (the organ with the further indication of registration for 4′ Gedackt).[2] With such means Bach mirrors not only the character of the primary theme of the Passion—the benefit of Jesus's sufferings for the faithful—but also that the scourging marks a major point of arrival in the structure, the culmination of the shift to flat keys for the beginning of the "symbolic trial." After the affirmation of Jesus's divine identity in the chorale "O großer König," the tritone shift that is completed with "Betrachte, meine Seele" has enormous significance, bringing out the sense of opposition between the physical events and their salvific meaning. Similarly, but with a different theological objective, the opposition between the viola da gamba solo and trumpet-like string writing in the aria "Es ist vollbracht," brings out two contrasted aspects of Jesus's death: its benefit for those in torment in the world ("O Trost für die gekränkten Seelen"), and its "cosmic" significance, in the sense of the Johannine portrayal of Jesus as *Christus Victor* ("Der Held aus Juda siegt mit Macht").

Examples of such usages could be multiplied virtually ad infinitum. Bach's instrumentarium is large and highly varied; and his concern with finding sonorous counterparts to his texts seems inexhaustible.[3] In many cases, such sonorities are immediately understood in terms of traditions that were both ancient and widespread. This is particularly true of the trumpets (with or without kettledrums), whose associations with military, triumphant, joyful, and eschatological themes are ubiquitous. In the case of other instruments their common associations—woodwind instruments with pastorale music, for example—may or may not be invoked, and other style features may or may not reinforce the instrumental associations. And, with the possible exception of the trumpets, we cannot expect that such associations will be invariable from work to work. There are no absolutes in this sphere.

Yet Bach often does assign certain of the instruments roles and associations that, although not immutably fixed, are consistent enough to suggest that he recognized those associations as a valuable means of projecting theological content, and the interrelatedness of ideas from work to work. This is particularly interesting when instead of drawing on widespread usages or associations, he "creates" ones of his own for particular purposes. In *Tonal Allegory in the Vocal Music of J. S. Bach* I described how Bach's introduction of oboes da caccia at several widely separated points in the *St. Matthew Passion* and the viola da gamba at two others reflect the

---

[2] Mendel, *Kritischer Bericht*, 89–99; summary on 88–89.

[3] The most recent and exhaustive study is Ulrich Prinz, *Johann Sebastian Bachs Instrumentarium: Originalquellen, Besetzung, Verwendung* (Kassel: Bärenreiter, 2005).

underlying theological message of the work.[4] In an immediate sense all the movements featuring those instruments provide meditative focus on the figure of Jesus at key points in the Passion: the oboes da caccia with his struggles in Gethsemane (the arioso, "O Schmerz"); his innocent suffering in the trial before Pilate ("Aus Liebe"); his suffering on the cross (the arioso "Ach Golgatha" and aria-dialog "Sehet, Jesus hat die Hand uns zu fassen ausgespannt"); and his burial (the aria "Mache dich, mein Herze, rein"); and the viola da gamba with his punishment first by the Jewish then by the Roman authorities. But behind the qualities of immediacy lie the primary theological concepts that are announced in the opening chorus of the work—love, *Geduld* (patience), and acknowledgment of guilt—whose affective characters are enhanced and their theological meanings linked by the special instrumental sonorities. The aria "Komm, süsses Kreuz," for bass, viola da gamba, and *basso continuo*, provides an outstanding instance of this quality, symbolizing the point at which the believer, in direct response to Jesus's suffering, voices the willing acceptance of the cross that constituted the core of the process of faith in Lutheran theology. In Bach's work, where concreteness is always of the highest value, all such instances (interpreted "theologically," of course) go hand in hand with others, such as tonal designs and musical styles, to make up the multifaceted character that is demanded of the conception of music as an aid to scripture interpretation. This involves his projecting qualities that are immediately audible, as well as those that require time and intellectual involvement. In this chapter I discuss, in quasi-narrative fashion, Bach's use of special instruments, especially the *violoncello piccolo*, in the cantatas for spring 1725 and indicate how their contribution to the musico-theological character of the works aids in articulating the role of the individual cantatas within the liturgical sequence.

The violoncello piccolo; "loud" and "soft" instruments

In the cantatas for spring 1725 Alfred Dürr and others have noted a tendency toward special sonorities and virtuoso writing in the woodwinds (especially oboes da caccia and recorders).[5] This is certainly true; as a group these cantatas exhibit a noticeable tendency toward chamber music, a quality that mirrors both the intimate surroundings of the Gospel narrative (Jesus and the disciples) and also the liturgical qualities associated with Pentecost. It might be added that one of the cantatas (BWV 42) for this time period features solo bassoon, whereas one or more trumpets sound in five cantatas, lending an obvious reminder of the *Christus Victor* theme, so prominent in the Easter cantata *Kommt, gehet und eilet*. Statistically far more remarkable than these instances, however, is the fact that Bach utilizes *violoncello piccolo* in five of these cantatas, whereas the instrument otherwise appears

[4] Chafe, *Tonal Allegory*, 346–59.
[5] Dürr, *Cantatas*, 34–35.

Good Friday	*St. John Passion*: 1st version: 1724; for the most part the same as the fourth (final) version	Violas d'amore (2) with lute in "Betrachte, meine Seele"; violas d'amore in "Erwäge"; viola da gamba and trumpet-like strings in "Es ist vollbracht"; oboe da caccias (2) in "Zerfliesse"
	2nd version: 1725	"Betrachte, meine Seele" and "Erwäge" replaced by "Ach, windet euch nicht so" (with oboes and b.c. only)
Easter Sunday	Cantata 249	Trumpets (3) and drums in 1, 3, 11; recorders (2) with strings in 7
Easter Monday	Cantata 6	Oboe da caccia solo in 1, *colla parte* in 2, 6; violoncello piccolo in 3
Easter Tuesday	unknown	–
Quasimodogeniti	Cantata 42	Obbligato bassoon in 1, 2, 3, 4
Misericordias Domini	Cantata 85	Violoncello piccolo in 2
Jubilate	Cantata 103	Piccolo recorder in 1, 3; trumpet and strings in 5
Cantate	Cantata 108	–
Rogate	Cantata 87	Oboes da caccia solo (2) in 3, as *colla parte* instrument(s) in 1 and 7
Ascension Day	Cantata 128	Horns (2) in 1, 5; trumpet with strings in 3; *colla parte* oboe da caccia in 1 and 5
Exaudi	Cantata 183	Oboes da caccia solo (2) in 1, 3, 4; *colla parte* in 5; violoncello piccolo in 2
Pentecost: Sunday	Cantata 74	Trumpets (3) and drums in 1; oboes da caccia solo in 1, 2, 6, 7; *colla parte* in 8
Pentecost: Monday	Cantata 68	Corno (= cornetto, *colla parte*) in 1; violoncello piccolo in 2; *colla parte* cornetto and trombones (3) in 5
Pentecost: Tuesday	Cantata 175	Recorders (3) in 1, 2, 7; violoncello piccolo in 4; trumpets (2) in 6
Trinity Sunday	Cantata 176	*Colla parte* oboe da caccia in 1, 4, 5

FIGURE 11.1 **"Special" instrumental usages in the first and second versions of the *St. John Passion* and the spring 1725 cantatas.**

only in some four other cantatas in his entire oeuvre. Figure 11.1 summarizes these instrumental usages.[6]

The instrument that Bach designates "violoncello piccolo" is one harboring considerable uncertainty and disagreement, centered mostly on whether it is simply a smaller cello than the normal one and featuring an extra string tuned a fifth above the a string, or an arm-held instrument, played like an oversized viola but with the same tuning as the smaller cello just mentioned. Adherents to the latter view have

[6] In the study of Ulrich Prinz, cited in n. 3 (see 601), the table of appearances of the *violoncello piccolo* in Bach's work is somewhat larger, owing to the inclusion of a few compositions that were not specified for the instrument by Bach, but which for various reasons (cleffing, for example) have been considered as possible candidates for the instrument. Prinz's references include most (if not quite all; see n. 7) of the significant literature on the question of the instrument's identification.

often linked the instrument to the "viola pomposa" that Bach supposedly invented, and about which Johann Nikolaus Forkel (1749–1818) has the following to say:

> [T]he former Cappellmeister in Leipzig, Mr. Joh. Seb. Bach, invented an instrument that he called *viola pomposa*. It is tuned like a violoncello but has one string more at the top, is somewhat larger than a viola, and is so attached with a ribbon that it can be held on the arm in front of the chest.[7]

Earlier in the same description Forkel makes clear that the invention of the *viola pomposa* arose out of the need to have an instrument to accompany the solo violin, one that would not obscure the violin, as was often the case with keyboard instruments, and that would neither be as distant in pitch from the violin as the normal cello nor conflict in register with the solo violin as a second accompanying violin would. If we follow his description strictly, then we know of no instances in which such an instrument is so used; furthermore Bach never uses the term *viola pomposa*. Nevertheless, there are instances where the *violoncello piccolo* functions as a kind of "mediator" between the *basso continuo* and the vocal soloist, both in range (which often splits into differentiated upper and lower registers, sometimes featuring wide-ranging scales that seem to join the two) and in its harmonic character. This kind of writing is much less characteristic of the normal cello. We can therefore not absolutely rule out the possibility that Bach *did* write for an oversized viola

---

[7] David, Mendel, Wolff, *New Bach Reader*, 368. The *violoncello piccolo* has prompted a considerable and often complex literature; see Prinz, *Bachs Instrumentarium*, 584–601; and for a more recent, divergent view, see Dimitry Badiarov, "The Violoncello, Viola da spalla and Viola pomposa in Theory and Practice," *Galpin Society Journal* 60 (2007): 121ff. It is possible that the instrument called *violoncello piccolo* by Bach was the same one referred to in 1790 in Ernst Ludwig Gerber's famous account of Bach's invention of the *viola pomposa* in 1724. Laurence Dreyfus, for example (*Bach's Continuo Group: Players and Practies in his Vocal Works*, Studies in the History of Music, 3:174 [Cambridge, MA: Harvard University Press], 1987) suggests that Bach invented the instrument "for his experimental set of demanding solos in the cantatas," while Winfried Schrammek ("Viola pomposa und Violoncello piccolo bei Johann Sebastian Bach," in *Bericht über die wissehschaftliche Konferenzzum III*, ed. W. Felix, W. Hoffmann, and A. Schneiderheinze, Internationalen Bach-Fest Leipzig 1975 [Leipzig 1977], 347–48), who views the *viola pomposa* principally as a chamber instrument, admits that it might have been the *violoncello piccolo* of the cantatas. Prinz argues that the instrument was a small cello held in the modern position, between the legs; excellent recordings have been made in this manner. But in recent years several scholars and performers have argued that the instrument was the "viola da spalla" of the Badiarov article cited above. The "viola da spalla," or "violoncello da spalla," was a small cello or very large viola held often as Forkel describes, across the chest (or on the shoulder), with a ribbon around the player's neck. The instrument might have had either four or five strings and would apparently have been played by a violinist. Whether this view is the last word may well be uncertain. But some of the foremost Bach performers have adopted it and produced excellent performances. See, for example, the Bach Collegium Japan recordings of Cantatas 68, 85, 175, and 183 (Bis records, 2008), with notes by Masaaki Suzuki and performances by Badiarov; also, the CD of Cantatas 18, 23, and 1 by *La Petite Bande*, directed by Sigiswald Kuijken, who argues for the "violoncello (or viola) da spalla" in his notes (Accent records 25306, 2008). At the 2008 annual meeting of the American Musicological Society in Nashville, Gregory Barnett ("The Violoncello da Spalla and the Eccentricities of Historical Performance Practice" [paper presented Nov. 7, 2008]) presented a historical summary of the instrument, arguing that it is unlikely to be the instrument Bach indicated with the heading *violoncello piccolo*.

(or small cello), that he called *violoncello piccolo* (or even, without our possessing a written document, *viola pomposa*).[8] This was, perhaps, the instrument that Bach intended for the sixth cello suite, and that instrument he certainly did not invent.

The most obvious features that distinguish the *violoncello piccolo* in relation to the normal cello are its upper register, due to the additional string, and its lighter sound, the result of its smaller size. Both qualities invite a style of writing that utilizes wide-ranging parts and agility of register shift, qualities that are very much in evidence in the sixth cello suite, but which is not specified for *violoncello piccolo*. In that work the upward extension of register owing to the additional e′ string, is not simply a transposition of the normal upper register up a fifth. The uppermost pitch on the a string in suites one through four is g′, and Bach very often treats that pitch as a climactic, structurally important tone. In the case of the fifth suite, whose a string is tuned down a whole tone, the highest *written* pitch is again g′, but owing to the *scordatura* tuning it sounds as f′. In contrast, however, the prelude to the sixth suite reaches much farther upward, to the pitch g″, notated in the soprano clef. This indicates a pitch an octave higher than the highest tone of the other suites and a perfect fourth higher than the equivalent notated pitch on the highest string of those suites. This extension of the register goes hand in hand with the "unearthly" quality that Peter Wispelwey finds in this suite and its D-major key.[9]

None of the *violoncello piccolo* parts in the cantatas features such a wide-ranging part as that of the sixth cello suite. The only solo to descend to the low CC is that of the aria "Mein gläubiges Herze" from Cantata 68, in which Bach introduces prominent scalar and arpeggio descent patterns when the voice cadences on "mein Jesus ist da," the downward plummeting motion suggesting, in light of the text, that Jesus's presence is a descent from above. The upper register (the register that exceeds the highest tones of the normal cello in the suites) is used sparingly and seems to have been introduced for the purpose of lending greater emphasis to the immediately following descent passages. Other *violoncello piccolo* parts do not exceed the viola register (those of Cantatas 180 and 49, for example) and are perfectly easily played on that instrument, while still others exhibit the kind of register dif-

---

[8] As Dreyfus indicates (*Bach's Continuo Group*, 257, n. 77), "Cantatas 6, 41, 49, 68, 85, 115, 175, and 183 have clearly designated *violoncello piccolo* parts, while the solo in Cantata 180, which survives only in score, may be for the viola" (whose range is not exceeded by the part in question). Note that Cantata 180 is the first appearance of the instrumental designation in Bach's work. Since Cantatas 180, *Schmücke dich, o liebe Seele*, and 49, *Ich gehe und suche mit Verlangen*, were both written for the twentieth Sunday after Trinity (in 1724 and 1726, respectively), and in both works the *violoncello piccolo* is associated with the allegorical representation of the longing of the soul (the bride) for union with Christ (the bridegroom), it seems likely that the instrument was indeed intended in Cantata 180. Bach's second use of the instrument came just two weeks after Cantata 180, in Cantata 115, *Mache dich, mein Geist, bereit*, for the twenty-second Sunday after Trinity, 1724. From this point on it utilizes the wider range and changing clefs that remain standard for Bach.

[9] Peter Wispelwey, liner notes for *Johann Sebastian Bach: 6 Suites per violoncello solo senza basso*, Channel Classics CCS 12298, 1998, 7.

ferentiation that offers the best explanation for why Bach used *violoncello piccolo* instead of either viola or normal cello. An aria from Cantata 41 provides the best example of the latter style. Because of these different characteristics among the various parts assigned to the instrument, it has even been suggested that the designation *violoncello piccolo* might refer to more than one instrument.

I do not propose to solve this riddle, or even to rehearse the various opinions that run throughout the literature. But when we investigate Bach's use of *violoncello piccolo* in the cantatas, of which there are a scant nine instances (with a few other possibilities among the unspecified instruments), five of them occurring in the spring 1725 cantatas, we certainly get a strong sense that Bach, at least in those five cantatas, used the instrument to project a set of interrelated theological themes. That sense is all the greater when we consider the individual cantatas as members of a sequence bound up with the character of the liturgical season from Easter to Pentecost. The pragmatic explanation for occurrences of this kind in Bach's cantatas (that Bach had a good player available for the time period in question) while obviously true, is unsatisfactory, since it neither accounts for the particular movements for which the instrument was chosen nor explains the uneven spacing of the movements with *violoncello piccolo*. The following discussion considers their liturgical, theological, and musical contexts, focusing on Bach's use of the instrument in the cantatas for spring 1725, but also includes the remaining secure appearances in cantatas for other occasions.

From their texts alone—taken in isolation from the cantatas in which they appear and the sequence as a whole—it is not immediately obvious that the movements with *violoncello piccolo* are theologically related to one another. But an overview of the liturgical occasions for which they were written is suggestive. In the spring 1725 cantatas the *violoncello piccolo* appears first in two early cantatas of the sequence, *Bleib bei uns* (BWV 6) and *Ich bin ein guter Hirt* (BWV 85), for Easter Monday and Misericordias Domini, the second Sunday after Easter, thirteen days apart. After Misericordias it does not sound again until the cantata for Exaudi, the Sunday after Ascension Day, four weeks later, *Sie werden euch in den Bann tun* (BWV 183), after which it sounds twice more in the cantatas for the second and third days of Pentecost, *Also hat Gott die Welt geliebt* (BWV 68), and *Er rufet seinen Schafen mit Namen* (BWV 175). These last two cantatas follow Cantata 183 by eight and nine days respectively. The remaining four uses of the *violoncello piccolo* within the cantatas occur at varied times between its very first appearance in an aria from Cantata 180, *Schmücke dich, o liebe Seele* (October 22, 1724) and its last, in an aria from Cantata 49, *Ich geh und suche mit Verlangen* (November 3, 1726). As it happens, those two cantatas were both composed for the same feast day, the twentieth Sunday after Trinity, an occasion that belongs in the context of the "eschatological" character of the ending of the liturgical year. The Gospel for that day, Jesus's parable of the king's wedding feast, is one of Matthew's eschatological parables of the Kingdom of God, emphasizing readiness for the afterlife. Cantatas 180 and 49, therefore, come at approximately the opposite time of the year from the spring cantatas. Yet they are very close to the latter in their subject matter. One of the possible instances of the *violoncello piccolo* appears in a cantata for the nineteenth Sunday after Trinity and another in one for the twenty-first Sunday after Trinity, although not in the same year as either of those just mentioned. Of the remaining two cantatas with *violoncello piccolo*, one, *Mache dich, mein Geist bereit* (BWV 115, for the twenty-second Sunday after Trinity, 1724, two weeks after Cantata 180), is based on another of Matthew's eschatological parables and has features in common with Cantatas 180 and 49. There may therefore be an association of the instrument with the latter weeks of the Trinity season.

Finally, Bach also used the *violoncello piccolo* in *Jesu, nun sei gepreiset* (BWV 41), for New Year's Day 1725, the year that saw six appearances of the instrument. In it the exceptionally wide-ranging *violoncello piccolo* part (in the fourth of six movements, an aria for tenor, *violoncello piccolo,* and *basso continuo*) depicts a point of great intimacy that contrasts with the much more extrovert and festive orchestration of the outermost movements (including three oboes, three trumpets, and kettledrums). Since Cantata 41 represents the all-encompassing nature of Jesus as Alpha and Omega, which it symbolizes by reiterating the trumpet motto of the opening chorus to close the cantata as well, the tenor aria, with its message of peace for the faithful, might well have been conceived as the "other side" of that representation. And it may be mentioned that Cantata 49, the last of Bach's cantatas with *violoncello piccolo,* is also one of the very small number to make direct reference to Jesus as "A" and "O."[10]

Thus the *violoncello piccolo* occurs in eight (perhaps even nine or ten) cantatas that come at the time periods that lead to the endings of the two "halves" of the liturgical year and one that begins the civil new year. Their placement suggests some connection to the eschatological character of those occasions. In the spring liturgy that theme arises within the context of Jesus's departure and the shift from anticipation of his return as a future event to emphasis on the coming of the Holy Spirit; in the late-Trinity season it arises from anticipation of the end of physical existence and what is to follow it (Matthew's future eschatology), whether joyful, as in Cantatas 180 and 49, or tinged with fear, as in Cantata 115.

And when we look more closely at the texts of the individual cantatas in which the instrument appears, we immediately find that the *violoncello piccolo* underscores certain theological and affective relationships among those works. Thus, in contrast to Charles Sanford Terry's view that the arias with *violoncello piccolo* exhibit no consistency whatever but take up completely variegated subject matter in their texts, study of the works in which the instrument appears from a broader liturgical standpoint suggests that there is a considerable element of theological consistency in their texts. That consistency, however, cannot be perceived if we take the aria texts in isolation and consider them as centered on poetic or affective

[10] Chafe, "*Anfang und Ende,*" 103–34.

rather than theological content, as Terry did.[11] In a sensitive study of this question, Miriam F. Bolduan suggests that in the nine arias in which the *violoncello piccolo* is specified Bach "presents the mystery of the integration of God and man in Jesus and the equally mystical relationship of Jesus and the believer," an assessment that brings up associations of Pentecost and the Holy Spirit, on the one hand, and the Eucharist, on the other. The former association is prominent in the 1725 post-Easter cantatas, whereas the latter appears in several of the cantatas for other occasions.[12] In the post-Easter cantatas the *violoncello piccolo* is associated with the believer's personal relationship to Jesus, who appears in three different but interrelated forms: as the resurrected Jesus, whom the disciples (= the church) urge to remain with them (Cantata 6); as the "good shepherd" and protector of his flock (Cantatas 85, 183, and 175); and as God himself, present through the "indwelling" of the Holy Spirit and the incarnation of Jesus in the human heart (Cantata 68). The most obvious of those relationships (the so-called authentic shepherding) occurs between Cantatas 85, *Ich bin ein guter Hirt*, and 175, *Er rufet seinen Schafen mit Namen*, for Misericordias Domini and the third day of Pentecost, two feast days whose Gospel readings formed a continuous segment from John 10 (but in reverse order: 12–16 for Misericordias Domini and vv. 1–11 for the third day of Pentecost). The focus on intimate contact with Jesus also underlies the cantatas for the twentieth Sunday after Trinity, where we find the instrument associated with the believer's longing for union with Jesus through the Holy Eucharist (BWV 180), and with his or her joyful anticipation of acceptance by Jesus, the "bridegroom" (BWV 49). The magnificent aria, "Ergieße dich reichlich, du göttliche Quelle," from Cantata 5 (*Wo soll ich fliehen hin*), for the nineteenth Sunday after Trinity, 1724, has no specific instrumental designation; but Alfred Dürr's suggestion that it might have been for *violoncello piccolo* is convincing in light of the tenor soloist's cry for the outpouring of God's forgiveness of sin through Jesus's blood, the outpouring

[11] See Charles Sanford Terry, *Bach's Orchestra*, 2nd ed. (London: Oxford University Press, 1958), 140, where Terry remarks that the *violoncello piccolo* "has no consistent characterization in his usage, and is associated with arias of diverse sentiment—with a picture of the Good Shepherd (Nos. 85 and 175), an evening scene (No. 6), a eucharistic hymn (No. 180), prayer (No. 115), a eulogy of peace (No. 41), a challenge to death (No. 183). Or it simply expresses care-free gaiety, as in No. 49, or light-hearted joy, as in the soprano aria, 'My heart ever faithful', of No. 68." The majority of Terry's individual characterizations are close to the mark (although some, such as Cantata 49, are not), but overly general (an "evening scene," a "eulogy of peace," "prayer"). Only the contexts permit us to perceive the connections.

[12] Miriam F. Bolduan, "The Significance of the *Viola Pomposa* in the Bach Cantatas," *Bach: Quarterly Journal of the Riemenschneider Bach Institute* 14, no. 3 (July 1983): 12–17. Bolduan points out that the nine arias with designated *violoncello piccolo* parts are all in quadruple meter, naming them all as *Allemandes* in terms of their style models and affective character. While I would not agree that all these arias are *Allemandes*, her observation is an interesting one that is certainly true in the most characteristic instance, the aria "Wofern du den edlen Frieden" from Cantata 41. The latter movement, in its highly polyphonic character bears a resemblance to the style of the aria "Komm, süsses Kreuz," for solo seven-stringed viola da gamba, from the *St. Matthew Passion*. "Komm, süsses Kreuz" also projects the sense of intimacy with Jesus, who helps the believer carry his own cross, that is shared by the arias with *violoncello piccolo*.

projected vividly by the unspecified string instrument.[13] Of the remaining two instances, Cantatas 41 and 115, the former appears, as mentioned earlier, in a context that is very much centered on the person of Jesus (a principal theme of New Year's Day), projecting a meaning that reappears in several of the 1725 post-Easter cantatas, while the latter suggests intimacy with God through prayer.

In terms of instrumental sonority, the starting point for the spring 1725 cantatas is the image of Jesus as *Christus Victor.* Adumbrated in the central section of "Es ist vollbracht," it emerges in all its glory on Easter Day in *Kommt, gehet und eilet*, whose opening movement complex (see ch. 8) comprises an entire three-movement concerto grosso complex. Its first and third movements are scored for three trumpets with kettledrums, oboes, bassoon, and strings with *basso continuo*; the third movement of the concerto, now with chorus, is the first texted movement of the cantata, to which style the final movement of the cantata returns. Within this framework, though, one aria is strikingly set apart in its sonority, Peter's solo, "Sanfte soll mein Todeskummer nur ein Schlummer, Jesu, durch dein Schweisstuch sein," which takes up the theme of the Lutheran sleep of death in a movement featuring the sound of two recorders and muted violins playing in slurred duplets throughout the movement (a characteristic of the vocal part as well), while the *basso continuo* generally plays slurred repeated notes, often functioning as pedal tones. As a result, the harmonic rhythm is unusually slow, the overall effect being that of a pastorale-style slumber song. And Bach creates the sense of a progression toward this movement in the preceding aria, scored for transverse flute or violin with pizzicato bass. The much more aggressive style of the aria that follows these two leads back toward the victorious tones of the final chorus, so that "Sanfte soll mein Todeskummer" seems to express a quality that is "contained" within the predominant affect of triumph.

In many ways the juxtaposition just described, which might be characterized generally as between "loud" and "soft" instruments, runs throughout the season, coinciding in many cases with turning points within the cantatas, and even with changes in tone between successive cantatas. Thus, on the following day *Bleib bei uns* strikes a completely different note for the second day of Easter, one that immediately marks a shift of perspective from the light and triumph of the resurrection to the darkness and anxiety of the world. Beginning with a minor-key introductory chorus in sarabande style, which seems to hark back in both its key (c) and style to the burial chorus of the *St. John Passion*, *Bleib bei uns* then continues, after the pattern described in chapter 8, with an aria and a chorale that center on paraphrases of the initial biblical motto, expanding its meaning gradually throughout the three-movement sequence that comprises the first "half" of the cantata. All three of those movements voice the basic prayer for Jesus to remain through the coming darkness. The alto aria "Hochgelobter Gottes Sohn" makes a personal plea for Jesus to remain the "light" of the faithful with the words "Bleib, ach bleibe unser Licht, weil

[13] Dürr, *Cantatas*, 580, n. 45.

die Finsternis einbricht," striking a tone of intimacy through its instrumentation, for oboe da caccia and pizzicato *basso continuo*.[14] The chorale that follows, "Ach bleib bei uns, Herr Jesu Christ," for soprano and *violoncello piccolo* solo, then characterizes the world as a place of darkness and tribulation (the "last troubled time") in which God's word provides the only light: "Dein göttlich Wort, das helle Licht, laß ja bei uns auslöschen nicht. In dieser letzt'n betrübten Zeit verleih' uns, Herr, Beständigkeit, daß wir dein Wort und Sakrament rein b'halten bis an unser End" (Do not let the bright light of your divine word be extinguished with us. In this last troubled time grant us, Lord, perseverance, so that we may preserve your word and sacrament pure until the end). In this context, both the oboe da caccia and the *violoncello piccolo* suggest the comfort of Jesus's presence (through word and sacrament) in a world of increasing darkness. The chorale "Ach bleib bei uns" is the focal point for the message of Cantata 6, linking the first three movements by means of motivic elements derived from the chorale (see ch. 9): its "message" is that Jesus's presence through "word and sacrament" is a point of stability, constancy, and light in a world dominated by their opposites. The *violoncello piccolo* solo is Bach's primary musical symbol of that presence.

We do not have the cantata that was heard on the following day, Easter Tuesday. The cantata produced one week later, however, BWV 42, *Am Abend, aber, desselbigen Sabbats*, is very different from *Bleib bei uns* in its musico-theological character, even though it shares some thematic ideas with it. And, as described in chapter 9, the tone is noticeably more militant, beginning, like BWV 249, *Kommt, gehet und eilet*, with a D-major concerto-like *Sinfonia*. This time, though, instead of the triumphant sound of trumpets and kettledrums, dialogs between strings and winds, and especially the prominence of solo bassoon in several movements, seem appropriate to the analogy between the persecuted disciples and the struggles of the faithful in the world.

When, therefore, the *violoncello piccolo* returns, along with the image of Jesus as good shepherd on the following week, we sense immediately that the tone has become softer and more consoling. Cantata 85, *Ich bin ein guter Hirt*, seems to hark back to *Bleib bei uns* in its C-minor tonality and its peaceful character. Whereas Bach uses oboes in the first and third movements, thereby underscoring both the pastorale and majestic associations of Jesus pronouncing himself the good shepherd (no. 1), coupled with the Trinitarian associations of the chorale paraphrase of Psalm 23 (no. 3: "Der Herr ist ein getreuer Hirt," sung to the melody associated with a German chorale paraphrase of the Gloria), Bach introduces the *violoncello piccolo* in the second movement in association with the *believer's* recognition of

---

[14] The oboe da caccia has particular connections to Bach, since its first known appearances come within certain cantatas of his first Leipzig cycle. For a recounting of the modern rediscovery of the oboe da caccia in exemplars made in 1724 by Bach's Leipzig instrument maker Eichentopf, see Nikolaus Harnoncourt, "Bach's 'Oboe da Caccia' and its Reconstruction," in *The Musical Dialogue: Thoughts on Monteverdi, Bach, and Mozart.*, trans. Mary O'Neill (Portland, OR: Amadeus Press 1989), 60–63.

Jesus as good shepherd: "Jesus ist ein guter Hirt."[15] The *violoncello piccolo* is used in much the same manner as in *Bleib bei uns*, perhaps to expand on the idea of Jesus's protection through the coming darkness (an association that Martin Moller brought out between the two Gospel readings). In Cantata 85 the character of that protection is connected more directly to love (expanded on in the second aria, "Seht, was die Liebe tut") than to the *Christus Victor* image.

The cantatas described to this point project two sides of John's view of the atonement as set forth by Gustav Aulén, Walther von Loewenich, and others: the triumphant image of the *Christus Victor* and the loving, protecting, good shepherd. Obviously, the trumpet is most closely associated with the former and the *violoncello piccolo* with the latter. Then the cantatas between Misericordias Domini and Ascension Day deal with the difficulty of life in the world and the anticipation of the coming of the Holy Spirit after Jesus's departure to lead the path of the faithful toward the desired haven, the "gewünschten Port." Perhaps because of the prominence of the theme of preparation for the time after Jesus's departure, these cantatas do not feature *violoncello piccolo*, and in them the references to seeing Jesus have an eschatological (future) character. Even the cantata for Ascension Day, *Auf Christi Himmelfahrt allein*, describes Jesus as seen from afar at the right hand of God. The intimacy of personal contact with Jesus that underlies the arias with *violoncello piccolo* in *Bleib bei uns* and *Ich bin ein guter Hirt* climaxes in Cantatas 68 and 175, in association with the coming of the Holy Spirit. The instrument's reappearance in the cantata for the Sunday after Ascension Day (Exaudi), *Sie werden euch in den Bann tun* (BWV 183), and the relatively close grouping of this cantata with the two others in which it appears, seem the more significant in light of the departure/return themes that preceded Ascension Day.

The cantatas between Jubilate and Ascension Day feature *other* instrumental usages that relate not only to the theological characters of the feast days in question but also to the main themes of the sequence as a whole. In Cantata 103, *Ihr werdet weinen und heulen*, Bach emphasizes Jesus's prediction of sorrow turning to joy by means of the instrumental character of the movements before and after the turning point, the former of which (excepting the recitatives) feature a solo *flauto piccolo* (a soprano recorder) while the latter feature solo trumpet. In the opening chorus the *flauto piccolo* is singled out as the principal instrumental soloist, playing the most prominent and climactic entrances of the tortured fugue theme, yet supplying also the music that most characterizes the rejoicing of the world. In the first aria, "Kein Artzt ist außer dir zu finden," it is an aural counterpart to the believer's forlorn longing for direct contact with the now-departed Jesus. In the middle section Bach introduces an idea echoed in later cantatas of the spring sequence, accompanying it here by the series of flat modulations (see ch. 10): Jesus's "hiddenness," alluded to in the phrase "verbirgst du dich, so muß ich sterben." The idea

[15] Bolduan ("The Significance of the *Viola Pomposa* in the Bach Cantatas," 13) makes this point in her association of these cantatas with the believer's response to the varied forms of God's presence.

that Jesus is "hidden" (*verborgen*) makes a link between the disciples, who are now without Jesus's physical presence, and the contemporary believer who has to find faith: the evidence of things not seen. After a recitative in which the believer proclaims trust in Jesus's word of promise, the overt triumph of the trumpet aria, "Erholet euch, betrübte Sinnen," castigates the senses for their dependence on physical qualities (such as sight), turning to expressions of joy in Jesus's promise of his return. This aria, marking the reappearance of the trumpet for the first time since Easter Day, introduces the turning point of the cantata by utilizing several of the instrument's chromatic out-of-tune partials in conjunction with the reappearance of chromatic harmony in the voice and strings (*betrübte Sinnen*). It thereby depicts all that the believer has to overcome, then turns to the triumphant-sounding triadic style familiar from *Kommt, gehet und eilet*. The symbolism of change is unmistakably indicated in the line "Laßt von dem traurigen Beginnen, eh' ich in Tränen untergeh'" and the extraordinary vocal melisma on "Freude" that overlaps with the final return of the material of the opening section, effecting the transformation to the joyful state of mind.

And—to leap ahead to a parallel point later in the season—in Cantata 175, for the third day of Pentecost, after two movements in which a choir of three recorders depicts the believer's longing for personal contact with Jesus the good shepherd, the tenor cries out in the second aria for Jesus, once again described as "hidden," to reveal himself: "Wo find ich dich? Ach! Wo bist du verborgen?" In that work Bach continues the desire for intimacy with Jesus in an aria with *violoncello piccolo* before creating another turning point, now with the aid of a second *dictum* from John that leads, as the second recitative did in Cantata 103, to a hortatory trumpet aria, "Öffnet euch, ihr beiden Ohren." This time it is reason that is castigated, in the recitative, while the trumpet aria urges the believer to open her ears to the word of promise, rooted in the resurrection. As in the *Easter Oratorio*, both Cantatas 103 and 175 set up an opposition between the recorder as symbol of the believer's longing for personal contact with Jesus and the trumpet as emblem of the universal triumph of Jesus's victory and its eschatological implications.

After *Ihr werdet weinen und heulen*, Cantata 108, *Es ist euch gut daß ich hingehe*, as the next cantata in the sequence, likewise features two biblical mottoes; and the role of the second in the overall design is once again a pivotal one. Here Jesus's return is presented in terms of the Holy Spirit; in the recitative that precedes the second motto the tenor cries out "Durch deinen Hingang kommt er ja zu mir, Ich frage sorgensvoll: Ach, is er nicht schon hier? Ach, ist er nicht schon hier?" The believer's anxious cry seems to arise from uncertainty as to how the presence of the Spirit will be recognized, or felt within. And since Lutheranism expressed suspicion of the reliance on mere feeling regarding the Spirit, the immediate response of the chorus, "Wenn aber jener, der Geist der Wahrheit, kommen wird," explains that the Spirit will lead the faithful to truth, not by speaking of himself but by bringing what he hears from above. The choral setting (described in ch. 9) mirrors the above/below theme in Jesus's words in a manner that suggests the doctrine rather than the personal aspect of the work of the Spirit. The subsequent aria, however, is once again an expression of intimacy and longing, ending now with anticipation of being in God's presence, "dass ich in der Ewigkeit schaue deine Herrlichkeit." Bach does not specify solo violin for the ornate first violin part; but it seems perfectly suited to the highly personal, chamber-music-like character of the solo, especially as a response to the tripartite choral fugue that precedes it. In this case, though, the instrumental character is, perhaps, less determining of that design than in the preceding and following cantatas. The solo motto with which it begins associates a florid oboe d'amore part with Jesus's words, but the second motto, set for chorus, seems to universalize the message of the coming of the Holy Spirit for the community as a whole. In their major keys the two mottos stand apart from the minor keys of the arias and chorale; this cantata is, in fact, dependent on tonal design and other stylistic qualities rather than its instrumental character.

In the third of the Ziegler cantatas, BWV 87, Bach brings back the oboe da caccia, heard previously in the aria "Hochgelobter Gottessohn" of *Bleib bei uns*. Bach's use of this instrument, in whose invention he might, in fact, have had some input, is nearly always for purposes of special intimacy, often in association with love.[16] In the third movement of *Bisher habt ihr nichts gebeten in meinem Name* Bach assigns a pair of oboes da caccia, often playing in parallel thirds and sixths, as the principal melodic figure—a slurred duplet, usually descending, associated with the word "Vergib" (forgive) in the soloist's petition to God: "Vergib, o Vater, vergib unsre Schuld, und habe noch mit uns Geduld, wenn wir in Andacht beten" (Forgive, O Father, forgive our guilt, and have patience with us if we pray devotedly). The pleading tone is bound up with the downward motion of the duplets, and often of the line in general, while in the *basso continuo* appears its complementary opposite: sequences of rising sixteenth-note arpeggios. "Vergib, o Vater" projects a striking sense of the dualism of petition and hope from a state dominated by consciousness of unworthiness. After a recitative that might have been added by Bach, the turning point is the second motto from John, "In der Welt habt ihr Angst; aber seid getrost, ich habe die Welt überwunden," the words that, as Walter Loewenich points out, were of special importance for Luther as the foundation of the meaning of the Gospel. In this case there are no special instruments; the bass voice, functioning as *vox Christi*, is accompanied by a quasi-ostinato *basso continuo* part, perhaps so as to let these pivotal words stand unadorned as the foundation in question.

Cantata 128, for Ascension Day, is the only cantata among those for spring 1725 to feature horns, a pair of which lend their majestic character to the opening chorale fantasia and the final chorale.[17] Then, after a recitative that juxtaposes worldly tribulation with the transfigured state of eternity, Bach gives us an aria for

---

[16] See Harnoncourt, "Bach's 'Oboe da Caccia' and its Reconstruction."

[17] Cantata 68 has the designation "Corne" as the instrument that doubles the soprano *cantus firmus* in the opening movement; on the basis of the style, the pitches required and the fact that the melody of the final chorale is played by cornetto, it is most likely that in this instance "Corno" is an abbreviation for cornetto.

trumpet, bass, and strings, in which the trumpet symbolizes Jesus's sitting at the right hand of God in majesty, while the dropping out of the trumpet from the middle section until the final ritornello just as clearly represents the text's emphasis on human inability to conceive of God's glory or to "build" knowledge of the deity on that glory. In this context the horns appear to represent Jesus's intrinsic majesty, as in the opening movements of Cantata 1, *Wie schön leuchtet der Morgenstern*, and Cantata 40, *Darzu ist erschienen der Sohn Gottes*, or the Quoniam tu solus sanctus of the *Mass in B minor*, whereas the trumpet is more closely linked to his victorious work. Thus the trumpet aria in Cantata 128 can be considered as a "stage" in the presentation of that work among the cantatas of the spring 1725 sequence, one that began in the *St. John Passion* with the trumpet style of the middle section of "Es ist vollbracht" ("Der Held aus Juda siegt mit Macht")—the cross as Jesus's "lifting up"—and was more explicitly expressed in the ending of Cantata 249 ("Der Löwe aus Juda kommt siegend gezogen"), a depiction of Jesus's triumphant return to the world "above." In Cantata 103 it expressed the believer's joy over the anticipation of seeing Jesus again. Now the hortatory tone of the trumpet aria in Cantata 128 carries it a step farther, urging the believer to envision and proclaim the image of Jesus at the right hand of God in glory: "Auf, auf mit hellem Schall verkündigt überall: mein Jesus sitzt zur Rechten."

On the Sunday after Ascension Day, Cantata 183, *Sie werden euch in den Bann tun*, marks a return to the tone of Jesus's prediction of the disciples' forthcoming persecution for their faith, while at the same time introducing the Holy Spirit as directing the path of the faithful and teaching prayer, themes carry forward from Cantatas 103, 108, and 87. After the seeing of Jesus from afar in Cantata 128, the change in sonority from the horns and trumpet of the earlier cantata to the softer, more personal oboes da caccia and *violoncello piccolo* seems very meaningful. The aria in which the instrument appears, "Ich furchte nicht des Todes Schrecken," reintroduces the theme of Jesus's protection ("Denn Jesus's Schutzarm wird mich decken") and now reappears for the first time since Cantata 85, four weeks earlier. Its affirming the believer's desire to follow Jesus ("ich folge gern und willig nach") bridges between the Holy Spirit's leading the faithful in Cantata 108 and the believer's willing following the Spirit in Cantata 175 ("Nun, werter Geist, ich folge dir"). Learning to follow the Spirit, in fact, bids to be considered the "goal" of the cantata sequence as a whole. Cantata 183 makes the all-important connection between Jesus's Spirit and that of the third person of the Trinity: after the expression of willingness to follow Jesus in the aria with *violoncello piccolo*, the second recitative addresses Jesus directly, "*dein* Geist wird bei mir stehen," after which the immediately following second aria addresses the Holy Spirit, "Höchster Tröster, heil'ger Geist." If the *violoncello piccolo* symbolizes Jesus's presence, which arguably underlies all the appearances of the instrument in these cantatas, then in the latter movement, and indeed throughout the remaining movements of the work, the presence of the Holy Spirit seems mirrored in the sound of the oboe da caccia. As the first aria of Cantata 183, "Ich fürchte nicht des Todes Schrecken" immediately follows the cantata's opening *dictum*, which introduces pairs of oboes d'amore and oboes da caccia in a very brief recitative setting of "Sie werden euch in den Bann tun," voicing once again the tribulation the disciples will suffer after Jesus's departure. The *dictum* describes a melodic motion from a′ to e″, cadencing after only five measures in e/E (E minor with a Picardy third), after which "Ich fürchte nicht," confirming e, provides a direct response from the believer who trusts in Jesus's protection and expresses willingness to follow. Quite possibly, the *violoncello piccolo* itself symbolizes that protection in this aria; its wide-ranging part surrounds the tenor voice in a manner suggesting an analogy to Mariane von Ziegler's using the word "Schützarm" (protective arm) to describe Jesus's "covering" the believer ("Denn Jesus's Schützarm wird mich decken"). In terms of register, "Ich fürchte nicht" is very similar to the arias from cantatas 6 and 85 (G–c″). But now Bach interrupts the style of continuous sixteenth notes, shared with those works, with passages in which the *violoncello piccolo* doubles the *basso continuo* exactly or near exactly in "walking" eighth notes, usually either in unison or at the octave above. The most conspicuous instances of this style appear at the outset, on "Ich fürchte nicht des Todes Schrecken" (the first two phrases) and in the "B" section, where the believer proclaims that owing to the protection of Jesus's "Schützarm" he will follow willingly and joyfully. As the tenor sings of following Jesus, the tonality shifts, to the sharpest key of the movement, f♯, cadencing in that key by means of the prominent "walking" bass, doubled by the *violoncello piccolo*. Soon afterwards Bach cadences in C, then in a, and, finally, G. These cadences, all of which feature the merging of *violoncello piccolo* with the *basso continuo*, complete the line "wollt ihr nicht meines Lebens schonen, und glaubt, Gott einen dienst zu thun: Er soll euch selber noch belohnen, wohlan, es mag dabei beruh'n" (If you do not want to protect my life, and believe you are doing God a service, he will reward you himself; it must be left at that). In this instance, a very uninspiring echo of the opening *dictum* is compensated for by the *violoncello piccolo*. The dual role of the *violoncello piccolo*—now playing in the melodically ornate style of the voice, now in the unadorned style of the *basso continuo*—seems to mediate between the believer's unavoidable troubles in the world and his reliance on God's support and promise. Rather than expressing the individual words or phrases of the text, the lower register of the instrument anticipates its next appearance (with the lowest pitch the instrument can play for "Mein Jesus ist da!") on the second day of Pentecost, the point in the spring cantata sequence when the "incarnation" of Jesus as the Spirit is directly expressed.

After "Ich furchte nicht des Todes Schrecken," Bach returns the focus of the sonority to the oboes da caccia, first in dialog with oboes d'amore in an accompanied recitative; there the oboes pick up the motive of the alto's opening words ("Ich bin bereit," an expression of faith and readiness to accept the Holy Spirit) and sound it throughout the entire movement. In the second aria, the oboes da caccia take the lead, playing in unison and concertizing with the first violin in a manner that was perhaps devised to depict the believer's awareness of the Spirit standing by in the protective role described for Jesus in the earlier aria. The oboe da caccia part at times merges with the violin, sounding an octave below, while at others it detaches itself, playing long lines that the violin punctuates with the head motive, associated with "Höchster Tröster, heil'ger Geist" in Cantata 183. Human weakness and need of support are also quite prominent in this movement and expressed, as we will see, by tonal means. In its sonorous dimension, however, we have, perhaps, an aural image of *Trost*.

For Luther, John was both the Gospel of *Trost* and the one that placed special emphasis on the person and words of Jesus. Like many commentators on John, before and since, Luther responded to John's emphasis on love and the special role of the Holy Spirit. In addition, Luther's incarnational theology and his Trinitarian doctrine drew much of their core from John's prologue and related passages from the Gospel and letters. Cantata 74, for Whitsunday, ties together many of the most characteristic ways that Luther viewed John; and Bach uses instrumental styles and sonorities to project their meaning. The initial motto, speaking of mutual love between the faithful and God, and the "indwelling" of Father and Son within the believer, is a classic statement on the Trinity, since the indwelling was widely interpreted as occurring through the Holy Spirit. Bach responds to the Trinitarian associations of this Johannine *dictum* in a familiar manner: three instrumental choirs of three trumpets, three winds, and three strings, all of which concertize separately and together as well as in various combinations of the individual members of each group throughout the movement. The Trinitarian symbolism recalls that of the Weimar cantata *Erschallet, ihr Lieder* (BWV 172), heard the preceding year, in which the same excerpt from John is preceded and followed by movements featuring three trumpets in the aria "Heiligster Dreieinigkeit," a petition to the Trinity. In both cantatas the tone then becomes more intimate, in the case of Cantata 74 with the aria "Komm, komm, mein Herze steht dir offen," for oboe da caccia solo and soprano with *basso continuo*, a depiction of the believer's readiness for the tropological incarnation of Jesus. The glory and majesty of God give way to his other side, the merciful, loving comforter of the faithful. The text of this aria expresses love, *Trost*, the hope that God's word will impact on the believer, and the believer's surety that his prayers will be heard, all themes that have run through the spring 1725 cantatas. Here the sudden shift in sonority after the splendor of the opening chorus makes an unforgettable impression. In concept the disparity between God and humankind and the miracle of God's choosing the human heart as his dwelling place are comparable (though realized entirely differently) to the sudden enharmonic change that expresses the same idea, in terms of the incarnation, in the Christmas cantata, "Christum wir sollen loben schon."

And, on the following day, Mariane von Ziegler's text for Cantata 68, *Also hat Gott die Welt geliebt*, portrays the coming of the Holy Spirit in terms that are strikingly reminiscent of a Christmas cantata: here the equivalent of Jesus's second, now spiritual incarnation, his rebirth within the soul bringing about the believer's own rebirth through the Spirit. That quality perhaps suggested pastorale elements to Bach, prompting him to turn to his earliest known secular cantata, the Weimar "Hunting Cantata" of 1713 (*Was mir behagt, is nur die muntre Jagd,*" BWV 208), for the models of the two arias of Cantata 68, "Mein gläubiges Herze" (which features the *violoncello piccolo* once again) and "Du bist geboren, mir zugute." Both arias deal with the effect of Jesus's coming into the world and to the human heart.

Cantata 68 weaves together the themes of love and the Holy Spirit (not mentioned directly but central to the second day of Pentecost) with Jesus's incarnation and its benefits for humanity, ending with a rather sober articulation of John's "realized eschatology"—that judgment and salvation take place in the present according to whether one believes in Jesus. The person of Jesus is the focal point of the work. Although the cantata does not refer directly to pastorale elements, as do Cantatas 85 and 175, Bach's turning to the Weimar "Hunting Cantata" as the source of his two arias suggests a resonance with the pastorale character of Cantata 175, performed the day after Cantata 68. The "Hunting Cantata" contained a substantial pastorale element, manifested above all in the well-known aria "Schafe können sicher Weiden," which describes the cantata's dedicatee, Duke Christian of Sachsen-Weißenfels, as a "good shepherd." Although Bach did not parody that aria in either Cantata 68 or 175, the latter work, which is directly concerned with the portrayal of Jesus as good shepherd, utilizes an aria of the same affective type and instrumentation (recorder choir) as "Schafe können sicher weiden." The qualities that led Bach to parody his 1725 "Shepherd Cantata" in the Easter Oratorio, *Kommt, gehet und eilet,* on Easter Day operate in Cantata 68 as well: the depiction of the Baroque ruler in both his majestic and his personal, caring aspects. The former quality emerges in Cantata 68 in the aria "Du bist geboren mir zugute," a parody of "Ein Fürst ist seines Landes Pan" in the "Hunting Cantata," and the latter in the aria "Mein gläubiges Herze," a reworking of the aria "Weil die wollenreiche Herden," sung in the "Hunting Cantata," as is "Schafe können sicher weiden," by Pales, god of shepherds.

In keeping with its pastorale background, Cantata 68 begins with a siciliano-style chorale setting, with winds and strings generally moving in unison and cornetto (or possibly horn, see ch. 12, n. 22) doubling the melodically decorated soprano chorale. Bach chose to vary the chorale melody extensively in this movement in order to bring out the melodic character that generally accompanies his Siciliano movements; the rising minor sixths of the first four lines, and, indeed, the entire melody of the first and third lines thereby evoke the melodic character of movements such as "Erbarme dich" of the *St. Matthew Passion.* The effect is that a tone resembling entreaty is embedded in the pastorale style, a reminder of the divine/human relationship.

Against this background, the aria "Mein gläubiges Herze" creates an unforgettable sense of direct unclouded joy and intimacy, qualities owing in large part to the freshness of Bach's youthful work. Its original form, "Weil die wollenreiche Herden," is a quasi-ostinato piece of unusually song-like melodic style dominated by the sevenfold ostinato-like reiteration of the joyful *basso continuo* phrase. In its original form, the leaping bass melody depicted the description of the sheep being driven joyfully out to pasture ("lustig ausgetrieben"). Bach reworked the aria substantially, completely replacing the vocal line, assigning the joyful figure to the *violoncello piccolo*, supplying a new, supporting *basso continuo*, and adding a dance-like instrumental postlude of twenty-seven measures on the joyful motive, now with the addition of two oboes to the *violoncello piccolo* and continuo. The result is a piece that perfectly represents joy in the presence of Jesus ("Mein gläubiges Herze, frohlocke, sing, scherze, dein Jesus ist da!"), the fulfillment of what the soprano cries out for in *Bleib bei uns*. If the *violoncello piccolo* also represents Jesus as mediator (as he is described in the following recitative), then the scalar descent of its lines to the low C at the ends of its phrases—joining the upper and lower registers—must have suggested to Bach the descent of Jesus into the believer's heart.[18] The dance-like character of the instrumental postlude projects a palpable sense of the believer's joy in that presence, extending the meaning of "mein Jesus ist da" to the idea that the presence of the Holy Spirit is equivalent to a second "incarnation" of Jesus, now within the human heart. As in all the other arias with *violoncello piccolo* from this period, the instrument symbolizes contact with Jesus; the instrumental postlude adds something of a sense that such joy goes beyond words (comparable, perhaps, to the dropping out of the trumpet in the aria "Auf, auf mit hellem Schall" from Cantata 128 as the text speaks of the inability of humanity to fathom God's greatness with the words "So Schweig' verweg'ner Mund," then the return of the trumpet and dropping out of the voice for the reprise of the opening material).

On the following day the last of the five arias with *violoncello piccolo*, "Es dünket mich, ich seh' dich kommen," from Cantata 175, relates to the aria in Cantata 85, "Jesus ist ein guter Hirt." The theme of Jesus as good shepherd is the principal link between the two cantatas, and one that emerges clearly in the two arias with *violoncello piccolo*.[19] Beyond that, the differences are interesting. In Cantata 85 the aria in question, "Jesus ist ein guter Hirt," is virtually a paraphrase, from the perspective of the believer, of the opening motto from John, which it directly follows. In Cantata 175, however, the aria with *violoncello piccolo* does not reiterate an idea already stated but voices the believer's very personal expression of recognition: he "sees" the shepherd approach, admits him through faith, "hears" his charming voice,

---

[18] We may be reminded of the plummeting C-major arpeggio in the cello that begins the ritornello of the aria "Johannes freudenvollen springen" in Cantata 121. There it follows an enharmonic modulation from the dominant of f♯ to C that expresses the miracle of the incarnation, after which the ritornello beginning describes the descent itself in the aforementioned arpeggio, while the upper strings depict the "joyful leaping" of the text.

[19] In Cantata 85 the text of the aria with *violoncello piccolo* (the second movement) is as follows: "Jesus ist ein guter Hirt; / Denn er hat bereits sein Leben/Für die Schafe hingegeben, / Die ihm niemand rauben wird./Jesus ist ein guter Hirt." That of the fourth movement of Cantata 175 runs: "Es dünket mich, ich seh dich kommen, / Du gehst zur rechten Türe ein. / Du wirst im Glauben aufgenommen / Und mußt der wahre Hirte sein. / Ich kenne deine holde Stimme, / Die voller Lieb und Sanftmut ist, / Daß ich im Geist darob ergrimme, / Wer zweifelt, daß du Heiland seist."

his "holde Stimme," with its tones of "Lieb und Sanftmut." The emphasis on the senses in this aria continues from the physical joy in Jesus's second incarnation through the Holy Spirit in the cantata of the preceding day, especially in the aria "Mein gläubiges Herze." And a similar idea perhaps underlies the circumscribed appearance of the bottom register in "Es dünket mich," whose lowest tones, A, G♯, G and F♯, sound at cadences involving the lines "[du gehst] zur rechten Thüre ein," "und musst der wahre Hirte sein," and "die voller Lieb und Sanftmut ist." In contrast to *Bleib bei uns* and *Ich bin ein guter Hirt*, the three cantatas with *violoncello piccolo* that come after Ascension Day all associate the lower register of the instrument with the very positive perception of the benefits of Jesus's presence. "Es dünket mich" caps a sequence of movements, two of which—the initial motto and the aria that follows it—feature the sound of a choir of three recorders (presumably a Trinitarian symbolism, since the instruments form countless full triads).

At this point Mariane von Ziegler placed a second Johannine motto, which voices the disciples' misunderstanding, then shifts suddenly to a warning against reliance on reason. In the preceding sequence of movements, seeing and hearing are described in unmistakably spiritual terms. But after the introduction of reason, one of the primary opponents of faith in the Lutheran worldview, the ensuing aria, "Offnet euch, ihr beiden Ohren, Jesus hat euch zugeschworen, dass er Teufel, Tod erlegt" brings back the trumpets, their last appearance in the 1725 cantata sequence, as if to overcome any lingering doubts arising from reason, to compensate for any inability to hear and understand the quiet inner message of the shepherd's voice represented by the initial sequence of movements. This aria forms part of the way in which Cantata 175 unites the figures of Jesus as good shepherd and *Christus Victor* with the coming of the Holy Spirit: accompanied by the "soft" instruments, in the initial movements the believer follows the shepherd; in the aria "Öffne dich," he follows the Jesus of the Passion and resurrection (the middle section proclaims that "Gnade, Gnüge, volles Leben will er allen Christen geben, wer ihm folgt, sein Kreuz nachträgt"); and in the final chorale, "Nun, werther Geist, ich folg' dir," he follows the Holy Spirit to the "other life" given through grace and the "light" of God's word ("hilf dass ich suche für und für nach deinem Wort ein ander Leben, das du mir willt aus Gnaden geben. Dein Wort ist ja der Morgenstern, der herrlich leuchtet nah' und fern": help me to seek for evermore according to your word another life, which you will give me through grace. Your word is the morning star that shines brightly near and far).

From this standpoint, the coming of the Holy Spirit is God's response to the prayer of *Bleib bei uns* for Jesus's presence through his word, "das helle Licht," as protection from the darkness of the world. In *Bleib bei uns* the chorale with *violoncello piccolo* capped an initial sequence of movements, all of which prayed for Jesus to remain, and the last of which gave particular emphasis to his presence through "word and sacrament." In Cantata 175 the theme of Jesus's leading the faithful through "green pastures" in the first aria recalls, of course, Cantata 85, while linking up with the textual background for "Mein gläubiges Herze" as well. After that

"Es dünket mich, ich seh' dich kommen," built almost entirely over a walking quarter-note bass line, depicts the security of the believer's seeing and hearing the shepherd as metaphors for the experience of the Holy Spirit within, the second incarnation of Jesus represented in Cantata 68, while at the same time recalling the following of Jesus described in Cantata 183 by the aria "Ich fürchte nicht des Todes Schrecken." In the recitative that follows, this unmediated awareness of the Spirit, equated with Jesus's words, is juxtaposed to reliance on reason, which leads the believer astray from the path of faith. The trumpet aria that follows then urges the believer to open her ears to the message of salvation spoken by Jesus in his *Christus Victor* portrayal. As in the opposition of trumpets and *violoncello piccolo* in Cantata 41, in Cantata 175 the *violoncello piccolo* represents its "other side."

While the spring 1725 cantatas are bound up with the character of that season, three (possibly four) of the cantatas *not* from spring 1725 in which the *violoncello piccolo* appears (BWV [5], 180, 115, and 49) reflect the eschatological character of the late-Trinity season for which they were written (i.e., the nineteenth, twentieth, twenty-first, and twenty-second Sundays after Trinity). In terms of the liturgical occasion the "earliest" is Cantata 5, *Wo soll ich fliehen hin*, which was composed as one of the chorale cantatas in 1724, for the nineteenth Sunday after Trinity. The third movement of this cantata, the tenor aria, "Ergiesse dich reichlich, du göttliche Quelle" (Pour out abundantly, you divine source), features an extraordinarily beautiful, active, and descriptive part that may be for viola, or for *violoncello piccolo*, as Alfred Dürr speculates.[20] Although we cannot base conclusions on Bach's use of the *violoncello piccolo* on a work for which the exact designation is lacking, we may note that the instrument in question was used in a manner that makes the most out of its capacity to depict the pouring forth of Jesus's redeeming blood, which in the cantata as a whole bridges between the Passion and the Eucharist.

The subject matter of Cantata 180, *Schmücke dich, o liebe Seele* (for the twentieth Sunday after Trinity, 1724), is derived from Matthew's parable of the kingdom of heaven as the royal wedding feast for which the invited guests were unworthy (Mt 22:1–14); the king therefore destroyed their city and invited instead anyone who could be found on the streets; the one guest who came without wedding garments was cast out into the darkness: "For many are called but few are chosen." The librettist based his chorale cantata text on a communion hymn ("Deck thyself, my soul, with gladness"), thereby making a traditional comparison between the king's wedding feast in the Gospel for the day, and the Last Supper as origin of the sacrament of Holy Communion. As a result, Cantata 180 closely parallels the themes that run throughout the spring 1725 cantatas: union with Jesus, who is present in word and sacrament, faith and the Holy Spirit; God's love figures especially prominently in movements four, six, and seven. Particular themes usually associated with John come into the foreground: the final chorale addresses Jesus as "bread of life," and the light/darkness metaphor appears in two movements to juxtapose the

[20] Dürr, *Cantatas*, 580, n. 45.

sinful world to Jesus. In striking parallel to Cantata 175, a recitative even juxtaposes reason, which cannot penetrate the "secret" of God's greatness, and the Holy Spirit, which teaches humanity through the word, faith, and love. Bach's setting features extensive use of "special" woodwind instruments and styles: recorders and oboes da caccia (plus strings) in two movements, recorders alone as accompanying parts in one recitative, a virtuoso transverse flute solo in another aria. The range of the *violoncello piccolo* in this movement (c–b′), chronologically its first appearance in Bach's work, does not exceed that of the viola. The instrument enters in the third movement, following six-and-a-half measures of recitative, to accompany the soprano solo chorale, "Ach, wie hungert mein Gemüte, Menschenfreund, nach deiner Güte." As the beginning of the recitative states, the gifts of the Eucharist ("des heilgen Mahles Gaben") are incomparably more precious than the "trinkets and vanities" the world holds dear. The chorale with *violoncello piccolo* voices the yearning of the believer's spirit for union with Jesus, ending "Wünsche stets, daß mein Gebeine mich durch Gott mit Gott vereine." In this work, therefore, the *violoncello piccolo* is associated especially clearly with the intimacy with God that comes through Jesus and the Holy Spirit.

Similarly, *Ich geh' und suche mit Verlangen* (BWV 49), for the same feast day two years later, expresses longing for union with Jesus in the form of a dialog cantata in which the soprano and bass soloists represent the soul and Jesus. The final movement assigns the last verse of Nicolai's chorale "Wie schön leuchtet der Morgenstern" with its address to Jesus as the "A" and "O," to the soprano solo, while the bass sings in language reminiscent of John, "Dich hab ich je und je geliebet, und darum zieh' ich dich zu mir." Intimacy between the bride/soul and bridegroom/Jesus sets the tone for the entire work. And Cantata 49 also has a very special instrumental character: with one exception, its closed movements (an introductory Sinfonia, the first aria, and the final duet with chorale) feature an obbligato organ part. The only other closed movement, the aria "Ich bin herrlich, ich bin schön," for soprano, oboe d'amore, *violoncello piccolo,* and *basso continuo* (the fourth movement), is in a sense the centerpiece of the cantata, since, preceded and followed by soprano-bass recitative dialogs, it represents the soul's expression of readiness for the heavenly banquet. The dialogue aspect of the other movements emerges now in the intertwining and close alternating of the oboe d'amore and *violoncello piccolo* parts. As the aria and subsequent dialog explain, the wedding clothes—represented, of course, by the attractive instrumental surface of the aria—signify the idea of justification by faith, the key to the soul's acceptance as a "guest" at the "Erlösungsmahl." In Bach's two Leipzig cantatas for the twentieth Sunday after Trinity, therefore, the *violoncello piccolo* even stands apart from the other "special" instruments, conveying particular qualities of the longing of the soul for union with Jesus. Since in these cantatas the instrument does not extend beyond the register of the viola, Bach must have been thinking primarily of the *sound* of the instrument as an analog of the wedding clothes of the Gospel parable and its figurative meaning: faith as the key to God's acceptance into eternal life.

Apart from Cantata 41, in which the *violoncello piccolo* is related to God's providing for both the physical and spiritual needs of humanity, the one remaining appearance of the instrument in Bach's cantatas took place two weeks after Cantata 180, on the twenty-second Sunday after Trinity, 1724. Cantata 115, *Mache dich, mein Geist, bereit*, based on another of Matthew's parables, takes up a very different aspect of the anticipation of eternity from Cantatas 49 and 180. Now it is readiness for the coming destruction of the world and the Last Judgment, rather than the heavenly banquet, that is urged on the believer. The believer's spirit prepares itself by watching, weeping, and praying in a world to which God has given his "Gnadenlicht" to aid only those with "offne Geistesaugen" to overcome the "Sünden Nacht." In the first aria, "Ach, schläfrige Seele, wie? wie?" instead of the comforting "sleep of death" that we saw in Peter's "Sanfte soll mein Todeskummer" from *Kommt, gehet und eilet*, or the secure sleep of the "sheep" under the watchful eye of the shepherd in Cantata 85, the pastorale style represents the link between the sleep of a sinful life (the "A" section) and the sleep of eternal death in the afterlife (the closing part of the "B" section). Between these two *Adagio* sections Bach placed a twenty-two-measure *Allegro* passage (the beginning of the "B" section) to represent the sudden awakening of humanity for God's judgment: "Es möchte die Strafe dich plötzlich erwecken und, wo du nicht wachest [the return of the *Adagio* style completes the sentence] im Schlafe des ewigen Todes bedecken" (Judgment may suddenly arouse you and, if you are not watchful, cover you in the sleep of eternal death). *Schlafe* and *Strafe* are juxtaposed, but express the same outcome. The first recitative adds a warning against Satan and the complete falseness of the world: "Des Satans List ist ohne Grund, die Sünder zu bestricken, brichst du nun selbst den Gnadenbund, wirst du die Hilfe nie erblicken. Die ganze Welt und ihre Glieder sind nichts als falsche Brüder; doch macht dein Fleisch und Blut hiebei sich lauter Schmeichelei" (Satan's deceit is without reason in its capturing the sinners; if you now break the bond of grace, you will never look upon the help. The entire world and its members are nothing but false brothers; yet in it your flesh and blood create pure flattery).

Within this context, the fourth movement, the aria "Bete aber auch dabei mitten in dem Wachen" (Pray, however, even there in the midst of your watching), for soprano, flute, *violoncello piccolo* and *basso continuo*, marks a turning point (expressed in the adversative conjunction "aber") from the warning character of the preceding movements to the promise of God's help in the recitative that follows. Most commentators on the movement have found it to project qualities of "exceptional fascination," (Dürr), "intimate emotion" (Terry), "sweet freshness" (Pirro), and the like.[21] The unusual *Molto Adagio* tempo and high degree of dynamic shifting, especially the *piano* indication for the solo instruments as the voice enters to reiterate the word "Bete" three times in rising sequences—the first two very slowly

[21] Ibid., 616; Terry, *Bach's Orchestra*, 87 (citing Pirro, *L'esthétique de Jean-Sébastian Bach* [Paris 1907, 223] as well).

and the last continuing with the normal rhythm of the instrumental part—give special attention to the character of prayer. At this point of unusual intimacy the *violoncello piccolo* departs from its role as equal partner in the instrumental duet texture and descends over a two-octave scale from d′ to D, changing from the usual alto clef to the bass clef, then returning to the upper register and clef as the voice quickens its rhythm. Bach utilizes this effect several more times throughout the aria, linking it in the same way with the first word, "Bitte," of the "B" section, and causing the *violoncello piccolo* to double briefly the *basso continuo* at important sectional cadences (at one of which it reaches its lowest tone in this movement, C♯). Although Bach might have had some ingenious "rhetorical" idea in mind (such as the symbolizing of the *Gnadenbund* of the recitative in the bond between registers), the immediate impact of these points of descent to the lowest register of the instrument is that of depth, a quality that suggests the humility and sincerity of praying (*Bete*) and beseeching (*Bitte*) God the judge from the depths of human guilt ("Bitte bei der grossen Schuld deinen Richter um Geduld, soll er dich von Sünden frei und gereinigt machen": Beg the judge for patience in your great guilt, that he will make you pure and free from sin). Mostly, however, the *violoncello piccolo*, although it does extend into the lowest register at times, participates in a chamber-music texture whose very attractive character offsets the dominant tone of warning in the text, so that its prayer for God's *Geduld* comes from one who, as in Cantatas 180 and 49, is prepared for God's acceptance.

The ensuing recitative indicates that God hears the prayer ("Er sehnet sich nach unserm Schreien": He longs to hear our crying), providing victory for the faithful who pray in Jesus's name. But the final chorale, in returning to the message of the opening movement and the anticipation of the last judgment, affirms the predominantly fearful tone of the work as a whole. The pleading character of the fourth movement therefore sets it apart not only from the overall warning character of the cantata but even from the depiction of God as judge of the guilty in its own text. Now the quality of intimacy and the attractive instrumental character combine to suggest all that the believer hopes for from his prayer.

The idea just mentioned underlies what is perhaps Bach's most interesting *violoncello piccolo* part in the cantatas, at least in terms of its instrumental character, that of the aria "Woferne du den edlen Frieden" from Bach's chorale cantata for New Year's Day 1725, *Jesu, nun sei gepreiset* (Cantata 41). I have discussed this cantata elsewhere, principally from the standpoint of its featuring a structure designed to articulate the metaphor of Jesus as Alpha and Omega, beginning and end, as the key to the community's hopes for the new year.[22] The outermost movements of Cantata 41 feature the very festive orchestra of three trumpets with kettledrums and three oboes in addition to the strings. Within these framing movements, however, Bach invokes the pastorale association of the oboes in an aria in which they function as a trio "choir" of homophonic and gently melodic character. And, in the

[22] See also Chafe, "*Anfang und Ende*," 103–34.

aria with *violoncello piccolo* he likewise invokes the quiet character associated with Jesus's bringing peace to the faithful. Now the instrument emerges in its most elaborate role, in an *adagio* solo in which Bach introduces the most agile and wide-ranging registral shifts of all the arias in which it appears. The notation, split according to register between treble and bass clefs (the former passages transposing down an octave in performance), helps underscore the meaning of the text: a prayer: whereas Jesus brings peace to the physical state of the community ("Woferne du den edlen Frieden vor unsern Leib und Stand beschieden"), he will also provide his word of blessedness for the soul ("so laß der Seele doch dein selig machend Wort"). With this "Heil" the community will be blessed on Earth and among the elect hereafter ("Wenn uns dies Heil begegnet, so sind wir hier gesegnet und auserwählet dort").

Behind this text lies the image of Jesus as Alpha and Omega, his hand held up in greeting and blessing (as is described in the preceding recitative). Once again, then, it was the personal contact with Jesus, bringing peace to the community, as in the post-Easter cantatas, that probably prompted the use of *violoncello piccolo*. And the wide-ranging character of the solo, with many disjunct leaps in register, emphasizing its dual roles as melody and bass instrument, mirrors the oppositions of physical and spiritual existence as well as Jesus's all-encompassing nature as Alpha and Omega. Jesus's divine nature underlies the festive scoring of the outer movements of the cantata, his portrayal as *Christus Victor* prompts a prayer from humanity to "tread Satan beneath our feet" in the second recitative, while his comforting presence offers peace and the promise of eternal life in more personal terms in the aria with *violoncello piccolo*.

If we project our knowledge of the ways that Bach uses the *violoncello piccolo* in the cantatas just discussed onto those for spring 1725, we see that in them Bach has devised a unique means of mirroring the positive appearance of Jesus in the world, not as judge or as the *Christus Victor* but as the "other side" of that portrayal, the good shepherd who brings peace, whose presence brings comfort and protection in times of darkness and fear, whose protective "arm" covers the believer, and whose incarnation through the Holy Spirit in the human heart brings boundless joy. In summary, whether the *violoncello piccolo* ought to be identified with the *viola pomposa* that Bach reportedly invented, the instrument has a role in the Bach cantatas that was principally motivated by musico-theological interests. Not only is the *violoncello piccolo* associated with various aspects of the presence and person of Jesus (i.e., union between the soul and Jesus in Cantatas 180 and 49; prayer for Jesus to remain in *Bleib bei uns*; the believer's experience of Jesus in the heart in Cantata 68; Jesus as good shepherd in Cantatas 85 and 175; Jesus's protective presence in Cantata 183), but its presence or absence also helps to define a large-scale pattern in the cantatas of spring 1725.[23]

[23] Bolduan makes several of these points in "The Significance of the *Viola Pomposa* in the Bach Cantatas."

Ascension Day is an ancient dividing point within the "great fifty days" in that it commemorates what John describes as the completion of Jesus's "lifting up," his return to the Father (thus in some traditions the time from Easter to Ascension Day was called the "great forty days," a designation that expressed an obvious juxtaposition of its character of celebration to the penitence of the forty days of Lent, which immediately preceded the Passion and Easter). Before Ascension Day Jesus's presence can be understood in the literal, physical sense; *Bleib bei uns* and *Am Abend aber desselbigen Sabbats* refer to Jesus's post-resurrection appearances, even though those narratives are extended figuratively to the later Christian community. After Ascension Day, however, Jesus's presence must be understood entirely as taking place through the Holy Spirit. The presence of the *violoncello piccolo* early in the sequence, then its absence and return after Ascension Day provides an aural counterpart to that pattern, which is described in the Johannine motto-texts of Cantatas 108 ("Est ist euch gut, daß ich hingehe; denn so ich nicht hingehe, kömmt der Tröster nicht zu euch. So ich aber gehe, will ich ihn zu euch senden") and 74 ("Ich gehe hin und komme wieder zu euch. Hättet ihr mich lieb, so würdet ihr euch freuen"). As we saw, Cantata 183 for the Sunday before Pentecost expresses the equivalence of Jesus's return and the coming of the Holy Spirit. The appearance of the *violoncello piccolo* in its first aria expresses a change in the understanding of worldly persecution. On the second day of Pentecost, Cantata 68 equates the coming of the Holy Spirit with Jesus's second incarnation, now within the human heart; the aria "Mein gläubiges Herze" draws the *violoncello piccolo* into the expression of joy that this event arouses in the believer. And on the third day of Pentecost the last of the five pieces with *violoncello piccolo* voices the believer's perception—through the metaphoric seeing and hearing—of Jesus's coming in faith as the good shepherd: "Es dünket mich, ich seh dich kommen, . . . Du wirst im Glauben aufgenommen . . . Ich kenne deine holde Stimme, die voller Lieb und Sanftmut ist, . . . wer zweifelt, daß du Heiland seist."

From Cantata 183, for Exaudi (the Sunday after Ascension Day), which is fully given over to anticipation of the coming of the Holy Spirit through the three days of Pentecost, the focus on special instrumental sonorities increases dramatically. While Easter (Cantata 249) and Pentecost (Cantata 74) feature the most outstanding instances of trumpet choirs, with the instrument used as soloist in Cantatas 103, 128, and 175, Cantata 183 for Exaudi is entirely given over to the "soft" instruments. Cantata 175, however, is the work that seems best to sum up their roles in the works of the preceding weeks. With its representation of two sides to Jesus's "word," that of the *Christus Victor* and that of the good shepherd, Cantata 175 brings together two types of instrumental sonority, *violoncello piccolo* and trumpets, which have run throughout the cantatas of spring 1725, both now heard for the last time. The recorders that sound at the beginning and end of the cantata, however, making their last and most conspicuous appearances in the spring 1725 sequence, establish a new framework, that of the comforting inner voice of the Spirit.

{12}

Exaudi and Pentecost: Cantatas 183, 74, 68, and 175

Sie werden euch in den Bann tun (BWV 183)

One of the most interesting features of the cantatas from Exaudi through Trinity Sunday is the reappearance of many of the themes of the cantatas for earlier weeks in the season, now in the context of the coming of the Holy Spirit, a quality that is mirrored musically in the noticeable increase of "soft" instruments, *violoncello piccolo*, oboes da caccia, and recorders (see fig. 11.1, ch. 11). *Sie werden euch in den Bann tun*, for the Sunday before Pentecost, exhibits several of these themes: worldly persecution, Jesus's protection of the faithful, anticipation of the coming of the Holy Spirit, prayer. Like Cantata 103, it begins with Jesus's foretelling the persecution of the disciples, "Sie werden euch in den Bann tun, es kömmt aber die Zeit, daß, wer euch tötet, wird meinen, er tue Gott einen Dienst daran" (They will put you under a bann [or "out of the synagogue"]; but there will come a time when whoever puts you to death will believe he is doing God a service therein). It may seem strange that, following the very positive framework of the cantata for Ascension Day, this cantata doubles back to such a theme directly before Pentecost. But, in fact, as Regin Prenter's seminal study of Luther's concept of the Holy Spirit makes clear, the work of the Holy Spirit is bound up with inner conflict. Its presence does not remove the individual to another, higher plane, in which he/she will be detached from the world forever. Just the opposite: the central idea, rather, is "conformity" to Christ, which means acceptance of worldly suffering and conflict as the will of God.[1] Although in Bach's time this view was tempered by increased emphasis on love and the feeling quality of faith and the Spirit, its theological core remained very much intact.

In fact, Cantata 44, of the preceding year, had begun with exactly the same motto (Jn 16:2), and had given far greater attention to the believer's conflict and struggle

[1] Prenter, *Spiritus Creator*, 3–27.

with the world than Cantata 183. In Cantata 44 Bach set the motto as an extended two-movement complex (87 + 35 measures), the first for tenor/bass duet and the second for full chorus, and its primary affect was one of lamentation. After that, the first aria had defined "true discipleship" for contemporary Christians in terms of persecution in the world (particularly by the Antichrist, widely considered by Lutherans to be the pope). Not until the end of the fourth movement did the librettist introduce any hint of the benefit of worldly suffering, offsetting the theme of persecution somewhat with that of God's watching over the church, and also a hint of the awaited blessed outcome for the faithful, but in no way replacing it. The last words "Es gehe, wie es gehe, dein Vater in der Höhe, der weiß zu allen Sachen Rat" (Let things go as they will go. Your Father in heaven knows what is appropriate for all situations) emphasize acceptance of God's will no matter where it leads.

Cantata 183 also gives expression to the necessity of leaving matters in God's hands. But it is not the final message of the cantata, which describes how the believer receives support from God in the present life. Thus, whereas Cantata 44 does not refer to the Holy Spirit at all, in Cantata 183 the experience of the Spirit is the main theme. The Johannine motto is now set as a scant five-measure solo for bass, with two oboes d'amore, two oboes da caccia, and *basso continuo*. And it serves as the introduction to a movement sequence of a very different order from that of its predecessor, so different, in fact, that we may consider that Bach and Ziegler might have deliberated on the difference and striven to represent another side of the meaning of the *dictum*. Moreover, in this different approach, Cantata 183 seems to have been designed to fit within the larger conception of the season as a whole as a transition from Easter to Pentecost. Despite its pessimistic initial pronouncement, Cantata 183 is not dominated by the idea of suffering in the world. Rather, owing in part to the fact that within John's Gospel the reading for Exaudi immediately precedes that for Cantate, two weeks earlier, it shares with Cantata 108 the theme of the Holy Spirit and how it will be experienced; this connection recalls Christian Marbach's perceiving a bond among Cantate, Rogate, and Exaudi. In the development of this theme Bach's conception goes beyond Mariane von Ziegler's text.

In the first aria, directly following the Johannine motto, the believer proclaims "Ich fürchte nicht des Todes Schrecken, ich scheue ganz kein Ungemach. Denn Jesus's Schutzarm wird mich decken, ich folge gern und willig nach" (I do not fear the horror of death, I do not shy away from hardship. For Jesus's protective arm will cover me, I will follow ready and willing). In Cantatas 44 of the year before and 42 earlier in the season, God's protection was of the church. Now the tone is more personal, implying that Jesus's longed-for return to the believer is at hand, while the willing following of Jesus echoes the many expressions of being directed by the Spirit in Cantata 108 and anticipates the ending of Cantata 175 for the third day of Pentecost (the chorale, "Nun, werter Geist, ich folge dir"). After this, the remaining three movements all introduce the Spirit directly, first as the anticipation of the presence of Jesus's spirit—"Ich tröste mich, dein Geist wird bei mir stehen" (I comfort myself, your Spirit will remain by me: accompanied recitative)—then in a direct address to the Holy Spirit—"Höchster Tröster, Heilger Geist" (Highest comforter, Holy Spirit: aria)—and finally, as a chorale summary of the role of the Spirit in enabling humanity to obtain help from God through prayer. Now the coming of the Spirit is not merely being foretold and anticipated (as in Cantata 108) but experienced within, a quality that Mariane von Ziegler introduced into her series *before* the narrative of the coming of the Spirit in the Gospel for Whitsunday. The effect is to broaden the meaning of the coming of the Spirit beyond the feast associated with its first historical manifestation, a very Johannine characteristic.

Bach's most immediate analog of this "spiritual" quality in Cantata 183 is the reappearance of oboes da caccia and *violoncello piccolo* (the first appearance of that instrument since Cantata 85, *Ich bin ein guter Hirt*), which introduce a tone that seems particularly appropriate to the intimate character of the Holy Spirit. Cantata 183, in fact, is very much a chamber-music conception, the chorus entering only for the final chorale. And in this conception the two arias are pivotal. The cantata has only five movements, of which the first and third are accompanied recitatives of only five and ten measures respectively. Since the first aria is marked *molt' adagio,* it can take well over seven minutes in performance, whereas the second aria takes less than half that time. In both arias, however, the relationship between the voice and the instrumental part/s seems to have been carefully calculated by Bach to project quailites related to the experience of the Spirit. In the first one the believer proclaims freedom from the fear of death because of Jesus's protective presence. The theme of freedom from fear does not mean, however, that the negative aspect of the Gospel reading has been forgotten or neglected, simply that it has been given a secondary position. Bach explores the nature of that freedom in the two arias.

The brevity of the opening *dictum* marks an enormous change from the tormented character of its setting in Cantata 44. The recitative in Cantata 183, set in A minor, is scored for bass with pairs of very slowly moving oboes d'amore and oboes da caccia above a pedal tone, A, that does not move until the cadence in the fifth and last measure. The uppermost melodic line for oboe d'amore, however, outlines a very direct stepwise ascent of a perfect fifth from a′ to e″. Diatonic at first, then chromatic as the motto refers to those who seek the believer's death, the rising-fifth line binds the locally dissonant but tonally logical series of harmonies into a shift from a to e (with the Picardy third). (See ex. 12.1) It appears as though the idea of change itself is central to the design, since Bach introduces the dominant of e right from the second measure, where it colors the sudden drop downwards in the voice for "Bann thun." After that, the harmony moves via the circle of fifths to the d harmony on "meinen" in the fourth measure. The diminished-seventh above the pedal on "tötet" is suddenly expressive. But the pedal A has not resolved, and the D-minor harmony (heard as the subdominant of a), moves, with "er thue Gott einen Dienst daran" to another diminished-seventh in the voice, now a tone higher, reintroducing the dominant of e, heard at "Bann thun," and now leading to the e/E cadence.

EXAMPLE 12.1 Cantata 183, *Sie werden euch in den Bann tun* *first movement*

Harmonically, the shift from a to e constitutes the "goal" of this movement, subordinating the various details in the voice, especially the diminished- or dominant-seventh descents (the first two of which leap back upward), to the cadence, where the voice moves upward to "Dienst" before the final drop on "daran." Thus the initial A minor gives way quickly to the key of the first aria, seeming in fact to direct the listener's thoughts to the aria's exploration of how, under Jesus's protection, the believer grapples with the horror of death. In this context, the meaning of the initial *dictum* is not merely that of the persecution of the disciples (now reinterpreted in terms of the contemporary believer), but of the carrying out of God's will, his alien work, embodied in the believer's "cross." Ziegler's and Bach's expansion on this idea in the E-minor aria with *violoncello piccolo*, "Ich fürchte nicht des Todes Schrecken," which follows immediately, makes this clear. Although the soloist proclaims his freedom from fear under Jesus's protective "Schutzarm," the movement is mostly elegaic in tone, not an expression of joy or freedom but rather of the acceptance of worldly persecution as the necessary "cross" of the world (see ex. 12.2). Throughout this magnificent movement Bach explores the character of that state of mind.

Ziegler's text divides clearly into two strophes of four lines each. Bach, however, makes the dividing point between the aria's two principal sections after the second line, thereby placing most of the weight of the movement on the believer's expres-

EXAMPLE 12.2 **Cantata 183, *Sie werden euch in den Bann tun*** *no. 2, aria "Ich fürchte nicht des Todes Schrecken," beginning*

sion of freedom from fear of death in the first two lines. And this section, as is usual in a *da capo* aria, has a rock-solid tonal structure involving modulation to the dominant (completed in m. 16 of its twenty-eight measures) and back, the whole framed by the tonic-key ritornello. Since the section repeats as a Da Capo, it represents fifty-six of the aria's seventy-four measures. Within the "B" section Bach sets the remaining six lines of the text, the first two of which—"Denn Jesus's Schutzarm wird mich decken, ich folge gern und willig nach" (lines 3 and 4)—are positive in tone, whereas the remaining four are much less so. Those lines first paraphrase the ending of the *dictum* of the first movement— "wollt ihr nicht meines Lebens schonen, und glaubt Gott einen Dienst zu thun" (if you do not want to preserve my life, and believe you are doing God a service)—then give the response, "Er soll euch selber noch belohnen, wohl an, es mag dabei beruhn" (He shall reward you himself; well then, it must rest with that). In making an uninterrupted sequence out of Ziegler's lines 3 through 8, Bach links Jesus's protection of the believer and the believer's willingness to follow to the theme of persecution with which the *dictum* ended and to the believer's leaving the outcome in God's hands.

Throughout the aria the ornate character of the principal melodic material and the slow sixteenth-note motion generate a very expressive Bachian line that seems designed to project the sense that the believer's confidence is under restraint or beset by worries and concerns. The minor character, amplified in the augmented seconds of the melody, prevents it from projecting a clear alternative to the fear of death that the believer claims freedom from in the opening lines. The "cross" of worldly life seems ever present. Nevertheless, in the changing roles of the *violoncello piccolo*—now playing the melodic line, now functioning as a bass line to the tenor—it appears that Bach might have intended the instrument to symbolize Jesus's supportive presence, while the sequential motion toward the cadences, where the *violoncello piccolo* always plays the bass line, suggests its leading the believer onward. As mentioned in chapter 11, expressions of the believer's reliance on Jesus's protection and her own willingness to follow lead in the middle section to the key of f♯ (m. 33), the farthest point in the sharp direction for the aria and the cantata as a whole. Usually the two styles in the *violoncello piccolo* are balanced. But here Bach extends the *violoncello piccolo*'s doubling of the bass to virtually the entire passage, creating a palpable association with the believer's reliance on Jesus's supportive presence through the adversities of life. In minor keys, Bach often associates modulation to the supertonic, which is outside the ordinary *ambitus* of the key and involves articulation of its dominant, still farther outside, with tormented states of mind, often suggesting the "difficult" way of the cross. As if to proclaim willingness to take that route, the tenor decorates the dominant on "gern" before the initial arrival on f♯, then sings an elaborate flourish on "folge" before the main cadence. And the following in question does generate an immediately positive effect, in that the music that sets the remainder of the text turns immediately to D and moves on through G to C major, settling on a long-held cadential c′ ("ruhn"), so that the textual reference back to the *dictum* that began the cantata voices the believer's intention to leave matters in God's hands. Now the conclusion "wohlan, es mag dabei beruhn," provides a decided sense that the outcome will be a positive one for the believer. And while the tenor holds the c′, the *violoncello piccolo* begins the main theme in C major. The cadence, however, is to A minor, after which the next phrase, after passing through e and b, moves to G major, closing the section in a more positive tone.

In the middle section the less-than-positive-sounding recall of the tone of the opening *dictum* is carried forward in the text so as to explore the impact of Jesus's protection in the adverse circumstances of life. The return to E minor for the repeat of the principal section, however, makes clear that the believer's proclaiming freedom from fear of the horror of death is a complex state of mind in which the liberating experience of faith (the positive "possessions" of faith, to use Walter von Loewenich's expression) do not yet fully overcome the opposition between faith and experience. Throughout, the aria depicts more the believer's direct response to the adverse circumstances than the avowal of freedom from fear of death with which it begins. Nevertheless, "Ich fürchte nicht des Todes Schrecken" mirrors, despite its elegaic tone, the beginning of the believer's understanding of the positive outcome of the torment predicted in the motto. The next stage in that understanding is the subject of the recitative and aria that follow.

Luther's commentary on the reading for Exaudi draws an analogy between the persecution of the disciples (that is, their being banned from the synagogue) and the excommunication of Lutherans by the pope. It develops the idea that the true church is the one that follows God's word regarding Jesus, rather than any accretions:

> On the other hand, if one abides by this article [the divinity of Jesus] diligently and earnestly, it has the grace to keep one from falling into heresy and from working against Christ or his Christendom. For the Holy Spirit is surely inherent in it, and through it illuminates the heart and keeps it in the right and certain understanding, with the result that it can differentiate and judge all other doctrines clearly and definitely, and can resolutely preserve and defend them. . . . Such a believer walks in simple faith, does not indulge in subtle disputes about God's Word, does not incite quarrels or foster doubt. And if someone assails one doctrine or another, a Christian is able to defend himself against these and to repel the attacks; for he has on his side the true Teacher, the Holy Spirit, who alone reveals this doctrine from heaven and is given to all who hear and accept this Word or sermon concerning Christ.[2]

While the minor key and predominantly sorrowful tone of "Ich fürchte nicht des Todes Schrecken" are reminders of the prediction contained in the Johannine *dictum* with which the cantata begins, the primary message of its text is the willing following of God's way under Jesus's protection. After its E minor, the G-major beginning of the subsequent alto recitative, setting the words "Ich bin bereit" (see ex. 12.3), is a special moment of faith, underscored by the fact that the motive associated with that phrase continues in dialog between the pairs of oboes throughout the entire movement. Now the alto solo proclaims complete trust in Jesus and an anticipation of the Spirit, still in the context of worldly suffering: "Ich bin bereit, mein Blut und armes Leben vor dich, mein Heiland, hinzugeben, mein ganzer Mensch soll dir gewidmet sein; ich tröste mich, dein Geist wird bei mir stehen" (I am ready to lay forth my blood and poor life before you, my Savior, my whole being will be dedicated to you; I comfort myself that your Spirit will stand by me). The affirmative character of the beginning expresses the believer's necessary conformity to the way of the cross and God's will, which may lead to tribulation she is unable to bear, as the final line makes clear: "gesetzt, es sollte mir vielleicht zuviel geschehen" (assuming that things should turn out to be too much for me).

In the context of the spring 1725 sequence, this movement carries the believer's anticipation of the coming of the Holy Spirit to a new level. While the instrumentation creates a bond with the opening motto, the ever present "Ich bin bereit" motive (which sounds in free inversion at "vor dich, mein Heiland") suggests a form of interior dialog. From the words "mein Blut und armes Leben" the harmony introduces the dominant- and diminished-seventh of e (reached on "mein Heiland, hinzugeben," then moves by circle-of-fifths motion toward D ("mein ganzer Mensch soll dir gewidmet sein; ich tröste mich, dein Geist wird bei mir [stehen]"), where it is suddenly deflected toward f♯, in preparation for the believer's final expression

[2] *Luther's Works*, vol. 24, *Sermons on the Gospel of St. John*, 320–21.

EXAMPLE 12.3 **Cantata 183, *Sie werden euch in den Bann tun*** *no. 3, recitative, beginning (m. 1) and ending (mm. 7–10)*

of weakness. As in other Bach cantatas, *O Ewigkeit, du Donnerwort* (BWV 60), for example, the "dissonant" motion to sharp-minor keys suggests the difficulty of the way of the cross. And for the ending Bach introduces a striking harmonic event. Using as a pivot the diminished-seventh chord on d♯ that had effected the shift to e in the opening *dictum*, the closing words, "gesetzt, es sollte vielleicht zu viel gesehehen" ("assuming that things should be too much for me"), make an enharmonic change from the sharp keys that have held until that point (an f♯ chord just before the point of change) to C minor, after which the recitative closes in C major, key of the aria that follows.

The sense of distance that underlies the f♯ and C cadences of the preceding aria seems compressed into this transformational event. We may be reminded of the enharmonic modulation from the dominant of f♯ to C major in Cantata 121, for Christmas Day, 1724.[3] There the transformation, associated with the miracle of the incarnation ("um zu den Menschen sich *mit wundervoller Art zu kehren*": so as *to turn* toward humanity *with miraculous art*), prepares for the C-major aria that follows, narrating the miraculous event of the incarnation in terms of John the Baptist's leaping in his mother's womb. It is an analog of the awareness of Jesus's presence, unmediated by anything of a rational character, exactly as it is here, where it mirrors the experience of the Spirit (longed for in Cantata 108) as if a second incarnation within the heart, coinciding with the believer's expression of his own weakness and need for aid from God. At the very point that the believer cries that things have become too much, the d♯′ changes to e♭′, while in the woodwinds, for the only time in the movement, the "Ich bin bereit" motive sounds simultaneously in both its original and its inverted forms.

Luther's concept of "conformity" (*Gleichförmigkeit*), set forth in his early writings and echoed by many subsequent Lutheran theologians, including some that Bach might have read, is explained by Regin Prenter in terms wholly applicable to this "turning point" in Cantata 183. Prenter emphasizes first that the work of conformity—rooted in inner conflict and tribulation as the result of God's "alien work," the cross laid by God upon the believer—is solely that of the Holy Spirit, whose presence in the believer must be viewed as a second, now spiritual (tropological) incarnation of Christ:

> Just as Christ is conceived by the Holy Spirit, so every believer is justified and regenerated not by the work of man, but by the grace of God alone and the work of the Spirit. It is the tropological exegesis which is used in such a way that the literal incarnation of Christ is interpreted as his *mystica incarnatio* by which he is spiritually born in the believer. Everything related about the first coming of Christ in the flesh may also be said about his spiritual coming.[4]

The closing words of Ziegler's recitative mirror Luther's proclaiming that the inner conflict associated with the cross will indeed be too much for the believer; and it is *there* that the Holy Spirit intercedes. In Regin Prenter's words:

> To endure the work of God in us during the infernal darkness of inner conflict is humanly impossible. Time and again it is emphasized that it is impossible to stand in the darkness of inner conflict. God the Holy Spirit alone can help us by interceding for us with groanings which cannot be uttered. . . . When the sinner groans for God with sighs that cannot be uttered in spite of

[3] See the discussion of this passage in Chafe, *Analyzing Bach Cantatas*, 142–43.

[4] Prenter, *Spiritus Creator*, 11.

> the darkness of trial, in the midst of the excruciating experience of the wrath of God and the terror of hell, and out through his rebellious blasphemy against God, then this greatest love to God, which groans for God, is not possible for man. It is not man himself who calls upon his last resources in a final religious effort, it is not man's inward soul that appears, but it is God himself who, as the subject of this greatest act of love, is truly present in us, it is the Holy Spirit himself who, as our helper and comforter, groans in us and for us.[5]

Prenter bases his understanding of the Holy Spirit, as did the Lutheran authors from the time of the reformer to Bach, on the classic text for Luther's understanding of the Holy Spirit in Romans 8:26:[6]

> Desgleichen hilft auch der Geist unsrer Schwachheit auf. Denn wir wissen nicht, was wir beten sollen, wie sich's gebührt; sondern der Geist selbst vertritt uns mit unaussprechlichem Seufzen.
>
> (Likewise the Spirit also helpeth our infirmities: for we know not what we should pray for as we ought: but the Spirit itself maketh intercession for us with groanings which cannot be uttered.)

Clearly, the tone of Luther's concept of conformity has greatly softened during the time between the reformer and Mariane von Ziegler. Her recitative does not expound on the conflict and torment that are often described so graphically and intensely in the earlier years of Lutheranism (and in other Bach cantatas). The concept of the spiritual or tropological incarnation of Jesus through the Holy Spirit as the means by which the willing but incapable believer may endure the cross of earthly suffering nevertheless underlies Ziegler's text for the aria "Höchster Tröster," which follows "Ich bin bereit," and whose middle section directly refers to Romans 8.

In Cantata 183, Bach uses the recitative "Ich bin bereit" to effect a turning point that introduces the coming of the Spirit. The a–e–G ascent through the movement keys from the initial motto to the "Ich bin bereit" that begins the recitative, and the move toward sharp-minor keys that turns around in the enharmonic change, symbolizes both the believer's readiness for the coming of the Spirit ("Ich bin bereit")—acceptance of adversity, or "Geduld" (patience) in the Lutheran frame of reference—

---

[5] Ibid., 16–17.

[6] Ibid., 18. As Prenter remarks, "the reference to Romans 8:26 is constantly repeated when Luther discusses the work of the Spirit in detail. This Scripture passage is Luther's center of understanding by which all his thoughts about the Spirit are orientated." In his double-chorus motet, *Der Geist hilft unser Schwachheit auf* (BWV 226), Bach set not only the twenty-sixth, but also the twenty-seventh verse of Romans 8: "And he that searcheth the hearts knoweth what is the mind of the Spirit, because he maketh intercession for the saints according to the will of God," concluding the motet with a verse of the chorale "Komm, heil'ger Geist." In light of the appearance of the verb "vertreten" (intercede) in both these verses its appearance in Cantatas 87 and 183 is noteworthy.

and the acknowledgment of weakness that is necessary to that event. The return through C major to A minor over the concluding sequence of movements describes prayer as the means by which the Spirit aids the believer in his weakness. The experience of the Spirit leads the believer from inner conflict to reliance on God's help.[7]

The character of the tonal transformation and the C-minor coloring at the close of the recitative, a sudden expression of weakness and reliance on the Spirit, prepare for the soprano's C-major aria, "Höchster Tröster, heil'ger Geist," in which, for the first time in the 1725 cantata sequence, the believer addresses the Spirit directly. In comparison to "Ich fürchte nicht des Todes Schrecken," "Höchster Tröster" projects much more of the positive impact of the Spirit on the believer. After the long-drawn-out expression of suffering and conflict in the earlier aria, this one is short and lively. Bach seems to describe the believer's experience of the Spirit in the relationship between the first violin and oboe da caccia parts, which sometimes merge into parallel octave or unison lines, whereas at others the oboe da caccia takes the melody, punctuated in the violin by the principal melodic figure, a turn followed by an upward leap. The complementary character of the two voices is one in which the oboe da caccia has the main melodic line, often suggesting a character appropriate to the believer's liberation from worldly torment. At the same time, it functions as a mediating middle voice between the first violin and the lower parts. The triple-meter dance-like character of the aria voices the believer's confidence, and the G-major close of the opening section lends an affirmative tone to her expressions of trust in the Spirit's direction: "Höchster Tröster, heil'ger Geist, der du mir die Wege weis'st darauf ich wandeln soll" (Greatest comforter, Holy Spirit, you who show me the way on which I must proceed). Nevertheless, in the middle section Bach moves progressively "down" through minor keys—d and g to c—indicating *piano* for the instruments whenever the voice is present, then closes in C. The sequence of ideas that prompted this modulatory design passes through expressions of human weakness and the inability to pray, paraphrasing Romans 8:26, and ending with an expression of trust in the Holy Spirit: "hilf meine Schwachheit mit vertreten, denn vor mir selber kann ich nicht beten, ich weiss: du [the "Höchster Tröster" of the first line] sorgest für mein Wohl" (Help my weakness by interceding, for on my own I cannot pray, I know that you look after my good). Since there is no textual *da capo* but only a return of the opening ritornello, the key of c, heard frequently in the cantatas of the preceding weeks, colors expressions of weakness that define the human condition; the change to C, echoing the ending of the preceding recitative, mirrors the transformation wrought by the Spirit but with instrumental music only, an allegory, perhaps, of the believer's silence, like that of the first aria of Cantata 128 (or the ending of the first aria of Cantata 68). The reference to the believer's inability to pray is, of course, a direct connection to the subject matter of Cantata 87 where the identical series of modulations—

[7] Ibid., 55–64.

through d (the initial motto) and g (the prayer for forgiveness in the aria with oboes da caccia) to c (the prayer, "drum suche mich zu trösten" (therefore seek to comfort me) had represented the "descent" that was turned around by Jesus's answer in the second motto.

In Cantata 183 the lively tempo, engaging melodic character, and major key of "Höchster Tröster" all project what the beneficial character of the Holy Spirit really means. And in the cantatas of the spring 1725 sequence that character is associated with music as a form of prayer. In chapter 10 I described how the theme of seeing Jesus culminates in Cantata 128 for Ascension Day, indicating that it is complemented by the theme of hearing in the cantatas for the latter part of the spring 1725 sequence. The first appearance of that theme is the reference to the Holy Spirit's communicating what he "hears" to the believer in the second *dictum* of Cantata 108 ("Denn er wird nicht von ihm selber reden, sondern was er hören wird, das wird er reden; und was zukünftig ist, wird er verkündigen"), implying, of course, the believer's *hearing* the Spirit, after which it is embodied in the theme of prayer, in Cantata 87, where it is associated with penitence. In Cantata 183 it reappears, now in the context of the Holy Spirit, who gives comfort, standing by the believer, whose weakness renders him/her unable to endure persecution. This is the meaning of the f♯/c enharmonic change and shift to C on "es sollte mir vielleicht zuviel geschehen" in the recitative third movement, after which the flat modulations leading to c/C in the second segment of "Höchster Tröster" introduce prayer as the answer to the believer's weakness: "hilf meine Schwachheit mir vertreten, denn vor mir selber kann ich nicht beten, ich weiss: du sorgest für mein Wohl." In the final chorale the initial lines, "Du bist ein Geist, der lehret, wie man recht beten soll" (You are a Spirit who teaches how one should pray properly) are then amplified by "Dein Beten wird erhöret, dein Singen klinget wohl" (Your praying will be heard, your singing sounds well), the allusion to music (*Singen*) suggesting a personal tone appropriate to the aforementioned liberating quality.

What I have just described appears in a treatise on singing in worship that was published in Leipzig just one year after Cantata 183 was written, Christian Marbach's *Evangelische Singe-Schule*.[8] In his first and third chapters, Marbach deals first with the relationship between singing and prayer, then with the Holy Spirit as the "Oberste Singe-Meister" who directs the furthering of our "Seelen-Heil" through prayer and music. In chapter 1 Marbach emphasizes the close relationship between prayer and singing, citing Luther's remark that "he who sings once prays twice," and making a special association of the two with the Sundays before and after Ascension Day, Cantate, Rogate, and Exaudi, the last of these crowning the meaning of the relationship:

> We see, therefore, that pious people seldom separate what God has joined together. And in public divine worship singing and prayer are *always* joined;

---

[8] Marbach, *Evangelische Singe-Schule.*

> there is also no doubt that that bond will also be inseparable in heaven and will remain indissoluble through eternity. Accordingly, therefore, here on earth the heart of a devoted Christian should be like the ark of the covenant: for as formerly on it two cherubim embraced one another, so here must singing and praying hold onto one another. Then there will always follow Cantate (singing) after Rogate (prayer) and Rogate after Cantate; the divine Exaudi, however, places the crown on both. For the Lord does what the God-fearing desire ("begehren") when they pray, and hears their crying when they sing, and helps them when he hears them. Psalm 145:19.[9]

Then in his third chapter Marbach draws the abovementioned analogy between the Holy Spirit and a music director, citing many of the passages from John and elsewhere in scripture that were widely associated with the role of the Holy Spirit in faith, including the one from Romans 8, cited earlier, that Mariane von Ziegler paraphrased in the text of "Höchster Tröster." In the second division of his chapter, titled "What does the Holy Spirit actually do then during the act of singing?" (Was der Heilige Geist denn eigentlich bey dem Singe-Wesen thue?), Marbach expands the analogy to seven subdivisions, citing Heinrich Müller's praise of singing in the fifth one, "the Holy Spirit sings with us and in us," and ending by proclaiming, as his seventh act of the Holy Spirit, that the Spirit

> highly recommends our songs in heaven, and through his support seeks to make them so pleasing that they may be heard with certainty and that our praying, beseeching and singing in Jesus's name must succeed well. For *he represents the holy*, according to the manner *that pleases God* (Romans 8:26), and therefore [makes them—the songs—so pleasing] that it pleases God. To this belong the words of the pleasing singer Paul Gerhard:
>
> You are a Spirit who teaches
> How one should pray properly.
> Your prayer is heard,
> Your singing sounds well.

---

[9] Ibid., 7:

> Wir sehen daher, daß fromme Leute das selten scheiden, was GOtt zusammen gefüget hat.Und im öffentlichen Gottesdienste wird auch Singen und Beten **allezeit** verbunden; es ist auch kein Zweifel, daß dieses Band im Himmel selbst wird unzertrennet bleiben, und durch die Ewigkeit erst recht unauflöslich werden. So soll demnach schon hier auf Erden das Herze eines andächtigen Christen wie die Bundes-Lade seyn: Denn wie sich auf jener ehemals zweyt Cherubim einander umfasseten; also müssen sich hier Singen und *Beten* an einander halten. Da folget denn immer *Cantate* auf *Rogate*, und *Rogate* auf *Cantate*, das göttliche *Exaudi* aber setzet beyden die Crone auf. Denn der HERR thut, was die Gottesfürchtigen begehren, wenn sie *beten*, und höret ihr Schreyen, wenn sie *singen*, und hilfft ihnen, wenn er sie *erhöret*. Psalm. 145, 19.

Psalm 145, v. 19 reads "He will fulfill the desire of them that hear him; he also will hear their cry, and will save them."

It ascends to heaven,
It ascends and does not cease
Until he has helped,
Who alone can help.[10]

This verse is the one chosen by Mariane von Ziegler as the final chorale of Cantata 183. For Marbach it summarizes how the relationship between singing and praying embodies the work of the Holy Spirit.

In the cantatas that follow, Mariane von Ziegler retains the themes of hearing and being heard, along with further allusions to music. One week later, in Cantata 74, for Whitsunday, the "indwelling" of God and the hope that his word will be internalized prompts the believer to an expression of faith: "Ich zweifle nicht, ich bin erhöret" (I do not doubt that I am heard). Later we hear the aria "Kommt, eilet, stimmet Sait und Lieder in muntern und erfreuten Ton" (Come, hasten, tune strings and songs in cheerful and joyful tone). And on the following day (Cantata 68) the rejoicing becomes still more overt: "Mein gläubiges Herze, frohlocke, sing, scherze, dein Jesus ist da" (My believing heart, rejoice, sing, play, your Jesus is here). It is Cantata 175, however, that ties together the themes of hearing and being heard in its juxtaposition of *violoncello piccolo* and trumpet for the shift from the believer's hearing the soft inner voice of the shepherd–"Ich kenne deine holde Stimme, die voller Lieb' und Sanftmut ist"–to his urging his ears to hear the word of promise: "Öffnet euch, ihr beiden Ohren." In such passages the theme of hearing and singing depicts the mutual exchange between the believer and God that comes through the Holy Spirit.

Wer mich liebet, der wird mein Wort halten (BWV 74)

In contrast to the other principal feastdays of the year, Pentecost celebrates an event that centers not on Jesus but on the disciples and, indeed, on the church and the individual Christian believer. As a feast celebrating the birthday of the church and marking, therefore, the transition to Christian life in the world, Pentecost is a focal point for the spiritual quality whose perspective dominates not only the liturgical year but the whole of Christian life. The coming of the Holy Spirit is not localized and unique in time, or historical, as are Christmas and Easter (and most of the

---

[10] Ibid., 22–23:

Endlich so bestehet das Amt des Heiligen Geistes auch darinnen, das er 7. *unsere Lieder aufs beste im Himmel recommandire,* und durch seinen Vorschub so angenehm zu machen suche, daß sie gewiß erhöret werden, und unser Beten, Flehn und Singen in JEsu Namen wohl gelingen müsse: Denn *er vertritt die Heiligen,* nach dem *das Gott gefälle,* Rom. 8, 26. und also, daß es GOtt gefällt. Hieher gehören des angenehmen Sängers, *Paul Gerhards* Worte: *'Du bist ein Geist der lehret,/Wie man recht beten soll:/Dein Beten wird erhöret,/Dein Singen klinget wohl;/Es steigt zum Himmel an,/Es steigt und läst nicht abe,/Biß der geholffen habe,/Der allein helffen kan.'"*

other feasts celebrated during the first half of the year). As a spiritual event whose external point of origin is bound up with the internalizing of God's word, it expresses the unique and universal means provided by God for the understanding of all other events.[11] Pentecost is the key to how all other events move from the realm of history to that of the faith experience of the individual believer. In this sense of transcending history, the coming of Jesus "in the Spirit" or, as Erdmann Neumeister put it, "in grace through word and sacrament," is just as appropriate to Advent and Christmas as to Pentecost. Spiritual understanding is therefore enshrined in the methodological understanding of scripture (hermeneutics) via the so-called spiritual senses, above all the tropological.[12] Thus between the epistles and the Gospels for the three days of Pentecost we perceive a division between the historical and spiritual sides of the coming of the Holy Spirit. The three epistles, all taken from the book of Acts, which is centered on history, narrate the coming of the Holy Spirit first to the disciples, then to gatherings at Caesarea and Samaria, the latter generally associated, like the coming of the Magi at Epiphany, with the gentiles. The Gospels for the three days of Pentecost, all from John, however, are not at all centered on events but rather on Jesus's words, the quality that Luther associated with John. The internalizing of those words is the tropological sense, the work of the Spirit.

Of those sayings of Jesus that foretell the coming of the Holy Spirit the best known is undoubtedly the opening motto of Cantata 74, "Wer mich liebet, der wird mein Wort halten, und mein Vater wird ihn lieben, und wir werden zu ihm kommen und Wohnung bei ihm machen" (Whoever loves me, he will keep my word, and my Father will love him, and we will come to him and make a dwelling place with him), since it describes love as the basis for the indwelling of Father and Son in the believer. Bach's first three Pentecost cantatas feature this statement as either the first or second movement. Its meaning is most directly expressed in Bach's first surviving cantata for Pentecost, BWV 172, *Erschallet, ihr Lieder, erklinget, ihr Saiten* (Sound forth, you songs, resound, you strings), written in 1714 to a text of Salomon Franck and performed repeatedly in Leipzig. After a festive introductory chorus for trumpets, strings, and winds, that work sets Jesus's words as a bass motto, followed immediately by an aria, "Heiligste Dreieinigkeit," for bass, three trumpets with kettledrums and *basso continuo* that proclaims the fuller understanding of the divine/human relationship that came through the Holy Spirit. "Heiligste Dreieinigkeit" beseeches God, the Trinity, to come to the human heart "in der Gnadenzeit," an expression that links the "tropological" or spiritual advent of Jesus to the time of the Spirit. And it makes clear the disparity between the Trinity and its dwelling place, the human heart: "Komm doch in die Herzenshütten, sind sie gleich gering und klein" (Come, however, in the humble abode of the heart, no matter how restricted and small it is). The remainder of Cantata 172 then turns

---

[11] On this aspect of Luther's view of the Holy Spirit, see Prenter, *Spiritus Creator*, 127.

[12] de Lubac, *Medieval Exegesis*, 2:127–78.

to imagery associated directly with the Holy Spirit, comparing the "wind" of Pentecost to the evening cool in the garden of Eden, the paradise of the soul (*Seelenparadies*) through which the Spirit of God moved (the tropological sense). A dialog between the soul and the Holy Spirit expresses the feeling associated with the Spirit.[13] All in all, Cantata 172 is the fullest expression of the relationship between Pentecost and Trinity in Bach's oeuvre.

In contrast to such a brilliantly focused expression of the meaning of Pentecost, Mariane von Ziegler's conception of the span that follows Ascension Day and ends with Trinity Sunday has a far more complex theological character. Instead of concentrating on the doctrine of the Holy Spirit, Ziegler follows the ideas presented in the Gospel readings, among which qualities of chronology and logical sequence are decidedly secondary to the anticipating, reiterating, and doubling back that characterize the nonlinear or "circular" meditative style associated with John. We have already seen that Ziegler's texts for Cantate, BWV 108, *Es ist euch gut, daß ich hingehe*, and Exaudi, BWV 183, *Sie werden euch in den Bann tun*, anticipate the theme of Pentecost, Cantata 108 raising the question of whether the Spirit is already present and Cantata 183 exploring one week before Pentecost how the Spirit aids the believer in dealing with persecution and fear of death. Her cantata text for Trinity Sunday entirely sets aside the festive, triumphant character generally associated with that feastday. The three cantatas for Pentecost introduce a range of ideas derived from the Gospel readings that explore different facets of the meaning of Jesus's presence through the Holy Spirit. Owing to the character of John's Gospel, those ideas generally reach out beyond the immediate theological context to express the unifying character of Pentecost. Since the most important point surrounding Pentecost is the understanding of God's presence through the Holy Spirit—God's spiritual rather than physical presence—the events of the scriptural narrative pivot around the relationship between Jesus's physical departure on Ascension Day and his return through the Spirit. As a result, Jesus's departure and return serves as a theme in several cantatas of the series. *Bleib bei uns* beseeches Jesus to stay; *Am Abend aber desselbigen Sabbats* describes his returning to protect the faithful; *Ihr werdet weinen und heulen* anticipates both the loss and return of Jesus in tropological terms; *Es ist euch gut, daß ich hingehe* takes up directly the themes of Jesus's going and the coming of the "Spirit of truth" (which is shared also by the Gospel for Pentecost); *Auf Christi Himmelfahrt allein* uses the *Haupt/Glieder* metaphor to poeticize the bond between Jesus, now ascended to heaven and his "members" below; and *Sie werden euch in den Bann tun* voices acceptance of the Holy Spirit as the means by which Jesus protects and teaches the faithful. That Mariane von Ziegler's cantata text for Pentecost, BWV 74, *Wer mich liebet, der wird mein Wort halten*, utilizes a motto from John in which Jesus predicts his coming and returning again—"Ich gehe hin und komme wieder zu euch. Hättet ihr mich

[13] The dialog in question resembles the "love duets" between Jesus and the soul in Cantatas 21 and 140.

lieb, so würdet ihr euch freuen" (I will go away and come again to you. If you loved me, then you would rejoice)—is what might from a linear standpoint be considered a redundancy is here entirely characteristic of the Gospel readings for the time between Easter and Pentecost. The quality of "atemporality" that many commentators have found in the Farewell Discourse is essential to the character of the season whose principal message is the means by which the events of Jesus's life and work move out of history to permeate the life of faith.

The Gospel reading for Whitsunday (Jn 14:23–31) is the earliest of the five readings from the Farewell Discourse within the Gospel itself, but the last in the sequence of spring readings drawn from those verses. That ordering enabled one of Jesus's earlier, more general discourses on the coming of the Holy Spirit to begin the sequence of Pentecost readings. The reading divides into three distinct parts (vv. 23–26, 27–29, and 30–31) that Mariane von Ziegler's text mirrors with the aid of two mottoes from John (vv. 23 and 28—movements 1 and 4), plus a third from Paul (Rom 8:1—movement 6). The first stage, in Cantata 74 (*Wer mich liebet, der wird mein Wort halten*), comprising the *dictum* of John 14:23 and followed by an aria and recitative, centers on the necessity of love and keeping God's word to the believer's state of readiness for reception of the Spirit. The second, the *dictum* of 14:28, plus a related aria, places Jesus's announcement of his departure and return in the context of that love and its implications of joy for humanity. And the third stage, the motto from Paul, followed by an aria and chorale, takes up the message of humanity's inheritance from Jesus's victory over Satan. In this sequence Ziegler's text seems to look *backwards* from the coming of the Spirit to Jesus's announcing his departure and return (the subject of Cantata 108), then to Paul's perspective on the resurrection. The effect is to suggest how the coming of the Spirit builds on, or follows from, the themes given earlier in the season.

Ziegler takes pains to bind these themes into a continuity by making the ending of each stage anticipate the theme of the next. Thus, after taking up love, God's word, *Trost,* and the certainty of being heard by God, all in the context of the readiness of the heart for God's dwelling place, her first stage leads into the theme of the second motto with the words "Drum laß mich nicht erleben, daß du gedenkst, von mir zu gehn. Das laß ich nimmermehr, ach, nimmermehr geschehen" (Therefore let me never feel that you might think of going away from me. That I will never more, Ah, nevermore allow to happen). In this way Ziegler establishes a tropological context for Jesus's announcement of his departure and return in the second motto. Likewise, the middle section of the second aria (no. 5) introduces the third topic of Jesus's discourse in the Gospel, the approach of Satan with the words "Der Satan wird indes versuchen, den Deinigen gar sehr zu fluchen. Er ist mir hinderlich, so glaub ich, Herr, an dich" (Satan will nevertheless seek utterly to curse your own. He is an obstacle to me, therefore I believe, Lord, in you) within the context of the believer's expression of joy over Jesus's return (the principal section). The third motto then affirms that the relationship between Jesus and the believer that results from Jesus's return renders the believer free from condemnation: "Es ist nichts Verdammliches an denen, die in Christo Jesu sind" (There is nothing to be condemned in those who are in Christ Jesus). The words "in Christo Jesu" express the idea of "indwelling" as set forth in the opening motto as a mutual one between God and the believer. And the aria that follows relates that quality to Jesus's victory over Satan in the Passion; Jesus's blood is the bond between him, and the believer, his suffering and death render the latter an inheritor of God's gifts.

Ziegler seems to have wanted to create a relationship between the two New Testament authors whose writings were central to Luther's thought, John and Paul. Her text, in fact, polarizes its first and third subdivisions, making the second motto into another "turning point": Jesus's departure and return symbolize the division between a group of ideas centered on intimacy with God (love and the "indwelling" of God in the human heart as told by John) and a group centered on the meaning of Jesus's defeat of the devil as proclaimed by Paul. Ziegler drew her third motto from Paul in order to emphasize an important dimension to the idea of "indwelling" that belongs to Pentecost: the gift of the Spirit is entirely unearned by humanity; only Jesus's Passion and the love that motivated it make it possible for humanity to receive the Spirit. The final chorale, "Kein Menschenkind hier auf der Erd' ist dieser edlen Gabe wert" (No child of humanity here on the earth is worthy of this noble gift), states that fact emphatically.

In keeping, perhaps, with its sounding on one of the three principal feast days of the liturgical year, BWV 74, *Wer mich liebet, der wird mein Wort halten,* utilizes the full *ambitus* of C/a in conjunction with its three biblical mottoes to represent different aspects of the Pentecost message. The first segment begins in the tonic, C, then shifts to the flat side of the *ambitus*: the subdominant, F, for the first aria, then to the supertonic, d, for the beginning of the ensuing recitative; the second aria shifts to the sharp, or dominant, side of the *ambitus*, with the second motto, now in e, and an aria in G; the third motto now turns back from e to the tonic region of the *ambitus*, with an aria in C and final chorale in a. Bach's choice of C major and C trumpets, instead of D, which would link up directly with the message of Easter, was perhaps made in conjunction with the fact that in its tonal design the cantata as a whole moves in three distinct key areas—the natural, flat, and sharp regions of the C/a *ambitus*—each one associated with a biblical *dictum*. Thus Bach mirrors the comprehensiveness of Ziegler's three divisions in his tonal structure.

In the opening movement five of the six keys appear, lending it a comprehensive as well as majestic tone. With its groups of three trumpets (plus kettledrums), three oboes (two oboes plus oboe da caccia), and strings, this movement expands the twofold groupings of voices (soprano/bass duet) and trumpets heard in its earlier version of Cantata 59. At first the chorus moves in duets: soprano and alto in mm. 10–15, tenor and bass in mm. 16–23, presumably a reference to the Father and Son of the *dictum* (as in Cantata 59). The three groupings of instruments, however, suggest a Trinitarian symbolism, especially when they concertize back and forth, as they frequently do.

EXAMPLE 12.4 **Cantata 74, *Wer mich liebet, der wird mein Wort halten*** *no. 2, aria, "Komm, komm, mein Herze steht dir offen," beginning*

Here, the direct shift to F for the first aria involves a striking change in tone as the oboe da caccia emerges from the oboe group to take on the role of the instrumental solo voice in the soprano's very personal plea to the deity: "Komm, komm, mein Herze steht dir offen, ach, laß es deine Wohnung sein! Ich liebe dich, so muß ich hoffen: dein Wort trifft itzo bei mir ein" (Come, come, my heart stands open to you, ah, let it be your dwelling place! I love you, therefore I must hope that your word will now penetrate into me). (See ex. 12.4) These lines voice the believer's response to the opening motto, while the lines "Ich zweifle nicht, ich bin erhöret, daß ich mich dein getrösten kann" (I do not doubt I am heard, that I can comfort myself with you) echo the linking of prayer and *Trost* in Cantata 87 and the ending of Cantata 183 ("dein Beten wird erhöret"). The beginning of the ensuing recitative then develops the theme of readiness voiced in the recitative "Ich bin bereit" of Cantata 183, in conjunction now with a move to the supertonic: "Die Wohnung ist bereit. Du findst ein Herz, das dir allein ergeben" (The dwelling place is ready. You find a heart that is given to you alone: D minor cadence). (See ex. 12.5) After the believer's rejection of his own thought of building a dwelling place for God in Cantata 128 (a worldly conception grounded in "works" and reason), this part of

EXAMPLE 12.5 **Cantata 74, *Wer mich liebet, der wird mein Wort halten*** *no. 3, recitative*

the cantata seems to associate the shift to the subdominant region of the *ambitus* (a "descending" sequence of keys) and the soft tone of the oboe da caccia with the "indwelling" of Father and Son within the human heart through love and the Holy Spirit, a conception shared by Cantatas 108 and 172.

The continuation of the recitative anticipates the theme of the second "division" of the cantata: "drum laß mich nicht erleben, daß du gedenkst, von mir zu gehn. Das laß ich nimmermehr, ach, nimmermehr geschehen." These lines shift immediately to A minor, bridging to the dominant side of the *ambitus,* which emerges in the E-minor second *dictum*, the aria "Ich gehe hin und komme wieder zu euch. Hättet ihr mich lieb, so würdet ihr euch freuen." Now love has the effect that Jesus's departure and return bring joy to the believer. Within the instrumental design of Cantata 74 this second motto can be described as the "center," in that its texture of intertwining vocal bass and *basso continuo* lines completes a progressive reduction in scoring (and lowering in pitch) throughout the sequence of movements to this point (after the motto the instrumentation increases again, mirroring the idea of departure and return). In the motto itself Bach describes Jesus's "going" and "returning" by means of an ascent/descent curve in both the quasi-ostinato bass and vocal melodies as well as modulation to G and back to e within the two segments of the piece (ex. 12.6). In comparison to the motto that begins Cantata 108, Jesus's going ascends rather than descends, and is complemented by a descent that mirrors his return through the Spirit. Even at Pentecost Jesus's going—that is, his ascension—is the necessary other side of the coming of the Spirit; hence the change in modulatory direction from the subdominant/supertonic region to the mediant/dominant for the second division of the work.

As in the first division, the second motto is followed by an aria that directly responds to its "word" of promise. In the earlier aria the benefit of love was *Trost*, represented in inner, intimate terms; now it is joy, pure and simple: "Kommt, kommt, eilet, stimmet Sait und Lieder in muntern und erfreuten Ton" (Come, come, hasten, harmonize strings and songs in joyful, rejoicing tone). Set in G, for tenor and strings with an ornate first violin part, this more extrovert hortatory aria completes the shift from the subdominant/supertonic area to the mediant/dominant, associating the concertizing of the tenor and first violin with the words "stimmet Sait und Lieder" and the dominant (G) with "in muntern und erfreuten Ton." The middle section, in e, offsets the tone of joy somewhat by a reminder that Satan will nevertheless attempt to "curse" the faithful ("Der Satan wird indes versuchen, den Deinigen gar sehr zu fluchen"); but, as the text asserts, faith provides the answer: "Er ist mir hinderlich, so glaub ich, Herr, an dich."

There is nothing at all casual about the change of tone for the middle section of the aria just described. The idea of Satan's "curse" and the turn to faith after the prominent emphasis on love in the opening movements is a key to the theological message of the work. For this cantata is unique among the series of spring 1725 in containing *three* successive motto/aria pairings; and, as mentioned earlier, the third motto, "Es ist nichts Verdammliches an denen, die in Christo Jesu sind," is no lon-

EXAMPLE 12.6 **Cantata 74, *Wer mich liebet, der wird mein Wort halten*** *no. 4, aria, "Ich gehe hin und komme wieder zu euch," beginning*

ger from John, as are the preceding two, but comprises instead the beginning of the eighth chapter of Paul's epistle to the Romans, in which the apostle describes the role of the life-giving Spirit of Christ in freeing humankind from the law of sin and death. As we have seen, Luther named the Gospel and letters of John and the epistle to the Romans as the principal books of the New Testament, designating the latter "the Gospel in its purest form." And his understanding of Pentecost was the result of Paul's discussions of the new law of the Spirit that the church celebrated as counterpart of the Jewish Pentecost.[14]

[14] See Luther, *Complete Sermons of Martin Luther,* vol. 4.1, *Sermons on Epistle Texts for Epiphany, Easter and Pentecost from the Kirchen-Postille* (Grand Rapids, MI: Baker Books, 2000), 330. Bach's most interesting setting of passages from Paul that set forth the ideas in question is the motet *Jesu, meine Freude,* in which verses from Romans 8 alternate with those of the chorale in an eleven-movement design.

Under the influence of Paul's words, the tone of the cantata from this point on changes substantially, so that we can speak of discrete "stages" in the theology of the work as a whole. John's presentation of the Spirit as *Tröster* (which underlies both the love in the first two movements and the rejoicing to which it leads in the tenor aria) gives way to an affective character that is closer to Paul's juxtapositions of spirit and flesh. Paul's reference to those who are "in Jesus" complements the "indwelling" of Father and Son in the human heart, as described in the opening motto. As if to ensure the sense of equivalence, Bach sets the motto from Paul, as he had the second one from John, for bass solo, now accompanied by two oboes and oboe da caccia. After the excursions to the subdominant/supertonic and mediant/dominant sides of the *ambitus* in the preceding movements, the third motto effects a return to the tonic region, beginning in e and moving progressively in the flat direction, inflecting its return to C major with a very expressive b♭ on "Jesu." The return to C and its message of mutual indwelling complete the idea of return proclaimed in the second Johannine motto.

The C-major *da capo* aria that follows the third motto, "Nichts kann mich erretten von höllischen Ketten als, Jesu, dein Blut" (Nothing can rescue me from the chains of hell, Jesu, other than your blood), seems to make direct reference to the ending of the recitative in the vocal phrase that ends each of its "A" sections. Although the return to C can be considered to mirror Jesus's return as described in the second motto, this one projects a very different character from that of the C major opening movement. Bach leaves out the trumpets and sets the aria in the style of a concerto for solo violin with separate string and wind choirs, deriving its extrovert militant character from the idea of Jesus's struggle with the forces of evil (ex. 12.7). The solo violin plays a remarkable arpeggiated part whose harmonic-chordal character frequently serves as bond (mediator, perhaps) between the wind and string bodies. In the middle section all the instruments unite for sharp punctuating chords on the words "Sterben" and "Erben": "Dein Leiden, dein *Sterben* macht mich ja zum *Erben*; ich lache der Wut" (Your suffering, your death, make me an inheritor; I laugh at the fury), making clear the idea of benefit for the believer as the outcome of Jesus's victory over death. Not only the solo violin but all the strings play aggressive triple stops at these points, while the solo violin plays a quadruple stop on the final chord of each of the ritornelli of the "A" section. Whereas the *violoncello piccolo* represents the comforting character associated with the image of Jesus as good shepherd, the solo violin of "Nichts kann mich erretten" depicts him as *Christus Victor*, the concertizing of strings and winds recalling the opening movements of Cantatas 42 and 103. The sense of struggle throughout this aria seems to join Paul's struggle between flesh and spirit to John's representation of Jesus's victory.[15]

[15] The salvific character of Jesus's blood, the subject of this aria, was associated with John as much as with Paul. Thus the tenth and last of Johann Arndt's preparatory sermons on the Passion from his

EXAMPLE 12.7 **Cantata 74, *Wer mich liebet, der wird mein Wort halten*** *no. 7, aria "Nichts kann mich erretten von höllischen Ketten," mm. 18–30*

After this aria, whose instrumentation and key balance to a degree the opening movement of the cantata, the final chorale ends the work in A minor instead of C, making the theological point that humanity is not worthy of (and has not in any way earned the benefits of) Jesus's sacrifice. Behind it lies Luther's and Paul's inveighing against "works righteousness," a tone that is removed from the direct optimism of the first, second, and fifth movements.

Postilla is devoted to this theme, titled "Erklärung von der Krafft des Bluts Christi" and taking John 1:7 as its text, "Das Blut JESU Christi machet uns rein von allen Sünden" (see Arndt, *Postilla,* 1:517–20).

In comparison to Bach's first Pentecost cantata, *Erschallet, ihr Lieder* (BWV 172), *Wer mich liebet* (BWV 74) is considerably more complex in its theological message. The earlier work is increasingly personal as it proceeds, a quality that is mirrored in its overall shift in the subdominant direction, from the dominance of trumpets in the instrumentation of its first and third movements to the intertwining of voices and oboe d'amore above a quasi-ostinato obbligato cello in the duet for the soul and the Holy Spirit that comprises its penultimate movement (the oboe d'amore playing a highly decorated version of the melody of the chorale "Komm, heiliger Geist"). The conspicuous flat modulations in the duet mirror as closely as possible the quality of increasingly personal experience as well as expressing human weakness in relation to the deity.[16] In *Wer mich liebet*, on the other hand, that quality emerges only in the first of its three subdivisions, the second one complementing it with a more extrovert quality of rejoicing and the third aria still more extrovert in nature but linked now to a message of militant "theological" character. In keeping with its depictions of Jesus in the role of the indwelling Holy Spirit, the comforter of the faithful and the *Christus Victor*, Cantata 74 separates its subdominant, dominant, and tonic tonal areas, placing them in the service of a comprehensive musico-theological message owing to the conjunction of mottoes from John and Paul.

Also hat Gott die Welt geliebt (BWV 68)

The third division of Cantata 74 utilizes a motto from Paul, rather than John, and reflects Ziegler's desire for comprehensiveness, a reminder of Walther von Loewenich's view that "for Luther the path to John went through Paul."[17] For the remainder of the spring cantata sequence the theological emphases return very solidly to John's perspective. The Gospel reading for the second day of Pentecost (Jn 3:16–21) is the ending of Jesus's discourse with Nicodemus (Jn 3:1–21), of which the preceding verses (1–15) comprise the Gospel reading for Trinity Sunday, six days later. Verses 1–15 take up the idea of rebirth through the Spirit, followed by Jesus's prediction of his "lifting up," whereas vv. 16–18 introduce the themes of God's love, faith as the key to salvation, and the question of judgment, and vv. 19–21 the very Johannine theme of light versus darkness. In her text for Cantata 68, however, Ziegler mirrors closely only the sequence of ideas in vv. 16, 17, and 18, leaving the three verses that deal with light and darkness for Trinity Sunday.

In Ziegler's text, "God so loved the world that he gave his only Son, so that all who believe in him should not be lost but have eternal life (Jn 3:16)," appears in the form of a chorale paraphrase, "Also hat Gott die Welt geliebt" (movement 1). "For

[16] See Chafe, *Tonal Allegory*, 145–47.

[17] Loewenich, *Luther und das Johanneische Christenthum*, 16.

God did not send his Son into the world to judge the world, but that the world should be saved by him (Jn 3:17)," is paraphrased as the final three lines of the only recitative (movement 3). And "Whoever believes in him will not be judged; whoever, however, does not believe, is judged already, for he does not believe in the name of God's only begotten Son (Jn 3:18)," appears as a direct quotation from the Gospel (the fifth and final movement). In addition, the recitative alludes to the epistle for the day (Acts 11:42–48), the ending of Peter's speech to Cornelius in Caesarea, which describes Jesus as judge of the living and the dead, offering forgiveness to all who believe in him, upon which the Gospel narrates that the Holy Spirit fell on all those who listened to the words, including the gentiles, who were then baptized by Peter in the face of astonishment from the Jewish Christians. The first half of the recitative, "Ich bin mit Petro nicht vermessen, was mich getrost und freudig macht, daß mich mein Jesus nicht vergessen" (Like Peter, I am not presumptuous; what gives me comfort and joy is that my Jesus has not forgotten me) makes a connection between the idealized believer of the cantata and Peter, who baptized all who responded with faith and on whom the Holy Spirit fell, whether Jew or gentile. The point is that the Holy Spirit makes distinctions only on the basis of belief or disbelief.

Thus Cantata 68 divides the world, whether Jews or gentiles, into those who hear the word, believe, and are possessed of the Holy Spirit, who therefore are not judged, or lost, but inherit joy and eternal life, and those who do not believe and are judged already in the present for their lack of faith. Judgment or lack of judgment is linked to the absence or presence of faith and the Holy Spirit. Ziegler's text is unusual in that instead of beginning with the biblical motto and progressing through processes of paraphrase and interpretation, ending with a chorale, it works backwards, from the chorale through the paraphrase to the biblical motto, becoming more severe at the end as it cites the scripture directly. The absence of a concluding chorale to put the ending in perspective is noteworthy. Presumably, the either/or character of the Johannine final chorus was intended to have a provocative effect: to provide food for thought for the congregation, so to speak, between the second and third days of Pentecost.

At the same time, however, Ziegler's text, which was composed, in the case of the two arias, so as to fit with preexistent festive music by Bach, gives ample attention to the joyful message of Pentecost. In this respect it has distinct affinities with the message of Christmas. Although the idea of rebirth through the Spirit belongs to the message of Pentecost, Ziegler's emphasis on *Jesus's* birth in Cantata 68 is remarkable (although it has a long pedigree in medieval exegesis). We find reference to Jesus's birth in the first and fourth movements in particular: chorale, no. 1: "Also hat Gott die Welt geliebt, daß er uns seinen Sohn gegeben." (God so loved the world that he gave us his son); "Wer glaubt, daß Jesus ihm geboren, der bleibet ewig unverloren" (Whoever believes that Jesus was born for him, he will never be lost, and aria, no. 4:"Du bist geboren mir zugute" (You are born for my benefit:). And, in addition, this cantata projects the joyful tone associated with the presence of Jesus at Christmas: the aria, no. 2: "Mein gläubiges Herze, frolocke, sing, scherze, dein Jesus ist da!" (My faithful heart, rejoice, sing, play, your Jesus is here). Thus, at the opposite time of the year from Christmas, *Also hat Gott die Welt geliebt* depicts the coming of the Holy Spirit as Jesus's second incarnation, within the heart, thereby completing the Christmas message and expanding on the indwelling of God as told in Cantata 74.

All of this analysis is central to Luther's concept of the Holy Spirit, as the following quotation from Regin Prenter, cited earlier in conjunction with Cantata 183, makes clear:

> Just as Christ is conceived by the Holy Spirit, so every believer is justified and regenerated not by the work of man, but by the grace of God alone and the work of the Spirit. It is the tropological exegesis which is used in such a way that the literal incarnation of Christ is interpreted as his *mystica incarnatio* by which he is spiritually born in the believer. Everything related about the first coming of Christ in the flesh may also be said about his spiritual coming.[18]

Although the Gospel for the second day of Pentecost is not drawn from the Farewell Discourse, as were those of the preceding two feast days, Cantata 68 balances the theme of the disciples' treatment by the world as narrated in Cantatas 103 and 183 by emphasizing a higher judgment. The Farewell Discourse is sometimes viewed as the equivalent for John of the "eschatological discourses" in Matthew, whose character influenced the ending of the other "half" of the liturgical year, the ending of the Trinity season. In her paraphrase of John 3:17, Mariane von Ziegler emphasized that Jesus came to the world "not *only* to judge" ("Er kam nicht *nur*, die Welt zu richten"). In an immediate sense, this was perhaps done so as to eliminate any sense of contradiction with v. 18 (and earlier verses of the same chapter), which ends the cantata with the clear message that Jesus *does* judge. But in terms of the coming Trinity season with its emphasis on Jesus's coming in judgment, it is the Johannine idea of judgment *in the present*—realized eschatology—that is the key to Ziegler's text.

Whereas all three cantatas for Pentecost 1725 center on the theme of love as the basis of the relationship between God and humankind, only Cantata 68 makes the point that it was God's love of the *world* that prompted the incarnation. This may seem at odds with the rejoicing of the world over the persecution of the disciples in Cantata 103. But, as Johann Arndt argues, in the second of his sermons for Pentecost Monday from the *Postilla*, God's love must be understood to embrace the entire world, and not, as some, especially the Calvinists, had argued, only the elect. Arndt supported this view through interpretation of the following words of the Gospel, "Das ist aber das Gericht, daß das Liecht in die Welt kommen ist, und die Menschen liebeten die Finsternüß mehr dann das Liecht" (That is then the judg-

---

[18] Prenter, *Spiritus Creator*, 11.

ment, that the light came into the world and humanity loved the darkness more than the light), which led him to conclude that human beings loved darkness more than light *by nature*. God's love was all the more to be praised, therefore, since it embraced even sinners and God's enemies. At the same time, human beings had to participate in this great love through their faith. Arndt cites Jesus's words from John 15:22 to illustrate the fact that Jesus's incarnation, in making sin known to humanity, removed the possibility of excusing or "cloaking" sin: "Wann ich nicht kommen wäre, und hätte es ihnen gesagt, so hätten sie keine Sünde. Nun ich aber kommen bin, können sie nichts fürwenden, ihre Sünde zu entschuldigen" (If I had not come and spoken unto them, they had not had sin: but now they have no cloak for their sin").[19] As great as God's love was, so great was his wrath, if one did not recognize and accept Jesus. Arndt explains John's reference to judgment "already" as God's means of identifying those who will be judged ultimately, as those who love darkness more than light and who are recognizable in the present through their evil works.[20] And for Arndt, the meaning of the words chosen by Ziegler to end Cantata 68 pivot around the acceptance or nonacceptance through faith of Jesus as the Messiah. In a sense, the ending of Cantata 68 raises a question that will be answered in the cantatas to follow. Ziegler's deferring all reference to the light/darkness theme of the Gospel for Pentecost Monday until Trinity Sunday, as we will see, enables Cantata 176 to take up these questions more fully.

The tonal design of Cantata 68 is rooted in ascent from its initial D minor (the chorale fantasia, "Also hat Gott die Welt geliebt") through F (the aria "Mein gläubiges Herze") and A minor (the first half of the lone recitative) to C (the recitative ending and aria "Du bist geboren mir zugute"), followed by descent through a back to d (the final chorus).[21] In this design, the chorale paraphrase that begins the cantata, "Also hat Gott die Welt geliebet," announces the potentially redeemed world as the "ground" and foundation for the believer's hopes. Bach molds the chorale into a siciliano-style melody, one that offers overtones of the pastorale as well as of entreaty. The instrumental scoring, for three oboes and cornetto (or horn), reinforces this impression.[22] The pattern of its cadences (d–F–[d, F]–a–a–F–d) is an ascent/descent curve within the tones of the triad, its "apex" the two A-minor cadences for the crucial phrases "Wer glaubt, dass Jesus ihm geboren, der bleibet

---

[19] Arndt, *Postilla*, 3:223, 245–46.

[20] Ibid., 246–57.

[21] Chafe, *Tonal Allegory*, 210.

[22] As Masaaki Suzuki points out ("The Wind Instrument in the First Movement of BWV 68") in his program notes for the Bach Collegium Japan recording of Cantatas 28, 68, 175, and 183 (BIS-SACD-1641, 2008, program booklet, 8), "there are some doubts regarding which instrument Bach intended for the wind part supporting the soprano in this movement. At the top of the part is the inscription 'Corne' and the part is notated at actual pitch. However, at the head of the fifth movement in the same part is the clear inscription 'Cornetto', and the music is notated a whole tone lower than the sounding pitch." Suzuki concludes "it is thus clear that in the fifth movement the cornetto would have been used together with the trombones tuned to the *Chorton* pitch, but it is most likely that a different instrument was envisaged for the first movement."

EXAMPLE 12.8 **Cantata 68, *Also hat Gott die Welt geliebt*** *no. 2, aria, "Mein gläubiges Herze," mm. 12–17*

ewig unverloren," an anticipation of the text of the last movement, making clear the crucial role of faith. Due to the repeated tones of the melody on the word "bleibet," the second of these phrases hovers on the dominant of a before making the fifth descent to a. The effect is to project this phrase as a point of attainment, after which the return through F to the tonic, d, is a palpable descent to the original level.

The aria that follows, "Mein gläubiges Herze" (soprano, *violoncello piccolo,* and oboe), is one of the greatest expressions of unmediated joy in Bach's oeuvre, its quasi-ostinato "leaping" melodic bass line originally associated in Cantata 208 with the line "weil die wollenreichen Herden durch dies weitgepriesne Feld lustig ausgetrieben werden" (while the flocks, rich with wool, are driven joyfully through this field, famous far and wide). (See ex. 12.8). The pastorale character suggested in the chorale fantasia now emerges in very personal, immediate terms, an analog of the joyful experience of faith, and a direct connection with the pastorale imagery of BWV 175, *Er rufet seinen Schafen mit Namen* (heard the following day) and, of course, BWV 85, *Ich bin ein guter Hirt.* Bach's ending "Mein gläubiges Herze" with a twenty-seven-measure instrumental postlude based on the joyful *basso continuo* melody of the aria, now set apart by its trio texture, depicts "joy to which nothing can be compared" as a joy that goes beyond words. It connects up with the several references to silence in the cantatas of the preceding weeks and it links up conceptually with the mistrust of reason that appears in a number of Bach cantatas, including *Er rufet seinen Schafen mit Namen*.

The first half of the recitative that follows then shifts to A minor, after which it settles on the dominant of C in preparation for the second aria. Drawing upon the majestic tone created for its original text, "Ein Fürst ist seines Landes Pan" (A prince is the Pan of his land), Bach's second aria, "Du bist geboren mir zugute," for bass, three oboes, and continuo, sensitively matches Ziegler's emphasis on Jesus's work of salvation over that of judgment in her paraphrase of John 3:17. The aria externalizes the message of joy presented in "Mein gläubiges Herze," representing the benefits of faith in the purpose of Jesus's incarnation as the "apex" of the tonal design, just as occurred with the phrase that referred to the meaning of Jesus's birth in the opening movement. The G-major close of the principal section is particularly striking, repeating the entire ritornello with the voice, in the dominant, to the text "das glaub' ich, mir ist wohl zumute, weil du vor mich genung getan" (I believe this, it uplifts my spirit, because you have done what is sufficient for me). The entire section then repeats once more, now in A minor, to the lines "Das Rund der Erden mag gleich brechen, will mir der Satan widersprechen, so bet' ich dich, mein Heiland, an" (The orb of earth may crumble immediately, Satan may speak out against me, but I will pray to you, my Savior), then in modified form, in e, to the same text. In this scheme the modulation to G in the first section has an unusually affirmative character, while the majestic style and oboe instrumentation lend the movement the character associated in the original with Pan, described in the text of Cantata 208 as the "illustrious" God who "makes the land so fortunate that forest, field and everything live and laugh."

After such an extrovert expression of joy, the motto from John that follows paints the ending of the work in sombre colors derived from the Gospel's alternative of judgment and salvation in the present life. Bach set the motto as a double fugue whose two subjects describe those alternatives: "Wer an ihn gläubet, der wird nicht gerichtet" (Who believes in him will never be judged) and "wer aber nicht gläubet, der ist schon gerichtet" (whoever does not believe is judged already). And he added a choir of three trombones and cornetto to the doubling instruments, lending the whole an unusually grave character that, owing to the absence of a concluding chorale, is in no way tempered by the perspective of the church. The A-minor beginning of the movement gives way to the tonic, d, in the answering voices, and an extensive element of flat modulating for "wer aber nicht gläubet" underscores the aspect of warning. It is noteworthy that until the final measures the principal theme of the fugue, more imposing than the others, due to its slower rhythm and wide intervals, sets only the text "Wer an ihn gläubet, der wird nicht gerichtet," whereas the more lively secondary themes set both the positive and negative pronouncements. When, near the end, a strong A-minor cadence is followed by the return to d for the final words of the motto "denn er gläubet nicht an den Namen des eingebornen Sohnes Gottes" (for he does not believe in the name of the only begotten Son of God), we hear, as the closing gesture of the movement, the line just cited sound to the principal theme in the soprano voice doubled by the cornetto, with all the other themes alluded to in the lower voices. More than any other gesture in the movement, this striking emphasis on the negative aspect of the text, places the joy of the preceding movements in a perspective that does not shy away from the fearful implications of John's mutually exclusive alternatives.

Er rufet seinen Schafen mit Namen (BWV 175)

On the second day of Pentecost Mariane von Ziegler's unusual either/or ending for Cantata 68 seems to leave something unsaid, to demand completion on the following day. Ziegler's text for that day, "Er rufet seinen Schafen mit Namen" makes the only explicit references to the Holy Spirit of the three 1725 Pentecost cantatas, ending with the chorale verse "Nun werter Geist, ich folge dir" (Now, worthy Spirit, I follow you). This verse characterizes the life of the Spirit as "another life" given by God in grace through his word ("hilf, daß ich suche für und für nach deinem Wort ein ander Leben, das du mir willt aus Gnaden geben"). And it alone suggests that Cantata 175 was conceived as a point of completion, returning to what was anticipated in Cantata 183, whose third, fourth, and fifth movements articulate a shift from third-person reference to Jesus to direct address, first to Jesus ("Ich tröste mich, dein Geist wird bei mir stehen"), then to the Spirit ("Höchster Tröster, heilger Geist," "Du bist ein Geist, der lehret"). The meaning of that shift, which describes a progression from the external word of scripture to the internal word of the Spirit, from history to faith, is duplicated in Cantata 175, in which the Word, given to the disciples by Jesus himself, is now given to the believer through the Spirit. All three of Ziegler's cantata texts for Pentecost emphasize that the Holy Spirit is a gift from God. The indwelling of Father and Son and the unworthiness of humanity for God's gifts expressed in Cantata 74 become joy over the spiritual "incarnation" of Jesus ("Mein gläubiges Herze") and recognition of his gifts ("Du bist geboren mir zugute") in Cantata 68. Cantata 175 views those benefits in light of Jesus's words, the comforting, personal voice of the good shepherd to his sheep as narrated in the Gospel for the day, now equated with the inner voice of the Holy Spirit.

The Gospel reading on which Cantata 175 is based (Jn 10:1–11) directly precedes that for Misericordias Domini (Jn 10:12–16) of five weeks earlier; thus, there is a direct link between Cantata 85, *Ich bin ein guter Hirt*, in which the image of the good shepherd was particularly prominent, and *Er rufet seinen Schafen mit Namen*, in which it merges into the Holy Spirit. The reverse ordering of the two readings was presumably conceived so that Jesus's generalizing the meaning of the analogy would be set forth earlier in the liturgical sequence; in addition, the verses for Misericordias bring out the theme of the good shepherd's laying down his life for the sheep, a parable of Jesus's Passion, commemorated just two weeks before. In

Cantata 85 the theme of love, which is prominent in all three Pentecost cantatas, is directly linked to Jesus's Passion; the second aria, "Seht, was die Liebe tut," relates Jesus's protection of "his own" to his having "poured out his precious blood on the cross." Jesus's suffering is equated to the shepherd's watching while the hired hands ("Mietlinge") sleep, his enabling the sheep to enjoy the pasture in peace.

The verses selected for the third day of Pentecost begin with the parable of the shepherd as the only one to enter the sheepfold by the door rather than "some other way," as the one whose voice the sheep recognize, who calls them by name and leads them forth (vv. 1–5). Its meaning has not yet been explained, and v. 6 narrates that Jesus's listeners (the Pharisees) did not understand what he said, prompting Jesus to explain (vv. 7–9) that he was the "door": "I am the door: by me, if any man enter in, he shall be saved, and shall go in and out, and find pasture" (v. 9), ending with "I am come that they might have life, and that they might have it more abundantly" (v. 11). With the next verse, "I am the good shepherd," Jesus provides the still more general basis for his explanation of the analogy to the "door," leading into the message of sacrifice that anticipated the Passion (but that in the liturgy followed it).

Mariane von Ziegler's text for Cantata 175 continues and develops these themes. The poem can be said to divide into two halves, each beginning with a motto from John. Ziegler follows the sequence of the Gospel reading closely, emphasizing first the personal relationship between the shepherd who knows the sheep "by name" and the sheep who respond only to the voice of the true shepherd (as opposed to the thief who enters the fold secretly). The first half takes up the believer's longing for the coming of the shepherd who is "concealed," embodying a sense of darkness awaiting light ("Ach, wo bist du *verborgen*? . . . Brich an erwünschter *Morgen*!": Ah, where are you hidden? . . . Break forth, awaited morning!), the time of faith (evidence of things not seen) and longing for fulfillment, as well as of comfort from the shepherd's voice. This is, of course, a poeticized expression of Christian life in the world after Jesus's departure, comforted by faith and directed by the Holy Spirit.

Up to this point, the believer responds to Jesus as shepherd. The first aria, "Komm, leite mich, . . . mein Hirte, meine Freude" (Come, lead me, . . . my shepherd, my joy), subtly equates the shepherd to the Holy Spirit by means of the "leiten" idea that figured prominently in Cantata 108. The "verborgen"/"Morgen" juxtaposition in the subsequent recitative anticipates the Spirit's revealing God's word as the "Morgenstern" in the final chorale. The second aria poeticizes the parable's description of the recognition of the shepherd by the sheep, the means of recognition shifting from the eyes at the outset—"Es dünket mich, ich seh dich kommen"(I think I see you coming)—to the faith that "hears" the shepherd's voice: "Du wirst im Glauben aufgenommen und mußt der wahre Hirte sein. Ich kenne deine holde Stimme, die voller Lieb und Sanftmut ist" (You are apprehended through faith and must be the true shepherd. I know your dear voice, which is full of love and gentleness). The qualities that run throughout this sequence of movements are the personal, hidden, quiet, and loving tones that characterize the shepherd. The theme of seeing Jesus, which runs throughout the Farewell Discourse, is reinterpreted in terms of the inner voice of the Spirit.

With v.6, however, John describes the immediate response of Jesus's listeners, who do not understand the parable: "Sie vernahmen aber nicht, was es war, das er zu ihnen gesaget hatte" (They, however, did not comprehend what it was that he had said to them: Jn 10:6). Ziegler introduces this verse as a second motto, the fifth of seven movements of Cantata 175, building it into a turning point by interpreting the failure to understand Jesus's words as a general quality of human nature shared by Jesus's historical audience and the contemporary community, that of reliance on reason or, we might say in this context, on the logic of ordinary direct discourse. And this becomes the theme of Jesus's dialog with Nicodemus in the Gospel for Trinity Sunday, five days later. John himself takes a generally pejorative view of reason that Luther also adopted, giving it particular emphasis in his sermons for Trinity Sunday. Ziegler brings it out in Cantata 175 by appending a passage of her own to the Johannine motto: "Ach ja! Wir Menschen sind oftmals den Tauben zu vergleichen: wenn die verblendte Vernunft nicht weiß, was er gesaget hatte. O! Törin [i.e., reason], merke doch, wenn Jesus mit dir spricht, daß es zu deinem Heil geschicht" (Ah, yes! We humans are often to be compared to the deaf: when our dazzled reason does not know what he has said. O foolish one, take note, when Jesus speaks to you, that it concerns your salvation).

After this condemnation of reliance on reason as a form of spiritual deafness, the believer urges his ears to hear the message of Jesus's promise to overcome death and the devil, providing grace, plenty, and full life to all who take up the cross and follow in the bass aria: "Öffnet euch, ihr beiden Ohren, Jesus hat euch zugeschworen, daß er Teufel, Tod erlegt. Gnade, Gnüge, volles Leben will er allen Christen geben, wer ihm folgt, sein Kreuz nachträgt" (Open up, ears, Jesus has sworn to you that he has put down death and the devil. Grace, benefit, full life he will give to all Christians who follow him and take up his cross). Making reference to the eleventh verse of the reading for the day ("I am come that they might have life, and have it more abundantly"), Ziegler binds it with the reference to the Passion that followed in the reading for Misericordias. The overt tones of victory that emerge in this aria mirror the fact that, liturgically speaking, the Passion, resurrection, and ascension are events that have *already* come to pass, proving the truth of Jesus's promise. But behind the juxtaposition of Ziegler's two contrasted aria texts lies the opposition of Luther's false *theologia gloriae*, which seeks to fathom God's greatness through reason, and the true *theologia crucis*, which runs contrary to human expectations; hence the disciples' misunderstanding and the struggle of the present day believer, needing to have God's promise trumpeted forth. In the final chorale the following of Jesus referred to in the aria's middle section is transferred to the Spirit in a direct address, "Nun, werter Geist, ich folg' dir." The Spirit's gifts of grace and the Word, the "morning star that shines gloriously near and far," lead to eternal life. Jesus, the Spirit, and the Word are bound together inseparably as the source of spiritual rather than rational enlightenment.

Thus *Er rufet seinen Schafen mit Namen* completes the message of Pentecost with a reminder of the Johannine portrait of Jesus, not only in the twofold form of the *Christus Victor* and good shepherd but also as the incarnate Word, a portrayal that underlies the theme of the shepherd's voice in the initial movement sequence, the misunderstood word of promise in movements five and six, and the word given by the spirit as "morning star" (*Morgenstern*, an expression that usually refers to Jesus) in the final chorale. The underlying theme of light and darkness, which Ziegler will bring out further in her text for Cantata 176, is bound up with this portrayal of Jesus's presence, testimony to Ziegler's understanding of the indebtedness of Luther's doctrine of the Spirit to John.

Within this framework, Cantata 175 makes reference to many themes of the cantatas for the preceding weeks. The theme of seeing Jesus runs through the season, from longing for Jesus's physical presence, interpreted eschatologically, in Cantata 249's duet recitative "Indessen seufzen wir . . . Ach, könnt es doch nur bald geschehen, den Heiland selbst zu sehen" (Ah, if only it could happen soon that I could see the Savior himself) to the seeing of Jesus in glory from afar in Cantata 128; Jesus's "hiddenness" echoes Cantata 103, in which the line "Verbirgst du dich, so muß ich sterben," is answered in the trumpet aria, "Erholet euch, betrübte Sinnen," in the lines "Mein Jesus läßt sich wieder sehen, O Freude, der nichts gleichen kann!" The need to find Jesus once more is, of course, completed at Pentecost. The theme of Jesus as good shepherd is a direct link with Cantata 85 (and an implied connection to Cantatas 183 and 68), while the depiction of Jesus as *Christus Victor* runs through the entire season; longing for the presence of the Spirit is shared with Cantata 108; Jesus as light is shared with Cantata 6, as is the description of the Word as light; the idea of following the Spirit echoes Cantata 183. Even the theme of misunderstanding echoes the anguished cry for Jesus to "speak no longer in proverbs" in Cantata 87, while the condemnation of reason harks back to Cantata 128. And, of course, the theme of discipleship, carried over into the Christian community, is virtually omnipresent.

Musically, Cantata 175 strikes another tone altogether from that of the ending of Cantata 68, turning to G and bringing back first the sound of recorders, not heard as a choir since Peter's "Sanfte soll mein Todeskummer" in Cantata 249, then of *violoncello piccolo*, heard the day before, in "Mein gläubiges Herze." In the introductory motto the recorders provide an undulating triadic sonority above a *basso continuo* that hardly moves from the tonic pedal except to cadence (ex. 12.9). The pastorale tone, heard in earlier cantatas of the sequence, predominates more than ever in the identically scored aria that follows (now for alto). Retaining the sound of parallel triads in the recorders, it turns to the $\frac{12}{8}$ meter and evenly flowing eighth-note melodic lines usually associated with pastorales, introducing its initial lines of entreaty ("Komm, leite mich, es sehnet sich mein Geist auf grüne Weide"—

EXAMPLE 12.9 **Cantata 175, *Er rufet seinen Schafen mit Namen* *first movement***

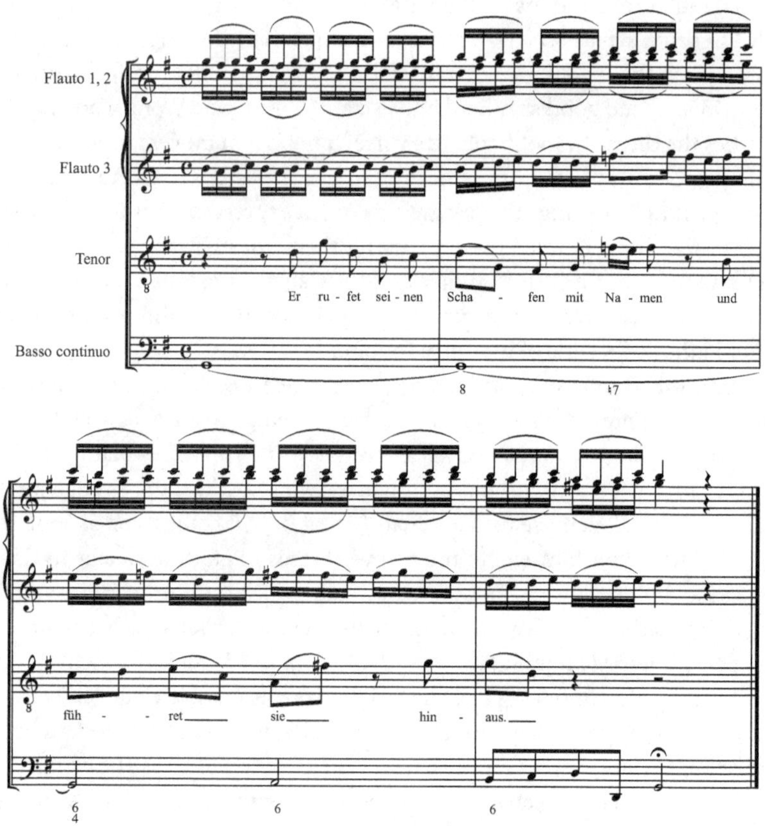

Come, lead me, my Spirit longs for green pastures) with the rising minor sixth, as did "Also hat Gott die Welt geliebt" in Cantata 68. Now the tonality shifts "down" from G to e, marking the beginning of a pattern of descent by thirds that will lead through C to a for the second recitative (ex. 12.10).

In the first recitative the believer cries out to the shepherd, who is "hidden": "Wo find' ich dich? Ach, wo bist du verborgen? O! Zeige dich mir bald! Ich sehne mich. Brich an, erwünschter Morgen!" (Where will I find you? Ah, where are you hidden? Oh! Show yourself to me soon! Break forth, awaited morning!). Bach describes the longed-for coming of the shepherd/Spirit by means of a descending circle-of-fifths motion that bridges from e to C (the dominants of a, d, G, and C in turn) for the second aria, "Es dünket mich, ich seh' dich kommen," for tenor, *basso continuo*, and *violoncello piccolo* (its last appearance in the cantata sequence). This aria projects the secure character demanded by such an expression of faith by means of a continually "walking" quarter-note bass line above which the *violoncello piccolo* plays nearly always in melodically flowing eighths, while all the parts

EXAMPLE 12.10 **Cantata 175, *Er rufet seinen Schafen mit Namen*** *no. 2, aria, "Komm, leite mich," beginning*

move in very balanced phrase groupings, usually of four measures (ex. 12.11). On a still larger level, the aria is strophic in design, mm. 1–32 repeating with new text and only slight musical modifications as mm. 33–64, both sections cadencing in the dominant, G, after which the remainder of the aria holds to the same style, cadencing first in a ("Ich kenne deine holde Stimme, die voller Lieb' und Sanftmuth ist"), then initiating the return to C with the line "daβ ich im Geist darob ergrimme" (so that I take offense in the Spirit) and completing it for the final words, "wer zweifelt daβ du Heiland seist" (with those who doubt that you are the Savior).

In this aria the depiction of Jesus as good shepherd, associated in Cantata 85 with the sound of the *violoncello piccolo,* coincides with modulation in the sub-

EXAMPLE 12.11 **Cantata 175, *Er rufet seinen Schafen mit Namen*** *no. 4, aria, Es dünket mich, ich seh' dich kommen," beginning*

EXAMPLE 12.12 **Cantata 175, *Er rufet seinen Schafen mit Namen*** *no. 5, recitative, mm. 1–8*

dominant direction (G–e–C), which Bach had introduced in Cantatas 249, 42, and 74 for arias of gentle character. The descent then continues with the shift to a for John's narrative of Jesus's audience's misunderstanding, which begins the subsequent recitative (ex. 12.12). In the middle section of the aria, the aforementioned move to a coincides with the description of Jesus's voice as full of love and gentleness. Now, in the recitative, it appears that these soft, intimate qualities are the very ones that prove an obstacle to understanding, on account of their conflicting with the human conception of God's glory. For, following the initial move to a ("Sie vernahmen aber nicht, was es war"), Bach shifts toward a quasi-Phrygian cadence to F♯ ("das er zu ihnen gesaget hatte"), in which the *basso continuo* moves from G up to A♯ instead of down to F♯, thereby highlighting the suddenness of the shift. Up to this point the instrumentation has reduced from three recorders and *continuo* to *violoncello piccolo* and *continuo*, then simply to *basso continuo* (all with voice). Now the strings enter with a sustained F♯^{6}, chord and the bass voice takes over with the pejorative characterization of reason ("Ach ja! Wir Menschen sind oftmals den Tauben zu vergleichen: wenn die verblendete Vernunft nicht weiss, was er gesaget hatte"). The strings then become much more animated as the text takes on a hortatory tone: "O Thörin! merke doch, wenn Jesus mit dir spricht, dass es zu deinem Heil geschicht." This point is one of the most striking of all the "turning points" in the spring 1725 cantata sequence, shifting the modulatory direction from "descent" to "ascent," and preparing, with its eventual cadence in D, for the subsequent trumpet aria. At the recitative turning point Bach perhaps intended the pivotal F♯ chord to suggest a symbol of disparity with the C major tonality of the preceding aria. Misunderstanding such as this verse describes is one of the most prominent features of John's Gospel, where it serves the double purpose of prompting further discourse from Jesus and emphasizing the split between all that is received through faith, the spiritual content that comes through Jesus from the world "above," and the inability of the world "below," due to its reliance on reason, to understand. John makes clear that such spiritual understanding is unmediated.[23]

After the quiet instrumental sonorities and the "descent" to the subdominant over the first four movements, the change within this recitative and the hortatory tone of the D-major aria for bass and trumpets that follows represent another "voice" altogether: that of Jesus's triumph over death and the devil, the *Christus Victor* image of the resurrection (ex. 12.13).

As in Cantatas 249 and 42, the descent to the subdominant and the aura of soft instruments are offset by shift to the dominant and a more extrovert tone. In the present context the descent/ascent tonal shape of Cantata 175, its utilizing a second Johannine motto as turning point, and its juxtaposition of arias with *violoncello piccolo* and trumpet all serve the purpose of joining the two aspects of Jesus that run throughout the cantatas of the preceding weeks, the good shepherd and the victor. In the *St. John Passion* these two sides emerge in the triumphant middle section of "Es ist vollbracht" and the pastorale character of the D-major dialog with chorale, "Mein teurer Heiland," that follows it. The main section of "Öffnet euch, ihr beiden Ohren" makes the point that the ability to hear and understand Jesus's promise is linked to faith in Jesus's overcoming the world (in the Passion

---

[23] See Loewenich, *Luther und das Johanneische Christentum*, 35, 42–51. As Loewenich indicates (46), Luther's response to the question of misunderstanding in John was to attribute it entirely to "unruly reason" ("unbotmäßige *ratio*"). See also Chafe, *Tonal Allegory*, 239–44.

EXAMPLE 12.13 **Cantata 175,** ***Er rufet seinen Schafen mit Namen*** *no. 6, aria, "Öffnet euch, ihr beiden Ohren," beginning*

and resurrection): "Jesus hat euch zugeschworen, dass er Teufel, Tod erlegt." This was the theme with which the spring 1725 series of cantatas began and that served Luther as key to John (and Bach as the turning point of Cantata 87). The middle section then confirms the benefits of the resurrection with a reminder of what "following" Jesus entails: "Gnade, Gnüge, volles Leben will er alles Christen geben, wer ihm folgt, sein Kreuz nachträgt."

The G-major chorale, "Nun werther Geist, ich folg' dir" (a verse of "Komm, heiliger Geist", prays that the Spirit, clearly equated with the resurrected Jesus of the aria "Öffnet euch," will help the individual to seek "according to your word another life, which you will give me through grace" ("nach deinem Wort ein ander Leben, das du mir willt aus Gnaden geben"). John's emphasis on the eternal life given to the believer in the present through his faith has the future orientation that is characteristic of Lutheranism; but there is a considerable sense of present experience, nevertheless. A second, varied *Stollen* describes the "Word" as the morning star that brings illumination, while the lines that precede the final Alleluja—"Drum will ich, die mich anders lehren, in Ewigkeit, mein Gott, nicht hören" (therefore in eternity I will not hear those who teach otherwise)—alludes to the division of the world into those who hear the word and those who do not (that is, those who "teach differently" and will themselves not be heard in eternity) as dramatized in the pivotal recitative with the second Johannine motto. In effect, with the aid of the return to G and the three recorders of the opening motto and aria, the ending of Cantata 175 affirms the role of the "inner" rather than "outer" word; its positive tone overcomes the rather grave view of division in the world that ended Cantata 68.[24]

In a sermon on the Gospel for Misericordias that he appended to his treatise on the blessedness of humanity in the present and in eternity, Johann Jacob Rambach discusses in detail the question of the mutual recognition of the shepherd and the sheep, explaining that on the part of the "sheep" that recognition was

---

[24] In his study of Luther's doctrine of the Holy Spirit, Regin Prenter (*Spiritus Creator*, 277) brings out the centrality for Luther of the distinction between "inner" and "outer" word, a distinction upheld by most later Lutheran theology.

no mere historical, but a spiritual and supernatural recognition, a fruit of the divine light, which penetrated into their understanding and drove the darkness out of it, and a working of the Holy Spirit. *For no man can say that Jesus is the Lord and shepherd but by the Holy Spirit. I Corinthians, 12:3.*[25]

Thus *Er rufet seinen Schafen mit Namen* completes the message of Pentecost with a work in which the overall framework is defined by the "soft" rather than "loud" instruments, the former associated with the intimate voice of the good shepherd who knows his "sheep" personally; throughout, this figure is equated with the inner voice of the Holy Spirit. At the beginning of the spring 1725 cantata sequence *Kommt, gehet und eilet* (BWV 249) had featured an aria with recorders and muted violins, Peter's "Sanfte soll mein Todeskummer nur ein Schlummer, Jesu, durch dein Schweißtuch sein," within the framework of a cantata of highly triumphant tone and prominent trumpet sonority. The sequence of movements that led from its introductory D-major "concerto" through a B-minor aria to Peter's G-major aria, constituted a progression in the subdominant direction whose theological goal, the believer's understanding of his death as a blessed sleep, is conveyed in the first word, "Sanfte." In Cantata 175 that tone returns in conjunction with another sequence that leads to the subdominant, the aria with *violoncello piccolo*, "Es dünket mich, ich seh dich kommen," whose lines "Ich kenne deine holde Stimme, die voller Lieb und Sanftmut ist" express the quality that enables faith to operate: "Du wirst im Glauben aufgenommen." Now the trumpet aria, "Öffnet euch, ihr beiden Ohren," with its recall of the *Christus Victor* imagery, is the one that stands apart from the predominant tone of the work as defined by the "soft" instruments. The basic theology is, of course, the same as that of *Kommt, gehet und eilet*, but the perspective has shifted from that of Easter and Jesus's victory to that of Pentecost and Jesus's return through the good shepherd and the Holy Spirit.

---

[25] Rambach, *Seligkeit der Gläubigen in der Zeit und in der Ewigkeit. . . nebst einer Predigt von der seligen Bekantschaft der Schafe Jesu Christi mit ihrem guten Hirten*, 72–73: "keine bloß historische, sondern eine **geistliche und übernatürliche Erkentniß,** eine Frucht des göttlichen Lichtes, welches in ihren Verstand eingedrungen, und die Finsterniß aus demselben vertrieben hat, und eine Würkung des heiligen Geistes. **Denn niemand kan JESUM seinen HErrn und Hirten nennen, ohne durch den Heiligen Geist, I Corinth. 12, 3.**"

{13}

Trinity Sunday: Cantata 176, *Es ist ein trotzig und verzagt Ding*

In Trinitarian doctrine, adopted by the church in the Middle Ages and retained by Luther for his church, God's threefold nature was attested to in certain scriptures, of which passages from the Gospel and letters of John were a mainstay.[1] In John such themes as the divinity of Jesus, the identity of Jesus and the Father, and the role of the Spirit, although not yet a doctrine, were viewed in Trinitarian light many centuries before Luther's time.[2] The prologue, in particular, with its copy of the beginning of Genesis and its identification of Jesus as the incarnate Word, was viewed as evidence of the Trinity for centuries, a tradition to which Luther held. And, as we have seen, the epistle for Quasimodogeniti was another such passage, linking the Trinity to the sacraments of baptism and the Eucharist, and thereby anticipating the coming of the Spirit at Pentecost. In the liturgy, Pentecost completes God's revelation of the Spirit with three days of epistle readings from Acts, which narrate the history of the coming of the Holy Spirit at various times and places, first to the Jews, then the gentiles; the Gospels, all drawn from John, provide the timeless, spiritual context and meaning of the Holy Spirit for humanity. The epistle for Trinity Sunday (Rom 11:33–36) then celebrates the depth of the wisdom and knowledge of God, his all-encompassing nature and glory, while the Gospel, taken from John's account of Jesus's dialog with Nicodemus, centers on the necessity of being born again through water and the Spirit to eternal life, ending with Jesus's prediction of his "lifting up" and the promise of eternal life to those who believe. With these readings Trinity Sunday marks the closure of the half of the year that centers on the life of Jesus, preparing the beginning of a new era in salvation history, the time of the church, which the liturgical year mirrors in the change of seasons.

While the epistle for Trinity Sunday is appropriate for the occasion (although it is still not the kind of passage that was traditionally cited as evidence of the Trinity),

---

[1] Loewenich, *Luther und das johanneische Christentum*, 20–22, 35–36.

[2] For a very readable survey of early Trinitarian thought see LaCugna, *God for Us*, 1–205.

the Gospel (Jn 3:1–15) has little to do with Trinity Sunday at all. Luther himself noted that fact, remarking "I don't know why this Gospel lesson was selected to be read on this Trinity Sunday, for it really doesn't deal with the subject of the Trinity."[3] Luther, therefore, does not attempt to relate the Gospel reading to the Trinity in any of his sermons for this occasion. The reason is presumably that the reading was set in place *before* that Sunday became associated with the Trinity. In the Roman Catholic liturgy it was Pentecost, not Trinity, that gave the numbering to the long sequence of Sundays that followed. And even in some Lutheran theological books of the seventeenth and eighteenth centuries the year was divided into a winter and a summer half, the former ending with Pentecost (or even Easter or Ascension Day), and the latter beginning with Trinity Sunday or before (or some related variant ordering).[4] Nevertheless, the long stretch of Sundays at the end of the year was almost invariably counted from the Sunday after Trinity, indicating that Trinity Sunday was truly a bridge between the two halves, based on a doctrine rather than an event, but a doctrine that followed logically from Pentecost.

The Gospel reading for Trinity Sunday forms a sequence (in reverse order from that of the Gospel) with that for the second day of Pentecost, six days earlier (Jn 3:16–21). Together they comprise Jesus's entire discourse with Nicodemus, which tells how Nicodemus, a prominent official among the Jews ("ein Oberster unter den Juden"), came to Jesus only by night (Jn 3:2). The main body of the dialog centers on the themes outlined earlier in this chapter. Then the reading returns to the light/darkness theme for vv. 19–21, expressing it in terms that seem to hark back to the prologue to the Gospel, which describes the light that came into the darkness of "the world," and the failure of "the world" to accept the truth, its preference for darkness over light. Thus John relates Nicodemus's coming to Jesus by night to one of the all-pervading "cosmic" themes of the prologue, traditionally associated with the Trinity.[5] But since these verses form part of the Gospel for the

[3] See the sermon for Trinity Sunday from 1532. Martin Luther, *Complete Sermons of Martin Luther,* vol. 6, *Sermons on Gospel Texts for Easter, Ascension Day, Pentecost Trinity, and the Fourteen Sundays after Trinity* (Grand Rapids, MI: Baker Books , 2002), 206.

[4] For example, Philipp Jacob Spener's *Die Evangelische Lebens-Pflichten in einem Jahrgang der Predigten bey den Sonn- und Fest-Täglichen ordentlichen Evangelien aus H. Göttlicher Schrifft* (Frankfurt am Main, 1702) is divided into two parts, the first ending with Pentecost and the second beginning (after a new title page) with Trinity Sunday; the same is true of August Hermann Francke's *Predigten über die Sonn- und Fest-Tags Episteln* (Halle, 1726). August Pfeiffer's *Evangelischer Schatz-Kammer* (Nuremberg, 1697) makes a division between Exaudi and Pentecost, setting the page numbering back to 1 at Pentecost and continuing from there to the end of the church year; Johann Arndt's *Postille* (Frankfurt, 1713) makes five major divisions with separate title pages for four of the five: (1) from Advent Sunday through Holy Week (preparations for the Passion), 1–522; (2) Meditation on the Passion (*Geistreiche Betrachtung über die ganze Passions-Historie*), 1–170, followed (without a new title page) by (3) Easter Day through the third day of Pentecost (i.e., the great fifty days), 1–264; and (4) for the Trinity season, beginning with Trinity Sunday, 358; and, finally, (5) the high feasts and "Apostel Tage," 1–210.

[5] As Loewenich indicates (*Luther und das Johanneische Christentum,* 36–37), for Luther John was "the great teller of the secret of the Trinity." Luther interpreted John's prologue as introducing two distinct persons who were nevertheless "one single, eternal natural God," explaining the expression "per-

second day of Pentecost, not Trinity Sunday, strict adherence to the Gospel readings would not make the connection of light and darkness to Trinity Sunday. As we saw, Johann Arndt takes the light/darkness theme as a key to his interpretation of the Gospel for Pentecost Monday. Mariane von Ziegler, however, used only vv. 16–18 in her text for Cantata 68, leaving the substance of vv. 19–21 for Trinity Sunday, giving them equal or greater prominence than those for the day (1–15). Thus she focused on the theme of light and darkness in her Trinity cantata, using that metaphor to set the glory of God apart from the weakness of human nature (another of the themes emphasized by Arndt in his Pentecost Monday sermons). Remembering, perhaps, that the story of Nicodemus has three stages in John (as August Hermann Francke brought out in the last of his lectures on John's Passion narrative), according to which Nicodemus increasingly emerges from the state of darkness and fear, Ziegler reinterprets his story in terms appropriate to the contemporary believer, thereby suggesting the believer's eschatological hopes—his rebirth to eternal life through the Spirit—as a symbolic emergence from darkness to light, and a logical context in which to introduce the Trinity.[6]

Bach produced four cantatas for Trinity Sunday that survive, two earlier and one later than *Es ist ein trotzig und verzagt Ding*. Of these cantatas, the first, *O heilges Geist- und Wasserbad* (BWV 165), centers on one of the themes of the Jesus/Nicodemus dialog, baptism through water and the Spirit, affirming the relationship to Pentecost; the second, *Höchsterwünschtes Freudenfest* (BWV 194), emphasizes God's greatness and glory, mirroring the tone of the epistle for Trinity Sunday.[7] In two movements, this cantata introduces the theme of darkness and light as a metaphor for the disparity between God's glory and human inadequacy in the aria "Was des Höchsten Glanz erfüllt, wird in keine Nacht verhüllt" (What the splendor of the most high fulfills will never be cloaked in night), and the following recitative "Wie könnte dir, du höchstes Angesicht, da dein unendlich helles Licht bis in verborgne Gründe siehet, ein Haus gefällig sein" (How could a house be pleasing to you, O highest countenance, since your infinitely bright light sees even into the hidden foundations). Cantata 194 has a very complex, and to a considerable extent unknown, history, involving parody, revisions, and performances, not only as a Trinity Cantata but also as a cantata for church consecration, to which the theme of God's house relates; nevertheless, it reminds us of the warnings against attempting to "build" a dwelling place for God (a metaphor for attempting to fathom God's glory) in Cantata 128, and the theme of the heart as God's dwelling place in Cantata 74, both of which emphasize the relationship of Jesus and the Father and the disparity between the human and the divine. In keeping with the primary charac-

---

son" (as distinct from "nature" or "*Wesen*") as hypostasis, the view that underlies the final line of *Es ist ein trotzig und verzagt Ding*.

[6] On Francke's view of Nicodemus, see ch. 7.

[7] Cantata 165 was presumably composed in Weimar, 1716 and perhaps re-performed in Leipzig 1724, while Cantata 194 has an unusually complex history of parody, multiple performances and revisions, including a performance on Trinity Sunday 1724. See Dürr, *Cantatas*, 719–20.

ter of Trinity Sunday, both these cantatas, as well as the cantata that Bach composed after 1725 to replace *Es ist ein trotzig und verzagt Ding* among the chorale cantatas, *Gelobet sei der Herr* (BWV 129), are festive in nature, and in major.

In relation to these works, though, Mariane von Ziegler's text for Cantata 176 takes a different approach altogether. Instead of beginning with a motto from John, Ziegler chose a verse from Jeremiah (17:9, somewhat modified) that makes a pejorative characterization of human nature—"There is a stubbornness and a despairing thing about all human hearts"—leaving all reference to the Trinity for the closing lines of the final two movements. Both her choice of introductory *dictum* and her emphasis on light and darkness in Cantata 176 might have been prompted in part by an intent to link up the text of her Trinity cantata with themes articulated in earlier cantatas of the spring 1725 season. The opposition of light and darkness as a metaphor for the presence of Jesus in "the world," as well as for human weakness and the need for God's protection, had already been introduced on Easter Monday, in *Bleib bei uns, denn es will Abend werden*. There the depiction of worldly darkness had sharply contrasted with the triumph of Bach's resurrection cantata, *Kommt, gehet und eilet*, heard the preceding day. Then, on Quasimodogeniti, six days later, *Am Abend aber desselbigen Sabbats* had emphasized the need of the faithful for Jesus's presence and protection from the fear of persecution that drove them to hide in darkness. Subtle, less direct references to the light/darkness idea emerge in a few later works such as Cantatas 85 and 175. There was precedence in the Lutheran authors for such a link: earlier, Martin Moller had introduced the passage from Jeremiah into his discussions of the Gospels for both Easter Monday and Misericordias, in both of which he had also taken up the theme of the darkness of the world.[8] Moller's explanations of the meaning of the passage suggest that qualities very similar to those exhibited by Nicodemus, in particular, the willful resistance to God's will, metaphorically the preference for darkness over light, underlay its association to the two earlier occasions. Aegidius Hunnius made an association between the verse from Jeremiah and the Gospel for Quasimodogeniti, bringing out the fact that the disciples' hiding from fear of the Jews exhibited the same qualities of *Trotz* and *Verzagtheit*. And Johannes Olearius, in his commentary on the verse, associated those qualities with darkness and light.[9] Mariane von Ziegler makes a similar association to Nicodemus. The concluding chorale verse has pronounced associations to baptism, which reminds us of the link to Quasimodogeniti (whose epistle reading brings out the theme of water and the Spirit, as does the Gospel for Trinity Sunday). It is significant then that only toward the end of the cantata does Ziegler make any reference to the Trinity: the aria "Ermuntert euch, furchtsam und schüchterne Sinne" (Arouse yourselves, fearful and downcast senses), begins by echoing the pejorative vision of human

---

[8] See Moller, *Praxis Evangeliorum*, 119, 152.

[9] Aegidius Hunnius, *Postilla* (Frankfurt, 1591), 57–58. Olearius, *Biblische Erklärung*, (Leipzig, 1679), 4:425.

nature that was announced in the opening *dictum* and ends with a proclamation of the Father, Son, and Holy Spirit as "dreieinig." And after that the concluding chorale (which takes its point of departure from the aria, as we will see) describes God as "ein Wesen, drei Personen" (one being, three persons). These lines make the only direct mention of the Trinity in the entire series of cantatas for spring 1725 as if, coming only at the end, those references mirrored the relatively late appearance of Trinity Sunday in the liturgy. Ziegler's decision to begin with a *dictum* from Jeremiah rather than John might well have reflected the shift to the Trinity season as the era of the church, beginning with a symbolic expression of human weakness. But, although the disparity between divine and human nature is Ziegler's starting point, with the ending of her text she articulates a kind of symbolic *Soli Deo Gloria* to the season as a whole. Owing to the character of the chorale melody that ends the cantata, however, Bach's setting shifts the perspective back to another solid reminder of the human/divine disparity; unlike Bach's other cantatas for Trinity Sunday, Cantata 176 begins and ends in minor (c).

Behind Bach's choice of key lies the opposition of light and darkness, first introduced in *Bleib bei uns*. Also, as mentioned earlier, the theme of *seeing* Jesus runs throughout the earlier part of the series as a whole, reaching its climax in Cantata 128 for Ascension Day. After that, the theme of *hearing*, even that of music, emerges in connection with the Holy Spirit. And Cantata 176 itself articulates a progression from the light/darkness theme to that of hearing and music, the latter themes emerging in the aria "Ermuntert euch, furchtsam und schüchterne Sinne, *höret euch, höret,* was Jesus verspricht," and the final chorale: "Auf daß wir also allzugleich zur Himmelspforten dringen und dermaleinst in deinem Reich *ohn alles Ende singen.*" Now the hearing of Jesus's word of promise through the Holy Spirit in the present leads over into the anticipation of the future manifestation of God's glory. Ziegler's passing over the light/darkness theme in her text for Cantata 68 and giving it unusual prominence in Cantata 176 might well have suggested to Bach that the ending of the season link up musically, through its C minor tonality, with what had been a prominent theme in *Bleib bei uns*, where it mirrored the concerns of the faithful in the world, as symbolized in the disciples' urging Jesus to remain. Now, however, its context is the acceptance of Jesus's physical absence, the presence of the Holy Spirit, and the hope of a fearful and timid humanity for eschatological fulfillment, mirrored symbolically in music.

Jesus's discourse with Nicodemus is entirely characteristic of John's style, in which particular individuals other than the disciples or the crowd at large (such as Pilate in the Passion) represent the worldly perspective, often failing to understand the spiritual character of Jesus's words. For Luther, Nicodemus's reluctance to come forth by day and his misunderstanding Jesus represented a failure to accept spiritual truth (light), on account of reliance on reason, which Luther linked with darkness rather than light. In choosing to begin her text with a motto that makes a pejorative characterization of human nature, Ziegler announced that her subject would be those qualities in human dealings with God that are stumbling blocks to understanding Jesus's words, as reason is described in Cantata 175.[10] Slightly, but significantly modifying the verse from Jeremiah, primarily with the addition of "um aller Menschen Herzen," Ziegler emphasizes the universality of stubbornness and timidity, qualities that were usually interpreted as, on the one hand, arrogance and aggressiveness, and on the other, fear and dejectedness.

In Ziegler's text, Nicodemus's reluctance to come to Jesus by day illustrates the meaning behind the word "verzagt," with which the contemporary believer identifies Nicodemus's fear of the day in the first recitative "Ich meine, recht verzagt, das Nikodemus sich bei Tage nicht, bei Nacht zu Jesu wagt" (I think, completely faint-hearted, Nicodemus did not dare to come to Jesus by day, but only by night). Here Ziegler introduces a reference to the story of Joshua's victory over the Amorites, in particular the sun's standing still in the sky until the battle was won (Josh 10:12–14), contrasting it with Nicodemus's longing for the sun to set. At the end of his treatise on Nicodemus, subtitled "Tractätlein von der Menschen-Furcht" (Little Treatise on Human Fear), August Hermann Francke includes fifty pages of excerpts from scripture "as much concerning human fear as the joy of faith." Among them are several passages in which God counsels Joshua with the expressions "Sey getrost und unverzagt" and "Fürchte dich nicht und zage nicht," which Joshua then repeats to his generals.[11] In this respect Joshua represented the opposite to Nicodemus. Whereas Nicodemus's longing for night inverts the believer's longing for the "erwünschter Morgen" in Cantata 175, becoming an expression of human weakness, Joshua's victory is, of course, a story of confidence, taking place in full sunlight. As the biblical narrative recounts, Joshua himself commanded the sun to stop, the only time, before or since, that God "hearkened unto the voice of a man." In medieval exegesis, whose principles of spiritual interpretation were still very much alive in the Bach cantatas, Joshua was thus a typological prefiguration of Jesus, his trumpet symbolizing God's word and his triumphantly leading the Israelites into the promised land as an allegory of the passing of scripture from the law to the Gospel.[12]

In Cantata 175 the "erwünschter Morgen" is the victory of God's word, which the trumpet aria, "Öffnet euch, ihr beiden Ohren" urges the believer to hear, and which is described in the final chorale as the "morning star that nobly illuminates near and far" ("Dein Wort ist ja der Morgenstern, der herrlich leuchtet nah und fern"). Since the light belongs to God alone, the "dazzled reason" ("verblendte Ver-

---

[10] Dürr, *Cantatas,* 370. See Chafe (*Tonal Allegory,* 225–53) for a discussion of Bach's treatment of the word "reason" (*Vernunft*), in particular Cantata 152, "Tritt auf die Glaubensbahn," in which reason is so described.

[11] Francke, *Nicodemus,* 207–9.

[12] De Lubac, *Medieval Exegesis,* 1:152. Johann Arndt (*Postilla,* 3:72–86) discusses Joshua as the last of three *Vorbilder* of Jesus and the Passion (the others being Jonah and Samson), bringing out the analogy between the sun, stopped in the sky until the victory, and Jesus's death and burial followed by the resurrection, the five kings defeated by Joshua as sin (coupled with the law), death, the devil, hell, and the world, the traditional opponents defeated by Jesus in the *Christus Victor* theory of the atonement.

nunft") that prevents the believer from understanding Jesus's words in Cantata 175 is equivalent to the daylight that prevents Nicodemus from understanding in Cantata 176. In the first aria of Cantata 176, "Dein sonst hell beliebter Schein," the believer voices an awareness that God's glory is "clouded over." For Ziegler, then, Nicodemus is in important respects a model for the contemporary believer, who, recognizing Jesus's divinity and her own inadequacy, takes comfort at night from Jesus's promise of eternal life for those who believe. That Ziegler specifies night as the time of comfort means, presumably, that it is to be understood as a metaphor for hearing and prayer, and this belonged to a state of humility involving rejection of the false *theologia gloria* and its association with reason, human aspiration to the sphere of God, and the like. It is also a metaphor for the world and the human perspective on the Trinity. Whereas, for Luther, Nicodemus's reliance on reason is a manifestation of the false *theologia gloriae*, an obstacle to faith, for Ziegler the believer's identification with Nicodemus, who does recognize Jesus's divinity and, although fearful, does come forth, is an expression of the true *theologia crucis*. The believer, by acknowledging his inadequacy before God, overcomes the "misunderstanding," associated with reason in Cantata 175, and profits from the injunctions against attempting to fathom God's glory—his hidden nature—in Cantata 128. Ultimately, the gradual revelation of the Trinity in Cantata 176 is linked with the acknowledgment of human weakness.

Cantata 176 follows a pattern similar to that of the four senses, with the motto from Jeremiah and the story of Joshua providing OT affirmations of the two sides of human nature, Joshua as a typological prefiguration of Jesus and his word as the light, after which the contemporary believer experiences the same sense of inadequacy before God as did Nicodemus. In this context Nicodemus represents a transition from the OT to the NT, similar to that of Joshua's leading the Israelites into the promised land. At the end of the cantata, the believer, as the result of acknowledging that weakness and trusting in God's word, anticipates eternity in the Spirit, proclaiming the glory of the Trinity. Although the Gospels for the third day of Pentecost and Trinity Sunday are not contiguous, in Ziegler's texts Cantata 176 responds to Cantata 175 in its thematic content. In Cantata 175 the turning point (the second motto) comes with the believer's rejection of reason, viewed as an obstacle to understanding Jesus's words, and his urging his ears to hear the word of promise, associated with Jesus's victory over death and the devil (the aria "Öffnet euch, ihr beiden Ohren"). And in Ziegler's text for Cantata 176 the second recitative is again a turning point, bringing out the believer's response to Jesus's promise ("So wundre dich, O Meister, nicht, warum ich dich bei Nacht ausfrage!": So do not wonder, O Master, why I question you at night), emphasizing acknowledgment of human weakness, and ending with the believer's trust in Jesus's leading his "heart" and "spirit" to [eternal] life. As a model for the contemporary believer, Ziegler's positive view of Nicodemus suggests an interpretation similar to August Hermann Francke's bringing out his threefold emergence from darkness to the light of faith. Francke linked this view with emphasis on human weakness and the rejection of reason (with particular reference to the burial scene of the *St. John Passion*).

The second recitative of Cantata 176 features a paraphrase from John 3:16 that does not appear in Ziegler's printed text; it is drawn from the Gospel for the second day of Pentecost and also paraphrased in the introductory chorale verse of Cantata 68: "weil alle, die nur an dich glauben, nicht verloren werden" (since all who believe only in you will not be lost).[13] This passage, which Bach sets in arioso style at considerably greater length than the entire remainder of the recitative, brings out the necessity of faith to salvation, as in Jesus's response to Nicodemus. It links up with the line "die ihm niemand rauben wird" (whom nobody will rob from him) from the first aria of BWV 85, *Ich bin ein guter Hirt* and "wer glaubt, daß Jesus ihm geboren, der bleibet ewig unverloren" (whoever believes that Jesus was born for him, he will never ever be lost) from BWV 68, *Also hat Gott die Welt geliebt.* And it appears near the beginning of the *St. John Passion* in conjunction with Jesus's protecting the disciples from the arresting party: "Auf dass das Wort erfüllet würde, welches er sagte: ich habe der Keine verloren, die du mir gegeben hast" (So that the scripture would be fulfilled in which he said: I have lost none of those whom you gave to me). We do not know whether the verse in question was inserted into Ziegler's text (either by Bach or by Ziegler herself) or belonged to it from the start and was later removed. It might even have been prompted by theological considerations that formed a part of Ziegler's "commission" rather than her own ideas. But its importance in the design of Cantata 176 is a very significant one.

In this cantata, the aria that follows the recitative just described—"Ermuntert euch, furchtsam und schüchterne Sinne" (Arouse yourself, fearful and timid senses)—recalls the nature of the human heart as articulated at the beginning of the work ("furchtsam und schüchterne" now substituting for "trotzig und verzagt"); it interprets Jesus's words to Nicodemus as the promise of heaven for all who believe: "erholet euch, höret, was Jesus verspricht: daß ich durch den Glauben den Himmel gewinne" (Pull yourselves together, hear what Jesus promises: that through faith I will win heaven). Ziegler's language here recalls that of the first of her hortatory arias, "Erholet euch, betrübte Sinnen," from Cantata 103 (Jubilate), the first of three trumpet arias, which, along with the second, "Auf, auf mit hellem Schall" from Cantata 128 (Ascension Day), emphasized the seeing of Jesus in eternity. After Ascension Day, the emphasis in Ziegler's texts shifted noticeably to *hearing* rather than *seeing*, to which the third such trumpet aria, "Öffnet euch, ihr beiden Ohren" (Cantata 176), gave voice. Now, in the aria "Ermuntert euch," not only is hearing Jesus's promise the key to the believer's praising the Trinity in the afterlife, but the aria reintroduces and transforms the thematic material of the opening movement of the cantata, now in E♭ rather than c, giving a positive interpreta-

[13] See Neumann, *Sämtliche von Johann Sebastian Bach vertonte Texte*, 365. The final lines in Ziegler's printed version of the recitative reads "Jedoch du nimmst mein zages Herz und Geist zum Leben auf und an," the word "zages" echoing the "verzagt" of the opening motto.

tion to the theme of human weakness as the outcome of the Holy Spirit. Arndt's arguments that humanity loved darkness *by nature*, which could be overcome through faith, echo here. As Cantata 175 had emphasized, belief (and therefore attaining eternal life) hinges upon hearing Jesus's words, the foremost attribute of John's Gospel for Luther. In Cantata 176 the darkness of night has eliminated the possibility of physical seeing; hearing the word—described in Cantata 175 as the "morning star that shines brightly near and far"—has therefore become the primary attribute of faith.

In "Ermuntert euch" the anticipation of eternity through faith culminates in the first explicit reference to the Trinity in Ziegler's cantata sequence: "Wenn die Verheißung erfüllend geschicht, werd ich dort oben mit Danken und Loben Vater, Sohn und Heilgen Geist preisen, der dreieinig heißt" (When the fulfillment of the promise occurs, I will glorify with thanks and praise the Father, Son and Holy Spirit, who are three-in-one). And the final chorale echoes it, ending the cantata with another address to the Trinity: "Gott Vater, Sohn und Heilger Geist, der Frommen Schutz und Retter, ein Wesen, drei Personen" (God Father, Son and Holy Spirit, the protector and savior of the pious, one being, three persons). In this ending we hear an echo of the theme of God's protection of the faithful that figured in a considerable number of the cantatas for spring 1725, beginning with *Bleib bei uns*. The relationship between an all-powerful, unfathomable deity and the "poor Christianity" that stands in need of protection (the ending of *Bleib bei uns* prays for Jesus, "der du Herr aller Herren bist" to "beschirm' dein' arme Christenheit, dass sie dich lob' in Ewigkeit") is very close to the core of Luther's doctrine of the Trinity, which was greatly indebted to John. Here, however, neither a chorale doxology nor Mariane von Ziegler's poetry can convey the subtlety of that relationship. Bach's music, on the other hand, proves capable in a variety of ways of leading the poetry to the articulation of new and often unsuspected levels of theological meaning.

That Bach returned to the key of c for *Es ist ein trotzig und verzagt Ding* is significant, given the role of that key at the close of the 1725 *St. John Passion* and in several of the cantatas that followed *Kommt, gehet und eilet*, beginning with *Bleib bei uns*. The turn to darkness and the juxtaposition of God's majesty to his "poor Christianity" in *Bleib bei uns* are paralleled by qualities in Bach's Trinity cantata, whose opening motto offsets the overt tones of triumph that had sounded in the D-major aria of Cantata 175 with another reminder of human finiteness. As a response to the cry of the believer in Cantata 175 for God (the shepherd) to reveal himself ("Wo find ich dich? Ach! wo bist du verborgen? O! Zeige dich mir bald! Ich sehne mich. Brich an, erwünschter Morgen!": Where will I find you? Ah! Where are you hidden? O show yourself to me soon! I am full of longing. Break forth, awaited morning!), Cantata 176 makes the point that God's revelation is made in the darkness of the world. Its C-minor tonality not only links up with *Bleib bei uns*, it can also be thought to follow logically from the G of *Er rufet seinen Schafen mit Namen* as a kind of symbolic cadence to the first half of the year. And so, after the D, G, and C of the cantatas heard on Easter Day, Ascension Day, and Pentecost, the

EXAMPLE 13.1 **Cantata 176, *Es ist ein trotzig und verzagt Ding*** *first movement, beginning*

c of *Es ist ein trotzig und verzagt Ding* represents a perspective dominated by the finiteness of the world, symbolized by Nicodemus, in relation to the glory of the Trinity: Jesus as "light."

The opening theme of Cantata 176 matches the character of the motto perfectly, not only in its striking opposition of the words "trotzig" (stubborn) and "verzagt" (timorous), but in its symmetrical ascent from and return to the C-minor triad (ex. 13.1). This portrayal of the human heart, symbol of human nature, in terms of both the minor key and a conspicuous element of chromaticism (on "verzagt") arises naturally from the allegorical associations of chromaticism and the minor triad in the Lutheran "metaphysical" tradition in seventeenth- and early-eighteenth-centuries music theory. The major triad was the foundation of that tradition because of its seeming to constitute an embedding of the idea of three-in-one in nature. Andreas Werckmeister's and Bach's canons on the *trias harmonicas*, often called *triunitas* in Lutheran music treatises, symbolize that association, which can be found in many of the Bach cantatas that assert the glory of God, the beginning of *Gott ist mein König* (Cantata 71), for example. The minor triad just as surely suggested the human sphere in many instances, especially when the two were contrasted. Recurrent associations of C minor throughout Bach's work, in particular to such ideas as Luther's concept of the "sleep of death," express what we might describe as an "eschatological" character, a depiction of the world awaiting redemption. In certain works juxtaposition of C minor and major, or progression from the one to the other, represent the opposition of a present life beset by tribulation and the future life of fulfillment (Cantata 21 is the most pronounced instance of this quality, since it articulates the c/C shift in terms of its beginning and ending), even of the sleep of death versus the resurrection (Cantata 127).

In Cantata 176 Bach is not concerned with offsetting the minor-key quality of the work with any direct emblems of glory. Instead, the antithesis between "trotzig" and "verzagt" led him to introduce a quality of assertiveness within the opening melodic gesture that is offset by the minor triad ("Es ist ein trotzig"), leading this in turn to a tone more nearly related to tribulation ("und verzagt Ding"). The line as a whole depicts the minor key as the bond between the seeming antithesis of stubbornness and fearfulness. The deeper antithesis, though, is between the complex of stubbornness and fearfulness together as a symbol of human finiteness and the qualities that belong to God alone. The dualism in question is one that emerges in various forms throughout Bach's work, where it mirrors the positive character of human intentions in combination with its negative other side: the inability to carry them out. A good example, in C minor, is the aria "Ich will bei meinem Jesu wachen" (I will watch by my Jesus) from the *St. Matthew Passion* (and its parodied form from the Köthen funeral music, "Geh, Leopold, zu deiner Ruh'": Go, Leopold, to your rest), where the quality of resolve in the text gave rise to a melodic head motive that were it in major would perfectly match the positive quality of the text; the minor key, however, undermines the resolve (as the fact that Leopold is dead undermines the otherwise positive gesture in the funeral music), so that the overall affect can be said to be rooted in opposition, the minor key reminding us of its major counterpart, of what it is *not*. Similarly, the two canons of the *Musical Offering* that bear inscriptions to the glory of Frederick the Great feature certain style elements that appear on the surface to proclaim that glory; yet the affective characters of those pieces run completely in opposition to such an idea; they confirm, in fact, the lamenting associations of the C-minor triad and the descending chromaticism within the theme itself. Thus the ascending modulations in the "Canon per tonos" of the *Musical Offering* (which Bach inscribed "As the modulation ascends so may the king's glory") can be interpreted in this light, while the "descent" in that work emerges in the return to the original key in a manner that confirms the finiteness of the ascent.[14]

[14] That is, the modulation ascends in pitch passing through the whole-tone sequence, c–d–e–f♯–g♯ (or a♭)–a♯ (b♭), and returning to c in the upper octave. For obvious reasons it cannot continue upward beyond the arrival on c. Such pieces, in fact, confirm the meaning of "glory" in Lutheranism: that it

So it is with *Es ist ein trotzig und verzagt Ding*. Like his eminent counterparts, Leopold of Anhalt-Köthen and Frederick the Great, Nicodemus (although "ein Oberster unter den Juden") is human, not divine. Behind the assertiveness of this first chorus, "Es ist ein trotzig," lies the fact that its minor key is an emblem of human weakness; following the C-minor triad, the upward-rushing scale creates the sense that it cannot pass beyond the d♭′, a minor ninth above the starting tone to which it leads and causes it to turn back on "und verzagt Ding" to reiterate the minor triad (now descending) on "Menschen Herzen." The overall shape of the work, viewed from the standpoint of its tonal plan, was perhaps designed so as to mirror the qualities suggested by the opening motto theme. The key scheme here is that of ascent from the initial C minor through g (the first recitative) to B♭ major for the first aria (exactly the keys of the first three movements of *Bleib bei uns*), followed by return through g for the second recitative, and E♭ for the second aria, to c for the final chorale.

In the opening phrase of Cantata 176, despite the antithesis of loud and soft, ascent and descent, the first violin line quickly attains its highest pitch c‴ in the opening measure, then descends to c′ over the course of the phrase, rapidly as it accompanies the word "trotzig," then slowly for "verzagt," a gesture that binds the oppositions within the basic framework of human weakness. Here, Bach's musical structure exhibits qualities that seem to derive from, or at the very least mirror, the sense of symmetry in the fugue theme. The pattern of voice entries is an ascending one, from bass to soprano, reaching the dominant with the completion of the soprano entry. These initial sixteen measures (the exposition) are then followed by eight in the dominant, in which we hear two further entries of the theme, the first beginning in c and shifting up a tone so as to end on the dominant of g, and the second beginning from g and merging into the return to c, three measures later. At the point of the shift up a tone in the first of these entries, attaining the sharpest point of the movement, an A–D progression, all four voices come together, note against note, for the only time in the movement, to give particular dramatic emphasis to the words "trotzig und verzagt." This is the beginning of a circle-of-fifths motion that not only leads back to c but immediately after turns even farther flat, to f, in which we hear two forceful cadences. There is a balance to this design, in that from the return to c until the end of the movement we have a sixteen- or

belongs to God alone; any human striving to fathom the glory of God brings only intensified suffering. Within this conceptual framework Bach's canons exhibit a dialectical character: those aspects that might be considered to represent glory, such as the "majestic" dotted and double-dotted rhythms in the "Canon per augmentationem" and the ascending modulations in the "Canon per tonos," are contradicted by the tremendously elegaic, dissonant and lamenting character of the one canon and the intensified chromaticism and registral finiteness of the other. Ursula Kirkendale's attempt to "read" the affective characters of these two canons in more literal, figural terms fails to take account of that dialectical quality, passing over the obvious chromatic, minor and dissonant aspects that easily overcome the superficial rhetorical "signs" of glory; see Ursula Kirkendale, "The Source for Bach's *Musical Offering*: The *Institutia Oratoria* of Quintilian," *Journal of the American Musicological Society* 33 (1980): 88–141.

seventeen-measure section in which the move to the subdominant can be considered the counterpart of the move to the dominant at the end of the first section. For the return to the tonic the soprano begins an entry in f before the f cadence, overlapping it with the return to c, as the tenor had overlapped the earlier return from g to c. The four measures that follow complete the return to c, but the strength of the subdominant in the final section cannot be denied; it is as if the subdominant, a mirror of human weakness, must be acknowledged to balance out the dominant, the one suggestive of *Trotz*, the other of *Verzagtheit*. In the key design of the cantata the idea of ascent is similarly balanced by that of descent; yet, as we will see, the subdominant, f, reappears toward the end of the final chorale as if to underscore the point that human weakness is the cantata's primary affective and theological sphere.

Seen this way it is significant that in the first recitative Bach moves from the initial dominant of g to a C-minor cadence for the narrative of Nicodemus's coming forth only by night, then on to F minor for that of the sun's standing still in the sky for Joshua's victory. This may seem the opposite of the usual association of F minor with tribulation. But, in fact, there is an inversion of meaning at play here, one that makes a point out of the positive value of Nicodemus's appearance. In fact, Johann Arndt interpreted the motionless sun in Joshua allegorically as Jesus's rest in the grave *before* the victory of the resurrection, a traditional view. Joshua himself commanded the sun to stop, but it was God who permitted it and gave the victory. Bach's move to F minor, therefore, does not mark the goal of the recitative. Whereas his setting binds the motionless sun and Nicodemus's fear into an ongoing tonal motion toward F minor, after the f cadence the music turn to g, in which it ends, for the narrative of Nicodemus's longing for the sun to *set*: "hier *aber* wünschet Nicodem: O säh' ich sie zu Rüste gehn!" The modulation has an "adversative" character, juxtaposing the a♮′ associated with Nicodemus's wish for the sun to set to the a♭′ of the preceding cadence to f, and setting up the B♭ of the aria that follows. After the F minor of Joshua's commanding the sun to stop, Nicodemus's wish for the sun to set projects a very positive character associated with his longing to see Jesus. Bach's allegory makes the point that Nicodemus's coming forth by night, his acknowledging his human weakness, does not mirror his fear but rather his faith.

This is confirmed by the B♭ aria that follows. Representing the voice of the contemporary believer, who imagines himself in Nicodemus's situation, it takes up the believer's recognition of Jesus's divinity in contrast to his own weakness. The message is basically the same as that underlying the *Soli Deo Gloria* that Bach placed on many manuscripts and the *Jesu Juva* that formed its counterpart. The aria is indeed positive in tone and detailed in its interpretation of the text. Over the course of the first three movements the overall tonal motion from C minor through g to B♭ can be said to describe an "ascent" that takes the question of light versus darkness out of its literal context, making the point that the spiritual meaning takes precedence. That spiritual meaning, given clearly in the B♭ aria, is the believer's recognition of the divinity of Jesus (with a hint of its Trinitarian implications in the line "Gottes Geist muss auf ihn ruh'n") and acknowledgment of one's own inadequacy before God.[15]

As the "apex" of the tonal ascent through the first three movements, the B♭ aria, "Dein sonst hell beliebter Schein soll vor mich umnebelt sein," confronts the opposition of the divine and the human, an extension of the encounter between Nicodemus and Jesus within the perspective of the contemporary believer. Bach sets the aria in what Alfred Dürr identifies as gavotte style, making the point that the predominant context is a worldly one. Jesus's "Schein" is clouded over for Nicodemus because he (Nicodemus) is human, not divine. And the melodic-figurational aspect of the movement is occupied entirely with the opposition of rising and falling sequences, high and low pitch spheres, sharpened and flattened accidentals, and triple and duple subdivision of the beat. One of the most unusual and striking devices is the contrast of passages with normal *basso continuo* and those in the so-called *bassetchen* texture (no *basso continuo*) in which the second violin and viola parts move into unison to provide a bass line in the upper register (the same as the earlier *basso continuo* line, but now an octave higher), and without any chordal realization of the harmonies. Bach introduces the *bassetchen* texture on the first phrase of the voice, "Dein sonst hell beliebter Schein soll vor mich umnebelt sein," underscoring the opposition of "above" and "below" by having the first violin articulate a rising arpeggio in triple subdivision of the beat followed by a drop of an eleventh and return to duple subdivision (ex. 13.2)

Bach makes his point—the opposition of God in himself versus the human perspective—at the beginning of the "B" section, where he retains the *basso continuo* for "Niemand kann die Wunder thun," switching to the *bassetchen* texture for "denn sein' Allmacht, und sein Wesen," and restoring the *basso continuo* for "scheint, ist göttlich auserlesen." Bridging the gap between the spheres of the divine and human is the descent of the Holy Spirit, which Bach describes in the descending violin line that accompanies these shifts, in the introduction of triplets in the voice for "Gottes [Geist muss auf ihn ruhn]," and in the dropping out of the *basso continuo* again as the voice cadences on "ruhn," which is held for five measures in the middle of which the *basso continuo* returns for a second cadence.

The surface detail of "Dein sonst hell beliebter Schein" is rooted in antitheses: loud versus soft dynamics, high versus low registers, ascending versus descending melodic lines, duple versus triple subdivisions of the beat, *basso continuo* versus *bassetchen* lines. However, just as these contrasts form part of a larger theological message under which they are subsumed, so the tonal structure of the aria is rock solid: tonic/dominant/tonic in the ritornello, and a very purposive modulation to the dominant to end the "A" section; modulation to the relative minor and back

[15] The phrase "Gottes Geist muss auf ihn ruh'n" refers, of course, to Jesus's baptism as told by all four evangelists (Mt 3:13–17; Mk 1:9–11; Lk 3:21–22; Jn 1:29–34). In the context of Cantata 176 they relate to Jesus's words to Nicodemus regarding rebirth through water and the Spirit as well as to their traditional Trinitarian interpretation.

EXAMPLE 13.2 **Cantata 176, *Es ist ein trotzig und verzagt Ding*** *no. 3, aria, "Dein sonst hell beliebter Schein," mm. 17–22*

to the tonic in the "B" section (which is then followed by the tonic/dominant/tonic of the ritornello again). Bach lavishes attention on the details, no matter how small, pointing up how the disparity between God and humankind—graphically described in the figural details—is bridged by the "resting" of the Spirit on humanity (also a reference to baptism). In this aria, as in the entire cantata, the ascent/descent shape can be considered to represent humanity's desire to approach God intermingled with awareness of human weakness. The idea of ascent, potentially a symbol of human aspiration toward the realm of God, and therefore an expression of the false *theologia gloriae*, emerges here as a positive quality because it is associated not with the believer's aspirations to the sphere of God but with his recognition of Jesus's divinity and his own inadequacy.

The bass recitative that follows is the turning point, voicing first the believer's awareness of his weakness as the reason behind his not approaching Jesus directly, "by day" ("So wundre dich, o Meister, nicht, warum ich dich bei Nacht ausfrage! Ich fürchte, dass bei Tage mein' Ohnmacht nicht bestehen kann": So do not wonder, O Master, why I question you by night! I fear that by day my weakness could not stand up), then continuing with a reference back to the timorous "heart" introduced in the opening movement: "doch tröst ich mich, du nimmst mein zages Herz und Geist zum Leben auf und an" (However you take my timid heart and Spirit up to you for life). Either Bach or Ziegler herself included the message of *Trost* at the beginning of these lines (the printed text begins simply "Jedoch du nimmst . . . "). Bach sets the first of these passages ("So wundre dich") with tonal motion from g to c, and the second ("doch tröst ich mich") with return to g for the extended arioso that paraphrases John's Gospel for the day: "Weil Alle, die nur an dich glauben, nicht verloren werden." Since this pronounced shift to g begins the return through E♭ to C minor for the final chorale, Bach can be considered to have extended his proclivity for making Johannine *dicta* into turning points in the tonal designs of the cantatas for this season to a text that, at least in Ziegler's printed version, did not have such a *dictum*.

As mentioned earlier, the E♭ alto aria, "Ermuntert euch, furchtsam und schüchterne Sinne," introduces direct reference to the Trinity in its final line. It is possible, therefore, that Bach embedded symbolic allusions to the Trinity in certain of the movement's most immediate features, such as the triple-meter time signature (in particular 3/8, which might be thought to mirror the idea of three-in-one more than the 3/4 of the preceding arioso), the three unison oboes that play the instrumental melody line (with significant exceptions), certain prominent triadic configurations within those lines and even, perhaps, the key of E flat (although it must be mentioned that Bach notates all movements of the cantata, including the E♭, with two rather than three flats, a feature that reflects some of the most important musical qualities of the work). More interesting than such partly inaudible devices, however, are the ways that Bach deals with Ziegler's reference back to the human qualities of the initial motto—now presented as "furchtsam" (fearful) and "schüchtern" (shy, timid) rather than "trotzig" und "verzagt"—and how they lead to anticipation of eschatological fulfillment and proclamation of the Trinity.

"Ermuntert euch" is another hortatory aria, the believer now urging his fearful, timid senses to arouse themselves to hear the word of promise, a message we have encountered in several earlier cantatas of the series. Nowhere in those works, however, did the idea of human weakness form such an obstacle; more often the obstacle was rooted in the presumptuousness of reliance on reason. Here, the stubbornly aspiring aspect of "trotzig"—the believer's resistance to God's will, mirrored in the futile ascent of the first theme of the cantata—must be denied; yet the believer must not be left in her *Verzagtheit*. The hortatory character of "Ermuntert euch" offers the alternative to the believer's stubbornness. As if to remind us of the "trotzig" and "verzagt" of the first movement, Bach takes, as his opening motive, a melody that quickly ascends, emphasizing the tones of the tonic triad to the high e♭″, then more slowly, and by step, descends to its starting point, passing through the flat-seventh degree, d♭″ as it turns downward (ex. 13.3).

This idea, as the subsequent entrance of the voice makes clear, mirrors the exhortation "Ermuntert euch" on the ascent and "furchtsam und schüchterne Sinne"

EXAMPLE 13.3 **Cantata 176, *Es ist ein trotzig und verzagt Ding*** *no. 5, aria, "Ermuntert euch, furchtsam und schuchterne Sinne," principal theme*

on the descent. In the initial phrase Bach develops the idea, introduced in the opening movement, that the flattened pitch marks the point of shift from ascent to descent; in both movements that pitch is d♭, the minor ninth above the tonic in the first movement, the flat seventh in "Ermuntert euch." Thus the idea of melodic descent is bound up with flatward motion, which in the opening movement led to emphasis on the subdominant, f, as we saw. To reinforce this point, Bach introduces, first to accompany the word "furchtsam," then directly before the second vocal phrase, a subtle reminiscence of the slurred duplets associated with the descent from d♭′ in the first movement. The idea is absent from the second section of the aria ("daβ ich durch den Glauben den Himmel gewinne. Wenn die Verheiβung erfüllend geschicht,"). With the sentence anticipating the glorious future in store for the believer left incomplete, Bach cadences in C minor. Then, as the voice drops out, oboes continue on, merging the beginning of the ritornello, now in C minor, with the beginning of the second half of the ritornello, Bach reintroduces the slurred-duplet pattern, extending it for several measures in which we hear an unmistakable reference back to the descending line that accompanied the word "verzagt" in the cantata's first movement. Derived from the descending "furchtsam und schüchtern" line of this aria as well, it makes a connection between the d♭′ that caused the line to pivot from ascent to descent on "verzagt" in the first movement. (ex. 13.4)

This event, however, does not determine the primary meaning toward which the aria moves. The purpose of the C-minor recollection of the first movement (as shown in example 13.4), is to remind us of the promise in C minor so that the return to the principal key, E♭, brings out the first reference to the Trinity as the believer anticipates seeing God in eternity. After the instruments cadence in C minor, the incomplete sentence continues with "werd' ich dort oben mit Danken und Loben Vater, Sohn und heil'gen Geist preisen, der dreinig heisst," now the third principal section of the aria. For the first half of the sentence, Bach had led the high tones of the vocal line upward in stages, through d♭″ to d♮″, then turned the line downward, through c″, b♭′, and a♭′ to the low c′ of the C-minor cadence. But,

EXAMPLE 13.4 **Cantata 176, *Es ist ein trotzig und verzagt Ding*** *no. 5, aria, "Ermuntert euch, furchtsam und schuchterne Sinne," oboe, mm. 66–70*

EXAMPLE 13.5 **Cantata 176, *Es ist ein trotzig und verzagt Ding*** *no. 5, aria, "Ermuntert euch, furchtsam und schuchterne Sinne," soprano, mm. 75–86*

for the second half, he changes its character, now continuing it with an extraordinary series of melismas on "Loben" und "preisen," and moving it upward, again by stages, through c″, d♭″, and d♮″ to the high e♭″. The pitch a♭′, which before had turned downward in the slurred duplets reminiscent of "verzagt" in the first movement, now continues upward (on "oben"), affirming all the more the E♭, instead of c. With the alto's arrival on the high e♭″ of "Vater," Bach introduces imperceptibly, and without any break, the reprise of the opening ritornello in the instruments, now with the voice making the explicit reference to the Trinity: "Vater, Sohn und heilgen Geist." There is a distinct sense that the Trinity emerges as the direct outcome of all that went before (ex. 13.5). Instead of proclaiming the Trinity from the outset as a given, Ziegler's texts center on scripture, reserving all reference to the Trinity for the end, as if mirroring the fact that the doctrine of the Trinity, rooted in scripture, came to the liturgy at a relatively late date. This quality fits, of course, with her unusual emphasis on human weakness throughout the cantata. Bach suggests that here the believer, like Nicodemus, attains through faith in Jesus's promise the capacity to recognize God. Since the movement has no textual reprise, the concluding instrumental version of the ritornello is now modified to end in E♭, seeming to confirm that recognition.

In the introduction to this book I mentioned that Bach's "Ziegler" cantatas often exhibited great subtlety. One quality that drew that quality from Bach was their relatively high number of movements, arias in particular, without textual reprises. I have discussed several of these, in which Bach overlaps the musical reprise with texts that were not heard earlier in the movements in question, sometimes with great ingenuity. In the aria "Erholet euch, betrübte Sinnen" from Cantata 103 (Jubilate) the reprise begins in the midst of the tenor's vocal roulades on the word "Freude" ("O Freude, der nichts gleichen kann"); in Cantata 108 for the following week (Cantate) the also soloist sings "through" the reprise, creating the effect of extending the phrase "daβ ich in der Ewigkeit schaue deine Herrlichkeit" beyond its expected ending point; in the aria "Auf, auf mit hellem Schall" of Cantata 128 (Ascension Day) Bach joins Ziegler's aria and recitative into one movement, ending with the recitative and featuring a musical reprise in which the trumpet reappears after its absence throughout the recitative, but without further text (mirroring the last line of the text "So schweig, verwegner Mund, und suche nicht dieselbe zu ergründen"). Now, in Cantata 176 Bach once again "sneaks in" the musical reprise during the last line of the aria "Ermuntert euch, furchtsam und schuchterne Sinne," reinforcing a text that has not been heard before. And, in common with several of the earlier ones it is a hortatory text and one whose final lines are eschatological in character. We cannot say, of course, whether Bach had any imput into the absence of textual reprises in Ziegler's texts. But breaking the familiar *da capo* pattern seems, in the cases just cited, to mirror the manner in which the texts move forward to anticipate ultimate things. In the case of "Ermuntert euch" the Trinitarian reference that emerges at the end of the aria anticipates the eschatological tone of the final chorale that follows.

In "Ermuntert euch" Bach binds together the melodic and tonal qualities of ascent and descent, hope for eschatological fulfillment, and awareness of human weakness, into a close mirroring of the theological implications of Ziegler's text. In fact, in every movement of the cantata, pitch juxtapositions and shiftings, usually between either a and a♭, or d and d♭, keep the basic dualisms surrounding the human and divine in our ears. In this aria another detail was added, after the score and parts were copied, which was perhaps intended to bring out the sense of intimacy that ran throughout the cantatas of the spring sequence in association with the "soft" instruments. In the two oboe parts long curved lines, first appearing with the words *piano tacet,* marked off passages in which apparently the two oboes were to drop out, leaving the oboe da caccia to play solo with the voice and the *basso continuo.* Although not identical in the two parts, they seem to indicate that for all the purely instrumental passages the two oboes played in unison with the oboe da caccia, whereas all the passages with voice were accompanied by *basso continuo* and oboe da caccia alone.[16] Along with a plethora of loud and soft dynamic markings, this indication invites consideration that it represents the hearing of the word of promise. In particular, the final twenty-measure vocal solo, beginning "werd ich dort oben" and concluding with the reference to thanking and praising God in eternity (mm. 74–94) is marked in this way in both oboe parts, along with the soft dynamic indication.

[16] As Robert Freeman, editor of Cantata 176 for the NBA, points out, Bach presumably indicated the pausing of the two oboes for the vocal solos in conjunction with a later performance (see Arthur Mendel, *Johann Sebastian Bach, Neue Ausgabe sämtlicher Werke,* Kritischer Bericht to NBA I/15 (Kassel: Barenreiter 1968), 59. It cannot be excluded, however, that it was an afterthought that belonged to the first performance as well. In any case, in light of the pronounced instrumental qualities of the spring 1725 cantatas (in particular the manner in which the oboes da caccia are used in Cantata 183; see ch. 12), this gesture is a very meaningful one.

That the final chorale of Cantata 176 returns to C minor is almost inevitable, given the extent to which this cantata, and the entire series of post-Easter cantatas, emphasize the perspective and concerns of humanity in the present world as their goal. It closes the cantata and the season with a hymn to the Trinity, the eighth and last verse of Paul Gerhardt's Trinitarian hymn, "Was alle Weisheit in der Welt," sung to the melody of "Christ, unser Herr, zum Jordan kam":

Auf daß wir also allzugleich	So that we shall, all together
zur Himmelspforten dringen	press forward to heaven's gates
und dermaleinst in deinem Reich	and one day in your kingdom
ohn alles Ende singen,	sing without end,
dass du alleine König seist,	that you alone are king,
hoch über alle Götter,	high above all gods,
Gott Vater, Sohn und heil'ger Geist,	God the Father, Son and Holy Spirit,
der Frommen Schutz und Retter,	protector and rescuer of the pious,
ein Wesen, drei Personen.	one nature, three persons.

This chorale exhibits several interesting features (ex. 13.6). First of all, its ninth and last line, "ein Wesen, drei Personen," stands apart from the *ababcdcd* rhyme scheme of the remaining eight lines, as if it were somehow different in nature. This quality is mirrored in the melody of the final phrase, which moves directly up an octave higher in pitch in relation to the penultimate phrase (from f′to f″), then cadences on c″ after a cadence to F minor at the end of the preceding phrase that sounds very much like the ending of the chorale. And this sense that the f of the penultimate phrase could easily have ended the chorale is one that arises in part from the given melody, which begins on f′ and cadences to C minor and F minor, respectively, for the two (repeated) phrases of the *Stollen*, the latter returning to end on the pitch f′. This alone suggests f rather than c as its key. This impression is then reinforced by lines 5 through 8 of the *Abgesang*, which cadence in c, c, c, and f. The curve of the line upward through phrases 5 and 6, then back down over more than an octave in phrases 7 and 8, first to the dominant of f (phrase 7), then to the low f′ with which the chorale began and the two *Stollen* ended (phrase 8), expands on the c and f cadences of the *Stollen* and would make a perfectly satisfactory and self-contained ending for the melody. In phrase 8, more than any earlier one, Bach introduces the pitch D♭ (and, of course, A♭ as well) into the harmony, reinforcing the sense of f as key. In contrast, the shift to A♮ and D♮ at the beginning of the final phrase (9) immediately indicates a change. Moreover, the starting pitch of phrase 9 an octave higher than the end of phrase 8, along with the fact that the phrase remains at high pitch, cadencing on c′, sets it apart from the curve of the melody over the preceding phrases. The final phrase is, in fact, a variant of phrase 6, which brings out the relationship between their texts: "hoch über alle Götter" and "ein Wesen, drei Personen," respectively. But phrase 6 marks, as I mentioned, the apex of a progressive ascent over the first two phrases of the *Abgesang*, after which the line makes a very pronounced complementary descent to the f′, thus

EXAMPLE 13.6 **Cantata 176, *Es ist ein trotzig und verzagt Ding* *final chorale***

ending phrase 8. Phrase 9, therefore, sounds like an "extra" phrase, but one whose meaning is drawn from within the remainder of the chorale.[17]

The quality in question is indebted to the chorale that is most widely associated with this melody, "Christ, unser Herr zum Jordan kam," which, owing to its theme of baptism has a distinct connection to the dialog between Jesus and Nicodemus.[18]

[17] Possibly the fact that each verse has nine lines is a mirroring of the Trinitarian associations of that number (i.e., 3 x 3), which can be found, for example, in the ninefold Kyrie, Christe, Kyrie settings of the third part of the *Clavierübung* ("Gott Vater in Ewigkeit," "Jesus Christus, unser Heiland," and "Gott Heilger Geist"). A similar purpose may also underlie the nine movements of the Credo of the *Mass in B minor*.

[18] As Martin Petzoldt brings out (*Bach-Kommentar.* Vol. 2, *Die Geistlichen Kantaten vom 1 Advent bis zum Trinitasfest*, [Kassel: Bärenreiter, 2007, 1074]), the textual *Abgesang* of this strophe is nearly

The traditional treatment of this melody was as one that ended in or on the dominant.[19] Bach's chorale cantata on "Christ, unser Herr" (Cantata 7), for example, is in E minor. But in the first movement the final phrase of the chorale ends on (but not in) the dominant, b, although the movement ends in e. The b ending of the chorale mirrors the fact that its final line introduces the idea of a "new life" given by baptism: "Das galt ein neues Leben." For the final movement of the cantata, however, Bach begins the chorale in E minor as usual, but this time ends the verse, and the cantata, in the dominant, B minor, thereby mirroring the opposition of Adam and Jesus in the final verse, and giving more pronounced emphasis to the idea of a new life.

Such an intricate mirroring of theological meaning is by no means unheard of, or even unusual, in Lutheran chorale melodies. And Bach is unusually sensitive to all such anomalies or quirks. The verse that ends Cantata 176 begins with the words, "Auf daß" (So that. . .), which mirrors Gerhardt's poem: the final verse is the logical outcome of the verses that precede it. In Cantata 176 the "auf daß" suggests that it follows directly from the Trinitarian ending of the aria "Ermuntert euch." Instead of beginning in f, therefore, Bach begins his harmonization with a B♭ chord, bridging between the E♭ ending of the aria and the f harmony that follows. Until its c cadence, this phrase might well suggest the key of E♭. The harmony binds the ending of the aria and the beginning of the chorale into a continuous reference to the Trinity. And Bach's continuing harmonization of the chorale emphasizes the subdominant f, as suggested by the melody itself, until the end. No phrase cadences on the dominant of c, so that along with the much higher pitch of the final line in relation to the penultimate one, the C minor cadence suggests the distance between the spheres of God and mankind, John's "above" and "below."

In the final analysis, it must be said that *Es ist ein trotzig und verzagt Ding* was crafted with immense care for its placement in the liturgical season and its unique treatment of the subject of the Trinity. The special qualities of this work involve both its music and its text (some aspects of which, such as the choice of chorale, might have been determined in large part by musical considerations), and thus it appears that Bach and Ziegler worked together in forming its conception. Those qualities suggest that the cantata was indeed intended to close out a series designed to lead to Pentecost and Trinity as both culminating and beginning points. The references to baptism signify, of course, entrance into the church, a new beginning. The emphasis on human weakness, evident in both text and music, echoes

identical to that of the first strophe of the chorale, suggesting that the choice of the chorale was indebted to its mirroring the catechism function of the chorale, while at the same time affirming the eschatological character of a doxology for the ending of the cantata.

[19] Georg Philip Telemann's setting in his *Fast allgemeines Evangelisch-Musicalisches Lieder-Buch* of 1730, for example, is in D minor ending on the dominant, as is that of the Freylinghausen *Geistreiches Gesang-Buch* (315). Both settings are notated in the "Dorian" key signature (without the flat). For Telemann see the facsimile edition in *Dokumentation zur Geschichte des deutschen Liedes*, vol. 3, ed. Siegfried Kross, 35 (Hildesheim: Georg Olms Verlag 1977).

the all-pervading theme of the world in the sequence as a whole, a theme that began with Cantata 6, *Bleib bei uns*. Although viewed primarily in pejorative terms throughout the sequence, the world is depicted as the object of God's love in Cantata 74, making the point of the transforming quality of the indwelling of God in the believer through the coming of the Holy Spirit. The emergence of reference to the Trinity at the end of "Ermuntert euch" suggests the confirmation of a doctrine that is reserved for the end. The same quality underlies the ending of the chorale, where the sense that the final phrase is set apart, both in pitch and in its suggestion of a dominant ending, serves as a reminder of the world above, a preparation for life in the world under the direction of the Spirit (the Trinity season).

{ 14 }

Spring 1725: The Cantatas and the Shape of the Liturgy

Because of the theological character of the season from Easter to Trinity Sunday, especially the prominence of Gospel readings from John, and the collaboration between Bach and Mariane von Ziegler on nine of the thirteen cantatas for that time period, we have a virtually unique opportunity to consider the composer's sustained response to a sphere of theological ideas that has long been known for its unity and distinctness. Not everything of John's celebrated literary and theological style was retained by Ziegler or by the librettists of the *St. John Passion* and the three surviving cantatas that followed it in 1725. But the texts in question certainly exhibit a degree of thematic interrelatedness that goes beyond that of any comparable sequence in Bach's oeuvre. It is, therefore, of a different order from the parallels among the chorale cantatas; these are rooted in a single set of musical and textual procedures according to which their forms were created but not particularly bound up with *thematic* connections of a theological kind from one cantata to the next. We do not find anything comparable, for example, to the appearance of the *violoncello piccolo* in the spring 1725 cantatas anywhere else in Bach's cantata output.[1]

If Bach and his librettists thought of the great fifty days as a theologically unified or at least consistent season as many theologians have over the centuries, then they might well have been concerned to articulate themes that express the transition from Easter to Pentecost, which, in fact, is exactly what we find in the 1725 cantata sequence. During that time frame, the shift of perspective from celebration of Jesus's completed work to the concerns of the faithful and the church without the physical presence of Jesus lends a sense of overall direction to the season.

[1] Another candidate might appear to be the prominence of obbligato organ in several cantatas for Trinity 1726, an occurrence that mirrors the eschatological character of many of the texts in which the instrument appears (including those for other years and seasons); it does not involve, however, cantatas for either a single season or for occasions that are thematically interrelated (apart from the eschatological association).

Given the many images of downward/upward motion associated with the Passion, resurrection, ascension, and coming of the Holy Spirit, images that permeate Jesus's words to the disciples in the Farewell Discourse, the great fifty days can be said to rotate around the idea of worlds "above" and "below," its overall motion primarily that of ascent followed by descent, but its individual stages continually reinterpreting those ideas on multiple levels.[2] John's depiction of Jesus as descending/ascending redeemer, discussed in chapter 8, pervades the great fifty days. Jesus's resurrection and ascension are the culmination of the upswing that begins with John's depiction of the cross as his "lifting up," whereas *Bleib bei uns* articulates the perspective of the world below, which culminates in the coming of the Holy Spirit. In its overall "direction," however, the great fifty days can be said to prepare for and finally to complete the return of Jesus through the Holy Spirit, a downward motion that leads to the perspective of the church on earth (as commemorated in the liturgy) awaiting the Second Coming, and in tropological terms mirrors the spiritual advent of Jesus through faith. That the concerns of the faithful during this time are rooted in the analogy with the disciples, now shorn of Jesus's presence and protection, mean that Jesus's last words to the disciples (the Farewell Discourse) become his message to the contemporary faithful regarding his spiritual presence.

In fact, the many oppositions we encounter throughout the spring 1725 cantata sequence—light/darkness, protection/persecution, faith/the world, sorrow/joy, redemption/judgment, and the like—all flow from the idea of Jesus's departure and return, his absence and presence, and the two directions, or worlds, associated with them: above and below. In music the allegorical representation of above and below generally involves temporal succession, since the simultaneity of high and low sounds is virtually ubiquitous. Thus Bach's use of the *bassetchen* texture makes its greatest impact in relation to the vastly more normal texture of music with *basso continuo* that surrounds it. Most forms of the above/below dualism, therefore, involve motion between the two. Such motion, described in the terms *anabasis* and *catabasis* of musical rhetoric, was so elemental as to be itself virtually ubiquitous.[3] Like the above and below of theology, descent/ascent qualities are extraordinarily simple in their reductive aspect, yet they are capable of generating highly intricate patterns of thought according to how they are "clothed" within the individual works and their particular contexts.

In the spring 1725 cantatas, the *violoncello piccolo* is Bach's most immediate means of suggesting aspects of Jesus's presence and person. It also provides a very subtle means of indicating not only Jesus's descent/ascent character but also his character as mediator, one that he shares with the Holy Spirit. Accompanied by that instrument, the believer first describes Jesus (in Cantata 6, *Bleib bei uns*) as

---

[2] The multiple levels arise from the ambiguity as to whether Jesus, in speaking of his return, is referring to the post-resurrection appearances, his Second Coming, or his coming through the Holy Spirit; similar ambiguities, or double meanings, surround his resurrection, ascension, even the crucifixion as an ascent.

[3] See Unger, *Die Beziehungen zwischen Musik und Rhetorik im 16.–18. Jahrhundert*, 36–37.

present through his word, a "bright light" for the faithful in the last dark and troubled times until the "end." After that, the instrument accompanies the description of Jesus as the good shepherd, who has already given his life to protect his "sheep" from danger (Cantata 85, *Ich bin ein guter Hirt*). And this protective, pastorale aspect is the association attached to the instrument when it returns after Ascension Day (in Cantata 183, *Sie werden euch in den Bann tun*), anticipating Jesus's return through the Holy Spirit. On the second day of Pentecost its appearance is bound up with the joy of Jesus's rebirth in the believer's heart (in Cantata 68, the aria "Mein gläubiges Herze, frohlocke, stets scherze, dein Jesus ist da.") And finally, one day later, the *violoncello piccolo* returns to the description of Jesus as good shepherd, adding the believer's seeing him and hearing his voice through faith (Cantata 175, *Er rufet seinen Schafen mit Namen*). We may not have enough information to settle decisively how the *violoncello piccolo* was held and played, or whether it bears any of the "mediating" associations Forkel attributed to the *viola pomposa*, but we can certainly conclude, on the basis of the foregoing outline, that Bach uses it in these cantatas to lead from the believer's need for Jesus's presence in *Bleib bei uns* to the certainty of his presence through faith and the Spirit in Cantatas 68 and 175. These two cantatas are the only ones in which the instrument descends below the G that is the lowest tone of the three earlier appearances of the instrument, the phrase "mein Jesus ist da" descending to the low C in what seems an obvious association between the bass register of the instrument and Jesus's tropological incarnation through the Spirit.

These occurrences suggest that the 1725 post-Easter cantatas were conceived as a sequence centering on the transition from the historical, physical presence of Jesus to the coming of the Holy Spirit. Taken in conjunction with the other instrumental qualities of these cantatas, they invite us to consider that Bach and Ziegler were concerned to present, and ultimately to unify, the various aspects by which Jesus appears to the believer—as the triumphant redeemer of the Passion, the loving good shepherd and protector, and the inner voice of the Holy Spirit. In relation to the equivalence of Jesus and the Father, as proclaimed in the *St. John Passion*'s first chorus, "Herr, unser Herrscher," and embodied in the resonance of the good shepherd portrayal with comparable depictions of God in the OT, the post-Easter cantatas project the kind of Trinitarian emphasis that Luther found in the Farewell Discourse. From the standpoint of the music, projecting those qualities—drawing an analogy between music and poetic texts, including the ideas "behind" them—involve reduction and patterning in the shapes of music. Melodies may make their primary impact as "pure" music, but if they are also to suggest extramusical *ideas* in a concrete manner their shapes need to be recognizable in extramusical *terms* (at least in a rationalistic era in which the analogy between music and language was widespread). The same is true of harmonies and harmonic sequences, even of tonal qualities, with the circle of fifths serving as the primary model. The ubiquity of circle-of-fifths progressions throughout Bach's music leaves little doubt that this is so.

The two musical directions that are embedded in the rationalistic fifth-based circle of keys (or circles of pitches, harmonies, or cadences, all of which were used by Bach and earlier composers with great frequency) were widely associated, though not with absolute consistency, with spatial directions, namely above (usually the sharp direction) and below (the flat direction). This quality is analogous to the widespread interpretation of scripture in terms of underlying shapes and directions, such as Luther's destruction/restoration dynamic, Rambach's "high" and "low" places in scripture, and August Hermann Francke's invoking the analogy between Jesus's death and resurrection and the act of immersion and reemergence from the water in baptism. The ubiquity of such images is undoubtedly why so many Lutheran chorale melodies exhibit phrase-patterning of similar kinds. Some also exhibit tonal anomalies such as the B♭'s in the G-Mixolydian chorale "Es ist die heil'gen zehn Gebot" or the D♯'s in the A-major chorale "Es ist genung" that point up the theological correlates of sharp and flat "events" with particular vividness.[4] More commonly, the patterns of accidentals that identify modal rather than tonal melodies—the flat second degree in the Phrygian mode, the flat seventh in the Mixolydian mode, the variable sixth degree in the Dorian mode, for example—were enormously stimulating to Bach in the devising of his large-scale designs for the cantatas, both of individual movements and of multimovement sequences. There may never have been any other composer who was so attentive to the structural, affective, and symbolic implications of pitches, accidentals, ambiguities of key, and the like.

In a considerable number of Bach's cantatas as well as in the two Passions, certain of the other oratorios, and the four *Missae Breves,* patterns of tonal ascent and descent (often reinforced, of course, by other musical parameters) are sufficiently clear—"straight line"—to enable them to be discussed as "tonal plan types": that is, as ascent/descent, descent/ascent, straight ascent, and straight descent. Interestingly, the cantatas that exhibit the most straightforward modulatory designs are those whose presentation of their theological content is also highly patterned according to the basic principles of Lutheran hermeneutics. Such patterning is quite prominent in many of Bach's early cantatas. The *Actus Tragicus* (descent/ascent, mirroring the opposition of law and gospel within the framework of salvation history, typological parallelism, and so forth); cantatas 12 (ascent: the *theologia crucis*); 172 (descent: the coming of the Holy Spirit); 21 (ascent: the relationship of OT and NT texts to the four senses, especially the progression to the final, eschatological state); and 61 (ascent: the direct presentation of the four senses) all provide outstanding instances, suggesting that in his earlier years as cantata composer Bach gravitated toward shapes that were directly modeled after those that underlay the principles of scripture interpretation.

The majority of the thirteen cantatas of spring 1725 feature shapes of these kinds, with the most common one being (surprisingly in light of its relative rarity

[4] This discussion and those that follow draw on Chafe, *Analyzing Bach Cantatas*, 161–74, 227–32; *Tonal Allegory*, 91ff.; and *Monteverdi's Tonal Language*, 234–46.

OCCASION	BWV	KEYS	AMBITUS	TONAL "SHAPE"
Easter Sunday	249	**D**, **b**, **D**, b, **b**, D–b, **G**, b–A, **A**, G–A, **D**	D/b	descent to G; return to D through A
Easter Monday	6	**c**, **E♭**, **B♭**, d–g, **g**, **g**	c/E♭ or B♭/g	ascent? or ascent/descent?
Easter Tuesday	–	–	–	–
Quasimodo-geniti	42	**D**, b, **G**, **b**, G–A, **A**, **f♯**	D/b	descent to G followed by A/f♯
Misericor-dias	85	**c**, **g**, **B♭**, E♭–A♭, **E♭**, **c**	c/E♭	ascent/descent
Jubilate	103	**b**, f♯–c♯, **f♯**, b–D, **D**, **b**	b/D	ascent/descent?
Cantate	108	**A**, **f♯**, b–D, **D**, **b**, **b**	D/b	descent
Rogate	87	**d**, g, **g**, d–c, **c**, **B♭**, **d**	g/B♭	descent/ascent
Ascension Day	128	**G**, e–b, **D**, **b**, **G**	G/e	ascent/descent
Exaudi	183	a–e, **e**, G–c/C, **C**, **a**	a/C	ascent/descent
Pentecost: Sunday	74	**C**, **F**, d–a, **e**, **G**, e–C, **C**, **a**	C/a	descent/ascent/descent
Pentecost: Monday	68	**d**, **F**, d–G, **C**, **a–d**	d/F	ascent/descent
Pentecost: Tuesday	175	G, **e**, a–C, **C**, a–D, **D**, **G**	G/e	descent to C/a; return to G through D
Trinity Sunday	176	**c**, g, **B♭**, g, **E♭**, **c**	c/E♭	ascent/descent

FIGURE 14.1 **Keys and tonal designs in the Cantatas for spring 1725** *Keys of closed movements in bold (column 3)*

among Bach's cantata oeuvre as a whole) the "ascent/descent" modulatory design: Cantatas 85, 128, 183, 68, and 176 exhibit this shape clearly, while others, such as Cantatas 6 and 103, feature it in part (fig. 14.1) Of the other types, Cantata 87 is a clear instance of the descent/ascent pattern, while Cantata 108 is a descent from beginning to end. Most of the other cantatas can be considered to mix the various types, several of them featuring pronounced descent patterns at the outset (249, 42, 74, 175), usually leading to the subdominant or the supertonic minor, then turning to the dominant region before returning to the tonic. This last type often suggests something of the I–IV–[ii]–V–I harmonic design, expanded out to the level of the key successions; it resembles the descent/ascent pattern.

In this context it is worth remembering that the close correlation between the musical designs of several of the Ziegler cantatas and the dual or multiple mottoes or motto paraphrases in their texts (Cantatas 108, 87, 74, 68, 175, and 176) suggests that Bach's input into the composition of the latter might have been greater than we know. Without ever composing a single line of any of the poetic texts, Bach might nevertheless have influenced Ziegler toward the introduction of biblical mottoes that would serve as cornerstones and turning points in his designs, just as many of his earlier cantatas feature turning points of similar kinds. It might not have been a question of influence but rather one of collaboration, even if only for a circumscribed time period. Whether or not we can attribute elements in some of the cantata texts to Bach's hand, the highly detailed manner in which he interprets the texts suggests that his own understanding was indeed quite specific, ultimately drawing every conceivable dimension of musical "allegory" into its sphere.

The preceding chapters have dealt with how the shapes of the spring 1725 cantatas mirror their individual texts. We now consider the extent to which these shapes and their placement in the entire series might also reflect the shape of the season as a whole: Jesus's resurrection and ascension followed by the descent of the Holy Spirit as the pivotal events, embedded increasingly within the perspective of the world that eventually comes to dominate life in the Trinity season. In some respects Bach's choice of keys, instrumentation, and styles for the successive cantatas of the 1725 post-Easter season articulate perhaps a coherent response to the character of that season: not a predetermined large-scale design and not a closed design such as we find with the six cantatas (performed on six separate feast days) of the *Christmas Oratorio*, but one whose meaning reflects the principles according to which Bach ordered and created relationships between the individual movements of his cantatas and oratorios. It might be viewed as a "loose" rather than "tight" conception of order and continuity. For instance, whereas a fugue, aria, or suite will nearly always begin and end in the same key, a cantata may not, though more often than not it will; an oratorio may or may not, depending on the degree of dramatic conflict involved (the *Christmas Oratorio* does, after making a substantial digression in its fourth cantata); and the two Passions do not, although there is a high degree of ordering of the keys of both works. On the scale of a cantata succession we could not expect a degree of ordering comparable even to that of the *St. Matthew Passion*, which begins in e and ends in c. I do not argue for a "grand design" that unites the works in question into anything resembling a closed musical succession. Rather, I view the ordering as somewhat analogous to Monteverdi's *Combattimento di Tancredi e Clorinda*, in which the beginning and ending D-minor key should not be considered in any sense as a "tonic" key but as the key chosen to articulate a frame of reference for the disparate events within the work. In this sense, its role in the design can be considered to derive historically from that of the first mode within a full modal spectrum. The tonality of the work is defined by the spectrum as a whole, which determines the key signatures (or transposition levels, of which there are two: the *cantus durus* and *cantus mollis*), and the range of individual modes. Anomalous tonal events may occur, but virtually everything can be rationalized within the large framework of the "two-system," four-hexachord paradigm.

In Bach's case the framework or paradigm is the circle of keys, within which the concept of *ambitus* regulates the relationships surrounding individual keys (in this case I refer specifically to Heinichen's "Musicalischer Cirkul," meaning keys and not just harmonies). In practical terms the range is that extending from four flats to four sharps, the range of the closed movements of the Bach cantatas and Passions, virtually without exception. Whether any one key emerges as an overall center is largely a factor of scale. Over the span of eight weeks we cannot expect anything of the kind; to argue for such a conception would be to falsify the entire theoretical framework itself. But within that framework we may find that particular keys, and their relationships to other factors, such as instrumentation, recur in similar contexts. Such is the case with the c/E♭ *ambitus* with which the *St. John Passion* ends, and especially with the key of the burial chorus, c, which is the same as that of the *St. Matthew Passion* and other cantatas dealing with similar subjects. Its recurrence in *Bleib bei uns* and *Es ist ein trotzig uns verzagt Ding* in association with darkness (versus light) may well remind us that the closing *ambitus* of the Passion takes the universal darkness that preceded Jesus's death as its point of departure. We cannot, of course, "prove" such associations, which must remain hypothetical in character.

In the *St. John Passion* I have argued for a large-scale quasi-symmetrical arrangement of key areas, or *ambitus*, according to which the flat regions are closely reflective of what John calls "the world [below]," whereas the sharp regions mirror its opposite, described by Jesus in the dialogs with Pilate as his kingdom, the realm of truth and of power, and associated particularly with ideas of freedom, redemption, and victory over death. The most characteristic *ambitus* for those two spheres are those of g/B♭ or c/E♭, on the one hand, and of D/b or A/f♯ on the other. These are also the two contrasting *ambitus* of the first six surviving cantatas of the spring 1725 sequence (see fig. 14.1), juxtaposed at first, as is the case between the ending of the *St. John Passion* (E♭/c) and the successive cantatas *Kommt, gehet und eilet* (D/b) and *Bleib bei uns* (E♭/c), then between *Am Abend, aber, desselbigen Sabbats* (D/b), *Ich bin ein guter Hirt* (E♭/c), and *Ihr werdet weinen und heulen* (D/b). With *Es ist euch gut, daß ich hingehe*, one week later, the D/b *ambitus* remains, perhaps as a reflection of the bond between the present and future eschatological aspects of *seeing* Jesus that is prominent in the texts of Cantatas 103 and 108. Between *Kommt, gehet und eilet* and *Bleib bei uns* the contrast resembles the affective spheres of the aria "Es ist vollbracht" and the final chorus "Ruht wohl" in the Passion, with the turn to flat keys after Easter Day associated particularly with the darkness of the world. In both *Bleib bei uns* and *Ich bin ein guter Hirt* the character of the music lends the C-minor tonality the sense of consolation that sounds in the burial chorus of the *St. John Passion. Bleib bei uns*, however, does not return to its initial c tonality but closes in g, whereas *Ich bin ein guter Hirt* ascends from c to g and B♭, for an expression of the glory of God before returning through E♭ to close in c. This may reflect the fact that *Ich bin ein guter Hirt* responds, especially in its final chorale (a paraphrase of Psalm 46), to the prayer that ends *Bleib bei uns*, for Jesus to manifest his power in protecting the faithful. This is the meaning of Martin Moller's citing the *dictum* that begins *Bleib bei uns* in his discussion of the Gospel for Misericordias. Whether Bach thought of it in such terms, the sense of closure that permeates the latter part of *Ich bin ein guter Hirt* is remarkable, projecting, in part by means of its tonal design, the security of Jesus's protection that is so prominent in the first three surviving post-Easter cantatas.

This initial group of Easter and post-Easter cantatas presents Jesus in two distinct aspects: the *Christus Victor* of the Passion and resurrection (especially in John), and the good shepherd of the tenth chapter of John. Jesus's protection of the disciples is prominent in both images. In these cantatas the trumpet style and the key of D are associated with the *Christus Victor* image, and the *violoncello piccolo* and the flat-key sphere, primarily c, with that of the shepherd. With the turn to readings from the Farewell Discourse, Ziegler places increased emphasis on the theme of the believer's longing to see Jesus, preparing for the third, and most essential aspect of Jesus's return, as the Holy Spirit. In *Bleib bei uns* seeing Jesus had been introduced by the unknown librettist as a natural consequence of the light/darkness theme, where it was associated with the bright light of the Word (the aria "Jesu, lass uns auf dich sehen, . . . Lass das Licht deines Wort's uns heller scheinen. . . "). After *Ich bin ein guter Hirt* the theme emerges more directly, now taking on an eschatological quality, first in Cantata 103 (*Ihr werdet weinen und heulen*), as the believer anticipates the joy of seeing Jesus in eternity. Then, after renewal of that longing in Cantata 108 (*Es ist euch gut . . .*), the latter cantata ends by associating the "way" to eternity with the Holy Spirit. These two cantatas bring out the sense that the world will be transformed by Jesus's return. Martin Moller viewed the Sundays for which they were composed as comprising an "octave," and between them there is a strong sense of tonal affinity rather than contrast. The earlier alternation of the flat and sharp *ambitus* now recedes, along with the theme of darkness. The two cantatas utilize virtually the identical set of keys, and both end with tonal descent to the concluding key, B minor. In Cantata 103 that descent takes the c♯ ending of the first recitative (the second movement) as its point of departure, passing through f♯ (the first aria) and D (the second recitative and aria), before turning to b. We have seen how the D-major aria projects an affect of joy in the anticipation of Jesus's return, after which the B-minor chorale emphasizes that the joy has a future eschatological character. After that, Cantata 108 is built entirely around the idea of descent from A through f♯, and D to b, which gives it the character of placing the message of Cantata 103 in a new context, that of anticipation of the Holy Spirit. Their tonal centers seem to bind the two cantatas into a sequence. Since their texts describe a shift from the faithful anticipating seeing Jesus in eternity to the coming of the Holy Spirit, it appears possible that the straightforward descent pattern of Cantata 108, like the many metaphors of direction in its text, should be understood as marking a shift from the antithesis of the disciples and the world in Cantata 103 to a more positive view of the world under the Spirit, which is the subject of the two *dicta* from John. Within that framework, the second *dictum* describes, in the contrasted tonal patterns of its ABA′ formal design, the juxtaposition of worlds above (associated with "truth") and below (the Spirit's revealing what he "hears" to humanity). The sense of directional patterning is a very palpable one.

After that, Cantata 87, *Bisher habt ihr nicht gebeten in meinem Namen*, can be said to mark a change, in that it introduces the theme of penitence, which is otherwise hardly present in the spring cantata sequence (see ch. 10). Its beginning with the negative formulation that begins Jesus's discourse to the disciples on prayer is a reminder of the change that comes with Jesus's departure: the juxtaposition of "bisher"—"up to now"—and the message of promise that pervades Jesus's words (and that Bach set in a more directly positive manner in the cantata produced one year before, *Wahrlich, wahrlich, ich sage euch,* BWV 86). In Ziegler's text the change in question is interpreted as the necessity of acknowledging guilt and sin as the route to the fulfillment of that promise. Cantata 87 therefore offers the clearest instance of a descent/ascent pattern in the entire series, associating the descent with anxiety in the world, which is bound up with the need for penitence and prayer, and the ascent with the transformation of worldly suffering into *Trost* and ultimately joy as the benefit of Jesus's overcoming the world. Here C minor is the "center" rather than the beginning or ending framework, which is assigned to D minor, possibly as the minor counterpart of the D major that was heard on Easter Day and within several later cantatas, where it served mostly as the expression of an affective sphere associated with Jesus's victory.

With Cantata 87 the D/b *ambitus* disappears altogether from the cantata sequence (other than as the keys of single movements, which are now no longer the principal keys). The sharpest key of the remaining cantatas of the season is now G, heard in Cantata 128 (*Auf Christi Himmelfahrt allein*) for Ascension Day and Cantata 175, for the third day of Pentecost. The G of Cantata 128 now features horns rather than the D trumpets of Cantata 249 (*Kommt, gehet und eilet*), a "softening" of the aura of victory that corresponds to the fact that Jesus's ascension is not a militant event as is the resurrection, but rather one of intrinsic majesty: remember that Cantata 249 ends with the line "Der Löwe von Juda kommt siegend gezogen" (the lion comes in victory), whereas Cantata 128 ends with anticipation of the believer's seeing Jesus's *Herrlichkeit.* Cantata 128 outlines the tones of the ascending/descending major triad in the keys of its movements, perhaps a Trinitarian symbol, as it was in the concept of the "harmonic triad" ("Triunitas") during Bach's time, and as it is in the chorale ("Allein Gott in der Höh' sei Ehr'") that supplied the melody of its opening movement, as well as that of the B♭ aria of *Ich bin ein guter Hirt.* As C minor was the nadir of the descent/ascent design of Cantata 87, now D major is the "apex" of the ascent/descent design of Cantata 128, serving as the key of a trumpet aria that articulates the opposition of the world "below" to the sphere of the resurrected and ascended Jesus. At the same time, however, the "Haupt"/"Glieder" metaphor that dominates the first movement, expresses the unity rather than the disparity of above and below, as the movement keys of the cantata describe the G triad.

On Ascension Day Cantata 128 completes the theme of the believer's longing to see Jesus. With Cantata 183 (*Sie werden euch in den Bann tun*), for Exaudi, Ziegler introduces a more direct anticipation of the Holy Spirit than that of Cantata 108. And Bach's choices of key and tonal shape seem again significant, especially seen in the recurrence of two themes from the preceding cantatas: Jesus's protection, voiced in the aria with *violoncello piccolo,* "Ich fürchte nicht des Todes Schrecken," and prayer, expressed first in terms of human weakness (the aria, "Höchster Tröster, heil'ger Geist"), then in terms of the coming of the Holy Spirit (the final chorale, "Du bist ein Geist, der lehret, wie man recht beten soll"). In this cantata the key element is the ascent, projected in the pure a′–e″ rising fifth melody of the opening movement, and picked up in the shift of key from a to e for the *violoncello piccolo* aria. When the "Ich bin bereit" of the third movement turns to G, key of the middle section of the preceding aria, the gesture seems a highly significant one, since it voices the believer's readiness for the coming of the Holy Spirit. The c/C gesture that ends the recitative follows from an enharmonic transformation from sharps to flats that appears to represent the sudden (tropological) advent of Jesus in the human heart via the coming of the Holy Spirit. The subsequent aria, "Höchster Tröster," then echoes that gesture at the cadence of its middle section, following modulation through d and g, as the believer voices first the human weakness that prevents true prayer, then the belief that God will care for her. In light of Ziegler's continuing the theme of prayer from Cantata 87, it seems significant that Bach duplicates the d–g–c pattern that had appeared in the earlier cantata, where it served both as the overall tonal sequence of the first through fourth movements, and also as the key sequence of the third movement (the recitative that set up the shift to c for the pivotal "central" movement). Since both Cantatas 87 and 183 echo the language of Romans 8, the connection suggests an association between the coming of the Holy Spirit and the C-major tonality of the latter work.

After *Bleib bei uns* and *Ich bin ein guter Hirt* the role of C minor lessens progressively in *Bisher habt ihr nichts gebeten* and *Sie werden euch in den Bann tun*, as the textual emphasis shifts from the sinful darkness of the world in *Bleib bei uns* to anxiety in the world countered by *Trost* in Cantata 87, then human weakness overcome by the Holy Spirit in Cantata 183. The appearance of C minor in Cantata 183 is momentary, a minor-mode coloring of C major, but when it reappears as the predominant tonal center of Cantata 176, it is developed as the symbol of human weakness, associated with the light/darkness antithesis once again. In Cantata 183 the C/a tonality can be said to bridge to Cantata 74 (*Wer mich liebet, der wird mein Wort halten*), where it centers an *ambitus* that features its subdominant-supertonic (F/d) and dominant-mediant (G/e) sides conspicuously as well. In its tonal design Cantata 74 resembles Cantata 249 in that after an initial festive articulation of the tonic major, with trumpets, oboes, and strings, the design turns in the subdominant direction as it describes a complex of ideas all suggestive of descent—the believer's open heart awaiting reception of God's indwelling, love, and the hope that God's word will impact on the believer, prayer, and *Trost* (the F-major aria, "Komm, komm, mein Herz steht dir offen"), followed by affirmation of the readiness of the human heart as God's dwelling place (the D-minor beginning of the recitative, "Die Wohnung ist bereit"). After that it turns in the dominant direction, first for the E-minor *dictum* from John, which describes the meaning of Jesus's going and returning in terms of the descent/ascent shape of its quasi-ostinato *basso continuo* and bass lines. The tonal curve of the movement sequence continues upward for the G-major aria, then returns through e and C, ending in a. Thus *Wer mich liebet* begins with a movement featuring signs of triumph, especially trumpets and kettledrums in C, but its theological character and overall tone incorporate a distinct focus on the human perspective, as befits its centering on the "descent" of God to the human heart. Its minor-key ending and reminder of human unworthiness offset the positive message of the benefits of Jesus's struggle and victory over death in the penultimate C-major "concerto" aria.

In terms of the sequence, the C/a tonality of *Wer mich liebet* can be viewed not only as mediating between the contrasted flat and sharp *ambitus* with which the post-Easter cantatas began, but also as the center of a new *ambitus* encompassing the keys of all the cantatas from Cantate to the third day of Pentecost: d (87), G (128), a (183), C/a (74), d (68), and G (175). The relatively uncomplicated major keys and triumphant affects of the Easter and Ascension Day cantatas mirror the fact that these cantatas were written for feasts whose Gospels are narrative in character and derive their theological messages from Jesus's triumph over the world rather than the character of life in the world itself. The large-scale "descent" from D and G to C in the cantatas for Easter, Ascension Day, and Pentecost can be considered to represent a shift in perspective from the triumphant completion of Jesus's work to the theme of humankind living in faith and the Spirit. Pentecost, anticipated several times in the post-Easter cantatas, is the spiritual "goal" of this series of cantatas. It is uniquely expressive of the content of John's Farewell Discourse, not only because the discourse weaves its way around the coming of the Spirit but also because John's *Tröster* embodies the foremost quality of the Gospel as Luther saw it. The ancient threefold view of Easter, Ascension Day, and Pentecost as depicting Jesus as *Überwinder* (overcomer, victor) and *Durchbrecher* (one who breaks through the separation of above and below), and the Holy Spirit as *Tröster* (comforter), applies here.

In relation to the C/a *ambitus* of *Wer mich liebet*, the d and G of *Also hat Gott die Welt geliebt* and *Er rufet seinen Schafen mit Namen* bring out qualities associated with the subdominant and dominant "sides" of the *ambitus* in Cantata 74. Those two works now feature the ascent/descent tonal type (d–F–C–a/d), followed by the descent/ascent type (G–e–C–a, then, following a sudden shift to sharps [cadences to f♯ and D in the recitative], an aria in D, and chorale in G). The key of C serves as the apex of the former cantata and very close to the nadir of the latter. That is, the key of C provides a bond between the subdominant/supertonic and dominant regions of Cantatas 74, 68, and 175. The "ascent" part of Cantata 68 progresses from a chorale statement of God's love of the world (the opening movement, "Also hat Gott die Welt geliebt," which features an ascent/descent articulation of the keys of d, F, a, F, and d in itself) and an affirmation of the presence of Jesus through faith (the first, aria "Mein gläubiges Herze") to an expression of the benefits of Jesus's incarnation (the C-major aria, "Du bist geboren mir zugute"). Following from a reference to the antithesis of judgment and salvation in the first recitative (a paraphrase from John), the closing choral motto sets forth John's either/or view of judgment and salvation in the present as a warning (reinforced by the lack of a concluding chorale).

Then *Er rufet seinen Schafen mit Namen*, heard on the following day, places the idea of division in the world in a broader and ultimately more positive perspective. Its descent/ascent pattern juxtaposes the inner and outer aspects of the message of salvation, setting the subdominant (C/a) and dominant (D) regions of the *ambitus* in opposition (as did Cantatas 249, 42, and 74), but an opposition that exists within the larger unity of the *ambitus* itself. The central recitative uses John's well-known emphasis on misunderstanding to issue a condemnation of reason (the turning point), which is then answered by the subsequent trumpeting forth of the message of Jesus's victory. The design as a whole equates the necessity of understanding the soft, personal voice of Jesus, the good shepherd (the subdominant region), both to the message of Jesus's victory (the dominant region) and to the Holy Spirit within (the tonic/relative minor region), completing the idea of "overcoming" the world through faith and the Spirit (as Cantata 128 did in terms of Jesus's physical ascension).

In relation to the positive tone of Cantata 175, its successor on Trinity Sunday, *Es ist ein trotzig und verzagt Ding*, returns to a pejorative view of human nature at the outset, setting it in opposition to the "light" associated with Jesus's presence. Its return to C minor, therefore, represents at one level a sudden change from the keys of the immediately preceding cantatas as its tone seems to turn away from their basic optimism. It might have been conceived by Bach as a counterpart to the C major of Cantata 74, in that it aids in differentiating the sphere of darkness and human weakness, on which the work centers, from that of Jesus. Its ending with a C-minor hymn to the Trinity is, in fact, a representation of the human perspective on the deity. Yet, the G/c succession between the keys of the final two cantatas of the spring sequence, even perhaps the C/a–d–G–c succession from *Wer mich liebet* to *Es ist ein trotzig und verzagt Ding*, may represent an aspect of continuity between Pentecost and Trinity, one in which Trinity Sunday, normally one of the most festive feasts of the year, represents the flawed and humble human dwelling place of God with the minor mode. Martin Moller's association of the motto that begins Cantata 176 with Easter Monday and Misericordias suggests that in this respect the c of Cantata 176 might have been conceived in relation to the c of *Bleib bei uns* and *Ich bin ein guter Hirt*, serving as a response to the prayer of the former work for God's presence in the world and a confirmation of the intimate relationship to God described in the chorale that ends *Ich bin ein guter Hirt*. Indeed, it might have been intended to link up with the C-minor portrayal of the world in Cantata 87 and the C-minor coloring of C major in *Sie werden euch in den Bann tun*. Like *Bleib bei uns* and *Ich bin ein guter Hirt*, *Es ist ein trotzig und verzagt Ding* modulates "upward" from its initial C minor to B♭, a progression that accompanies an increasingly positive tone among the "ascending" sequence of movements and that lends the work as a whole an "ascent/descent" shape. The B♭ aria, with its many sets of oppositions centered on the juxtaposition of Jesus as "light" and human weakness as "darkness," is then followed by a recitative that accepts the implications of those oppositions and pivots around *Trost* for the faithful. From this point the return through the E♭ of the second aria to the C-minor ending of the cantata represents the idea of life in the world as one in which the believer, accepting his human frailty and awaiting the future fulfillment, enjoys the benefits of faith and the Holy Spirit in the present life.

The theme of "the world" in the Bach cantatas is a very broad and complex one, not limited to any particular season or scriptural source. The value of studying the cantatas produced in spring 1725 is bound up with their reflecting the character of a season whose principal aim is to show how faith and God's gift of the Holy Spirit enable humankind simultaneously to live in and "overcome" the world. Love, the working of the Spirit, the balance between rejection of the world, and the benefits provided by faith in present life—themes forming what Walther von Loewenich calls the realization of faith in experience—offset what Loewenich calls the "negative delimitation" of faith, that is, faith "in opposition to experience," bringing us closer to the experience of the world in the orthodox Lutheranism of Bach's time and surroundings. That experience must have featured a considerable degree of the qualities of conflict and tension that Lutheranism views in terms of the antithesis of faith and experience. That Bach expressed his "final purpose" in terms completely other than Mariane von Ziegler did hers, that he underlined in his *Calov Bible* many passages suggestive of a personal struggle with authority, are facts that attest to such conflict. Apparently he sought some form of resolution in the view that one must accommodate oneself to God's will. In some respects religious life in Leipzig exhibited considerable resistance to Enlightenment ideals (as demonstrated in the negative attitude toward reason in the Bach cantatas), while at the same time harboring prominent individuals such as Gottsched, Ernesti, Christian Wolff, and Mariane von Ziegler, who espoused those ideals. Yet the collaboration of Bach and Ziegler to produce a group of works whose theological message goes well beyond the antitheses that figure so prominently among its individual themes provides an appropriate close to a double series of works—the first two Leipzig cantata cycles—that began soon after Bach's arrival there in Pentecost 1723 with two cantatas, the second of which ends with John's message of brotherly love (Cantatas 75 and 76). However ideal a message, it reflected the purpose of the liturgical year itself: to use the life and work of Christ as meditated upon in the first half of the year to aid the faithful in the struggle to overcome the world.

BIBLIOGRAPHY

Ainsworth, Maryan W., and Maximiliaan P. J. Martens. *Petrus Christus: Renaissance Master of Bruges.* New York: Metropolitan Museum of Art, 1994.

Althaus, Paul. *The Theology of Martin Luther.* Translated by Robert C. Schulz. Philadelphia: Fortress Press, 1966.

Ambrose, Z. Philip. "'Weinen, Klagen, Sorgen, Zagen' und die antike Redekunst." *Bach-Jahrbuch* 69 (1983): 34–35.

Arndt, Johann. *Auslegung des gantzen Psalters Davids des Königlichen Propheten. . . .* Jena, 1624.

Arndt, Johann. *Paradiesgärtlein.* Züllichau, 1734.

Arndt, Johann. *Postilla: Das ist Auslegung der Sonn- und Fest-Tags Evangelien durchs gantze Jahr. . . .* Frankfurt, 1713.

Arndt, Johann. *Sechs Bücher Vom Wahren Christenthum. . . . Nicht allein mit beygefügten Gebetern, Anmerkungen, Lebenslauf des Auctoris, und gewönlichen Registern; Sondern auch mit ganz neuen und an einander hangenden Accuraten Summarien jedes Capitels, Einem neu-verfertigten besonders brauchbaren Sonn- und Fest-Tages-Regiwster; Und einer Catechetischen Einleitung von 288 Fragen versehen. Nebst dem Paradies-Gartlein, In groben Druck heraus gegeben Mit einer historischen Vorrede Herrn D. Johann Jacob Rambachs.* Züllichau, 1734.

Arndt, Johann. *Vier Bücher Von wahrem Christenthumb: Die erste Gesamtausgabe (1610).* Herausgegeben von Johann Anselm Steiger. 3 vols. Hildesheim: Georg Olms Verlag, 2007..

Arnold, F. T. *The Art of Accompaniment from a Thorough-Bass.* London: Oxford University Press, 1931. Reprint, New York: Dover Publications, 1965.

Aulén, Gustav. *Christus Victor.* Translated by A. G. Hebert. New York: Macmillan, 1969.

Axmacher, Elke. *"Aus Liebe will mein Heyland sterben." Untersuchungen zum Wandel des Passionsverständnisses im frühen 18. Jahrhundert.* Beiträge zur theologischen Bachforschung. Neuhausen-Stuttgart: Hänssler Verlag, 1976.

Axmacher, Elke. "Bachs Kantatentexte in auslegungsgeschichtlicher Sicht." In *Bach als Ausleger der Bibel,* edited by Martin Petzoldt, 15–32. Göttingen: Vandenhoeck & Ruprecht, 1985.

Axmacher, Elke."Ein Quellenfund zum Text der Matthäus-Passion." *Bach-Jahrbuch* 54 (1978): 181–91.

Axmacher, Elke. *Praxis Evangeliorum: Theologie und Frömmigkeit bei Martin Moller (1547–1606).* Göttingen: Vandenhoeck & Ruprecht, 1989.

Badiarov, Dimitry. "The Violoncello, Viola da spalla and Viola pomposa in Theory and Practice." *Galpin Society Journal* 60 (2007).

Barnett, Gregory. "The Violoncello da Spalla and the Eccentricities of Historical Performance Practice." Paper presented at the Annual Meeting of the American Musicological Society, Nashville, 2008.

Benjamin, Walter. *The Origin of German Tragic Drama*. Translated by John Osborne. London: New Left Books, 1977.

Blankenburg, Walter. "Die Symmetrieform in Bachs Werken und ihre Bedeutung." *Bach-Jahrbuch* 38 (1949–50): 24–39.

Bolduan, Miriam F. "The Significance of the Viola Pomposa in the Bach Cantatas." *Bach. Quarterly Journal of the Riemenschneider Bach Institute* 14, no. 3 (July 1983): 12–17.

Bornkamm, Heinrich. *Luther and the Old Testament*. Translated by Eric W. Gritsch and Ruth C. Gritsch. Edited by Victor I. Gruhn. Philadelphia: Fortress Press, 1974.

Brecht, Martin ed., *Geschichte des Pietismus 1: Der Pietismus vom siebsehnten bis zum frühen achtzehnten Jahrhundert*. Göttingen: Vanderhoeck & Ruprecht, 1993.

Breig, Werner. "Zu den Turba-Chören von Bachs Johannes-Passion." In *Geistliche Musik: Studien zu ihrer Geschichte und Funktion im 18. und 19. Jahrhundert*, edited by Constantin Floros, Hans Joachim Marx, and Peter Petersen. Hamburger Jahrbuch für Musikwissenschaft. Laaber: Laaber-Verlag, 1985.

Brockes, Barthold Heinrich. *Irdisches Vergnügen in Gott: bestehend in Physicalisch- und Moralischen Gedichten, Vierter Theil*. Tubingen, 1753.

Brockes, Barthold Heinrich. *Der für die Sünde der Welt gemarterte und Sterbende Jesus*. Hamburg, 1715.

Brown, Raymond E. *The Death of the Messiah*. 2 vols. New York: Doubleday Anchor Books, 1994.

Brown, Raymond E. *The Gospel According to John I–XII*. Vol. 29a. Anchor Bible Series. New York: Doubleday, 1966.

Brown, Raymond E. *The Gospel According to John XIII–XXI*. Vol. 29b Anchor Bible Series. New York: Doubleday, 1966.

Brown, Raymond E. *An Introduction to the New Testament*. New York: Doubleday, 1996.

Bugenhagen, Johannes. *Historia des leidens und Aufferstehung unsere Herrn Jesu Christi / aus den vier Evangelisten*. Wittenberg, 1530.

Bukofzer, Manfred. *Music in the Baroque Era*. New York: W. W. Norton, 1947.

Bultmann, Rudolf. "Die Bedeutung der neuerschlossenen mandäischen und manichäischen Quellen für das Verständnis des Johannesevangeliums." *Zeitschrift für die Neutestamentliche Wissenschaft und die Kunde der älteren Kirche* 24 1925: 100–146 Reprint, *Exegetica*. Tübingen: Mohr, 1967.

Bultmann, Rudolf. "Johanneische Schriften und Gnosis." *Orientalische Literaturzeitung: Zeitschrift für die Wissenschaft vom ganzen Orient und seinen Beziehungen zu den angrenzenden Kulturkreisen* 43. 1940. Reprint, *Exegetica*. Tübingen: Mohr, 1967.

Bultmann, Rudolf. *Theology of the New Testament*. Translated by Kandrick Grobel. Vol. 2. New York: Charles Scribner's Sons, 1955.

Burmeister, Joachim. *Musica Poetica*. Rostock 1606. Facsimile reprint edited by Martin Ruhnke. Kassel: Bärenreiter, 1955.

Butt, John. *Bach's Dialogue with Modernity: Perspectives on the Passions*. Cambridge: Cambridge University Press. 2010.

Buttstett, Johann Heinrich. *Ut, Mi, Sol, Re, Fa, La, Tota Musica Et Harmonia Aeterna*. Erfurt, 1715.

Calov, Abraham. *Die Heilige Bibel nach D. MARTINI LUTHERI Deutscher Dolmetschung und Erklärung*... 3 vols. Wittenberg, 1681–82.

Calvin, John. *John*. Edited by Alistair McGrath and J. I. Packer. Wheaton, IL: Crossway Books, 1994.

Cannon, Beekman. *Johann Mattheson: Spectator in Music.* New Haven, CT: Yale University Press, 1947.

Cannon, Beekman. "Johann Mattheson's 'Inquiring Composer.'" In *New Mattheson Studies*, edited by George J. Buelow and Hans Joachim Marx. Cambridge: Cambridge University Press, 1983.

Chafe, Eric Thomas. "Allegorical Music: The 'Symbolism' of Tonality in the Bach Canons." *Journal of Musicology* 3 (1984): 340–62.

Chafe, Eric Thomas. *Analyzing Bach Cantatas.* New York: Oxford University Press, 2000.

Chafe, Eric Thomas. "*Anfang und Ende*: Cyclic Recurrence in Bach's Cantata *Jesu, nun sei gepreiset* BWV 41." In *Bach Perspectives 1*, edited by Russell Stinson. Lincoln: University of Nebraska Press, 1995.

Chafe, Eric Thomas. "Bach's Ascension Oratorio: God's Kingdoms and Their Representation." In *Bach Perspectives 8: J. S. Bach and the Oratorio Tradition,* edited by Daniel R. Melamed, 122–45. Urbana: University of Illinois Press, 2011, .

Chafe, Eric Thomas. "Bach and Hypocrisy: Truth and Appearance in Cantatas 136 and 179." In *The Century of Bach and Mozart: Perspectives on Historiography, Composition, Theory and Performance*, edited by Sean Gallagher and Thomas Forrest Kelly, 121–43. Cambridge, MA: Harvard University Press, 2008.

Chafe, Eric Thomas. *Monteverdi's Tonal Language.* New York: Schirmer Books, 1992.

Chafe, Eric Thomas. *Tonal Allegory in the Vocal Music of J. S. Bach.* Berkeley: University of California Press, 1991.

Chemnitz, Martin. *Examination of the Council of Trent.* Translated by Fred Kramer. Parts 1-4: St. Louis: Concordia, 1971, 1978, 1986.

Chemnitz, Martin. *The Two Natures in Christ.* Translated by J. A. O. Preus. St. Louis: Concordia, 1971.

Chemnitz, Martin, Johann Gerhard, and Polycarp Leyser. *Die Harmonie derer Heiligen vier Evangelisten, angefangen vom D. Martinus Chemnitius, fortgesetzet vom D. Polycarpus Lyserus, und zu Ende gebracht vom D. Johann Gerhard.* Translated by D. Otto Nathanael Nicolai. Vol. 1. Magdeburg und Leipzig, 1764.

Chemnitz, Martin, Polycarp Leyser, and Johann Gerhard. *Echt evangelische Auslegung der Sonn- und Festtags-Evangelien des Kirchenjahrs.* 7 vols. St. Louis : Druckerei der Synode von Missouri, Ohio und anderen Staaten, 1872.

Chemnitz, Martin, and Polycarp Leyser. *Harmoniae Evangelicae: A praestantissimo Theologo D. Martino Chemnitio Primum Inchoatae, Et per D. Polycarpum Lyserum Continuatae, Libri Quinque.* Frankfurt, 1622. English translation of book 1, "Dedicatory Epistles and Chapters 1–16." In *The Harmony of the Four Evangelists,* vol. 1, book 1, edited by Richard J. Dinda. Malone, TX: Center for the Study of Lutheran Orthodoxy, 2009; Vol. 1, bk. 2, chs. 17–33 (2011); Vol. 1, book 3, Part One (2012).

Cobb, Peter G. "The History of the Christian Year." In *The Study of Liturgy*, edited by Geoffrey Wainwright, Edward Yarnold, Paul Bradshaw, and Cheslyn Jones. Oxford: Oxford University Press, 1992.

Conzelmann, Hans. *The Theology of St. Luke.* Published as *Die Mitte der Zeit* in 1953. Translated by Geoffrey Buswell. Philadelphia: Fortress Press, 1982.

Cox, Howard, H., ed. *The Calov Bible of J. S. Bach.* Translated by Ellis Finger. Ann Arbor: UMI Research Press, 1985.

Cullmann, Oscar. *Christ and Time.* Published as *Christus und die Zeit* in 1946. Translated by Floyd V. Filson. 3rd rev. ed. London: SCM Press, 1965.

Cullmann, Oscar.*The Johannine Circle*. Translated by John Bowden. London: Westminster Press, 1976.

Dahlhaus, Carl. *Untersuchungen über die Entstehung der harmonischen Tonalität*. Kassel: Bärenreiter, 1968.

Dammann, Rolf. *Der Musikbegriff im deutschen Barock*. Cologne: Arno Volk Verlag, 1967.

Das Privilegirte Ordentliche und Vermehrte Dresdnische Gesang-Buch. Dresden and Leipzig, 1735.

David, Hans T., Arthur Mendel, and Christoph Wolff, eds. *The New Bach Reader: A Life of Johann Sebastian Bach in Letters and Documents*. New York: W. W. Norton, 1998.

De Lubac, Henri. *Medieval Exegesis: The Four Senses of Scripture*. Translated by Mark Sebanc and E. M. Macierowski. 2 vols. Grand Rapids, MI: Wm. B. Eerdmans, 1998–2000.

Dilherr, Johann Michael. *Heilige Sabbaths Arbeit*. 2nd ed. Nuremberg, 1674.

Dilherr, Johann Michael. *Weg zu der Seligkeit*. Nuremberg, 1655.

Dilherr, Johann Michael, and George Philipp Harsdörffer. *Drei-ständige Sonn- und Festtag-Emblemata, oder Sinne-bilder* [ca. 1660], *mit einem Nachwort von Dietmar Peil*. Facsimile ed. Hildesheim: Georg Olms, 1994.

Dix, Dom Gregory. *The Shape of the Liturgy*. London: Dacre Press, 1945.

Dodd, C. H. *The Interpretation of the Fourth Gospel*. Cambridge: Cambridge University Press, 1960.

Dreyfus, Laurence. *Bach's Continuo Group: Players and Practices in His Vocal Works*. Vol. 3. Studies in the History of Music. Cambridge, MA: Harvard University Press, 1987.

Dreyfus, Laurence. "The Triumph of 'Instrumental Melody': Aspects of Musical Poetics in Bach's *St. John Passion*. In *Bach Perspectives 8: J. S. Bach and the Oratorio Tradition*,, edited by Daniel R. Melamed, 96–121. Urbana: University of Illinois Press, 2011.

Dürr, Alfred. *Johann Sebastian Bach's "St. John Passion": Genesis, Transmission, and Meaning*. Translated by Alfred Clayton. New York: Oxford University Press, 2000.

Dürr, Alfred. *Die Kantaten von J. S. Bach mit ihren Texten*. 6th ed. Kassel: Barenreiter-Verlag, 1995. English edition, *The Cantatas of J. S. Bach*. Revised and translated by Richard D. P. Jones. Oxford: Oxford University Press, 2005.

Dürr, Alfred. "Zu den verschollenen Passionen Bachs." *Bach-Jahrbuch* 64 (1957): 5–162.

Düwel, Klaus, ed. *Epochen der deutschen Lyrik*. Vol. 3, *Gedichte, 1500–1600*. Munich: Deutsche Taschenbuch Verlag, 1978.

Emans, Reinmar, and Sven Hiemke, eds.. *Bachs Passionen, Oratorien und Motetten: Das Handbuch*. Laaber: Laaber-Verlag, 2009.

Erasmus. *On the Freedom of the Will (De Libero Arbitrio)*. Edited and translated by E. Gordon Rupp in collaboration with A. N. Marlow. In *Luther and Erasmus: Free Will and Salvation*. Philadelphia: Westminster Press, 1969.

Fischer, D. Albert, and W. Tümpel. *Das deutsche evangelische Kirchenlied des siebzehnten Jahrhunderts*. 5 vols. Gütersloh: C. Bertelsmann, 1904–11.

Francke, August Hermann. *August Hermann Franckens / . . . Sonn- und Fest-Tags-Predigten*. Halle, 1724.

Francke, August Hermann. *CHRISTUS / Der Kern heiliger Schrifft / Oder / Einfältige Anweisung / wie man Christum / als den Kern der gantzen heiligen Schrifft / rech suchen / finden / schmäcken / und damit seine Seele nähren / sättigen und zum ewigen Leben erhalten solle*. Halle, 1702. Reprint, in English translation as *Christ; The Sum and Substance of all the Holy Scriptures in the Old and New Testament*. London, 1732.

Francke, August Hermann. *Das Abendmahl des Lammes / In einer Predigt Uber das Evangelium Luc. XIV, vers. 16–24*. Halle, 1699.

Francke, August Hermann. *Einleitung zur Lesung der H. Schrifft / insonderheit des Neuen Testaments* 3rd ed. Halle, 1699.

Francke, August Hermann. *Nicodemus / Oder / Tractätlein / von der Menschen-Furcht*. 3rd ed. Halle, 1727.

Francke, August Hermann. *Oeffentliche Reden über die Paßions-Historie / Wie dieselbe vom Evangelisten Johanne im 19. u. 19. Cap. beschrieben ist*. 1716. 2nd ed., Halle, 1719.

Francke, August Hermann. *Predigten über die Sonn- und Fest-Tags Episteln*. Halle, 1724.

Franklin, Don. "The Libretto of Bach's John Passion and the Doctrine of Reconciliation: An Historical Perspective." In *Das Blut Jesu und die Lehre von der Versöhnung im Werk Johann Sebastian Bachs*, edited by A. A. Clement. Proceedings of the Royal Netherlands Academy of Arts and Sciences, no. 164. Amsterdam: North-Holland, 1995.

Frei, Hans W. *The Eclipse of Biblical Narrative*. New Haven, CT: Yale University Press, 1974.

Freiesleben, Gerhard. "Ein neuer Beitrag zur Entstehungsgeschichte von J. S. Bachs Weihnachtsoratorium." *Neue Zeitschrift für Musik* 83 (1916).

Freylinghausen, Johann Anastasius. *Geist-reiches Gesang-Buch*. Halle, 1721.

Freylinghausen, Johann Anastasius. *Grundlegung der Theologie*. Halle, 1703. Facsimile ed. by Matthias Paul. Hildesheim: Olms-Weidmann, 2005.

Freylinghausen, Johann Anastasius. *Das Hohepriesterliche Gebeth unsers hochgelobten Heilandes JEsu CHristi aus dem XVII Capitel Johannis. . . .* Halle, 1719.

Freylinghausen, Johann Anastasius. *Neues / Geist-reiches / Gesang-Buch / auserlesene / so / Alte als Neue / geistliche / und liebliche / Lieder / Nebst den Noten der unbekannten Melodeyen / in sich haltend / Zur Erweckung heiliger Andacht und Erbauung in Glauben und gottseligen Wesen / herausgegeben / von / Johann Anastasio Freylinghausen*. Halle, 1713.

Friedrichs, Henning. *Das Verhältnis von Text und Musik in den Brockes-Passionen Keisers, Händels, Telemanns und Matthesons*. Musikwissenschaftliche Schriften, Vol. 9. Munich and Salzburg: Katzbichler, 1975.

Gardiner, John Elliot. *Music in the Castle of Heaven*. London: Penguin Books, 2013 and New York: Knopf, 2013.

Gassmann, Michael, ed., *Bachs Johannes Passion: Poetische, musikalische, theologische Konzepte*. Internationale Bachakademie Stuttgart Schriftenreihe Band 17. Kassel: Bärenreiter, 2012.

Gerhard, Johann. *Erklährung der Historien des Leidens und Sterbens unsers Herrn Christi Jesu nach den vier Evangelisten (1611)*. Edited by Johann Anselm Steiger. Stuttgart-Bad Cannstatt: Frommann-holzboorg, 2002.

Gerhard, Johann. *Postille, das ist Auslegung und Erklärung der sonntäglichen und vornehmsten Fest-Evangelien über das ganze Jahr . . . Nach den Original-Ausgaben von 1613 und 1616. Vermehrt durch die Zusätze der Ausgabe von 1663*. Berlin, 1870.

Götze, Johann Melchior. *Der Weit-berümte MUSICUS und ORGANISTA / Wurde / Bey Trauriger Leich-Bestellung / Des Weyland / Edlen und Kunst-Hoch-erfrhren / HERRN / ANDREAE / Werckmeisters . . . In einer Stand-Rede dargestellet / Von / Johann Melchior Götzen*. 1707.

Grimm, Jacob, and Wilhelm Grimm. *Deutsches Wörterbuch*. Vol. 10. Bearbeitet von Moriz Heyne. Leipzig, 1877. Munich: Deutscher Taschenbuch Verlag, 1999.

Hamann, Johann Georg. *Poetisches Lexicon*. Leipzig, 1737.

Harnoncourt, Nikolaus, and Reinhard G. Pauly. "Bach's 'Oboe da Caccia' and its Reconstruction." In *The Musical Dialogue: Thoughts on Monteverdi, Bach, and Mozart*, 60–62. Portland, OR: Amadeus Press, 1989.

Haselböck, Lucia. *Bach Textlexikon: Ein Wörterbuch der religiösen Sprachbilder im Vokalwerk von Johann Sebastian Bach*. Kassel: Bärenreiter 2004.

Heermann, Johann. *Crux Christi, Das ist: Die schmertzliche und traurige Marter-Woche, unsers hochverdienten Heylandes JEsu Christi, ...* Braunschweig, 1668.

Heermann, Johann. *Heptalogus Christi, Das ist: Die Allerholdseligsten Sieben Worte Unsers treuen und hochverdienten Heylandes JESU CHRISTI, Mit welchen Er am Creutze sein Leben geendet hat*. Braunschweig, 1670.

Heermann, Johann. *Labores Sacri. Geistliche Kirch Arbeit. In Erklärung aller gewöhnlichen Sontags und vornehmsten Fest Evangelien*. Leipzig, 1726.

Heinichen, Johann David. *Neu erfundene und Gründliche Anweisung zu vollkommener Erlernung des General-Basses*. Hamburg, 1711. Reprint, facsimile edited by Wolfgang Horn. Documenta Musicologica, Erste Reihe. Vol. 40. Kassel: Bärenreiter, 2000.

Heinichen, Johann David. *Der Generalbaß in der Komposition* (Dresden, 1728). Facsimile ed. Hildesheim: Georg Olms Verlag, 1994.

Herberger, Valerius. *Das Himmlische Jerusalem*, 1609. Reprint, edited by Friedrich Ahlfeld. Leipzig: Ernst Bredt, 1858.

Herberger, Valerius. *DE JESU, Scripturae nucleo & medulla, Magnalia Dei. Das ist: Die grossen Thaten GOTTES / von JEsu / Der gantzen Schrifft Kern und Stern / Nebst beygefügtem Psalter-Paradise*. Leipzig, 1700.

Herberger, Valerius. *Epistolische Herz-Postilla*. Leipzig, 1736.

Herberger, Valerius. *Evangelisches Herz-Postilla*. Leipzig, 1668.

Herberger, Valerius. *Paradies Blümlein*. 1598. Reprint, *Paradies-Blümlein aus dem Lustgarten der 150 Psalmen. . . Mit einem Vorwort von C. W. Otto, . . . Neue wortgetreue Ausgabe*. Halle, 1857.

Herz, Gerhard. "Toward a New Image of Bach." *Bach: Quarterly Journal of the Riemenschneider Bach Institute* (1970).

Hildesheimer, Wolfgang. *Der ferne Bach*. Frankfurt am Main: Insel Verlag, 1983.

Hindermann, Walter. *Die nachösterlichen Kantaten des Bachschen Choralkantaten-Jahrgangs*. Hofheim am Taunus: Friedrich Hofmeister, 1975.

Hoffmann-Axthelm, Dagmar, "Bach und die *Perfidia Iudica*—Zur Symmetrie der Juden-Turbae in der Johannes-Passion," *Basler Jahrbuch für historische Musikpraxis* 13 (1989): 31–54.

Hofmann, Klaus, "Zur Tonartenordnung der Johannes-Passion von Johann Sebastian Bach," *Musik und Kirche* 62 vol. 2 (1991): 78–86. Reprinted in *Bachs Passionen, Oratorien und Motetten. Das Handbuch*, edited by Reinmar Emans and Sven Hiemke, 179–91. Laaber: Laaber Verlag, 2009.

Holborn, Hans Ludwig. "Bach and Pietism: The Relationship of the Church Music of Johann Sebastian Bach to Eighteenth-Century Lutheran Orthodoxy and Pietism with Special Reference to the *St. Matthew Passion*." PhD diss., School of Theology at Claremont, CA, 1976.

Hunnius, Aegidius, *Postilla / Oder / Außlegung der Sontäglichen Episteln und Evangelien / von Ostern an biß auff den Advent*. Frankfurt, 1591.

Hunnius, Nicolaus. *Epitome Credendorum Oder Innhalt der gantzen Christlichen Lehre . . .* Wittenberg, 1719.

Jablonski, Daniel-Ernst. *Oeconomia Scholae Crucis, GOTTES Kreutz-Schule* (Cölln an der Spree, Berlin, 1694).

Käsemann, Ernst. *The Testament of Jesus: A Study of the Gospel of John in Light of Chapter 17*. Translated by Gerhard Krodel. Philadelphia: Fortress Press, 1968.

Kempis, Thomas à. *Imitatio Christi.* German edition by Johann Arndt: *Von der Nachfolge Christi*, in *zwey alte und edle Büchlein, Das Erste. Die Deutsche Theologia . . . Das Ander, Die Nachfolgung Christi, . . . jetzt . . . an den tag gegeben / Durch Johannem Arndten. . . .* Magdeburg, 1605.

Kevorkian, Tanya, *Baroque Piety: Religion, Society and Music in Leipzig, 1650–1750*. Aldershot: Ashgate, 2007.

Kirkendale, Ursula. "The Source for Bach's Musical Offering: the Institutio oratoria of Quintilian." *Journal of the American Musicological Society* 33 (1980): 88–141.

Köstenberger, Andreas J. *A Theology of John's Gospel and Letters: the Word, the Christ, the Son of God.* Biblical Theology of the New Testament. Andreas J. Köstenberger, general editor. Grand Rapids, MI: Zondervan, 2009.

Kuhnau, Johann. Preface to *Texte zur Leipziger Kirchen-Musik*, 1709. Reprinted in B. F. Richter. "Eine Abhandlung Joh. Kuhnau's." *Monatshefte für Musik-Geschichte* 34 (1902): 148–54.

Kuhnau, Johann. *Musicalische Vorstellung / Einiger / Biblischer Historien / In 6. Sonaten / Auff dem Claviere zu spielen / Allen Liebhabern zum Vergnügen versuchet von Johann Kuhnauen.* Leipzig, 1700. New edition in facsimile, edited and with introduction in English translation by Kurt Stone: *Six Biblical Sonatas, for Keyboard, 1700*. New York: Broude Brothers.

Kuijken, Sigiswald. Liner notes to *J. S. Bach / La Petite Bande: S. Kuijken: Cantatas for the Complete Liturgical Year. 20 CD-Edition, 2006–*.

Kysar, Robert. *John, the Maverick Gospel.* Atlanta: John Knox Press, 1976.

LaCugna, Catharine. *God for Us: The Trinity and Christian Life.* San Francisco: HarperCollins, 1991.

Lange, Joachim. *Evangelisches Licht und Recht, Oder Richtige und Erbauliche Erklärung der heiligen Vier Evangelisten, und die Apostel-Geschichte, ...* Halle, 1735.

Lange, Joachim. *Oeconomia salutis evangelica.* Halle, 1728.

Leaver, Robin. "Bach, Hymns and Hymnbooks." *Hymn* 36, no. 4 (October, 1985): 7–13.

Leaver, Robin. *Bach's Theological Library.* Neuhausen-Stuttgart: Hänssler, 1983.

Leaver, Robin. "J. S. Bach and Scripture: Glosses from the Calov Bible Commentary." St. Louis: Concordia, 1986.

Leaver, Robin. *Luther's Liturgical Music: Principles and Implications.* Lutheran Quarterly Books. Grand Rapids, MI: William B. Eerdmans Publishing Company, 2007.

Leisinger, Ulrich. *Bach in Leipzig, Bach und Leipzig: Konferenzbericht Leipzig 2000.* Leipziger Beiträge zur Bach-Forschung. Hildesheim: G. Olms Verlag, 2002.

Lester, Joel. "The Fux-Mattheson Correspondence: An Annotated Translation." *Current Musicology* 24 (1977): 37–62.

Levenson, Jon. D. *The Death and Resurrection of the Beloved Son: The Transformation of Child Sacrifice in Judaism and Christianity.* New Haven, CT: Yale University Press, 1993.

Loewenich, Walther von. *Luther's Theology of the Cross.* Translated by Herbert J. A. Bouman. Minneapolis: Augsburg Publishing House, 1976.

Loewenich, Walther von. *Luther und das Johanneische Christentum.* Munich: Chr. Kaiser Verlag, 1933.

Lösecke, Albrecht. *THEOLOGIA-FOEDERALIS-OECONOMICA, Die Haushaltung u. Wege GOttes mit den Menschen / Darin Die Lehre von den Bündnissen GOttes mit den Menschen verhandelt / die Theologie u. Ordnung des Heyls / wie alle Glaubens-Artickel in Biblischer Folge, Kettenweise an einander hangen, gezeiget, Die Vorbilder Altes Testaments in ihrem Gegen-Bilbe erkläret, und die Kirchen-Historie von Anbegin der Welt bis an die gegenwärtige Zeit nebst dem allmähligen Anwachs der Ceremonien, vorgestellt wird.* Halle, 1724.

Lütkemann, Joachim. *Apostolischer Hertzens-Wekker.* Stade, 1736.

Lütkemann, Joachim. *Harpffe / Von zehen Seyten / Das ist: Gründliche Erklärung / Zehen Psalmen Davids.* Frankfurt and Leipzig, 1674.

Lütkemann, Joachim. *Vorschmack der göttlichen Güte.* Wolffenbüttel, 1653.

Luther, Martin. *Das XIIII und XV Capitel S. Johannis / durch D. Mart. Luther: Gepredigt und ausgelegt.* Wittemberg, 1539.

Luther, Martin. *Das XVI und XVII: Capitel S. Johannis: Gepredigt und ausgelegt durch D. Mart. Luther.* Wittemberg, 1538.

Luther, Martin. *Das siebenzehend Capitel Johannis / von dem gebete Christi: Gepredigt und ausgelegt durch D. Mart. Luth.* Wittemberg, 1534.

Luther, Martin. *Der XC. Psalm: das Gebet Mose / durch D. Mart. Luther in Latinischer sprach ausgelegt / und verdeudscht / Durch M. Johann Spangenberg. Mit einer Vorrede Doctoris Georgij Maioris.* Wittemberg, 1548.

Luther, Martin. *First Lectures on the Psalms (1–75).* Edited by Hilton C. Oswald. Vol. 10. *Luther's Works.* St. Louis: Concordia Publishing House, 1974.

Luther, Martin. *Lectures on Genesis, Chapters 1–5.* Edited by Jaroslav Pelikan. Vol. 1, *Luther's Works.* St. Louis: Concordia Publishing House, 1958.

Luther, Martin. *Lectures on Genesis, Chapters 6–14.* Edited by Jaroslav Pelikan. Vol. 2, *Luther's Works.* St. Louis: Concordia Publishing House, 1960.

Luther, Martin. *Lectures on Isaiah, Chapters 1–39.* Edited by Jaroslav Pelikan. Vol. 16, *Luther's Works.* St. Louis: Concordia Publishing House, 1969.

Luther, Martin. "A Meditation on Christ's Passion, 1519." In *Luther's Works.* Vol. 42, *Devotional Writings 1.* Translated by Martin H. Bertram. Edited by Martin O. Dietrich, 3–14. Philadelphia: Fortress Press, 1971.

Luther, Martin. *Kirchenpostille,* "Second Sermon for Exaudi." *Luther's Works.* Vol. 2.1, 259–71. English edition.Grand Rapids, MI: Baker Book House Company 2000. Reprint of *The Precious and Sacred Writings of Martin Luther.* Vol. 12, edited by John Nicholas Lenker. Minneapolis: Lutherans in All Lands, 1907.

Luther, Martin. *On the Bondage of the Will (De Servo Arbitrio).* Edited and translated by Philip S. Watson in collaboration with B. Drewery. In E. Gordon Rupp and P. S. Watson, *Luther and Erasmus: Free Will and Salvation.* Philadelphia: Westminster Press, 1969.

Luther, Martin. *Sermons on Epistle Texts for Epiphany, Easter and Pentecost.* Vol. 4.1, *The Complete Sermons of Martin Luther.* Grand Rapids, MI: Baker Books, 2000.

Luther, Martin. *Sermons on Gospel Texts for Easter, Ascension Day, Pentecost, Trinity, and the Fourteen Sundays after Trinity.* Vol. 6, *Complete Sermons of Martin Luther.* Grand Rapids, MI: Baker Books, 2002.

Luther, Martin. *Sermons on the Gospel of St. John*. Edited by Jaroslav Pelikan and Daniel E. Poellot. Translated by Martin H. Bertram. Vol. 24, *Luther's Works*. St. Louis: Concordia Publishing House, 1961.

Luther, Martin. *Word and Sacrament I*. Edited by E. Theodore Bachmann. Vol. 35, *Luther's Works*. Philadelphia: Muhlenberg Press, 1960.

Marbach, Christian. *Evangelische Singe-Schule*. Breslau and Leipzig, 1726. Reprint, Facsimile ed. Hildesheim: Georg Olms Verlag, 1991.

Marissen, Michael. "The Character and Sources of the Anti-Judaism in Bach's Cantata 46." *Harvard Theological Review* 96, no. 1 (2003): 65–99.

Marissen, Michael. *Lutheranism, Anti-Judaism, and Bach's "St. John Passion."* New York: Oxford University Press, 1998.

Marshall, Robert L. *The Compositional Process of J. S. Bach*. 2 vols. Princeton, NJ: Princeton University Press, 1972.

Mathesius, Johann. *DILVVIUM, das ist, Historia von der Sündflut, dadurch Gott der Herr zum schrecklichen exempel seines zorns wider die sünde, zu Noah zeiten, die erste unbußfertige Welt erseufft, und nicht allein die menschen, sondern alles was odem gehabt, vertilget hat*. Nuremberg, 1587.

Mattheson, Johann. *Critica Musica. Des fragende Componisten/Erstes Verhör/über ein gewisse Passion* (Hamburg, 1725). Facsimile ed. Amsterdam: F. Knuf, 1964.

Mattheson, Johann. *Das forschende Orchestre*. Hamburg, 1713.

Mattheson, Johann. *Der vollkommene Capellmeister* (Hamburg, 1739). Facsimile ed. Edited by Margarete Reimann. Kassel: Bärenreiter, 1954.

Mattheson, Johann. *Grosse General-Bass Schule Oder: Der Exemplarischen Organistenprobe* (Hamburg, 1731). Facsimile reprint Hildesheim: Georg Olms Verlag, 2004.

Mattheson, Johann. *Kern melodischer Wissenschaft*. Hamburg, 1737.

Mattheson, Johann. *Kleine Generalbaß-Schule* (Hamburg, 1735). Facsimile reprint with an introduction by Sven Hiemke. Laaber: Laaber-Verlag, 2003.

McGrath, Alister E. *Luther's Theology of the Cross: Martin Luther's Theological Breakthrough*. Oxford: Blackwell, 1985.

Meeks, Wayne A. "The Man from Heaven in Johannine Sectarianism." *Journal of Biblical Literature* 91, no. 1 (March, 1972): 44–72.

Melamed, Daniel R. *Hearing Bach's Passions*. New York: Oxford University Press, 2005.

Mendel, Arthur. *Johann Sebastian Bach, Neue Ausgabe sämtlicher Werke*. Series 2, vol. 4 (*Johannes-Passion*). Kassel: Bärenreiter, 1973–74.

Mendel, Arthur. *Johann Sebastian Bach, Neue Ausgabe sämtlicher Werke*. Series 2, vol. 4 (*Johannes-Passion*). Kritischer Bericht. Leipzig: VEB Deutscher Verlag für Musik, 1974.

Minear, Paul. "J. S. Bach and J. A. Ernesti: A Case Study in Exegetical and Theological Conflict." In *Our Common History as Christians: Essays in Honor of Albert C. Ousler*, edited by John Deschner, L. T. Howe, and K. Penzel. New York: Oxford University Press, 1975.

Minear, Paul. "Matthew, Evangelist, and Johann, Composer." *Theology Today* 30 (1973): 243–55.

Moller, Martin. *Praxis Evangeliorum: Einfeltige erklerung und nützliche betrachtung der Evangelien / so auff alle Sontage und vornemesten Fest Jährlich zu predigen verordnet sind*. Görlitz, 1614.

Moller, Martin. *Soliloquia de Passione Jesu Christi, Das ist: Heilige Betrachtung deß Leidens und Sterbens unsers HErrn und Heilandes JEsu Christi*. Lüneburg, 1730.

Müller, Heinrich. *Apostolischer Schluß-Kette*. Frankfurt, 1671.

Müller, Heinrich. *Evangelischer Herzens-Spiegel, und Paßions-Predigten; Imgleichen D. Joachimi Lütkemanns, . . . Apostolischer Herzens-Wecker, . . .* . Stade, 1736.

Müller, Heinrich. *Geistliche Erquick-Stunden, oder Dreyhundert Hauß- und Tisch-Andachten*. Hamburg, 1736.

Müller, Heinrich. *Geistliche Seelen-Music*, Rostock, 1659.

Müller, Heinrich. *Geistlicher Danck-Altar / Zum täglichen Beth- und Lob-Opffer / In dem Hertzen der Christen aufgerichtet, . . . Auch mit fernerer Anweisung Gottseliger Sing- und Bibel-Andacht zu einem erbaulichen Communion-Buch vermehret, und mit nöthigen Registern versehen, nebst einer Vorrede Hn. D. Michael Heinrich Reinhards*. Hanover, 1724.

Müller, Heinrich. *Himmlischer Liebeskuß oder Übung des wahren Christenthumbs*. Rostock 1659. Rev. ed., *Göttliche Liebes-Flamme Oder Auffmunterung zur Liebe Gottes*. Frankfurt, 1676.

Müller, Heinrich. *Thränen- und Trost-Quelle, Bey Erklärung der Geschichte, von der Großen Sünderin, Luc. VII. V. 36. 37. Etc.* Hanover, 1724.

Neumann, Werner. *J. S. Bachs Chorfuge: Ein Beitrag zur Kompositionstechnik Bachs*. 3rd ed. Bach-Studien, vol. 3. Leipzig: Breitkopf & Härtel, 1953.

Neumann, Werner ed. *Sämtliche von Johann Sebastian Bach vertonte Texte*. Leipzig, 1974.

Neumann, Werner, and Hans-Joachim Schulze, eds. *Bach-Dokumente*. Vol. 2, *Fremdschriftliche und gedruckte Dokumente zur Lebensgeschichte Johann Sebastian Bachs, 1685–1750*. Kassel: Bärenreiter, 1969.

Niedt, Friedrich Erhard. *Musicalische Handleitung*. Teil 1– 3 in einem Band (1710, 1721, 1717). Facsimile ed. Hildesheim: Georg Olms Verlag, 2003.

Nicolai, Philipp. *Freudenspiegel des ewigen Lebens*. Facsimile reprint of the 1st ed. (Frankfurt, 1599), edited with a forword by Dr. Reinhard Mumm. Soest: Westfälische Verlagsbuchhandlung Mocker & Jahn, 1963.

Nicolai, Philipp. *Praxis vitae aeternae: Beschreibung deß gantzen geheimnisses von Christlicher ubung / Auch rechter fahrt und wandel zum Ewigen leben / worvon ordentlich in fünff Büchern gehandelt wird*. Hamburg, 1619.

Nicolai, Philipp. *THEORIA VITAE AETERNAE: Historische Beschreibung desz gantzen Geheimnisses vom Ewigen Leben*. Hamburg, 1628.

Nicolai, Philipp. *Von Christo Jesu dem Bawm des Lebens und seinen edlen Früchten: Eine Christliche Predigt uber die Wort des HErren. Mose. 14. Ich wil sein wie ein grünende Tanne / etc.* Hamburg, 1607.

Olearius, Johann. *Biblische Erklärung Darinnen / nechst dem allgemeinen Haupt-Schlüssel Der gantzen heiligen Schrifft* . . .5 vols. Leipzig, 1678–81.

Olearius, Johann Christoph. *Evangelischer Lieder-Schatz*. Jena, 1706.

Pelikan, Jaroslav. *Bach Among the Theologians*. Philadelphia: Fortress Press, 1986.

Penna, Lorenzo. *Li Primi Albori Musicali*. Bologna, 1684. Reprint ed., Bibliotheca Musica Bononiensis Collana diretta da Giuseppe Vecchi dell'Universitá degli Studi di Bologna. Agosto: Arnaldo Forni Editore, 1996.

Peters, Mark. A. *A Woman's Voice in Baroque Music: Mariane von Ziegler and J. S. Bach*. Aldershot and Burlington, VT: Ashgate, 2008.

Petzoldt, Martin. *Bach-Kommentar, Band 1: Die Geistlichen Kantaten des 2. Bis 27. Trinitatis-Sonntages*. Internationale Bachakademie Stuttgart. Kassel: Bärenreiter, 2004. *Band 2:*

Die Geistlichen Kantaten vom 1. Advent bis zum Trinitatisfest. Kassel: Bärenreiter, 2007.

Petzoldt, Martin. "Theologische Überlegungen zum Passionsbericht des Johannes in Bachs Deutung." In *Johann Sebastian Bach. Johannes-Passion, BWV 245*. Kassel: Schriftenreihe der Internationalen Bachakademie Stuttgart, 1994.

Petzoldt, Martin. "Zur theologischen Petrus-Existenz in Bachs Johannes-Passion." In *Bachs Johannes Passion: Poetische, musikalische, theologische Konzepte,* edited by Michael Gassmann. Bachakademie Stuttgart Schriftenreihe Band 17. Kassel: Bärenreiter, 2012.

Pfeiffer, August. *Antimelancholicus oder Melancholey Vertreiber.* Leipzig, 1688.

Pfeiffer, August. *Evangelische Erquickstunden.* Leipzig, 1753.

Pfeiffer, August. *Evangelisches Schatz-Kammer.* Nuremberg, 1697.

Pfitzner, Victor C. "Luther as Interpreter of John's Gospel: With Special Reference to His Sermons on the Gospel of St. John." *Lutheran Theological Journal* 18, no. 2 (1984): 65–73.

Prenter, Regin. *Spiritus Creator.* Translated by John M. Jensen. Philadelphia: Muhlenberg Press, 1953.

Prinz, Ulrich. *Johann Sebastian Bachs Instrumentarium: Originalquellen, Besetzung, Verwendung.* Kassel: Bärenreiter, 2005.

Rambach, Johann Jacob. *Ausführliche und gründliche Erläuterung über seine eigene INSTITUTIONES HERMENEUTICAE SACRAE, . . . aus Licht gestellet von D. Ernst Friedrich Neubauer.* 2 vols. Gießen: Johann Philipp Krieger, 1738.

Rambach, Johann Jacob. *Betrachtung des Geheimnisses Jesu Christi in dem Vorbilde der Ehernen Schlange und der Frey-Städte Israels/ in einigen öffentlichen Reden angestellet.* Halle, 1726.

Rambach, Johann Jacob. *Betrachtungen über das gantze Leiden Christi.* Jena, 1730.

Rambach, Johann Jacob. *Betrachtungen über den Rath Gottes von der Seeligkeit der Menschen, wie solche von dem seligen Auctore in der Stadt-Kirche zu Giessen in den ordentlichen Donnerstags-Predigten vorgetragen worden; nunmehro in zweyen Theilen ans Licht gestellet von Johann Philip Fresenius, . . .* Giessen, 1737.

Rambach, Johann Jacob. *Betrachtungen über die Sieben Letzten Worte des Gecreutzigten JEsu.* Halle, 1728.

Rambach, Johann Jacob. *Christus in Mose . . .* frei bearbeitet von J. Rächele. Cleveland: Lauer & Yost, 1886.

Rambach, Johann Jacob. *Christus in Mose, oder Betrachtungen über die vornehmsten Weissagungen und Vorbilder in den fünf Büchern Mosis auf Christum . . . zum Druck ausgefertigt . . . von Johannes Philipp Fresenius.* Frankfurt and Leipzig, 1736–37.

Rambach, Johann Jacob. *COLLEGIUM HISTORIAE ECCLESIASTICAE VETERIS TESTAMENTI, oder Ausführlicher und gründlicher Discurs über die Kirchen-Historie des alten Testaments von Erschaffung der Welt bis auf die Geburt Christi. . . Franckfurth, 1737.* Frankfurt, 1737.

Rambach, Johann Jacob. *Dogmatische Theologie / oder / Christliche / Glaubens-Lehre / Vormals in einem Collegio thetico / Uber des / Hochberühmten Herrn D. Joachim Langens, . . . OECONOMIAM SALUTIS / DOGMATICAM.* Frankfurt and Leipzig, 1744.

Rambach, Johann Jacob. *Erbauliche Betrachtungen über die Heils-Güter in Christo / Nach Anleitung des von dem sel. D. Philipp Jacob Spenern herausgegebenen Tractätlein, Die lauter Milch des Evangelii genannt: Vormals in einigen Erbauungs-Stunden auf dem*

Wäysenhause zu Halle angestellet; nun aber, als / Der andere Theil / Von des sel. Auctoris Betrachtungen über die Ordnung des Heils. Frankfurt und Leipzig, 1737.

Rambach, Johann Jacob. *Evangelische Betrachtungen über die Sonn- und Fest-Tags-Evangelia des gantzen Jahrs.* Halle, 1732.

Rambach, Johann Jacob. *Martini Lutheri Herrliches Zeugniß von Christo dem einigen Wege zur Seligkeit, über Joh. 14, 5–9. Mit einer Vorrede von der genauen Verbinding des Verdienstes und Exempels Christi heraus gegeben von Johann Jacob Rambach ed., D. Martini Lutheri Auserlesene erbauliche Kleine Schriften, aus seinen grossen Tomis genommen . . . von D. Johann Jacob Rambach,* 1743.

Rambach, Johann Jacob. *Seeligkeit der Gläubigen in der Zeit und in der Ewigkeit. . . . Anhang / einer Predigt von der Seeligen Bekantschaft der Schafe Jesu Christi mit derem guten Hirten; welche in der Schul Kirche in Halle am Sontage Misericordias Domini Anno 1729 gehalten worden.* 1729.

Robichaux, Kerry S. "The Divine Economy." *Affirmation & Critique* 4, no. 1 (1999): 3–12.

Scheide, William H. *Johann Sebastian Bach as a Biblical Interpreter.* Princeton Pamphlets No. 8. Princeton, NJ: Princeton Theological Seminary, 1952.

Scheide, William H. "Johann Sebastian Bachs Sammlung von Kantaten seines Vetters Johann Ludwig Bach (1)." *Bach-Jahrbuch* 46 (1959): 52–94; (2) *Bach-Jahrbuch* 48 (1961): 5–24.

Schmidt, Sebastian. "Anhang. Des Sel. Herrn Sebastian Schmidts *PARAPHRASIS oder Kurtze Erklärung des XVII Capitels Johannis.*" In *Das Hohepriesterliche Gebeth Unsers Hochgelobten Heylandes JEsu CHristi / Auß Dem XVII Capitel Johannis,* edited by Johann Anastasius Freylinghausen, 677–93. Halle, 1719.

Schrammek, W. "Viola pomposa und Violoncello piccolo bei Johann Sebastian Bach." In *Internationales Bach-Fest 3,* edited by W. Felix, W. Hoffmann, and A. Schneiderheinze. Leipzig, 1975.

Scriver, Christian. *Heilige und GOtt wohlgefällige Haushaltung / Aus denen gewöhnlichen Sonn- und Festtäglichen Evangelischen Texten des Jahres.* Magdeburg and Leipzig, 1717.

Scriver, Christian. *Müßige Land-Stunden.* Königsberg, 1698.

Scriver, Christian. *Seelen-Schatz. Fünff Theile.* Schaffhausen, 1738.

Semrau, Max. *Die Kunst der Renaissance in Italien und im Norden.* Vol. 2 of Wilhelm Lübke, *Der Kunstgeschichte,* newly revised by Max Semrau. Stuttgart: Paul Neff Verlag, 1905.

Smalley, Stephen S. *John Evangelist and Interpreter.* Exeter: Paternoster Press, 1978.

Smend, Friedrich. "Bachs Matthäus-Passion." *Bach-Jahrbuch* 25 (1928): 1–95.

Smend, Friedrich. *Bach-Studien.* Edited by Christoph Wolff. Kassel: Bärenreiter, 1968.

Smend, Friedrich. "Die Johannes-Passion von Bach." *Bach-Jahrbuch* 23 (1926): 105–28.

Smend, Friedrich. *Joh. Seb. Bach: Kirchen-Kantaten, Heft 6.* Berlin: Der Christliche Zeitschriftenverlag, 1947.

Spener, Philipp Jacob. *Die Evangelische Glaubens-Lehre / In einem Jahrgang der Predigten / Bey den Sonn- und Fest-täglichen / Ordentlichen / Evangelien / Auß heiliger Göttlicher Schrifft.* Frankfurt, 1710.

Spener, Philipp Jacob. *Der Evangelische Glaubens-Trost / Aus den Göttlichen Wohlthaten / Und / Schätzen der Seligkeit in Christo / In einem Jahr-Gang der Predigten / Uber die ordentliche / Sonn- und Fest-Tägliche / Evangelia.* Berlin, 1727.

Spener, Philipp Jacob. *Die Evangelische Lebens-Pflichten in einem Jahrgang der Predigten bey den Sonn- und Fest-Täglichen ordentlichen Evangelien aus H. Göttlicher Schrifft.* Frankfurt am Main, 1702.

Spitta, Philipp. *Johann Sebastian Bach: His Work and Influence on the Music of Germany, 1585–1750.* 2 vols. Translated by Clara Bell and J. A. Fuller-Maitland. London and New York: Breitkopf und Härtel, 1889. Reprint, New York: Dover Books, 1951.

Steiger, Lothar. "'Wir haben keinen König denn den Kaiser!' Pilatus und die Juden in der Passionsgeschichte nach dem Johannes-Evangelium. Oder die Frage nach dem Antijudaismus in Bachs Johannes-Passion." In *Internationale Arbeitsgemeinschaft für theologische Bachforschung, Bulletin 5: "Wie freudig ist mein Herz, da Gott versöhnet ist": Die Lehre von der Versöhnung in Kantaten und Orgelchorälen von Johann Sebastian Bach,* edited by Renate Steiger, 25–36. Heidelberg, 1995.

Steiger, Lothar, and Renate Steiger. "Die Passions theologie der Bachzeit, ihr Predigttypus und der Text der Johannes-Passion." In *Johann Sebastian Bach: Johannes-Passion BWV 245,* edited by Ulrich Prinz, 8–43. Vorträge des Meisterkurses 1986 und der Sommerakademie J. S. Bach 1990, edited by Ulrich Prinz, 8–43. Kassel: Bärenreiter, 1993.

Steiger, Renate. "'Bisher habt ihr nichts gebeten in meinem Namen.' Die Kantate BWV 87 und das Vaterunser. Eine Antwort an Ulrich Konrad." In *Gnadengegenwart: Johann Sebastian Bach im Kontext lutherischer Orthodoxie und Frömmigkeit.* Stuttgart-Bad Canstatt: Friedrich Frommann Verlag, 2002.

Steiger, Renate. "'Die Welt ist euch ein Himmelreich': J. S. Bach's Deutung der Pastoralen." *Musik und Kirche* 41 (1971): 1–8, 69–79.

Steiger, Renate. "'O schöne Zeit! O Abendstunde!': Affekt und Symbol in J. S. Bachs Matthäuspassion." *Musik und Kirche* 46 (1976): 15–22.

Steinberg, Leo. *Leonardo's Incessant Last Supper.* New York: Zone Books, 2001.

Steinberg, Leo. *The Sexuality of Christ in Renaissance Art and in Modern Oblivion.* 2nd ed. Chicago: University of Chicago Press, 1996.

Stiller, Gunther. *Johann Sebastian Bach and Liturgical Life in Leipzig.* Translated by Herbert J. A. Bouman, Daniel F. Poellot, and Hilton C. Oswald. Edited by Robin A. Leaver. St. Louis: Concordia, 1984.

Stoeffler, F. Ernest. *German Pietism During the Eighteenth Century.* Leiden: E. J. Brill, 1973.

Stoeffler, F. Ernest. *The Rise of Evangelical Pietism.* Leiden: E. J. Brill, 1971.

Suzuki, Masaaki. Liner notes to *Johann Sebastian Bach Cantatas 28, 68, 85, 175, 183.* CD, Bach Collegium Japan. Bis SACD 1641 (2008).

Talley, Thomas J. *The Origins of the Liturgical Year.* Collegeville, MN: Liturgical Press, 1986.

Tauler, Johann. *Das Buch von geistlicher Armuth.* Edited by P. Fr. Heinrich Seuse Denifle. Munich, 1877.

Tauler, Johann. *The Following of Christ.* Translated by J. K. Morell. London, n.d.

Tauler, Johann. *Predigten auf alle Sonn- und Festtage im Jahr. . . .* nach den Ausgaben von Joh. Arndt und Phil. Jac. Spener. Edited by Eb. Kuntze and J. H. R. Biesenthal. Berlin: August Hirschwald Verlag, 1841.

Telemann, Georg Philipp. *Lukaspassion 1728.* Edited by Hans Hörner and Martin Ruhnke, Georg Philipp Telemann, Musikalische Werke Vol. 15. Kassel: Bärenreiter, 1964.

Terry, Charles Sanford. *Bach's Orchestra.* 2nd ed. London: Oxford University Press, 1958.

Unger, Hans Heinrich. *Die Beziehungen zwischen Musik und Rhetorik im 16.–18. Jahrhundert.* Musik und Geistesgeschichte: Berliner Studien zur Musikwissenschaft, Bd. 4. Hildesheim: G. Olms, 1969.

Unger, Melvin P. *Handbook to Bach's Sacred Cantata Texts: An Interlinear Translation with Reference Guide to Biblical Quotations and Allusions.* Lanham, MD: Scarecrow Press, 1996.

Walter, Meinrad. *Johann Sebastian Bach, Johannespassion: Eine musikalisch-theologische Einführung*. Stuttgart: Carus-Verlag, 2011.

Weise, Christian. *Der grünen Jugend Nothwendige Gedancken*. Leipzig, 1675.

Weiss, Dieter. "Zur Tonartengliederung in J. S. Bachs Johannes-Passion." *Musik und Kirche* 40 (1970): 33.

Werckmeister, Andreas. *CRIBRUM MUSICUM Oder Musicalisches Sieb*. Quedlinburg and Leipzig, 1700.

Werckmeister, Andreas. *Erweiterte und verbesserte Orgel-Probe* (Quedlinburg 1698). Facsimile reprint edited by Dietz-Rüdiger Moser. Documenta Musicologica, Erste Reihe, 30. Kassel: Bärenreiter, 1970.

Werckmeister, Andreas. *HARMONOLOGIA MUSICA Oder Kurtze Anleitung zur Musicalischen COMPOSITION*. Frankfurt and Leipzig, 1702. Facsimile ed. with an introduction by Dietrich Bartel. Laaber: Laaber-Verlag, 2003.

Werckmeister, Andreas. *Hypomnemata Musica*. Quedlinburg, 1697. Facsimile ed. Hildesheim: Georg Olms, 1970.

Werckmeister, Andreas. *Musicae mathematicae hodegus curiosus, oder Richtiger Musicalischer Weg-Weiser*. Frankfurt and Leipzig, 1687. Facsimile ed. Hildesheim: Georg Olms Verlag, 1972.

Werckmeister, Andreas. *Musicalische PARADOXAL-DISCOURSE Oder Ungemeine Vorstellungungen . . . .* Quedlinburg, 1707. Facsimile ed. with an introduction by Dietrich Bartel. Laaber: Laaber-Verlag, 2003.

Werthemann, Helene. *Die Bedeutung der alttestamentlichen Historien in Johann Sebastian Bachs Kantaten*. Tübingen: J. B. Mohr, 1960.

Wispelwey, Peter. Liner notes to *Johann Sebastian Bach: 6 Suites per violoncello solo senza basso*. CD, Channel Classics CCS 12298, 1998.

Wolff, Christoph. *Johann Sebastian Bach: The Learned Musician*. Oxford: Oxford University Press, 2000.

Wustmann, Rudolf. *Johann Sebastian Bachs Kantatentexte*. Vol. 14/1. Veröffentlichungen der Neuen Bach-Gesellschaft. Leipzig: Breitkopf & Härtel, 1913.

Wustmann, Rudolf. "Zu Bachs Texten der Johannes- und der Matthäus-Passion." *Monatsschrift für Gottesdienst und kirchliche Kunst* 15 (1910): 126–31, 161–65.

Yearsley, David. *Bach and the Meanings of Counterpoint*. Cambridge: Cambridge University Press, 2002.

Zander, Ferdinand. "Die Dichter der Kantatentexte Johann Sebastian Bachs: Untersuchungen zu ihrer Bestimmung." *Bach-Jahrbuch* 54 (1968): 25.

Zahn, Johannes. *Die Melodien der Deutschen Evangelischen Kirchenlieder*. 6 vols. Gütersloh, 1889. Reprint, Hildesheim: Georg Olms Verlag, 1963.

Ziegler, Christiane Mariane von. *Versuch in Gebundener Schreibart*. Vol. 1. Leipzig, 1728.

{ INDEX }